S0-AXX-646

BUSINESS DATA PROCESSING

BUSINESS

Prentice-Hall, Inc., Englewood Cliffs, New Jersey

DATA PROCESSING

FOURTH EDITION

ELIAS M. AWAD

George Ball Distinguished Professor of Business, Ball State University

Library of Congress Cataloging in Publication Data

Awad, Elias M
Business data processing.

Bibliography: p.
1. Electronic data processing—Business.
2. Punched card systems. I. Title.
HF5548.2.A9 1975 651.8 74–11201
ISBN 0–13–093864–5

BUSINESS DATA PROCESSING, fourth edition
Elias M. Awad

Printed in the United States of America

10 9 8 7 6 5 4 3

Prentice-Hall International, Inc. *London*
Prentice-Hall of Australia, Pty. Ltd. *Sydney*
Prentice-Hall of Canada, Ltd. *Toronto*
Prentice-Hall of India Private Limited *New Delhi*
Prentice-Hall of Japan, Inc. *Tokyo*

to FREDERIC K. EASTER, Jr.

contents

PART ONE

COMPUTER-PROCESSING—AN OVERVIEW

PART TWO

CHARACTERISTICS AND INTERNAL OPERATION OF A BUSINESS COMPUTER

PART THREE

COMPUTER SYSTEMS AND DEVICES

PART FOUR

COMPUTER APPLICATION DEVELOPMENT AND PROGRAMMING

PART FIVE
DATA-PROCESSING MANAGEMENT

PART SIX
APPENDIXES

preface

The maintenance, stability, and growth of today's business organization depend largely upon the quality of its information and the effectiveness of its data processing system. The advent of the electronic computer has projected the manager into the role of a full-time decision maker by freeing him from the drudgery of routine processing tasks. This "Second Industrial Revolution" is now an integral part of every field—business and scientific—and affects the lives of millions. With this orientation, the study of business data processing becomes increasingly important, especially to students majoring in business management, business organizations, accounting, data-processing systems, or business economics.

This new edition follows a pattern similar to the previous three in terms of lucidity, consistency, and currency of the subject areas appropriate for a basic text in business data processing. Some of the major features or changes are as follows:

1. Each chapter begins with a general outline and ends with a summary, a glossary of basic terms, questions for discussion, and suggested readings.
2. Problems and exercises underscoring key features of each chapter are available in *Concepts in Business Data Processing: Student Guide,* which accompanies this text and contains solutions to even-numbered items.
3. *Issues in Business Data Processing: A Reader* is a new addition, designed to supplement the text with readings and issues related to key aspects of computer processing and management.
4. Major reorganization of the sequence and content of the text. Punched card data processing devices are deleted except for the keypunch, which is still in use as a computer input preparation device.

4. Part One, Computer Processing—An Overview, includes a major revision of Chapter 1 with emphasis on the growing importance of management information systems and a discussion of computer growth. Chapter 2 clarifies the systems concept as it relates to business organizations and shows how information flows throughout the system for effective decision making. Chapter 4 includes a section on developments of computer languages.

5. Part Two, Characteristics and Internal Operation of a Computer System, includes updated presentation of the makeup and characteristics of today's business-oriented, digital computers (Chapter 5). Chapter 6 describes and illustrates the concept and structure of *virtual memory.* Chapter 7 is a summary of computer number systems and arithmetic. It can be deleted without sacrificing the continuity of the text matter.

6. Part Three, Computer Systems and Devices, includes major emphasis upon direct data-entry devices in Chapter 8, with a section on *intelligent terminals* and an illustration of the use and importance of POS systems in retailing. Chapter 9 discusses the latest input/output devices available for computer processing. Chapter 10 explains the *microfiche concept*—a new technique in microfilm. Chapter 12 includes a new section on *virtual time sharing* and another section on the structure and design of the *computer data base.* Finally, Chapter 13 presents an overview of the IBM system 3/15.

Part Four, Computer Applications Development and Programming, begins with a new chapter (14) which explains the stages involved in designing and developing systems projects. Once learned, the succeeding chapters (15–20), related to tools for program planning and the use of various languages, begin to make sense. Chapter 19 is a new chapter introducing BASIC. The use of this language is gaining in importance among time-sharing users, especially in schools that maintain an ongoing time-sharing facility.

8. Part Five, Data Processing Management, presents principles applicable to the planning, organization, and management of a data-processing department.

This edition is dedicated to Frederic K. Easter, Jr., Assistant Vice President of Prentice-Hall, Inc., whose foresight of the need to introduce basic data processing to the academic business program was reflected in his publication of the first edition of this text in 1964. His continued support and dedication to advancing the cause of data processing made the succeeding publications possible.

Special thanks go to Burt Gabriel, the text editor, whose creative talent and wealth of pertinent information, as well as the many hours he devoted in guiding my thoughts through the preparation of this edition, shall always be appreciated. I also appreciate the interest and dedication of Fred Dahl, production editor, whose professional touch in coordinating the various aspects of the manuscript are reflected in the finished product.

I am indebted to many individuals and organizations whose cooperation helped in the preparation of this edition – Professor William C. Akin, Southwest Texas State University; Professor Joel Darrow, Pace University Graduate School; Professor Thomas G. DeLutis, Ohio State University; Professor Elmer C. Laedtke, Northern Virginia Community College; and Dr. Melvin Morganstein, Nassau Community College. My thanks go to IBM and other computer manufacturers for permission to use and adapt the copyrighted photographs of the equipment and schematics presented in the text; to Marjorie Homan for typing the final draft from a virtually handwritten copy; and to Rita Putko of Burroughs Corporation for expediting the availability of technical information against a tight deadline.

I am personally indebted to Mr. Arthur M. Wirtz for providing use of the library facilities and privacy of the Ivanhoe Farms where the bulk of this edition was written. His special interest in my work was a strong motivator behind each publication. My wife, Sandy, deserves most credit for her patience, constant encouragement, and for the many family hours sacrificed in the revision process.

ELIAS M. AWAD

COMPUTER PROCESSING— AN OVERVIEW

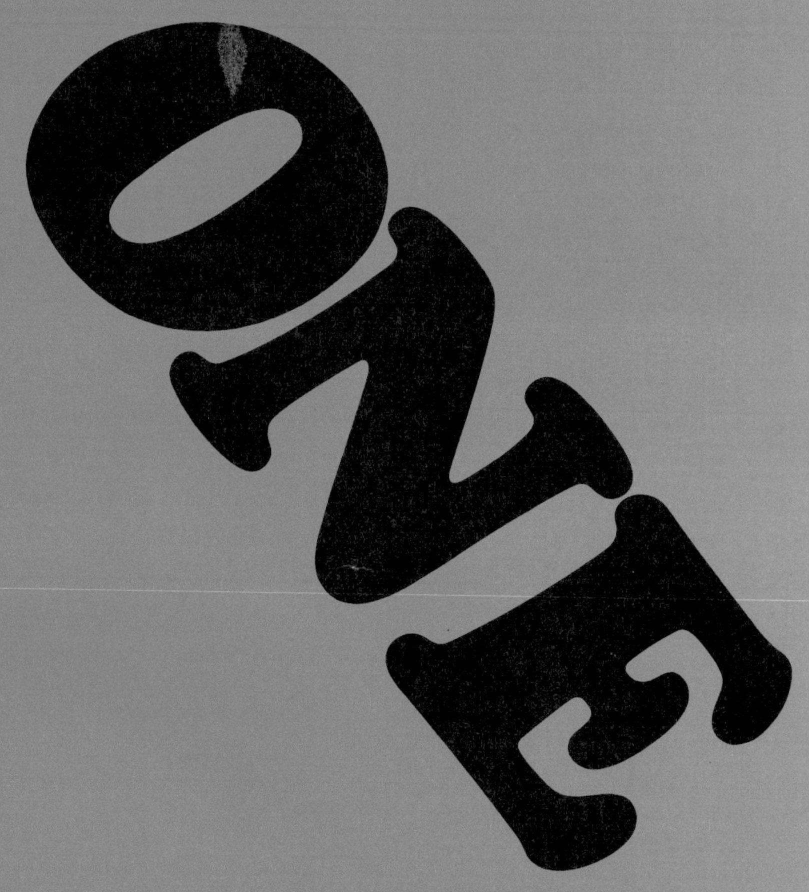

management information and data processing

1

MANAGEMENT INFORMATION VERSUS DATA PROCESSING

Data Processing

Pressures for Management Information

environmental and organizational factors

accuracy factor

timeliness and speed factors

cost factor

METHODS OF DATA HANDLING

Electronic Data Processing

COMPUTER APPLICATIONS

Basic Applications

record keeping

payroll

production scheduling

order writing

customer billing

financial accounting

inventory control

Since the beginning of time, man has manipulated data, and by using the communication methods and devices available to him, has passed useful information to other men. In ancient caves we find carved wood pictures, hieroglyphics on stone tables, and maps of battles. All illustrate man's early efforts to process and transmit information. Man recognized early the value of developing tools to help in physical and mental work. Thus, the axe became an extension of the hand by increasing the effective force of the hand; the telescope, an extension of the eye in identifying faraway objects; the bicycle, an extension of the leg; and the telephone, an extension of the ear.

As civilization progressed, man's genius for devising ways of harnessing the forces of nature, thus replacing animal power by engine power, resulted in revolutionary environmental changes, which have molded us into a highly sophisticated and technologically advanced society. During World War II, for example, scientists tested the atomic bomb and developed the ballistic missile, which now act as deterrents to outside attack; breakthroughs in electronics led to the use of radar in airports, on ships, and in advanced weapons. Since then *the electronic computer, an extension of man's brain,* has made possible a multibillion dollar space exploration program that has landed men on the moon. In the words of Whisler, "Older technologies are [an] extension of man's hands and muscles and were his tools and servants while modern information technology is an extension of man's brain and is his partner—or even his master."

One of the "marvels of the age," modern computers work so rapidly that most people are blinded with admiration for their performance; they really believe that the machines think for themselves and thus will revolutionize in some unexplained way the whole structure of business. Just how a "hunk" of metal encasing electronic circuits can accomplish this is not considered by the uninitiated. One should realize from the beginning that these machines are to be regarded as tools which aid in mental work of a repetitive and decision-making nature. They can do nothing that a human being does not instruct them to do in the first instance.

MANAGEMENT INFORMATION VERSUS DATA PROCESSING

Many computer texts loosely interchange the use of terms such as "information processing," "data processing," "management information," and the like. In the interest of clarity, it is important to recognize that the term *data* has to do with facts or informational raw materials which, when put through a specified transformation process, becomes useful information for management. *Management information* is the output of a particular data-processing operation and is intended to serve a specific purpose. In Fig. 1-1, the transformation process begins with informational raw data that are submitted to a specific processing routine, which results in management information ready to be communicated to the user.

Data Processing

Data processing, then, consists of producing and reporting meaningful information. Everybody must process data, whether performing a decision-making function as an individual, a head of a family, a student, a leader of a social or political organization, or an owner of a business—large or small. In most cases, pencil and paper have been and still are used as manual aids in problem solving. In the distant past, under a barter system, the environment in which a businessman operated did not require visual evidence of his work or elaborate mental calculations. Calculations

FIGURE 1-1. *Transformation process of data*

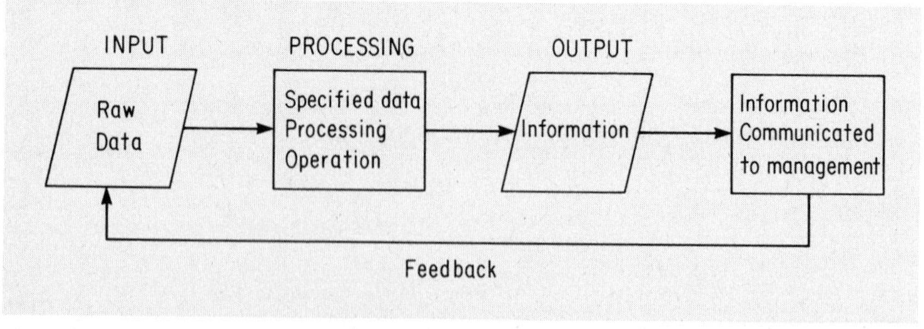

were so few that he could perform them mentally as quickly as a sophisticated computer performs electronically the greater volume of such calculations today. As communities expanded, and the barter system was replaced with monetary systems, the basis of business relationships changed also from an intimate, personal one to an impersonal one. This change required businessmen to record their activities in writing and to retain records for analysis and for future reference.

Understanding of the past often is a prerequisite to planning future endeavors and guiding men in their present actions. For example, credit buying, with its attendant need for keeping records on accounts receivable and accounts payable, illustrates one reason data processing has become so important in economies where business life is conducted primarily on the basis of "man's faith in man."

Pressures for Management Information

The competitive nature and complexity of today's business make it necessary that executives have access to the right kind of information for effective decision making.[1] Data from within and from without the firm must be processed with emphasis on accuracy, timeliness, speed, and cost. Each of these factors will be discussed briefly.

Environmental and Organizational Factors. Pressures exerted from without and from within business firms generate increased paperwork, making the use of data processing a "must." External factors include, among others, billing. Some customers purchase merchandise for cash; most purchase on account. For the latter, billing is required at the end of a specific period after adjustments, returned items, and discounts are taken into consideration. This creates assets in the form of accounts receivable on the seller's books. Suppliers, too, ship merchandise to the seller on account, creating a liability in the form of accounts payable on the books of the seller. Once received, items have to be counted and recorded. They have to be listed and checked (i.e., inventoried). The supplier has to be paid, after allowance for returned or defective merchandise (if any) and cash or quantity discounts are taken into consideration. Owners (stockholders, single proprietors, or partners), on the other hand, require periodic reports of the current status and business activities of their firms. Such information is needed to determine whether a profit is being made, which in turn guides the decision of whether to continue

[1] Managers utilize information differently, depending on their level in the organization and the task they are assigned. Upper management generally needs information for developing policies and working out long-range plans. They have more use for environmental information (about customers, suppliers, etc.), and spend more time in planning than does lower management. Given the time pressures, upper management would more likely require information presented in condensed (summarized) form. Lower management, on the other hand, needs detailed internal information for making day-to-day decisions, and spends more time in organizing and implementing the policies developed by upper management.

to operate the business, to invest more money in it, or to sell out. Quality information contributes to good decisions, which lead to successful management performance and goal achievement. Quality information is the element that holds together an ongoing organization.

In addition, the government requires a multitude of reports from business firms. Taxes have to be paid and supporting statements produced concerning realized net income, the specific tax-deductible expenses incurred, and the periodic report of Social Security payments withheld. Many other statements are also required for various reasons.

Internal factors also create the need for a host of records. Pressures within the firm necessitate the processing of all types of expenses and revenues in a predetermined order. For example, payroll and payroll taxes, revenue from sales, the updating of inventory, and the handling of receivables and payables all need processing. These and many other activities require a data-processing system efficient enough to present all necessary reports accurately and economically, with as little waste of time as possible.

ACCURACY FACTOR. Once learned, most basic steps in analyzing any transaction become routine and, consequently, require little creative thinking. However, because it is man's nature to think and make decisions when performing each step, there is a wide margin for error, especially if the steps involve some exceptions. Errors occur and perhaps multiply with prolonged work on the same application, because of carelessness, boredom, and environmental conditions such as pressure for deadlines. In common terms, the mental fatigue resulting from a repetitious clerical job can be likened to the physical fatigue resulting from a repetitious physical exercise, such as touching your toes with your hands 20 to 50 times or repeating push-up exercises 100 times.

TIMELINESS [2] AND SPEED FACTORS. In addition to the need for accurate information, effective day-to-day "on the spot" decision making requires that such information also be received on time. The business environment in the United States is one that stresses time and its cost very heavily. As a result, competition becomes more intense, because the aim of most business firms is to produce more and to produce it efficiently, that is, in less time. Firms have become quite cost conscious as a result of their interest in mass producing quality products at the lowest price possible.

COST FACTOR. The time element and timing are important, as many business organizations have abandoned price competition in favor of cost

[2] Also referred to as response time—the amount of time it takes processed information to reach its intended user. We discuss response time in Chapter 20.

competition. A business firm may be able to compete more successfully by practicing efficiency through reduction of its operating costs rather than of its retail prices. In other words, firms that are "low cost" and produce a quality product are those that are likely to command the markets for particular products. Furthermore, factors such as technological change, innovation, and growth in size and complexity justify the need for and the importance of cost control. Business data processing plays a major role in this respect by reducing the amount of time taken to produce necessary records and reports accurately and quickly in situations where volume is the rule rather than the exception.

Although it is desirable to be cost conscious in operating a business, it is also important to consider the economics of information acquisition. The computer is not necessarily the most economical means of producing management information. Given the computer's cost and size, each organization should examine its own set of needs, the managerial level at which information is needed, and its time and speed factor requirements before deciding on the type of data-processing system or, in the case of a computer, the size and level of sophistication of the computer system needed for the job.

From the foregoing, it can be concluded that, for a business to survive in a competitive system, executive decisions have to be made fairly rapidly and on as sound a basis as possible. Many "split-second" decisions are required daily. These decisions demand reliable, accurate, and concise information presented in an understandable form when needed. Because the slower manual approach is no longer considered satisfactory in meeting this demand, machines that can do significant repetitive jobs fast, with a high degree of accuracy, obviously are needed. Once this is understood, the role of high-speed computer systems in business becomes clear.

METHODS OF DATA HANDLING

Data are handled manually, by punched cards, or by electronic data-processing methods. Although the principles used in each system are essentially the same, electronic data-processing systems are not only faster but also differ in the method of data handling from punched-card systems. Although certain equipment is commonly used in both, each system uses certain other equipment peculiar to its needs. Recent developments, however, clearly indicate a significant drift from punched-card systems into electronic systems, with punched-card components used in a peripheral data-preparation capacity. The advent of the minicomputer and other related computer systems leaves no doubt that the computer is the system to adopt for producing all kinds of business information for management decision making.

In the early 1920s, the word *robot* was introduced by the Czech author Karel Čapek in his play *R.U.R.* (Rossum's Universal Robots); the word is used today to describe modern computers, because a computer under human control is capable of repeating an operation for the one hundredth time as accurately and quickly as for the first time, no matter how routine or boring it may be. Provided the source data are prepared correctly, processing them by computer can be done very quickly and with a degree of accuracy close to perfection. Otherwise, the computer comes up with inaccurate results, since it can be no more accurate than the person who prepares the data for its use. Preparation of instructions for computer processing is called *programming*. People who do it, called *programmers*, must be trained especially for the job.

Figure 1-2 outlines the work done by humans in preparing a problem and feeding relevant information to a computer system for processing. Note that the number of people needed match, approximately, the number of machines used. If these data were to be processed manually, probably about 10 or 20 times this number of people would be required, depending on the type of machines, input and output devices, or other supporting equipment available.

In explaining the work performed by computers, we need to distinguish two types of human thinking. *Creative* thinking demands imagination and insight. It is the type of thinking done by a composer when he composes a symphony or by a mathematician when he develops a new formula or theory. No definite set of rules exists for attaining such results. *Routine* thinking, on the other hand, is the habitual, perfunctory approach to performing work that is based on a definite set of rules, and requires essentially little talent other than following proper instructions. The computer is primarily designed to do this routine "thinking" in order to reserve human time and energy for creative thinking. Implied in this statement is the fact that, although computers exceed man in terms of accuracy and speed in processing data, they lack inherent advantages (such as intelligence), which makes them dependent on man for efficient functioning. Thus, for optimum output, it seems proper to expect a man–machine team effort, where each side is assigned the type of tasks for which it is best trained. Man is best at innovating and learning from his mistakes or the mistakes of others; the computer excels man in being fast, accurate, tireless, and a perfect follower of instructions. What man is good in doing acts as a limitation for the computer, and vice versa.

We have already emerged into the "thinking machine" era in which computers are *programmed* to do well what man does badly or is unable to do at all. To those who understand its makeup and characteristics, the computer has become a source of high hopes. To the uninitiated it has become a source of deep fears of being enslaved to an ultraintelligent

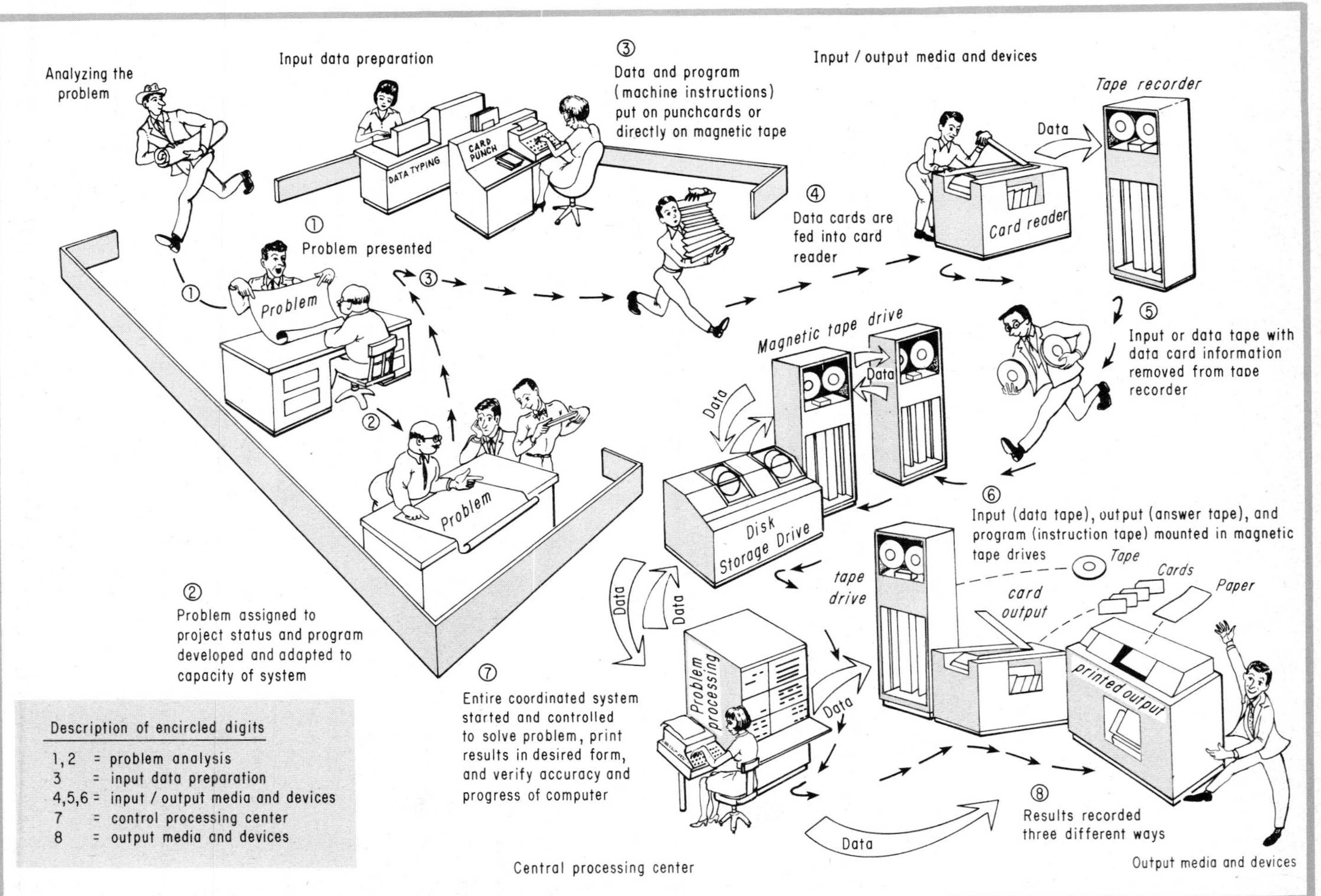
Analyzing the problem
Input data preparation
DATA TYPING
CARD PUNCH
③
Data and program (machine instructions) put on punchcards or directly on magnetic tape
Input / output media and devices
Tape recorder
Data
Card reader
④
Data cards are fed into card reader
①
Problem presented
Problem
⑤
Input or data tape with data card information removed from tape recorder
Magnetic tape drive
Data
Data
②
Problem
Disk Storage Drive
⑥
Input (data tape), output (answer tape), and program (instruction tape) mounted in magnetic tape drives
Tape
Cards
Paper
tape drive
card output
printed output
②
Problem assigned to project status and program developed and adapted to capacity of system
Data
Data
Problem processing
Data
⑦
Entire coordinated system started and controlled to solve problem, print results in desired form, and verify accuracy and progress of computer
Description of encircled digits
1,2 = problem analysis
3 = input data preparation
4,5,6 = input / output media and devices
7 = control processing center
8 = output media and devices
⑧
Results recorded three different ways
Data
Central processing center
Output media and devices
FIGURE 1-2. *Typical business application of an electronic data-processing system*

robot who would replace their productive endeavors and threaten their freedom. The human imagination and creativity used in designing and building computers go unnoticed, while the necessary impersonal numeralization and standardization of information are pointed to as "dehumanizing" the business world.

Man, the shallow sophisticate infers, has become a number at the mercy of machines.[3] However, one should realize that it is man who creates the machines, not vice versa. The "dehumanization" has been balanced by a corresponding "humanization" inherent in the construction and design of the "robots." One can reason that the effort and time that were once spent on processing data manually are now spent in devising ways, systems, and machines to process them electronically. From this viewpoint, man spends his time thinking creatively instead of routinely. Over the last century, the substitution of machines for labor has benefited human beings by creating jobs rather than allowing them to be destroyed by starvation.

Much of the terminology used to describe the component parts and functions of computers has been indiscriminately borrowed from the fields of engineering, mathematics, and psychology. Computer designers and users, for example, speak of computer "memory," computer "language," computer "logic," and even computer "intelligence." Adoption of such terms may lead to confusion and misunderstanding, as it is unlikely that computers can be transformed into humans merely by believing and describing them in terms of human qualities. As mentioned earlier, a computer's main role is to do well those chores that man does poorly or is unable to do at all. Unless we are careful in the way we name computer activities and operations, we could very well underestimate their potential and confound their role with that of man.

COMPUTER APPLICATIONS

Asking what the computer does is like asking where the automobile can go. Since the early 1950s when computers became commercially available, hundreds of applications have been developed in virtually every field. In fact, there are enough currently operational applications to fill a

[3] The theory that computers contributed to mental illness by the depersonalization effect of numbers was recently tested and appeared to be unsubstantiated. A leading psychologist at the UCLA Neuropsychiatric Institute reported that disturbed people do not seem to have fantasies about computers (in spite of the threats of depersonalization and "magic brains"), probably because they still know very little about them. Doctors, however, are believed to have a phobia about computers dehumanizing conventional diagnosis. Even after orientation lectures, many doctors still fail to realize that computers are programmed by humans and are used primarily to aid and not to replace man.

large volume. Some of the key business applications[4] are (1) basic applications, (2) management decision making, and (3) real-time applications.

Basic Applications

RECORD KEEPING. Cognizant of the expenditure of large sums for maintaining and updating various records, business organizations earmark a substantial portion of computer time for record processing and maintenance.

PAYROLL. In payroll, for example, a computer uses payroll data in allocating and distributing various costs among selected projects or among the departments involved.

PRODUCTION SCHEDULING. The computer determines the number of men needed, the required raw materials, and the loading requirements of each machine. The goal is to develop a production schedule that will minimize cost and provide the best allocation of the available human and material resources.

ORDER WRITING. A computer can be programmed to prepare several copies of shipping orders from data available in sales orders. One copy goes to the order picker, a second is packed with the shipment, and a third is mailed to the customer, acknowledging the receipt of the order.

CUSTOMER BILLING. When the status of thousands of accounts must be updated daily and the speed of receiving cash owed by the customer determines the amount of purchases the company can make, the use of the computer is an absolute necessity.

FINANCIAL ACCOUNTING. Financial accounting is processed by a computer at a slightly higher cost than traditional accounting methods. Materials, personnel time, and other charges are keypunched, sorted, and posted in the required formal ledgers.

[4] Other business applications include (1) sales forecasting and control (ideal for the marketing department), (2) a general ledger system, where the computer handles the printout of journal entries, profit and loss statements, balance sheets, etc., (3) cost accounting routines involving computerized reports on production cost (by product, by department, or by division), manpower cost allocation and analysis, etc., and (4) assignments for a given assembly line, which determines labor, material, and equipment requirements for the company's products, and produces follow-up cost information that is feedback to management.

Inventory Control. Inventory control involves handling of receipts and disbursements of inventory items on hand, as well as computation of their cost. A computer system is used to record and account for incoming and outgoing items, to keep continuous track of the items on hand, and to compute current stock levels, safety stock demands, and optimal order size. An automated inventory control has been credited with altering the elements leading to the high and low points in the economic cycle. It results in reduction in the average inventory level and substantial capital saving.

Inventory management faces constant functional changes that result from production, sales, and customer demands. These changes are met by (1) developing centralized inventory control routines, with emphasis on statistical analysis for more accurate forecasting, and (2) establishing systems that aid in developing relationships between financial, marketing, production, and inventory activities. Some systems are used in forecasting short-term variations in consumer demand, in determining economic order quantities, and in resource allocation. The system simulates inventory levels, and determines the location and number of additional required warehouses for a given time period.

Management Decision Making

Linear Programming. Linear programming is commonly used in many organizations as a quantitative approach for finding an optimum solution (such as minimizing costs or maximizing profits) to specific problems. Given the resources, requirements, and their constraints, the relationship among these factors is expressed in terms of a set of linear equations. The equations can then be solved to determine the outcome of any combination of requirements.

Linear programming is used in solving a wide range of problems. Industrial plants, for example, must schedule their machines or production lines to meet their share of the market demand. Bus lines program movements of buses and drivers according to predetermined bus schedules. In such problems, the primary goal is to attain the desired level of efficiency by minimizing the cost of meeting the demand. The more successful the company is in controlling cost, the more likely it will be able to survive its competition and pursue its growth objectives.

Simulation. Classic applications (e.g., inventory control or customer billing) generally work with a clearly defined problem, available input data, and known cause-and-effect relationships. Many business problems, however, do not quite provide clear-cut information with known cause-and-effect relationships for processing. Lack of knowledge of the variables involved often makes it impossible to proceed in developing such projects as building a plant or mass producing a giant passenger airliner. To minimize risks, then, a *simulation* (model representation) of the essence of the project is initially constructed. The model can be physical (e.g., an airplane) or mathematical (a set of equations is developed to study a given system).

In computer-oriented simulation, years of operation can be evaluated in a matter of minutes. Thus, this technique offers a basis for "low-cost" decisions and wise planning for projects that often involve millions of dollars in potential investments. To initiate a simulation routine, the problem is defined and the relationships among key variables are established. Since the designer is working with a model rather than a real situation, certain assumptions governing the relationships incorporated in the model are spelled out, and all possible factors, major and minor, are also considered. The closer the model approaches reality, the more accurate and reliable the results will be.

The airlines are among the established industries that rely on simulation in many areas of endeavor. Simulation, for instance, helps airlines in training pilots. Over $1 million has been spent on one flight simulator. Each simulator consists of a cockpit (showing an airport and its runway) and all necessary controls. A computer makes the controls react as they would in a real airplane. Airlines have also used simulation in purchasing new planes and planning new routes. A computer is fed key specifications (such as weight, fuel consumption, and overall performance within the flight patterns of the existing make), operating maintenance and overhaul costs, out-of-pocket depreciation, and other predictable expenses to be incurred throughout the life span of the aircraft. The final printout tells management about the economy of the plane, the break-even point, and other related figures needed for final decisions.

Thus, simulation by computer provides a wide range of answers to real problems that cannot be effectively worked out in real life. It is used to model projects ranging from computer construction to railroads, warehouses, and production lines in many industries. To perform such simulation studies, special languages have been developed. The most commonly used languages are General Purpose Simulation System (GPSS) and SIMSCRIPT. Designed by IBM, GPSS is a language that lessens programming effort, is easy to learn and use, and is available on most currently used computers. The cost of doing a simulation study using this language varies with the complexity of the problem, but can easily exceed $10,000. This estimate includes the cost of data collection, development of the basic model, and computer running time.

One of the most powerful simulation languages is SIMSCRIPT. Developed in 1963 by The RAND Corporation under the sponsorship of the U.S. Air Force, it was first used in simulating aircraft maintenance routines; since then several versions have evolved into SIMSCRIPT I.5, SIMSCRIPT II, and SIMSCRIPT II PLUS. Unlike GPSS, this language allows itself to be tailored to the system, but requires more programming knowledge and effort. The analyst studies the proposed system by running the model as it exists over a simulated run time. He then introduces change in the logic aspects of the model and observes the effects. He continues this routine until the model runs as anticipated.

PROJECT MANAGEMENT (CPM AND PERT). When large-scale construction projects are planned, some form of control over their progress becomes mandatory. With a given deadline, the relationship of a project's many interdependent activities requires a way of measuring the progress of the activities performed and finding the *critical path* of those activities.

Project management involves the use of CPM (critical-path method) and PERT (program evaluation and review technique), which are graphical approaches to planning large development and construction projects. PERT was originally developed by the Defense Department to measure project progress, and received wide publicity after it was successfully used in the development of the Polaris Weapon System. The technique kept tabs on the progress of contractors, subcontractors, and system managers. Although some authors refer to CPM as emphasizing the activities and PERT the events, in practice the distinction has all but disappeared. Therefore, PERT is used here to refer to the entire task, and the *critical path* is shown to indicate its importance in the PERT network.

Figure 1-3 shows five alternative paths to the end event. The time unit (duration) for this analysis may be the number of hours, days, weeks, months, or years, whichever is appropriate. The critical path, shown by the heavy line, indicates the route through the PERT network that takes the most time.

FIGURE 1-3. PERT network with activity durations entered for each activity. Critical path is shown in heavy arrows

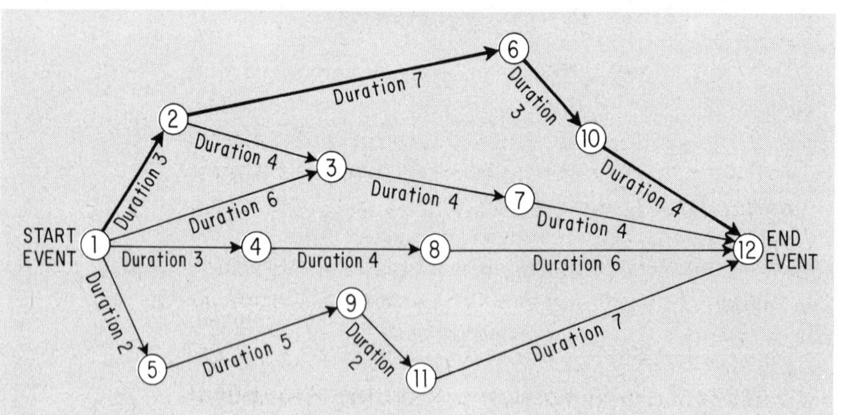

In developing a PERT network, the following items are basic:

1. Each individual task must be shown in the network as comprising both activity and event.
2. Successor events are completed only after predecessor events have been handled.
3. The time interval can be only an estimate, since most episodes in real life are based on decisions made under some degree of uncertainty. It is preferred that someone familiar with the activity make the time estimate.
4. Computer programs may be used for analyzing activities in order to compute the critical path and its subcritical paths.

MANAGEMENT GAMES. A management game is a small-scale simulation of the decisions made in a real-life business situation. Many educational institutions require their business students to participate in a management game to help them understand better the interrelationships among key business areas (such as accounting, finance, marketing and production), and to integrate what they have learned into a high-level management viewpoint. Likewise, large organizations use the game as an effective tool in their executive-development programs for the same purposes. Complex games are normally played with the assistance of the computer for handling the required calculations.

To play the game, several teams represent the management of hypothetical companies. Each team is given information about its company, its assets, and production details. The management decisions to be made may relate to product pricing, volume of production, sales volume, and so forth. The objective is to improve the competitive standing of the team's company in relationship to the other companies represented in the game. When decisions are made, they are fed into a program-controlled computer system, which prints out the results of each team's decision or decisions. Repetitive feedback from the different decisions fed into the computer should help each team improve its decision-making ability or competitive techniques.

COMPUTER-ASSISTED INFORMATION STORAGE AND RETRIEVAL. The increasing complexity of our socioeconomic environment and the masses of information generated daily in scientific and business operations suggest an urgent need for an efficient and rapid systematic method of collecting, storing, and providing access to information of various types. The development of larger and faster computers, low-cost mass-information storage devices, and efficient input–output display terminals, such as the cathode-ray tube display stations, has had a profound impact on the information storage and retrieval effort.

Unlike a traditional data-processing system, the computer-assisted information-retrieval system is a responsive system; it responds to the user's inquiries about the available collected data.[5] Factors that should be considered regarding the use of an information-retrieval system include frequency of use, ease of access, and safeguards against possible duplication of information. To facilitate information storage and the use of an information system, especially one that contains large volumes of information, the system involved is expected to have direct-access devices that would provide random-access features and high-speed access. In doing so, not only can management be provided with a greater amount of information on a selective basis, but also with better information for decision making.

The development of new classification and indexing [6] techniques now permits selected information to be arranged in mass-storage devices in a format more amenable to interaction with the users. The availability of sophisticated input–output display terminals and time-sharing systems means that interaction between man and the machine is now more feasible and, indeed, vital for the proper responsiveness of the retrieval system.

Information retrieval is more widely used in scientific than in business areas. Transcribing and storing original documents in a form understandable to the computer is costly. In the use of a computer for information retrieval, the file containing the original documents must first be referenced through an abstract, which, in turn, identifies the location of the file. The computer then retrieves the original document from the file and prints out a copy. However, the computer retrieves only those documents that fit the exact description. Such inflexibility, added to the high cost of information storage and abstract preparation, discourages many business concerns from setting up a full-fledged information-retrieval system. Further development of current mass-storage devices and better use of microfilm could expand the use of such a system and justify the investment.

MANAGEMENT INFORMATION SYSTEM. As computers continue to demonstrate their utility in the business environment, management looks expectantly to the future. Advances in computer technology, such as multiprogramming, multiprocessing, real-time and time-sharing capability, and practical mass-storage devices, have increased management expectations as to what can be done with computers.

[5] For example, a life insurance user may ask, "What information is available regarding the number of deaths from lung cancer in the state of Kentucky?" To answer the question, a computer searches an index file (abstracts on original documents prepared and stored in advance) for such terms as "deaths," "lung cancer," and "Kentucky." The entry that contains all these terms is identified, or a printout is made of the original documents stored in the file.

[6] An index is used here to refer to a shorthand representation of the original information, which assists in the location of a given transaction or record. It is generally made up as an index term that describes the record and a record address that identifies the storage location of the record in the files.

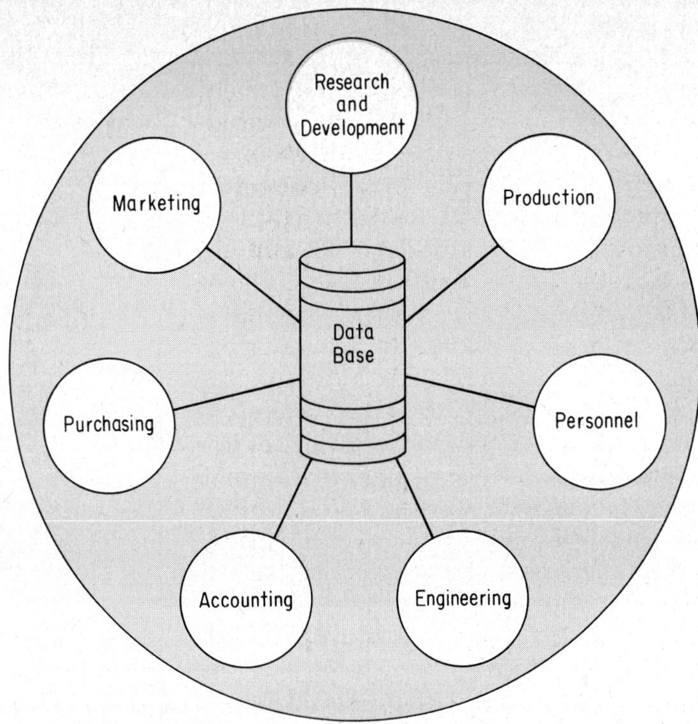

FIGURE 1-4. Computer-based management information system

One particular development receiving widespread attention is the *management information system (MIS)*—an all-inclusive computer-based information system designed to provide instantly the information that management needs for effective decision making. To do so, it must operate in a real-time mode. That is, data must be processed as received and in time to affect a decision (Fig. 1-4).

The *data base*, a major component of MIS, is an area containing all the information and decision rules used by a business organization, in a format applicable to any user's needs and immediately available when needed. The job of assembling in a single location all pertinent information used by a given organization poses great difficulty, since it involves detailed analysis of that organization.

In addition to a data base, other characteristics of MIS include

1. Instant recording of business transactions and incidental changes in the data.
2. Regular evaluation and monitoring of the events (internal as well as external) and the elements that have a bearing on the existing data.
3. Man–machine interaction available for looking into possible relationships in the existing files.
4. The availability of periodic reports and special informational reports when needed.

Although the idea underlying MIS is feasible, system designers face several hurdles. First, each managerial level has certain expectations and requires information unique to that level. For example, upper management requires information related to the organization's competitors and environment in general for modifying existing policies and developing strategies for future action. The type of information needed at that level is quite different from middle management's need for in-house information to help implement existing policies. The need of lower management (foreman, first line supervisor, etc.) for detailed information affecting their particular departments represents another level.

In addition to the complex problem of providing information to serve each managerial level, a computer-based MIS system is also expected to provide specialized information to managers according to their areas of concentration. For example, a production manager may require specialized information about the availability of raw materials, the status of certain material in stock, the volume of production at a given moment in time, and any sales activity that might have a bearing on his decision to maintain a desired production capacity. This type of information is naturally different from information needed by the personnel manager, the sales manager, and others in the organization.

Thus, an ideal all-inclusive management data base should be designed to serve management regardless of the level of responsibility or area of concentration. To do so means to build in great flexibility, a task so intricate and time consuming that by the time the system is operational it would probably be out of date.

For larger organizations, MIS invariably requires large, high-speed computers with mass auxiliary storage devices and real-time input–output capability.

Real-Time Applications

Real-time applications pertain to situations where the computer produces given results almost instantaneously, allowing immediate control over the project under study. One early use of real-time programs was in monitoring the performance of astronauts at every phase and every stage of their flight. This allows instant decisions to be made to minimize wide deviations from the planned course and to correct likely errors, a flexibility that is not possible if any other computational technique is used.

Most airlines handle reservations on a real-time basis. Passenger specifications (e.g., early Friday morning, first class, nonstop jet flight from Chicago to New York) are entered into a keyboard by the receiving branch. The central computer system receives the messages, checks the status of the closest flight, searches for available seats, verifies, and reserves a space for the customer in a matter of seconds.

Another interesting real-time application involves a "talking" computer that answers stock data inquiries. In the spring of 1965, the Quotation Service of the New York Stock Exchange's Market Data System installed an IBM computer system to aid subscribers in receiving instantaneous data on stock prices, quotations, and volume via telephone. For information regarding a given stock, the broker dials a four-digit number that connects him with the computer system. The computer searches for the data and collects the answer from a *voice answer back* unit, which stores a 126-word vocabulary on a recording drum. Additional information can be obtained by adding 3 to the first four-digit code. For example, if the code of the stock involved is 5427 and the broker desires more information on it, he dials 8427.

In the summer of 1967, a part of the first meeting of the Congress on Medical Electronics and Biological Engineering produce a first in intercontinental medical communications. Two electrocardiographs were recorded in Tours, France, and were transmitted (by RCA communication channels, via satellite) to the computer complex at the U.S. Health Service's medical systems development laboratory in Washington, D.C.; minutes later, the findings were relayed back to Tours.

Some Areas of Computer Use

EDUCATION (COMPUTER-ASSISTED INSTRUCTION). The educational system's growing complexity and class size, and the divergent aptitude and achievement levels, background, and capabilities of students, make it difficult for the traditional instructor to reach all students and meet their needs satisfactorily.[7] Consequently, a lecture geared to the slow learner tends to frustrate the more intelligent learner, and vice versa. The *computer-assisted instruction (CAI)* method uses the computer to tutor a a number of students working simultaneously at specialized input–output display terminals,[8] where they interact independently with the computer on a self-paced basis. The scheduling of computerized lessons is not limited by the presence of the instructor.

A typical lesson begins with a short tutorial section at the student's level, followed by problems and questions on the material covered. The student's answer is graded for conceptual validity and computational accuracy; if it is correct, the computer presents the next, higher-level text, and so on, until the lesson is completed. Otherwise, a remedial section of greater depth and clarity is presented for better understanding of the subject matter.

[7] Other weaknesses of the traditional instructional approach include the instructor's limited background in certain areas, his occasional poor preparation of the assigned material, and his prejudices and subjectivities.

[8] The most basic terminal used is the low-cost teletypewriter. The lesson is presented as a printed alphanumeric set of lines; student responses are entered through the keyboard. A more effective terminal is the graphic display unit with light pen, a keyboard, an audio tape feature, and an image projector.

In preparing CAI lessons,[9] several specialists are involved. The subject-matter expert specifies the lesson text and associated problems; the educational psychologist works on developing the supportive teaching strategies; the programmer converts the lesson details and the accompanying problems into appropriate computer language; and an evaluation expert (or a team) pretests the complete system for validity and reliability before it becomes available to students.

The CAI endeavor today is a small segment of the total CAI market. Approximately 1,000 CAI systems are already in operation[10] at public school systems and various military and industrial training facilities. Some obstacles to CAI are operational costs, the restricted processing performance of the equipment when interacting with the student, fear of change and reduction of personnel, lack of high-quality lesson material, and the need to secure the support of educators for its wide-scale adoption. Once adequate funds become available and the obstacles are removed, education will be available to thousands of citizens through terminals in the home, school, and industry.

MEDICINE. Great advances have been made in the field of medicine through computers. Physicians can now diagnose, test, and evaluate various human ailments by computer. Recently, an entire poison control center has been computerized. When an emergency poison case arrives in the hospital, a nurse keys in the suspected brand of poison, and within seconds a computer located in a remote area transmits pertinent information for treatment. Another health center uses a computer program designed to predict a potential health problem for an individual based on the profile information he submits in advance. El Camino hospital in Mountain View, California, installed terminals and printers at strategic locations throughout the hospital into which doctors, nurses, and administrative personnel feed medical information to update patients' records.

Medicine is a major industry with a real need for the kind of services offered by computers. In 1970, less than 10 percent of the approximately 8,600 hospitals in this country had computers, and they were used primarily for traditional business applications. No major efforts were made for developing the types of applications that would automate the information-handling details connected with the patient and his doctor. One major obstacle is the language barrier between doctors in general and the computer specialist; another is the doctors' inherent distrust in com-

[9] CAI lessons are generally classified either as tutorial, drill, or dialogue. A tutorial lesson usually serves students in engineering, mathematics, accounting, economics, medicine, and languages. A drill lesson is prepared for those in language skills. A dialogue lesson is geared for industrial training, medical, and military programs. Special lessons have even been written to help handicapped students.

[10] The three largest CAI systems in use today are the ARPANET system, supported by the Department of Defense, the PLATO system at the University of Illinois, and the TICCIT system at the Mitre Corporation. The last two systems are subsidized by the National Science Foundation.

municating vital medical data to computers. An obvious remedy would be to educate each group about the needs and area of specialization of the other.

GOVERNMENT OF THE PEOPLE, FOR THE PEOPLE, BY THE COMPUTER. The government and its associated substructure have applied the computer to applications ranging from budget control to aerospace techniques.[11] On the local level, for instance, early in 1970, an Eastern state developed a computer-assisted management system to analyze expenditures by function rather than by department. The state and local government is a $100 billion per year industry. Budgets now can be functionally oriented, with each department's budget dependent on the public services it performs. Consequently, the departments should operate with the efficiency and cost effectiveness of a private enterprise, since the intended computer plan is to determine what service is provided and the cost of each service. Once known, loopholes and unnecessary expenditures can be eliminated.

In aerospace techniques, the role of the computer is obvious. Since the inception of the space program, thousands of technical organizations and scientists have pooled their talents and efforts to explore outer space and put a man on the moon. Christopher C. Kraft, Jr., Director of Flight Operations at the NASA Manned Spacecraft Center, has remarked:

> If I had to single out the piece of equipment that, more than any other, has allowed us to go from earth-orbit Mercury flights to Apollo-linear trips in just over seven years, it would be the high-speed computer.

The initial mathematical calculations for the space effort were phenomenal and would have required hundreds of man-years of manual effort. In fact, no space flight would have been possible without the split-second calculations necessary for maintaining a 25,000-mph spacecraft on course.

THE COMPUTER INDUSTRY

Computer Growth

Technological changes over the past two decades have been most obvious in the computer's capacity to handle voluminous data at high speed, which has resulted in a growing demand for computer installations.

[11] The government constituted the second largest computer user in the late 1960s. Production firms, government agencies at the federal, state, and local levels, and insurance and financial firms make up roughly 65 percent of the total computer users. Educational institutions, transportation firms, and public utilities represent 25 percent; the balance is represented by retail firms, mining, construction, and others.

Year	Number of Computer Systems Installed	Average Sale Price	Percentage of 1951 Sale Price	Average Cost per 1 million Calculations($)	Total Cost of Writing Program Instruction($)
1951	10	3,000,000	100.0	250.00	NA
1953	50	2,750,000	91.8	250.00	4.00 (est)
1955	244	2,250,000	75.0	165.00	4.20
1959	3,000	1,225,000	41.8	20.00	4.50
1965	23,000	700,000	23.3	2.75	5.50
1969	59,500	400,000	13.3	0.25	6.75
1971	82,000	375,000	12.5	0.10	7.30
1972	100,420	350,000	11.7	0.09	7.50
1975 (est.)	150,000	300,000	10.0	0.08	8.00

FIGURE 1-5. Decreasing cost of computers and computation

In the early 1950s, first-generation computers processed data at millisecond (one thousandth of a second) speeds, whereas in the early 1960s, second-generation computers operated in the microsecond (one millionth of a second) range. Since 1965, third-generation and other computers have been operating at nanosecond (one billionth of a second) speeds, 900 times faster than the first-generation models. Advanced computers in the third- and fourth-generation [12] category can process data at nanosecond and even picosecond (one trillionth of a second) speeds. Increased speed of calculation has resulted in lower computation costs, and the larger production volumes of computers of various sizes [13] has resulted in a lower sale price per component, as shown in Fig. 1-5.

The general factors indicated in Fig. 1-5 are as follows:

1. The number of computer installations has increased from 10 systems in 1951 to a staggering 82,000 installations in 1971, to 100,420 installations in 1972, and an estimated 150,000 in 1975.[14] Com-

[12] The generation progression is applied arbitrarily by the computer industry. For example, although the new IBM 370 and the Burroughs 7600 systems are not claimed by either company as exclusively fourth-generation systems, these new lines have been received in many quarters of industry as a new generation of computer systems.

[13] Computer sizes have also changed. The primary computer storage area holds program instruction and the data to be worked on. In first-generation computers, primary storage capacity was 4,000 words or less; in second-generation computers, it was up to 30,000 words; and in third-generation computers, upward of 100,000 words. The larger fourth-generation computers are capable of storing over 1 million words in primary storage.

[14] On an international level, U.S. computer manufacturers and their subsidiaries have 85.1 percent of the free-world computer market, followed by West Europe (8.3 percent) and Japan (6.6 percent). Of the U.S. share, IBM has installeed 55 percent of the total U.S. computers, followed by Univac, Burroughs, Control Data, National Cash Register, Honeywell, and Xerox Data systems. Source: *Infosystems,* March 1973, pp. 56–59.

puter installations in 1971 and 1972 are broken down by size as follows [15]:

Computer Size	1971	1972	Percentage Increase	Percentage of Total 1971	1972
Minicomputer	33,020	53,895	63.2	40.3	53.7
Small	36,636	29,252	20.2 dec.	44.7	29.1
Medium	10,645	14,872	39.7	13.0	14.8
Large	1,680	2,401	42.9	2.0	2.4
Total	80,981	100,420	22.5	100.0	100.0

It should be noted that minicomputer installations lead other systems in the number and percentage of increase in installations. They rose 64 percent in 1972 over 1971 and account for 54 percent of the total installations in 1972, compared to 40 percent in 1971. By contrast, small computer installations decreased 20 percent in 1972 over 1971 and represent 29 percent of the total installations in 1972, compared to 44.7 percent in 1971.

2. Although the number of computers has increased, the average price of each computer has decreased. The average price of a computer dropped from $3 million in 1951 to around $350,000 in 1972; $300,000 is estimated for 1975, 10 percent of the price of the 1951 computer.
3. A decrease in the price of computers and a steady increase in their processing speeds mean a proportionate decrease in the cost of computation. It cost, on the average, $250 per 1 million calculations on the 1951 computers, compared to 9 cents on today's computer. For these calculations to be performed manually, it would cost approximately $5,500, signifying the tremendous cost effectiveness of today's computer.

Given the total cost of a computer installation, the use of computers, then, should result in greater cost effectiveness, the greater the volume, through expected reduction in handling, administrative, and other related costs. Figure 1-6 illustrates the relative economic advantage of computers compared to manual or punched-card systems. Intersection point A' indicates the break-even total cost of processing volume A through manual and computer systems. According to the chart, it would be more economical to process manually when the volume is below A. Similarly, intersection point B' indicates the break-even total cost of processing volume B through punched-card and computer systems. If processing volume is below B (but above C), a punched-card system

[15] Source: Diebold Computer Census published in part by *The Office*, Feb. 1973, p. 64.

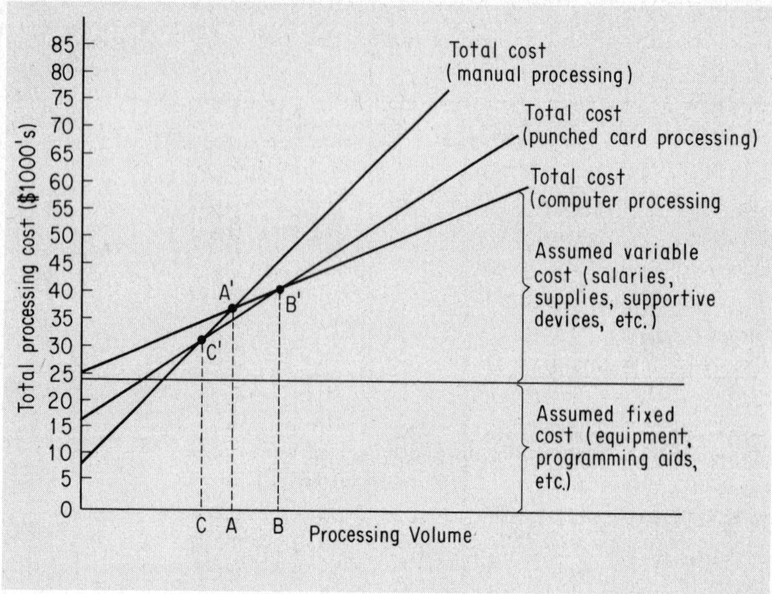

FIGURE 1-6. Cost effectiveness of processing methods—a hypothetical example

would be more economical. Processing volume above *B* favors the computer method.

4. While the average cost of computation has decreased, the total cost of writing one computer instruction has steadily increased. As shown in Fig. 1-5, the total cost of writing a computer instruction has increased from $4 in 1953 to an estimated $7.65 in 1973, and can be expected to reach $8 per instruction by 1975. The primary reasons for this increase are (a) the rising cost of skilled labor, and (b) the excess of demand over supply of qualified designers and programmers, especially to work with the latest equipment. These two factors prompted a large insurance company to seek and hire systems talent from England to fill 27 openings in its systems planning department.

The cost of programming and systems analysis will continue to rise unless improved technology, better ways of using current technology, or more sophisticated systems analysis methods are developed. Such a possibility is unlikely to materialize before the mid- or late 1970s.

Bridging the Generation Gap

In the past, a switchover from a computer of one generation to one of another often required major modifications in existing applications programs for proper compatibility with the newer system. More recently, manufacturers of third- and fourth-generation computers have built their systems so that they are hardware compatible (language instructions of one computer are accepted for execution by another computer) and software[16] compatible (a higher-level computer program of a computer is accepted by another computer with little or no modification). For example, the IBM 360 user who is switching to the newer IBM 370 system can use many of the existing programs in the latter system without any change.

In addition to compatibility between computers of a given manufacturer, an increasing number of computer makers are designing their systems tc be compatible with systems produced by others. The user now can drop one computer make in preference to another without a major rewrite of or modification in existing programs. This freedom of choice also means that the user need not feel tied to the manufacturer of his existing system for a more advanced replacement. Furthermore, IBM's unbundling policy, in effect since January 1970, means that the user is no longer limited in his choice of software and supportive services, which were once provided in the computer manufacturer's "bundle." A system can be designed to include components made by different manufacturers and can be operated without any difficulty by software provided by an independent agency.

The Seething Seventies—An Outlook

When viewing the computer industry in restrospect, one is justified in referring to the past two decades as the *Revolutionary Fifties* and the *Sensational Sixties*. The advent of the electronic computer in the 1950s brought revolutionary changes in commercial operations and the manner in which managers made their key decisions. The 1960s brought a major change—a transition from second- to third-generation equipment with sensational increases in the speed and number of computers in operation, while the price of many computers dropped below $5,000. Over 70 percent of the approximately 115,000 computers in operation today were installed in the 1960s. Administrative managers were exposed to and shared responsibility over data-processing operations. The 1960s indeed gave us unique and powerful tools and transformed our jobs and thinking in ways that we still cannot fully grasp.

With the introduction of the fourth-generation series of computers, the minicomputer, and many other expected developments, it seems appropriate to refer to this decade as the *Seething Seventies*. Among the key expected developments are the following:

1. *Data transmission via satellite,* by which organizations will exchange operating data with affiliating organizations and provide government agencies pertinent reports.

[16] Software refers to programs and supportive aids that are needed for computer processing; hardware refers to physical components making up the computer. Software is explained further in the latter part of Chapter 4.

2. *Cryogenics,* which reduces the sensitivity of computers by controlling their temperature close to absolute zero.
3. *Fluidic computers,* which are expected to be cheaper and easier to maintain, will use fluid instead of electronic circuits.
4. *Various types of terminals,* which would allow virtually every user to have direct access to a computer.
5. A *laser computer,* capable of processing data at 10 trillion bits per second.
6. *Electro-optical memories,* to be made from a layer of a thin rare-earth ferroelectrical crystalline material, will be capable of erasing data and changing their condition at the speed of light.
7. A *microcomputer,* which has up to 16,000 words of storage on a single chip. Much progress has been made toward its development. Commercially available units should be on the market before 1980, selling under $50. Such a pocket-sized computer would be as common as the typewriter, and would deemphasize the need to teach students the operating mechanics of arithmetic in favor of training in "thought" mechanics in solving problems at all levels. The microcomputer could serve as a credit card, storing a customer's credit history, which would then be available when making purchases. The idea underlying computer miniaturization is beginning to appear in automobiles for monitoring the performance of critical components, and microcomputers could soon appear as the integral monitor in devices such as television, kitchen appliances, and clothes washers. They could also be programmed to monitor cleaning and maintenance chores, keep track of home improvement expenses, record all kinds of tax-deductible bills and details, tutor children during specified periods, and record and even answer telephone messages by voice-response touch-tone.

The 1970s should also produce electronic instead of embossed credit cards, designed to activate terminals that would feed into fund-transfer computers. The computer would have the account number and other details of customer records. It could allow a customer in a given bank to transfer money to pay a retailer whose account is in a different bank. This method would make obsolete today's clearing-house methods. Although fund-transfer terminals are available today, they are not capable of being activated by an electronic card.

In a continuing effort to acquire information quicker and cheaper, the "talking computer" is beginning to take roots. Sometimes called a voice-response system or audio response, this relatively unique approach is the answer to accurate and fast information retrieval. Speed of acquisition is as fast as the human voice. The system consists mainly of a 12-button phone and a speaker, which responds with a human voice to a dialed number. It is suitable primarily for short interrogations, and several banks use it for inquiring about the status of loans, checking accounts, and mortgage transactions. Retailers can use it to provide a

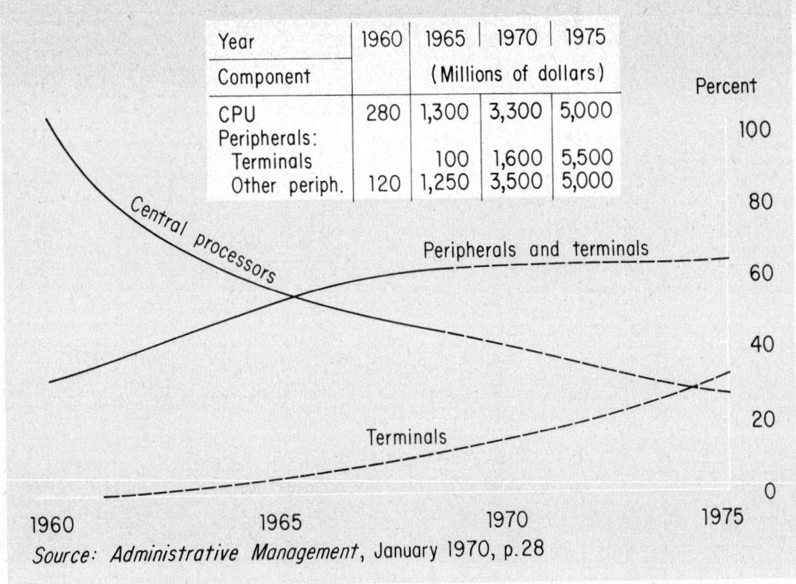

Year	1960	1965	1970	1975
Component	(Millions of dollars)			
CPU	280	1,300	3,300	5,000
Peripherals:				
Terminals		100	1,600	5,500
Other periph.	120	1,250	3,500	5,000

FIGURE 1-7. Projection of hardware components as a percentage of the total system cost

private answer concerning slow-paying credit customers or misuse of credit cards. The job is done cheaply, quickly, and continuously.

The talking computer has been available since the early 1960s, but only recently has it been gaining popularity. The main objections to its use are (1) the accessibility of received information to the worker in charge of the system, and (2) the limited speech capacity (50 to 2,000 words) of most systems. How fast the market grows depends on how quickly the users accept its unique advantages.

The foregoing predictions are partly substantiated by the steady, increased investment in data terminals and peripherals over central processors (Fig. 1-7). Although by 1975 we anticipate twice the volume of today's computer-related sales, the value of peripherals and terminals is expected to be double that of central processors, and the number of terminals is expected to be close to 2 million units (valued at approximately $5½ billion) and to account for one half the total peripheral market. Items such as the television-like cathode-ray tube (CRT) display terminal will be as common in business as are typewriters or dictating machines today. Only 10 years ago the computer industry was a $1 billion industry with an average delivery of 1,000 computer systems per year. In 1970 the industry delivered close to 20,000 computer systems, and by 1975 deliveries are expected to reach 45,000 units annually.

In all, it can be safely concluded that, unlike the 1950s, the 1970s will bring changes in computers that are profound, but more evolutionary than revolutionary, with emphasis on communication more than on computational capabilities, and on the individual and his information needs. The businessman can turn to pictorial rather than printed representation of the data he needs. Thus, the visual display terminal with its multiaccess facilities represents a major breakthrough in computer technology by enabling man to interact with the machine more directly and effectively, and in a manner unmatched to date. But, with all that, man is still considered the master, and the computer, the spearhead of the information revolution, the slave.

SUMMARY

In this chapter we have presented an overview of data processing. Data were distinguished from information, in that they are the informational raw material which, through a processing routine, are transformed into information for management use. Data processing consists of producing and reporting meaningful information.

As an operating system, an ongoing organization receives inputs and encounters pressures from its environment as well as from within. Considering the timing and competitive factors surrounding their decisions, management finds it increasingly important to have immediate access to accurate, reliable, and concise information for effective decision making. The time allotted to management for reacting to events is constantly shrinking, and, considering the accelerated level of risk accompanying each decision, the commitment to use a computer is made with the expectation that the system will be capable of producing quality information accurately, economically, and at the time it is needed.

Data are handled manually, by a punched-card system, or by electronic computers. The method used depends on the company's size, the number of applications that involve repetitive computation, the volume of activities in each application, and management's response-time requirements for certain information. Although more and more organizations are switching from noncomputer to computer systems, the trend in itself is not necessarily an indication that the computer is the solution to all problems. Each organization should evaluate its own needs and determine its requirements before deciding on committing its resources to a computer system of any size.

In explaining the work performed by computers, a distinction was made between routine and creative thinking. A computer's primary role is to handle the routine phase of man's tasks. Consequently, man can apply his creative abilities to contribute to the organization's present and future growth plans.

Basic, advanced, and real-time computer applications were briefly discussed. Among the basic applications are record keeping, payroll, production scheduling, order writing, customer billing, and financial accounting. Advanced applications include linear programming, project management (critical-path analysis), simulation, information retrieval, and management information systems.

Among the general areas of computer use are (1) education, where computer-assisted instruction is gaining in popularity. The student's interaction with the computer when learning well-programmed lessons in his area of interest is generally far superior and more effective than the traditional instructor–student relationship, especially in large classes; (2) medicine, for diagnosing, testing, and evaluating various human ailments. Medicine is a major industry, but only in the past few years has it begun to adopt and apply the use of computers to serve its needs. Bridging the communication gap between the doctor and the computer professional is needed for proper functioning; (3) government, where the computer has been successful in analyzing expenditures at the federal, state, and local levels. Of significance is the direct, positive contribution of computers to putting man on the moon.

The computer industry is a growing industry. New and more advanced computer systems continue to appear on the market. Technological breakthroughs contributed to the steady decrease in the cost of producing computers and to their miniaturization. The availability of the microcomputer at below $50 is expected by 1980.

The 1970s have been seething with computer developments that promise to improve man's lot and contribute to his comfort and growth. One side effect of this is man's vulnerability in terms of the availability of private information now stored in data banks, which is often accessed by unauthorized institutions and government alike. To control this informational leak requires societal support through new laws to safeguard man from undue harassment and return to him the privacy that he once enjoyed.

Terms to Learn

Practitioners, professionals, and scientists use a language unique to their respective fields for effective communication. As a new area of specialization, data processing has its own language, which includes a set of unique terms to facilitate communication among its members and interaction with the computer. Students are well advised to review the terms listed at the end of each chapter and to look up their meaning in the glossary at the end of the text.

- Business data processing
- Delayed time
- Electronic data processing
- Management information system
- Programming
- Punched-card data processing
- Real-time
- Simulation
- Standardization
- "Thinking" machine

QUESTIONS

1. Historically, man has developed tools and devices to multiply his physical strength and others to extend the power of his brain. How do these tools differ in terms of their contribution to man's progress? Which set of tools is the more complex? Why?
2. In view of the historical developments regarding man's achievement in producing tools to help realize his goals, what future developments in data processing do you believe are likely to take place? Point out valid reasons to support your answer.
3. What aspects of man's brain (creative versus routine) have been served by the computer? Can you think of services or functions for which computers now substitute for man? Discuss.
4. "Information is the basic element that glues an organization together." Do you agree with this statement? Explain.
5. How is management information related to data processing?
6. What type of information is expected by upper and lower management? How does such information contribute to effective decision making?
7. Why is speed an important factor in data processing? Would the speed factor be equally as important for a small as a large firm? Why?
8. Electronic systems with robot-like functioning have been called "thinking" machines. Compare them with human capabilities and limitations.
9. Referring to the methods and steps in data processing (Fig. 1-3), how would one determine the proper method for a given firm?
10. What are the key elements that make up a PERT network? How does such a network help management make effective decisions?
11. Explain briefly the role of the computer in
    a. Simulation
    b. Management games
    c. Computer-assisted instruction
    d. Management information system
12. Explain an application not previously mentioned that can be handled effectively by a computer system.
13. Visit a computer installation in a neighboring firm and report on the
    a. Specific components that make up the system.
    b. Types of documents and finished reports produced.
    c. Size of the staff and the general types of functions they perform.
14. If you were asked to point out the significance of electronic computers in industrial organizations, what would you specify as the single most important contribution? In answering this question, indicate the reason(s) that might convince upper management to consider the adoption of a computer.

SUGGESTED READING

CHAPIN, NED. *Computers—A Systems Approach.* New York: McGraw-Hill Book Company, 1971, pp. 2–10.

CLARKE, A. C. "Are You Thinking Machines?" *Industrial Research,* XI, March 1969, pp. 52–55.

"Crystal Balling: More Thoughts About the 70's . . . and Beyond," *Infosystems,* Feb. 1973, pp. 48–49ff.

"Crystal Balling: The Corporate Computer in the 70's," *Infosystems,* Jan. 1973, pp. 24–25ff.

DIEBOLD, JOHN. *Beyond Automation.* New York: McGraw-Hill Book Company, 1964.

HAMMEL, D. G. "An Introduction to Computer-Assisted Instruction," *Modern Data,* Oct. 1973, pp. 42–43.

JORDAIN, P. B., ed. *Condensed Computer Encyclopedia.* New York: McGraw-Hill Book Company, 1969.

LANDERS, R. R. *Man's Place in the Dybosphere.* Englewood Cliffs, N. J.: Prentice-Hall, Inc., 1966.

"Look Out—Here Comes 1973," *Modern Data,* Jan. 1973, p. 45.

NORTON, J. H. "Information Systems: Some Basic Considerations," *Management Review,* Sept. 1969, pp. 2–8.

RATHE, A. W. "Projection 1976: New Demands on Management," *Michigan Business Review,* May 1968, pp. 21–24.

SOOD, J. H. "Shopping the World Computer Market," *Infosystems,* March 1973, pp. 56–59.

"Talking Computer . . . What . . . How . . . Who," *Infosystems,* July 1972, pp. 36–38.

TRIBUS, MYRON. "Simulation: Management's Risk Reducer," *Business Automation,* April 1971, pp. 18–21.

TURING, A. M. "Can a Machine Think?" *The World of Mathematics,* Vol. IV. New York: Simon & Schuster, Inc., 1956, pp. 2099–2133.

WEIK, M. H. *Standard Dictionary of Computers and Information Processing.* New York: Hayden Book Company, Inc., 1969.

WITHINGTON, F. G. "Trends in MIS Technology," *Datamation,* Feb. 1970, pp. 108–110ff.

the systems concept and information flow in business organizations

2

SYSTEMS VIEW OF BUSINESS ORGANIZATIONS

Systems Levels and Linkage

SYSTEMS CONCEPT OF DATA PROCESSING

INFORMATION FLOW

Purchasing

Receiving

Disbursements

Stockkeeping

Production

Sales

Billing and Collection

Delivery

Interdepartmental Disbursements

Preparation of Reports

ROLE OF THE SYSTEMS ANALYST

An information system is as critical to a business organization as the nervous system is to the human body. Business organizations cannot function without information. Limited information or the absence of useful information can determine the difference between successsful and unsuccessful decisions for organizational functioning. Thus, before any discussion can be made regarding methods and techniques of producing useful information, it is essential to have an overview of the type and flow of key information that binds various areas of the organization. This chapter explains the systems concept and how a business organization functions as an ongoing system. Within this framework, we go on to illustrate information flow and the role of various types of information for proper functioning.

SYSTEMS VIEW OF BUSINESS ORGANIZATIONS

The term *system* has been subject to a great deal of misunderstanding and indiscriminate use. For some time, most developmental work related to this concept has been done by management scientists, who have drawn upon work previously done by others. Biologists refer to a "system" as a complex of elements standing in interaction. A nation is a system composed of its people, the government, and various institutions; the human body is a system composed of many interrelated parts. Likewise, a business organization is a system composed of many interrelated activities or components. Each component, called a *subsystem,* interacts with other components (subsystems) to contribute toward the realization of preplanned goals. As in the human body, the failure of one subsystem could conceivably hamper the functioning of others in the system.

Systems Levels and Linkage

From the foregoing, it can be suggested that the systems concept stresses (1) an ongoing, dynamic state, (2) compatible relationships and interaction within and between subsystems, and (3) the influence these relationships have on the behavior and performance of the total system for goal accomplishment. If we consider a typical manufacturing organization as an ongoing system, each of the seven inner circles in Fig. 2-1 constitutes a subsystem, which, while carrying out its own system as an entity, generates information to help the other six subsystems function. For example, the accounting department is an organizational subsystem; it consists of a complete information system in terms of the various operations that it must perform to produce accounting data and reports. Implied in this activity is the fact that each subsystem has its own objective within the guidelines and expectations of the organization—the macro system.

An important point to remember is that the areas of operation within each subsystem level are linked together and work toward accomplishing the subsystem objective, while each subsystem level is linked to a higher subsystem level so that the total performance is a direct contribution to meeting the needs of the macro system—the organization. These relationships follow a pattern such as the production employees' (minor subsystem) involvement in producing the goods demanded by middle management (intermediate subsystem) for fulfilling the directives and policies of upper management (major subsystem). It is this type of linkage that molds a system together and contributes to its survival and future success.

SYSTEMS CONCEPT OF DATA PROCESSING

The systems concept of data processing deals with developing the most efficient system with the following characteristics:

1. A dynamic system capable of *adapting* itself and *responding* to the changing environment.
2. *Interdependence* among subsystems.
3. Subsystem *compatibility* and linkage for ensuring an ongoing relationship within the system.
4. The availability of a *feedback* mechanism that relays timely information to all managerial levels.

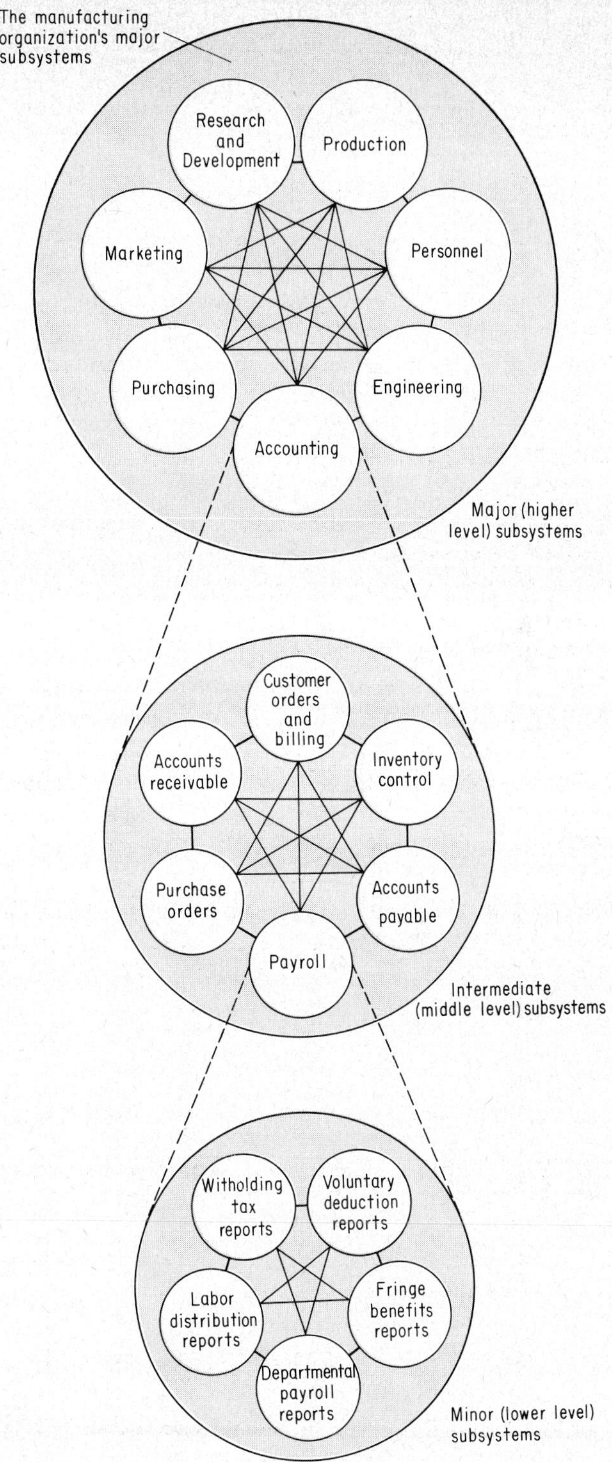

FIGURE 2-1. A manufacturing organization's main subsystems

A more encompassing *total systems* concept of data processing is one that views the organization as a single system consisting of many interrelated subsystems, and exercises proper interrelationship between the system producing information and the system producing decisions. In an ideal structure, the total systems structure has access to and manipulates all the firm's inputs and outputs automatically. From an operational view, however, the total system has been an ideal sought throughout the 1960s, but it has seldom been achieved. Although computers make possible the integration of various subsystems to form an information system, questionable definition of the concept makes it difficult to effect its use for business application. The recent trend toward establishment of data banks and data bases is viewed as an extension of the idea underlying the total system or the information-producing system.

To illustrate the systems concept, let us look into the primary information requirements of a business organization.

INFORMATION FLOW

The information system of a business organization is the pattern of information flow and processing operations that is carried out within its boundary. It is a study of how information is communicated and processed to optimize management effectiveness and attain organizational goals. Information determines the degree of successful decision making, which, in turn, contributes to a lasting business operation. Most information a business organization receives, especially a manufacturing firm, is generated as a result of day-by-day operations and the firm's interaction with the environment. No business is designed to survive and grow without active and constant dealings with various external and internal groups.

Figure 2-2 is a schematic diagram of eight key operations (source and flow of information) of a manufacturing firm.[1] Because these operations are interrelated, they generate masses of data throughout the organization. Information derived from various operations results in records and reports to be used by management in making the decisions necessary for running the organization, and management is the process of converting information into action.[2] The primary function of data processing in a setup such as this is to make all the information flow available to the appropriate subsystem at the designated time.

[1] Note that the source of information emphasized in this chapter is within the organization. Some information also comes from external sources as the organization interacts with other organizations. Thus, decision making depends on external as well as internal sources of information. Information generated from the manager's decisions is fed back for further modification or control. This feedback loop (concept) is critical to any dynamic, ongoing organization.

[2] These operations are interconnected by a communication system (telephones, messengers, etc.) that facilitates the transmission of information between and among the organization's subsystems.

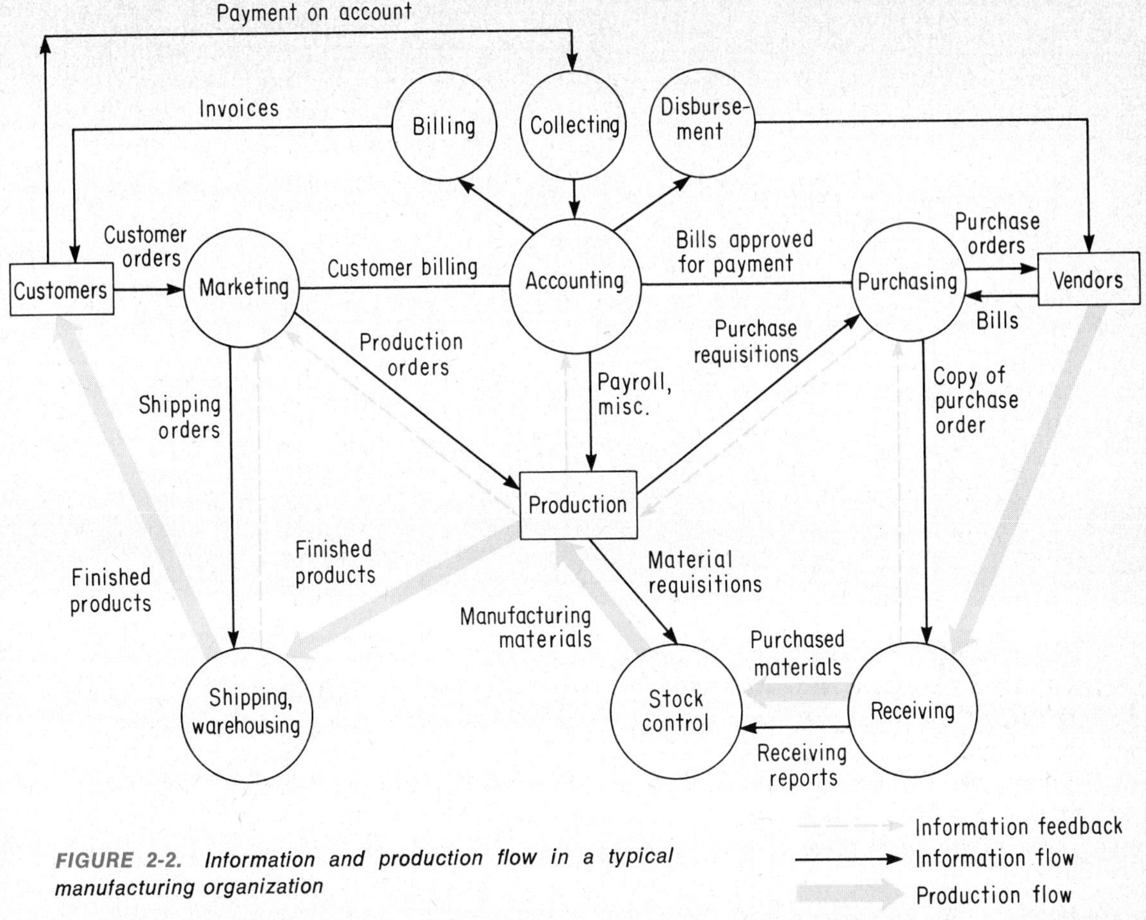

FIGURE 2-2. Information and production flow in a typical manufacturing organization

Purchasing

Purchasing consists of the procurement of raw materials, equipment, and supplies to meet the needs of the various departments of the organization. In a medium-sized to large manufacturing firm, the purchasing function is centralized in the purchasing department. After the decision has been made regarding the type and quantity of product to be manufactured, a final quota is determined based on past sales volume, quantity on hand, and an estimate for next year's sales. The sales department has data available to furnish production-planning personnel with any or all information about actual and predicted sales.

Once a production quota has been approved and authorized, the stockroom is checked for the available amount of supplies. For example, assume that the production-planning department of the American Manufacturing Company has decided to stock 2,000 units of a given item for the year ending December 31, 1974. If the company has followed a policy of ensuring a minimum "safety stock" of 400 units to prevent a total shutdown, then the net amount to be purchased will be 1,600 (2,000 — 400). Next, the net quantity of items needed is requisitioned by filling out a *purchase-requisition* form, which requests the purchasing department to place an order for the needed supplies. The purchasing department, in turn, locates and determines the suppliers from whom the order is to be filled, and follows this by drawing up a purchase order.

The *purchase order* is made in three copies: the original, which goes to the supplier from whom the goods are to be purchased; the first carbon, which is retained by the purchasing department; and the second carbon, which is sent to the receiving department. Figures 2-3 and 2-4 involve a purchase requisition and a purchase order. In Fig. 2-3 Jim Adams approved the purchase requisition. Mr. Mabbs, the purchasing agent of the company, followed up the requisition by signing a purchase order to procure the 1,600 items from Bennett Electronics (the supplier).

Purchasing is a specialized function involving an up-to-date knowledge of the quality and various competitive brands available on the

AMERICAN MANUFACTURING COMPANY
4813 Dempster Street,
Skokie, Ill.

Requisition No. M110 Date August 30, 197X

Please purchase for delivery . . . . Before Sept. 30

Quantity	Description	
200	Transformers	392K
300	Switches	410A
100	Capacitors	17 Z
400	2 ft.-wires	1 S
600	Reactors	007J

Requisitioned by E.M. Walters Approved by Jim Adams

Purchasing Agent Memorandum of Order

Purchase order no. 1704 Issued to Bennett Electronics

Date of Order Aug 20 Evanston

FIGURE 2-3. Purchase requisition —from production department to purchasing

PURCHASE ORDER

No. 1704

AMERICAN MANUFACTURING COMPANY
4813 Dempster St.,
Skokie, Ill.

To: BENNETT ELECTRONICS
312 Church St.,
Evanston, Ill.

Date Aug. 30, 197X
Deliver Before Sept. 30
Ship via Best way
f.o.b. ______
Terms 2/10, n/30

Quantity	Description	Price
200	Transformers 392K	4.00
300	Switches 410A	2.00
100	Capacitors 17A	4.00
400	2 ft. - wires 1S	.50
600	Reactors 007J	10.00

AMER. MFG. CO.

Req. No. M110 By Richard Mabbs
purchasing agent

FIGURE 2-4. *Purchase order—from purchasing department to vendor*

market. The purchasing agent not only needs to satisfy the specifications of the department regarding the materials, but is also expected to procure the materials at the best possible price. To do so means sampling several competitive brands, and sending a *request for quotations* or *bids* for similar-quality products. After the source of supply has been determined, a purchase order is prepared.

Receiving

As soon as the shipment is received, it is checked and verified (against a copy of the original purchase order) by the receiving department. The receiving clerk (1) inspects the merchandise to make sure that it is in good condition; (2) counts and weighs the merchandise, determines the quantity received, and records the quantity on his copy of the purchase order; and (3) initials the copy of the purchase order and forwards it to the purchasing department to be filed in the "receiving" records.

BENNETT ELECTRONICS
312 Church St.,
Evanston, Ill.

Invoice No. 2390

Customer's Order No. 1704
and Date 8/30/7X

Requisition No. M110

Contract No. ____

Sold to: AMERICAN MANUFACTURING CO.
4813 DEMPSTER ST.,
SKOKIE, ILL.

Date Shipped: Sept. 8, 197X from Evanston

How shipped & Route Eastern Trucking

Terms: 1/10, n/30

FOR CUSTOMER'S USE ONLY

Register No.	Voucher No.
f.o.b. checked	
Terms approved	Price approved E.D.M
Calculations checked C.R.D.	
Materials received 9/16/7X (date) Moe (signature) Rec. Clerk (title)	
Satisfactory & approved	
Adjustments	
Accounting Distribution	
Audited J.K.M.	Final Approval K.C.

Quantity	Description	Unit Price	Amount
200	Transformers 392K	4.00	800.00
300	Switches 410A	2.00	600.00
100	Capacitors 17Z	4.00	400.00
400	2 ft.-wires 1S	.50	200.00
600	Reactors 007J	10.00	6,000.00
			$8,000.00

FIGURE 2-5. *Sales invoice—from vendor to purchasing department*

Goods Checked to Invoice	
Invoice Checked to Purchase Order for:	
Merchandise	CQ
Prices	CQ
Discount Terms	CQ
Freight Terms	CQ
Invoice Footings and Extensions Checked	
Approved for Payment	Frank Eisenbach
Paid by Check No. 1400	Date Sept 16, 197X

FIGURE 2-6. Check sheet

When the sales invoice is received by the purchasing department, a checklist is used to verify the data it contains. The invoice describes the merchandise shipped, shows the amount charged, and provides other important information. In our example (Figs. 2-3 to 2-7), the purchasing department of the American Manufacturing Company received a sales invoice for 1,600 units ordered from Bennett Electronics (Fig. 2-5).

Upon proper inspection of the merchandise by the receiving department, a purchasing department clerk initials the check sheet on the "goods checked to invoice" line (Fig. 2-6). Next, the clerk checks the invoice against the first carbon copy of the purchase order for details regarding the merchandise ordered, prices, and discount and freight terms. If they are correct, he places his initials on the "invoice footings and extensions checked" line of the check sheet. Finally, the purchasing department approves payment and sends the invoice to the accounting department for disbursement.

Disbursements

The terms of the invoice received from Bennett Electronics were 1/10, n/30, meaning 1 percent cash discount will be allowed if the purchaser (American Manufacturing Company) pays the invoice within 10 days from its date. Otherwise, the purchaser is expected to pay the full amount (in our example, $8,000) within 30 days. Cash discounts are a common practice used by vendors to encourage prompt payment. When the accounting department receives the invoice, the treasurer approves payment by placing his initials on the check sheet on the "approved for payment" line. The cashier then draws a check and gives it to the treasurer for his

Date	Invoice	Amount
9/16/7X	2390	8,000.00
Total		8,000.00
Discount		80.00
Net		7,920.00

SECOND NATIONAL BANK

No. 1400

Chicago Sept. 16, 197X

Pay to the Order of BENNETT ELECTRONICS $ 7,920.00

EXACTLY $ 7,920.00 AND 00 CTS. ---------- dollars

AMER. MFG. CO.

Frank Enenbach

Treasurer

FIGURE 2-7. Payment check—from accounting department to vendor

FIGURE 2-8. Bookkeeping entries for invoice

ACCOUNTS PAYABLE

197X		Description	√	Debit		197X		Description	√	Credit	
Sept	16	Bennett Electronics		8,000	00			Bennett Electronics		8,000	00

CASH

197X						197X					
Jan	1	Balance		20,000	00	Sept	16	Bennett Electronics		7,920	00

CASH DISCOUNT

197X		Description		Credit	
Sept	16	Bennett Electronics		80	00

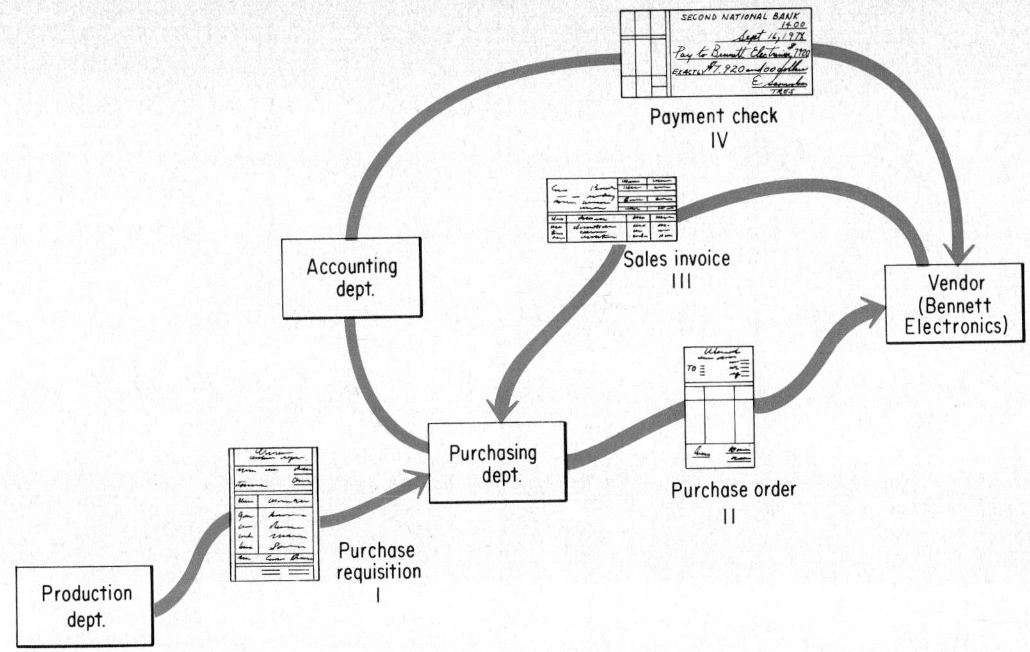

FIGURE 2-9. Summary of purchasing operation

signature (Fig. 2-7). The invoice is sent to the bookkeeper, who makes entries debiting (reducing) the *accounts payable* account by $8,000, crediting (reducing) the *cash* account by the amount of the check ($7,920), and crediting (increasing) the *cash discount* account by $80.00 (1 percent of $8,000) (Fig. 2-8). A summary of the foregoing activities is shown in Fig. 2-9.

Stockkeeping

In addition to the information relayed to the purchasing department, the receiving department sends the stockkeeping department a receiving order, showing the quantity and source of the supplies received. The incoming raw materials and supplies, then, are stored by the stockkeeping department, which in turn updates its *stock records* to indicate the net amount of such supplies available. Future *material requisitions* received from the production department necessitate a credit entry by the amount requisitioned, thus showing the amount remaining on hand. The stock clerk sees that the production and other departments get what is needed to prevent any stoppage for lack of materials.

Production

Producing a finished good requires preplanning of several elements:

1. Design and development of the product(s) under consideration.
2. Procurement of machines and tools to manufacture the product.

3. Selection and training of personnel to supervise and handle the machinery and tools.
4. Requisitioning of an adequate quantity of raw and other materials and supplies to initiate and continue production.
5. Provision of quality control and maintenance of the production facilities.

The foregoing elements are vital steps, whether the company in question manufactures products by special order or in advance of anticipated sales. In the former case, a copy of a sales order initiates production. The latter case is the more common type of production. Manufacture of merchandise is initiated by a *production order,* usually originated by the production-planning department. The production-planning department, in cooperation with the sales department and other involved departments, gathers, evaluates, and forecasts the volume of units to be produced. Once the order is received, the production department requisitions the purchase of needed raw materials, which reactivates a series of steps involving the purchasing department, suppliers, receivers, and stockkeeping personnel.

Sales

Finished goods are shipped from the production department to a warehouse, where they are temporarily stored. They are later packed and shipped upon the receipt of a sales invoice, shipping order, or the like. A sales invoice is a standard form used by the sales department to indicate the type, quantity, and price of merchandise ordered by the customer. An order involves the following general steps:

1. The files are checked for the availability of the desired merchandise.
2. A copy of the sales order is handed to the customer as an acknowledgment.
3. A copy of the sales order is sent to the warehouse or the shipping department to authorize delivery of the merchandise involved. A shipping order also can be used.
4. The sales department keeps the original copy of the sales order on file for future reference.
5. A copy of the sales invoice is sent to the accounting department for billing.

Billing and Collection

Billing may be a manual, punched-card, or electronic operation, and involves primarily the preparation of customers' invoices and the charges connected with them. An invoice contains the necessary information to support the seller's claims for the amount for which the customer is being billed. The general steps in billing include

1. Recording descriptive details in a coded form and the quantity and unit price of each item.
2. Calculating the total price of each item by multiplying unit price times quantity.
3. Adding the "total price" column.
4. Adding shipping costs and local and state taxes, if any.
5. Adding steps 3 and 4 to the invoice.

Once completed, the invoice is mailed to the customer for collection. When the amount is received, the accounts receivable clerk makes an entry on the books crediting the customer's account, which until then has shown a debit balance by the amount of the invoice. Such information later becomes a part of the profit-and-loss statement under *sales*. Debit balances of *accounts receivable* accounts are shown in the balance sheet under *current assets*.

Delivery

Once authorization to ship a given order has been received, the shipping department packs and transports the goods to the proper destination. The department follows this action by sending a notification of shipment to the sales department or other departments concerned.

Interdepartmental Disbursements

In addition to the billing and collecting functions, the accounting department also performs a disbursing role in connection with the employee payroll. In a practical application, permanent files containing data, such as rate of pay and number and type of deductions to be made, are used in connection with the data from time cards to compute employees' earnings. The *earnings record*, which lists cumulative earnings, deductions, and other relevant data for each employee, is used to prepare such statements as Social Security reports and income tax reports.

A payroll application is a separate function. Depending on the number of employees, the number of shifts per day, the union–company labor agreements, the number and type of deductions, and the method used in the preparation of the payroll, payroll may constitute a full-time job, which justifies its assignment to a subdepartment, called the *payroll department*.

Preparation of Reports

Business reports are statements used by management to control and conduct business operations. They are a key source of information, and provide feedback to various internal and external sources, such as owners, managers, creditors, and government agencies.

AMERICAN MANUFACTURING COMPANY Income Statement For the year ended 12/31/7X			
Net sales			$100,000
Cost of goods sold:			
Beginning inventory (12/31/7X)		$15,000	
Net purchases		8,000	
Cost of goods available for sale		$23,000	
Ending inventory (12/31/7X)		11,000	
Cost of goods sold			12,000
Gross Profit on Sales			$ 88,000
Selling expenses	$11,000		
General expenses	14,000		
Total operating expenses			25,000
Net income before taxes			63,000
Income tax			21,000
Net income			$ 42,000

FIGURE 2-10. *Income statement*

The foregoing sources of data generate a manufacturing and distribution cycle that begins with the production of goods and ends in their sale and delivery. This cycle continues as long as the company operates. Since profit is the primary objective, earnings are periodically prepared in the form of a profit-and-loss or *income statement* (Fig. 2-10). This statement contains information regarding income from sales, cost of goods sold, and general, selling, and federal income-tax expenses.

ROLE OF THE SYSTEMS ANALYST

One critical role performed by management is synchronizing the overall activities of the organizational subsystems. For several years there has been increased reliance on the emerging systems analyst to optimize team effort and to evaluate the operation of the entire information flow and decision-making processes of the organization. As a staff officer of a formal data-processing department, he advises managers (users) on particular projects and, using various tools, develops new procedural and administrative methods of implementing these projects. He determines what is being done now, what should be done to improve the existing subsystem, and how to carry out the steps that lead to a predetermined solution. Since people are involved, he can be best described as a salesman who must know how to sell what he perceives as an ideal constructive change to management and to those who must live with the proposed change. Details on systems analysis and design are covered in Chapter 8.

At this point, it can be concluded that the proper functioning of an an organization's information system requires the joint effort of its human, procedural, and physical components, which generate and feed desired information to and from areas such as production, purchasing, personnel,

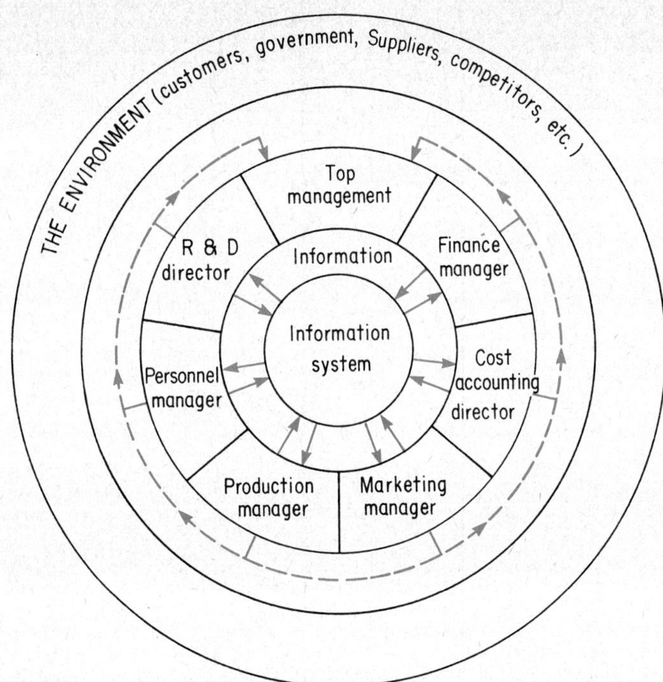

FIGURE 2-11. Formal information system

sales, distribution, and accounting. The details of the income statement indicate the type and volume of routine and repetitive information that flow through other areas (departments). Integration of these areas and the data they generate into a data-processing system is a challenge in itself. When properly done, it should minimize processing costs and produce highly effective reports for management decision making at all levels.

As shown in Fig. 2-11, an information system, whether manual or electronic, forms a central source of all needed reports and, because of its special-purpose role, it is expected to provide all departments with the best service at minimum cost. These factors will be reexamined in later chapters.

SUMMARY

Information flow in business organizations was explained by use of the systems concept—that is, a business firm is an ongoing system made up of various subsystems working interdependently and interacting in such a way that the total effort is a direct contribution to a profitable and lasting operation.

A functioning organization generates and manipulates various types of information at all levels. In the case of a production organization, for instance, the resulting information system handles and communicates data from one department to another. It requires the joint efforts of the human, physical, and procedural elements of such departments as production, purchasing, accounting, distribution, and sales. Each department receives, processes, selects, and transmits a unique set of information and operates in a way compatible with the expectations of other departments. As illustrated in this chapter, information flows into and out of each department in an organized and orderly manner, and the system is expected to be efficient in terms of the total information-processing cost and to produce highly effective reports for management decision making at all levels.

TERMS TO LEARN

Disbursements	Receiving
Income statement	Sales invoice
Material requisition	Stockkeeping
Production	Subsystem
Purchase order	System
Purchase requisition	Total systems concept
Purchasing	

QUESTIONS

1. What is a system? A subsystem?
2. Your school may be viewed as a formal educational system. Illustrate the elements involved and the components that are within its structure. What type of information flows from its boundary? Explain.
3. Explain briefly the information flow that takes place in a manufacturing organization. Relate information flow to each key operation.
4. Distinguish between the following operations:
   a. Purchase requisition versus material requisition
   b. Shipping order versus purchase order
   c. Stockkeeping versus receiving
   d. Production order versus purchase order
   e. Purchase requisition versus purchase order
   f. Accounts payable versus disbursement
   g. Billing versus invoice payment
   h. Production order versus shipping order

the data-processing cycle

3

Each organization, large or small, whether it is a sole proprietorship, partnership, or corporation, must process data regularly. The processing may be as simple as writing up a credit memorandum or as complex as preparing the payroll of General Motors. Depending on the size of the firm, the volume and frequency of data involved, the repetition of applications, and the internal and external contacts, a business firm must choose whether to process data manually, electromechanically, or electronically.

All factors being equal, a small-sized establishment (e.g., an ice cream stand or a grocery store) would probably find manual–electromechanical means of data processing adequate, in contrast with large firms (e.g., Ford Motor Company or Eastman Kodak), which find it almost imperative to utilize computers for handling large volumes of data. Figure 3-1 serves as a general illustration.

Other than volume, one wonders what it is about data processing that takes so much time. The answer lies in the matter of procedure. Chapter 2 presented the types, makeup, and sources of information flow generated by a business firm. To process the data related to this information flow, five separate phases, called the data-processing cycle, are usually required. This cycle consists of

1. Data origination
2. Data input
3. Data processing
4. Data reporting and communicating
5. Data storage and retrieval

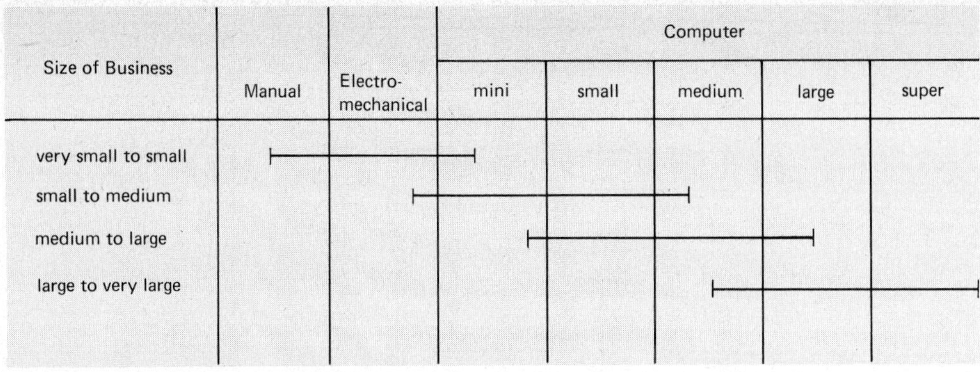

FIGURE 3-1. Data-processing needs by size of business

Although shortcuts may be used to complete each phase, as well as the work between phases, the overall sequence is, nevertheless, fixed.

DATA ORIGINATION

Raw data for processing business information are found in original papers (handwritten or typed) called *source documents.* Examples include time cards, sales orders, deposit slips, and purchase orders. What types of source documents were generated in the illustration of the American Manufacturing Company in Chapter 2? The production department initiated a purchase requisition, the purchasing department made up a purchase order, the receiving department activated a check sheet, the accounting department received a sales invoice, and the sales department wrote up a sales order and transferred related information to the accounting department for billing and collection; all this information constitutes source data, which are later used for verifying the transactions involved and processing them for further action (either manually by a journal entry on the books or electromechanically by recording them on a punched card or a magnetic tape to be run on a computer).

In many organizations, payroll processing begins with time cards as source data. Payment for the total time reported is based on a fixed hourly rate for the regular working day, plus additional payment (usually $1\frac{1}{2}$ times the hourly rate) for overtime. As we see in Fig. 3-2, Sam Elliott worked a total of 50 hours during the week beginning December 3, 1973. If the regular work week is 40 hours, his overtime is 10 hours.

DATA INPUT

Input data consist of original or source transactions that require processing. Source data are recorded either manually (e.g., by pencil) or by

Employee No. *4012*
Employee Name *Sam Elliott*
Dept. *Data Processing* Week Beginning *Dec. 9, 197X*

	A.M.		P.M.		EVE.	
MON	8:00	12:00	1:00	5:00	6:01	7:31
TUES	8:00	12:01	1:00	5:00		
WED	8:15	12:01	12:50	5:04	5:30	8:00
THUR	7:55	12:00	1:00	4:50		
FRI	8:00	12:10	12:55	5:00	6:13	7:43
SAT	8:00	12:30				
SUN						

FIGURE 3-2. Data origination—a time card

a mechanical device. In manual data recording, a pencil serves as both an input and output device, since it is used for recording the original data and for listing the results obtained from the computations.

Proper recording of data involves (1) *editing*—that is, deciding on the kind of data that require processing; and (2) *verifying*, or checking on the validity and accuracy of such data. In the example of Elliott's time card, the timekeeper would need to compute the total amount of regular time and overtime worked and verify any related figures before the time card can be used as part of the payroll data for further processing.

When editing input data, one should condense (code) as much of it as possible. Coding reduces the amount of data to be recorded and processed and is a means of identifying different classes of data. It can be alphabetic, numeric, or alphanumeric (using both numbers and the alphabet). In Fig. 3-2, Elliott's employee number is 4012. The first two digits denote the department where he works. The last two digits represent a serial number. Regardless of the type of data-processing equipment used, reading a number is more convenient and more accurate than reading a name, since a given name might occasionally belong to two or more employees in the same department.

To illustrate the procedure used in carrying out data origination and the remaining phases of the cycle, let us assume a manual approach in processing and preparing checks of hourly employees. Payroll is one of the most important recurrent events in business organizations; it is prepared once a week, once every other week, or once a month, depending on the employer's established routine. A business organization employs wage earners who receive a fixed salary and hourly employees whose gross income is based on the amount of time shown on their time cards.

The time card in Fig. 3-2 serves as a complete record of Elliott's work week. On Monday, December 3, 1973, he reported to work in the marketing department by punching in at 8:00 A.M. He punched out at 12:00 for lunch, returning at 1:00 P.M., and punched out again at 5:00 P.M. He worked 1½ hours of overtime in the evening. Basic payroll *data*, therefore, *originate* on the time card for a large part of the work force.

From the foregoing discussion, it can be concluded that the source document represents input to a data-processing system. Under a manual data-processing system, at the end of the last day of the week the payroll department collects employee time cards from all departments. The remaining steps are then taken to process the data and prepare employee paychecks.

DATA PROCESSING

Processing is the actual work performed on data and involves the following steps: (1) classifying, (2) sorting, (3) calculating and recording, and (4) summarizing.

Classifying

After data have been secured, they are identified and grouped into categories or classes. One way recorded data are classified is by department. Elliott's time card is among other time cards handled by the data-processing department. Assume that there are two other departments: production (with employee numbers ranging from 5001 to 5025) and purchasing (whose employee numbers range from 6001 to 6040).[1] To classify the whole set of time cards by department, we rearrange them as shown in Fig. 3-3.

Sorting

Sorting involves sequencing information in a predetermined order (alphabetic or numeric) to facilitate processing. Once the time cards have been classified by department, sorting each of the decks of the three depart-

[1] Bear in mind that the first two digits (high-order digits) of each employee's number denote his department.

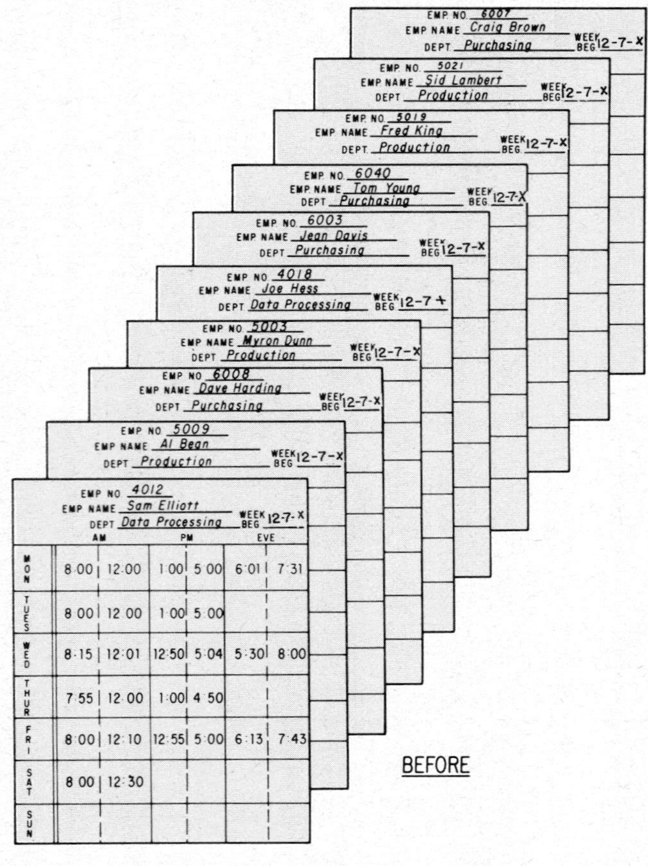

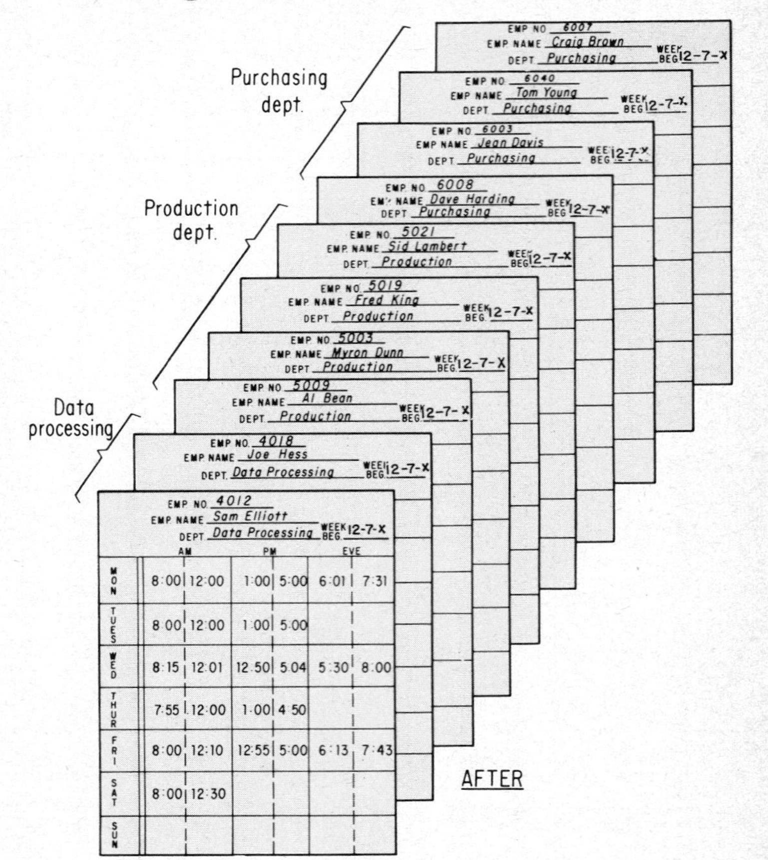

FIGURE 3-3. *Classifying by department*

ments simplifies the completion of the job and facilitates future filing chores (Fig. 3-4). After the deck has been sorted, the payroll clerk can handle each group separately, compute the amount of time worked, and calculate the earnings of each employee.

Manual sorting is time consuming, and although it is practiced by many small business establishments, it is not an efficient way of manipulating data for larger firms. As they seek accuracy, economy, and speed, larger firms use the more efficient and sophisticated electromechanical or, more commonly, electronic sorting techniques.

Calculating and Recording

Calculating and recording involve reconstruction of data through the arithmetic processes of addition, subtraction, multiplication, and/or division. It is the most crucial phase of data manipulation, since it is at this step that most of the work is done to arrive at a meaningful solution to the problem—in our example, the correct amount of the paycheck after deductions.

Thus, the sorted set of time cards is used in determining gross pay, amount of deductions, and take-home (net) pay of each employee. Gross pay is computed by multiplying the number of hours reported on the time card by the hourly rate. In Fig. 3-2, Elliott worked 40 regular and 10 overtime hours. For a 5-day work week (at the rate of $4 per hour), then, his gross regular pay would be as follows:

Regular payment	40 × $4 =	$160
Overtime payment	10 × $6 =	60
Total gross pay for the week		$220

Net pay is computed by subtracting federal withholding tax, Social Security tax (F.I.C.A.), union dues, health insurance premiums, and other deductions from the total gross pay. The take-home pay figure is printed on the right-hand section of a two-part *check*. Details of the deductions are shown on the stub (the left part of the check in Fig. 3-5). The payroll department records payroll data of all employees in a special journal to be used later in preparing income tax and other reports.

Summarizing

Summarizing is compressing a mass of data into a meaningful and usable form. It involves listing (tabulating) related information and figuring out its total. Management finds summarized reports more helpful and timesaving for decision making than detailed reports. In a payroll report, for example, an administrator might need specific figures regarding the total amount paid in wages and salaries for a given week. Payroll details

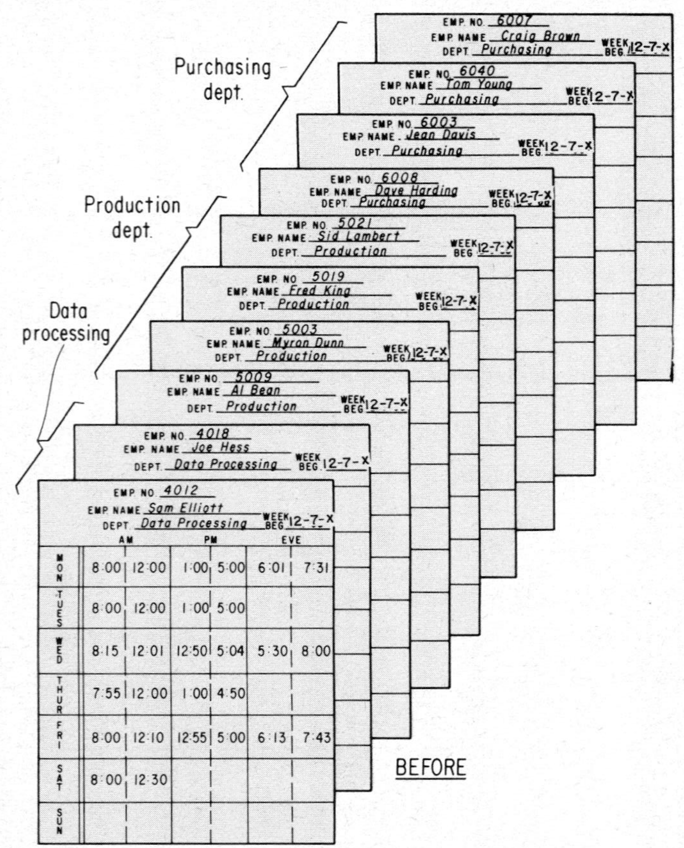

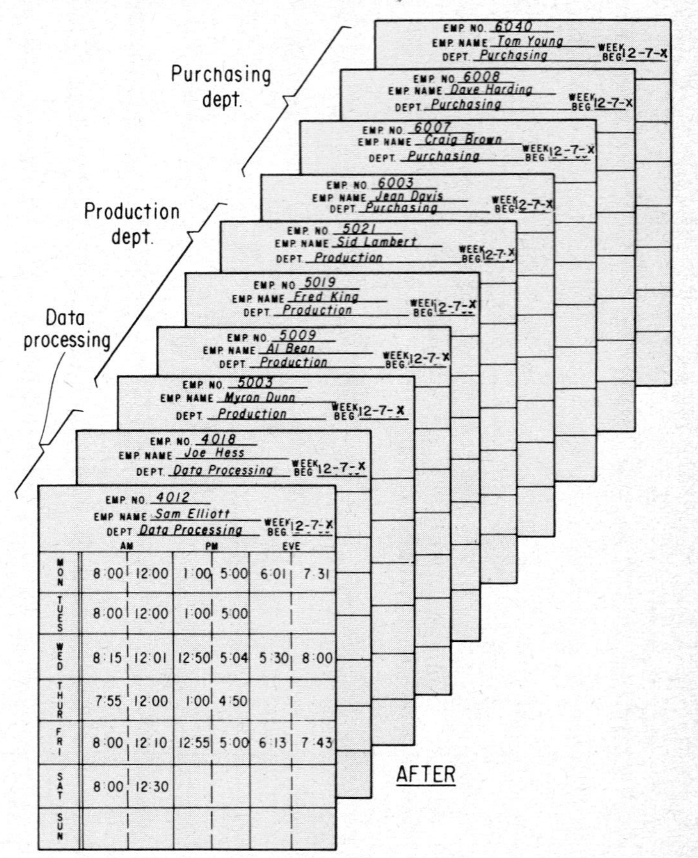

FIGURE 3-4. *Sorting classified data*

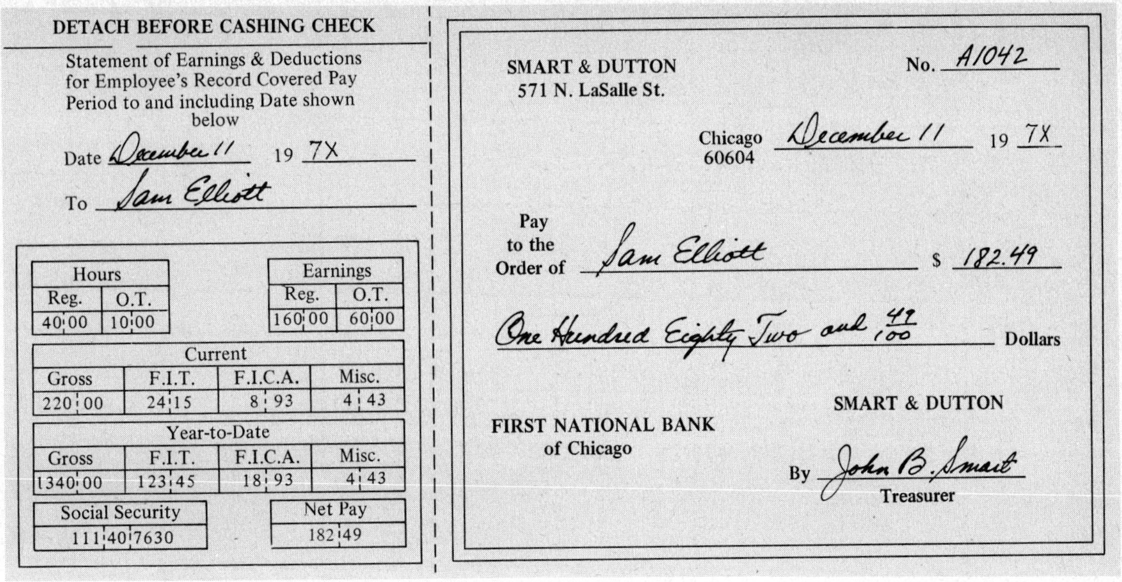

DETACH BEFORE CASHING CHECK

Statement of Earnings & Deductions for Employee's Record Covered Pay Period to and including Date shown below

Date *December 11* 19 *7X*

To *Sam Elliott*

Hours		Earnings	
Reg.	O.T.	Reg.	O.T.
40.00	10.00	160.00	60.00

Current			
Gross	F.I.T.	F.I.C.A.	Misc.
220.00	24.15	8.93	4.43

Year-to-Date			
Gross	F.I.T.	F.I.C.A.	Misc.
1340.00	123.45	18.93	4.43

Social Security	Net Pay
111-40-7630	182.49

SMART & DUTTON
571 N. LaSalle St.

No. *A1042*

Chicago 60604 *December 11* 19 *7X*

Pay to the Order of *Sam Elliott* $ *182.49*

One Hundred Eighty Two and 49/100 Dollars

FIRST NATIONAL BANK
of Chicago

SMART & DUTTON

By *John B. Smart*
Treasurer

FIGURE 3-5. *A paycheck*

are used to prepare such a report. Payroll reports indicate, by department, who earned what amount, but generally delete mention of deductions, amount of time worked, and the like. The detailed payroll data could be *summarized* into totals that offer useful information.

DATA REPORTING AND COMMUNICATING

Once summaries of data have been prepared, they represent output information and are reported to the users. No output is useful unless it is communicated promptly and effectively to the people involved. Failure to do so is as wasteful and useless as for a college student to take courses for credit but ignore the exams.

One major output of a payroll application is the employee paycheck. Figure 3-5 shows Elliott's net pay of $182.49. He detaches and cashes the check, while retaining the stub for reference.

DATA STORAGE AND RETRIEVAL

Storage of existing data for future retrieval[2] terminates the data-processing cycle (Fig. 3-6). Data storage can be made *manually* (e.g., in

[2] Methods of retrieval range from manually pulling a given record from file to electronically retrieving information from a mass-storage device through a computer terminal. The terminal could be located in the computer center or hundreds of miles away.

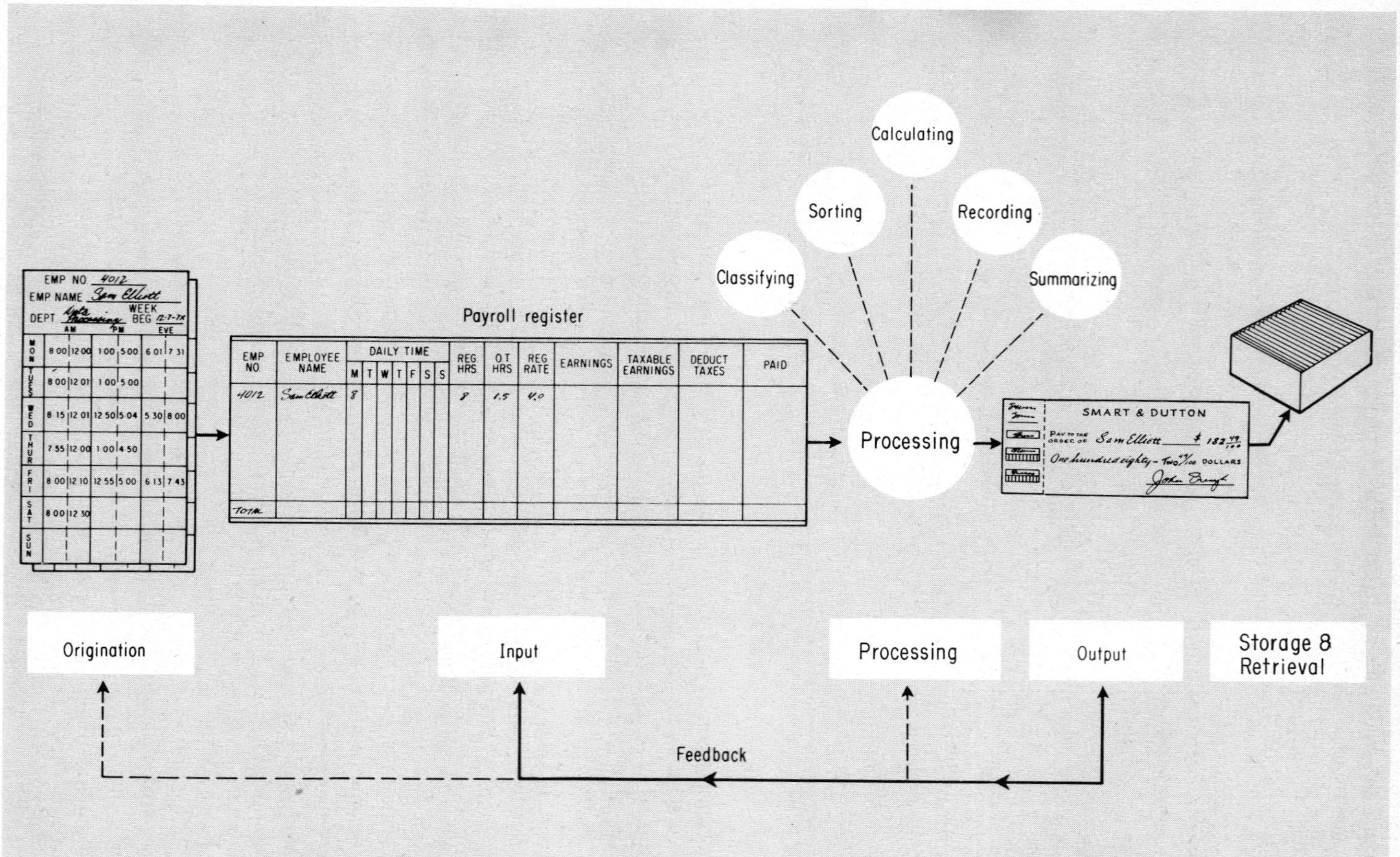

FIGURE 3-6. *Summary of data-processing cycle*

ledger books), *electromechanically* (in punched cards), or *electronically* in a computer memory.

Before stored data are used again, a comparison is made between the initial objectives and the output. Any discrepancy is analyzed, corrected, and fed back to the proper stage in the cycle. This action is referred to as the *feedback concept* of control. It is a vital step in following up on essential information, and helps to ascertain consistency and accuracy of the information sought.

In recycling an operation, the output of the previous machine run often becomes the input (raw) data of a new run. This is analogous to the unsold (ending) inventory of a retail store at the end of the year becoming the beginning inventory available for sale on the first day of the next year.

The steps that make up the data-processing cycle, shown in summary form in Fig. 3-6, are basic to the use of any system of data processing. They must be performed whether the approach used is manual, electromechanical, or electronic.

PUNCHED-CARD DATA PROCESSING

Briefly, a punched-card system prepares business reports by a routine that begins with the recording of source documents on standard-sized cards designed for this purpose. The cards, each containing a single transaction (unit record), are then fed through various equipment for classifying, calculating, and producing final reports. For example, suppose that on January 1, a customer purchases an item from a retail store for $100 on account, with payment to be made in two equal installments, the first payment being due by January 15; general information, such as the customer's number, name, and address, in addition to the amount of $100, is first punched in a card to record the necessary data for reference. Next the card is fed through an accounting machine, which reads and interprets the holes in the card and, on a statement form, prints the account number, name, and address of the customer, the item purchased, and its cost. This statement is mailed to the customer. On January 15, the customer pays his first installment of $50. Upon receipt of the check, the name, address, and account number, along with the amount of $50, are punched in a card called the *payment card*.

The calculator first reads the initial card containing the $100 debit and then the payment card containing the first installment of $50. On the payment card, it punches the remainder (the balance of $50), along with the other necessary information, and the payment card becomes the customer's updated record. On January 31, when the second installment is received, a new card is punched to record all the necessary information

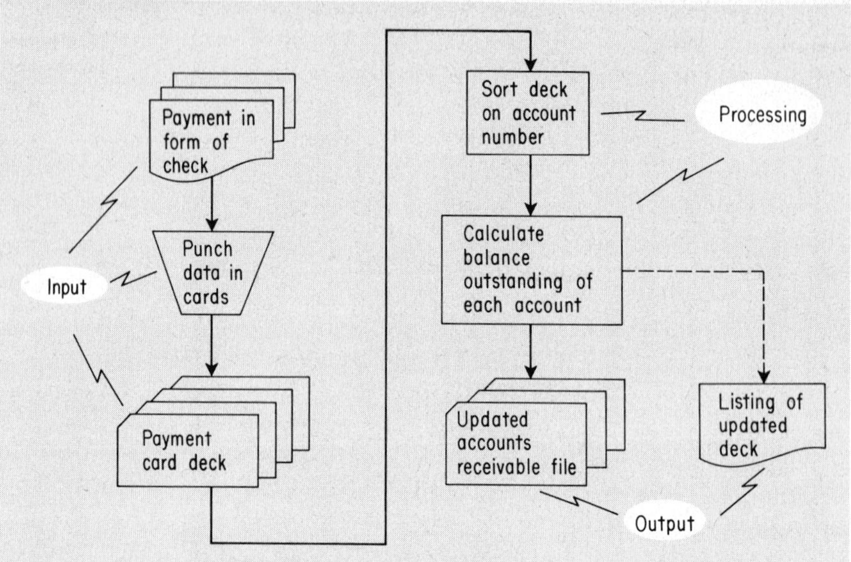

FIGURE 3-7. Punched-card data processing—general handling of payment in an accounts-receivable routine

and the final payment of $50. It is then merged with the updated record of January 15, and the $50 payment is subtracted from the $50 balance to show that the account has a zero balance (Fig. 3-7).

From this illustration we can see that a data-processing system consists of input, processing, and output, and the tasks involve the basic steps of originating, classifying, sorting, calculating, summarizing, storing, and communicating. This simple transaction, when multiplied many times during the week, requires a host of punched cards, as well as a number of punched-card machines set up to work as a team in processing the desired data and preparing needed reports (Fig. 3-8).

COMPUTER PROCESSING

Although punched-card data processing is a major improvement over manual systems, it has some limitations. Intercommunication between the machines in the system is somewhat limited. The machines are not capable of handling exceptions within a normal routine, so a firm must occasionally return to manual processing. The punched-card system is also limited because of its inability to "make decisions" in the course of processing. Complex problems must be solved in pieces, or fractions, rather than in one continuous process.

Processing can be accomplished more effectively and, especially in larger organizations, more efficiently through a computer system. A basic

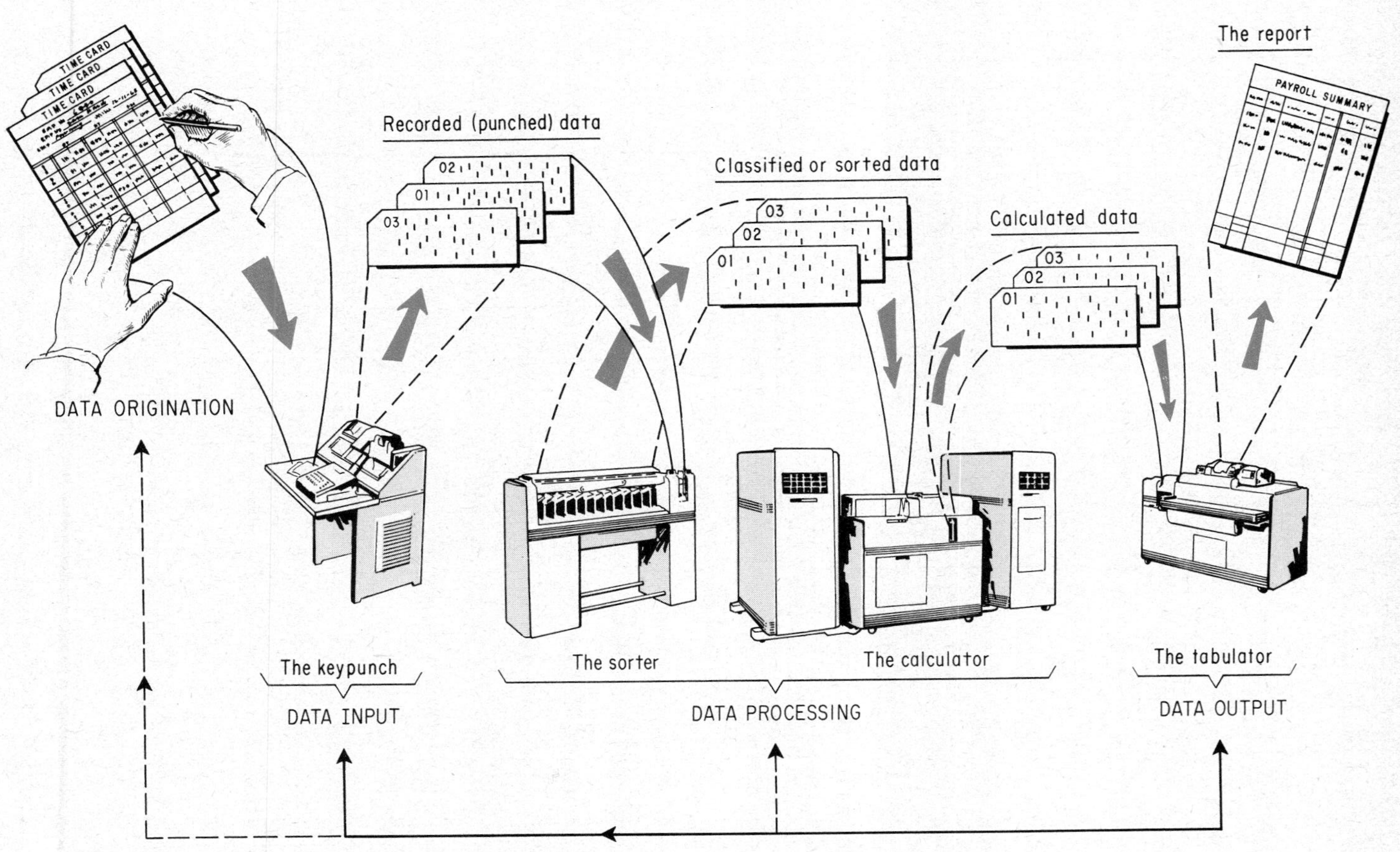

FIGURE 3-8. *Punched-card data-processing cycle*

computer systems consists of three primary components: a *central processing unit (CPU)*, an *input* device, and an *output* device. The CPU is the heart of the total system and is comprised of an arithmetic section for computation, a main storage section [3] for holding the program and related data for processing, and a control unit for supervising the sequence of execution of the program instructions and for directing supportive devices to perform designated functions.

Although the number of additional, supportive components and the degree of sophistication of computer systems vary,[4] the input–processing–output cycle remains the same. A computer-oriented data-processing cycle begins with an input medium (such as punched card, magnetic tape, or punched paper tape) that holds source data for processing. When fed into an appropriate input device, the data are read into the computer's main storage for processing based on a program already available in main storage. Then the computer passes the processed results (output) to a printer in the form of a report or to another output device in a machine-readable form for future processing.

The computer system, then, is more flexible. The punched-card system has to read, sequence, and accumulate the cards, and finally print out summary reports. The computer system, on the other hand, performs the same routine, but has greatly extended capabilities. It can add, subtract, multiply, and divide; verify the accuracy of incoming information; reject certain cards if they contain invalid coding; and use a preplanned set of logic to deal with output data before a final printout is made.

Electronic data processing is accomplished either in batch or in real-time mode, depending on the configuration and capabilities of the system. *Batch* processing relates to the manipulation of data accumulated in batches over a period of time; *real-time* processing handles transactions as soon as they are received. Real-time is superior to batch processing, especially in such applications as airline reservations, where immediate response to inquiries is critical. For organizations that have no in-house computer system, *time-shared* systems (systems shared by many organizations) are an alternative solution for electronic data processing.

SUMMARY

In the foregoing presentation we discussed a data-processing cycle that provided a regular, orderly way of preparing the weekly payroll. Payroll originated on the employee time cards and was classified into arbitrary

[3] Secondary (auxiliary) storage units are also used in support of the computer's main storage. Details on this and other devices are presented in Chapters 9 & 10.

[4] Details on input-output and peripheral devices are explained in Chapters 9 & 10.

groups or classes. Next, the amount of hours worked was computed, and, using the hourly rate, the gross pay of each employee was calculated. Gross pay was reduced by the total amount of deductions, leaving the net pay. A check, showing all pertinent details, was drawn and handed to the employee concerned. Finally, follow-up reports were prepared and communicated to management, and any pertinent data were placed in storage for future reference.

The data-processing cycle employed in a punched-card data-processing system simulates the cycle used in the manual system, except that data are processed by means of punched-card machines which are electromechanical in nature. The punched-card data-processing cycle goes through the following phases:

Phase 1: Data origination and input. Source documents such as time cards or sales invoices are prepared manually (using a pencil and paper or a typewriter) and are recorded on punched cards or punched paper tape.

Phase 2: Data processing. Once input cards are prepared, input machines (e.g., a card sorter, collator, or punched paper-tape reader) read and manipulate (sort, classify, calculate, and summarize) the data the cards contain.

Phase 3: Data output. The result of data manipulation is meaningful output in the form of a printed report or a general summary.

In a computer system, the foregoing phases are referred to as input, processing, and output, respectively.

TERMS TO LEARN

Data input
Data manipulation
Data origination
Data processing
Data-processing cycle
Editing
Gross pay
Net pay
Paycheck
Payroll
Sorting
Source document
Stub
Summarizing

QUESTIONS

1. What general factors determine the choice of the type of data-processing system? Relate your ideas to a specific organization. List your assumptions, and explain the reason(s) for your choice.

2. What procedure is involved in carrying out the data-origination phase? What other phases are involved in a data-processing cycle?
3. What is the difference between data origination and data input?
4. What operations are generally included in data manipulation? Explain the role of data manipulation in the preparation of an income statement.
5. What elements constitute a paycheck? Who is involved? What is involved? What payroll data are made available with the check?
6. Contrast the steps involved in a manual cycle and a punched-card data-processing cycle. What differences (if any) exist between the two cycles? What possible advantages does each cycle provide? What type or size of firm is likely to adopt each system?

developments in data processing

4

EARLY METHODS OF CALCULATION

Finger Counting

The Abacus

DEVELOPMENTS IN MANUAL AIDS TO WRITTEN CALCULATIONS

Double-Entry Bookkeeping

The "Grating" Method

The "Bones" Method

The "Sluggard" Method

DEVELOPMENTS IN MECHANICAL AIDS TO WRITTEN CALCULATIONS

Numerical Wheel Calculator

"Four-Function" Machines

Key-Driven Calculating Machines

DEVELOPMENTS IN PUNCHED-CARD PROCESSING

Joseph Marie Jacquard

Developments in the United States

Developments in England

COMPUTER DEVELOPMENT

Origin of the Digital Computer (1812–1937)

the difference engine
the analytical engine

Origin of the Analog Computer

THE COMPUTER INDUSTRY

Developments in Universities

First-Generation (Vacuum Tube) Computers (1946–1959)

Second-Generation (Transistorized) Computers (1959–1965)

Third-Generation Computers (1965–1970)

Fourth-Generation Computers (1970–1977 est.)

KEY DEVELOPMENTS IN SOFTWARE

Developments in Programming Languages

FORTRAN
COBOL
PL/1

Man has always been challenged by mathematics and the need to solve mathematical problems. To most people, however, the job of solving a formula is both boring and time consuming. For this reason, attempts have been made since the beginning of history to make calculating less tedious and much faster.

Historical developments in data processing are a compilation of man's continuing effort to find better and more efficient ways of gathering and processing useful data as his business life accelerated both in size and in complexity. In the process, man had to adapt his needs to the advancing technological levels of his environment. Technological advancements involving better ways of processing data, however, did not always render older methods obsolete. Instead, man, in several cases, continued using some of the older methods of data processing (in either original or modified form) while also making use of later developments.

KEY DEVELOPMENTS IN SOFTWARE

Until the nineteenth century, people found business calculations a very complex job, because they had to be done "in the head." Writing materials were very scarce and therefore expensive to use for ordinary purposes. Paper was probably made by the Chinese before the time of Christ, but not until the thirteenth century A.D. did the science of paper making spread into Europe. We are told that paper manufacturing was originated by the moors in Spain early in the twelfth century. Large-scale paper manufacturing in Italy occurred in 1276. Later, paper mills began to spread into countries such as England, France, and Germany. Paper made from pulp, however, was an invention of the nineteenth century. Not until relatively recent times has paper been available on a mass-production basis.

Finger Counting

Lack of paper caused early man to do most of his calculations mentally, with the aid of his fingers. Each finger might represent one of the animals he owned or a measure of stored grain. Simple additions were carried out by finger tallying. For example, to add 5 and 2, one held up 2 fingers, then 5 more fingers, and counted the total number of upraised fingers to get the result of 7. When more complex forms of calculation were devised, they were initially performed by the use of fingers. Finger counting techniques were so important that they were taught in Roman schools, and various methods were devised to do "advanced" operations, such as multiplication and division. For instance, the student was required to learn the multiplication table only up to 5×5. His fingers took over in figuring out the product of any numbers between 5 and 10. Suppose that we wish to multiply 9×7. We would raise four fingers on one hand, representing 6, 7, 8, and 9, and two fingers on the other hand, representing 6 and 7—that is, the numbers over 5 (Fig. 4-1). The product is obtained as follows: The sum of the fingers raised (i.e., $4 + 2 = 6$) determines the value of the tens position, and the product of the fingers not raised ($1 \times 3 = 3$) determines the value of the units position: thus, 63. Try this method, using different numbers between 5 and 10, and see how easy it is to multiply. Also, try to visualize how long the average-sized firm of today would take, using this method, to calculate customer bills at the end of each day.

The Abacus

Man was limited in how far he could go with his finger-counting techniques. His ingenuity later led him to overcome these limitations by using pebbles and other similar small objects for counting.

The verb *calculate* is derived from the Latin *calculus*, which means "pebble" or "a small piece of marble." Experienced calculators of early

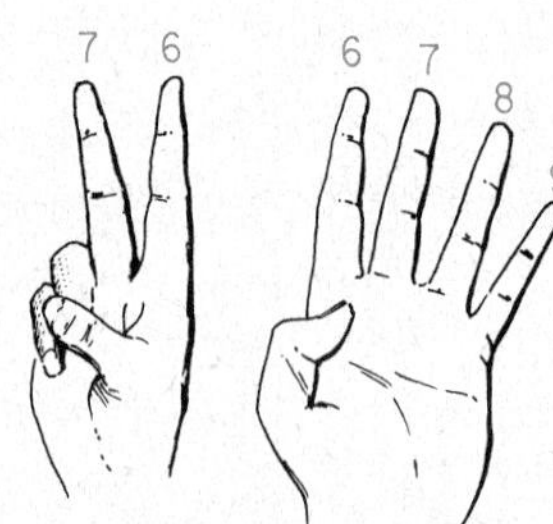

FIGURE 4-1. *Finger multiplication*

times performed their calculations by the use of a manual counting board called an *abacus,* which contained pebbles placed in grooves or beads strung on a string. In the typical abacus, the beads are strung on strings in the form of rows. Each row contains 10 beads, representing the 10 fingers. The position of the row represents the decimal value of the beads. Performing calculations on the abacus is a manual operation. Beads must start in the left part of the device, and addition, the most common arithmetic function performed, is accomplished by successively adding values represented by beads in the different rows. The abacus was used efficiently in addition and subtraction, and limited historical data show that many people have also used the abacus for multiplication and division, performing multiplication by repeated addition and division by repeated subtraction.

The abacus was used until comparatively recent times, partly because of the scarcity of writing materials and partly because of the lack of a practical numbers method. Even after written methods of calculation were devised, the influence of the abacus still remained. Today, its influence is seen in the use of the word *calculate,* as well as in the use of the term *buying over the counter.* The latter is derived from the Middle Ages, when merchants used boards or counting tables to compute their customers' accounts.

Some question exists concerning the origin of the abacus. Although several nations claim to have originated it, the idea probably developed in many nations and was carried into other parts of the world by merchants and travelers. Its original home is believed to have been Egypt or Babylon. The ancient Hindus used one type of abacus called the *sand tray* or *dust board,* which was also common in both the Roman and Greek civilizations. Some scholars trace the origin of the term *abacus* to the Semitic *Abai,* meaning "dust." However, others believe that the Greek *abax,* which means "tablet," is a more likely origin. Other types of abaci include the Chinese *Suan-pan,* the Japanese *Soroban,* the Russian *S'choty,* the Armenian *Choreb,* and the Turkish *Coulba.*

DEVELOPMENTS IN MANUAL AIDS TO WRITTEN CALCULATIONS

Double-Entry Bookkeeping

Sketchy historical data suggest that the birth of double-entry bookkeeping occurred in Italy in the fourteenth century. A double-entry ledger dating from 1340 and showing a merchandise account for pepper was found in Genoa. The account was debited with various expenses and credited with receipts. The balance was transferred to a "profit-and-loss" account.

In 1494, Luca Paciolo of Venice published his book, *Everything About Arithmetic, Geometry, and Proportion.* He summarized the existing routines of bookkeeping, and pointed out that the chief objective of bookkeeping was the preparation of key information on assets and liabilities. He emphasized the use of (1) a memorial (daybook), (2) a journal (formal debits and credits in Italian currency), and (3) a quaderno (ledger).

Between the early 1400s and the 1800s, record-keeping methods were developed and expanded, but little was done to speed up the process of recording business transactions, calculating various amounts, or producing business reports.

The "Grating" Method

Arab, Hindu, and European calculators were the first to develop techniques of written calculations. The Arabs originated a "grating" method, which was used by the Hindus in multiplication. This method requires a tablet consisting of a number of squares with diagonals. The multiplicand is placed on top of the tablet with its high-order position over the top left column. The multiplier is placed to the left side of the tablet with its high-order position in the upper left corner (Fig. 4-2). The square holds the product of the digits to the top and left of it. For example, assume the multiplication of 217 × 14. The number 217 is placed at the top of the tablet with the 2 over the left corner, the 1 over the middle column, and the 7 over the right column. The number 14 is placed on the left side of the tablet with the 1 (the highest power) to the side of the top left corner.

The lower halves of the upper three squares show the product of multiplying 217 × 1. The bottom three squares display the product of multiplying 217 × 4. Notice that the 2 in 28 (the product of 7 × 4) is displayed in the upper half of the square which shows the 28. The product of 217 × 14 is attained by adding diagonally, as shown in Fig. 4-2.

The "Bones" Method

The preceding "table" approach was used later in 1617 in Napier's "bones." John Napier, of Merchiston, Scotland, attempted to reduce tedious calculations involving large numbers. His "bones," or rods, made a great impression on Europeans and Chinese. Each rod is divided into

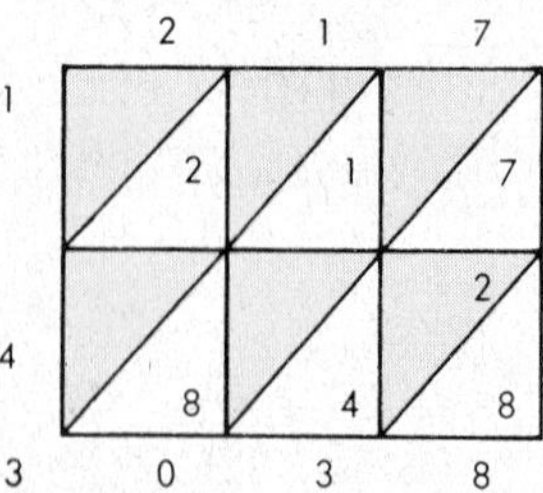

FIGURE 4-2. "Grating" method of multiplication

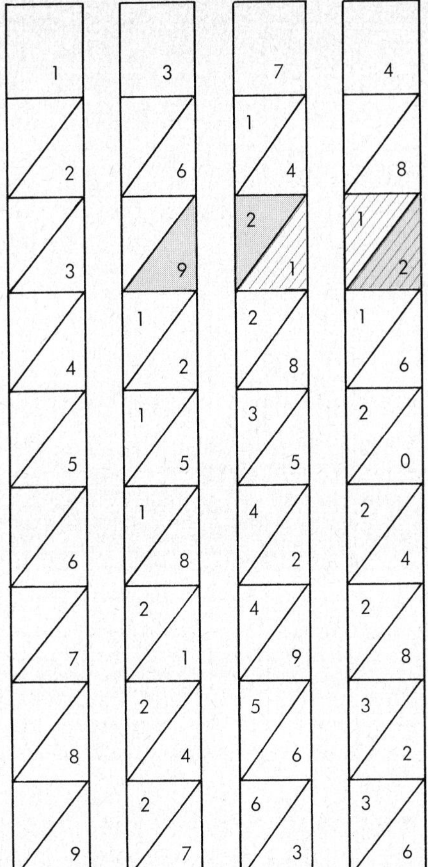

FIGURE 4-3. *Napier's bones*

nine squares; eight squares are divided diagonally. The top square holds a digit (i.e., a number from 1 to 9). The remaining eight squares in the rod hold the product of multiplying that number by 2, 3, 4, 5, 6, 7, 8, and 9. The rods for multiplying 3, 7, and 4 are shown in Fig. 4-3. Once the table is set up, one can easily obtain the product of 2 × 374 or 5 × 374 or any other numbers from the top squares and the left rod, because the numbers in the middle are used to obtain the product only. For example, in order to get the product of 3 × 374, we add diagonally the values in the third square of each of the rods of the multiplication, as illustrated in Fig. 4-3.

The "Sluggard" Method

The Arabs and the Hindus rarely used any multiplication tables. But in the sixteenth century, when written calculations became more and more common, calculators introduced a written method that would obtain

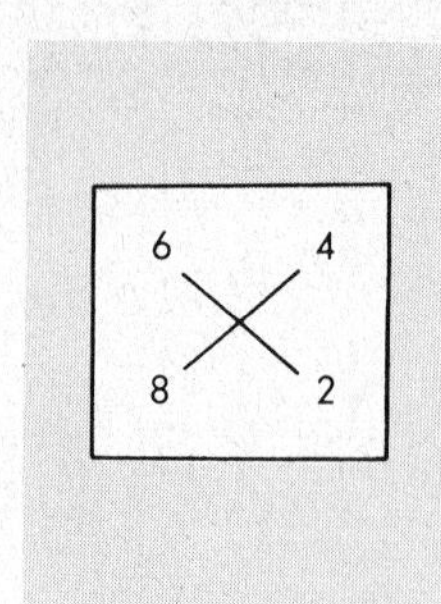

FIGURE 4-4. *The "sluggard" method*

the product of numbers up to 10 × 10, similar to the Roman approach using the fingers. In this method, called the "sluggard" method, the multiplication table of 5 × 5 had to be learned. For example, in multiplying 8 × 6, the numbers 6 and 8 are recorded in the manner shown in Fig. 4-4. Opposite these two digits, their differences from 10 are written. The tens position of the product is obtained either by subtracting 2 from 6 or 4 from 8 (i.e., 4). The *units position* of the product is obtained by multiplying the 4 and 2 (i.e., 8). So, the product of 6 × 8 is 48.

DEVELOPMENTS IN MECHANICAL AIDS TO WRITTEN CALCULATIONS

Numerical Wheel Calculator

Widespread use and knowledge of the Arabic system of numeration began in Christian Europe about the thirteenth century. Later, mathematicians began to develop computing devices to calculate at a much higher level than that of the abacus. The first of such devices was the numerical wheel calculator (the world's first adding machine) made around 1642 at the age of 18 by *Blaise Pascal,* one of the seventeenth century's greatest mathematician–philosophers. Pascal built his calculator because he wanted to aid his father, who at that time was the superintendent of taxes in Rouen, France. His calculator (Fig. 4-5) was capable of registering decimal value by the rotation of a cogwheel gear by one to nine steps, with a carry lever to operate the next higher digit wheel as a given cogwheel exceeded ten units of registration. This is considered the first real calculating machine to be developed. The present-day odometer is an example of a machine that applies Pascal's use of a series of cogwheels to calculate data.

"Four-Function" Machines

In 1673, *Gottfried Wilhelm von Leibniz,* a philosopher and mathematician, showed how a mechanical multiplier could be made. He felt that multiplication could be treated like addition. For example, multiplying

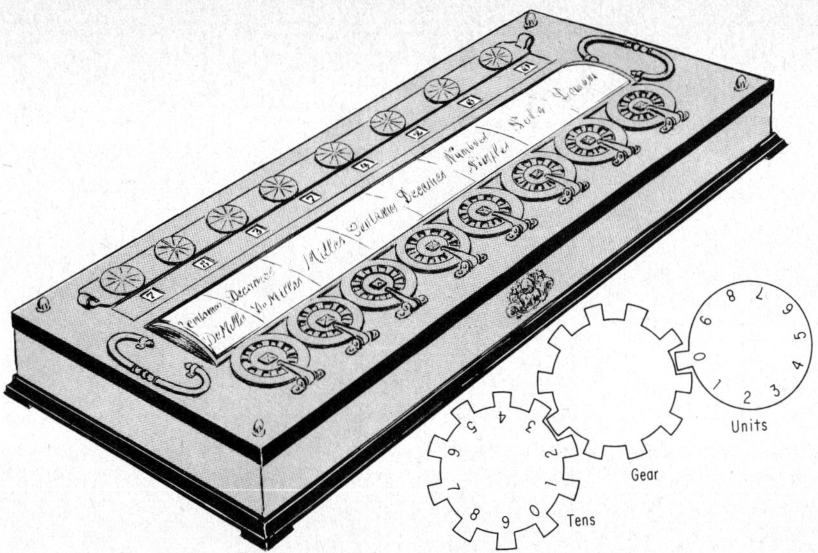

FIGURE 4-5. *Numerical wheel calculator*

5 × 4 means 5 added to itself four times or 4 added to itself five times. In this case, two counters would be needed: one to perform the addition, and the other to show when addition should stop. Division was looked upon as the reverse of multiplication, and subtraction was adding the second quantity in reverse. Thus, these four basic arithmetic operations were based on counting. Leibniz built his "stepped-wheel" machine when he was about 25 years old. It was later manufactured in 1694. However, this machine, as well as that of Pascal, was not considered dependable in its operation.

One of the more dependable and successful calculating machines was developed in 1820 by *Charles Xavier Thomas,* of Colmar, France. It performed the four functions of arithmetic. In 1872, *Frank Stephen Baldwin,* of the United States, introduced a principle in his calculating machine different from the one on which the Thomas machine was based. He began building his machine a year later, thus marking the beginning of the calculating-machine industry in the United States.

Key-Driven Calculating Machines

The invention and development of key-driven devices and machines, such as the typewriter and the cash register, played a major role in the advancement of data processing, particularly in the recording and reporting functions. In 1887, Dorr Eugene Felt patented his comptometer (known then as the "macaroni box"). Improved versions of Felt's machine are still in wide use today. In 1890, W. S. Burroughs, a bank clerk, invented a key-set adding–printing machine geared to minimize the drudgery of bookkeeping. The machine, operated by a crank, was designed to record, summarize, and calculate.

About 1911, Jay R. Monroe and Baldwin introduced the Monroe calculator, the first commercially successful keyboard machine.

Accounting machines were not developed until after World War I. These were machines capable of printing values in a columnar arrangement, in addition to performing the functions of recording, calculating, and summarizing, which are common characteristics of most adding machines. Included in this category are billing machines, which automatically extend amounts on invoices, and payroll machines that handle tax and other deductions in arriving at net pay, while simultaneously providing copies or registers for accounting purposes.

Although electric motors provide greater speed and facility, all devices classified as adding machines, calculators, or accounting machines are considered "nonautomatic" equipment. All require a human worker to control and operate each step of processing.

DEVELOPMENTS IN PUNCHED-CARD PROCESSING

Joseph Marie Jacquard

Punched-card methods have been in wide use since the early 1930s. Their history, however, dates back to 1801, when a Frenchman named Joseph Jacquard perfected the first punched-card machine, a loom to weave intricate designs into cloth. The outstanding feature of this machine was its ability to follow a set of instructions punched into cards. Because of the "fear of machines," Jacquard had difficulty gaining public acceptance for its use. In the city of Lyons, he was physically attacked and his machine destroyed. Through Napoleon's support, he rebuilt his machine and proved its usefulness in weaving. Lyons' prosperity in the mid-1800s was attributed largely to the success of Jacquard's loom.

Developments in the United States

The history of punched cards and electromechanical punched-card machines dates from the late 1800s. It started because the pressing demands of the U.S. Bureau of the Census created a need for developing better and faster methods of processing census data. During the nineteenth century, the population increased greatly in the United States. The information of a more complex nature that was demanded at every census made the manual method impractical. By the time the desired information was ready for publication, it was old and useless. To combat this situation, the Census Bureau sought the aid of Herman Hollerith, a noted statistician, as a special agent for the 1890 census. At that time, Hollerith was experimenting with punched-card components in the hope of producing a machine that would process census data faster and more efficiently than the manual system. The 1880 census took 7½ years to finish, a total time considered by Hollerith as a tremendous waste.

Hollerith completed a set of machines in time to process the 1890 census. It was the first large-scale punched-card data-processing machine installation. It included a card punch (a keyboard invented by Hollerith) that punched holes in 3- by 5-inch cards to record data, manually fed electromagnetic counters, and a sorting box. In operation, a punched card was placed in the pin press, and a hinged box was lowered to activate a counter and open the lid of a sorting slot. Cards were deposited at a speed of 50 to 80 a minute. A test tabulation of 10,000 returns showed that the enumeration time was three fourths and the tabulating time was one eighth of that required for earlier systems. The census job was completed in 2½ years, despite an increase in population from 50 million in 1880 to 63 million in 1890, a saving of over 5 years' time.

In 1896, Hollerith formed the Tabulating Machine Company (absorbed in 1911 by International Business Machines), where he developed his machines for commercial sale. His first customers were the railroads, which used his machines for computation of freight statistics. IBM's real name at that time was the Computing-Tabulating-Recording Company. It was changed officially to IBM in 1924.

In 1905, after Hollerith had resigned, S. N. D. North, Director of the U. S. Census Bureau, hired James Powers (a comparatively little-known statistician from New Jersey) to develop more equipment in a new mechanical laboratory subsidized by Congress. Powers developed several tabulating and other punched-card machines, which were used successfully in the 1910 census. He developed the *simultaneous-punching* principle, which involves the keying in of all information to be punched in a card. Then, by depression of a certain key, the information is punched simultaneously. This technique has the advantage of allowing the keypunch operator enough time to ascertain that the data to be punched are correctly keyed in. This is in contrast with the *serial technique* of punching, which causes a character to be punched in a column each time a key is depressed.

Powers resigned his job with the Census Bureau in 1911 to form the Powers Accounting Machines Company in order to capitalize on his sorter and punching machines. His company was merged in 1927 with other office supply companies to form the Remington Rand Corporation. Presently, data-processing equipment is marketed through the Univac Division of Sperry Rand Corporation.

Developments in England

In 1926, the work of mechanizing calculations on navigational tables was initiated by L. J. Comrie, another pioneer in the field of computation, who was the deputy superintendent of the Nautical Almanac Office in England. Astronomical data were often faulty and unreliable because of the many mistakes resulting from the use of manual computation. Combie applied Hollerith's system for preparing the tables for the Nautical Almanac. Pertinent data were punched on cards in order to compute the position of the moon daily at noon and midnight from 1935 to 2000 A.D. From the results of the computations, the tables of the Nautical Almanac were prepared by the National Cash Register Company's accounting machines—hooked up in pairs and operated from a single shaft—a modern version of the Babbage difference engine.

COMPUTER DEVELOPMENT

Origin of the Digital Computer—(1812–1937)

Automatic computation began in 1812 with Charles P. Babbage, an English mathematician who thoroughly mastered the basic fundamentals of digital computers, to the marvel of those associated with him. Born in 1792 in Devonshire, England, Babbage became wealthy when his father (a banker) died and left him a sizable inheritance. He received a formal education interrupted by many personal factors. He taught himself enough mathematics to find out later at Cambridge University that what he knew was far beyond the background of his teacher. With two of his friends, George Peacock and John Herschel (whose father discovered the planet Uranus and who himself later became a noted astronomer), he formed the Analytical Society. In 1828, with no scholarly distinction, Babbage was elected to the Lucasian Chair of Mathematics (Newton's Chair) and held it for 11 years, an unprecedented event in view of the fact that he had not delivered even one lecture at the University.

THE DIFFERENCE ENGINE. One of the better-known contributions of Babbage was the "difference engine" (Fig. 4-6). In 1812, while looking at a table of logarithms full of mistakes, he began to think in terms of a machine capable of computing mathematical tables. The French government had already used several computers, which could only add and subtract. The job performed on the tables was initially divided into simple operations, each of which was assigned to a separate computer. Babbage firmly believed that he could develop a special-purpose machine capable of doing the computations automatically. Figure 4-7 presents the main idea of computing tables. It is centered around the fact that the level

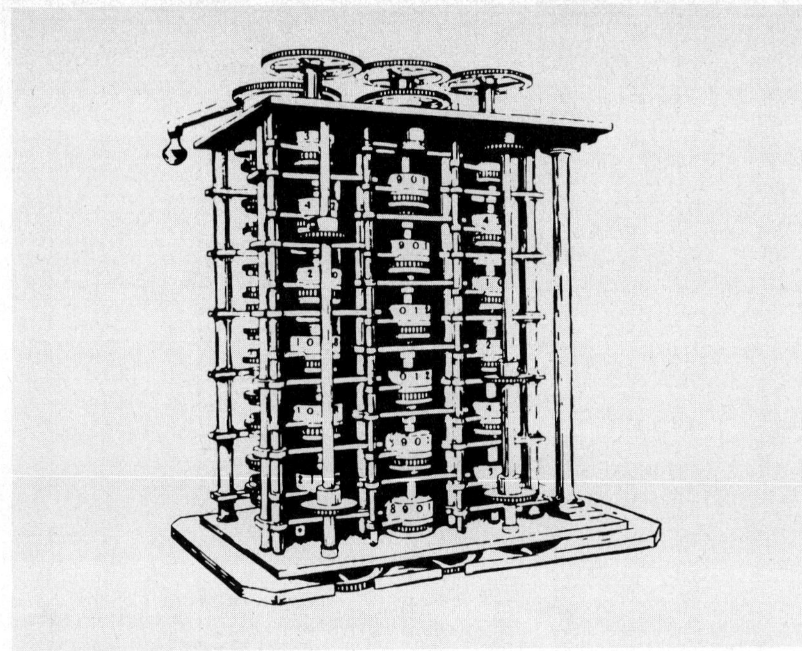

FIGURE 4-6. *Babbage's difference engine*

When A is		B would be =	1st. diff. D 1	2nd. diff. D 2	3rd. diff. D 3
0	then	0			
			1		
1		1		6	
			7		6
2		8		12	
			19		6
3		27		18	
			37		6
4		64		24	
			61		
5		125			

FIGURE 4-7. *Computing tables*

difference between values computed for a formula remains the same. Once the difference has been achieved, the subsequent values themselves can be produced by addition alone. Figure 4-7 shows the level difference of A^3 in the formula $B = A^3$.

The third-level difference corresponds to the third power of A in $B = A^3$ and is constant. If we wish to compute any other value of A, it can be done by addition alone. For example, in computing the value of $A = 6$, we would add $6 + 24 + 61 + 125$ to give us the sum of 216. Additional numbers in column D 2 can be found by simple addition—that is, 30, 36, 42, and so forth. From these numbers, the numbers of the second column (D 1), and ultimately those of the first column, can be found.

The foregoing idea was demonstrated in a model of the difference engine that Babbage made in 1822. It was received with such great interest and enthusiasm that the Royal Society promised to subsidize his project for developing a larger machine. The British government built a workshop for him, as well as a special fireproof vault to safeguard the blueprints of his engine. However, Babbage took more time than anticipated to complete his model, for he became interested in a new idea involving a machine of fantastic capabilities that he wanted to build instead. This "defection" led, in 1842, to withdrawal of government support for the project, which forced Babbage to give up its construction. A model of the difference engine built in 1859 for the Registrar General was later adopted by life insurance companies for computing life tables.

THE ANALYTICAL ENGINE. In 1833, while the difference-engine project was suspended for a year, Babbage conceived the idea of building an analytical engine that would be capable of performing any calculation. It was to be the first general-purpose digital computer. Babbage worked on it for the remaining years of his life and financed it completely from his own funds. He died in 1871 with the job undone, a disappointed man, although he left thousands of drawings that outlined the details of building the engine. Later his son, H. P. Babbage, took up his father's project and succeeded in completing part of the arithmetic unit.

Babbage's plan to build what seemed to his colleagues to be "Babbage's folly"—a fantastically large engine—at a time when such a machine was beyond the grasp and comprehension of the majority of mathematicians probably hampered the serious development of his ideas for over 100 years. Once he developed the idea of the analytical engine, he virtually abandoned the rather simple and useful difference engine. The analytical engine was to contain a memory unit, automatic printout, a sequential program control, and would accept arithmetic input from punched cards, such as those invented by Joseph Marie Jacquard. The engine fascinated Babbage, but his impatience with his staff and his failure to properly express himself made him a poor salesman of his ideas. Because of his limited success, he became a frustrated and unhappy man; he once told a friend that he could not remember a single completely happy day in his life. He seemed to feel that mankind was against him, and especially the English people and the British government. Despite his failure to "sell" his ideas, we may still think of Babbage as one of the great pioneers in the field of computation. He was a philosopher, a mathematician, a professor, and the writer of over 80 books and papers. He was a man of vision who possessed the foresight, courage, and imagination to work on and develop what he believed was possible and helpful to mankind.

Origin of the Analog Computer

All the foregoing counting machines were digital, in that they essentially performed counting operations. Many analog devices were known in the early history of Western Europe, and the first analog computation is believed to have been the use of graphs to solve surveying problems.

The first extensively used analog computer was the slide rule, developed in the early 1600s. Among other arithmetic functions, multiplication and division are performed simply by subtracting or adding the distance on the frame to that on the slider.

One of the earliest large-scale analog computers was built by Lord Kelvin in 1872 to predict the height of tides in English harbors. The action of its pulleys and weights acted to simulate the effect of the moon, sun, and winds on tides. The changes caused by the impact of these factors, combined with complex formulas stored inside the machine, produced graphs that indicated the degree of change of tides. Although this particular machine was bugged with imperfections, it nevertheless is considered a significant accomplishment in the development of analog computers.

THE COMPUTER INDUSTRY

Developments in Universities

Over 100 years passed before another machine similar to the one visualized by Babbage was developed. In 1937, Howard G. Aiken,[1] a professor of applied mathematics at Harvard University, developed some ideas involving mechanical calculations. Through E. Brown, who then was a consultant to International Business Machines (IBM) and a professor at Harvard, Aiken sold IBM his ideas, which resulted in a research grant to Harvard for developing a sequential computer. Seven years later (May 1944), through Aiken's efforts, the first large-scale electromechanical computer (named the Harvard *Mark I*) was put into service. Its calculating elements consisted of mechanical counters driven through electromagnetic clutches controlled by electromechanical relay circuits. It adds, subtracts, multiplies, divides, and compares quantities. It has the ability to refer to any tables stored in it for solving specific problems, and can be adapted to solve various kinds of problems for engineers, physicists,

[1] Possibly because of the early uses of the computer in World War II in solving secret wartime problems, Aiken voiced concern for the applications chosen for computers. At a testimonial dinner in 1961, he emphasized the hope that computers would be used for the benefit of man and not to his detriment. Aiken died in 1973 at the age of 73.

and mathematicians. It was the first machine to do long series of arithmetic and logical functions. After the Mark I, the Mark II, Mark III, and Mark IV were constructed by Aiken.

In the early 1940s, John W. Mauchly of the University of Pennsylvania became aware of the need for a high-speed electronic device able to do great quantities of statistical calculations for weather data. During World War II, a contract for the project was made between the University of Pennsylvania and the U.S. government.

In 1945, Mauchly and Presper Eckert used the facilities of the Moore School of Electrical Engineering to build a large general-purpose computer, called the ENIAC[2] (Electronic Numerical Integrator And Calculator). This machine was *the first all-electronic computer.* The ENIAC was considered very fast in working out long calculations. Initially, it was used primarily for solving mathematical problems in the areas of ballistics and aeronautics. Its main drawback was its having been designed for a special set of problems, thus making any change of programming relatively slow. The ENIAC was moved to Aberdeen Proving Grounds in Maryland in 1947 and continued in operation until October 2, 1955.

Also in the mid-1940s, J. von Neumann, another pioneer, issued a report to a group connected with the Moore School of Electrical Engineering at the University of Pennsylvania in which he described the *basic philosophy of computer design.* His stored-program concept replaced the wiring board that was used to program earlier computers. This concept has been incorporated in today's computers. Von Neumann himself did not believe that all his theories were practical, but with today's advanced technology almost everything he described in his theoretical paper has become reality. One often hears of computers designed on the "von Neumann concept."

As a result of von Neumann's paper, the Moore School of Electrical Engineering took over the project of developing the EDVAC (Electronic Discrete Variable Automatic Computer) for Aberdeen Proving Grounds. The EDVAC was then the prototype stored-program computer. It used punched paper tape for input and a program (which controlled the sequential operations) was placed in the memory of the machine. It was the *world's first commercial electronic data-processing machine.*

First-Generation (Vacuum-Tube) Computers (1946–1959)

In 1946, Eckert and Mauchly left the University of Pennsylvania, negotiated a contract with the National Bureau of Standards, and formed the Eckert–Mauchly Corporation. They started to develop the UNIVAC (uni-

[2] The ENIAC contained 19,000 vacuum tubes, weighed 30 tons, and occupied 1,500 square feet of floor space. It did in 1 day what once took 300 days to perform, thus outperforming electromechanical devices 300 to 1.

versal automatic computer), which was delivered to the Bureau of the Census on June 14, 1951, and was used continuously 24 hours a day for 12 years. The UNIVAC is well known for having predicted the victory of President Dwight D. Eisenhower in the 1952 election.[3] The Eckert–Mauchly Corporation later became a division of Sperry Rand Corporation.

Other computer manufacturers who developed first-generation computers were IBM, Burroughs, Honeywell, and Radio Corporation of America (RCA). IBM built the Mark Computer Series in the mid-1940s, delivered the 604 Electronic Calculating Punch in 1948, and the 702, 704, 705, and 709 commercial computers in the 1950s; the latter were sold in various modified versions through 1958. In 1953 IBM also delivered and sold over 1,000 IBM 650 magnetic drum computers. In 1957, Burroughs built a magnetic drum computer, the E101; Honeywell delivered its Datamatic 1000 late that year. RCA, on the other hand, was probably the first manufacturer to build an operational magnetic core memory, which was incorporated in its business-oriented, variable-word-length BIZMAC. The BIZMAC was already outmoded by the time it was delivered in 1956.

Since 1959, hundreds of large and small computers have been made available for commercial purposes. Well over 200 firms now manufacture computers and related products. Among them are The IBM Corporation, General Electric Corporation, Sperry Rand Corporation, Minneapolis-Honeywell, Inc., Burroughs Corporation, National Cash Register, and Control Data Corporation.

Compared to later computers, first-generation computers were bulky in size, somewhat inflexible, and demanded strict observance of air-conditioning requirements. They were made of vacuum tubes and relays, and had limited memory. However, they had advantages over the electromechanical data-processing machines. Their increased speed was attributed to the use of vacuum tubes for switching, and they were also the first practical systems to allow internal-type programming. It was this latter feature that provided comparison and "logical decisions" ability to be applied during calculations of data, and which, since then, has led to computers being referred to as "thinking machines."

Second-Generation (Transistorized) Computers (1959–1965)

The second-generation stage was marked by the advent of large-scale computers with large memories and microsecond access time. Solid-state

[3] On November 4, 1952, the UNIVAC computer on CBS was assigned the task of making hourly estimates of the number of states and the total electoral and popular votes to be carried by Stevenson and Eisenhower. At 9:15 that evening, with 3,398,745 votes in, UNIVAC predicted 5 states, 93 electoral votes, and 18,986,436 popular votes for Stevenson and 43 states, 438 electoral votes, and 32,915,049 popular votes for Eisenhower. Soon afterward, Stevenson conceded. This was the general public's first exposure to the uses and capabilities of the electronic computer. Source: *Computers and Automation,* Dec. 1967, p. 26.

components, such as diodes and transistors, replaced the vacuum tube, shrinking the physical size of the computer without decreasing its effectiveness. Greater computing capacity was realized through the use of magnetic cores for internal storage of data and instructions. Processing speed was increased, and scores of medium- to large-scale computers with built-in error detection and correction devices were designed to handle data at millisecond speeds. Air-conditioning requirements became less strict, and peripheral equipment also improved. High-speed printers and readers made on-line data processing possible. More sophisticated software (programs) and programming techniques became available.

Computer manufacturers who introduced business-oriented, second-generation computers were IBM, Minneapolis-Honeywell, Burroughs, National Cash Register, RCA, Philco, Univac, and Control Data Corporation. In 1959, IBM produced the 7070, 7080, and 7090 series; in 1960, the 1400 and 1600 series; and in 1962, the popular 7040 and 7044 computers. The IBM 1400 computer was the most popular second-generation system—nearly 15,000 units were produced.

Minneapolis-Honeywell brought out its Model 800, while in 1963 Burroughs unveiled the Burroughs 5000 (later modified under B5500) computer system. National Cash Register, one of the first companies to abandon the vacuum-tube computer market, produced the all-transistorized 304 computer. About the same time, RCA built its transistorized 501. In 1957, Philco produced the Philco 2000, a high-speed binary computer with capability for automatic switching for all tapes at all available channels. Univac introduced the UNIVAC III in the early 1960s and the 1107 thin-film computer in 1962. Control Data Corporation, formed in 1957 by a group of Univac employees, delivered its first 1604 computer in 1960 and the 600 model in 1963. This corporation is the Cinderella of electronic computers manufacturers. It has grown at a phenomenal rate, producing computers ranging from very small ones to the 6000 supercomputer series. The CDC 6600 supercomputer executes approximately 3 million operations per second; most large-scale computers installed in the mid-1960s were 6600's. In 1968, Control Data Corporation started delivery of a still more powerful CDC 7600 computer system, which executes instructions at the rate of 20 to 25 million instructions per second.

Third-Generation Computers (1965–1970)

The transition from the second- to the third-generation stage is fuzzy. Most computers placed on the market after 1964 are labeled third-generation computers. Third-generation computers make up the bulk of today's computers. They are characterized by monolithic integrated circuits, time-sharing terminals, multiprogramming (executing several programs in parallel style) and multiprocessing capability, real-time processing, and greater miniaturization of hardware.

More effective use of input–output devices and random-access devices (e.g., disk memory) now enables an organization to store virtually all its operating and functional data. Data-communication equipment facilitates transmission of data from any area to computer storage, connects operating facilities between two or more computers, and allows high-speed recording or inquiries to the computer system from remote stations. Optical scanning and MICR (magnetic ink character recognition) also are widely used in business organizations such as banks and insurance companies. The nanosecond processing speed is here to stay.[4]

The IBM 360 system [5] is believed to be the first commercially available data-processing system with a design based on the use of IBM's solid logic technology (SLT). The circuits of the arithmetic unit perform calculations in billionths of a second. They are smaller than transistor circuits, process information in less space, and transfer the results much faster. Because of these miniature-sized circuits, we now have smaller-sized computers with the capabilities of large-scale second-generation computers. Development of the computer industry by generations is presented in Fig. 4-8.

[4] The ENIAC (the first electronic computer) exhibited a processing speed factor of 10,000 over earlier computing methods. Twenty-five years later, through three successive generations, data-processing speed has gained 10,000 times or roughly 100,000 times the speed of the ENIAC. Although these figures are somewhat inaccurate, they give us an idea about the direction and rate of development in business data processing.

[5] Soon after the introduction of the IBM 360, RCA announced the availability of its Spectra 70 series, which is compatible with the 360 series. In December 1963, Minneapolis-Honeywell produced the Honeywell 200 and a whole line ranging from the small 100 to the very large 1200 computer. Other third-generation computers include Burroughs 6500, 7500, and 8500 large computers, Univac's 9000 series, National Cash Register's Century series (1968), and Control Data Corporation's new medium-priced 3000 series.

FIGURE 4-8. *Development of the computer industry by generations*

Item	First generation	Second generation	Third generation	Fourth generation
	4 4 4 4 5 5 5 5 5 5 5 5 5 5	6 6 6 6 6	6 6 6 6 6 7	7 7 7 7 7 7 7
	6 7 8 9 0 1 2 3 4 5 6 7 8 9	0 1 2 3 4	5 6 7 8 9 0	1 2 3 4 5 6 7 ---
Vacuum tube computers				
On-line, real-time processing				
Transistorized computers				
Multiprocessing concept				
Integrated circuitry				
Mass memory				
Time shared computer				
Microprogramming				
Display terminals				
Plated wire memory				
Mgt. information center				
Data banks				
Voice-picture data communication				

——— historical range of use
– – – – projected range of use

From the foregoing accomplishments, the greater flexibility and reliability of mass-storage devices and extensive use of communication terminals indicate a trend toward a single line of hardware and a total information system for business organizations. Scientists continue to probe into finding new ways of building computers that will be faster, smaller, more efficient, less costly, and more reliable than computers built to date. The fourth-generation series is just a beginning.

Fourth-Generation Computers (1970–1977 est.)

The end of 1970 marked the beginning of a family of new-generation computers, produced by IBM, NCR, Burroughs, and others with subtle but profound changes in data computations. What does fourth-generation computer mean and how does it alter existing data-processing systems? From a *design viewpoint,* this new breed will offer users increased input–output capability (or a separation of input and output functions from processing), longer component life, and greater system reliability.

From a *functional viewpoint,* we can now have powerful new languages that broaden the use of multiprogramming and multiprocessing, and a major shift from batch to on-line, remote, interactive processing. Whereas on-line processing has increased from 4 to 15 percent since 1965, the new line of fourth-generation computers is expected to boost this rate to 50 percent by the mid-1970s.

From a *managerial viewpoint,* fourth-generation computers are expected to make the manager's job easier and more efficient. With the availability of a management-oriented language and a network of compatible computer systems at central, divisional, and individual user locations, linked together by a remote terminal and a data-voice concept, the manager now can make direct man–machine communication for information acquisition and feedback more readily and efficiently than ever before. A management information center as such offers groups of managers physical interaction with the system. Furthermore, data banks and central computer-based files containing key information will allow management not only immediate access to the information it needs but also (1) realization of time saving, which can be devoted to the decision-making effort, (2) constructive changes in the manager's work habits, (3) a shorter distance between managerial levels, (4) lower user organization costs, (5) slow but significant replacement of traditional files and information storage, and (6) constructive changes in decision making. The electronic computer would be expected to do more communicating than computing. The mysterious punch-card holes representing data and the invisible evidence of data on magnetic tapes are now clarified through display terminals. Over 20,000 such devices are in use today, and close to 200,000 additional units are expected to be in operation by the mid-1970s.

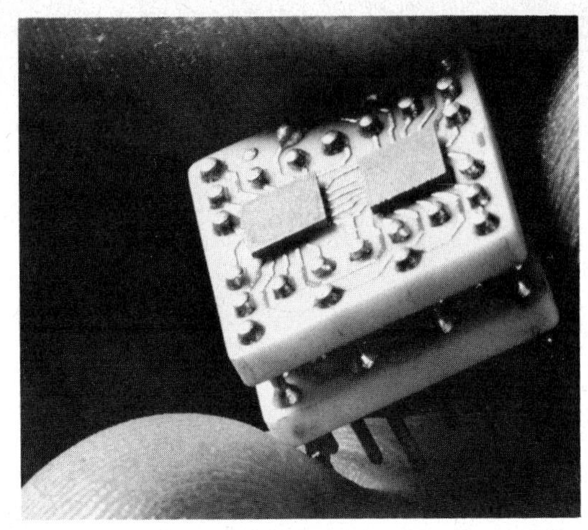

FIGURE 4-9. A magnified representation of a silicon chip used in advance supercomputers.

The IBM new-generation series, for example, is characterized by a variable micrologic concept used for instructions and execution in processing high-speed buffer memories, increased ease of diagnosing component breakdowns, and built-in communication capabilities between man and machine (Fig. 4-9). Variable micrologic is unique in the way it alters an instruction set through programming. For example, the logic of a MULTIPLY instruction can be altered to produce different results from the same available data. Furthermore, micrologic programming is designed so that any second- or third-generation computer logic can be duplicated and made compatible with new hardware. Thus, going from one system to another is now more reliable and effective than ever before.

With regard to size and type of internal memory, memory size ranges from 32,000 (32K)[6] to 2 megabytes, or 2 million bytes of storage. Internal memory is packaged in convenient sizes for future up-grading and is made up of ferrite core memory and a relatively faster MOS (metal-oxide-semiconductor integrated circuit) buffer memory where instruction and data are initially stored. During processing, the computer is designed to run at the higher speed rate of the buffer memory.

In addition to the availability of remote terminals for time sharing and conversation, interacting with a data base, and data entry and retrieval, other characteristics of the new generation of computers include

1. Increased use of multiprogramming (concurrent operation of two or more programs).
2. Increased availability of the computer system (reduction of the duration and frequency of interruptions to the system functions).
3. Shared memory storage (emergence of multiprocessor units).

[6] K = 1,000 storage locations.

4. Operation of the central processing unit of the computer in more than one mode (increasing the systems overall processing performance).
5. The use of newly developed software (programs and other related packages), which increases the system's reliability and effectiveness.

The fourth-generation computer, although considered more evolutionary than revolutionary, will cause several repercussions in the data-processing market. First, many leasing firms will encounter difficulty in allocating new customers to take over third-generation systems released by users moving into fourth-generation hardware. This means that an abundant supply of used computer systems will be available at a substantial discount from equipment owners and leasing firms. Second, there will be greater competition among computer manufacturers, especially with IBM, for a share of the new-generation market. Historically, other companies tend to imitate IBM in producing similar hardware and supportive software, with prices and terms essentially the same. A third factor will be top management's involvement in better, in-depth understanding of the electronic data-processing field. An organization will be expected to upgrade, replace, or retain an existing computer system based more on professional, technical knowledge of the hardware than the former impulsive, hasty commitment to any given computer make or system.

The foregoing innovations and developments point to a trend in the direction of using the computer as an agent of change and as a tool for channeling and manipulating such change, because change has become a dominant factor in our modern free world. Failure to harness this unique technology might lead to a breakdown rather than a breakthrough. The transition to the fourth-generation stage is being made more quietly than the transition from the second- to the third-generation stage, but the demand on the human side is for greater efforts, clearer thinking, and more sincere devotion to the cause of the organization and, in the long run, to the society of which we are a part.

KEY DEVELOPMENTS IN SOFTWARE

The term software refers to the computer programs, procedures, and specialized aids (e.g., compilers and library routines) that contribute to the operation of a computer system. The rate of progress in this area has not been as impressive as that of hardware. Much of the problem encountered in using computer systems for producing useful managerial information has been traced to software constraints. In some instances the use of advanced computer hardware is hampered by the inefficient or unfinished software package used to run the system. Consequently, more investment is being made in programming and other software aids than ever before.

Two recent developments in software worth noting are packaged programs and operating systems. Computer manufacturers and various software companies have been producing generalized programs for standardized applications, such as payroll, accounts receivable, and inventory control. Business firms, especially organizations that follow similar accounting procedures, no longer have to commit their programmers to the time-consuming production of such programs. Instead, programmer time can now be devoted to special-purpose applications unique to the firm in question.

The growing popularity of packaged programs has much to do with the shortage of qualified programmers and the fact that a well-written packaged program may be more efficient and less expensive than a similar program written by the traditional programmer. The primary drawback occurs in situations where a packaged program may require extensive modifications before it begins to operate properly for a given user. Even then, not all programmers might have the proper background in making required changes.

An operating system is a collection of specialized routines for operating the computer at maximum efficiency. Among the functions it performs are job scheduling, program and file loading, supervising program execution, allocating storage, coordinating interaction between man and computer, and controlling input and output operations and the functions in a time-sharing and multiprocessing mode. Multiprogramming refers to the concurrent execution of two or more programs by the computer. Details on operating systems and multiprogramming are covered in Chapter 12.

Developments in Programming Languages

A programming language is a key tool used in manipulating an electronic computer, as well as a means of communicating a problem to the computer for processing. It involves a formal description of the problem and a set of required instructions to the operating system. First-generation computers executed sets of symbols in a coded, *machine-oriented language.* Soon it was found that further use of machine language would be unwieldy. Each instruction had to be written in binary form, making it time consuming and, therefore, impractical for programming business problems. Furthermore, a program written for one computer did not run on another computer, and addition or deletion of one instruction could affect other instructions in the program.

When second-generation computers were introduced in 1959, the programming-language problem was alleviated by the development of *symbolic assembly language* in the form of symbolic codes. These languages (e.g., the autocoder) were easier to write than the machine language. However, the growing demands of computer programmers put a damper on symbolic languages in general. Differences in symbolic notation among symbolic programs of similar applications made it difficult to piece subprograms together or to use another person's program without major rewriting.

Later effort led to the development of *higher-level languages*, which offer better notation, are independent of the computer on which they are run, require of the programmer no particular understanding of the machine code or the characteristics of the computer used, and facilitate understanding, coding, debugging, documenting, and maintaining the program once it has been written. The program is finally translated into machine language by a special program, called a *compiler*, for processing.

Higher-level languages have several limitations.

1. Compilation takes time and is generally more time consuming on "one-shot" problems than would be the case in assembly-language programming. Furthermore, recompiling must be carried out every time a change is made in the source program.
2. Some compilers do not provide the proper diagnostics. A programmer with limited knowledge in machine code may find it more difficult to debug a higher-level language program than an assembly-language program.
3. Occasionally, a problem may require certain operations that cannot be performed without resorting to machine code. In this case, choice of the proper programming language to match the existing computer is very important. The user should also investigate the chosen language in terms of its (a) suitability to the types of problem area he is involved in, (b) efficiency of implementation, (c) potential in expanding its use to other application areas, and (d) ease of use and documentation.

Among the most commonly used higher-level languages are COBOL, FORTRAN, and PL/1; all are designed for specific application areas. COBOL (COmmon Business-Oriented Language) deals with business and financial applications; FORTRAN (FORmula TRANslation) deals with numerical, scientific (and more recently, nonscientific) applications; PL/1 (Programming Language 1) is aimed at wide data-processing application areas. Figure 4-10 summarizes the categories of languages written to date. Over 100 programming languages have been written to date; approximately 20 languages are obsolete, 75 are little used or only used on special applications, and 15 are presently active, including COBOL, FORTRAN, and PL/1.

FORTRAN. FORTRAN has had more impact on data computation than any other single development. It is a product of the Programming Research Group, Applied Science Division, of IBM. Specifications were submitted in November 1954 to allow the IBM 704 to process a problem in the form of a mathematical notation. In 1955, a working group, headed by John Buckus of IBM, completed the first FORTRAN manual, whose specifications were essentially the same as FORTRAN specifications set

- I. Languages for Numerical Scientific Problems
  - A. Early Systems
    - SHORT CODE
    - A-2 and A-3
    - BACAIC (Boeing Airplane Company Algebraic Interpretive Coding System)
    - PRINT (PRe-edited INTerpreter)
  - B. More Widely Used Systems
    - MATH-MATIC
    - UNICODE
    - IT (Interval Translator)
    - FORTRANSIT (FORTRAN and IT)
    - GAT (Generalized Algebraic Translator)
    - ALGOL (ALGOrithmic Language) 58, 60, 6X
      - Extensions of ALGOL
        - LISP2 (LISt Processing)
        - AED (Automated Engineering Design)
        - SFD-ALGOL
        - SIMULA (SIMUlation LAnguage)
        - DIAMAG (on-line extension of ALGOL)
        - GPL (Generalized Programming Language)
  - C. FORTRAN (FORmula TRANslator)
    - Extensions of FORTRAN
      - FORMAC (FORmula MAnipulation Compiler)
      - QUIKTRAN
      - GRAF (GRaphic Additions to FORTRAN)
      - DSL/90 (Digital Simulation Language on 7090)
  - D. On-Line Systems
    - JOSS (JOHNNIAC Open Shop System)
    - QUIKTRAN (on-line version of FORTRAN)
    - BASIC (Beginner's All-purpose Symbolic Instruction Code)
    - CPS (Conversational Programming System)
    - MAP (Mathematical Analysis without Programming)
    - APL/360 (A Programming Language on IBM 360)
    - DIALOG
    - AMTRAN (Automatic Mathematical TRANslation)
  - E. Languages with Fairly Natural Mathematical Notation
    - COLASL
    - MADCAP
    - MIRFAC (Mathematics In Recognizable Form Automatically Compiled)
- II. Languages for Business Data-Processing Problems
  - A. Early Languages
    - FLOW-MATIC (implemented on UNIVAC I)
    - AIMACO (AIr MAterial COmmand Compiler)
    - FACT (Fully Automatic Compiling Technique)
    - GECOM (GEneralized COMpiler)
  - B. COBOL (COmmon Business-Oriented Language)
- III. Storing and List Processing Languages
  - IPLV (Information Processing Language V)
  - L^6 (Bell Telephone Laboratories Low-Level Linked Languages)
  - LISP 1.5 (LISt Processing)
  - COMIT
  - SNOBOL
  - TRAC (Text Reckoning And Compiling)
- IV. Formal Algebraic Manipulation Languages
  - ALGY
  - FORMAC (FORmula MAnipulation Compiler)
  - MATHLAB
  - ALTRAN (extension to FORTRAN)
  - FLAP (for symbolic mathematics)

FIGURE 4-10. *Summary of computer languages*

- V. Multipurpose Languages
  - JOVIAL (Jules' Own Version of IAL)
  - PL/1 (Programming Language 1)
  - Formula ALGOL (extension of ALGOL)
  - LISP2
- VI. Specialized Languages
  - A. Languages for Special Application Areas
    1. Machine-tool control
       - APT (Automatically Programmed Tools)
    2. Civil engineering
       - COGO (COordinate GeOmetry)
       - STRESS (STRuctural Engineering Systems Solver)
       - ICES (Integrated Civil Engineering System)
    3. Logical design
       - APL (A Programming Language)
       - LOTIS (LOgic TIming, Sequencing)
       - LDT (Logic Decision Translator)
       - SFD-ALGOL (System Function Description)
    4. Digital simulation of block diagrams
       - DYANA (DYnamics ANAlyzer)
       - DYSAC (DigitallY Simulated Analog Computer)
       - DAS (Digital Analog Simulator)
       - DSL/90 (Digital Simulator Language on IBM 7090)
    5. Compiler writing
       - CLIP (Compiler Language for Information Processing)
       - TMG
       - COGENT (COmpiler and GENeralized Translator)
       - META 5
       - TRANDIR
       - FSL (Formula Semantics Language)
       - AED (Automated Engineering Design or ALGOL Extended for Design)
  - B. Specialized Languages Across Application Areas
    1. Discrete simulation
       - DYNAMO
       - GPSS (Generalized Purpose Systems Simulator)
       - SIMSCRIPT
       - SOL (Simulation Oriented Language)
       - MILITRAN
       - SIMULA (SIMUlation LAnguage)
       - OPS (On-Line Process Synthesizer)
    2. Query
       - COLINGO and C-10 (Compile On LINe and GO)
       - 473L Query
       - ADAMS (A DAta Management System)
       - BASEBALL (data-base system containing information about baseball)
       - DEACON (Direct English Access and CONtrol)
       - AESOP (An Environment System for On-Line Processing)
    3. Graphic and on-line display languages
       - GRAF (GRaphic Addition to FORTRAN)
       - PENCIL (Pictorial ENCodIng Language)
       - Graphic
       - DOCUS (Display-Oriented Computer Usage System)
       - AESOP (An Evolutionary System for On-Line Processing)
    4. Computer-aided design
       - AED

Source: Jean E. Sammet. *Programming Languages: History and Fundamentals.* Englewood Cliffs, N.J.: Prentice-Hall, Inc., 1969.

FIGURE 4–10. *(cont'd)*

in 1954. Later in 1957, Buckus presented the first paper on this most widely used higher language before the Western Joint Computer Conference.

Following FORTRAN I, FORTRAN II was released in 1958 as a new version with significant additions. It was designed for the IBM 709 and 650 computers. FORTRAN III became known in 1960 and was used in programming the 7070 and 1620 computers. In 1962, FORTRAN IV was released on the IBM 7070 and, with periodic improvements, it has been used ever since.

Although this artificial language was initially developed for scientific computations, it has been used recently in business data processing. It can be learned quickly, a FORTRAN program can be written in a relatively short time, and the computer can quickly translate it into an object program that works well for most problems. FORTRAN will be discussed fully in Chapter 18.

COBOL. In May 1959, the Pentagon called a meeting of 40 representatives from computer users, computer manufacturers, and government installations to discuss the feasibility of developing a common business-oriented language adaptable to computer data processing and independent of any computer make or model. Late that year a committee made up of members from six major computer manufacturers [7] and two government agencies met to study the status of existing business computers. After several meetings, the committee adopted the name COBOL for a language oriented strictly to solving business problems. After some revision and editing, the language was approved and, in April 1960, was published by the U.S. Government Printing Office. Changes and modifications were introduced each year, resulting in a successive yearly publication of an updated version of COBOL.

As will be discussed in Chapter 17, COBOL is a natural, hardware, English-like language, which offers readable and understandable program details and which can be used as direct input to the computer. Its conversion from one computer to another is quite simple, and its highly readable form is most appreciated by programmers with limited experience and users who wish to examine the program content.

Standardization of COBOL began in January 1963 under the United States of America Standards Institute (USASI). A voluntary federation of about 150 trade and professional associations, USASI facilitates the development of voluntary standards. The COBOL standard, which was approved by committee consensus, gained wide acceptance. The implementation of COBOL has been carried out by every computer manufacturer, as pressure was exerted both from customers and, in particular, from government agencies, which require the use of COBOL on federal projects.

[7] IBM, Burroughs, RCA, Sylvania Electric, Minneapolis-Honeywell, and the Remington Rand Division of Sperry Rand Corporation.

PL/1. A relatively new language, PL/1 has established stable roots since its inception. FORTRAN's limited capability in handling alphanumeric data and its lack of adaptability to various programming techniques and equipment led IBM late in 1963 to form an Advanced Language Development Committee to develop a language that would alleviate these problems. After a year of revisions and editing, a modified version of what is now called Programming Language 1 (PL/1) was presented. Early in 1965, a PL/1 department was formed within IBM to manipulate all activities related to this language. The first compiler for the IBM 360 was released in August of the following year.

PL/1 is a very general language with notations closer in succinctness to FORTRAN than to COBOL. A FORTRAN programmer should find no difficulty learning PL/1, since it was meant to be applied in areas designed for FORTRAN and COBOL. Because several manufacturers have expressed interest in the potential use of PL/1, teams have been formed within these firms to study the language and pass judgment to management regarding its implementation. Thus, within 5 years from the beginning of the project, PL/1 has had a positive effect on the electronic data-processing industry. Although its future is unclear, it could very well replace major languages such as COBOL and FORTRAN.

SUMMARY

Developments in data processing date back to the beginning of mankind. Historical records show finger counting was used in Roman schools, and the abacus was an early manual calculating device. Double-entry bookkeeping started in Italy in 1340, and the "grating," Napier "bones," and the "sluggard" methods were developed in an attempt to establish manual aids to written calculations. In 1642, Pascal built the first mechanical calculator. In 1873, Baldwin built the first calculating machine, which marked the beginning of the calculating-machine industry in the United States.

Punched-card data processing began in 1801 with Jacquard's perfection of a punched-card-operated machine for cloth weaving. In 1890, Herman Hollerith completed a punched-card system to process the 1890 U.S. census. The company he formed in 1890 was absorbed in 1911 by IBM. In 1905, James Powers took over as director of the U.S. Census Bureau. The punched-card machine he developed was successful in processing the 1910 U.S. census. The company he formed in 1911 was merged in 1927 with other companies to form the Remington Rand Corporation.

The digital computer originated with Babbage's development of the analytical engine in 1833. In 1944, Aiken of Harvard developed the Mark I; next, in 1945, Mauchly and Eckert produced the ENIAC—the first all-electronic computer. During this time, von Neumann's stored-program concept helped build the EDVAC—the world's first commercial electronic computer.

The computer industry underwent four generations of technological change. First-generation computers, exemplified in the UNIVAC, were made of vacuum tubes and relays and had limited memory. Second-generation computers were transistorized, less bulky, had large memories, and operated at microsecond speed. Third-generation computers, exemplified by the IBM 360 line, are characterized by monolithic integrated circuits, time-sharing terminals, multiprogramming and multiprocessing capability, real-time processing, and greater miniaturization of hardware. Today's fourth-generation computer handles data at the nanosecond speed, and offers increased input–output capability, longer component life, and greater system reliability. It is characterized by a variable micrologic concept used for instruction and execution in processing high-speed buffer memories and built-in communication capabilities between man and machine.

Software developments include the availability of packaged programs and operating systems. Programming languages have also evolved from machine language, to assembly language, to higher-level languages, which offer better notation and are machine independent. Among the widely used higher-level languages are FORTRAN, COBOL, and PL/1. FORTRAN is a problem-oriented language that is quite convenient for many business applications. COBOL is used exclusively for programming business applications. PL/1 is a relatively new language combining some of the best features of other languages.

TERMS TO LEARN

Abacus
Analytical engine
COBOL
Difference engine
EDVAC
ENIAC
FORTRAN
Fourth-generation computers
Mark I
Numerical wheel calculator
PL/1
Second-generation computer
Serial-punching principle
Simultaneous-punching principle
Third-generation computers
UNIVAC

QUESTIONS

1. What is an abacus? Discuss its origin.
2. What is the "grating" method? Who originated it? Explain its operation.
3. Explain briefly the way Napier's "bones" perform the multiplication function.

4. Show how multiplying 7×9 is done by the use of the "sluggard" method.
5. State briefly the main ideas of Leibniz. What were the results of these ideas?
6. Summarize the main idea underlying Babbage's difference engine. How is it different from the analytical engine?
7. What is the main contribution of Howard G. Aiken to the computer industry?
8. What factors were responsible for the initiation and, later, the development of punched-card data processing? Explain.
9. Describe the main contributions of Herman Hollerith and James Powers to punched-card data processing. What organizations developed from their work?
10. In what respect is a slide rule similar to an analog computer?
11. What is meant by a second-generation computer? Discuss the differences between first-, second-, third-, and fourth-generation computers.
12. Summarize the distinguishing features of higher-level programming languages. Which language would you choose for ease of programming business applications? Why?
13. What is a packaged program? How is it different from an operating system?

SUGGESTED READING

BERKELEY, E. C. *Giant Brains or Machines That Think.* New York: Science Editions, Inc., 1949.

BUDD, A. E. *A Method for the Evaluation of Software: Procedural Language Compilers*—Particularly COBOL and FORTRAN, MITRE Corp., (DDC), AD651142, Commerce Department Clearinghouse, Springfield, Va., April 1966.

CHAPIN, N. "What Choice of Programming Languages?" *Computers and Automation,* XIV, Feb. 1965, pp. 12–14.

HOPPER, G. M., and J. W. MAUCHLY. "Influence of Programming Techniques in the Design of Computers," *Proceedings of the IRE,* XLI, Oct. 1953, pp. 1250–1254.

JEQUIER, NICOLAS. "Computer Industry Gaps," *Science and Technology,* Sept. 1967, pp. 30–39.

Management Operating System: Inventory Management and Materials Planning. Detail, IBM Corp., E20-0050-0, Data Processing Division, White Plains, N.Y.

ROSEN, SAUL. "Electronic Computers: A Historical Survey," *Computing Surveys,* I, March 1969, pp. 7–36.

ROSENBERG, J. M. *The Computer Prophets.* New York: Macmillan Publishing Co., Inc., 1969.

SAMMET, JEAN. *Programming Languages: History and Fundamentals.* Englewood Cliffs, N.J.: Prentice-Hall, Inc., 1969, pp. 2–61.

SCHWARTZ, J. I. "Comparing Programming Languages," *Computers and Automation,* XIV, Feb. 1965, pp. 15–16, 26.

SHAW, C. J. "Assemble or Compile?," *Datamation,* X, June 1964, pp. 34–35.

VON NEUMANN, JOHN. *The Computer and the Brain.* New Haven, Conn.: Yale University Press, 1950.

WHITEMAN, I. R. "New Computer Languages," *International Science and Technology,* April 1966, pp. 62–68.

CHARACTERISTICS AND INTERNAL OPERATION OF A BUSINESS COMPUTER

business computer systems— an overview

5

WHAT IS A BUSINESS COMPUTER SYSTEM?

THE MAKEUP OF A BUSINESS COMPUTER SYSTEM

Hardware

primary operations of a computer system

Software

Peopleware

USES AND CAPABILITIES OF BUSINESS COMPUTERS

LIMITATIONS OF BUSINESS COMPUTERS

Inability to Handle Unprogrammed Information

Inability to Make Decisions Independently

Occasional Breakdowns

Impracticality of Use on Nonrecurring or Nonrepetitive Calculations

DATA-PROCESSING METHODS

CLASSIFICATION OF BUSINESS COMPUTER SYSTEMS

Purpose

special-purpose computers
general-purpose computers

Type

hybrid computers

Capacity

minicomputers
small-sized computers
medium-sized computers
large-scale computers

Punched-card data-processing systems and the equipment associated with them are in limited use today, as they are being rapidly replaced by computers of various sizes and types. This dramatic transition is explained by the operation of a relatively advanced processing routine that involves the use of electronics. Such a routine is designed to serve business firms in a much more efficient, accurate, and economical manner than the punched-card routine. Although computer methods provide cheaper handling once the system has been installed, initial costs must be justified on the basis of the nature of the operations to be performed and the data to be gathered.

The development of computer systems for business data processing is a perfect example of the rapid technological change manifested in the adage, "What is new today may become obsolete tomorrow." Research, experimentation, and the actual size of the "new" systems increase in those industries that find electronic systems economical. The "new" improves on the basic ideas behind the "old" punched-card processing, just as the once-"new" punched-card systems supplanted the "old" manual methods.

Thus, to give students a well-rounded picture of developments in the business data-processing field, a description and analysis of the development of the "Babbage" ideas in modern computer systems are essential. When today's students enter business, they will probably find themselves involved either in the actual operation or in the consideration of a computer installation. Hence, their need for understanding the ideas involved in both punched-card and electronic systems stands out in clear relief.

The purpose of Part II is to instill an understanding of the overall functioning of electronic data-processing systems. A clear-cut picture of the computer's basic elements, its language, the means by which it calculates and processes data, and how instructions are written so that it can perform its various calculations should enable students to think intelligently, rather than "awesomely," about these machines and their purposes in business.

WHAT IS A BUSINESS COMPUTER SYSTEM?

A business computer system is one that manipulates business data within its main unit, based on a predetermined series of steps or set of instructions, with a minimum of human intervention. A more specific description is "automatic high-speed electronic business data-processing digital computer."

Automatic is synonymous with *self-directing*. Once the computer receives a set of instructions that tells it what to do and how to produce the desired results, it performs all the required work independently of human intervention. Its self-direction is limited, however, by the instructions made available to it by a human programmer.

High-speed refers to the ability of the computer to perform required operations at speeds ranging from a minimum of 1,000 operations per second to around 1,000,000 per second. A few computers operate beyond this limit.

Electronic explains how a computer is able to operate as a high-speed machine. Electronics relates to the flow of electrons behaving as signals in the circuitry of electronic equipment. These signals are manipulated to represent numeric, alphabetic, or special codes. The electrical pulse's high speed permits electronic computers to operate efficiently, with information flowing thousands of times faster than it does through electromechanical or other machines.

Business data processing refers to the manipulation of given business facts to obtain a desired result in the form of printed financial reports or other business statements.

Digital defines the type of computer. Such a computer utilizes counting devices and numbers to express variable quantities and for calculations. By contrast, the analog computer transforms physical flows, such as temperature or pressure, into electrical quantities to solve a problem.

Computer refers to a machine capable of solving problems in their entirety, and not merely the arithmetic operations that can be performed on any calculator. Although referred to as a "human brain," a computer is no more human than an electric saw or automobile. It is assembled from many different parts. However, the manner in which a computer processes data is seemingly "human," primarily because it is designed to follow the same routine that a human being would have to follow in solving the problem. It simulates the patterns of human thought, but does not do the thinking.

THE MAKEUP OF A BUSINESS COMPUTER SYSTEM

An ongoing computer data-processing system requires the functioning of (1) primary and supportive *hardware,* (2) *software,* and (3) *"peopleware."* Each of these areas is special purpose but integral in orientation, and must function in line with the overall design and demands of the system. Details on hardware are covered in Chapters 8 to 13, software is discussed in Chapters 16–20, and peopleware in Chapters 21 and 22.

Hardware

The term *hardware* generally refers to the equipment that prepares and reads input data, the central processor, which stores, computes, and controls the data it receives, and the printing devices, which print out the results arrived at by the central processor. Auxiliary hardware such as the key punch, which operates independently and is detached from the main computer system, is called *off-line* equipment; subsystems such as the card reader and the printer, which are directly connected to the computer system, are called *on-line* equipment. A summary of the type of hardware used in various capacities is presented in Fig. 5-1.

Data Preparation	Input	Processing	Output
Key punch devices Verifiers Paper tape punch devices Paper tape to magnetic tape converters Paper tape to punch card converters Magnetic tape encoders	Punched card reader Paper tape reader Magnetic tape unit Magnetic ink character reader Optical scanner Console typewriter	Central processing unit (primary storage, arithmetic, control)	Card punch Paper tape punch Visual display Line printer Audio response Console typewriter

FIGURE 5-1. Function of key computer components

Primary Operations of a Computer System. The primary operations of a computer system are analogous to the human thought process of communicating, holding information, choosing among selected alternatives, calculating, and producing a result. For example, in determining the current cash balance of the ABC Company (adding the previous balance of $30 to today's receipts of $5), the elements required for a correct solution are as follows:

1. **Communicating.** The correct answer cannot be produced without communicating relevant data. The instruction implying addition of the previous balance of $30 to today's receipts of $5 must be accessible and properly visualized.
2. **Holding information and making decisions.** After the instruction (add) and the amounts to be added (30 and 5) are visualized or read, they are retained in the mind or memory. Memory stores the desired data as long as they are needed. It is also the area where logical decisions are made concerning the problem. The person checks for positive signs in both amounts, ascertains that no fractions are ignored, and decides whether the amounts in memory are sufficient data for producing a satisfactory answer.
3. **Calculating.** The next step is to add 30 plus 5 to get the sum of $35—the new cash balance.
4. **Producing a result.** Upon arriving at the sum ($35), the answer is written down on paper with the proper description.

The foregoing human thought process points out that the brain cannot work effectively without the aid of its auxiliary units or organs. The eyes, for instance, read the data written on the blackboard and communicate (transport) the instruction (add) and the amounts (30 and 5) to be added to the brain. After addition, the hand communicates the answer to the user by writing it on paper. Like the human brain, the business computer cannot function effectively without the aid of its auxiliary units. That is the reason why we speak in terms of a computer system rather than of a single computer. The operations comprising any business computer system are as follows:

1. **Input.** For a computer system to process business problems, it must be capable of receiving business data in an orderly manner. Business data, called *input,* are placed in a device called an *input device,* which is the "eye" of the computer. The device reads the desired data and communicates them (through cables) to the memory unit of the computer (middle square of Fig. 5-2).
2. **Processing.** The elements involved in processing are primary storage, "decision making," computations, and the stored program. The data read by the input device are transferred to the primary storage section of the computer (called memory) and are held there until arithmetic is performed. Primary storage is the heart of the com-

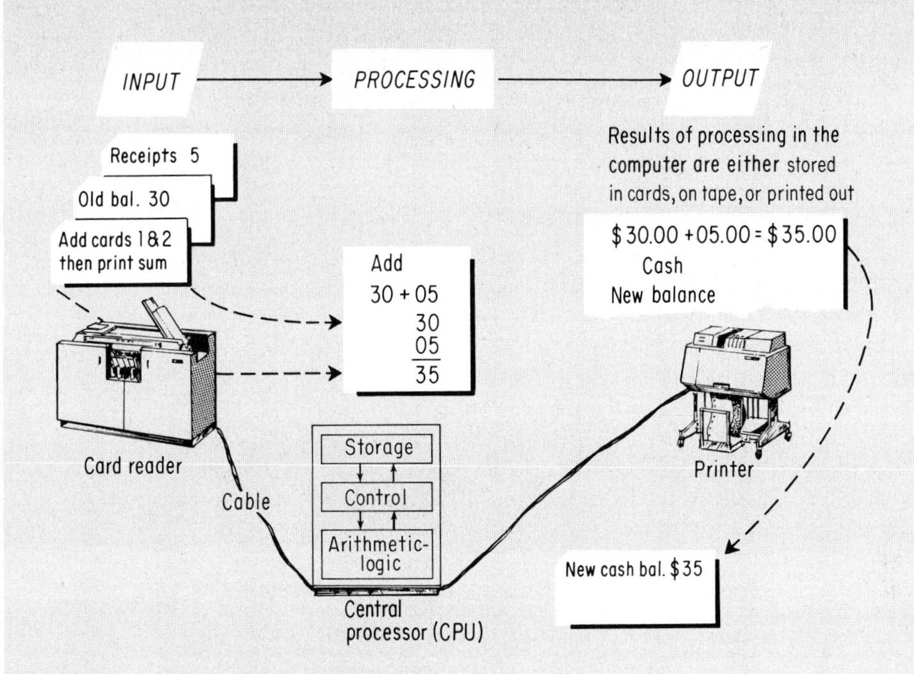

FIGURE 5-2. Functional organization of a business computer system, using card reader and printer as examples of input and output devices

puter and is analogous to the "human brain" (middle square in Fig. 5-2).

The arithmetic-logic unit is designed to do arithmetic, compare values, "logically" to determine their equality, to distinguish between a positive and a negative value, and to determine whether a number is greater than, equal to, or less than zero. Arithmetic is performed by reading numbers into registers that are added, subtracted, or operated on. Once completed, the computer result is either temporarily stored for later use or is produced in the form of printed output.

The control unit establishes order by policing the operation of the computer system. It determines the time when input data are read into storage, when arithmetic operation is performed on selected stored data, and when output information is printed out. Thus, stored program instructions are first fed in a predetermined sequence into the control unit, where they are interpreted before any "authorization" is transmitted to the system device involved for action.

3. **Output.** The final element of a computer system is the preparation of information resulting from the computations made in the central processing unit. Referred to as *readable output,* this step usually

occurs in the form of a punched card or magnetic tape. In certain systems, punched paper tape is also available as a form of output. In the example involving the human thought process, the paper is the output medium and the pencil is the output unit or device.

Software

For the computer to read, remember, make decisions, calculate, update files, and write in proper sequence, it must have access to prewritten, stored programs designed for that purpose. *Software* commonly refers to such programs, as well as to operating aids (usually made available to the user by the manufacturer) that extend the capabilities of the computer system. A stored program contains instructions that tell the computer what steps to take, what data to work on, and what to do with the results. In the computer a control element instructs the central processing program, which causes all other subsystems to operate in the correct manner and contribute to obtaining the desired results.

Peopleware

The term *peopleware* encompasses the data-processing staff that designs, programs, and operates the many facets of a computer installation. Among others, the staff consists of systems analysts, programmers, and console operators, who perform special-purpose tasks under the supervision of a manager especially trained for his role.[1] These people all work as a team to operate the system by the following steps:

1. **Problem definition**—deciding on the information requirements of the proposed system.
2. **System analysis and design**—planning and organizing the procedural aspects and logic of the proposed system.
3. **Program development**—preparing clearly defined instructions in machine-readable format.
4. **Input data preparation**—coding or storing input data in a suitable medium for processing.
5. **Program loading**—storing the program in the central processing unit in preparation for a "live" run and output acquisition.

USES AND CAPABILITIES OF BUSINESS COMPUTERS

Digital computers used in business are built to aid man in doing the many repetitive tasks that make up the course of his business. They boost his productivity and improve the quality of his output, regardless of whether

[1] Details on each specialty are explained in Chapter 22.

this output is a tangible product or an intangible service. Business computers do this in several ways:

1. By processing a greater number of items per second, the exact amount depending upon the type and size of the computer. Because the speed of the electronic computer is measured in thousandths, millionths, or billionths of a second,[2] it is faster than any other type of machine designed to do similar work. With this capability, a business firm can conveniently update each and every record, because actual calculations take very little time.
2. By processing business data more accurately than alternative methods. A clerk, *at his best,* makes at least one error per 100 manual calculations, whereas the computer's rate of error is a fraction of 1/10,000th of 1 percent, or 99.999+ percent accuracy. A punched-card system operates with a much higher degree of accuracy than any manual system, but it cannot operate with as much accuracy as an electronic system, because it is composed mostly of mechanical parts. Although electricity is used to operate most punched-card systems, the fact that they are mechanical makes them subject to greater error than a computer system, which operates by means of electronic circuitry.
3. By allowing time for creative and intelligent planning. A computer's greater versatility in tirelessly performing millions of operations frees great amounts of time for more productive use.
4. By lowering processing costs. In general, the cost of each application processed by a computer is lower than alternative machine methods. Although the initial cost of obtaining the computer is high, the saving resulting from its speed and accuracy in many cases justifies the decision to install it.

Among the chief capabilities of business computers are the following:

1. **Ability to handle repetitive tasks.** A business computer is designed to handle any repetitive, recurring problem using different data as long as it has access to prescribed procedures.
2. **Self-operational ability.** The business computer is capable of storing (temporarily or permanently) the data and the program that tells it what to do. The program is loaded in primary storage for effecting direct access to the data and for providing a self-operating situation with a minimum of human intervention.
3. **Ability to communicate effectively.** A business computer is capable of accepting information and, after performing the desired routine, of giving correct results.

[2] Although this speed is fantastic, a few of the latest supercomputers perform at the picosecond level (one trillionth of a second), a breakthrough in electronic computation.

4. **Ability to "make decisions."** A computer cannot do anything a man could not do if he had the time. A digital computer is capable of following instructions stored in it and of modifying any of those instructions if necessary. In other words, the computer is present so that it can choose between alternative courses of action to perform the right routine. In this respect, the act is referred to as "decision making." However, the choice between alternatives is limited to those prepared for it by the programmer. The computer can decide on the correct sequence of steps necessary to solve a given problem on the basis of conditions occurring in the interim. In computer terminology, this is referred to as *feedback*.
5. **Ability to check on the correctness of its own work.** A business computer is capable of checking on the accuracy of its own work by means of a parity check. In this, the computer counts the number of characters it has in storage and keeps track of every character resulting from an arithmetic or other operation. Details on parity check are covered in Chapter 6.
6. **Ability to do new and additional tasks.** A computer can be instructed to do additional tasks, such as printing an order every time the stock level of a given item falls below a desired minimum. By the same token, it can print a list of all the items currently available in stock by color, size, and/or other specifications. It can tabulate or summarize quantitative information more effectively than any human clerk, because it is not subject to "boredom."

Interest in the practical use of electronic systems developed for various reasons. One hundred years ago, electronic computers were not really needed for the relatively slow pace of events characteristic of an agricultural economy. If they had been, there would have been interest in building them, because the ideas governing their operation and behavior were already known (see Chapter 4). However, as economies were transformed from basically agricultural to predominantly manufacturing or industrial ones, the need for machinery and the adoption of automated techniques to mass produce for expanding markets became more and more apparent. Business executives became very conscious that, if they were to compete in rapidly growing competitive markets, they must have essential business data about their products as quickly as possible and in usable form. Therefore, the elements of time, speed, and accuracy in data preparation become more important as economies grow and markets expand.

The saving of time by speed can be, and is, solved by increasing clerical help to process and handle paperwork. However, increasing the clerical staff results in the generation of new problems:

1. A firm must hire supervisors to organize and direct the many plans and procedures handled by clerks, and this results in an increase in the cost of data-handling tasks.
2. Morale problems increase with an increase in human help. Many

office workers become bored with the repetitive nature of their work, and its monotony causes them to brood about many things, at the expense of their accuracy and efficiency.

3. Storage becomes a problem, because all business data must be filed regularly.

Even though the problems of time and speed are solved in this manner, the high costs associated with such a solution are illustrated by the fact that clerical workers receive approximately $1 out of every $8 paid for wages and salaries in the United States. Thus, the basic problem of lowering the cost of data handling and data processing remains. To solve it, some industries have moved ahead successfully into the area of electronic data processing. The banking industry, for instance, processes well over 10 billion checks every year. Each check is handled several times and must go through a long routine before it is finally paid and returned. At present, most large banks are using magnetic character sensing by reader–sorter machines, which read the depositor's account number and other related data printed in magnetic ink on the face of the check. Checks are sorted into the desired classifications or sequence in a fraction of the time that would be needed to do this manually.

LIMITATIONS OF BUSINESS COMPUTERS

Inability to Handle Unprogrammed Information

A computer can manipulate the business information it has been programmed to handle and communicate it to the user. It is incapable of handling almost anything beyond this level. In other words, it cannot make a decision in situations where *qualitative* factors are involved. A computer, for instance, can show certain expense items that exceed a desired maximum, but it cannot take action to stop the expense.

Computers have been employed to compose music, write poetry (with laughable results), and play chess; but so far these activities are relatively limited and involve "thinking" in a very restrictive sense. They are still subject to human direction and control. However, these accomplishments present all kinds of new opportunities for computer scientists and users.

Inability to Make Decisions Independently

A computer can neither make its own program nor determine its own course of action. Because of the way it is designed, it has to be told in a very detailed manner how to do any given job. All alternative courses of action are predetermined and stored as a part of the program by a human programmer. The computer can choose a desired routine only if it is provided for in the program.

Occasional Breakdowns

Even though a computer processes business data in a manner close to perfection, it cannot be perfect. Anything made by man is subject to occasional breakdowns. It has been estimated that up to 10 percent of scheduled computer time may be lost due to computer failure, power failure, or the failure of some related supportive hardware.

A computer occasionally develops "bugs." A story is told of a digital computer that sold the wrong stocks because of a slipped cog. Another concerns a computer operated by the Army that ordered millions of dollars' worth of items shipped to Europe that were never requested. These stories, although anecdotal, do point out that environmental, technical, and human factors can contribute to the failure of a computer. All manufacturers prescribe the manner in which their computers are to be treated by outlining a workable series of steps for proper operation. When the instructions are followed exactly by the user, a computer's accuracy, compared with that of a human being, is perfect. Some computers built today can perform over 9 billion operations without an error.

Impracticality of Use on Nonrecurring or Nonrepetitive Calculations

The best justification for the use of a computer in business lies in its application to routine, continuous, repetitive tasks. A computer should not be expected to perform nonrecurring or nonrepetitive calculations on small amounts of data. As was previously mentioned, every application requires the preparation of a program to tell the computer what to do and how to go about reaching a solution to the problem. Considering the amount of human effort and time expended in program preparation, it is normally anticipated that the application will be used over and over again. The many hours involved in writing the program become only a matter of minutes to the computer when it processes the complete application. Therefore, programming effort should be applied toward recurring, routine applications and not toward those jobs that involve one-time exceptions or infrequent processing.

DATA-PROCESSING METHODS

Data are processed either in batches or on line (immediately) as they are received. Batched data are usually accessed sequentially through such storage devices as magnetic tape or punched cards. No record in the file can be read without scanning through the records preceding it. However, batched data are accessed at random when they are stored in direct-access storage devices, such as magnetic disks or magnetic drums. In this approach any record can be processed without having to scan over the records preceding it.

On-line processing is ideal in production and inventory control, airline and hotel reservation systems, and savings and loan account routines when the records of the transactions and the bank records must be kept current. Batch processing is ideal for payroll, accounts receivable, and other applications when there is obvious saving of computer time if the transactions are accumulated and periodically processed in batches, rather than on line. Often the entire master file is on magnetic tape and is put through the computer every time it needs updating. Prior to the actual computer run, the batch of transactions involved is first sorted and sequenced in the same order as the master file. When the operation begins, the computer reads each transaction and locates the corresponding record on tape, and so on, until the entire tape is updated. A new, updated master tape is written and used for the next updating operation.

Cost savings and efficiency of operation are also realized when transactions are processed in batches through direct-access file storage devices. Although not mandatory, sequencing a large volume of input transactions prior to the actual computer run results in a faster and less costly operation. In the case of only a few transactions, sequencing might not be necessary, as it often takes more time to put them in sequence than the extra time taken by the movement of disks to locate the appropriate records.

CLASSIFICATION OF BUSINESS COMPUTER SYSTEMS

The first computer was made commercially operational in the early 1950s. Today, over 100,000 computer systems, with a value of over $25 billion, are processing data each day. Business computer systems are generally classified by (1) purpose (i.e., whether the computer is a special-purpose or a general-purpose computer), (2) type (analog or digital), and (3) capacity (or the amount of work it can handle).

Purpose

SPECIAL-PURPOSE COMPUTERS. Special-purpose computers are designed to solve specific types of problems and usually are tailored to the specific needs of a single customer. Some computers have detailed instructions built into them to do the specialized job efficiently and economically. The main drawback, however, is limited versatility, especially in terms of handling different jobs. Many special-purpose computers

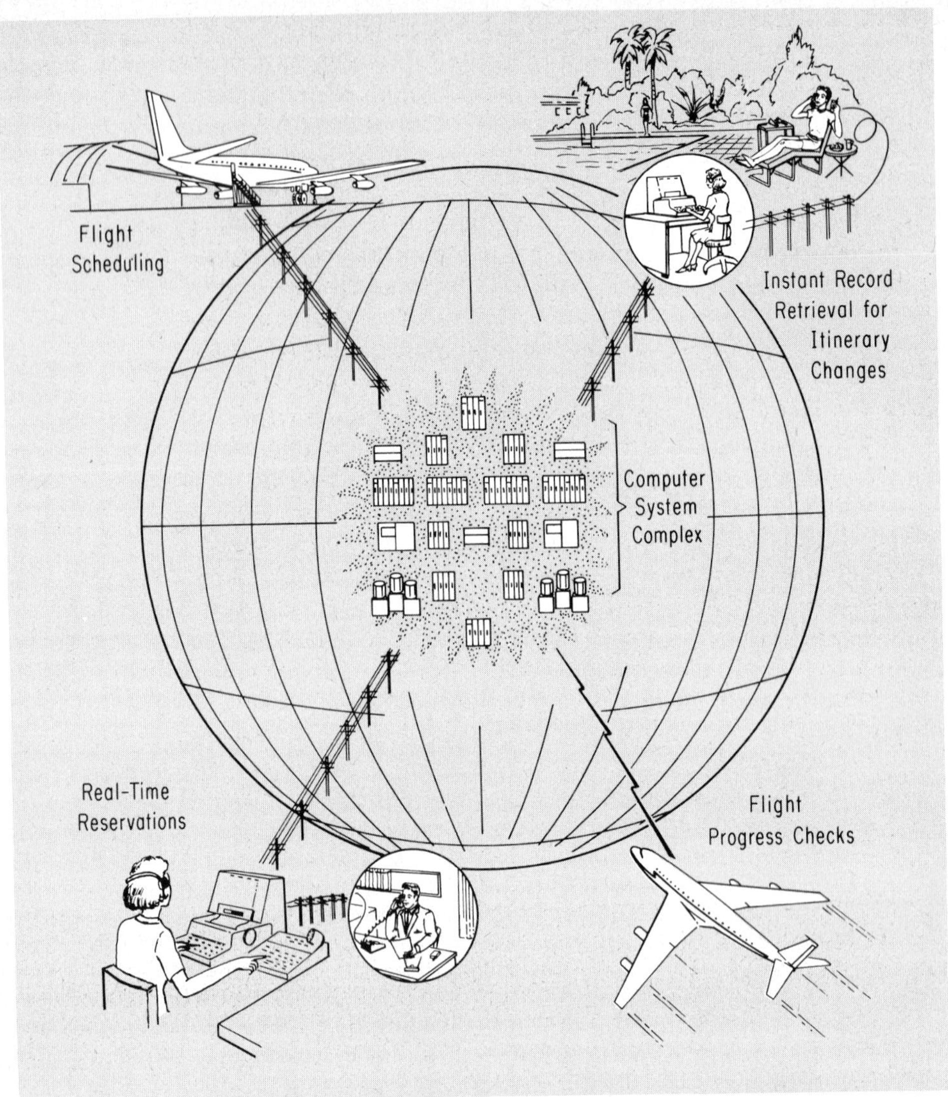

FIGURE 5-3. Airline reservation system

are built for the airlines and the military. Examples include computers used for traffic control, airline reservation systems (Fig. 5-3), satellite tracking, and collection of highway tolls.

General-Purpose Computers. General-purpose computers are built for handling a variety of jobs by executing sets of stored-program instructions. Although this characteristic permits more versatility in working out diversified routines, such as payrolls, sales analysis, accounts receivables, and inventory control, diversification means some sacrifice in speed and some limitations imposed by the size of the computer's primary storage.

Type

Computers fall into two classifications: *digital* and *analog*. In a digital computer, all arithmetic computations depend eventually on counting, in the same manner as an abacus depends on the counting of beads for similar functions. By contrast, there is no counting of unrelated or discrete quantities in an analog computer. Thus, it can be said that digital computers *count*, whereas analog computers *measure*.

The idea behind an analog computer was developed by Vannevar Bush of the Massachusetts Institute of Technology, who was the first to build such a machine. The machine was called the differential *analyzer*. Early analog computers represented occurrences by the length of a rod or the rotation of a shaft. They were not always very accurate, since their mechanical moving parts wore down in time. The present use of transistors makes the more recent versions of analog computers more accurate, faster, and more dependable than their predecessors (Fig. 5-4).

The name *analog* comes from the word *analogous* or *similar*. The thermometer, for instance, records various mercury levels based on

FIGURE 5-4. *Analog computer (Courtesy Electronic Associates, Inc.)*

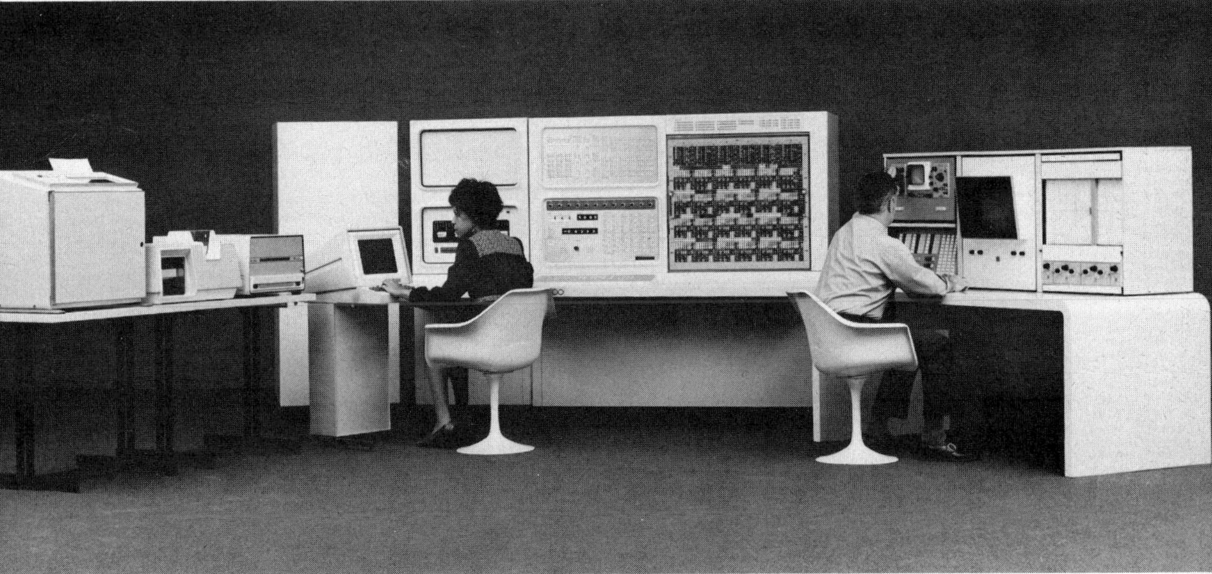

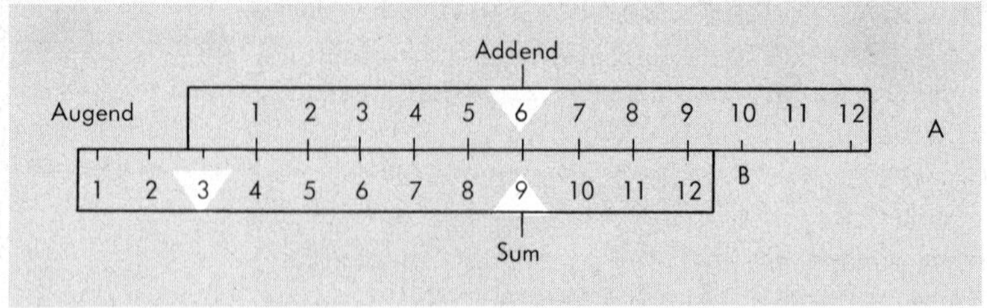

FIGURE 5-5. Two rulers as an analog computer

changes in temperature. When the temperature rises, the mercury level rises; when the temperature falls, so does the mercury level. That is, changes in temperature are shown by analogous or like changes in the level of the mercury in the thermometer. The same principle of similarity is used by analog computers in performing arithmetic functions with measurements. Numbers are represented by physical quantities. Measurements are made, with results displayed and later used in various arithmetic operations to generate similar new data.

The analog computer, then, is a mathematical instrument, one example of which is the slide rule. In fact, two rulers can simulate the operation of an analog computer (Fig. 5-5). For instance, in adding 6 + 3, ruler A is first placed on top of ruler B. Ruler A is moved to the right until its left edge is on top of the number 3 on ruler B. The sum 9 is now displayed immediately under the number 6 on ruler A. A physical quantity was used to represent a number. In fact, we represented each of the two numbers by a length on a ruler. The sum was obtained simply by adding the lengths. Try different examples and see how simple this operation can be.

Both digital and analog computers have been used in solving business and scientific problems more quickly and more accurately than man is able to do acting alone. However, statistics indicate a greater demand for digital computers than for analog computers. In terms of accuracy, the results shown by an analog computer contain systematic errors that must be allowed for; that is, its instruments are apt to show a value of a given quantity slightly different from the true value. The true value of 199 volts in a circuit, for instance, might be shown as 200 volts on the dial. Such a systematic error will affect the final results by the same amount of deviation.

By contrast, the digital computer does not commit errors as such, unless there is a major flaw caused by faulty current flow. The most expensive analog computer is reported to be accurate to within 0.0001 of 1 percent. Results derived from a digital computer are 100 percent accurate if the data fed into it describe accurately the conditions of the problem under discussion.

Probably the most important reason for the wide use of the digital computer is its flexibility in handling various types of problems. To solve a problem on an analog computer, a set of electrical components must be wired and placed in the right position. Solving a different problem means a rewiring process, which is time consuming. On the other hand, loading a new program into the input component of the digital computer is all that is required for solving a different type of problem. Although an average program takes several days to prepare, the preparation is less time consuming in that the program can be used indefinitely to work out different solutions to the same type of problem.

From the foregoing, we can conclude that each type of computer is designed to handle a particular set of problems. Analog computers are ideally used for scientific and engineering problems, when physical measurements are manipulated as data for arithmetic operations, when the solution of the problem involved needs one cycle of operations, and when a high degree of accuracy is not critical. When 100 percent accuracy is demanded, and repetitive, routine mathematical operations are involved, the digital computer is the one to use. Since business demands are of the latter type, the greater demand for digital computers is accounted for.

HYBRID COMPUTERS. Although both analog and digital computers have been extensively used and widely accepted in various industries, an attempt has been made to design a computer that combines the best features of both types. This special-purpose machine, called a *hybrid computer,* combines the measuring capabilities of the analog computer and the logical and control capabilities of the digital computer. It offers an efficient and economical method of working out special types of problems in science and various areas of engineering. Among the applications are space-vehicle simulations and the training of space pilots, analysis of signals received from special sensors attached to humans and animals in laboratories, and the solving of differential equations for chemical reactors.

Capacity

Computer capacity refers to the volume of data the computer can handle. The capacities of earlier computers were a function of their physical size: the larger the computer, the more volume of work it was expected to handle. Today, technological advances in the miniaturization of the modern computers' primary storage permit us to measure a computer's capacity by the volume of work it can process. With that in mind, computer systems are classified as minicomputer, small-sized, medium-sized, or large-scale computers. Size is determined primarily on the basis of the processing speed and size of primary storage. Monthly rental prices have been considered by the industry as an acceptable measure of the computer size. The rental price is roughly one fiftieth of the average sale price. Figure 5-6 serves as a guideline.

Computer Size	Average Monthly Rental Price Range	Sale Price Range
Minicomputers	$ 550–$ 2,000	$ 13,000–$ 100,000
Small-scale	2,000– 10,000	100,000– 500,000
Medium-scale	10,000– 25,000	500,000– 1,250,000
Large-scale	25,000– 75,000	1,250,000– 3,750,000
Super-sized	$75,000–$250,000	$3,750,000–$12,500,000

FIGURE 5-6

MINICOMPUTERS. Since 1965, a new system has been marketed for the small businessman—the compact, low-cost minicomputer, which can be operated by just one person. Although small in size and low in cost, the minicomputer can be big in performance, depending on the supportive hardware included. For example, the IBM System/3 [3] prepares reports by reading data cards, punching predetermined results, printing detailed output, collating and reproducing selected data, and performing arithmetic calculations, using only one unit called the multifunction card unit. Such a combined operation makes obsolete the punched-card system it was designed to replace. Details on minicomputers are discussed in Chapter 13.

SMALL-SIZED COMPUTERS. The distinction between minicomputers and small computers is vague; some users refer to minicomputers as small computers, and vice versa. Generally, small computers are fast, versatile, and powerful processing systems that have more efficient input–output media and devices than minicomputers. Small computers were originally built to do the job of punched-card systems by replacing most of the sorters, collators, and accounting machines. As programmable tabulators and superior calculating punches, they provide the advantage of stored programming to users who are ready to change from a punched-card system to a more flexible and powerful solution to their problems (Figs. 5-7 to 5-9). However, since the minicomputer has also moved in to replace the punched-card system, the trend has been to expand the capabilities of the small computer.

Card-oriented systems batch process transactions that are sequenced on sorters and collators in advance of the computer run; magnetic-tape systems batch process transactions that are sequenced in the same order as the master file for updating. Small-sized systems using magnetic

[3] The IBM System/3 is considered to be between a true minicomputer and a small-sized computer. Details are discussed in Chapter 13.

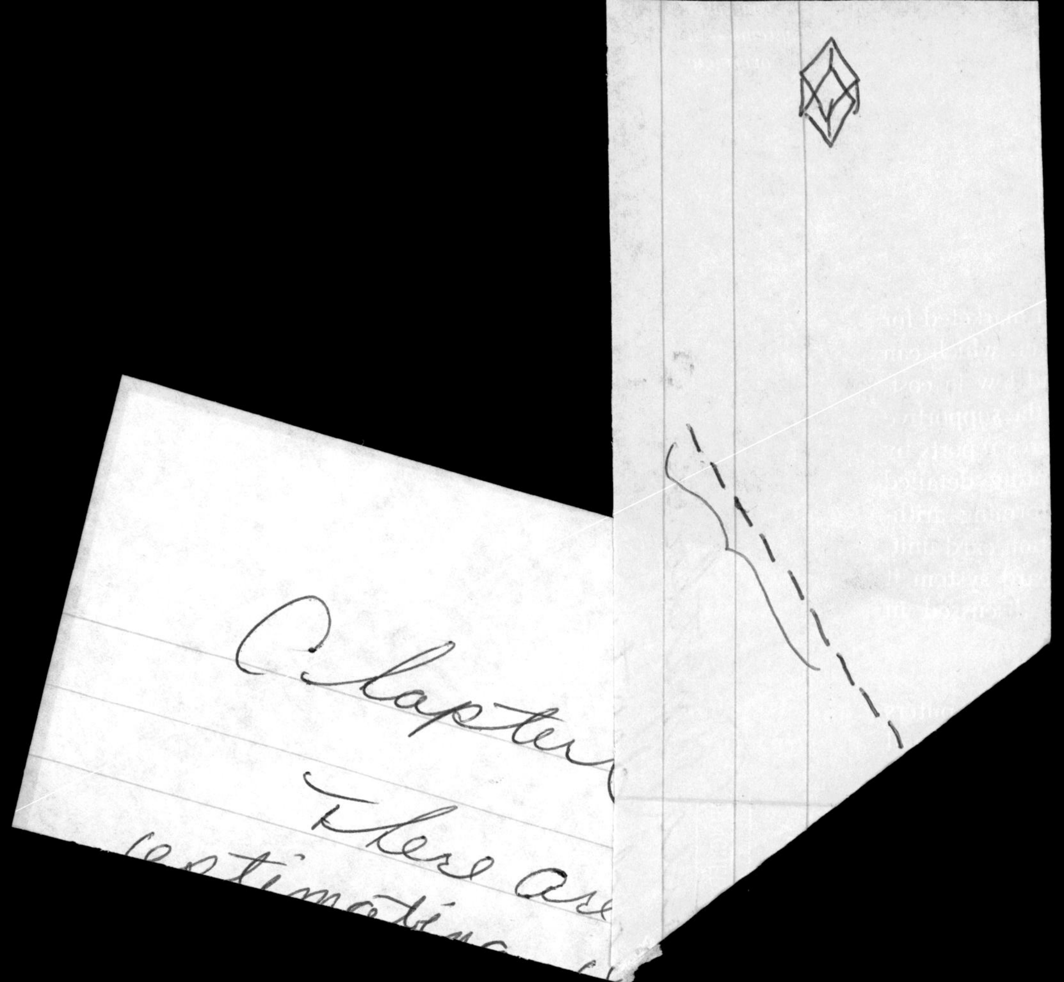

Chapter
Here are
estimating

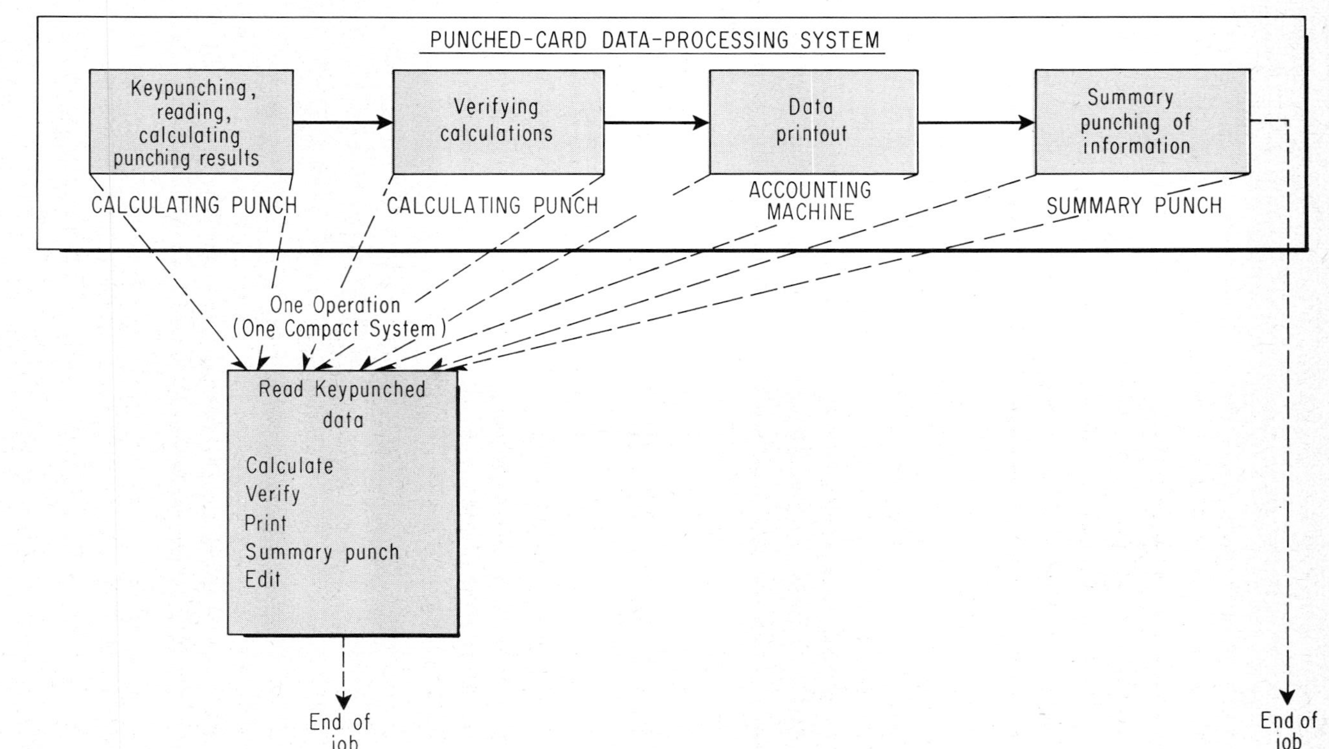

FIGURE 5-7. *Advantage of a small computer system over conventional punched-card data-processing systems*

FIGURE 5-8. UNIVAC 9200 system (Courtesy Rand Corporation)

FIGURE 5-9. IBM 360, model 20 (Courtesy IBM)

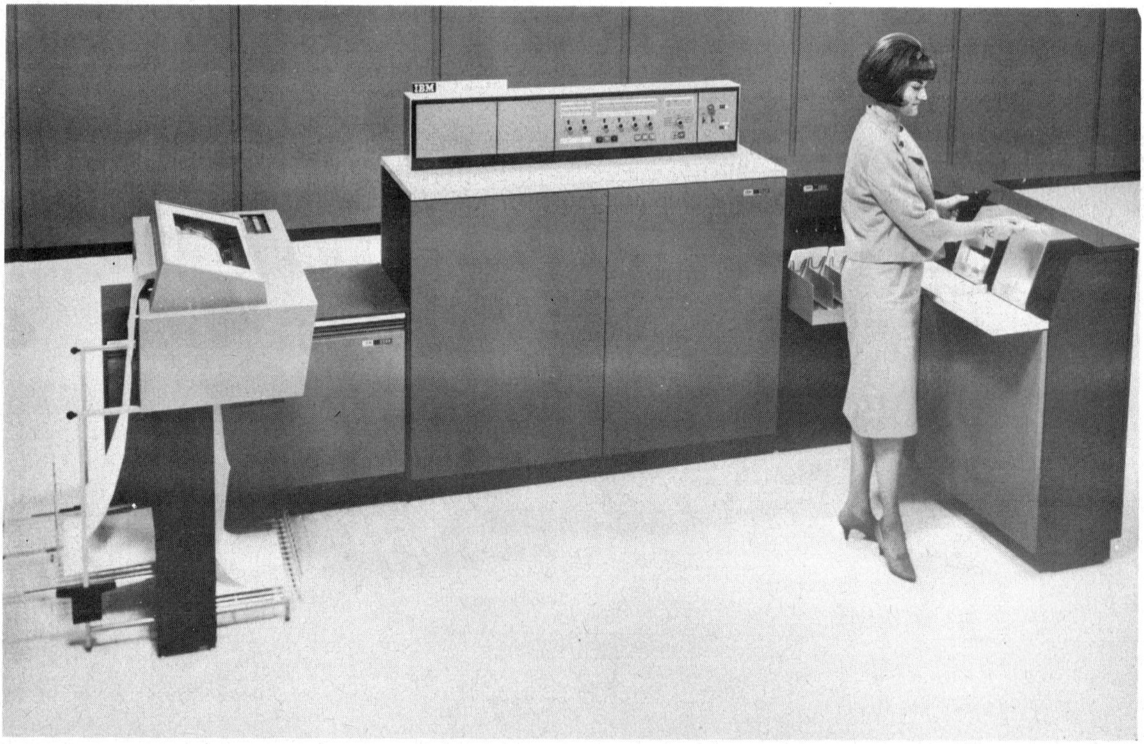

disks are capable of processing data either in batches or, more commonly, randomly. In either case, two or more magnetic-disk drives are required.

The small-sized computer system consists mainly of a central processing unit (core storage capacity from 4,096 to 20,000 positions), a punched-card input–output device, two to four magnetic tape units (optional), and a printer. Depending on the optional features included, monthly rental ranges from $1,200 to $4,000 for the small, card-oriented system and from $3,000 to $5,000 for the small, magnetic-tape-oriented system.

MEDIUM-SIZED COMPUTERS. Compared to small computer systems, medium-sized installations provide the advantages of (1) faster operating speeds, (2) larger memory capacity (between 16,000 and 250,000 positions), (3) faster input–output devices (usually magnetic-tape units) for efficient handling of data, and (4) printers for producing reports at high speeds. The Burroughs 3500 computer system and the IBM 360, model 30, are examples (Figs. 5-10 and 5-11).

LARGE-SCALE COMPUTERS. Large-scale computers incorporate the features of medium-sized computers, but have separate consoles to ma-

FIGURE 5-10. Burroughs 3500 computer systems (Courtesy Burroughs)

FIGURE 5-11. IBM 360, model 30 (Courtesy IBM)

nipulate the system and its peripheral equipment, more optional features, faster input–output devices, faster and larger processing units, and a storage capacity between 131,000 and 1,000,000 positions, which are capable of handling random processing. Monthly rental is over $20,000 (Figs. 5-12 and 5-13).

The expense incurred in large-computer rental creates a problem for the user—efficient utilization of computer time. Once it becomes available, the system must be employed profitably every single second on all applications. Incompatibility of the peripheral devices accompanying the system often accounts for waste. While the card reader feeds data into the central processing unit, while the tape drive is receiving or giving out information, or while the printer is listing results, the arithmetic unit is idle. To make up for the relatively slower operation of these devices, various programming "tricks" have been developed. One is the employment of an off-line or "interrupt" connection, where magnetic tapes are used as intermediate data carriers, releasing the computer from dependence on card readers and high-speed printers. Briefly, data punched in cards are copied electronically (away from the computer) on magnetic tapes (or magnetic disks), which, in turn, are used as the primary input medium. On output, the data from the computer are written on magnetic tapes, and the printer is then fed the required information for final printout. In this approach the magnetic tape performs the role of a buffer.

Another way of maximizing the use of large-computer-system time is the "satellite" way. Provided there is enough work to do, one or more small computers are incorporated around the large computer to form a

FIGURE 5-12. Burroughs 6500 computer system (Courtesy Burroughs)

FIGURE 5-13. IBM 360, model 65 (Courtesy IBM)

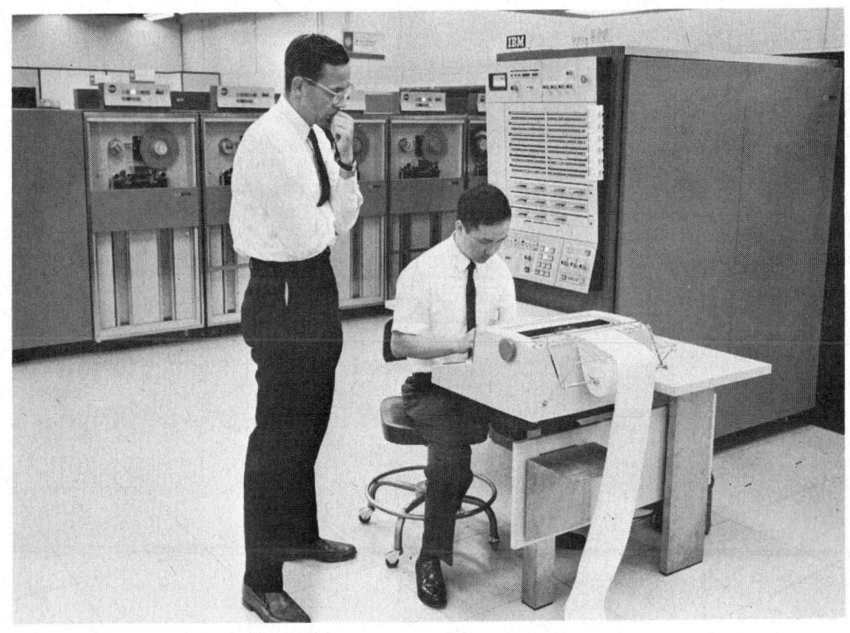

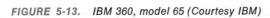

satellite that takes over the duties of preparing magnetic tapes for processing, testing, merging, and other similar tasks. This approach has proved its overall economy of operation in many large installations.

The most recent approach to utilizing the large computer's time to its fullest is called *multiprogramming*—the processing of several programs simultaneously. The multiprogramming system eliminates any slack in processing. For example, after a particular phase of the first program has been acted upon and is being handled by a peripheral device (such as the printer), the computer acts on the second program, processing it until an instruction is received from the peripheral device, which notifies the computer of the completion of that phase of the first program. This interrupt instruction causes the computer to revert to the first program, execute more instructions, actuate the printer, and handle the second and, eventually, succeeding programs with virtually no waste of processing time. Thus, although such computer systems are extremely expensive, large companies find them worth the expense, since they are in a position to provide both skilled programmers and continuous applications involving thousands of employees and hundreds of thousands of customer accounts on a daily basis. Computers responsible for such volume and scope of operation are rightly included in the "millionnaire" club.

SUMMARY

A business digital-computer system manipulates business data based on a predetermined set of stored-program instructions with minimum human intervention. Business computer systems are classified as special-purpose or general-purpose; analog, digital, or hybrid; or by size as minicomputer, small-sized, medium-sized, or large-scale computer. The computer used for processing business applications is invariably general-purpose (capable of handling a variety of jobs) and digital (performs computations through counting); the size varies with the requirements and needs of the particular organization.

Among the uses of business computers are (1) the processing of a greater number of items at high speed, (2) the processing of data more accurately than alternative methods, (3) to allow time for creative and intelligent planning, and (4) to lower processing costs. Among its chief capabilities are its ability to

1. Handle repetitive tasks.
2. Operate on its own with minimum human intervention.
3. Communicate effectively.
4. Make logical choices among available alternatives.
5. Check on the correctness of its own work.
6. Do new and additional tasks.

The chief limitations of a business computer are its

1. Inability to handle unprogrammed information.
2. Inability to make decisions independently.
3. Occasional failure and physical breakdown.

Computers process data in batches or on line. Batch processing saves computer time, since transactions are accumulated and processed in batches. On-line processing is ideal for applications when the records must be kept current.

A computer system consists of a central processor, one or more input and output devices, and other supportive devices. The processor includes main storage, arithmetic and logic, and control units. In addition to hardware, a stored program and programming aids are needed for directing the system to perform required tasks. Programmers and systems analysts determine the procedures and the software that effect each application.

TERMS TO LEARN

Code check
Digital computer
Feedback
General-purpose computer
Input
Logic
Memory
Microsecond
Millisecond
Nanosecond
Output
Program
Special-purpose computer

QUESTIONS

1. What is meant by the term "computer"? What is meant by the term "digital"?
2. List the components and explain in detail the makeup of a business computer system.
3. "A computer cannot do anything a man could not do if he had the time." Do you agree with this statement? Defend your answer.
4. In what respect is a computer referred to as "making decisions"?
5. What is meant by parity check?
6. What are the limitations of a digital computer? Explain.
7. What is the difference between batch and on-line processing?
8. What elements constitute the central processing unit?
9. What does an electronic data-processing installation normally consist of, if it is to operate as a functioning system? Why? Explain.

10. Does a stored program differ from control? Explain.
11. What are the three classifications of business computers? Explain each briefly.
12. What distinguishes a small-sized computer from a minicomputer? a medium-sized computer from a small-sized computer? a large-scale computer from a medium-sized computer?

SUGGESTED READING

BEKEY, G. A., and W. J. KARPLUS. *Hybrid Computation.* New York: John Wiley & Sons, Inc., 1968.

CHAPIN, NED. *Computers—A Systems Approach.* New York: Van Nostrand Reinhold Company, 1971, pp. 22–24.

FEIGENBAUM, E. A., and JULIAN FELDMAN, eds. *Computers and Thought.* New York: McGraw-Hill Book Company, 1963.

HELLWIG, JESSICA. *Introduction to Computers and Programming.* New York: Columbia University Press, 1969.

VON FOERSTER, HEINTZ, and J. W. BEAUCHAMP, eds. *Music by Computers.* New York: John Wiley & Sons, Inc., 1969.

primary storage and information retrieval

6

PRIMARY STORAGE

Characteristics of Primary Storage

immediate access to data stored in memory
reusability
permanent recording of data already in storage
automatic or self-checking ability
durability
compact size

MAGNETIC CORE STORAGE

Advantages of Magnetic Core Storage

BINARY-CODED ALPHANUMERICS

Six-Bit Code

Eight-Bit Code

Check Bits

OTHER TYPES OF PRIMARY STORAGE

Planar Thin-Film Memory

Semiconductor Memory

Cryogenic Memory

Photodigital Memory

Electro-Optical Memory

Laser Holographic Memory

Bubble Memory

VIRTUAL STORAGE—AN OVERVIEW

Basic Structure

STORED-DATA RETRIEVAL

Fixed- and Variable-Word-Length Computers

Arithmetic–Logic Unit

Registers

Computer Operating Cycle

The central processing unit is the heart of a computer system. It is the center of all data computations; without it, processing cannot be done. Its role in a computer system can be compared to the relation of human memory to man, or of the engine to the automobile. All computations and decisions affecting the daily activities of a person are made in memory. In the case of a computer, the primary difference is that the computer must be instructed in detail by a human programmer before it can act like a human brain. The term *memory* is arbitrarily used to describe the central processing unit's primary function.

A storage device is any unit capable of retaining information until it is needed and producing it on demand. Storage of data in the central processing unit is called main memory, internal storage, or *primary* storage; storage of data elsewhere is referred to as external, or *secondary*, storage. To illustrate the difference between primary and secondary storage, let us take a look at the storage of merchandise in retailing. A retailing firm generally orders merchandise in quantities that exceed its immediate needs or anticipated volume during a given period. Seasonal drops in the price of the merchandise or price discounts on quantities over a certain limit (say 100 items) often induce the retailer to order in large quantities. A common procedure involves filling the shelves on the sales floor to capacity and storing the rest in a stockroom. Merchandise placed on the sales floor is viewed as *primary storage,* whereas the extra merchandise available in the stockroom is said to be in *secondary* storage. Should a customer want an item in secondary storage, the salesman must call for its transfer from the stockroom before the sale can be made. This process, although workable, is impractical because it takes extra time and prolongs the sales process. Obviously, efficiency is at its best when the merchandise is directly accessible for immediate turnover.

Like the retail store, the central processing unit must have direct access to needed data in primary storage before any computations or other processing can be done. Initial data are received from an input device in the same manner as the one by which the salesman on the sales floor receives merchandise from the stockroom during the business day as it is needed. The average time the computer requires to locate or recall data from any memory location is called *average access time.* Average access time is less for data in primary storage than in secondary storage, because data in primary storage are already within the computer and, therefore, take less time to be reached.

The "stockroom" of the central processing unit can be *on-line* devices (e.g., magnetic disk) that provide direct access to selected records, or *off-line* devices such as punched card readers or magnetic tape drives, where records are stored in sequential order.

In determining the computer's primary and secondary storage requirements, the data-processing manager should take into consideration factors related to processing speed, storage capacity, and data accessibility. The processing speed expected of the system depends on the company's requirements. If processing speed is extremly important, primary storage should be large enough to accommodate all the necessary data. A cost-conscious manager, however, would compromise the speed factor in preference for an overall combination of primary and secondary devices that produce the best package.

The computer's storage capacity should then meet the company's present and future needs. Many fourth-generation computers offer over 3 million bytes (storage locations) of primary storage. On-line storage devices with much greater storage capacity are also available. Finally, data accessibility has to do with a choice between batch-sequential versus on-line, direct-access processing. In the final analysis, the manager should decide on a system that combines the foregoing factors in such a way as to meet most economically the organization's immediate and long-term data-processing needs.

PRIMARY STORAGE

Characteristics of Primary Storage

IMMEDIATE ACCESS TO DATA STORED IN MEMORY. For the arithmetic and logic units to operate efficiently, stored information should be directly accessible at high speed. In other words, access time to data in primary storage should be as close to zero as possible in order to maximize the speed of data delivery. Some processors access data in less than 1 microsecond; secondary direct-access devices generally access stored data in milliseconds.

REUSABILITY. A primary storage device should be capable of erasing unneeded data and storing new data in its place. In many respects it is like a tape recorder designed to erase previous recordings every time a new recording is made on the same tape. Most primary storage devices have this characteristic.

PERMANENT RECORDING OF DATA ALREADY IN STORAGE. The computer's primary storage unit should be designed to retain stored data intact in the event of electrical failure. Loss of data should occur only at the discretion of the programmer or the console operator to allow room for incoming data or to clear storage of unwanted details. Most primary storage devices used in commercial computers retain data permanently.

Technically, destructive readout occurs momentarily in some primary storage devices when data are read from storage to be used elsewhere for processing. Since the devices are designed to retain the original data permanently and accurately, they also restore the original data automatically as it is being "read out."

AUTOMATIC OR SELF-CHECKING ABILITY. To verify the accuracy of the data represented in storage, a primary storage device should have an automatic self-checking feature, called a *parity check*. The computer counts the number of bits of data in storage and, upon the destruction or loss of any single bit, signals on the console that an error has been made. The operator then determines the type of error and its location by manipulating certain switches.

DURABILITY. Unlike punched cards, which wear out in time, primary storage devices are built to last permanently in spite of the constant storing and re-storing of data in them. It would be inconvenient and expensive to replace or frequently repair a primary storage device.

COMPACT SIZE. Because space is always at a premium, a primary storage device should be physically small, yet capable of storing a large volume of data.

MAGNETIC CORE STORAGE

Vacuum tubes were an early primary storage unit in the ENIAC. Their bulky size and storage limitations (1 bit of information per tube) accounted for the slow processing of applications at that time. In the

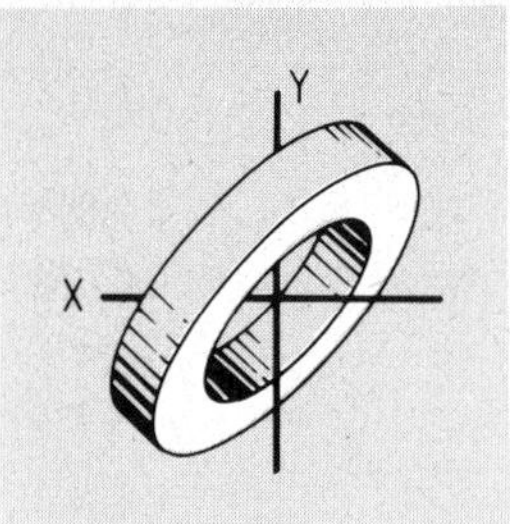

FIGURE 6-1. Magnetic core with x and y wires

mid-1950s, IBM introduced the use of magnetic drums as the primary storage device in its IBM 650 computers. The later introduction of the high-speed magnetic core in the IBM 704 and most of the computers that followed left the magnetic drum virtually obsolete, except as a secondary storage device. Improvements in production techniques over the past decade have resulted in reducing the size of the magnetic core from $\frac{1}{8}$ to 18/1,000 inch and access speed from 2 microseconds to 290 nanoseconds. Production cost has also dropped considerably.

Magnetic core devices are very popular and effective storage units and are used in most commercial computers. They consist of a doughnut-shaped ring of ferromagnetic material. *Ferro* denotes the presence of iron and *magnetic* indicates the ability of the material to be magnetized. A magnetic core can be magnetized quickly and is highly retentive. Unless it is demagnetized, it is capable of retaining its magnetism almost indefinitely.

Because of the importance of speed, cores are made very small, which means that faster switching and less magnetizing force are required to change their status. The magnetizing force is generated by running a heavy current through two wires, usually called X and Y, passing through the core (Fig. 6-1).

Advantages of Magnetic Core Storage

1. **Dependability.** A magnetic core can be easily magnetized to represent data. It is called "nonvolatile," meaning that once information is stored in core it cannot be destroyed except by human command.
2. **Durability.** A magnetic core does not wear out or deteriorate with age, because it is an immovable part and does not rely upon physical motion for its operation.
3. **High-speed access.** Fast access time of magnetic core memory is attributed to its unique design and fast switching capabilities. Each bit of information is stored in a separate magnetic core, ready to read or write through switching.
4. **Low-cost operation.** The operating cost of a magnetic core is relatively low. It does not use any power to retain the data it

stores. The only time it uses power is when new data are being stored.

5. **Large capacity.** Because each magnetic core measures about $\frac{1}{16}$ inch, there are a great number of cores in the primary storage of the computer. Memories with 100,000 to over 1 million bytes (each byte representing eight data cores plus a parity check core) are not uncommon in medium- to large-sized computers.
6. **Low heat dissipation.**
7. **Adaptability to word-oriented or character-oriented computers.**

The magnetic core has only two definite states: the 0 state and the 1 state. It can store either a 1 bit [1] or a 0 bit of information. If values greater than 1 are to be stored, more than one core is needed. For example, to store a decimal value of 2, two cores are needed: one to represent the 0 bit and one to the left of the first to represent a 1 bit, because 2 in decimal is 1 0 in binary.

Cores are arranged in a matrix strung on a screen of wires, which form a core plane (Fig. 6-2). Each core has an X and a Y wire running through it at right angles. It can be set to a 1 state by sending one half the total required current through the X wire from left to right and the other half through the Y wire from top to bottom (Fig. 6-3). The core can be set to a 0 state by sending the flow of current through the X and Y wires in the opposite directions (Fig. 6-4). The polarity of the core in a specific direction, then, is determined by the direction and amount of current flowing through the X and Y wires.

Reading a magnetic core. When a particular core is read, one half the total amount of necessary current is sent through each of the X and Y wires. In Fig. 6-5, one half the current was sent through the X wire, and one half through the Y wire. *Only the core at the intersection of the two*

[1] Data stored in magnetic core are referred to as *bits*. The word bit is an abbreviation of the words *binary digit*.

FIGURE 6-2. Magnetic core plane (Courtesy IBM)

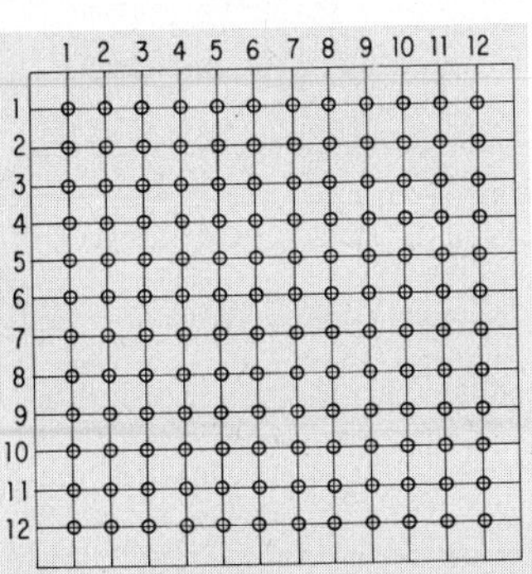

FIGURE 6-3. Magnetic core in a one-bit status

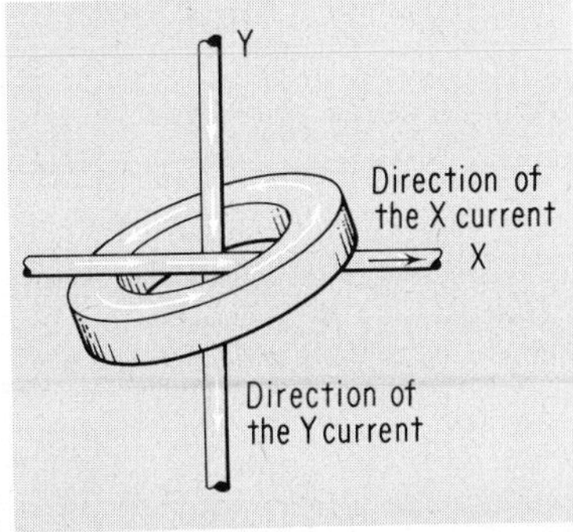

FIGURE 6-4. Magnetic core in a zero-bit status

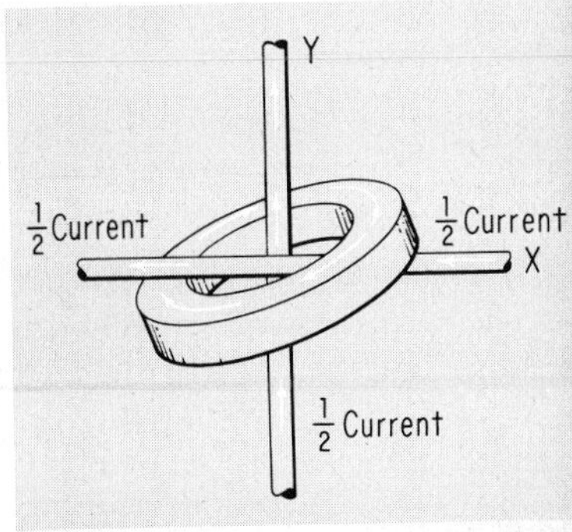

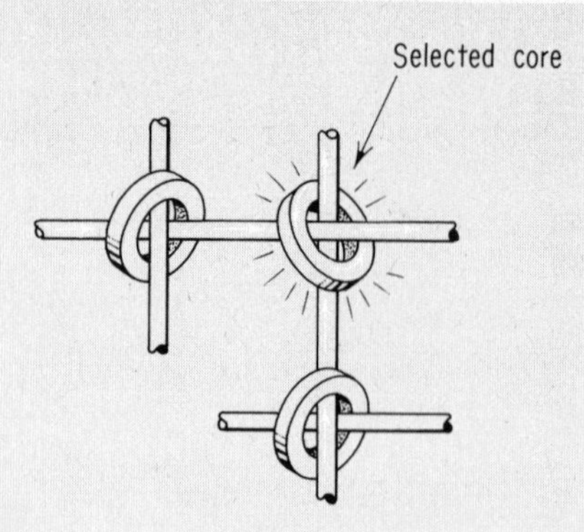

FIGURE 6-5. Selected core

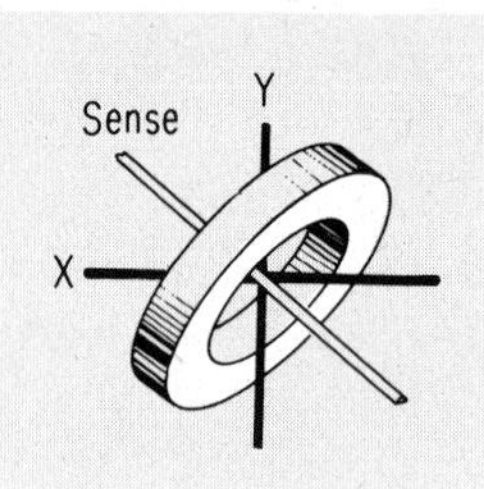

FIGURE 6-6. Magnetic core showing the x, y, and sense wires

wires receives the full current. That particular core is said to be *selected.* All other cores strung on the X wire are *half-selected.* They retain their status because each of them receives only one half the current necessary to magnetize them—that is Y current only.

The destructive aspect of the readout process requires the use of a third wire (inserted through each core) called a *sense wire* (Fig. 6-6). When a particular core (representing a 1 bit of data) is read, it clears to 0. This action induces current in the sense wire, which signals that the 1 bit should be restored to that particular core. Then the circuitry immediately writes in the 1 bit by reversing the current flowing through the X and Y wires of that core, so that the core is once again magnetized in a clockwise direction. However, if the selected core originally stored a 0 bit, no current enters the sense wire, and the core retains its status. The sense wire is activated only in a reading operation when a magnetic core originally representing a 1 bit is cleared to 0 as a result of readout.

Writing in a magnetic core. The process of writing data in a magnetic core is somewhat more complex. Writing in a core involves either re-storing the information previously stored in it or replacing the data with new 1's. When data are written in a core, one half the necessary current is sent through each of the X and Y wires in *exactly the opposite direction from that used in readout.*

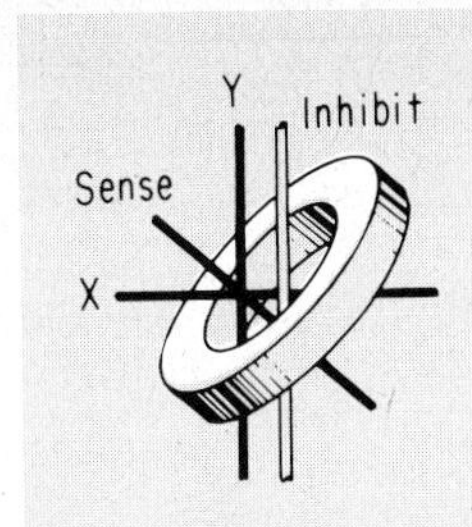

FIGURE 6-7. Magnetic core showing the inhibit wire

The X and Y wires cannot distinguish between 0's and 1's. They merely carry current. Because at times certain cores must be coded to represent a 0 bit, a technique is required to keep these cores in this state. This necessitates the addition of a fourth wire, called the *inhibit* wire (Fig. 6-7). It is inserted parallel to the Y wire and extends through every core in storage. Its main function, if activated, is to maintain the status of the 0-bit cores by preventing 1 bits from being written in them, as would be done normally if the procedure were not interfered with. To accomplish this, the computer passes one half the amount of necessary current through the inhibit wire, thus neutralizing the one half current flowing through the X wire, with the result that the 0 cores have only the current from the Y wires flowing through them. Because this is not sufficient to disturb their original magnetization as 0 bits, this procedure preserves them as 0-bit cores. If it were not used, they would become 1-bit cores (Fig. 6-8).

FIGURE 6-8. The presence of an inhibit current (left); the absence of an inhibit current (right)

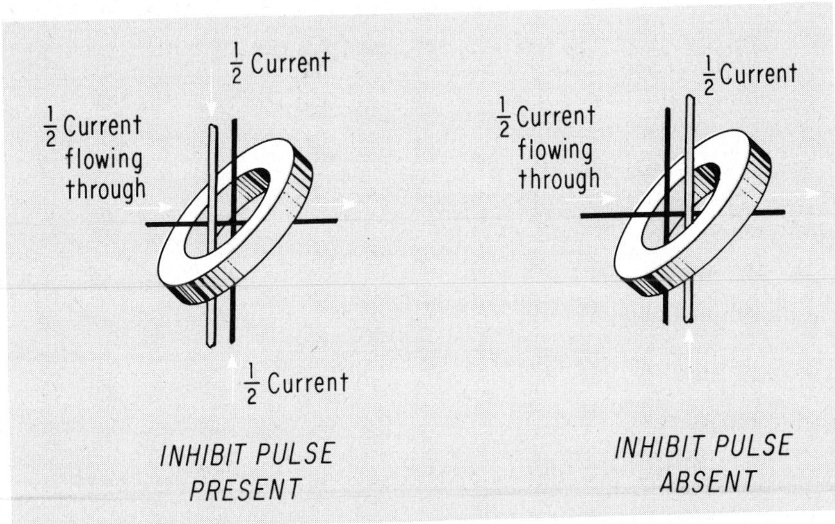

In summary, the function of the four wires is as follows:

1. X and Y wires are used for readout and/or writing in magnetic cores.
2. The sense wire is used only in a read operation to determine if a given core is in a 1-bit or a 0-bit state.
3. The inhibit wire is used in the write operation only if it is decided that a given core is to represent a 0 state.

BINARY-CODED ALPHANUMERICS

Six-Bit Code

In electronic data processing, the need for primary storage to represent alphabetic as well as numeric data is very important. Each of the 56 different characters (10 numeric, 26 alphabetic, and 20 special characters) is represented in two electronic states: 0 bit and 1 bit. An internal coding scheme is developed so that each character is represented by a combination of 0- and 1-bit sets. The number of combinations of 0 and 1 bits in a set is determined by raising 2 to an exponent equal to the number of 0 and 1 bits in the set. For example, a 3-bit set has 8 (2^3) different 0 and 1 combinations [2]; a 4-bit set (called *binary-coded decimal* or *BCD*) has 16 (2^4) different 0 and 1 combinations [3]; and so on. For representing 56 alphanumeric characters, then, a minimum of a 6-bit set (2^6) is needed for storing and processing (Fig. 6-9).

Although the specific combination of 0 and 1 bits per set assigned to represent alphanumeric characters varies with different computer makes, one 6-bit coding scheme calls for the use of the BCD code (8421) and two additional bits (A and B). Numeric characters are represented by the BCD section only; the alphabetic and special characters are encoded by a combination of BCD bits and A and B zone bits. The first nine letters (A to I) are represented by one A and one B bit in addition to the use of the numeric BCD bits 1 to 9. The next nine letters (J to R) are represented by one B bit each, in addition to the use of the numeric BCD bits 1 to 9. The last eight letters (S to Z) are represented by one A bit each, in addition to the numeric BCD bits 2 to 9 (Fig. 6-9). Any part of the 6-bit set that is not a 1 bit is set to 0. Coding of special characters, such as blanks, commas, and asterisks, is arbitrarily established by the computer manufacturer.

[2] A 3-bit set is adequate for encoding each single octal (base 8) character; they are combined in eight different ways to encode the eight octal characters.

[3] A 4-bit set is used in encoding each of the 16 hexadecimal (base 16) characters. Details on the hexadecimal system are covered in Chapter 7.

	Alphanumeric representation		Numeric (BCD)			
e.g.	B	A	8	4	2	1
2	0	0	0	0	1	0
A	1	1	0	0	0	1
⋮						
I	1	1	1	0	0	1
J	1	0	0	0	0	1
⋮						
R	1	0	1	0	0	1
S	0	1	0	0	1	0
⋮						
Z	0	1	1	0	0	1

FIGURE 6-9. Six-bit coded data representation

Eight-Bit Code

In addition to expanding the BCD-bit set to include data coding, a method used in third- and fourth-generation computers is to extend the coded binary sets from 6 to 8 bits per set. The 8-bit set, called a *byte*, ranges in decimal notation from 0 to 255 (2^8). This extension not only allows up to 256 characters to be handled by the computer, but also forms binary-coded hexadecimals, which simplifies the conversion routine for arithmetic operations.

That is, an 8-bit byte can be used to represent two binary-coded hexadecimal digits. In problems involving only numeric digits, the 8-bit byte can be divided into two four-digit (BCD) sets packing two decimal digits and representing a hexadecimal digit in BCD form. However, for encoding alphanumeric data, one 4-bit set codes the numeric digits, and the other 4-bit set codes the zone digits. In Example 2 of Fig. 6-10, the

FIGURE 6-10. Special character byte representation

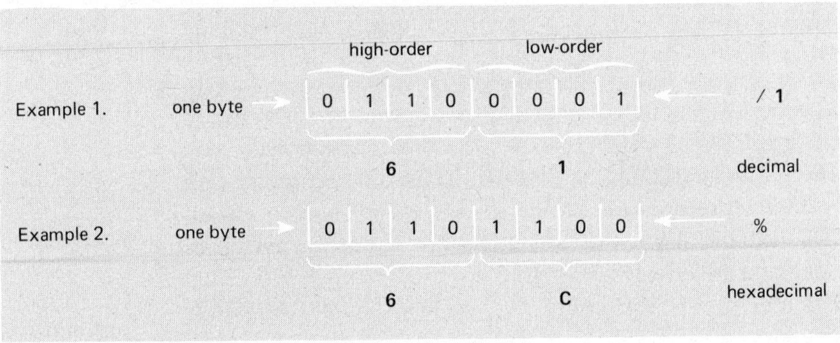

		high-order				low-order				
Example 1.	one byte →	0	1	1	0	0	0	0	1	← / 1
		6				1				decimal
Example 2.	one byte →	0	1	1	0	1	1	0	0	← %
		6				C				hexadecimal

Character	EBCDIC Bit Representation	ASCII-8 Bit Representation
0	1111 0000	0101 0000
1	1111 0001	0101 0001
2	1111 0010	0101 0010
3	1111 0011	0101 0011
4	1111 0100	0101 0100
5	1111 0101	0101 0101
6	1111 0110	0101 0110
7	1111 0111	0101 0111
8	1111 1000	0101 1000
9	1111 1001	0101 1001
A	1100 0001	0101 0001
B	1100 0010	1010 0010
C	1100 0011	1010 0011
D	1100 0100	1010 0100
E	1100 0101	1010 0101
F	1100 0110	1010 0110
G	1100 0111	1010 0111
H	1100 1000	1010 1000
I	1100 1001	1010 1001
J	1001 0001	1010 1010
K	1001 0010	1010 1011
L	1001 0011	1010 1100
M	1001 0100	1010 1101
N	1001 0101	1010 1110
O	1001 0110	1010 1111
P	1001 0111	1011 0000
Q	1001 1000	1011 0001
R	1001 1001	1011 0010
S	1110 0010	1011 0011
T	1110 0011	1011 0100
U	1110 0100	1011 0101
V	1110 0101	1011 0110
W	1110 0110	1011 0111
X	1110 0111	1011 1000
Y	1110 1000	1011 1001
Z	1110 1001	1011 1010

FIGURE 6-11

8-bit byte represents special character (0/0), but when it is handled as two 4-bit sets, it represents hexadecimal digits 6C in binary-coded form.

Currently, there are two 8-bit codes used in most third- and fourth-generation computers: the Extended Binary-Coded Decimal Interchange Code (EBCDIC), developed by IBM, and the American Standard Code for Information Interchange (ASCII) (Fig. 6-11). EBCDIC employs an 8-bit unit byte for data representation and is used in the primary memory of IBM 360 and 370 systems. As mentioned earlier, the 8-bit format offers the advantage of packing two decimal digits in each byte, since a decimal digit can be represented by a 4-bit code. The *packed-decimal* format is

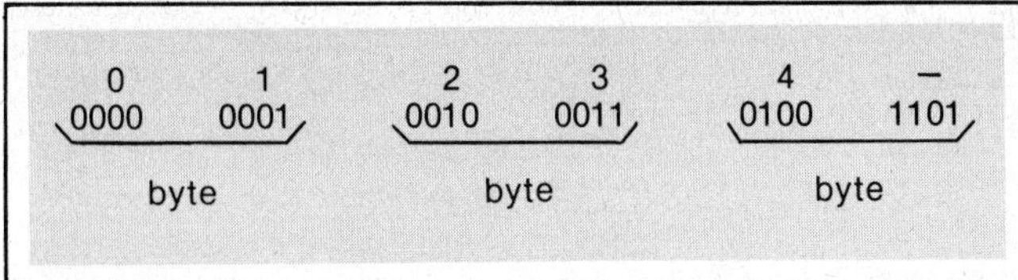

FIGURE 6-12. Decimal value — 1234 represented in packed-decimal format

designed to reduce storage requirements for decimal data. The leftmost 4 bits are used to represent the decimal digit, and the rightmost 4 bits are used for decimal digit or for sign designation (Fig. 6-12).

In EBCDIC, an unsigned digit is assumed positive and is represented by 1111 in the leftmost 4 bits. The 1111 format was chosen to make certain that numeric characters would be the highest in the collating sequence of characters. In the packed format, the sign occupies the least significant (rightmost) 4 bits, and all other sign designations are eliminated.

ASCII was originally in the form of a 7-bit standard code promulgated by the American Standards Association (now the American National Standards Institute) in 1966 to provide a standardized machine-to-machine and system-to-system communication medium. Today's version of ASCII is a modification of the 7-bit standard code by IBM, which uses 8 bits in its IBM 360 and 370 systems. The concept and advantages of 8-bit ASCII are identical to those of EBCDIC. The difference lies in the bit configurations chosen to represent alphabetic, numeric, and special characters.

Check Bits

A typical computer operation involves constant movement of a large volume of data during processing. Regardless of the quality and reliability of the computer's design, it is conceivable that some errors might occur or information might be lost during this phase. Computer designers alleviate the problem by using an error control mechanism referred to as a *parity bit* or a *binary check bit.*

The *check bit* is a binary digit that is added to the bit configuration representing data in a specific computer. A 4-bit code becomes 5 bits; a 6-bit alphanumeric code totals 7 bits, and an 8-bit alphanumeric code will have a total of 9 bits. The error control mechanism counts the 1 bits of the character-bit set and adds a check bit to the sum to make the total number of 1 bits odd or even, depending on the computer design. In computers specifying *odd parity,* for example, a check bit (1 bit) is attached to the character-bit set when the total number of 1 bits is even. Otherwise, no check bit (0 bit) is recorded. In computers specifying

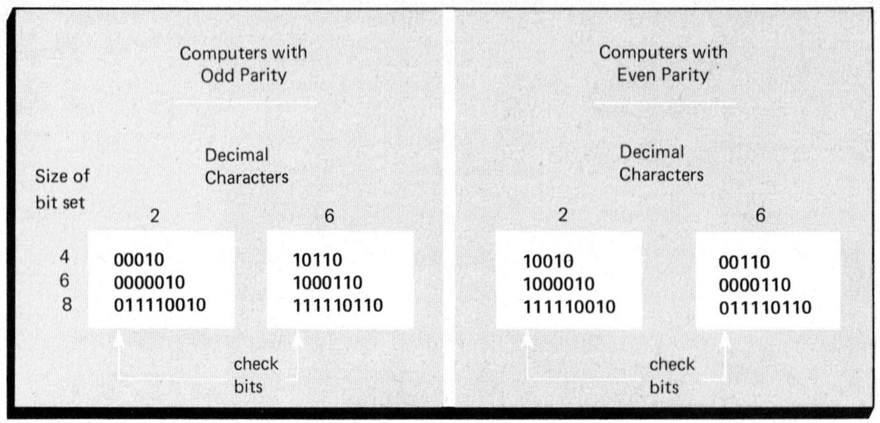

FIGURE 6-13. Examples of odd and even parity

even parity, a check bit is attached when the total number of 1 bits is odd. Otherwise, no check bit is recorded (Fig. 6-13).

In the absence of a proper check bit, the computer behaves in a predetermined way depending on its design and the operation undertaken. Some computers are designed to turn on an error light and stop automatically; others signal the programmer for instructions regarding the error. Some computers have an automatic error-correcting device to handle the matter.

OTHER TYPES OF PRIMARY STORAGE

Planar Thin-Film Memory

A very rapid and reliable storage device, magnetic thin-film memory, is a recent attempt at faster access to and miniaturization of primary storage. It was developed by the process of depositing a nickel ferrite substance on a nonconductive base, such as glass or plastic. These metallic spots or rectangles are connected by ultrathin, etched copper wires, and make up planes of memory cores that are much smaller than the doughnut-shaped magnetic core (Fig. 6-14). Each spot performs in the same manner as the magnetic core, requiring only two wires. A current is applied to rotate the polarity of a particular spot, indicating whether a 1 or a 0 is stored. Polarity is returned to its original state by a pulse digit that reverts the spot's status to 1 or 0. Initially, thin-film planes were made by hand. The substandard quality of a single bit could cause rejection of the entire plane of 768 rectangles. New techniques of vacuum depositing have brought the present cost of making thin-film memory within a practical price range. Further improvements and miniaturization are likely to continue.

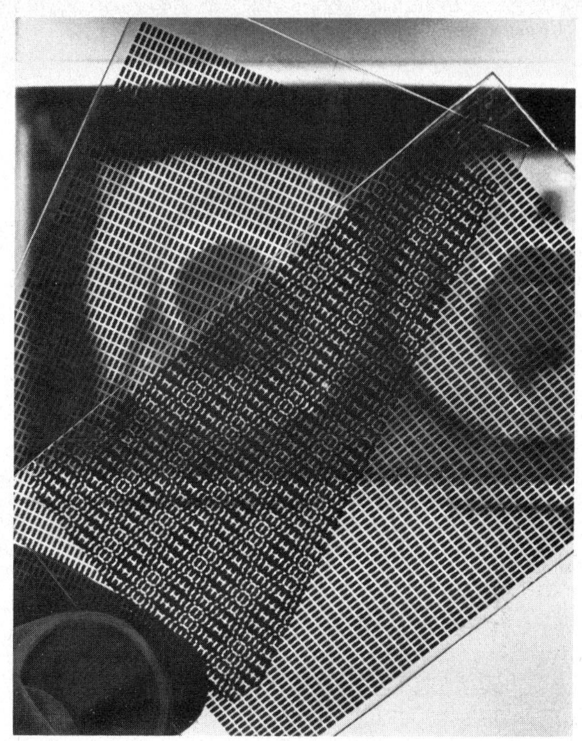

FIGURE 6-14. Magnetic thin-film memory (Courtesy Burroughs)

Semiconductor Memory

Semiconductor memory is a term coined by IBM; it was used for the first time early in 1971 to indicate the main memory of the IBM 370, Model 145, business computer system. This unique memory system is produced in modules; each memory module consists of two silicon (monolithic integrated circuit) chips. Each silicon chip contains 128 memory circuits and designated support circuits in an area of about $\frac{1}{8}$ inch. The primary advantage of this system is faster memory access, with memory size reduced by at least 50 percent (Fig. 6-15).

FIGURE 6-15. Semiconductor memory (Courtesy IBM)

Since its inception, the magnetic core has remained the primary memory medium, owing to its lower cost and reliable storage. The continuing quest for lower cost and higher performance has led manufacturers to examine or develop many alternative technologies for memories. Today, some argue whether and when semiconductor memory will replace magnetic-core memory. Although the market for semiconductor memory is expected to reach $200 million by 1975, its price must come down drastically for it to replace magnetic cores. In 1967, semiconductor memory cost around 50 cents per bit of storage. In 1972 the cost dropped to 10 cents. It is predicted that by 1975 the price will be 0.1 to 2.5 cents per bit of storage. Memory prices in the IBM 360 computers today run between 17 and 40 cents per bit of storage.

At present, semiconductor memory is much more cost-effective than magnetic core for computer systems with main memory capacity of less than 10,000 bits, since their cost is proportional to the storage size. By contrast, magnetic core memory requires a high overhead for its addressing electronics.

Cryogenic Memory

Still relatively new, the cryogenic-memory technique deals with superconducting memory set at a very low temperature, which makes it extremely fast and small. Development of a technique to reduce production cost is needed before it can be made commercially available.

Photodigital Memory

Designed by IBM for the U.S. Atomic Energy Commission, photodigital memory employs an electron beam to record binary data on 1.3- by 2.7-inch pieces of film. The film then is developed by an internal automated "film laboratory," transported in plastic cells through a series of pneumatic tubes, and filed for future retrieval. This unique and extremely costly form of data memory indicates the possible direction and breakthroughs in memory research and development.

Electro-Optical Memory

A small research and development firm located in Las Vegas is feverishly working on a film medium that could become the standard memory unit of future-generation computers. With a million dollar investment and a group of 20 engineers, technicians, and other highly qualified specialists, the firm is developing a product that hinges on the principle of the polarization of light; light is captured in the same way that electric charges are captured to control the direction of a ferromagnetic core. With this electro-optical memory, it would be feasible to store data at *greater densities* and process them at the *speed of light*.

This unique memory design is based on a film made of crystal layers (derived from a rare-earth ferroelectric crystalline material) with different polarizations of opposite surfaces at different points. When these differently polarized layers are properly sandwiched, they can be used to store, reshuffle, and erase the information they hold in the same manner as electronic computers.

When this memory device becomes operational,[4] it could revolutionize the entire data-processing makeup. Since there are no moving parts to wear out and light beams are used instead of electricity, a computer using this concept could last as long as the telephone, and would be quite inexpensive to build. The operating cost is expected to be around 0.0002 cent per bit with a 50-nanosecond access time, in contrast to IBM's 360/96 computer, which costs around 5 cents for each of its 300,000 bits of memory, with an access time of 500 nanoseconds.

Laser Holographic Memory

The laser holographic memory system, still in an experimental stage, uses a special optical plate of multilayered thin film of cerium oxide evaporated on a glass substrate through a variety of randomly patterned screens. The plate, called a random phase shifter, disperses laser beams as they pass through it. A Japanese firm is developing a high-density unit capable of storing 20,000 bits in a circular space ½ millimeter in diameter—about 1,000 times the storage density of integrated-circuit memory systems. On that basis, a holographic memory system containing 10,000 units on a 5- by 5-centimeter plate would have a storage capacity of 2 trillion bits, with a unit readout speed of a few microseconds.

During the spring of 1972, RCA built for the National Aeronautics and Space Administration the first full-cycle, all-optical, 1-million-bit laser memory. In this system, a laser beam first passes through two accoustoelectric, electronically controlled crystals, which deflect the beam in direct proportion to the frequency of sound waves made to pass through them. The deflected beam then strikes one of many different holograms (optical interference patterns) in a flat array, called a *hololens*. The hololens splits the beam so that one part passes through, while the other part is made to fall on a flat plane composed of liquid crystal cells. The cells are tiny areas that can be made reflective (dark) or transparent (light). The cells introduce digital information into the laser beam in the forms of tiny dark areas and tiny light areas, which correspond to the binary (1, 0) code used in computers and represent the data to be written into memory.

Bubble Memory

In electronics, induced resistance to electric current increases with increased wiring. The thousands of wires needed to interconnect the active logic components in core memories limit the maximum speed that can be

[4] A prototye demonstration was held early in 1970.

achieved by the computer's electronic circuitry. Magnetic bubble memory is a revolutionary alternative to core memory. Since no wires are used, bubble memory would be easier to produce and miniaturize and offers hope for greater reliability and longer life.

Bell Laboratories and IBM have been working on the application of magnetic bubble material in computer memories. Bell researchers have developed a method for growing crystal substrate for bubble; IBM has developed noncrystalline or amorphous materials and a way of sensing the bubbles. Using the phenomenon of magnetoresistance, the new sensors are tiny strips of magnetoresistive material—the magnetization changes when a magnetic bubble is nearby. The presence of a bubble is transformed into an electrical signal compatible with the computer's electronic circuitry.

The bubbles (each measuring 1/10 micron in diameter) are negatively magnetized cylindrical islands in a positively magnetized film made of amorphous material. They appear when an amorphous film is exposed to a uniform magnetic field of a specified critical intensity. If the applied magnetic field is increased beyond the critical intensity, the differentiated magnetic character of the bubble disappears, and vice versa. This phenomenon provides the basis for bubble memory to function in binary mode; the appearance of a bubble represents a binary bit 1 and its absence represents a binary bit 0. The number of bubbles that can be created or erased in a given microscopic-sized area provides the basis for developing computer storage beyond today's computer memories.

Bell Laboratories demonstrated the feasibility of bubble memory in 1969, and followed this in 1973 with an operational prototype with a 16-million-bit capacity. By 1980, it is expected that bubble storage devices may hold more than 1 billion bits of data per square inch.

Among the attributes of bubble memory are

1. Nonvolatility, which assures the retention of data during power loss.
2. Nondestructive readout.
3. A 100-fold improvement in access time.
4. Capacity to operate at any speed for any length of time (virtually maintenance free) and to reverse the direction of data flow when necessary.
5. Low operating costs, since very little electric power is needed to induce the magnetic field in manipulating the bubbles.

The future of bubble memory lies in data storage and high-volume data handling. An obvious use in data storage would be for bubble memory to replace established storage media, such as the magnetic disk, tape, or drum. The final proof depends on the development of hardware for the proper application of this phenomenon.

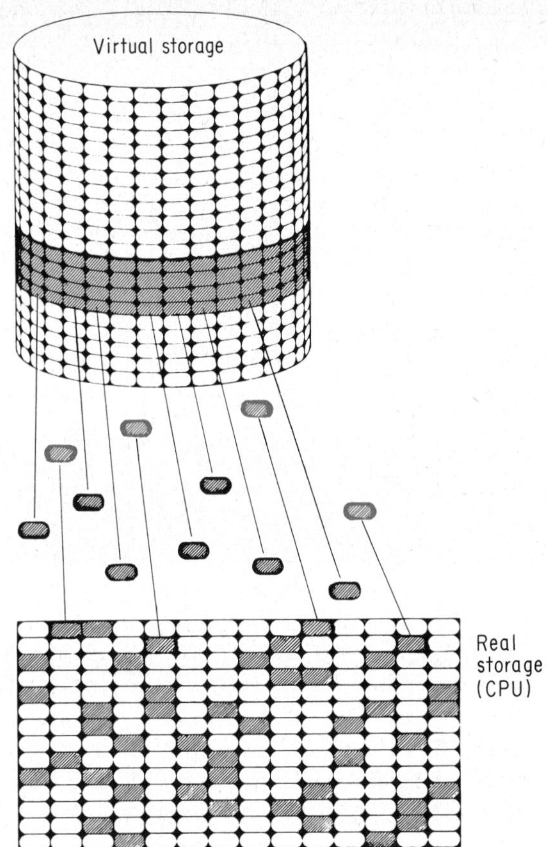

FIGURE 6-16. Virtual storage

VIRTUAL STORAGE—AN OVERVIEW

Conceptually, programmers often view primary storage as independent of secondary storage devices. With the advent of more sophisticated software and hardware, primary storage is now conceived as a large, simulated real storage, which is virtually unlimited in its capacity to store data (hence the phrase *virtual storage*). This allows data, including the program, to be moved or changed between primary and secondary storage.

Virtual storage involves the use of a high-capacity, direct-access device such as magnetic disk or drum as though it were an expanded primary storage (Fig. 6-16). It requires no major reprogramming, minimizes the storage constraints, and makes more efficient use of the computer's primary storage. The concept is not new. The British first used it in the late 1950s on their Atlas computer. Various versions are presently available at extra cost on Burroughs 500 and 700 series, Univac 70 series, and Control Data's larger computers.

The announcement by IBM of its System 370 series in 1970, however, was accompanied by renewed emphasis on a concept of memory management—a new, long-term strategy for increasing the potential of the computer programmer. Steady application growth has traditionally led to increased demand for more freedom in application design. The introduction of the IBM 360 series, for example, allowed programmers freedom in developing application without much concern for computer power. But primary storage constraints were a barrier to designing and developing applications. The advent of the IBM 370 computer offers the programmer relatively larger primary storage, and the virtual-storage option increases real storage by more than 400 percent.

Virtual storage offers several advantages:

1. A programmer need no longer be concerned with program size. He is free to concentrate on problem solutions and laying out a well-designed efficient program.
2. The computer's primary storage need not hold the entire program throughout its execution. The rest of the program is kept on disk for immediate use. This means more efficient use of primary storage.
3. It increases the computer system's total storage by as much as four times its real main storage. For example, the primary storage of the IBM 370, Model 135, is about 245,000 bytes and Model 168 (the new model) is about 4 million bytes. With the virtual-storage feature, the total available storage appears to be 1 million and 16 million bytes, respectively.
4. In the case of the IBM 370 system, virtual storage makes the system more versatile and responsible, broadens the range of applications, and allows more jobs to run concurrently.
5. Elaborate applications can be tested and debugged during prime time by giving each application to be tested a low priority so that it can be done during slack periods without interfering with the normal load.

Of the virtual storage techniques available, IBM uses what is called the "page concept." The program is broken into multiple, equal-sized, 2K or 4K blocks called pages which are stored in direct-access device(s) and recalled into primary (real) storage as needed. Managing the transfers is the task of the computer's operating system. One drawback of paged virtual memory is that individual programs may require more time for execution. The system may make frequent page swaps (also called thrashing or churning) between real storage and virtual storage to the point where it compromises the efficiency of the system. One approach to minimizing thrashing is to use a priority scheduling algorithm, which allows paging of only the highest priority jobs. Another remedy is to select a page size appropriate to the computer's operating system. In any case, the true contribution of virtual storage appears to be controversial and may be subject to further refinements.

The size of virtual storage can be determined by the programmer and, in the case of the IBM 370 system, may be up to 16,777,216 bytes. This much capacity contains storage space for the computer program and the system control programming (SCP). Virtual storage is divided into contiguous (linear), fixed-sized segments determined by the SCP and controlled with a CPU hardware feature called a *dynamic address translation (DAT)*. Each segment is further divided into smaller increments, called *pages*, the size of which is also determined by the SCP and controlled by the system's hardware. Although the computer program does not have to be organized into page-size groupings, optimum performance can be achieved by grouping related data and their instructions in the same page format.

Real storage is also divided into fixed-sized increments called pages, which are always the same size as the virtual storage page, so that proper fit can be made for a given page of data or instruction that might be transferred from virtual storage to real storage for processing. It should be kept in mind that such structure is internal and, as far as the programmer is concerned, he is unaware of either the size or the content of real storage (Fig. 6-17).

A processing routine normally begins when a programmer feeds in his program via a terminal or keypunches it into cards, which are then read into memory. The compiler or assembler translates the program into machine language (called object program) and places it in program library in auxiliary storage, called external page storage (Fig. 6-17). The object program is executed by first moving it into virtual storage. The page containing the first phase of the program is assigned to an available page frame in real storage. As program execution begins, more program pages are transferred from virtual storage to real storage until the entire program is available for continuous execution.

The number of required page frames in real storage for a program's

FIGURE 6-17. *Virtual-storage structure*

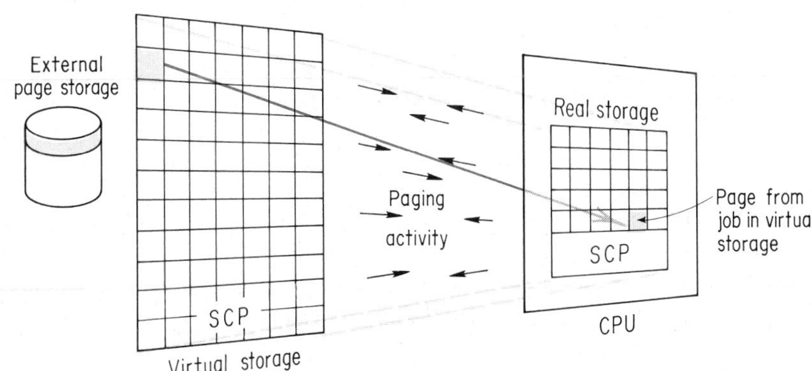

continuous execution is called the program's working set. For optimum performance, the working set of pages should be adequate to accommodate the program for the time interval it is being used. For example, if a given program occupying 50,000 bytes in virtual storage has less than 50,000 bytes of real storage, it could still run successfully, but would require more running time. The increased running time is due to the computer's need to wait for more pages to be transferred into real storage for continued execution.

It should be remembered that virtual memory provides a solution to certain types of problems, but not all. It takes time and know-how to minimize inefficiency resulting from excessive thrashing. Furthermore, since additional equipment (and therefore, more investment) is generally needed for an efficient virtual memory, attention should be given to planning and reviewing the user's program designs to determine the proper utilization of real memory. Advance planning to determine the types and size of both programs and hardware components is also important.

STORED-DATA RETRIEVAL

For a computer to process a problem, it must be able to retrieve or have direct access to the data and instructions stored in magnetic cores, thin film, or other primary-storage devices. The storage unit of the central processor includes areas for working storage and for storing input data, program instructions, and output data. The working-storage area is used by the stored program to store semiprocessed data, the input-storage area for holding incoming data for processing, the program-storage area for storing the program instructions, and the output-storage area for holding processed information. The size of each storage area is flexible and is determined by the programmer (Fig. 6-18).

As shown in Fig. 6-18, program instructions move to the control unit, which manipulates the processing procedure. The frequency and number of instructions involved depend on the complexity of the application. Once initiated, data flow from the input-storage area to the arithmetic–logic unit for actual processing. Intermediate results or semiprocessed data are temporarily held in the working-storage area until needed. They can be recalled by the arithmetic–logic unit as many times as necessary until processing is completed. The finished output is then transferred to the output-storage area to be read out to the user.

Stored-data retrieval is accomplished by assigning a location number, called an *address*, to each storage location in memory. The assignment of the addresses, which are arranged in sequential order, is analogous to a coat checkroom. A checkroom consists of several racks, each rack is assigned a number (the address) that is printed on a ticket to be handed to the coat owner. Without this system of identification, the coat-check

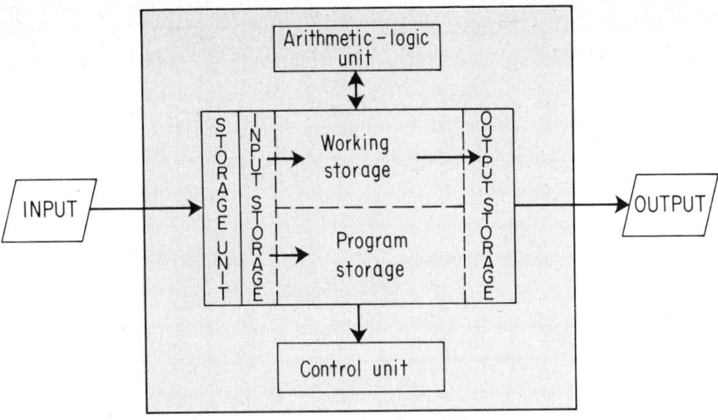

FIGURE 6-18. Computer processing unit

girl would have difficulty returning the proper coat to its rightful owner. After all, who would accept a $60 coat as a substitute for a $300 tailor-made imported cashmere!

Likewise, computer memory is referenced by a set of storage locations or addresses. The address remains unchanged and is independent of the data it contains. In magnetic core, storage is made up of a set of stacked planes; core bits from each plane are combined to represent an alphabetic, numeric, or special character, which is referenced by an address (Fig. 6-19). This example is geared to individually addressable (variable-word-length) computers; however, some addresses refer to a

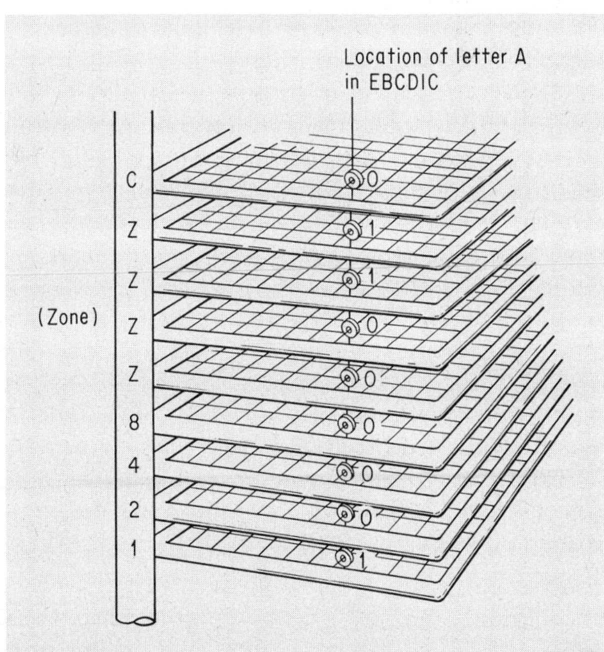

FIGURE 6-19. Location of the letter A in EBCDIC

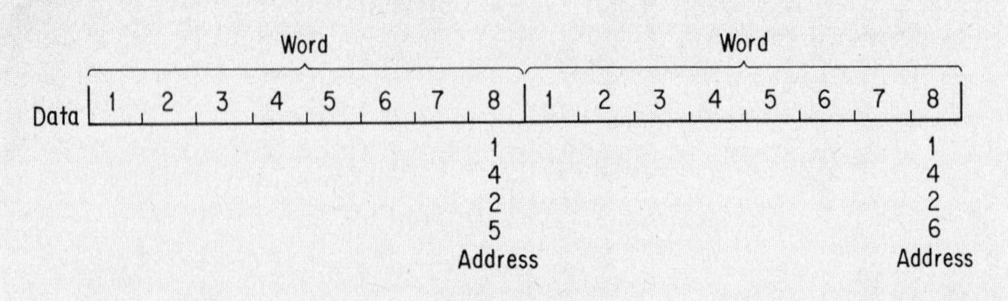

FIGURE 6-20. Fixed-word-length storage

fixed number of characters (word) in what is called fixed-word-length computers. Thus, the size of the data stored or retrieved by a given address depends on whether the computer in question is a variable-or fixed-word-length computer.

Fixed- and Variable-Word-Length Computers

In a fixed-word-length computer, the number of characters making up a word is fixed in length and is handled as a group. Each group has only one address, is picked up as a unit, and contains as many characters as every other word. For example, the numeric characters in Fig. 6-20 make up two eight-character words. The first word is referenced by one address (1425) and the second word by another address (1426). When the contents of the first word (12345678) must be printed, for example, the programmer instructs the computer to print 1425 (the address of the word). The computer will interpret the instruction to mean that it should print the contents of address 1425.

For arithmetic and other operations, a fixed-word-length computer has several addressable general- and special-purpose registers where instructions or specific data are moved in parallel, later moving back to regular storage. Parallel transfer of data means speed of movement to and from the designated registers. Once this step is completed, the next sequential step of the program is carried out, and so on until the entire program has been executed.

In a variable-word-length computer, there is no limit to the size or number of characters making up a word in storage. Each character is individually addressable (having a specific address) and can be retrieved from primary storage and processed with other characters through proper programming instructions (Fig. 6-21).

How does a variable-word-length computer retrieve a specific value composed of two or more characters as a unit? A common approach used in many modern computers (e.g., IBM 370 system) refers to an instruction that specifies the length of the word. The instruction indicates the leftmost

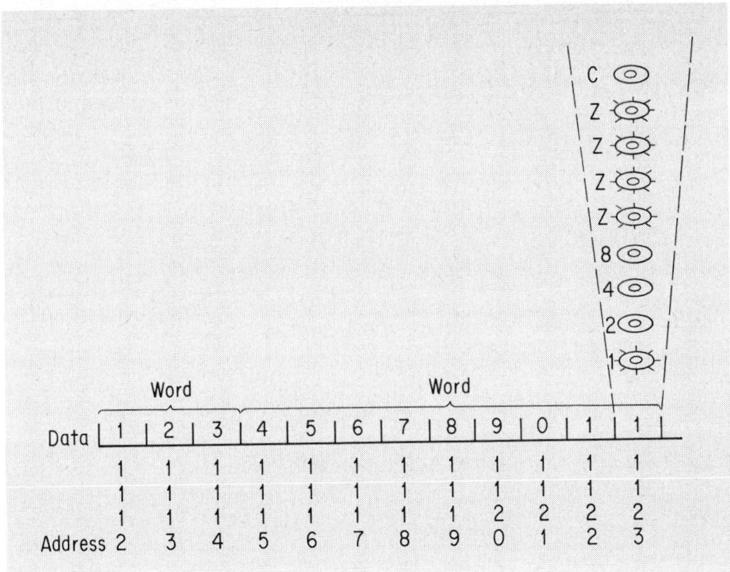

FIGURE 6-21. Variable-word-length storage

address of the particular word and specifies the number of address locations (and, therefore, the word length) to be included. Data retrieval, then, begins with the leftmost address and continues from left to right until all the characters specified by the instruction are picked up.

Variable-word-length computers perform arithmetic serially, one position at a time; fixed-word-length computers compute in parallel, handling any two data words in one cycle regardless of the size of each word. The relatively greater speed of fixed-word-length computers, however, requires more complex circuitry and a higher cost than variable-word-length computers.

Many third-generation computers can accept fixed and variable words by *byte-addressable* instructions. In a byte-addressable computer such as the IBM 370, a fixed binary word is made up of 8-bit bytes and is retrieved by the address of the first byte. Although certain instructions specify half a byte or a double byte, an instruction referencing this address will cause the computer to retrieve four consecutive bytes automatically. However, the variable-word-length approach is accomplished through an instruction that references the address of the first byte and the number of succeeding bytes in a given word.

Arithmetic–Logic Unit

As mentioned earlier, the arithmetic–logic unit handles the processing (arithmetic calculations and logical comparisons) of actual data. Computer logic is relatively simple compared to the complex logical thinking of the human brain. However, the speed of computer logic, and its capacity for "remembering" former steps in problem solution, compensates for the basic simplicity of its logical operations and makes it efficient in the processing of data.

Registers

Unlike the computer's passive main storage, registers are active storage areas designed to hold data or a limited number of words. Some registers are used by the control unit and some by the arithmetic–logic unit; others are used as temporary storage areas. Some registers are used automatically by the computer and, therefore, are not addressable; other registers may be addressed by the programmer for specific work designated in the program.

Addressable registers are general-purpose registers that require words of fixed length, as they are designed to store a specific number of bits until needed. When the job is completed, the stored data are returned to main storage. Third-generation computers, such as the IBM 360 and the new IBM 370 series, are designed to have several general-purpose registers for handling fixed-word-length instructions.

In addition to general-purpose registers, the CPU contains special-purpose registers reserved for special jobs. They include the accumulator, address, instruction, and storage registers. The *accumulator* register is used in addition. It retains the result of an arithmetic operation until it is needed. For example, when two numbers are added, an accumulator register is cleared, and the first number is stored in it. Through the adder, the second number is added to the value stored in the accumulator. When the final total is reached, the sum is moved back to computer memory.

The function of the *address* register is to hold the location number specified by the program instruction. The *instruction* register holds one instruction at a time until it is executed, and the *storage* register stores the data needed for the next processing step.

Computer Operating Cycle

In dealing with problems processed in the CPU, two elements are stressed: the operation to be performed (e.g., ADD, SUBTRACT, COMPARE, MOVE DATA) and the data that will be operated on. The operation to be performed is called *operation code;* the location of the data to be operated on is called the *operand.* Each program instruction consists of at least an operation code (op-code) and a reference to an operand. Most instructions include two operands (A and B). The data represented by operand A and operand B are processed in different ways, depending on the op-code.

Most computers in use today provide for a fixed time interval for each operation and, in this respect, determine the beginning of the next operation. To determine the exact timing for each operation, electronic control circuitry emits a pulse that indicates the end of one operation and the beginning of another. Pulse times in larger computers can range in millions of pulses per second.

Program execution goes through an instruction (I) cycle and an execution (E) cycle. The two cycles are synchronized by pulses emitted by the electronic clock circuits. During the I cycle, the program instruction is moved from main storage to a storage register; the operation code is stored in the instruction register and the operand(s) is stored in the address register. The op-code, then, is transformed into the proper circuitry to do the operation. During this cycle, the instruction address counter is incremented by one, which indicates to the computer the location of the next instruction.

Actual data processing takes place in the execution (E) cycle. The data specified by the operand(s) are moved from storage to the proper registers (and vice versa) for arithmetic and other operations. The results are held in appropriate registers or storage areas until needed. Once completed, the CPU proceeds to handle the details required by the next instruction.

SUMMARY

Data computations are made in the central processing unit. Processing requires the accessibility of data in primary storage. The total storage capacity required of a computer system is determined to a large extent by a company's needs in terms of processing speed, storage capacity, and data accessibility. An ideal system is one that combines these factors in such a way as to meet the company's immediate and long-term data-processing needs most economically.

The main types of primary storage devices are as follows:

1. **Magnetic core storage.** Consists of doughtnut-shaped rings of ferromagnetic material. This form of storage is highly dependable, durable, provides high-speed data access, low-cost operation, low heat dissipation, and adaptability to word-oriented or character-oriented computers.
2. **Planar thin-film memory.** A very rapid and reliable storage device, which is gaining popularity with further improvements in miniaturization; its production is likely to continue.
3. **Semiconductor memory.** Representative of the IBM system 370 main memory, this type of memory is more cost-effective and provides faster memory access than magnetic core memory.
4. **Cryogenic memory.** Deals with superconducting memory set at a very low temperature.

5. **Photodigital memory.** A unique form of data memory. It is relatively limited in use owing to present high production cost.
6. **Laser holographic memory.** Still in the experimental stage, but making headway for future full-scale operation.
7. **Bubble memory.** A recent technique for miniaturizing data memory with the major objective of storing more than 1 billion bits of data per square inch of space.
8. **Virtual memory.** A large simulated real storage that relieves the programmer from being concerned about program size and allows him to concentrate, instead, on problem solution.

Data retrieval is accomplished by assigning addresses to each storage location in memory. The storage unit contains areas for working storage, storing input data, and program instructions. The control unit monitors the processing procedure; the arithmetic–logic unit handles processing of actual data through the use of general-purpose and special-purpose registers. Instructions are also loaded and executed using special registers; the computer programmer may take many alternatives in handling program execution. The key idea behind the operating cycle remains the same. There is an instruction cycle to set the processing phase in motion and an execution cycle to execute the necessary steps. Both cycles are controlled by timing circuits to move instructions and data.

TERMS TO LEARN

Accumulator	Parity check
Address	Primary storage
Binary-coded decimal byte	Register
Cryogenics	Secondary storage
Inhibit wire	Self-checking code
Logic	Sense wire
Magnetic core	Software
Operand	Thin-film memory
Operation code	Virtual storage
Packed decimal	

QUESTIONS

1. Explain the difference between primary and secondary storage. Give an example to illustrate this difference.
2. What are the characteristics and primary areas of primary storage? Explain each briefly.
3. "A magnetic core has only two definite states." What are they? Explain. What advantages does magnetic core offer as primary storage?

4. What is the difference between a 6-bit and an 8-bit code? Explain.
5. How can a given magnetic core be set to a 0 state? to a 1 state?
6. If the X and Y wires are used to carry current, what is the purpose of the sense wire?
7. How are data read from and written in magnetic cores?
8. What is the difference between thin-film and cryogenic memory? Explain.
9. Explain briefly (a) photodigital memory, (b) electro-optical memory, (c) bubble memory, (d) semiconductor memory, (e) holographic memory.
10. Explain the difference between fixed- and variable-word-length computers.
11. How does the arithmetic–logic unit differ from the control unit?
12. What is the difference between an address and a register?
13. What functions do general- and special-purpose registers serve? Explain.
14. Explain briefly the operating cycle related to program execution.
15. What are the advantages and drawbacks of virtual storage?
16. Explain briefly the basic concept and structure of virtual storage.

SUGGESTED READING

BERGSTRESSER, R. V. "Virtual Storage Operation," *Datamation,* Feb. 1973, pp. 57–59.

CHAPIN, NED. *Computers—A Systems Approach.* New York: Van Nostrand Reinhold Company, 1971, pp. 300–338.

DAVIS, G. B. *Computer Data Processing.* New York: McGraw-Hill Book Company, 1973, pp. 118–140, 144–159.

"How to Think About Virtual Storage," *Infosystems,* Nov. 1972, pp. 44–45ff.

"How IBM Talks About Virtual Storage," *Infosystems,* Oct. 1972, pp. 26–28.

Introduction to Virtual Storage in System 370. IBM Manual No. GR20-4260-0.

"Magnetic Bubbles Place Seen Between Core and Disk," *Computerworld,* Sept. 27, 1972, p. 24.

MEETHAM, ROGER. *Information Retrieval.* Garden City, N.Y.: Doubleday & Company, Inc., 1970.

computer number systems and arithmetic

7

Octal Arithmetic

octal addition
octal subtraction
octal multiplication
octal division

Hexadecimal Arithmetic

hexadecimal addition
hexadecimal subtraction
hexadecimal multiplication
hexadecimal division

For many centuries early man functioned without a standardized method of counting or a means of communicating data to his fellowman. Stones, pebbles, sticks, and other physical objects were used to represent quantities. In the earliest system, the written form of a unit was represented by a single mark: | . Other marks were added as more units were counted. Roman numbers are refined forms of this early numbering system. Each number retains a fixed value regardless of its position. For example, the Roman symbol V represents decimal 5; symbol VI is 6; symbol VII is 7; and so on. Later we shall see that in modern systems a number is determined more by its position than absolute value, and the number of symbols used depends on the base of the particular system.

Over the succeeding centuries, the Egyptians, Chinese, Hindus, and other civilizations developed many number systems, which complicated communication flow; the absence of standardization also limited the application and spread of sciences such as mathematics. Eventually, the use of the decimal (base 10) system of counting (believed to have developed from man's use of his 10 fingers) became the standard in the world and evolved as the most efficient system handled manually by man.

During the past decade, however, greater emphasis has been placed on *man-to-machine* communication than on *man-to-man* communication. Electronic computers were developed to simplify the handling of numeric and alphabetic data. For the convenience of the user, especially in business data processing, input to the computer is written in standard decimal or alphabetic form. Before processing, these characters are converted into codes by the computer, based on a binary number system. The coded

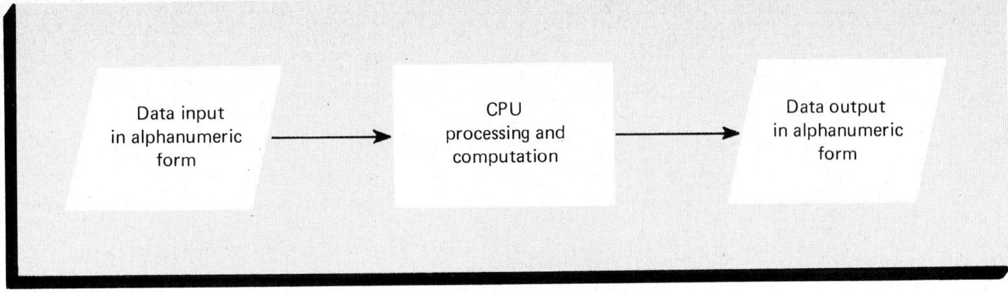

FIGURE 7-1. Conversion routine in computer processing

data are reconverted to decimal and/or alphabetic characters upon print-out (Fig. 7-1). Although few people besides the microprogrammer[1] need to work in terms of a binary code, it is helpful to understand something about the nature of this number system and its ability to represent data in computer storage.

THE CONCEPT OF A NUMBER SYSTEM

A number system involves a base (radix), an absolute digit, and a positional (or place) value. The base defines the maximum number of digits used in the system; positional value represents the radix and the power[2] of that position. The value of a given digit is computed by multiplying the digit by its positional value. The sum of the digits' products gives us the final value. Figure 7-2 illustrates this concept by using two examples in decimal notation.

In the examples in Fig. 7-2, it can be seen that in the decimal system the radix used is 10. With whole numbers, the value attributed to a decimal digit is determined by its position. The first position to the right has a value of 1; the second to the left, 10; the third to the left, 100; and so forth. Note that as each position is added it is placed to the left of the preceding one.

[1] A microprogram is a special control program stored in a special control storage area for initiating the execution of a sequence of "micro instructions" for each machine-language instruction. Microprogramming is a very specialized activity used for expanding the versatility of many computer systems.

[2] For review purposes, two facts must be remembered:

a. A digit raised to power 0 is always equal to 1. For example, $1^0 = 1$, $7^0 = 1$, etc. In number systems, the positional value of the low-order digit is the base of the number system raised to power 0.
b. A number with a minus exponent is interpreted as a fraction. For example, $10^{-1} = 1/10$; $10^{-2} = 1/10^2$ or $1/100$. The base point is located between power 0 and the power -1. In the decimal system, the base point is called the decimal point.

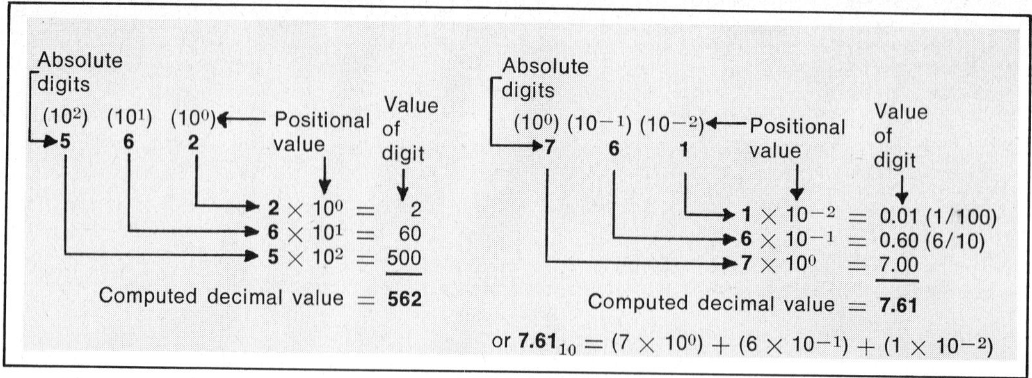

FIGURE 7-2. Examples of the decimal system

Several number systems have been developed, each having a different base and set of absolute values. Fifteen number systems are listed in Fig. 7-3. This chapter is primarily concerned with the binary, octal, and hexadecimal systems—the three key number systems for today's computers.

THE BINARY NUMBER SYSTEM

Because the decimal system is the most commonly used system for arithmetic operations, we have learned to add, subtract, multiply, and divide according to its rules. In fact, until recently, it has been the only system

Name	Base (Radix)	Absolute Values
binary	**2**	**01**
ternary	3	012
quarternary	4	0123
quinary	5	01234
senary	6	012345
septenary	7	0123456
octenary (octal)	**8**	**01234567**
nonary	9	012345678
denary (decimal)	**10**	**0123456789**
undenary	11	0123456789A
duodenary	12	0123456789AB
tredenary	13	0123456789ABC
quatuordenary	14	0123456789ABCD
quidenary	15	0123456789ABCDE
hexadenary (hexadecimal)	**16**	**0123456789ABCDEF**

FIGURE 7-3. Fifteen number systems and their absolute values

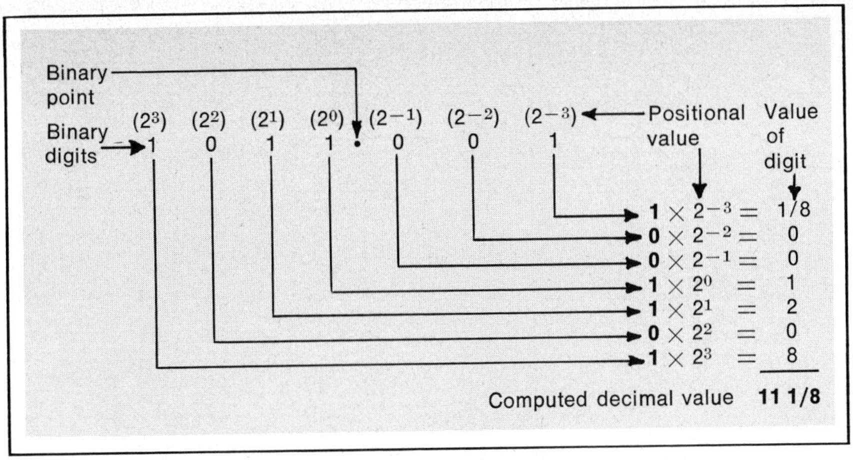

FIGURE 7-4. Computing the decimal equivalent of a binary number

taught in schools. Many call it "ten-finger arithmetic." Unfortunately, however, "ten-finger arithmetic" does not lend itself readily to the operation and use of electronic digital computers. For one thing, computers made of electronic components and switching devices are *bistable*, or have two definite states. They are either energized (on) or deenergized (off). For electronic devices used in computers, 10 defined states, then, are not feasible. Instead, the bistability of electronic components makes it simpler to use a binary (two-state) number system, which lends itself more easily and economically to the design and function of digital computers.

The binary system uses radix 2, or two absolute values (0 and 1), and positional values in powers of 2. The value of each position doubles as it is added from right to left—that is, 1 (2^0), 2 (2^1), 4 (2^2), 8 (2^3), 16 (2^4), 32 (2^5), and so forth. As is true in the decimal system, the decimal equivalent of a binary number is the sum of the product of its absolute and positional values (see Fig. 7-4).

Binary-to-Decimal Conversion

Unlike businessmen, whose primary interest is handling input and output data in decimal form, computer personnel have a special-purpose orientation. They are often involved in handling data in different number systems. Since they work with computers, they need to understand these systems and know how to convert a number in one system to a number in another system. A binary-to-decimal conversion method less cumbersome than the one in Fig. 7-4 calls for multiplying each binary digit (beginning with the left digit) by 2 and adding its product to the next digit until the entire binary number is added (see Fig. 7-5).

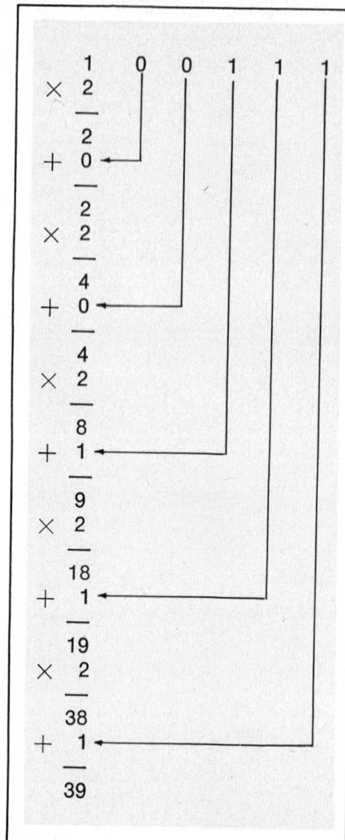

FIGURE 7-5. Conversion of a binary number to a decimal

A binary fraction is converted to a decimal fraction as follows: Beginning with the first binary digit to the right of the binary point, each numerator is multiplied by 2, and the product is added to the next numerator. The denominator, however, begins with 2 for the first position and doubles for each succeeding position. Conversion of the binary fraction .001 (Fig. 7-4) to a decimal fraction is shown in Fig. 7-6.

Binary fraction	.0	0	1
Decimal fraction	0/2	0/4	1/8

FIGURE 7-6. Conversion of a binary fraction to a decimal fraction

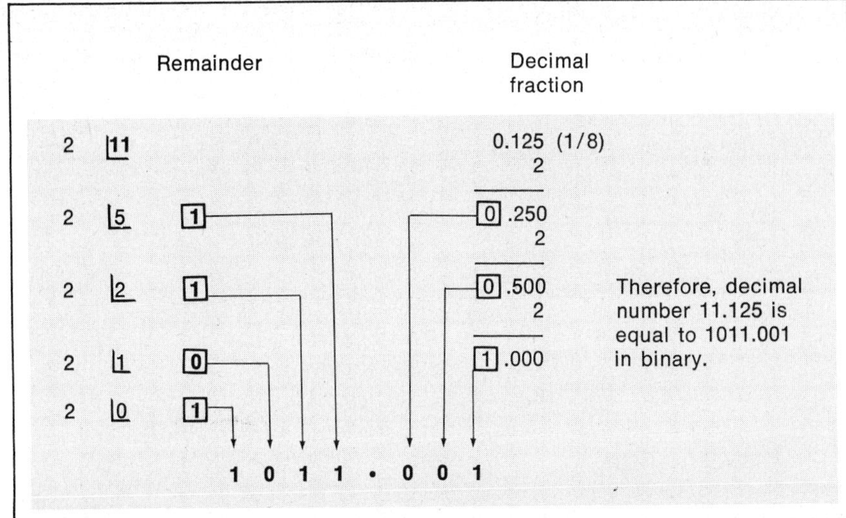

FIGURE 7-7. Conversion of a decimal number to a binary number

Decimal-to-Binary Conversion

One method of converting an integer number to a binary number is to divide it successively by 2. The remainder of each division becomes a part of the binary number. A decimal fraction, on the other hand, is converted to a binary fraction by multiplying it successively by 2. The digit to the left of the decimal (0 or 1) produced after each multiplication forms a part of the binary fraction. Figure 7-7 shows the conversion of decimal number $11\frac{1}{8}$ (Fig. 7-4) to a binary number.

BINARY-BASED NUMBER SYSTEMS

The discussion presented thus far indicates that any number must be represented by a set of binary digits, since the foundation of almost all computers lies in the binary system, and binary bits 0 and 1 can be reliably represented in the computer's switching complex and storage structure. However, because of the design and circuitry of various computers, the number of binary digits assigned to represent a number must be specified either in terms of a fixed number of bits (fitting the description of a fixed-word-length computer) or a variable number of bit sets (fitting the description of a variable-word-length computer). Each bit set ranges in size from 4 to 8 bits per set.

In representing numbers by a fixed set of bits, the computer operator often finds it cumbersome to work with or read a series of binary digits. Thus, more effective computer notations have been developed. The ones currently emphasized are the octal and the hexadecimal number systems. On the other hand, numbers represented by a variable number of bit sets refer to a binary-coded decimal—a binary-based system of coding. These systems and their arithmetic operations constitute the remainder of this chapter.

Binary-Coded Decimal (BCD)

Even though most computers operate in the binary mode, only some of them use straight binary representation as a coding system. A straight binary machine represents data by translating a decimal number, regardless of its size, into one binary combination. For example, a decimal value of 954 is symbolized by the straight binary representation shown in Fig. 7-8.

Positional value	512	256	128	64	32	16	8	4	2	1	
Binary Equivalent	1	1	1	0	1	1	1	0	1	0	= 954

FIGURE 7-8. *Straight binary representation*

For purposes of facilitating arithmetic computations, straight binary representation is more suited to scientific calculations than to commercial data processing. In business-oriented computer systems, each code digit should be instantly recognizable; therefore, a special coding technique is required. For easy representation of decimal digits, coded-decimal techniques are more popular. The most popular coded-decimal technique is referred to as the *binary-coded decimal* or *BCD code.*

USES AND LIMITATIONS. The BCD code is used in computers that are a compromise between pure binary and pure decimal computers. The technique simply takes each decimal digit and codes it in a set of four binary digits. Given the 10 decimal digits, a combination of 2 one-binary bits (1 1) will represent only a maximum decimal equivalent of 3. A combination of 3 one-binary bits (1 1 1) will represent a maximum decimal equivalent of 7. Therefore, 4 one-binary digits (1 1 1 1) are needed to represent any one of the one-decimal digits (0 through 9). The BCD code of the 10 decimal digits is shown in Fig. 7-9.

Decimal Digit	Binary Coded Decimal
0	0 0 0 0
1	0 0 0 1
2	0 0 1 0
3	0 0 1 1
4	0 1 0 0
5	0 1 0 1
6	0 1 1 0
7	0 1 1 1
8	1 0 0 0
9	1 0 0 1

FIGURE 7-9. BCD code of the 10 decimal digits

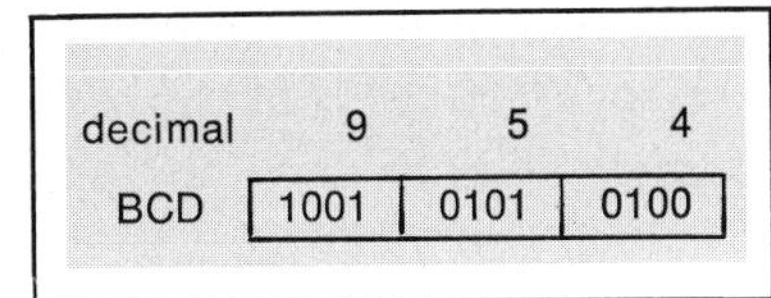

decimal	9	5	4
BCD	1001	0101	0100

FIGURE 7-10. BCD value of 954

Using the information in Fig. 7-9, we see that a fixed number of 4 binary bits, or digits, is needed every time a decimal digit is represented. Figure 7-10 shows the decimal value 954 represented in BCD.

The main advantage of the BCD technique is that the binary coding of decimal digits is easily and clearly understood. Anyone who has an understanding of the binary values of the 10 decimal digits can recognize and interpret the decimal equivalent of any specific BCD number.

The primary disadvantages of the BCD are (1) its inefficiency, (2) the difficulty in doing arithmetic when compared with the binary system, and (3) the need to perform two types of arithmetic in each arithmetic operation.

1. The BCD system is inefficient because, although the four fixed binary digits (8, 4, 2, 1) can represent up to the decimal equivalent of 15, they are employed to represent only the first 10 decimal digits.
2. In arithmetic operations, the BCD encounters difficulty with regard to the decimal carry. When an addition requiring a carry is made, it does not provide a carry. Instead, it represents the sum of two or more decimal digits in one-binary combination. An example is given in Fig. 7-11.
3. The arithmetic section must perform the double function of binary and decimal arithmetic—in other words, binary addition within those binary digits being added, and decimal addition when the number of decimal digits added exceeds two.

Decimal	BCD
9	1001
+ 4	+ 0100
13	**1101**

FIGURE 7-11

Decimal	BCD
6	0110
+ 3	+ 0011
9	**1001**

FIGURE 7-12

We can see that the BCD does not provide for the required decimal carry. In the number 13 in Fig. 7-11, the sum 3 (0 0 1 1) and a carry should be obtained. Instead, the system represents the whole sum (13) in one decimal digit. Computers that use the BCD code need some corrective techniques to represent the desired carry.

When no carry is required, however, addition in the BCD is very easy and convenient. An example is $6 + 3 = 9$ (Fig. 7-12). The decimal sum in this example does not require a carry. The sum is one digit. The BCD system works well because the sum represents only one decimal digit.

Binary-Coded Octal

The octal number system or base 8 is most commonly used in scientific-oriented computers. It uses the bits 4, 2, and 1 to represent a maximum decimal value of 7. Thus, the octal code is similar to the BCD code (8, 4, 2, 1), except that the fourth bit (8) is not used. Decimal numbers from 8 up are represented by adding an octal digit to the left of the previous one. Each octal digit is a multiple of 8 (positional value) and is similar to the binary digit, which increases by a multiple of 2 (base 2), and the decimal digit, which increases by a multiple of 10 (base 10). Figure 7-13 shows a comparative representation of decimal digits in BCD and octal codes.

FIGURE 7-13. Binary-coded octal and an example

Octal Digit (Absolute Values)	Binary-Coded Octal	Decimal Value		Octal Positional Value $8^2 8^1 8^0$	Octal Notation	Explanation
0	000					
1	001					
2	010					
3	011	14	=	1 6	16_8	$(1 \times 8^1) + (6 \times 8^0) = 14$
4	100	15	=	1 7	17_8	$(1 \times 8^1) + (7 \times 8^0) = 15$
5	101	16	=	2 0	20_8	$(2 \times 8^1) + (0 \times 8^0) = 16$
6	110	75	=	1 1 3	113_8	$(1 \times 8^2) + (1 \times 8^1) + (3 \times 8^0) = 75$
7	111					

Subscript 8 indicates that the number 113 is an octal number

```
octal    4   6   7
        ×8
        32
        +6
        ---
        38
        ×8
        ---
       304
        +7
        ---
decimal  311
```

FIGURE 7-14

Octal-to-Decimal Conversion

Octal-to-decimal conversion is done by multiplying each octal position (beginning with the left octal digit) by 8 and adding its product to the next number, and so on, until the last digit is added (but not multiplied). For example, 467 in octal is converted to decimal as shown in Fig. 7-14.

Octal-to-decimal conversion can also be performed by multiplying each octal absolute value by its positional value. Using the same example, Fig. 7-15 shows the conversion of octal number 467 to a decimal number.

A decimal number is converted to an octal number simply by dividing it successively by 8. The remainder of each division forms a part of the octal number (see Fig. 7-16).

Binary-Coded Hexadecimal

Large numbers in binary are often cumbersome to interpret and to manipulate. The hexadecimal system has the capacity to handle large binary as well as BCD numbers, since each hexadecimal digit represents four binary bits (Fig. 7-17).

The hexadecimal numbering system uses base 16 (positional values), unlike base 10 of the decimal system, base 8 of the octal, or base 2 of the binary system. Since the decimal system provides only 10 digits to repre-

FIGURE 7-15

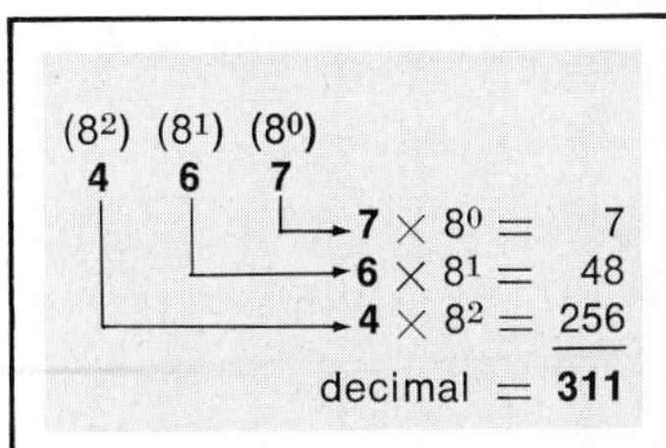

FIGURE 7-16

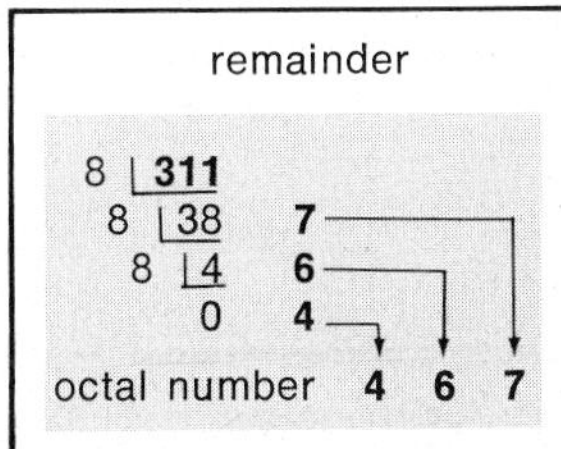

Hexadecimal Digit	Binary-coded Hexadecimal
0	0000
1	0001
2	0010
3	0011
4	0100
5	0101
6	0110
7	0111
8	1000
9	1001
A	1010
B	1011
C	1100
D	1101
E	1110
F	1111

FIGURE 7-17

sent the first 10 values of the hexadecimal system (0 to 9), the remaining six hexadecimal values are arbitrarily represented by the first six letters of the alphabet, A, B, C, D, E, and F. Thus, the entire symbolic set of the hexadecimal numbering system consists of 0, 1, 2, 3, 4, 5, 6, 7, 8, 9, A, B, C, D, E, F. In this sequence, A represents a decimal value of 10; B, a decimal value of 11; . . .; and F, a decimal value of 15 (Fig. 7-17). When the decimal number 10 is reached, note that a carry to the next most significant position takes place. In the case of the hexadecimal system, when the hexadecimal number 16 is reached, there is also a carry to the next most significant position.

Since a hexadecimal digit represents a fixed set of four binary digits, the conversion of hexadecimal to and from binary is relatively simple. Hexadecimal-to-binary conversion is made by replacing each hexadecimal digit by the equivalent set of four binary digits. To illustrate, hexadecimal number E 7 A is converted to a binary number as shown in Fig. 7-18.

A binary number is converted into a hexadecimal number by separating the binary digits (starting with the rightmost digit) into fixed sets of four digits. If the last set is less than four digits, leading zeros are

Hexadecimal	E	7	A
Binary	1110	0111	1010

FIGURE 7-18

Binary	0101	1100	1011
Hexadecimal	5	C	B

FIGURE 7-19

added. Once this is established, the equivalent hexadecimal digit for each set is substituted. For example, the binary number 010111001011 is converted to a hexadecimal number as shown in Fig. 7-19.

A decimal number is converted to a hexadecimal number by dividing successively by 16. The remainder of each division stands for a hexadecimal number. The remainders 10 through 15 must be converted to their hexadecimal notation of A through F, respectively. For example, the decimal value 1970 is converted into a hexadecimal number as shown in Fig. 7-20.

Conversion from hexadecimal to decimal is simply performed by a series of multiplications and additions:

1. Multiply the most significant (leftmost) hexadecimal digit by 16.
2. Add the next most significant hexadecimal digit to the product, and multiply the sum by 16.
3. Continue the add and multiply procedure until the least significant (rightmost) hexadecimal digit has been added to the last product.

Using the hexadecimal result (7 B 2) in the example given in Fig. 7-20, we proceed as shown in Fig. 7-21. From that illustration, we see that 7 B 2 is the hexadecimal value of 1970.

FIGURE 7-20

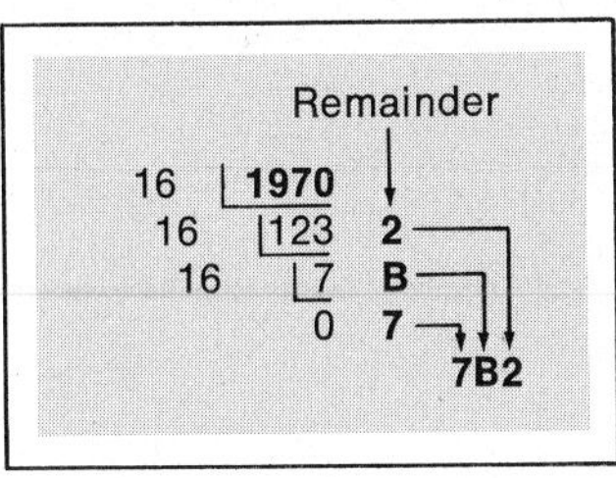

FIGURE 7-21

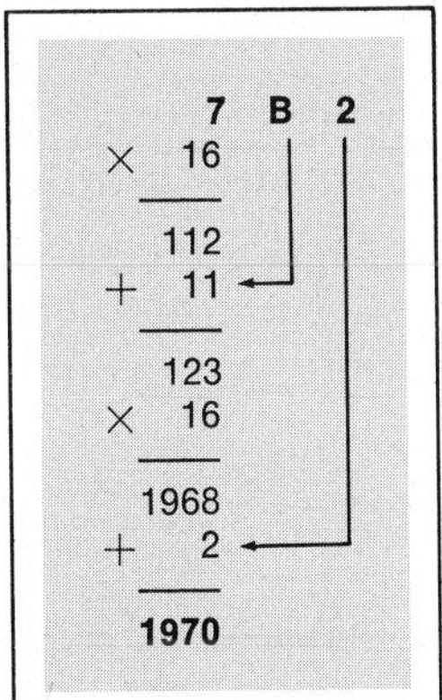

Computer programmers rarely ever do binary arithmetic, but a general knowledge of this area is helpful background for understanding digital computers. Therefore, this section is a brief coverage of computer arithmetic and may be deleted without breaking continuity.

The computer's primary storage has been shown to store data for processing and retain output information until needed. Output information is developed through the arithmetic unit, which consists of electronic devices such as adder circuits [3] and accumulator registers. These devices perform addition, subtraction, multiplication, division and logical functions under the direction of the control unit.

Adders are either serial or parallel. *Parallel adders* add several bits simultaneously, using a different adder for each pair of digits. A parallel adder is effective in fixed-word-length computers, which deal with information in groups of several digits at a time. It is capable of (1) adding a full word of digits to another full word of digits, (2) allowing the result to be accumulated at the same time, and (3) taking care of the carryover from one decimal position to another.

With variable-word-length computers, parallel adders are impractical. Since fields are of varying lengths, there is no requirement for a specific number of digits to be handled by the parallel adder. Therefore, a serial or one-digit adder is more appropriate.

A *serial adder* adds successive pairs of digits one digit at a time. Beginning in the low-order position, the first pair of digits is added and the sum is put back directly into the low-order position of the area in computer memory reserved for storing the sum. This routine is applied on each succeeding added-to-storage pair of digits until all the digits have been added, making the need for an accumulator unnecessary.

Serial addition takes more time than parallel addition, as time usage depends primarily upon the number of places used, and they require less hardware then those which utilize parallel addition. To add two three-place numbers in parallel addition, for example, would require the use of three one-position adders, which would operate simultaneously. Serial addition of the two three-place numbers would require the use of one adder, which would handle the three consecutive steps needed to add the positional values of the two numbers.

Binary Arithmetic

Binary and Decimal Addition. Nearly all arithmetic operations are performed by computers through addition. In decimal addition, one

[3] Other related devices include an inverter circuit, which produces the proper complement in binary subtraction, and a comparator, which determines the larger of two binary values. As an electronic device, an adder circuit produces a sum and carry, if any, from each pair of bits and relays the carry to the next pair of bits to be added.

	Binary	Decimal
	1110	14
	+ 0101	5
Carry	1	
	10011	19

FIGURE 7-22. *Binary addition*

number is placed under another number and the two are added. We carry a number from one column to the next when the sum of the first column exceeds 9. In binary addition, we carry a number from one column to the next when the sum of the first column exceeds 1 (Fig. 7-22).

As you can see, the addition rules in binary are few and simple. They are summarized as follows:

$1 + 1 = 0$ and carry 1 to be added to the next column; i.e., $1 + 1 = 10$
$1 + 0 = 1$
$0 + 1 = 1$
$0 + 0 = 0$

Binary and Decimal Arithmetic with Complements. There are two complements of interest associated with a decimal digit. One complement method is related to the base of the decimal system and is called the *tens complement;* the other complement method is identified by the base of the decimal system less 1, and is called the *nines complement.*

The decimal tens complement method. The tens complement of a number is the amount that must be added to that number to make a total of the appropriate power of 10. The tens complement of the subtrahend is determined and added to the minuend and any end-around carry is replaced with a plus sign. The complement of 4 is 6 ($10 - 4 = 6$). The complement of 19 is 81 ($100 - 19$); of 10, 90 ($100 - 10$); and so forth. To illustrate, subtraction of 3 from 9 is handled as follows:

1. Complement the subtrahend (3). The tens complement of 3 is 7.
2. Add the minuend (9) to the complement 7. The carry resulting from the sum is replaced by a plus sign.

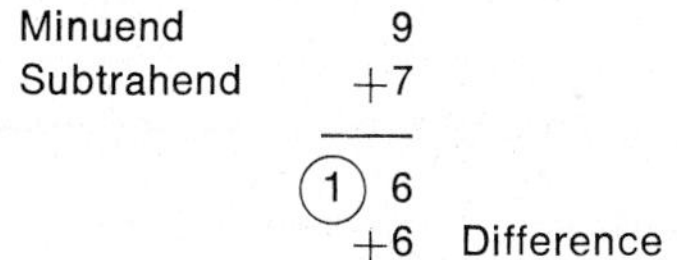

+6 Difference

Failure to develop a carry means that the remainder is in complement form, and the final answer is negative. When the remainder is in complement form, it is not the true remainder and must be recomplemented. For example,

Minuend	4
Subtrahend	—7
Difference	—3

1. Complement the subtrahend (7). The tens complement of 7 is 3.
2. Add 4 to the complement 3. 4 + 3 = 7.
3. Since there is no carry, 7 is in complement form. The tens complement of 7 is 3, and its sign is negative. The answer, then, is —3.

The decimal nines complement method. In the nines complement method, the complement of the subtrahend is the amount that must be added to that number to make a total of 9. That is, each decimal digit in the subtrahend is first subtracted from 9. For example, the complement of 5 is 4, the complement of 3 is 6, that of 62 is 37 (99 — 62), that of 621 is 378 (999 — 621), and so forth. For example, subtraction of 32 from 61 is handled as follows.

1. Take the nines complement of the subtrahend (32). The nines complement of 32 is 67 (99 — 32).
2. Add the complement (67) to the minuend (61), giving a total of 128.
3. A carry in the high-order position of the sum is added to the units digit, and the total value is given a plus sign. Therefore, the remainder of 61 — 32 is +29.

Minuend	61
Nines Complement	67
	(1) 28
	→1
	+29

However, if no carry develops, the sum is in complement form and is also negative. A recomplement is necessary to obtain the true remainder. For example, 64 — 78 = —14 is derived as follows:

1. Take the nines complement of the subtrahend (78). It is 99 — 78, or 21.
2. Add the complement (21) to the minuend (64), giving a total of 85.
3. Since no carry develops, recomplement the sum (85) and add a minus sign to the true remainder. The nines complement of 85 is 14. The true remainder, then, is —14.

BINARY SUBTRACTION. *Binary subtraction—the ones complement method.* Binary subtraction is performed by reversing the subtrahend to its opposite state (giving us the ones complement), adding it to the minuend, and adding any resulting carry to the sum. For example,

Minuend	1 0 0 1	9
Subtrahend	−0 1 1 0	−6
Difference	+0 0 1 1	+3

1. Complement the subtrahend (reversing its digits) and add:

Minuend	1001
Subtrahend in complement form	+1001
	(1)0010
	→ 1
	11 (3 in decimal)

2. Add the end-around carry to the units position.

If no carry develops, the result is a negative remainder in a complement form. It must be recomplemented and a negative sign added to get the right answer. For example,

Binary	***Decimal***
0111	7
−1011	−11
−0100	−04

1. Complement the subtrahend (lower value) and add:

```
 0111
+0100
 ----
 1011
```

2. Since no carry develops, the result in step 1 is recomplemented and given a negative sign. So, 1011 becomes −0100 (−4 in decimal).

Note that in binary subtraction both the minuend and the subtrahend must have an equal number of digits. The shorter number is filled with zeros, as shown in the preceding examples.

Binary subtraction—the twos complement method. This method of binary subtraction is performed by taking the ones complement of the subtrahend, and then adding 1 to the low-order digit. Any end-around carry is replaced by a plus sign. If no carry occurs, the result is recomplemented and given a minus sign.

To illustrate, suppose that we wish to subtract 0 1 0 0 (4) from 1 0 0 1 (9). We proceed as follows:

1. Determine the ones complement of the subtrahend, add 1 to the low-order position, and add:

Subtrahend	0100	1001 (9)
Ones Complement	1011	→ 1100
Add 1	+ 1	(1) 0101
Twos complement	1100	+0101 Difference

The encircled digit is an end-around carry and is changed to a plus sign. Therefore, the true remainder becomes +0 1 0 1.

If no carry develops, however, the remainder must be recomplemented and given a negative sign. Let us reverse the example by subtracting 9 from 4.

1. Determine the twos complement of the subtrahend and add.

Subtrahend	1001	0100 (4)
Ones complement	0110	0111
Add 1	1	1011
Twos complement	0111	

The absence of a carry leads to recomplementing the remainder (reversing the digits and adding 1 to the low-order digit) and adding a negative sign. So the true remainder becomes —0101.

$0 \times 0 = 0$
$0 \times 1 = 0$
$1 \times 0 = 0$
$1 \times 1 = 1$

Binary Multiplication. The binary multiplication table involves the four basic steps shown in the margin. In the binary mode, multiplication is done by one of two methods: (1) the decimal method, or (2) the shift method.

Decimal method of binary multiplication. The decimal method simply utilizes the technique we follow when we multiply manually, using pencil and paper (Fig. 7-23).

Decimal	Binary
5	101
× 3	× 11
15	101
	101
	1111

FIGURE 7-23. Binary multiplication—the decimal method

Shift method of binary multiplication. When using the shift method, multiplication is performed by multiplying the multiplicand by the first left-hand bit of the multiplier and then shifting left one position and adding 0. The same procedure is followed on the second-position bit of the multiplier, and so on, until the operation is completed. For example, multiplying 11 × 11 (3 × 3 in decimal) involves the following steps:

1. Multiply the multiplicand by the first left-hand bit of the multiplier:

   1 1

   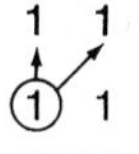

   1 1 Product of the first multiplier
2. Shift left one position by adding 0 to the right; the product (1 1) of step 1 becomes 1 1 0.
3. Multiply the multiplicand by the next bit of the multiplier:

   1 1

   1 (1)

   1 1 Product of the second multiplier
4. Add the product obtained in step 3 to the shifted product in step 2. Or

```
   1 1 0
+    1 1
  ------
 1 0 0 1   Final product
```

Multiplication on a computer is performed in a similar way. A device called an *accumulator* is used to record the steps illustrated.

Binary Division. Division is a series of successive subtractions, just as multiplication is a series of successive additions. The quotient tells us the number of times the divisor was subtracted from the dividend. In subtraction, however, the complementing routine is done first, followed by additions.

Like decimal division, binary division is performed on the basis of the following table:

$1 \div 0 = 0$
$0 \div 1 = 1$
$1 \div 1 = 1$

Assuming that complementing is done every time subtraction is made, an example of a division is

```
         1001
  11  ) 11011
        11
        00011
           11
           00
```

Octal Arithmetic

Octal Addition. Octal addition is similar to decimal addition except that digits 8 and 9 are not used. The next digit after octal 7 is 0 with a carry of 1. Thus, $3 + 4 = 7$, and $3 + 5 = 0$ and 1 carry or 10 (8 in decimal). Figure 7-24 is a 7×7 octal addition table. The sum of an

Augend Digits \ Addend Digits (+)	0	1	2	3	4	5	6	7
0	0	1	2	3	4	5	6	7
1	1	2	3	4	5	6	7	10
2	2	3	4	5	6	7	10	11
3	3	4	5	6	7	10	11	12
4	4	5	6	7	10	11	12	13
5	5	6	7	10	11	12	13	14
6	6	7	10	11	12	13	14	15
7	7	10	11	12	13	14	15	16

FIGURE 7-24. Octal addition—the unshaded area shows the sum of $3 + 5$

addend digit and an augend digit is located at the intersection of their respective columns. Our example of 3 + 5 is shown in Fig. 7-24.

OCTAL SUBTRACTION. Octal subtraction is carried out either by borrowing or by using the sevens complement and the end-around carry. Using the latter method, subtracting octal 14 from octal 62 involves the following routine:

1. Find the sevens complement of the subtrahend (14) and add it to the minuend.

77 − 14 = 63

Minuend	62
Sevens complement of 14	+ 63
	(1) 45
End-around carry	→ 1
True remainder	+ 46

The end-around carry is added to the low-order digit, and the final sum is given a positive sign.

However, if no end-around carry is developed, the remainder must be recomplemented and given a negative sign. Let us reverse this example by subtracting octal 62 from octal 14:

1. Determine the sevens complement of the subtrahend (62):
   77 − 62 = 15.
2. Add the complemented subtrahend to the minuend (14):

Minuend	14
	+ 15
	+ 31

Since there is no end-around carry, octal 31 is recomplemented and given a negative sign. The remainder is —46, or —38 in decimal.

OCTAL MULTIPLICATION. Octal multiplication is somewhat more complex than binary multiplication. By the shift method we obtain the partial product of each multiplier digit by using a 7 × 7 octal multiplication table (Fig. 7-25). The partial products are shifted to the left and

×	0	1	2	3	4	5	6	7
0	0	0	0	0	0	0	0	0
1	0	1	2	3	4	5	6	7
2	0	2	4	6	10	12	14	16
3	0	3	6	11	14	17	22	25
4	0	4	10	14	20	24	30	34
5	0	5	12	17	24	31	36	43
6	0	6	14	22	30	36	44	52
7	0	7	16	25	34	43	52	61

FIGURE 7-25. Octal multiplication

added. The shift method is implemented as follows: Beginning with the right-hand multiplier digit,

1. Multiply each multiplier digit by the multiplied digits (shifting to the left after each multiplication) and add to obtain the partial products.
2. The partial products in step 1 are added (by shifting) to arrive at the final product. Figure 7-26 illustrates the multiplications of octal 236 by octal 25.

OCTAL DIVISION. The two common methods of division are (1) long division and (2) repeated subtraction. The method of long division is the same as that used in decimal division. In the repeated-subtraction method, we repeatedly subtract the divisor from the dividend until there is no remainder. The total number of subtractions denotes the quotient. Division of octal 310 by 62 is illustrated in Fig. 7-27.

FIGURE 7-26. Shift multiplication

Conventional Method

Multiplicand	236
Multiplier	× 25
First partial product	1426
Second partial product	474
Final product	6366

Shift Method

Step 1	Step 2	
236	236	
× 2	× 5	
14	36	
6	17	
4	12	
474	1426	Partial product of right-hand digit plus
	+ 474	partial product of left-hand digit
	6366	Final product

```
                 4 Quotient
Divisor    62 ⌐ 310 Dividend
                310
                ---
                000 Remainder
```

Octal	No. of Subtractions
310	
− 62	1
226	
− 62	1
144	
− 62	1
62	
− 62	1
0	4 Quotient

(a) Long Division (b) Repeated Subtraction

FIGURE 7-27. *Octal division*

Hexadecimal Arithmetic

HEXADECIMAL ADDITION. Hexadecimal addition is governed by the same rules that apply to decimal and binary addition. Basically, the primary difference among the three types of addition is the point at which carry occurs. In performing decimal addition, when the sum of a series of decimal digits exceeds 9, there is a carry to the next higher-order digit position. A carry in binary addition takes place when the sum of binary digits exceeds 1. In hexadecimal addition, the carry takes place when the sum of digits exceeds F (equivalent to 15 in decimal). For example, 7 + 8 = F (not 15), 7 + 9 = 10 (equivalent of decimal 16), and B + 4 = F in hexadecimal. Figure 7-28 presents the hexadecimal addition of a 15 by 15 matrix, or 225 entries.

FIGURE 7-28. *Hexadecimal addition matrix*

	1	2	3	4	5	6	7	8	9	A	B	C	D	E	F
1	02	03	04	05	06	07	08	09	0A	0B	0C	0D	0E	0F	10
2	03	04	05	06	07	08	09	0A	0B	0C	0D	0E	0F	10	11
3	04	05	06	07	08	09	0A	0B	0C	0D	0E	0F	10	11	12
4	05	06	07	08	09	0A	0B	0C	0D	0E	0F	10	11	12	13
5	06	07	08	09	0A	0B	0C	0D	0E	0F	10	11	12	13	14
6	07	08	09	0A	0B	0C	0D	0E	0F	10	11	12	13	14	15
7	08	09	0A	0B	0C	0D	0E	0F	10	11	12	13	14	15	16
8	09	0A	0B	0C	0D	0E	0F	10	11	12	13	14	15	16	17
9	0A	0B	0C	0D	0E	0F	10	11	12	13	14	15	16	17	18
A	0B	0C	0D	0E	0F	10	11	12	13	14	15	16	17	18	19
B	0C	0D	0E	0F	10	11	12	13	14	15	16	17	18	19	1A
C	0D	0E	0F	10	11	12	13	14	15	16	17	18	19	1A	1B
D	0E	0F	10	11	12	13	14	15	16	17	18	19	1A	1B	1C
E	0F	10	11	12	13	14	15	16	17	18	19	1A	1B	1C	1D
F	10	11	12	13	14	15	16	17	18	19	1A	1B	1C	1D	1E

In using the table, two hexadecimal digits (one digit in the top row and another digit in the left column) are selected. The sum is found at their intersection. For example, the sum of F + F = 1E (intersection). 1E is equal to $(1 \times 16) + 14 = 30$ in decimal.

HEXADECIMAL SUBTRACTION. Hexadecimal subtraction follows a routine similar to that of decimal and binary subtraction. The primary difference relates to the point that a carry of 1 in hexadecimal represents decimal 16. The following examples illustrate two ways in which subtraction is performed:

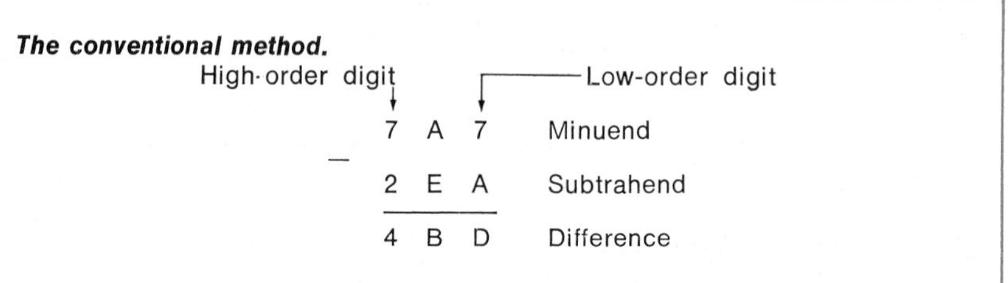

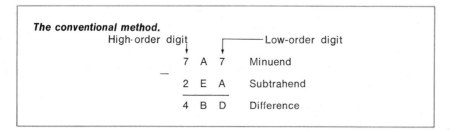

1. Begin with the low-order (right) digit and subtract A from 7. Since A (equivalent of decimal 10) is greater than 7, 1 (equivalent of decimal 16) is borrowed from A, increasing 7 to 17 (equivalent of decimal 23). Now subtract A from 17. The remainder is D (equivalent of decimal 13). A (having been decreased by 1) becomes 9.
2. Subtract E (14 in decimal) from 9. Since E is greater than 9, 1 is borrowed from 7 (third hexadecimal digit), increasing 9 to 19. Now subtract E from 19. The remainder is B. The high-order digit 7 becomes 6.
3. Subtract 2 from the high-order digit 6, leaving 4. Therefore, the final remainder is 4 B D.

The paycheck method.

	2	5	2	B	1	Minuend
−		D	3	2	C	Subtrahend
	1	1		1		Carry
	1	7	F	8	5	Difference

1. Begin with the low-order digit and subtract C from 1. Since C (equivalent of decimal 12) is greater than 1, 1 is borrowed from B, increasing 1 to 11 (equivalent of decimal 17). Now subtract C from 11. The remainder is 5.
2. Add a carry of 1 to 2 (the next higher-order subtrahend), making it 3. Subtract 3 from B. The remainder is 8.

3. Subtract 3 from 2. Since 3 is greater than 2, 1 is borrowed from 5, increasing 2 to 12 (equivalent of decimal 18). The remainder is F.
4. Add a carry of 1 to D, making it E. Subtract E from 5. Since E is greater than 5, 1 is borrowed from 2, increasing 5 to 15 (equivalent of decimal 21). The remainder is 7.
5. Subtract a carry of 1 from 2. The remainder is 1.

Hexadecimal Multiplication. Hexadecimal multiplication is subject to the same rules that apply to decimal and binary multiplication. To simplify the complex procedure followed, a hexadecimal multiplication table is presented in Fig. 7-29.

The following example illustrates the procedure used in hexadecimal multiplication:

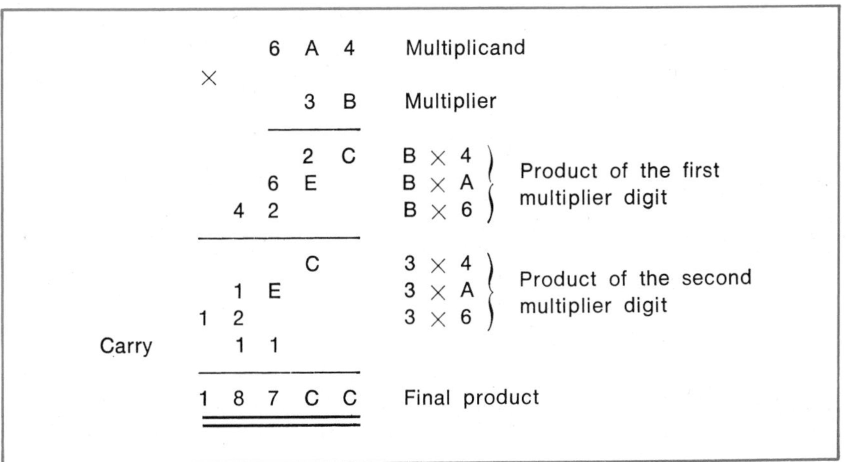

6 A 4 Multiplicand
× 3 B Multiplier
2 C B × 4
6 E B × A
4 2 B × 6
Product of the first multiplier digit
C 3 × 4
1 E 3 × A
1 2 3 × 6
Product of the second multiplier digit
Carry 1 1
1 8 7 C C Final product

FIGURE 7-29. Hexadecimal multiplication matrix

1	2	3	4	5	6	7	8	9	A	B	C	D	E	F
2	04	06	08	0A	0C	0E	10	12	14	16	18	1A	1C	1E
3	06	09	0C	0F	12	15	18	1B	1E	21	24	27	2A	2D
4	08	0C	10	14	18	1C	20	24	28	2C	30	34	38	3C
5	0A	0F	14	19	1E	23	28	2D	32	37	3C	41	46	4B
6	0C	12	18	1E	24	2A	30	36	3C	42	48	4E	54	5A
7	0E	15	1C	23	2A	31	38	3F	46	4D	54	5B	62	69
8	10	18	20	28	30	38	40	48	50	58	60	68	70	78
9	12	1B	24	2D	36	3F	48	51	5A	63	6C	75	7E	87
A	14	1E	28	32	3C	46	50	5A	64	6E	78	82	8C	96
B	16	21	2C	37	42	4D	58	63	6E	79	84	8F	9A	A5
C	18	24	30	3C	48	54	60	6C	78	84	90	9C	A8	B4
D	1A	27	34	41	4E	5B	68	75	82	8F	9C	A9	B6	C3
E	1C	2A	38	46	54	62	70	7E	8C	9A	A8	B6	C4	D2
F	1E	2D	3C	4B	5A	69	78	87	96	A5	B4	C3	D2	E1

Note that one multiplier digit is handled at a time, and, by shifting, the products of the two multiplier digits are added as shown.

HEXADECIMAL DIVISION. Like octal or decimal division, hexadecimal division can be performed by long division or by repeated subtraction. The repeated-subtraction method can be cumbersome, depending on the size of the divisor and the dividend. The quotient is the number of subtractions made. Remainders are treated in the same manner as decimal and binary remainders.

Decimal equivalent		Long division	
	18		12
11	198	B	C6
	11		B
	88		16
	88		16
	00		00

SUMMARY

A number system involves a base, an absolute digit, and a positional value. The base defines the maximum number of digits used in the system; the positional value represents the radix and the power of that position. A digit's value is derived by multiplying it by its positional value.

The three number systems covered in this chapter are the binary, octal, and hexadecimal systems. The binary system uses base 2 (values 0, 1); the value of each position doubles as one moves from right to left. Conversion to decimal involves multiplying each binary digit by 2 and adding its product to the next digit until the entire binary number is added. Conversely, a decimal digit is converted into binary by dividing it successively by 2. Any remainder becomes a part of the binary number.

The Binary-Coded Decimal (BCD) code is a derivative of the binary system. The code simply takes each decimal digit and codes it in a fixed set of four binary digits.

The octal number system uses base 8 (values 0 and 1 to 7); the value of each position increases by a multiple of 8 as one moves from right to left. Conversion of octal to decimal is done by multiplying each octal position by 8 and adding its product to the next number until the entire octal number is added. Conversely, a decimal digit is converted into octal by dividing it successively by 8. The remainder of each division becomes a part of the octal number.

The hexadecimal system uses base 16 (0, 1 to 9, and A to F); the value of each position increases by a multiple of 16 as one moves from right to left. Conversion to binary is made by replacing each hexadecimal digit by the equivalent set of four binary digits. A decimal digit is converted to a hexadecimal number by dividing it successively by 16. The remainder of each division stands for a hexadecimal number.

Nearly all arithmetic operations are performed by computers through addition. Binary subtraction is performed by a ones complement routine by reversing the lower value and adding its complement to the upper value. The end-around carry is converted to a plus sign, which becomes a part of the remainder. Absence of a carry means recomplementing the difference and labeling the true difference as negative. Binary multiplication is a series of successive additions and is essentially performed by the traditional decimal method or the shift method. Binary division is a series of successive subtractions.

Octal and hexadecimal arithmetic follow essentially the same routines as decimal and binary arithmetic, keeping in mind that the octal uses base 8 and the hexadecimal uses base 16.

TERMS TO LEARN

Accumulator	Ones complement
Binary	Parallel addition
Binary-coded decimal	Serial addition
Byte	Tens complement
Hexadecimal	Twos complement
Octal	

QUESTIONS

1. What is a number system?
2. What is the difference between straight binary and binary-coded-decimal representation?
3. "The decimal system uses base 10, whereas the binary system uses base 2." Explain.
4. Why are four binary bits used in the BCD code to represent the decimal digits?
5. What procedure is used in converting values from binary into decimal? Give an example.
6. Using the 6-bit alphanumeric code, encode the following data:
   a. 14728
   b. Business education
   c. Product number 6K 4821

7. Convert the following numbers to decimal numbers:
   a. 81_{16} f. BD_{16}
   b. $.101_2$ g. 764_8
   c. 121_8 h. $1C_{16}$
   d. 100_{16} i. 101010_2
   e. 11.111_2 j. 101_2
8. What is the octal code? How is it different from the binary code? The decimal code? Give an example illustrating the method used in converting an octal value into these two codes.
9. Explain the binary-coded hexadecimal. Show how a hexadecimal digit is converted to decimal and binary.
10. Convert the following decimal numbers to the number system indicated:
    a. 9 to binary
    b. 16 to hexadecimal
    c. 15 to hexadecimal
    d. 384.5 to binary
    e. 84 to octal
    f. 296 to octal
    g. 209 to BCD
11. Convert the following binary numbers to octal and hexadecimal numbers:
    a. 101011001 e. 10101010
    b. 10010011 f. 1010101
    c. 1110011 g. 1010101001
    d. 11100 h. 110110110
12. Convert the following hexadecimal numbers into decimal and binary numbers:
    a. E f. 17
    b. DD g. DB
    c. BA h. FF
    d. 1B i. AC
    e. 71
13. Represent the following alphanumeric values in a 6-bit code:
    a. 125 e. J15Z
    b. A56 f. SUN5
    c. ALPO g. JUDY
    d. BITS h. 143K
14. Add a binary digit to the left of the answers in question 13 to represent odd parity.
15. Explain and illustrate the difference between a parallel adder and a serial adder.
16. Add the following values in binary. Check by converting to decimal.

a. 100	c. 101	e. 101	g. 10111	i. 10111
011	011	100	11011	01011
___	___	___	___	___
b. 011	d. 101	f. 111	h. 11011	j. 11111
101	110	111	11110	11111
___	___	___	___	___

17. Subtract the following values in binary. Check by converting to decimal.

a.	c.	e.	g.	i.
10	11	101	1011	1111
01	01	100	0100	1000

b.	d.	f.	h.
11	01	010	0100
10	10	101	1101

18. Multiply the following values in binary. Check by converting to decimal.

a.	c.	e.
100	111	1011
11	11	1101

b.	d.
101	111
11	111

19. Multiply each problem in Question 18 by using the shift method.
20. Divide the following binary numbers:
    a. 100 ÷ 10 c. 111 ÷ 10 e. 10010 ÷ 11 g. 11101 ÷ 101
    b. 110 ÷ 10 d. 1001 ÷ 11 f. 11110 ÷ 110
21. Add the following octal numbers:

a.	c.	e.
243	777	1007
435	123	6661

b.	d.	f.
460	177	321
457	621	465

22. Use the sevens complement method to subtract the following octal numbers:

a.	c.	e.
71	57	1144
–27	–23	–666

b.	d.	f.
61	1143	646
–17	–367	–677

23. Multiply the following octal numbers:

a.	d.	g.
12	311	325
17	77	36

b.	e.	h.
7	77	3251
7	66	16.1

c.	f.	i.
25	76	3765
17	7	453

24. Show the repeated-subtraction method in dividing the following octal numbers.
    a. 416 ÷ 132 c. 17 ÷ 5 e. 144 ÷ 31
    b. 75 ÷ 13 d. 66 ÷ 6 f. 67 ÷ 13
25. Divide octal number 3362634 by 6057 by the long-division method.

26. Perform the following hexadecimal additions:
    a. 16 + F d. A + BB
    b. BA + C e. D + E + FD
    c. E + FF f. DE + 10 + 1A
27. Perform the following hexadecimal subtractions:
    a. FF — E c. 74 — 4A e. CC — D
    b. 16 — A d. 4A — 4C f. FB — BF
28. What is the sixteens complement of the following hexadecimal numbers?
    a. E c. AB e. 1
    b. 9 d. 5 f. F
29. Perform the following hexadecimal multiplications:

a. 4A	b. A4	c. FE	d. 17
3E	C2	EF	7A
—	—	—	—

SUGGESTED READING

CROWDER, N. A. *The Arithmetic of Computers.* Garden City, N.Y.: Doubleday & Company, Inc., 1960.

FLORES, WILLIAM. *The Logic of Computer Arithmetic.* Englewood Cliffs, N.J.: Prentice-Hall, Inc., 1963.

KNUTH, D. E. "The Evolution of Number Systems," *Datamation,* Feb. 1969, pp. 93–97.

MAYNE, DAVID. "What's Next in Memories?", *Datamation,* Feb. 1968, pp. 30–32.

RICHARDS, R. K. *Arithmetic Operations in Digital Computers.* New York: Van Nostrand Reinhold Company, 1955.

COMPUTER SYSTEMS AND DEVICES

input preparation and direct data-entry devices

8

RECORDING INPUT DATA

The 80-Column Key Punch

Data Verification

The 96-Column Key Punch

DIRECT DATA-ENTRY DEVICES

Intelligent Terminals

Key-to-Tape Devices

data recorder

modes of operation

pooling and communicating

Key-to-Cassette/Cartridge Devices

Key-to-Disk Devices

Key-to-Diskette System

IS THE KEY PUNCH OBSOLETE?

ELECTRONIC POINT-OF-SALE TERMINALS

Case Illustration

problem definition and testing

Business data processing was centered initially around punched-card equipment, but now is centered around the electronic computer. Even with the greater emphasis on computer processing, most smaller computer systems are card oriented and rely in some capacity on the traditional input media and devices, such as the punched card and the key punch. Today, over 500,000 key-punch machines are in operation, and the key punch probably will continue to be in use for some time.

More recently, direct data-entry devices are being offered as a replacement for the key punch and card input preparation. This chapter discusses this area as a key element in operating a computer system.

THE 80-COLUMN PUNCHED CARD

People who have not come into contact with punched cards are rare or nonexistent. Such cards are used extensively for paychecks, time cards, soap coupons, gas credit cards, utility bills, BankAmericard or *Time* magazine bills, and even as tickets for use on turnpikes. High schools, colleges, and universities use them as class admission cards. Most smaller-sized computers rely on punched cards for receiving input data or computer instructions for processing.

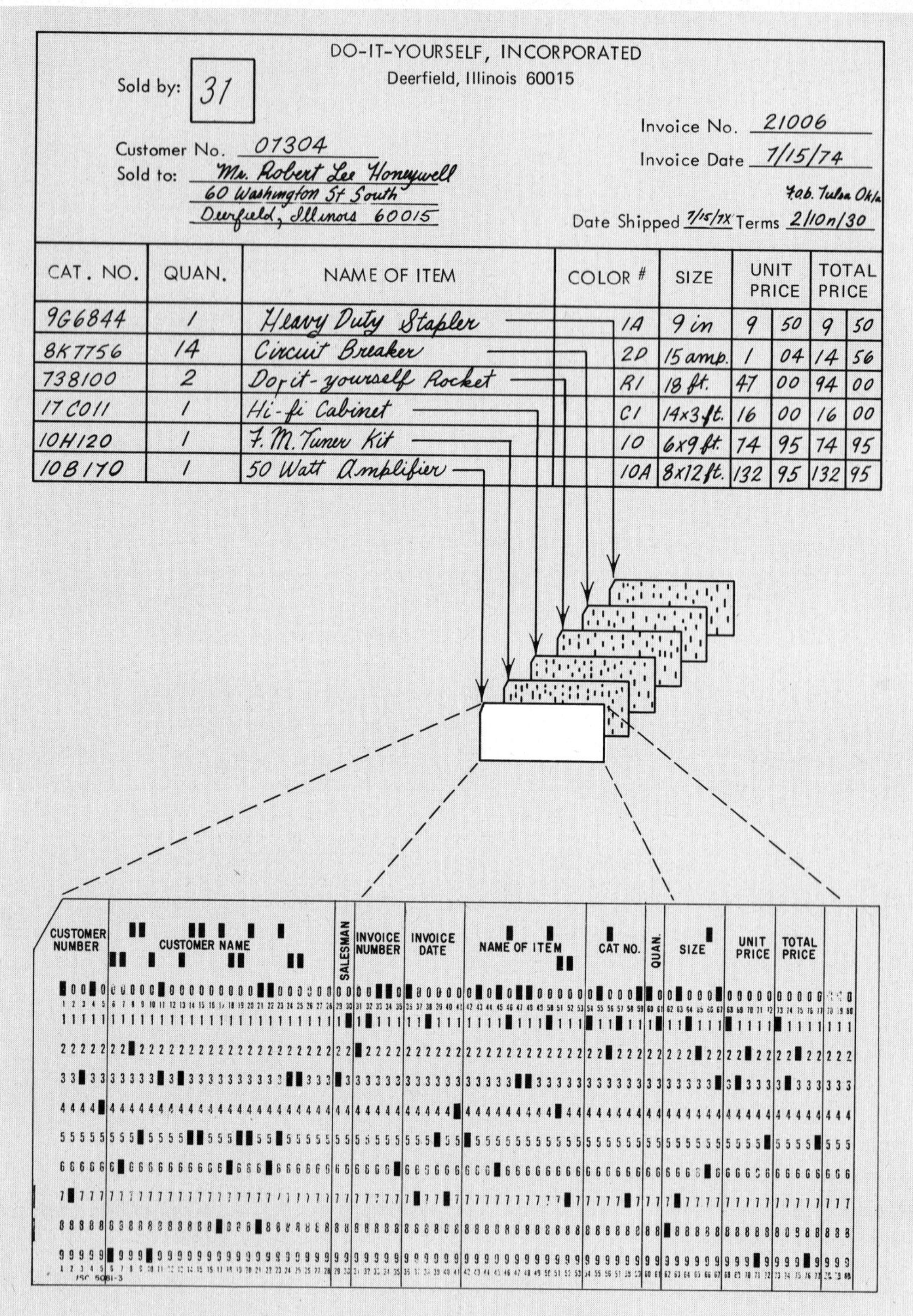
DO-IT-YOURSELF, INCORPORATED
Deerfield, Illinois 60015

Sold by: 31

Invoice No. 21006
Invoice Date 7/15/74

Customer No. 07304
Sold to: Mr. Robert Lee Honeywell
60 Washington St South
Deerfield, Illinois 60015

f.o.b. Tulsa Okla
Date Shipped 7/15/7X Terms 2/10n/30

CAT. NO.	QUAN.	NAME OF ITEM	COLOR #	SIZE	UNIT PRICE		TOTAL PRICE	
9G6844	1	Heavy Duty Stapler	1A	9 in	9	50	9	50
8K7756	14	Circuit Breaker	2D	15 amp.	1	04	14	56
738100	2	Do-it-yourself Rocket	R1	18 ft.	47	00	94	00
17C011	1	Hi-fi Cabinet	C1	14x3 ft.	16	00	16	00
10H120	1	F.M. Tuner Kit	10	6x9 ft.	74	95	74	95
10B170	1	50 Watt Amplifier	10A	8x12 ft.	132	95	132	95

FIGURE 8-1. A partial invoice—the unit-record principle

Punched cards are of two types [2]: (1) the widely used 80-column IBM card or (2) the 96-column card designed primarily for the IBM System/3 computer.

The punched card is a *unit record,* because *only the data related to one transaction* are recorded on a given card. Because it is mobile, the card can also be merged with cards containing different information for calculating or summarizing data. Figure 8-1 illustrates an invoice containing six transactions between Do-It-Yourself, Inc., and Mr. Robert Lee Honeywell. The 50-watt amplifier transaction is used to demonstrate how each transaction is entered on a separate card. For this invoice, six cards would be required to record all the information, because in actual future processing, each transaction must first be punched in a card in the same manner as has been done for the one involving the 50-watt amplifier.

Basically, the 80-column card (also called a *tab card*) is a rectangular pasteboard of high-quality paper able to resist contraction or expansion caused by temperature or humidity. It measures $7\frac{3}{8}$ inches long by $3\frac{1}{4}$ inches wide by 0.007 inch thick. In Fig. 8-2, the upper right corner of the card has been cut as a visual aid to assure the machine operator that all cards in the deck are facing the same direction. Although most unit-record machines do not sense corner cuts, some specially designed machines halt automatically upon detection of a cut in the wrong position. Colored and striped cards and cards with round corners are also used to identify a particular deck of cards or to facilitate overall card handling.

The 80-column card is divided into 80 vertical spaces called *columns.* The columns are numbered (left to right) from 1 to 80. In each column,

[2] Late in 1966, the Univac Division dropped the 90-column round-hole design and discontinued production of related equipment. The new Univac punched-card line is an 80-column (rectangular-hole) card, making it more adaptive to the IBM card system.

FIGURE 8-2. *IBM card—one third of actual size*

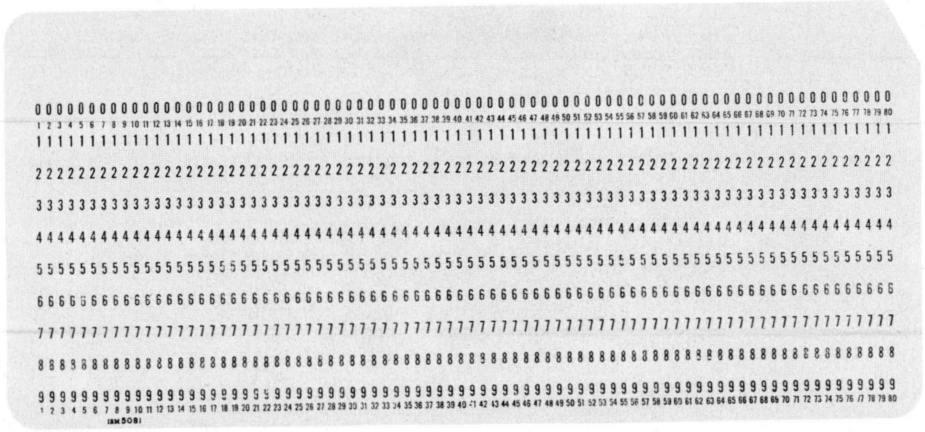

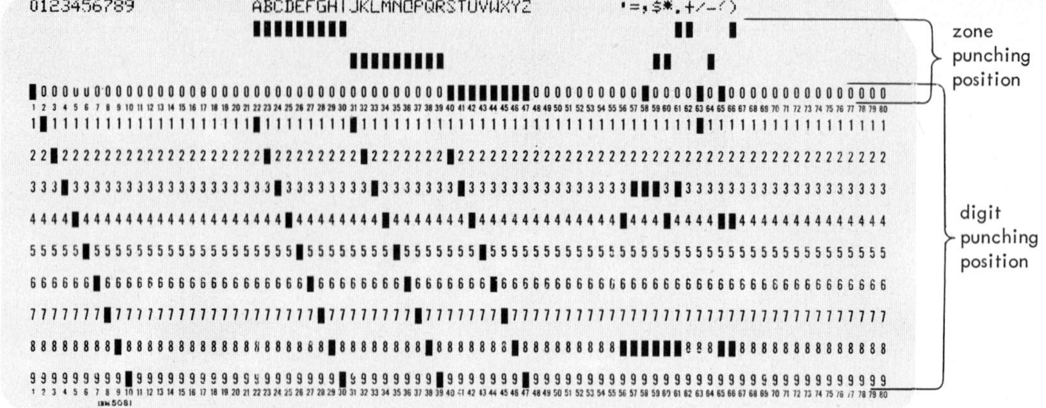

FIGURE 8-3. Punching positions of an IBM card

one letter, one digit, or a special character can be punched; a card can thus store a total of 80 characters. For example, punching employee number 40875 in a card would require five consecutive columns. If we decided to reserve the first five columns for that purpose, digit 4 would be punched in column 1, digit 0 in column 2, digit 8 in column 3, digit 7 in column 4, and digit 5 in column 5.

The 80-column card is also divided into the zone punching position and the digit punching position. The zone punching position consists of three horizontal rows, two of which are located in the top gap of the card for zone punching only. The first row from the top is *row 12.* The next is *row 11,* or the X *row.*[3] The third row is known as the *zero row* and can be used as *either* a zone punching position or a digit punching position (Fig. 8-3).

The digit punching position consists of 10 rows to accommodate digits 0 to 9. Row 0 accommodates digit 0; row 1, digit 1; row 2, digit 2; and so forth.

A punched card's top edge is called the *12-edge;* the bottom edge is called the *9-edge* to identify it with row 9. These terms are used to identify the edge of the card that should be fed into the machine. Some machines accept data cards when fed 12-edge first and others when fed 9-edge first. *Face up* means that the printed side of the card faces up when placed in the feed hopper. *Face down* means the opposite. Thus, if a machine processes a data card "12-edge first, face up," the printed side of the card is up and the edge that is closest to row 12 is fed first.

[3] A punch, called the X punch, can be punched in any of the 80 columns of row 11 to distinguish a given card or cards from the remaining cards of the deck.

Data recording is accomplished by key punching in accord with a coded arrangement of rectangular punched holes [4] in 80-column cards. Once data have been punched, the card becomes a permanently stored reference and can be duplicated when desired. It becomes a medium of communication between the operator and the machine(s) involved in the system. In other words, punched cards enable men to feed certain input information to the computer for processing so that the computer can *feed back* accurate answers as output.

In *numeric data recording*, the numbers are recorded by punching *one hole* in a column for each digit. If we need to punch the number 14036 in columns 13 to 17, for example, five consecutive holes would be required in the digit punching position of these columns (Fig. 8-4).

Alphabetic data recording requires *two holes* in any column for each alphabetic character. One hole must be in the *zone* punching position and the other in the *digit* punching position. Because there are three zone rows for punching alphabetic characters (i.e., rows 12, 11, and 0), the alphabet is divided into three parts, each part containing letters equal to the number of rows in the digit punching position. Depending upon the letter in mind, one of the two holes must be in row 12, 11, or 0, and the other hole must be in one of rows 1 to 9.

[4] The machine code used to store information on an 80-column card is referred to as the *Hollerith code.* Herman Hollerith devised the technique of storing data in a standard-sized card by following a predetermined code to punch holes in specific locations on it.

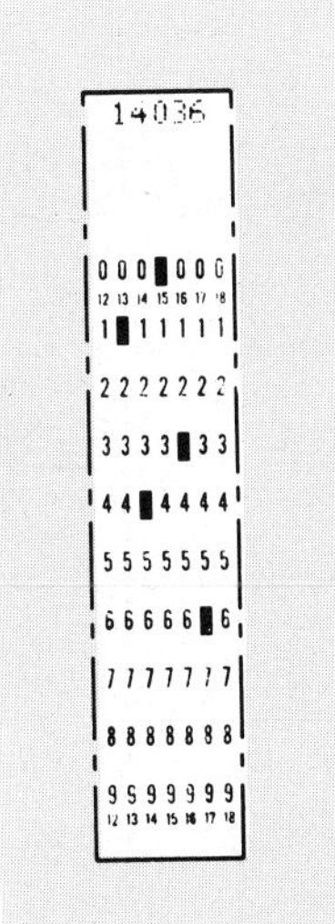

FIGURE 8-4. Coding 14036 in columns 13 to 17

Letter	Zone Pch. Pos.	Digit Pch. Pos.
A	12	1
B	12	2
C	12	3
D	12	4
E	12	5
F	12	6
G	12	7
H	12	8
I	12	9

FIGURE 8-5. Coding letters A through I in columns 16 to 21

Letter	Zone Pch. Pos.	Digit Pch. Pos.
J	11	1
K	11	2
L	11	3
M	11	4
N	11	5
O	11	6
P	11	7
Q	11	8
R	11	9

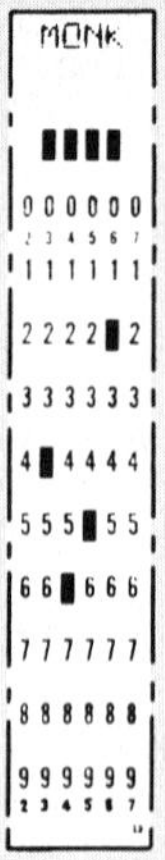

FIGURE 8-6. Coding letters J through R in columns 2 to 7

Letter	Zone Punching Position	Digit Punching Position
S	0	2
T	0	3
U	0	4
V	0	5
W	0	6
X	0	7
Y	0	8
Z	0	9

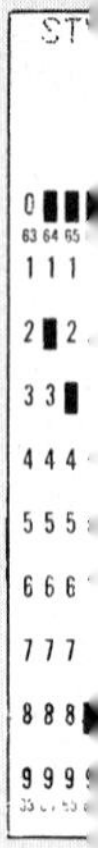

FIGURE 8-7. Coding letters S through Z in columns 63 to 68

The three parts of the alphabet are A to I (first nine letters), J to R (second nine letters), and S to Z (remaining eight letters). Letters A to I are each coded by punching a hole in row 12 and another hole directly below in rows 1 to 9, respectively. For example, letter A would be coded by a hole in row 12 and a hole in row 1 directly below. Letter B would be coded by a hole in row 12 and a hole in row 2 directly below, and so on for the remaining letters to I (Fig. 8-5).

At this point, as is apparent, the letter I occupies the last usable row on the card. To code the second group of letters, J to R, we must start with row 1 again, and use row 11 for the zone punch, instead of row 12, and rows 1 to 9 for the digit punch (Fig. 8-6).

Letter R now occupies the last row on the card. To code the remaining letters, S to Z, we must, therefore, start over again, using row 0 for the zone punch and rows 2 to 9 for the digit punch (Fig. 8-7). Note that there are only eight letters left in the third alphabetic group, and rows 2 to 9 are used for the digit punch instead of rows 1 to 8. This is done, possibly, to avoid punching holes too close to each other, as would be the case if rows 0 and 1 were used. In the early machines, accuracy was sometimes lost if holes were punched too close together. For this reason, a gap was decided upon and has become a part of the standard procedure, even though modern key-punch machines have been improved to such an extent that the proximity of holes no longer makes any difference.

The preceding predetermined code is built into present-day key-punch machines so that all an operator must do is press the proper letter of the alphabet on the keyboard and the holes will appear in the card as described.

Card Layout Requirements

The cards themselves must be of a predetermined format so that each unit of information occupies the same position on all cards representing any given transaction. If the customer's number occupies columns 1 to 5, for example, it must always be punched in that location, and the area should not be used for any other data. *Standardizing* the *location* of all data in a card is as important as standardizing the signature location to the bottom right side of a check or the location of a postage stamp on the upper right corner of an envelope. This leads us to the important concept of *field.*

Any one transaction contains a certain number of details called *units of information.* A *field* is a group of consecutive card columns reserved for a *specific unit of information.* In Fig. 8-1, for example, because the punched card contains 11 units of information related to the last transaction on the invoice, 11 fields are used, occupying 77 of the 80 columns available. The length of the field depends on the maximum anticipated length of the unit of information. The minimum length of a field is one column, and the maximum is the size of the card, or 80 columns.

Identifying Marks

A card may be identified by format, color, corner cut, horizontal color stripes, or control field. The *format* shows how the various fields are arranged on a card and distinguishes the card from others that enter the processing routine. For example, in a banking application, a name-and-address card may have, basically, a customer-number field, name field, home-address field, and business-address field, whereas a loan card may have a customer-number field, name field, amount-of-the-loan field, number-of-payments field, and amount-of-each-payment field. In addition to having a different format, the name-and-address card may be visually distinguished by a blue stripe and the loan card by a yellow stripe. On the other hand, cards of different *colors* may be used to designate the different types.

A *control field* aids in the *location* and *reassembly* of a group of cards that has previously been merged with other groups of cards containing all kinds of information for processing. You frequently hear of × punch in column 80 or × punch in column 27. This denotes that only certain cards in a group have an × punched in column 80 or in column 27. To illustrate, assume that a group of cards contains information on managers, foremen, and rank-and-file employees. Assume further that, at the end of the year, the board of directors decides to grant a $500 bonus to managers only. To enable the machine to select the managers' cards out of the deck, some distinctive code must be placed on the managers' cards that would not appear in any other group of cards.

Usually, this coding is done by punching an X in a column reserved for that purpose. In this example, let us reserve column 80 as the X column. Once X has been punched in column 80 of each manager's card in the group, the process of picking out these cards by machine becomes a simple matter. Every time the machine reads X in column 80, it ejects the card into a pocket, leaving the remaining cards to drop undisturbed into another pocket.

Uses of Punched Cards

Punched cards have several uses, depending on the reports and procedures required. Five common uses are discussed next.

APERTURE CARDS. Aperture cards, most commonly used for storing engineering sketches and blueprints, are regular 80-column cards with rectangular spaces for accommodating microfilm frames (Fig. 8-8). The data representing the microfilm frame can be key punched and interjected and later sorted or reproduced, like any ordinary data card.

DETAIL CARDS. Detail cards are commonly used in inventory control. Each item in stock is represented by a punched card containing reference and quantitative data. The card at the bottom of Fig. 8-1 is a detail card. It can also be called a *transcript card* if the key-punch operator has punched its content from a source document.

MARK-SENSED CARDS. Mark-sensed cards are usually used in reproducing small quantities of numeric information; they are punched

FIGURE 8-8. Aperture card

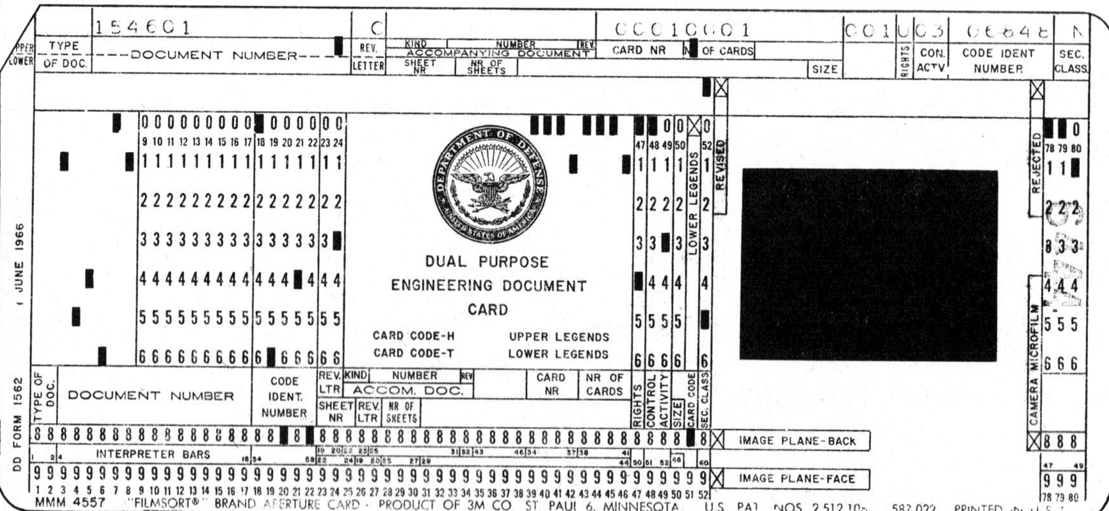

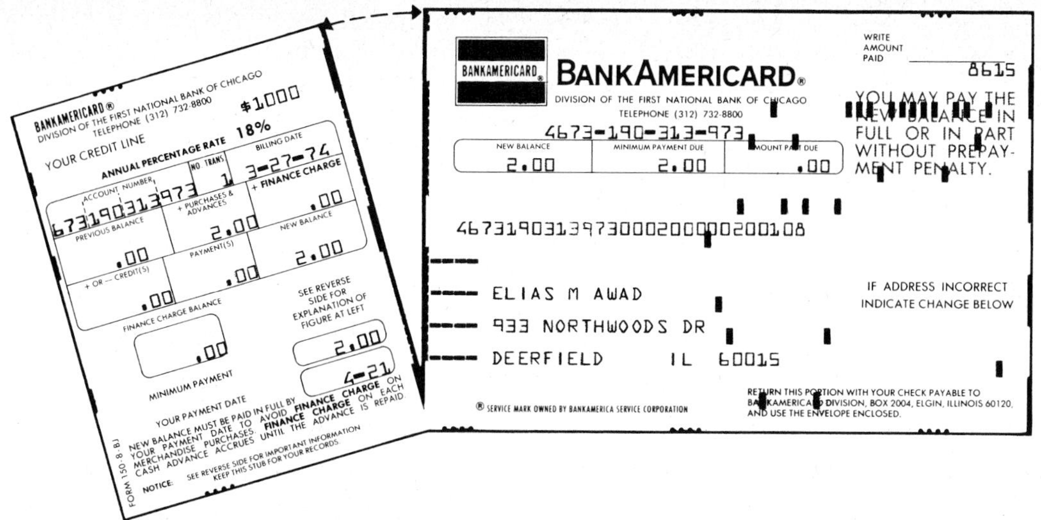
BANKAMERICARD®
DIVISION OF THE FIRST NATIONAL BANK OF CHICAGO
TELEPHONE (312) 732-8800
YOUR CREDIT LINE $1000
ANNUAL PERCENTAGE RATE 18%
ACCOUNT NUMBER 4673190313973
NO. TRANS. 1
BILLING DATE 3-27-74
PREVIOUS BALANCE .00
+ PURCHASES & ADVANCES 2.00
+ FINANCE CHARGE .00
+ OR — CREDIT(S) .00
PAYMENT(S) .00
NEW BALANCE 2.00
FINANCE CHARGE BALANCE .00
SEE REVERSE SIDE FOR EXPLANATION OF FIGURE AT LEFT
MINIMUM PAYMENT 2.00
YOUR PAYMENT DATE 4-21
NEW BALANCE MUST BE PAID IN FULL BY YOUR PAYMENT DATE TO AVOID FINANCE CHARGE ON MERCHANDISE PURCHASES. FINANCE CHARGE ON EACH CASH ADVANCE ACCRUES UNTIL THE ADVANCE IS REPAID.
NOTICE: SEE REVERSE SIDE FOR IMPORTANT INFORMATION. KEEP THIS STUB FOR YOUR RECORDS.
FORM 150-8-BJ

BANKAMERICARD BANKAMERICARD®
DIVISION OF THE FIRST NATIONAL BANK OF CHICAGO
TELEPHONE (312) 732-8800
WRITE AMOUNT PAID 8615
YOU MAY PAY THE NEW BALANCE IN FULL OR IN PART WITHOUT PREPAYMENT PENALTY.
4673-190-313-973

NEW BALANCE	MINIMUM PAYMENT DUE	AMOUNT PAST DUE
2.00	2.00	.00

467319031397300002000200108
ELIAS M AWAD
933 NORTHWOODS DR
DEERFIELD IL 60015
IF ADDRESS INCORRECT INDICATE CHANGE BELOW
® SERVICE MARK OWNED BY BANKAMERICA SERVICE CORPORATION
RETURN THIS PORTION WITH YOUR CHECK PAYABLE TO BANKAMERICARD DIVISION, BOX 2004, ELGIN, ILLINOIS 60120, AND USE THE ENVELOPE ENCLOSED.

FIGURE 8-9. Stub card

automatically by the reproducer when it senses the marks made with an electrographic pencil in designated locations on the face of the card.

STUB CARDS. Stub cards are adapted to situations in which stubs substitute for a receipt. Most bills (e.g., water and telephone bills) have a perforated card, which, when torn off, leaves a 51-column card to be mailed back with the payment. The stub (a 29-column section with key information) is retained by the customer (Fig. 8-9). Banks have made wide use of this type of card for loan payments. The number of prepunched perforated cards represents the installments a borrower agrees to pay. The set is stapled on the left stub edge in booklet form.

SUMMARY CARDS. Summary cards represent totals or accumulated results of data read from detail cards. An accounting machine is connected to a reproducer and is wired to allow summarized information to be punched.

THE 96-COLUMN PUNCHED CARD

A radical departure from the traditional 80-column card, a new compact 96-column card, which is used with IBM's System/3 computer, was announced in July 1969 to meet the needs of small business. Slightly larger than a standard wallet-sized credit card, the 96-column card measures 2.63 by 3.25 inches, holds 20 percent more data than the 80-column card, and provides greater efficiency in data storage and handling. The use of optical readers to sense punched characters results in a more economical

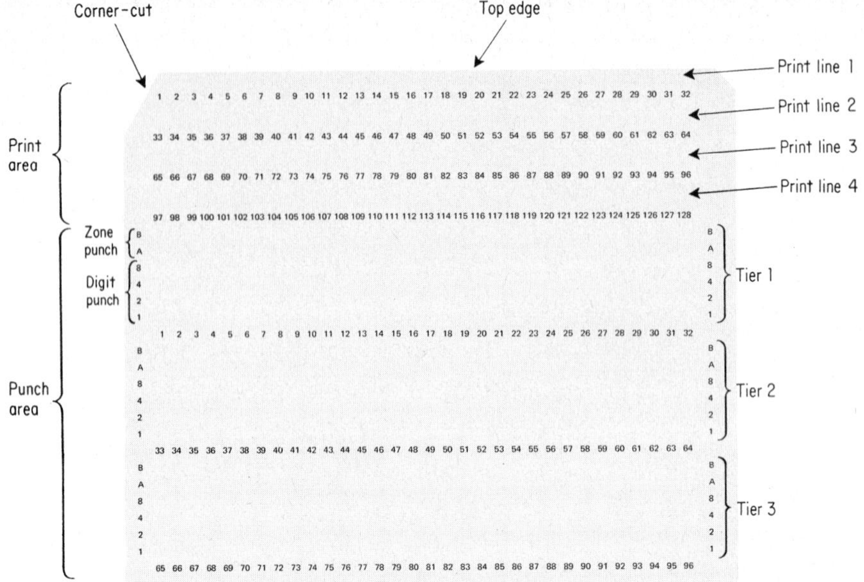

FIGURE 8-10. Ninety-six-column card

and effective operation. Furthermore, this card concept provides the unique feature of one-time punching and verifying of data, thus eliminating clerical errors caused by transcription.

Physical Characteristics

Figure 8-10 shows a blank 96-column card with two sections. The upper section is the print area, and the lower section is the punch area. The *print area* is reserved for four print lines to help the user read what is punched in the card. The first three print lines are numbered from 1 to 96, and 96 alphabetic characters can be printed to correspond with the 96 columns in the punch area. The fourth print line, numbered 97 to 128, does not correspond to any punched area, but may also be used for printing.

The *punch area* is divided into upper, middle, and lower tiers, with 32 columns in each tier. The upper tier (tier 1) contains columns 1 to 32; the middle tier, (tier 2), columns 33 to 64; and the lower tier (tier 3), columns 65 to 96. Since each column can be punched to represent one character, a maximum of 96 characters can be punched in the card.

Data Representation

A character is coded in a card column by a fixed combination of holes. In processing punched data, the computer can distinguish one character from another by the specific punch combination. Each tier has a 6-bit

			Numeric Characters									
			0	1	2	3	4	5	6	7	8	9
Punch Positions	Zone	B										
		A	A									
	Digit	8									8	8
		4					4	4	4	4		
		2			2	2			2	2		
		1		1		1		1		1		1

FIGURE 8-11. Numeric coding—IBM 96-column card

BCD format to represent any of the 32 possible characters. As indicated in Fig. 8-10, the two topmost punch positions, B and A are called the zone punch portion, and the remaining four punch positions, 8, 4, 2, and 1, are called the digit punch portion. Numeric coding is accomplished by punching in the digit portion of a column the position or combination of positions that add up to the desired digit. For example, digit 8 consists of a hole in the 8 punch position; digit 7 consists of one hole in each of the 4, 2, and 1 punch positions (Fig. 8-11).

Alphabetic and special-character coding combine the zone and digit punch positions for each punched character. The first nine letters (A to I) are coded by holes in the A and B positions, plus the appropriate hole configuration for digits 1 to 9. The second nine letters (J to R) are coded by a hole in row B and the appropriate hole configuration for digits 1 to 9. The remaining eight letters (S to Z) are coded by a hole in row A and the appropriate hole configuration for digits 2 (for letter S) to 9. Special characters are coded by various other combinations of six punch positions in a column (Fig. 8-12).

FIGURE 8-12. Alphabetic and special-character coding—IBM 96-column card

Alphabetic Characters

			A	B	C	D	E	F	G	H	I	J	K	L	M	N	O	P	Q	R	S	T	U	V	W	X	Y	Z
Punch Positions	Zone	B	B	B	B	B	B	B	B	B	B	B	B	B	B	B	B	B	B	B								
		A	A	A	A	A	A	A	A	A	A										A	A	A	A	A	A	A	A
	Digit	8								8	8								8	8							8	8
		4				4	4	4	4						4	4	4	4					4	4	4	4		
		2		2	2			2	2				2	2			2	2			2	2			2	2		
		1	1		1		1		1		1	1		1		1		1		1		1		1		1		1

Special Characters

			}	¢	.	<	(	+	|	!	$	*	)	;	¬	-	/	&	,	%	—	>	?	:	#	@	'	=	"	b
Punch Positions	Zone	B	B	B	B	B	B	B	B	B	B	B	B	B	B	B														
		A	A	A	A	A	A	A	A								A	A	A	A	A	A	A							
	Digit	8		8	8	8	8	8	8	8	8	8	8	8	8			8	8	8	8	8	8	8	8	8	8	8	8	
		4				4	4	4	4			4	4	4	4					4	4	4	4			4	4	4	4	
		2		2	2			2	2	2	2			2	2			2	2			2	2	2	2			2	2	
		1			1		1		1		1		1		1		1		1		1		1		1		1		1	

Card Fields and Layout

As with the 80-column card, items of information are recorded in the 96-column card in groups of consecutive columns called fields. A field may vary in size from 1 to 96 columns, depending on the amount of data to be included in each group. When deciding on the length of a given field, allowance should be made for future expansion by punching present field data in the rightmost columns. Any unused columns should be filled with zeros. Card layout forms, such as the one shown in Fig. 8-13, are often helpful in planning the length and sequence of the fields related to the project under consideration.

ADVANTAGES AND LIMITATIONS OF THE PUNCHED CARD

The use of the punched card in information processing offers the advantage of *standardization of data* for more efficient handling. Although it store only 80 or 96 characters, each character can be a code that actuates a machine to perform a specific function or a series of functions. Other advantages include *ease of storage and assembly, ease of reassembly for various routines,* and *low cost per unit of information.*

The primary limitation of the punched card is its physical makeup. It may not be folded, spindled, mutilated, or stapled at all. Any change in the overall smoothness of the card could jam the machine used in processing the data it contains. Its size is a further limitation; the 80-column card, for instance, has a maximum storage capacity of 80 characters, which is inefficient when up to 2,000 characters can be "typed" on it.

Requiring data to be punched in specified fields also limits the number of characters that can be stored. For example, assume that the first six card columns are a customer's account number, and that, in most current accounts, customers' account numbers range four to five columns in length. In such cases, the sixth column (column 1) has to be left blank or punched with zero for consistency, and it cannot be used for other purposes. Since applications involve thousands of customer accounts, much waste results from rigid standardization of data location.

STATUS OF THE PUNCHED CARD

Much controversy is going on regarding the status of the punched card in computer data processing. Although major attacks have been leveled against its practical use, the use of the card continues to grow, especially as an output medium. Card output in the form of turnaround documents (particularly invoices) is gaining in popularity. Such computer-punched documents permit convenient, relatively economical input with minimal need for human handling and rekeying. Thus, the increased use of

IBM

CARD

Card Name ______________________

	1	2	3	4	5	6	7	8	9	10	11	12	13	14	15	16	17	18	19	20	21	22	23	24	25	26	27	28	29	30	31	32	33	34	35	36	37	38	39	40	41	42	43	44
Print																																												
Print Line 1 / Tier 1																																												
Punch	EMPNO			NAME (maximum of 15 characters)															DATE						TOTAL																			
Program Control Card	N	N	N	A	A	A	A	A	A	A	A	A	A	A	A	A	A	A	N	N	N	N	N	N	N	N	N																	

N = Numeric

A = Alphabetic

Card Name ______________________

	1	2	3	4	5	6	7	8	9	10	11	12	13	14	15	16	17	18	19	20	21	22	23	24	25	26	27	28	29	30	31	32	33	34	35	36	37	38	39	40	41	42	43	44
Print																																												
Print Line 1 / Tier 1																																												
Punch																																												
Program Control Card																																												

Card Name ______________________

	1	2	3	4	5	6	7	8	9	10	11	12	13	14	15	16	17	18	19	20	21	22	23	24	25	26	27	28	29	30	31	32	33	34	35	36	37	38	39	40	41	42	43	44
Print																																												
Print Line 1 / Tier 1																																												
Punch																																												
Program Control Card																																												

FIGURE 8-13. Card layout form

punched cards is based on economic and human-oriented considerations. As long as customers are invoiced by mail, the punched card will very likely remain the major medium. A decade ago the growth rate was at about 5 percent per year. Today, it is estimated to be between 10 and 20 percent a year.

Newer applications, especially those using minicomputers and data terminals, are likely to find the 96-column card the dominant form of card input. The 96-column card offers the following advantages over the 80-column card:

1. Its smaller size produces easier physical handling.
2. It has the capacity to hold more information.
3. It has space allocated for both printing and punching.
4. Its coded data are more easily manipulated and converted by the computer.
5. It involves simpler equipment with higher reliability at lower cost. It is believed to be less costly to engineer and manufacture a punch and die to produce a round hole than a rectangular hole (80-column card characteristic).

In certain applications, however, where the size of the document (such as a payroll check) is important, the use of the 80-column card is very likely to continue. Whether the 96-column card will replace the 80-column card in other applications is not yet certain. There are over 500,000 80-column key punches in use today, and such a large base cannot disappear. On the other hand, with IBM committed to making the 96-column card the primary source of original data for its System/3 computer, and the popular acceptance of this system, as evidenced by a backlog of orders for 10,000 units, the 96-column card stands a fair chance of eventually becoming the primary input-data medium in card-oriented computer systems.

RECORDING INPUT DATA

The 80-Column Key Punch

Card-input data preparation is performed by the key punch. The key punch has a keyboard containing numeric, alphabetic, and special characters.[5] The mere depression of a key causes the character it represents to be punched. One character at a time is punched as the card moves through the key punch from right to left. Figure 8-14 shows the IBM 029 key punch,[6] which prints or interprets directly over the columns as it punches holes in the card.

[5] Some earlier key-punch machines have numeric keyboards only. They are still available and are used when the alphabetic requirement does not exist.

[6] One 96-column and four 80-column key punches are the most common in use today:

IBM 024—punches data but does not print what it punches.
IBM 026—punches data and prints their interpretation on top of card.
IBM 029—has extended code to accommodate the IBM 360 computer system.
UNIVAC 1701–04 Verifying Punch—allows operator to rekey data before final punching.
IBM 5496 Data Recorder—punches 96 round holes in a new 96-column card and allows operator to rekey data before final punching. Burroughs Data Recorder offers similar features.

Several other companies now make 80- and 96-column key punches.

FIGURE 8-14. IBM 029 printing card punch

The keyboard is normally in alphabetic mode. Shifting it into numeric mode is done manually by depressing the numeric shift key. For keypunching a large volume of numeric data, automatic shifting of the keyboard into numeric mode is actuated by a coded program card, which is inserted in the key punch for that purpose. The program control unit contains the coded IBM program card that causes the key punch to duplicate, skip, or shift automatically[7] (Fig. 8-15). The card is wrapped around a drum and placed in position before keypunching begins (Fig. 8-16). In this way, repetitive information in a deck of cards is

[7] *Skipping* is initiated by an 11 punch (one hole in row 11) in the far left column of the skip field. The size of the skip field is determined by a 12 punch in each consecutive field column (Fig. 8-15, columns 61 to 80). *Numeric punch* is programmed by leaving blank the far left column of the numeric punch field, followed by a 12 punch in each consecutive field column (Fig. 8-15, columns 1 to 5 and 49 to 60). *Alphabetic punch* is programmed by a 1 punch in the far left column of the alphabetic punch field, followed by an A punch in each consecutive field column (Fig. 8-15, columns 45 to 48). *Duplicating numeric* is programmed by a 0 punch in the left column and a 12 punch in each of the consecutive field columns (Fig. 8-15, columns 6 to 23). *Duplicating alphabetic* is programmed by 0 and 1 punches in the left column, followed by an A punch in each consecutive field column (Fig. 8-15, columns 24 to 44).

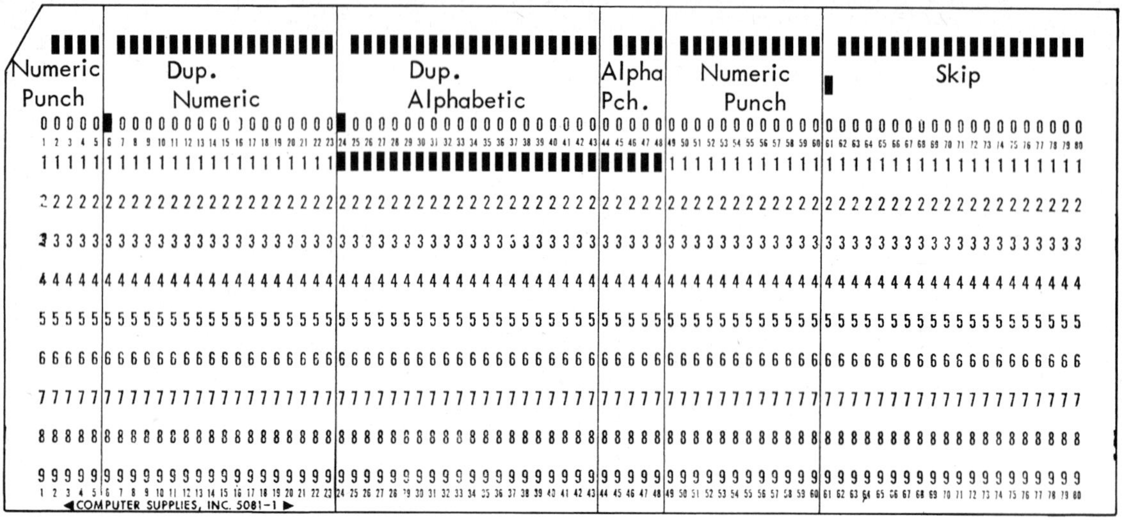

Numeric Punch | Dup. Numeric | Dup. Alphabetic | Alpha Pch. | Numeric Punch | Skip

COMPUTER SUPPLIES, INC. 5081-1

FIGURE 8-15. Program card

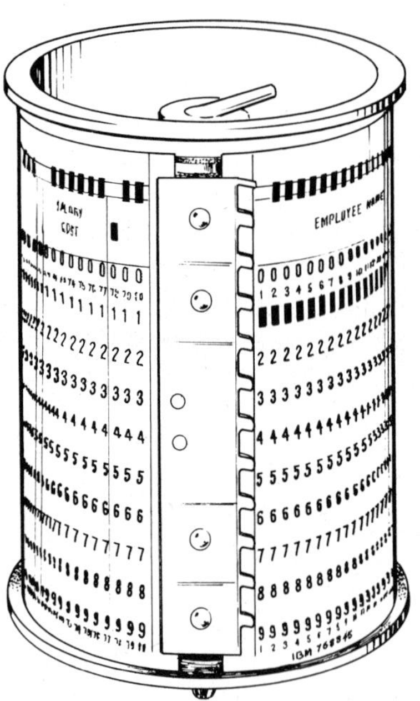

FIGURE 8-16. Program control unit

duplicated in approximately one sixth the time taken by the key-punch operator to do the job manually. Also, accuracy is increased by the substitution of machine operation for human operation.

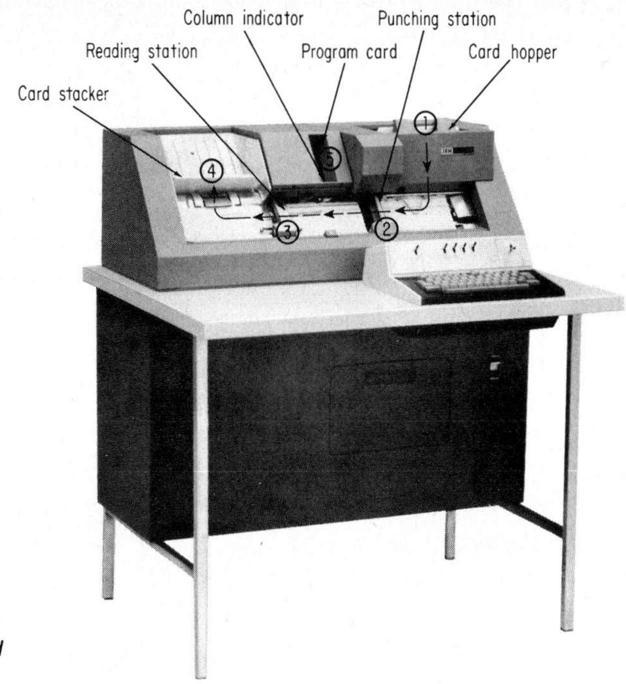

FIGURE 8-17. Path of the card through the key punch

In addition to the keyboard, the other components of the key punch are (1) the *card hopper,* (2) the *punching station,* (3) the *reading station,* and (4) the *card stacker* (Fig. 8-17).

The function of the *card hopper* is to hold approximately 500 cards (9-edge first) and to facilitate feeding one card at a time as needed. Cards move through the key punch from right to left as columns 1 to 80 are being punched. Upon the depression of a *feed* key, the first card drops to the card bed. The feed key is depressed a second time to cause the second card to drop to the card bed; the first card then moves to the *punching station* while the second card waits at the card bed. As soon as column 80 of card 1 passes the punching station and begins to move under the *reading station,* card 2 moves to the punching station. This causes another card to drop automatically from the card hopper to the card bed. Thus, the blank cards in the card hopper move continuously on their way through the punching and reading stations for data recording and, finally, to their destination in the *card stacker.*

The punching station contains 12 punch blades positioned in the same sequence as the vertical layout of the card. The top three punch blades are for the zone punching positions (12, 11, and 0), and the remaining nine blades are for the digit punching positions (1 to 9) (Fig. 8-18).

Occasionally, the user is faced with the need to duplicate certain repetitive information into one or more cards. The *reading station* per-

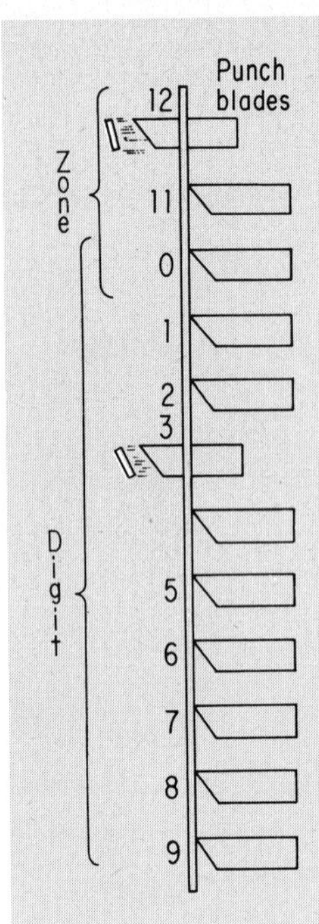

FIGURE 8-18. Letter C in the card column

forms this task by sensing the data that move underneath it and, when the duplicate ("Dup") key is depressed, by actuating the punching station to place holes in the card under it in the same location as those in the sensed card. The synchronized card movement in both stations facilitates the duplicating function.

Manual keypunching is a slow and time-consuming job. Punching input-data cards proceeds at an average speed of 160 keystrokes per minute with accuracy dependent upon the time allowed for the job and the legibility and accuracy of the source documents themselves. Either factor contributes to keypunching errors. Errors discovered during processing cause frustrating interruptions; the time needed to locate them depends on the type of error made and the complexity of the system itself. Efficiency is drastically reduced and costs can easily mount.

Data Verification

The formal routine in error detection requires the use of an 80-column verifier, which senses the characters punched in the card and compares them with the information keyed in through the keyboard. If the sensed holes match the keyed-in data, a notch indicating the correctness of the data is punched on the right edge of the card, opposite row 1. However, if any discrepancy is detected, an error is indicated by a notch on the top of each incorrectly punched column.

FIGURE 8-19. IBM 5496 data recorder (Courtesy IBM)

The 96-Column Key Punch

Data are punched in the 96-column card by the IBM 5496 data recorder. Similar to the 80-column key punch, the recorder consists of a 64-character keyboard, a card hopper, a punching station, a reading station, a printing station, and a card stacker (Fig. 8-19).

The recorder is best described as a "delayed" serial machine, for one of its outstanding features is a buffered input–output area. Input data are held in the machine's key entry area until all data for a card have been keyed, thus providing the operator ample time to verify and rekey any number of characters, if necessary. When all the data have been keyed, a release key is depressed, and the characters are electronically read from the verifier and punched into the card serially. While the data for a given card are being punched, data for the next sequential card can be keyed. Such overlapping of punching and keying functions increases the performance of the recording phase.

Data verification is done on the same unit. The flip of a switch converts the data recorder into a verifier. The same routine followed on the 80-column verifier is applied. Detection of an error turns on a warning light and causes the machine to lock. The operator then attempts to verify the card. If the error light comes on and the keyboard locks three times, the mistake is verified.

For automatic data recording, up to four prepunched program cards are read by the recorder and stored in the on-line storage unit. Selection of one of four program cards speeds up the recording process and offers versatility of field controls within the job at hand. Data verification takes almost as much time as the actual punching of the data. Despite this fact, it should be patiently done, because errors are less costly to locate now than at a later stage.

DIRECT DATA-ENTRY DEVICES

For two decades, punched-card data entry has been the traditional, accepted method of converting human-collected (source) data into machine-readable form. The standard 80-column IBM card has the psychological advantage of being a visual and an understandable physical record. It has been the mainstay as an input medium for many reasons, including its high level of accuracy and flexibility with regard to correcting errors, and is an ideal method of data entry for applications, such as billing, that require a return record. The key punch, in turn, has proved itself to be a rugged, highly reliable, economical data-entry device.

Data-entry problems can be overwhelming. Over $1.50 billion was spent in 1973 for input-data preparation. Over one third of a computer system's expense is generally earmarked for data preparation. Given these pressures and the fact that business operations have required increased data-input speed to facilitate the processing of large volumes of data within critical deadlines, the punched card has proved deficient in speed of processing, owing to the manual labor involved in punching the data, verifying and correcting them, and the physical handling of bulky stacks of punched cards. Also the punched card is easily damaged. The alternative solution to this problem was the development of a data-input device that would eliminate the key punch and would record source documents *directly* on magnetic tape or magnetic disk.[8] Such devices, called data-entry devices, speed up the data-preparation process and allow a record to be corrected while being verified, resulting in minimum physical movement for both the operator and the machine.

Intelligent Terminals

The direct data-entry devices presented in this section are key-to-tape, key-to-cassette/cartridge, key-to-disk, and key-to-diskette terminals. Each unit offers unique features and is designed to meet certain data-entry specifications. Some of these terminals are referred to as intelligent terminals. An *intelligent* terminal is generally one containing an integral processor and memory; it is capable of editing, recalling constant information, error detecting, and the like, independent of the CPU. In some

[8] Details on magnetic tape and magnetic disk are covered in Chapter 9.

operations, such terminals are capable of functioning as limited "satellite" processors, in addition to functioning as interactive terminals to a central computer system.

Accuracy is the primary asset of intelligent terminals, and this factor outweighs most every other factor in justifying their selection. By their use, error rate in many firms has been reduced by over 90 percent. Also, editing capability allows a firm to use non-data-processing personnel responsible for source documents to do data-entry work. This could mean lower data-entry preparation costs and the release of data-processing personnel to concentrate on the more challenging aspects of the data-processing function.

Key-to-Tape Devices

Generally, a key-to-tape device offers, among others, the following advantages:

1. It is faster than the key punch, since it is electronic, whereas the key punch is electromechanical.
2. Greater flexibility in input format can be made with transactions that exceed the 80-column-card constraint.
3. It provides for error correction simply by backspacing. Unlike the case with keypunching, where error correction requires replacement of the card containing the error with another blank card, the operator of a key-to-tape device simply backspaces to the location of the error and then inscribes the correct character. Thus, error handling at the source means elimination of future problems and additional costs.
4. The tape drive, being a more efficient device than the card reader, is not as likely to encounter the kind of problems that the card reader often does when processing a mutilated, stapled, or spindled card. Furthermore, one key-to-tape machine performs the functions of both the key punch and the verifier more efficiently.
5. Elimination of punched cards means elimination of the card cost and the expense of training key-punch operators, a reduction in manual handling, and an approximate 25 percent increase in throughput over the key punch, as data are read directly from tape. The saving becomes more obvious with a larger volume of source-data entry and a better-organized overall data-entry process.
6. With the tape as a medium, recorded data cannot get out of sequence.

DATA RECORDER. Representative of direct source-data devices is the data recorder, first pioneered in 1965 by Mohawk Data Sciences.[9] Its two

[9] In 1968, Honeywell, Inc., became the first major computer manufacturer to compete with Mohawk Data Sciences for the key-to-tape market. Honeywell's 50 some models offer varied features and capabilities.

FIGURE 8-20. Mohawk Data Sciences' 6401 data recorder (right, Courtesy Mohawk Data Science) and Honeywell's Key-to-tape system (Courtesy Honeywell)

models, the 1101 and the 6401, handle the dual function of keying in and verifying source data directly on magnetic tape (Fig. 8-20). The procedure is simple. A software or hand-wired control package links a keyboard to a tape drive. Signals from keystrokes transform source characters into magnetic tape codes understandable to the computer. Over the past 10 years, many improved versions have been developed, with over 50 companies involved in their production or marketing. The key differences among these devices lie in tape-recording codes and densities.

The data recorder consists of (1) a keyboard of the type used in IBM's 80-character key punch, (2) a control panel, (3) a small (80- to 120-character) magnetic core memory and electronic logic, and (4) a handler for $\frac{1}{2}$-inch magnetic tape. Depending on the manufacturer and model, the data recorder encodes keyed-in data through core storage in seven tracks at a density of 200 bits per inch, or in nine tracks at 556 or 800 bits per inch.

Modes of Operation. The data recorder can be operated in one of three modes: (1) entry, (2) verify, and (3) search modes. Changing from one operating mode to another simply involves setting a designated switch or switches.

In the *entry* mode, source data are keyed and entered into the recorder's core memory.[10] When the record is complete, it is extracted (either by manually depressing a key or automatically) from core memory and written on magnetic tape. The written record is automatically backspaced and read by the machine to compare its content with that of core memory for parity. During this phase, the keyboard is locked to prevent entry of additional data. When the record is found correct, the keyboard is unlocked and the operator begins keying the next record. However, if an error is detected, the entire record or any part of it can be rewritten (Fig. 8-21).

The *verify* mode is used when a batch of records already written on tape must be verified, character for character, for accuracy. During this mode, the data recorder reads into memory one record at a time. The verifier operator keys in the source record used by the entry operator.

[10] Other features of the data recorder include skipping and duplicating certain information through a program prepared in advance by the operator.

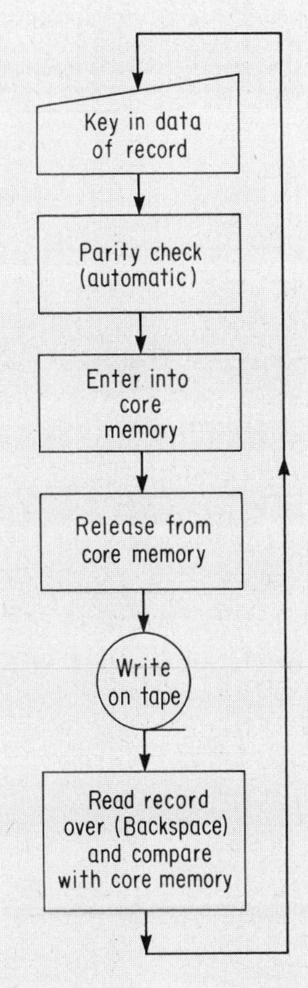

FIGURE 8-21. Sequence of primary steps in the data entry mode

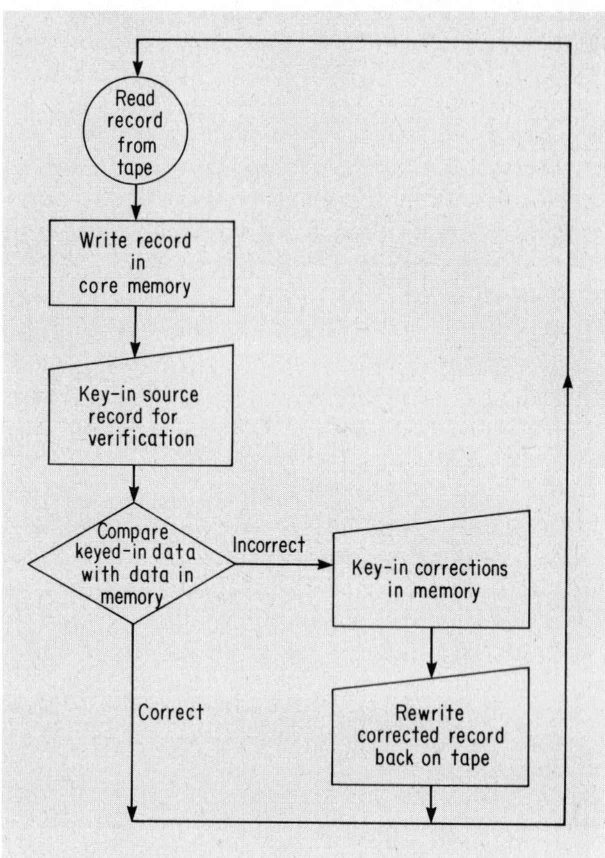

FIGURE 8-22. Sequence of primary steps in the data-verify mode

When the verification is complete and no error is detected, the data recorder reads in the next record in sequence, until every record is verified.

However, if an error is found in a given record, the unit locks and a red indicator flashes. At that time, the verifier operator rekeys the source record. If, after the third try, the error is still indicated in core memory, the operator makes a correction by depressing the "Corr" key and keying the correct characters into memory. The now-accurate record in memory is rewritten on tape (by depressing the "Release" key), followed by an automatic backspace-and-read verification of the rewritten record (Fig. 8-22).

The *search* mode is used to locate a particular record on tape. When search is initiated and the data recorder locates the record, it halts, allowing the operator to change, add to, or delete whatever information is required.

Pooling and Communicating. When several key-to-tape devices are used, data records are often combined through a pooler. The *pooler* is designed to pool several magnetic tapes into one for verification or for direct entry into computer memory under the control of read and write programs.

Most key-to-tape systems also provide for data communication with other key-to-tape systems or with a remote computer facility over a leased voice-band line. The current trend is toward decentralizing data-processing facilities through remote batch terminals (RBTs) linked via communication lines to a central computer system at another location. This allows the remote user (e.g., salesman) direct access to and the convenience of using a central computer from the data source.

Key-to-Cassette/Cartridge Devices

Since 1965, when key-to-tape devices were first introduced, a new type of input medium, called key-to-cassette or key-to-cartridge input system, was developed. The system uses a cassette or a cartridge for storage of input data. Data are recorded directly on a small magnetic cassette tape or on a cartridge, and are later converted to a full-sized magnetic tape for computer processing (Fig. 8-23). The unique advantage is simplicity of operation and the ability to capture data anywhere they originate. In large organizations, for example, district or regional offices use the cassette

FIGURE 8-23. *IBM's tape cartridge and reader (Courtesy IBM)*

or cartridge device, and later the data are transmitted over telephone lines or by mail to high-level offices for processing.

The tape cassette generally measures $2\frac{1}{2}$ by 4 inches and contains two reels for tape feed and take-up. The $\frac{1}{4}$-inch tape may have from two to eight tracks and can store about 200,000 characters. The tape cartridge, on the other hand, is sprocket driven, which allows for accurate positioning of the tape on the read–write head of the unit. The tape ranges from 100 to 120 feet in length, with a capacity of approximately 28,000 characters.

Compared to the traditional $\frac{1}{2}$-inch magnetic tape, cartridges or cassettes offer three unique advantages:

1. More economical storage and easier handling. No spooling or tape loading is necessary, since this phase of the operation is virtually automatic.
2. A convenient method of maintaining batch control. In a banking application involving the processing of rejected checks, the average batch of 250 80-column records is easily stored on the cartridge's capacity of 28,000 characters.
3. Protection from dirt. Each cartridge or cassette is placed in a plastic housing to prevent dirt or human mishandling from distorting the data stored in it.

In magnetic tape recording and processing, the effectiveness of a tape system depends on its performance characteristics, intended usage, and maximum error rate. In terms of performance characteristics, the system's specified bit density and tape speed have direct bearing on its reliability. The higher its packing density (bits per inch), the greater the error rate caused by dust particles or by possible deficiencies in the tape. Even if the track width is increased so as to increase the tape's effective contact with the read–write heads, angular misalignment resulting from this attempt could take place. Furthermore, increasing tape speed brings with it the problem of controlling proper tension, especially during start–stop operations.

Consideration of the life of the tape is also important. Key-to-tape systems that record data once for future reference do not require high tape life. On the other hand, if the data recorded will be used over and over, high tape life is extremely critical.

Like that of other entrants to the direct data-entry equipment field, the market for key-to-cassette devices is still in its infancy. As the unit price decreases, the number of installations is expected to increase dramatically. In 1972 about 42,000 units were in operation. One research firm predicts that between 100,000 and 125,000 key-to-cassette units should be in operation by 1975, with an estimated price tag for the lower-priced terminals at $12,000—40 percent of today's price.

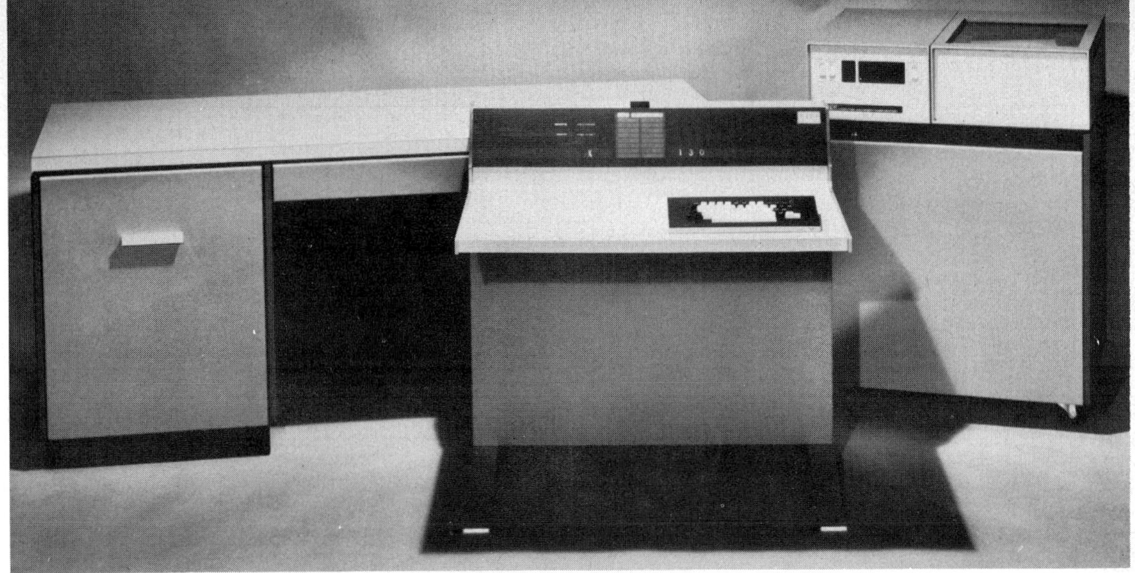

FIGURE 8-24. Key-to-disk method of data input (Courtesy Computer Machinery Corporation)

Key-to-Disk Devices

Unlike the key-to-tape or key-to-cassette/cartridge devices, the key-to-disk system (also called *shared processor*) is a pioneering step toward data-input automation. First developed in 1967 by the Computer Machinery Corporation, the system consists of a magnetic disk, a set of key stations (ranging from 8 to 64), a small-sized computer, a control package, and a tape unit. The procedure involves keying in the input data, which are first edited by the small computer prior to their temporary storage on a random-access storage disk or drum. The "loaded" disk or drum (output) is then read out on computer-compatible magnetic tape for processing (Fig. 8-24).

Several unique features are provided in the key-to-disk system, some of which are as follows:

1. The *stored format.* As the input data are keyed in, they are arranged in predetermined formats. Several formats can be stored in the system and made available through a selected key on the keyboard. This stored-format concept is a timesaving feature compared to the stand-alone units, which may be slowed down because of the need to change program formats or, in the case of the key punch, the need to change a program card for each format.
2. Decreased error rates. A character-display panel on many systems is useful for sight verification purposes. The panel indicates to the operator the last character or even the entire record entered or verified, depending on the make. This feature reduces verification strokes and improves the operator's overall efficiency in handling the system.

3. Most key-to-disk systems provide, as a by-product, production figures for each key-station operator. In addition to its editing function and control of data flow and stored programs between the key station and the disk, the computer also maintains a historical file on each operator, in terms of the number of keystrokes made and the jobs processed. Some systems even count the number of errors made and the time it took the operator to enter and verify the source data. The computer can easily determine the operator's efficiency and effectiveness for feedback to lower-level management.
4. Simultaneous verification with data entry. Visual verification through display devices is also available on some systems.
5. Elimination of tape handling, which is the core in key-to-tape or key-to-cassette systems.
6. Convenient location and accessibility of stored program formats for use by all key stations.
7. Reduced hardware requirements. In one installation, a nine-station key-to-disk system replaced 16 key-punch machines.[11]
8. Key-station operator acceptance of the system, because it provides total operator–system interaction at a mental level of activity that has been shown to increase productivity. Furthermore, operators now work with a system much quieter than the key-punch machine and thus in a more pleasant working environment.

Key-to-Diskette System

A newcomer into the data-entry industry, the IBM 3740 Data Entry Diskette System has been touted as the beginning of IBM's formal attack on the punched card and the key-punch market.[12] Although there might be some truth to the idea of exploring more direct ways of preparing data for input, this new system can be objectively viewed as a contribution to remote data capture; therefore, it is most efficiently used in a decentralized data-entry environment (Fig. 8-25).

The basic 3740 system consists of an *operator key station* and a *data converter* for converting the diskette output to a nine-track magnetic tape for processing. The operator key station consists of a key-punch-type keyboard, a display that shows 240 characters of status data, a controller,

[11] In 1971, the regional Internal Revenue Service, Andover, Massachusetts, installed a direct data-entry system (DDES), which eliminated the use of the punched card. With this system, the center's capacity increased from a reported 130,000 to 200,000 returns a day during a peak season. In addition to the increased saving in cost of operation and the improvement in service, the system eliminated the need for handling an estimated 68 million cards each year. Furthermore, the required number of key-station terminals to handle the total task was slightly more than half the number of key-punch machines formerly used for the job.

[12] IBM's introduction of the 3740 key-to-diskette entry system is interpreted by many users as an endorsement of the concept of direct data entry. It also serves (psychologically) to encourage the use of direct data entry as an alternative to the key punch. See *Computerworld,* Jan. 1, 1973, p. 21, and Jan. 31, 1973, pp. 1 and 3, for details.

FIGURE 8-25. IBM 3740 data station (Courtesy IBM)

and a small, Mylar, record-like *floppy disk*, called a *diskette*, which can store up to 1,898 128-character records, or the capacity of 3,000 80-column punched cards. Data are recorded and read serially, and either transmitted over communications lines (model 2 version of the system) directly to an IBM 360, 370, System/3 facility, or the recorded diskette is placed in a data converter for converting its content to a nine-track magnetic tape.

IS THE KEY PUNCH OBSOLETE?

In determining which type and model of source-data device is the best, the prospective user must look into his own application needs, the volume of data input, and cost considerations. Nearly all models are believed to be close to 98 percent accurate. The key-to-disk system is generally competitive with card-oriented systems using 12 key-punch machines or more, and thus is ideally designed for installations where large volumes of data are prepared for input. Although more expensive to install and operate than other devices, it provides more efficient and effective performance in meeting the demands of most larger installations. The growth market rate is not as high as for some other direct data-entry devices; however, key-to-disk annual sales are expected to increase from $25 million in 1971 to an estimated $140 million by 1976. Figure 8-26 gives data-entry and data-conversion costs.

Favorable user response explains to some degree the growing popularity of the key-to-tape device. Part of the success of this concept stems from the similarity between the key-to-tape device and a company's key-punch operation, its reliability, the ease of operator training, and the efficiency of data preparation, especially in smaller installations requiring no more than three to eight key stations. Although most key-to-tape devices rent for more than twice the key punch, savings because of fewer units

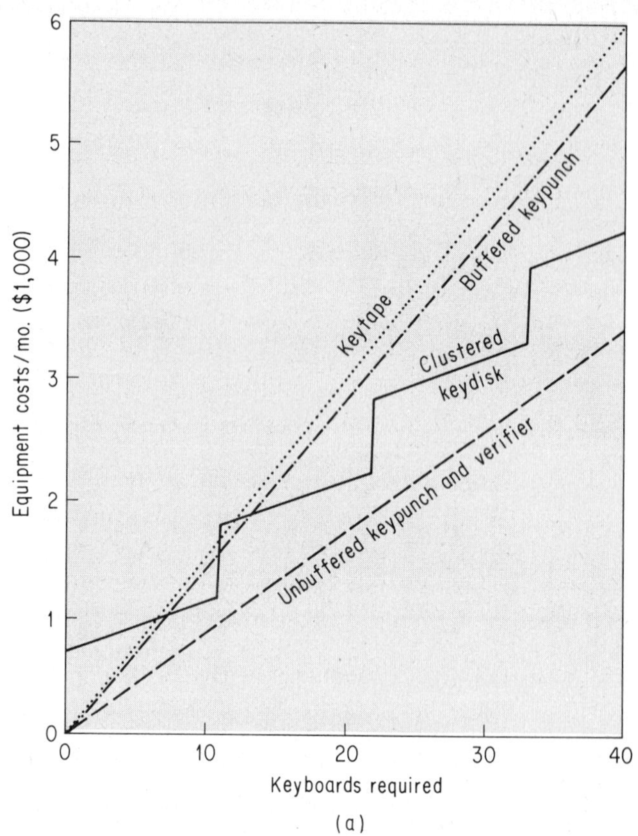

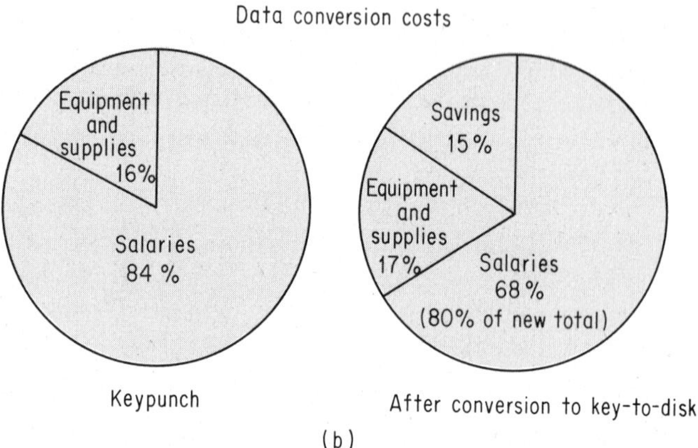

FIGURE 8-26. *Data-entry and source-data conversion costs: (a) relative costs of keyboard entry systems over a range of unit requirements (the key-to-disk system becomes economically competitive at a level of six keyboards if an improvement in throughput of 30 percent is realized); (b) the 1 percent increase in the cost of equipment and supplies for key-to-disk systems is more than offset by an increase in efficiency and throughput.*

These charts were taken from "Data Entry, Keying for Profits," prepared by Samson Science Corp., a subsidiary of Quantrum Science Corp.

and operators more than compensates for the difference. In 1965, around 600 stations were installed. In 1973, the number of installations increased to 40,000. With this steady, accelerated increase and the continued shift from keypunching to key-to-tape,[13] it is very likely that the figure will exceed 60,000 by 1975. By contrast, there are over 500,000 key punches and verifiers in use, with an estimated increase of 50,000 units per year.

The likelihood of the key-to-tape device pushing the traditional key punch off the market is questionable. Several indicators point to a continued adoption of the key punch: (1) the used key-punch market offers IBM models 024 and 026, but very few model 029 key-punch machines. The implication is that users with the latter machine are more likely committed to its use. (2) Many owners of older-model key-punch machines are updating them with newer ones, probably indicating reluctance to switch from a card-oriented system to any other form of data-preparation system. (3) The key-punch service bureaus keep a full-time schedule, leading one to believe that the key punch as a primary data-preparation device is still "alive and well."

The long-term outlook, however, may not be as promising for the key punch. Organizations with large, centralized in-house input-generation areas could easily switch to a key-to-tape, key-to-disk, or optical recognition system (to be explained in Chapter 10) when the price of such devices decreases. When that takes place, the use of the key punch will be primarily in hotel computer systems, schools, and smaller organizations. A schematic of the alternative data-entry methods is presented in Fig. 8-27.

ELECTRONIC POINT-OF-SALE TERMINALS

It has been estimated that over 75 percent of the information required by retailers can be captured at the point of sale, and the retail industry is beginning to use a new type of direct data-collection hardware to do so. Point-of-sale (POS) terminals, often referred to as "intelligent cash registers," have built-in sequence control and instruction routines that offer the following key benefits:

1. They help the salesman in handling the details of each transaction at the time it occurs, eliminating the need for other input devices.
2. Reduction of sales staff, resulting from the increased efficiency by automated entry of item and price data, automatic computation of sales tax, entry of discounts, and the like, and the step-by-step procedure offered the clerk in handling each sales transaction.
3. Reduction in inventory personnel, since a POS terminal handles inventory records automatically through data collection and processing.

[13] Buffered key-punch machines have put a damper on the competitive edge of key-to-tape devices. However, since they rent for over twice the rent of the non-buffered models, a cost consideration remains an issue.

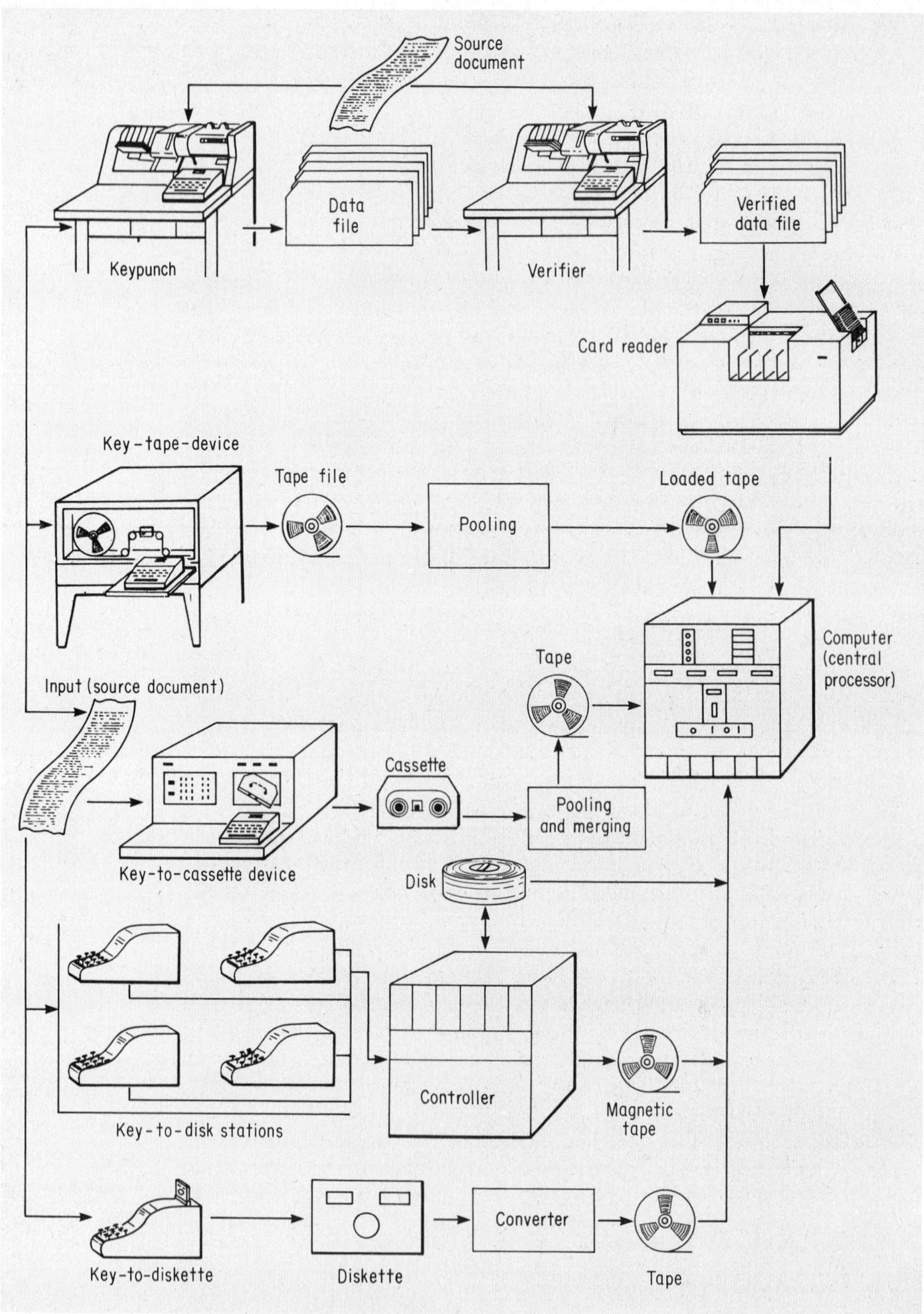

FIGURE 8-27. *Alternative methods of data entry*

4. Automatic updating of customer accounts.
5. Reduction of bad credit-risk accounts and credit-authorization personnel through an automated credit-authorization system.
6. Shorter period to train clerks to operate a POS terminal than a conventional cash register.

Point-of-sale data collection dates back to the early 1950s, when machine-readable tags were used to encode inventory information. When an item was sold, the tag was saved, and tags were later sent in batches to a central data-processing facility where they were converted to a faster input medium for processing.

Unlike the batch-processing method, the use of POS terminals involves a more efficient approach to the handling of direct tag reading. In some of today's modern terminals, the salesclerk simply follows lighted legends, accompanied by specific instructions. The terminal can handle as many as 12 different transactions, including information related to such categories as discounts, uneven trade, and down payment on merchandise purchased. Some terminals even validate a customer's credit status, enabling him to move through the checkout counter at top speed. Such capability simplifies the clerk's functions and allows him to concentrate on the needs of the customer.

Although the majority of POS systems share similar characteristics, the approach they use in capturing the data may be *electromechanical, optical,* or *magnetic*. The electromechanical approach involves a hand-held device or a reader for reading the traditional perforated tapes. The optical and the magnetic approach involve a portable "wand" reader, which scans the price and stock number on the tag with foolproof accuracy. The price of the terminal ranges from $2,800 to $3,500.

The three major POS manufacturers are Singer, NCR, and the Uni-Tote division of General Instrument Corporation (Fig. 8-28). Uni-Tote's lead in the field dates back to 1966, when it installed 350 POS registers in Joseph Magnin's 35-store chain. Since then, it has installed hundreds of similar systems in major retail chains throughout the country. In 1971, it introduced the Series 300, a third-generation electronic POS system that can be connected to a central computer system via telephone lines. It has guide lights that indicate the sequence of data entry and a drum printer that produces a two-part journal: one part is a permanent journal tape, and the other, a customer receipt.

The optical approach is exemplified by NCR's optical wand, which reads color-coded data and emits an audible "beep" with each wave of the wand to tell the salesclerk that the data are entered correctly (Fig. 8-28). This innovation minimizes keying errors and allows various levels of authorization for selected transactions. While NCR's system visually displays the sequence of operator instructions, Singer's approach is to light up each key in its proper sequence. Both systems, however, are considered highly accurate.

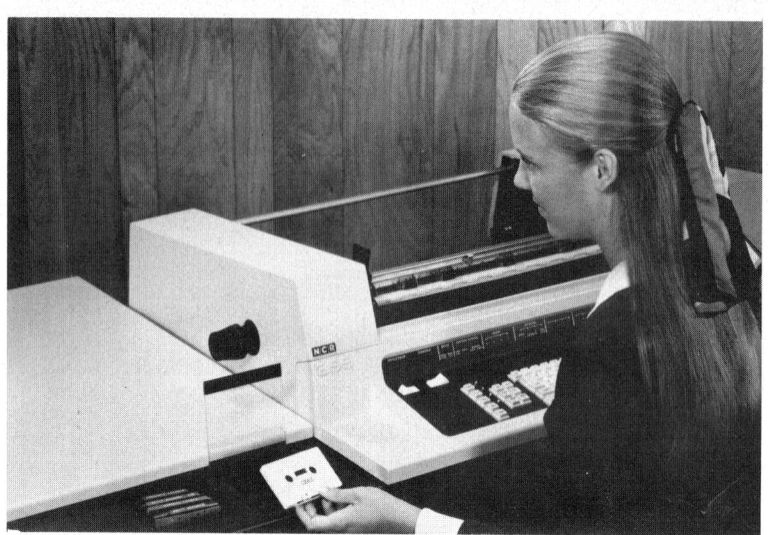

FIGURE 8-28. Examples of leading POS systems. On the right, the NCR 280 terminal retail. Above, the NCR 399 self-contained cassette can be used for input or output of systems information; data can be placed on the cassette as a by-product of posting. Below, the NCR 399 serves as an intelligent terminal that can provide editing, formating, validating, and batching of input data for transmission to a data center or another computer (Courtesy NCR).

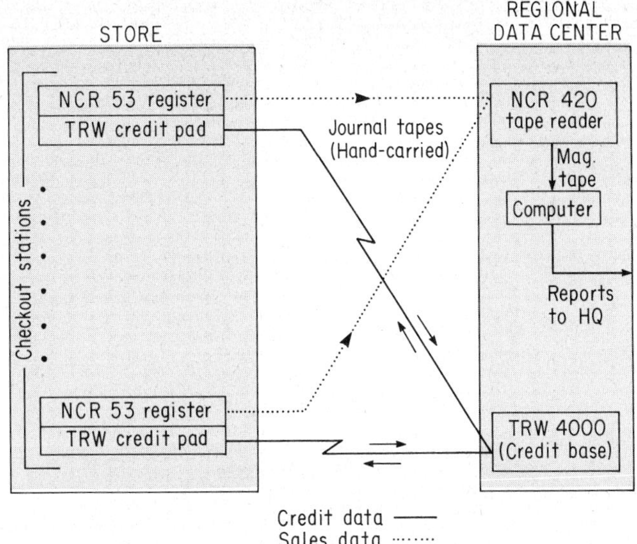

FIGURE 8-29

Case Illustration [14]

Perhaps the most significant POS system installation to date is the one to which Montgomery Ward—one of the largest retail store chains—is committed. In 1973, the firm placed an order with National Cash Register for 11,000 additional NCR[15] 280 POS terminals to be used in its 450 stores throughout the United States. When final installations are made, Montgomery Ward will have installed 16,000 POS units valued at $60 million.

Problem Definition and Testing. As will be explained in Chapter 21, Montgomery Ward conducted a study of the feasibility of putting into operation a totally integrated POS system. Prior to 1968, Montgomery Ward had 15,000 registers, 10,000 of which were the conventional electromechanical type that performed sales transaction routines. The main problems were automated recording of item sales card inventory, greater data accuracy, and better and faster customer service.

In 1968, cash registers were upgraded in selected stores by the introduction of NCR Model 53 automation registers, on which clerks could record merchandise and transaction information at the point of sale. The journal tape produced by each register was sent daily (by messenger service) to the data center to be written on magnetic tape for computer processing. Credit authorization for each transaction was handled by a credit authorization system next to each register and a credit data base processor at the data center (Fig. 8-29).

[14] This illustration was adapted from *Modern Data,* June 1973, pp. 30–32.

[15] John Patterson, the founder of National Cash Register, first developed and distributed the cash register in 1884. NCR now controls 75 percent of the market.

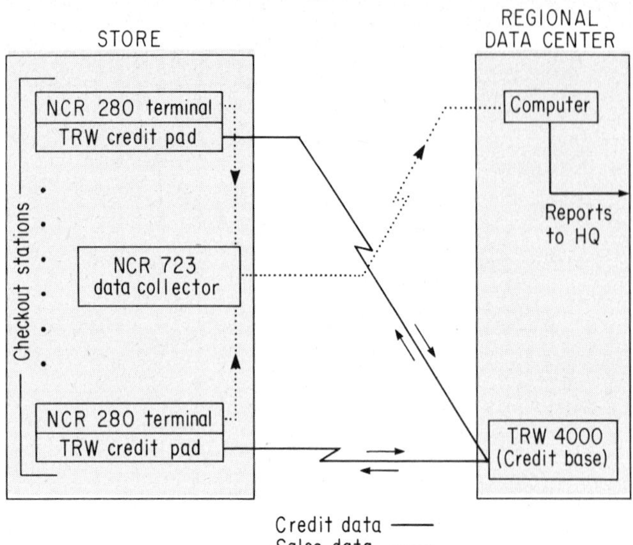

FIGURE 8-30. Present NCR 280 system (Courtesy NCR)

By 1971, management realized that even with improvements in mechanizing sales and account reporting, the need for more timely information pointed to a data terminal rather than an automated register. This prompted a commitment to an NCR 280 POS system that provided its own calculation capability and printers for customer receipts, sales check, and sales transaction journal. Furthermore, every terminal had an in-store data collector that automatically received data from the terminal at the end of each sales transaction. In the evening, the regional computer polled the data collector for data access and processing (Fig. 8-30).

Compared to the past system, the present NCR 280 system resulted in 10 to 15 percent fewer registers and faster and more efficient data entry. It also increased production by 50 percent over the conventional cash register. By the end of 1973, Montgomery Ward is expected to have 2,500 terminals and eight NCR 725 minicomputers in operation. By 1978, an additional 5,000 terminals will have been installed (Fig. 8-31).

Thus, the ultimate goals of such integrated POS systems are total control of the entire retail operation through automation of merchandise inventory, customer billing, and credit authorization, a variety of management reports to aid decision making, and faster and better customer service. That is what POS is all about.

SUMMARY

In this chapter we discussed card input media and devices and key direct data-entry devices. The most commonly used medium in card-oriented computers is the 80-column or the 96-column punched card. Either type

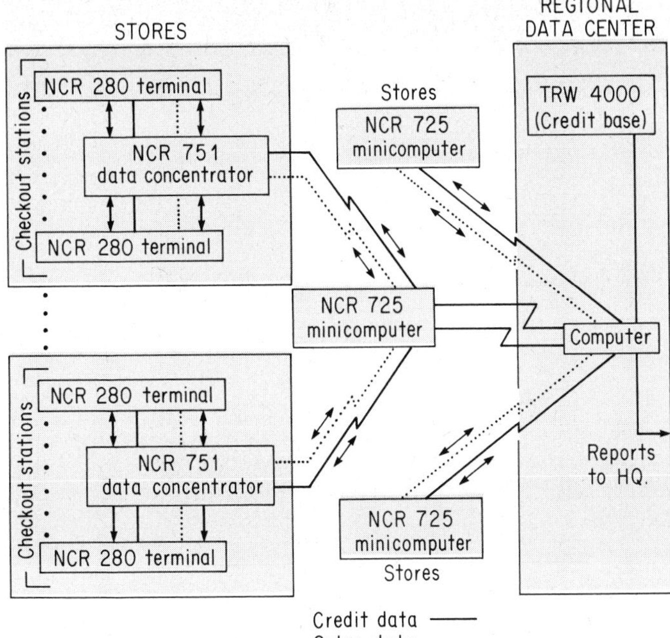

FIGURE 8-31. Eventual NCR 280 system (Courtesy NCR)

is designed to store in coded form a transaction or a program instruction. The data it stores may be alphabetic, numeric, or alphanumeric. The data must be in a predetermined format so that each unit of information (field) occupies the same position on all the cards in the deck. Among the commonly used types of cards are the aperture, detail, mark-sensed, and stub cards.

The punched card offers the advantage of data standardization for efficient processing, ease of data storage and assembly, and low-cost storage per unit of information. Among its limitations are its physical makeup; it cannot be spindled, folded, or stapled, or it might jam the machine. Its size further limits the amount of data that it can store. Compared to the 80-column card, the 96-column card offers the advantages of easier physical handling, greater information capacity, and the use of simpler and more reliable equipment at lower cost.

Each type of card uses its respective key punch for data recording. Automatic (programmed) keypunching is achieved through a coded program card, which guides the key punch to do such jobs as skipping, punching, or duplicating numeric and alphabetic data.

The primary direct data-entry devices are the key-to-tape, key-to-cartridge/cassette, key-to-disk, key-to-diskette, and point-of-sale terminals. The growing popularity of these devices poses a real threat to the future of the key punch, and they are very likely on the way to becoming the standard method of preparing data for processing. Generally, they offer the following advantages:

1. Improvement in operator throughput (efficiency) by the simple elimination of the physical movement of punched cards and the easier, quieter, and faster operation of direct data-entry devices.
2. Reduced cost of media and personnel. Input data, especially in high-volume application, that once required tens of thousands of punched cards can now be stored on tape at a fraction of the cost. Furthermore, improved efficiency of direct data-entry devices means fewer operators (therefore, greater savings) to do the same job.
3. More efficient and easier data verification and correction routines. The use of visual display of keyed data on some data-entry devices eliminates the need to verify the same data on separate machines. In the event of error, the operator simply backspaces to the error location and keys in the correct data.
4. Operator statistics collected as a by-product of some direct data-entry devices (e.g., key-to-disk system) give the manager real facts about the operator's performance and offer a good basis for determining bonus payments, salary increases, or development of a training program to correct weaknesses. Operators, on the other hand, are likely to accept more readily the report the system gives them on their own performance, as they know that they are getting a more objective evaluation than from a supervisor.
5. Operators view themselves in a more "professional" light. Operating noisy key-punch machines and handling bulky stacks of punched cards often give the impression of working in a factory. By contrast, the relatively quiet atmosphere of a direct data-entry system gives the operator the feeling of being an integral part of the computer world. This state of mind contributes to higher morale on the job and better cooperation with management.

In determining which terminal best suits a given application, users who need to translate source documents into computer input from remote locations will find terminals such as the IBM 3741 system appropriate. For users with source documents in one location, key-to-disk is a proper choice. However, users with high-volume, fast-turnaround requirements will find optical-character-recognition (OCR) equipment the ideal choice. Finally, users whose applications work best on an interactive basis might find on-line (direct) entry devices offering the best potential. In any case, the final decision to move to a new form of input-preparation device should be based on the real need to improve the efficiency of the input-preparation phase for the particular application(s) at the lowest cost possible.

TERMS TO LEARN

Data inscriber	Output device
Data recorder	Peripheral equipment
Detail card	Point-of-sale (POS) system
Disk pack	Pooling
Field	Program card
Hollerith code	Punched card
Input	Read check
Input device	Stub card
Keyboard	× punch
Mark-sensed card	Wire matrix printer

QUESTIONS

1. Describe the 80-column and 96-column punched cards. Give two examples of their use.
2. Why is a standard punched card necessary? Explain briefly.
3. What is the unit-record principle? The Hollerith code?
4. What is meant by "9-edge first, face down"? What is meant by "12-edge first, face up"?
5. How is alphabetic recording of data different from numeric recording in the 80- and 96-column cards?
6. An order form contains seven different types of merchandise ordered by a given customer. How many cards would be required to record the orders for further processing?
7. What is a field? Explain. Give an example.
8. How many different ways may a card be identified? Explain each briefly. For what reason is a control field used? Give an example.
9. Explain briefly the primary types of punched cards.
10. Summarize the advantages and limitations of the punched card.
11. Discuss the similarities and differences between an electric typewriter and a key punch.
12. What is a program card? How does it differ from a regular punched card? Why is a program card used?
13. Suppose that you have 200 blank cards in which student number 0561 is to be punched in columns 1, 2, 3, and 4 of each card. You have only an 80-column key-punch machine at your disposal. What is the most efficient method of punching the number in the cards?
14. How does the key-to-disk system differ from the data recorder?
15. What is the difference between key-to-disk and key-to-diskette terminals?

16. In view of the latest developments in direct-input and other devices, what is your assessment of the future of the key punch? Do you agree with the argument in this chapter? Why?
17. Explain briefly the procedure underlying a POS input system.

SUGGESTED READING

ENG, FRANK. "Key-to-Disk Data Entry," *The Office*, Feb. 1973, pp. 55–57.

FIELDMAN, L. A. "A Primer on Source Data Automation," *Data Processing Magazine*, Sept. 1969, pp. 26–29ff.

———. "The Coming of Keyboard-to-Disk Systems," *Modern Data*, March 1973, p. 30.

FRANK, R. A. "Simple Terminals May Be Trend of the Future," *Computerworld*, Feb. 9, 1972, p. 8ff.

GRUNBLATT, STANLEY. "Delete Delays and Dollars with Direct Data Entry," *Infosystems*, Sept. 1972, pp. 20–25.

"How Union Carbide Kicked the Keypunch Habit," *Infosystems*, Dec. 1972, pp. 26–29.

"Keypunch Falling—Key–Disk Terminals Seen Input Kings," *Computerworld*, March 22, 1972, p. 29.

"Key-to-Magnetic Data Entry Systems at Work," *The Office*, Feb. 1973, pp. 50–53.

SALZMAN, R. M., and A. S. NISKOVEN. "Data Entry Systems," *Modern Data*, Feb. 1973, pp. 28ff.

STENDER, R. C. "The Future Role of Keyboards in Data Entry," *Datamation*, June 1970, pp. 60–62.

input-output and secondary storage media and devices

9

The central processing unit cannot function alone. Although it is the heart of a computer system, its performance depends largely on the types and capabilities of the system's input and ouput devices. *Input devices* are needed for transferring machine-readable data directly or indirectly (from secondary storage) to the central processing unit for processing. *Output devices* are needed for receiving processed (*output*) information from the central processing unit and making it available to the user on request. This chapter explains how data are transferred into the central processing unit from input media such as punched cards, magnetic tape, and magnetic disk, and how output data are written from primary storage via an on-line printer or back onto tape or disk. Input–output and storage devices are also included. To produce meaningful information, a computer system requires that its input–output and other peripheral devices function with the central processing unit in a compatible manner. Input and output devices are manipulated by a control unit that decodes instructions from the central processing unit and initiates the operation of the designated devices. A channel connects the control unit to the central processing unit and performs a control function for many input and output devices. The sequence of steps for input entry is as follows:

1. The computer executes a program instruction to read a record held in an input device.
2. The control unit receives a signal to initiate the operation of the input device.

3. The input device reads the record and converts it into electrical pulses or signals.
4. The signals are checked by the control unit.
5. A data channel facilitates the transmission of data signals into memory for processing.
6. The central processing unit is activated to begin operation on the data received.

This six-step cycle also applies for output entry.

Coded input data first are read by an input device and then are transferred to the computer for processing. If the output is needed immediately by management, it is converted into human language by an output device called the printer. On the other hand, if the output is to be stored for future processing, this can be done on output media such as punched cards, punched tape, or magnetic tape.

Each type of computer has its own individual machine language and utilizes different input and output devices. We must examine these devices in order to comprehend more fully the implications involved in the various processing systems and to understand how "garbage in, garbage out" can be prevented from occurring. The primary input–output devices discussed in this and succeeding chapters are presented in summary form in Fig. 9-1.

Input and Output Devices

DEVICE	INPUT	OUTPUT	MEDIUM USED	SPEED RANGE Low	High	
Card reader	X		Punched card	100	2,000	cards per minute
Card punch		X	Punched card	100	500	cards per minute
Tape reader	X		Paper tape	10	2,000	characters per second
Tape punch		X	Paper tape	20	300	characters per second
On-line printer		X	Special paper	300	2,500	lines per minute
Magnetic ink reader	X		Special ink	750	1,600	documents per minute
Optical scanner	X		Special paper	100	2,400	characters per second
Console typewriter	X	X	Special paper	6	30	characters per second
Cathode-ray tube display	X	X	Cathode-ray tube	250	10,000	characters per second
Computer output microfilm		X	Microfilm	30	500	characters per second

FIGURE 9-1. Input–Output and Secondary Storage Devices

Secondary Storage Devices

DEVICE	MEDIUM USED	STORAGE CAPACITY	DATA TRANSFER RATE (CHARACTERS PER SECOND)
Magnetic tape drive	Magnetic tape	1 to 20 million chars. per tape	15,000 to 800,000
Magnetic disk pack	Magnetic disk	2 to 100 million chars. per pack	100,000 to 800,000
Magnetic drum unit	Magnetic drum	1 to 4 million chars. per drum	275,000 to 1,200,000
Magnetic strip unit	Magnetic strip	100 to 400 million chars. per handler	25,000 to 45,000
mass core unit	Magnetic core	1 to 2 million chars. per unit	250,000 to 2,000,000

FIGURE 9-1 (cont'd)

BUFFERING VERSUS MULTICHANNEL SYSTEMS

Some older computers have separate buffers for temporary storage of information being transmitted between secondary and primary storage or between input–output devices and primary storage. An unbuffered system performs a read–compute–write cycle in series, that is, one operation after another (Fig. 9-2); a buffered system allows the three operations to overlap, as shown in Fig. 9-3. In an overlapping procedure, the total

FIGURE 9-2. The roles of unbuffered input and output devices in computer processing

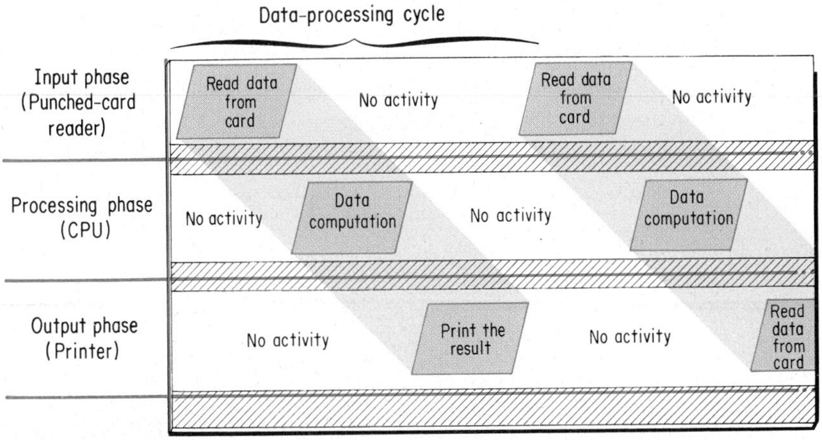

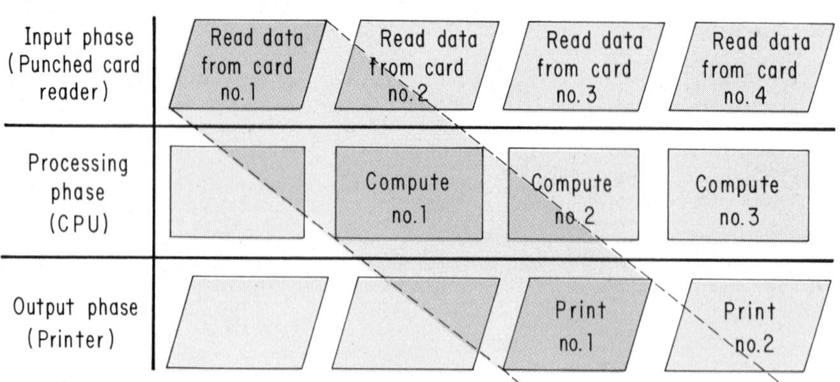

FIGURE 9-3. *The roles of buffered input and output devices in computer processing*

time for handling a transaction is the time it takes to handle the longest operation (i.e., input, processing, or output) versus the total time of the three operations in the unbuffered system. Thus the buffered system contributes to more efficient computer processing.

The need for input–output overlapping operations is readily apparent when the timing of a computer system is considered. Today's electronic computers execute instructions at microsecond speeds, whereas most input and output equipment, being largely electromechanical, still operates relatively slowly. There is no compatibility, for instance, between a computer that executes an instruction in 10 microseconds and a card reader that reads input data to the computer in 75 milliseconds, or 7,500 times as slow. An overlapping operation serves to compensate for this imbalance and to cut down on idle time.

To illustrate the role of a buffer when integrated into a computer system, consider the following steps, which use punched cards as input and printed data as output:

1. Input deck is fed into the card reader.
2. Data from the first card go automatically into the input buffer.
3. The stored program calls for a card to be read. Data from the input buffer are transferred to memory.
4. Data from card 2 begin to transfer automatically to the input buffer.
5. Card 1 is being processed while the input buffer contains the data from card 2.
6. Processed information from card 1 is sent to the output buffer.

7. The stored program calls for another card to be read. Data from the input buffer (card 2) are transferred to memory.
8. Data from card 3 begin to transfer automatically to the input buffer.
9. Output buffer is automatically sending the processed data from card 1 to the printer.
10. Information from card 2 is processed, while the input buffer is filling with the next card's contents.

At the end of this processing, card 1 has been completely read, processed, and printed. The information from card 2 is ready to be sent to the output buffer, and the data of card 3 are available in the input buffer. The process between steps 6 and 10 continues until the entire deck of cards is processed. You will note that at the input stage a card is always being prepared ahead of time by moving it into the input buffer, while the card ahead of it is being processed. Likewise, at the output phase, a card is always in the process of being printed while the card preceding it is being processed. Through the use of such overlapping made possible by buffers, a great deal of total processing (throughput) time is saved.

Buffers are expensive and have a fixed length, which limits the size of the input or output block(s) that can be handled. In the more current, sophisticated systems, especially in those utilizing several input–output devices, a data channel separates the function of input–output from that of the central processor, thus allowing overlapping operations. Such systems use primary storage areas for input and output buffers, and manage the movement of data between primary storage and input–output devices independently of the computational phase of the central processor. Each data channel is activated by an input–output instruction that tells it what to do. Once activated, the processor proceeds in its processing routine, and is interrupted only when the data channel needs to receive data from (or bring data into) primary storage or when an error ocurs. In the former case, the data channel functions simply by delaying the processor for one cycle. In the latter case, a preestablished error-check routine is carried out for the channel signals in the order in which they are received.

Whereas high-speed input–output (e.g., magnetic tape unit or disk storage unit) often monopolizes a separate *selector* channel (sometimes referred to as a "burst" mode), traditionally slower units, such as card and punch devices, are hooked up to a *multiplexor* channel made up of many subchannels to accommodate overlapping operations. They are served in sequence independently of one another (Fig. 9-4). The multichannel approach has led to the use of input–output control systems (IOCS), which allow the programmer to use macro-instructions rather than the traditional symbolic or machine instructions required on older

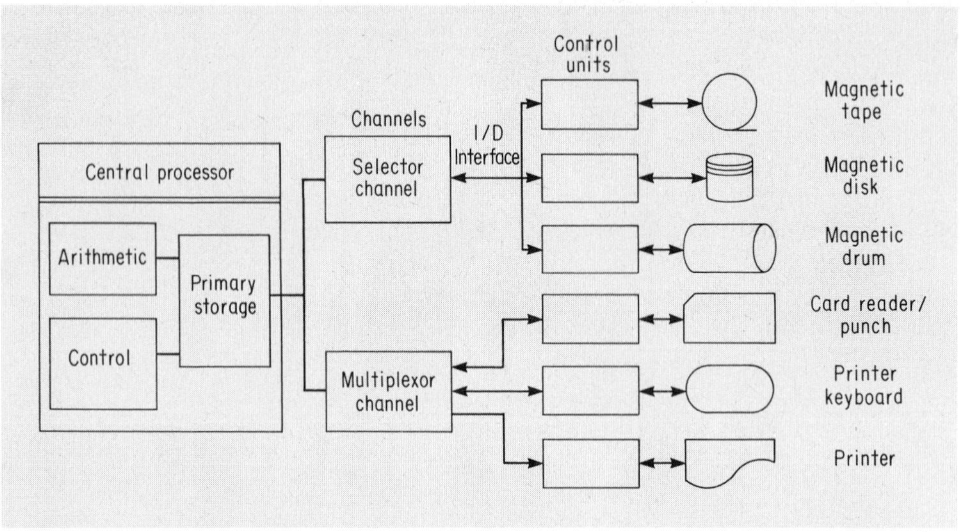

FIGURE 9-4. Use of data channels for input/output

computer systems. Through an assembly program, each macro-instruction is substituted for by a set of equivalent machine instructions, which are given to the computer for processing. Details on multichannel systems are presented in Chapter 12.

INPUT–OUTPUT PROGRAMMING

The instructions written for input–output devices to cause them to perform various functions vary in complexity, depending on the flexibility of the particular computer system. One approach uses symbolic instructions in cases where the computer has limited input–output capabilities. Another, newer approach relies on macroinstructions, which are either supplied by the manufacturer or written by the user's programming staff. Macroinstructions preclude the need for extensive coding of input and/or output operations; when the macroinstructions and related specifications have been written, an assembler substitutes a set of prewritten instructions in the object (final) program for each macroinstruction.

The IOCS is a standard routine designed to simplify input–output programming. It initiates and manipulates the input–output operations of a computer system. IOCS implementation simply involves writing specific macro-instructions. An OPEN macro-instruction, for example, initiates the use of a given file; a CLOSE macro-instruction specifies the termination of that file. To process a specific file record, the input GET (plus the name of the file) is all that is needed to carry out the operation. Writing a record requires a PUT (plus file name) instruction to do the job. This

File definition [1]		(written once at the beginning of the operation)
OPEN	________ file name	(written once at the beginning of the operation)
GET	________ file name	
•		(written once for each record to be processed)
•		
•		
PUT	________ file name	(written once for each record to be written)
•		
•		
•		
CLOSE	________ file name	(written once at the end of the operation)

[1] File definition generally includes specifications regarding the type of file and the device used, whether the file record to be processed is fixed or blocked, and the location in storage to which it should move.

FIGURE 9-5

approach simplifies input–output programming and yields the same results as if the input–output records were read or written individually. The sequence of macro-instructions used for a given file is shown in Fig. 9-5.

READING AND PUNCHING DEVICES

Punched-Card Reader

The punched-card reader is one of the more popular input devices used in small- to medium-sized systems. It is designed to read punched data, which are directly transferred to the central processing unit for processing. Once it is read, each card drops in its respective stacker to be picked up by the operator for later use (Fig. 9-6).

The two types of punched-card readers are (1) the brush type and (2) the photoelectric type. Figure 9-6 shows a brush-type punched-card reader that reads one card at a time. A stack of cards is first placed in the read hopper 9-edge first, face down. The first card in sequence passes underneath the first set of 80 reading brushes, called the *read–check* station (see Fig. 9-7). The brushes take a *hole count* to keep track of the number of holes in the card for checking purposes. The same card moves underneath the next set of 80 read brushes, which, after verifying the hole count made by the read-check brushes, directs the data electrically into the central processing unit. The card then drops into the stacker marked "normal read." The second card in sequence goes through the same procedure, and so forth, until the whole file is read.

FIGURE 9-6. *IBM 2450 brush-type card reader (right) and card punch (left)*

FIGURE 9-7. *Punched-card "read" and "punch" schematic of brush-type reader*

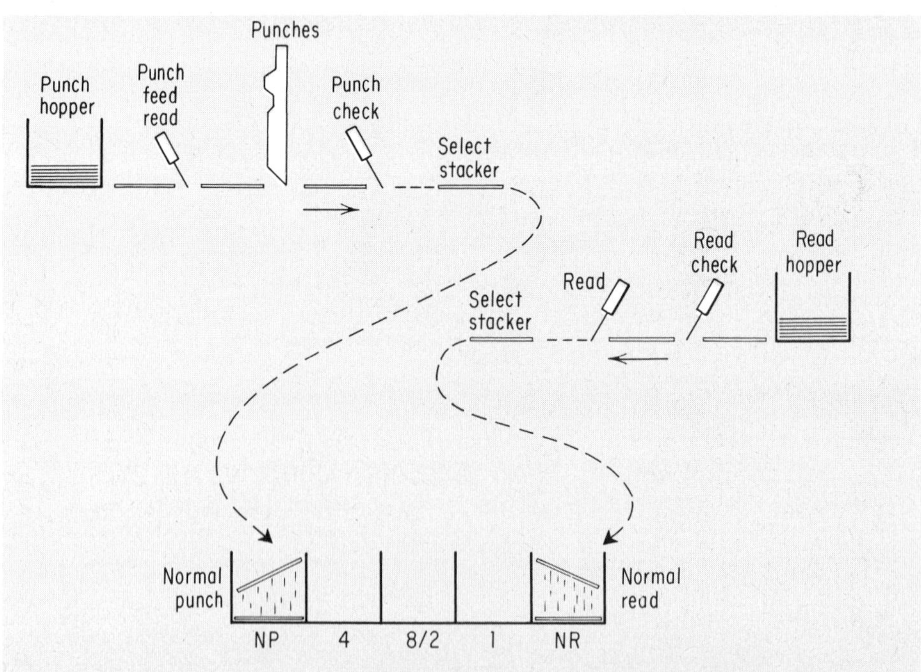

The photoelectric-type punched-card reader is the same as the brush type in that both machines sense holes in a card. The main difference lies in the method of sensing. The latter machine uses brushes to sense holes in a card; in the former, 80 photoelectric cells are activated as the punched card passes over a main light source. Figure 9-8 presents the IBM 3505 card reader, which reads cards *serially* (column by column) by a light-sensing unit and is capable of detecting invalid, off-punched, and mispositioned codes. This input device can be used with the IBM System 360 and System 370 series.

The left side of the punched-card reader (Figs. 9-6 and 9-7) is used for punching output information from the central processing unit into blank cards stacked in the punch hopper. A blank card moves automatically under the punch dies and the output is punched. The punched card then moves under a set of 80 brushes, which check on the accuracy of the punch dies. If they are correct, the card is ejected into the radial stacker below it. Otherwise, the machine stops, indicating an error. The IBM 2540 punches up to 300 cards per minute. Faster machines especially designed for card punching are also available.

Paper-Tape Reader

A paper-tape reader provides direct input to a computer by reading prepunched data in paper tape. It also provides output from a computer by punching output information in the same medium. Paper-tape systems are used most often in systems where information is received over wire communication circuits and in scientific applications involving limited

FIGURE 9-8. *IBM 2501 card reader (left) and schematic of light sensing (right)*

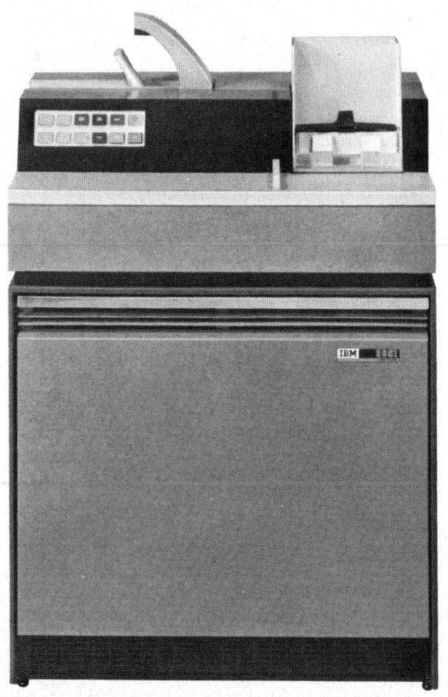

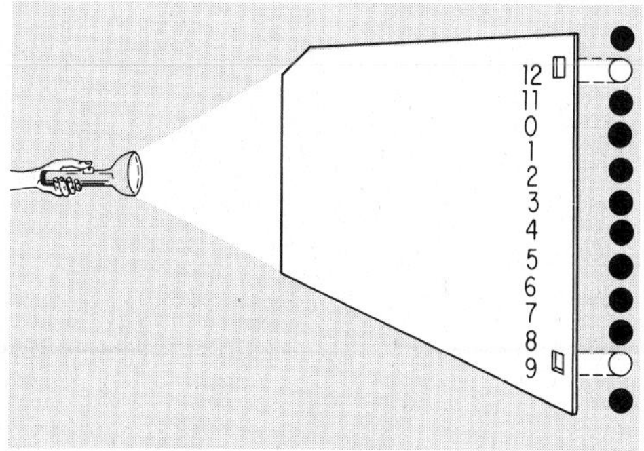

FIGURE 9-10. Paper tape to magnetic tape converter

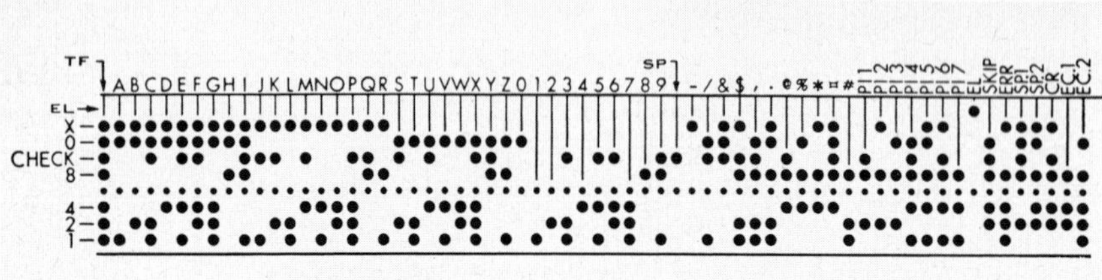

FIGURE 9-9. Paper tape 8-channel code

input and output. In the past, paper tape has not been widely used as an input–output medium because of the lack of tape-preparation devices. Most tapes had to be prepared manually or, in some cases, punched by units that provided limited flexibility. Currently, this difficulty has been overcome with relative success through the introduction of better punching devices. Although still comparatively less popular than other input–output media, paper tape is now being used more effectively than in the past.

Recording on paper tape is done by machines that punch data received by a direct connection to a typewriter or a key punch. Other machines may then transmit the data punched into the paper tape over telephone or telegraph lines in order to produce a duplicate tape at the other end of the line, where the duplicate can be used for further processing.

Data stored on paper tape are recorded in patterns of round punched holes located in parallel tracks (channels) along the length of the tape. Paper tapes vary according to the number of channels they contain. Most are either five or eight channels wide. Figure 9-9 shows the more common, eight-channel tape. A channel is an imaginary line that runs parallel to the edge of the tape. From the bottom, the channels are 1, 2, 4, 8, K, 0, and X. A numeric, alphabetic, or special character is represented by one or a combination of holes in a given vertical column.

There are many paper-tape readers, punches, and combination devices available. More recently, some manufacturers are offering paper tape to magnetic tape converters (Fig. 9-10). Punched paper tape has the advantage of easy and relatively compact storage. It takes less space for storage than does the punched card. Being light in weight, it is easier to handle and cheaper to mail. Also, it is more economical to use than punched cards because of the low cost of the tape and the transport units.

Compared to more advanced media, however, punched paper tape has been found to be very slow and as impractical as the punched card. The manual punching of coded information allows considerable possibility of error. Because it is made of paper, it is more likely to break during processing (giving rise to the expression a "torn-tape system"). Other disadvantages include the fact that paper tape cannot be split apart for sorting, collating, and other related operations as can a set of punched cards. Visual reading of punched paper tape is a problem for someone who is untrained, although there are certain machines that can interpret and print the characters from the paper tape in the same fashion that cards may be interpreted.

PRINTERS

Output information can be presented in many forms, depending on the output device or the user's requirements. One such device, the printer, is commonly used in business applications for providing a permanent visual record of the information generated by the computer. Depending on the type of printer, printing speed varies from 10 to 2,000 characters per second or up to 2,500 lines per minute.

Character-at-a-Time (Impact) Printers

TYPEWRITER. Computers are designed to print out data in several ways. Some employ serial (character-at-a-time) printing, whereas others use line-at-a-time printing. The electric typewriter is the simplest means of serial printing. Compared to other printing methods, however, the typewriter is very slow, printing at most 16 characters per second.

The typewriter can be used either as a remote terminal or, when it is linked on-line to a computer console, as a monitor printer. By typewriter, the computer is occasionally interrupted during the processing of given data. An inquiry may be made by "asking" it to disclose the balance or other data concerning a specific account. "Asking" the computer is done by keying in a code that tells it what to do and where to find the desired information. With the manipulation of certain switches or buttons, the inquiry is carried out and accurate results obtained. Other on-line uses of the typewriter include giving the computer proper substitutions for invalid data, inserting missing or new operating instructions into the stored program, resetting the system when an error condition causes the computer to halt, and instructing the console to select different input–output devices. The usefulness of the typewriter as an on-line device, then, lies in the fact that it can notify the computer of these conditions and exceptions (Fig. 9-11).

FIGURE 9-11. On-line typewriter used with the IBM 360 system

MATRIX PRINTER. In the matrix printer, small wires are arranged in the form of a rectangle, usually in a 5 by 7 matrix (Fig. 9-12). The matrix moves along the line of the paper to print alphabetic, numeric, or special characters. The ends of the selected wires are pressed by a hammer against an inked ribbon, resulting in the printing of the data on paper.

TELETYPE PRINTER. Another character-at-a-time printer, the teletype printer employs a type square (a matrix) that contains the necessary alphabetic, numeric, and special characters. As the matrix stops at each character, a hammer behind the designated character strikes it against an inked ribbon, which in turn imprints it on the paper. Maximum operational speed for this type of printing is 10 characters per second.

FIGURE 9-12. Arrangement of wire-matrix printer—digit 5

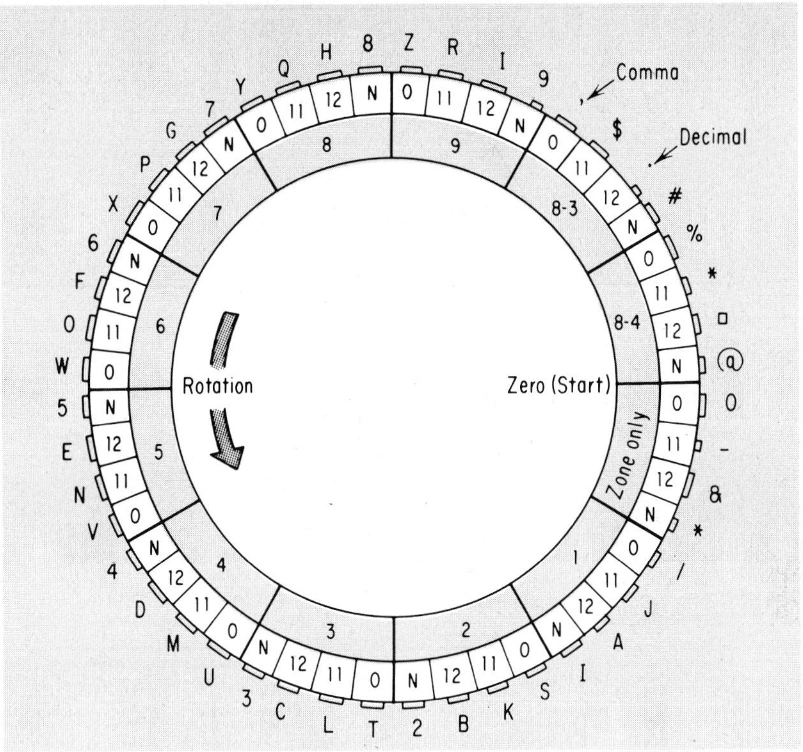

FIGURE 9-13. *Printwheel*

Line-at-a-Time (Impact) Printers

Wheel Printer. The wheel printer consists of 120 printwheels, each containing 10 digits, 26 letters, and 12 special characters (Fig. 9-13). The printwheels are aligned horizontally along the width of the paper and are positioned to print simultaneously. This means that a parallel method of printing is used and that up to 120 characters can be printed on a given line at a rated speed of 150 lines per minute.

Chain Printer. The chain printer is an electromechanical printer that utilizes five sections connected together to form a chain. Each section has the capacity to print 48 characters—10 digits, 26 letters, and 12 special characters (Fig. 9-14). The chain revolves horizontally and is positioned behind the inked ribbon. The hammers, upon firing against the back of the paper, cause a character in the chain to press against the ribbon, which results in the printing of that character on the form. Figure 9-14 shows the IBM 3211 printer, which is ideally suited for the IBM 370 system printout.

Unlike other printers, line printers offer the features of accuracy and speed. Each line printer has an error-check indicator that stops and signals

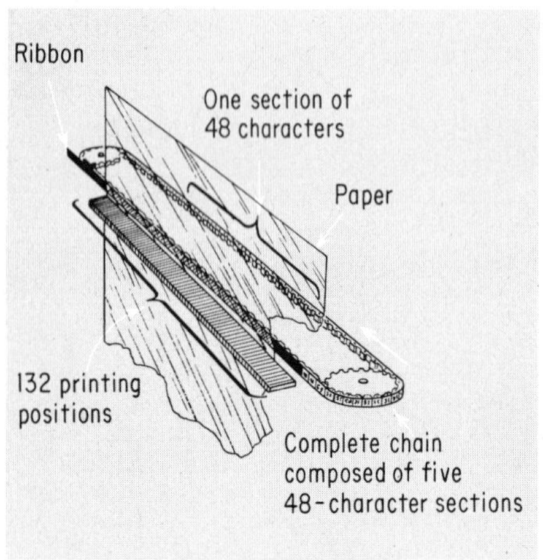

FIGURE 9-14. IBM print chain (left) and the IBM 3211 chain printer (Courtesy IBM)

to the operator in the event of inaccurate printing of the data received from the central processing unit. The same error indication is also signaled on the computer's console. In terms of speed, many line printers have been operating at 1,000 or more lines per minute. The new IBM 3211 printer is capable of printing 2,500 lines per minute. This means that $1\frac{1}{2}$ million pages can be printed [2] on a three-shift, 600-hour-per-month basis. This much output serves as a warning to management of the obvious waste of computer time and system effectiveness that will occur unless proper planning and justification of computer use are made in advance.

Xerographic and Electronic Printers

From the foregoing discussion, it can be concluded that the hammer impact action of line printers is quite an improvement over the action of serial printers in terms of accuracy and speed. However, despite the recent improvement in speed, the relatively slow mechanical action of the hammers is incompatible with the much greater speed and efficiency of

[2] The answer is derived as follows:
Size of paper form = 10 × 14 inches
Number of lines per inch = 6 (or 60 lines per page)
2,500 × 60 = 150,000 lines per hour
150,000 = 2,500 pages per hour
60 (lines per page)
2,500 × 600 hours = 1,500,000 pages per month

the computer. To bridge the speed gap, xerographic and electronic printers have been developed.

In xerographic printing, small ferrite particles are deposited on a special paper by the action of an electronic signal. The process follows steps similar to those used in Xerox copying machines in common use in many business offices.

An electronic printer functions on the principle of shooting an electronic beam through a mask containing various alphanumeric characters. On the opposite side of the mask, a photographic film captures the characters projected by the electronic beam. A developing device later is used to convert the film data into hard copy. This electronic printing device has a speed of close to 64,000 lines per minute, or some 38 million (64,000 × 600 hours) pages of output per month.

Although electronic-beam printing is the fastest method available, it does not compete with line printing for quality of output or convenience when several copies are required. Since electronic printing is one-copy printing, the procedure has to be repeated from the beginning for more copies of the same output data.

SPECIAL-PURPOSE OUTPUT DEVICES

Various specialized projects require attachment of an output device especially designed for the job. One device, known to civil engineers and draftsmen, is the *graph plotter,* which produces free-form [3] pictorial configurations under the direct control of the computer (Fig. 9-15).

[3] The other type of graph plotter plots a diagram with the constraint of *X* and *Y* coordinates. This is called an *X–Y* plotter.

FIGURE 9-15. *A graph plotter*

A graph plotter is simply a paper-holding drawing board with a mechanical pen suspended over it. When plotting begins, the pen is lowered to the surface of the paper and makes various lines in different locations. Recently, an attempt has been made to plot dress designs through the computer. When the plotter has completed its pictorial representation of the proposed dress, the picture is fed into the computer for evaluation. The plotter is then directed to plot separate sewing, cutting, and related diagrams for each dress size.

Plotters are not only used in civil engineering, drafting, and dress design, but they are also becoming popular in medicine. They have been successfully utilized to plot human brains and skeletons with a high degree of accuracy. There is also an increasing trend toward the use of plotters for graphic output in oil, geophysical, and oceanographic applications, and in computer art.

Generally, graph plotters plot limited amounts of information, are slow, and require the manual replacement of paper after every diagram has been completed.

In addition to graph plotters, computer-output-to-microfilm (COM) and voice-response devices (especially display boards) have been popular. Voice-response devices generate human voice from a prerecorded set of words stored in memory. They are essential in man–machine communication and in future audio-response systems. Display boards have become common fixtures in such places as brokerage houses and airline and bus terminals. Their appeal is primarily due to their ability to project immediate output concerning the desired information or the particular situation at hand. Details on the devices are covered in the next two chapters.

MAGNETIC TAPE INPUT AND OUTPUT

Business data-processing applications involve thousands of transactions and a large volume of related data. A large-scale computer is not designed to store such volume in memory and still provide enough room for processing. Although access time would improve significantly, the cost of building a computer large enough to eliminate the need for secondary storage would be prohibitive. Thus, secondary storage media, such as magnetic tape and magnetic disk, are essential for efficient functioning, especially in larger-sized computer systems. In the following sections we discuss secondary storage media and devices, and provide an overview of magnetic drum, magnetic strip and card, and laser memory devices.

Primary Characteristics of Magnetic Tape

Magnetic tape is a widely used secondary storage medium. In addition to its high-speed read-in and write-out, it offers the unique advantage of storing hundreds of characters on 1 inch of tape. Like the tape used in home tape recorders, data on computer tape may be erased and the tape reused repetitively, thus making it one of the most economical and versatile forms of storage.

Today's magnetic tape is manufactured to meet rigid specifications. It is made of plastic, coated on one side with a metallic oxide.[4] The oxide can be easily magnetized and retains its magnetism indefinitely. Bits of data in the form of magnetic *spots* are recorded on the oxide side of the tape by the read–write heads of the tape unit. The spots, which are invisible to the human eye, are placed across the width of the tape on parallel tracks running along the entire length of the tape. Although the tape length of each reel varies from system to system, it is usually either 2,400 or 3,600 feet. Tape width varies also; however, $\frac{1}{2}$-, $\frac{3}{4}$-, and 1-inch widths are the most popular.

Magnetic tape is a *sequential* file storage medium, which means that the first record written on it must be read or scanned before the second record, the second before the third, and so forth. Sequential file storage is ideal when regular updating of applications such as accounts receivable is required. Time is not wasted, because the computer does not have to search for a specific record; each customer's account is in sequential order. In applications that require the reading of records scattered throughout the tape, access time is slower and the use of magnetic tape is impractical.

Data Representation

Data are usually recorded on magnetic tape in seven or nine parallel tracks or channels. In either case, the pattern of magnetized spots across the width and along the length of the tape is a *coded representation* of the data stored on it. These spots are magnetized in one of two directions of polarity, indicating either a 0 bit or a 1 bit to correspond to the pulses received from the computer.

In the *seven-channel code*,[5] the first six channels (tracks) across the width of the tape represent one column of data (frame) or one character. In Figure 9-16, a dash stands for the presence of a magnetic spot or 1 bit and a blank represents a 0 bit. The 1 and 0 bits are used together to code alphabetic, numeric, or special characters.

Most third-generation computers use a nine-channel code, or the extended binary-coded decimal interchange code (EBCDIC), as shown

[4] In a more expensive tape, a very thin coat of polyester on top of the oxide inhibits wear. Despite this added protection, a certain amount of wear occurs over time.

[5] The 7-bit code has been explained in more detail in Chapter 7.

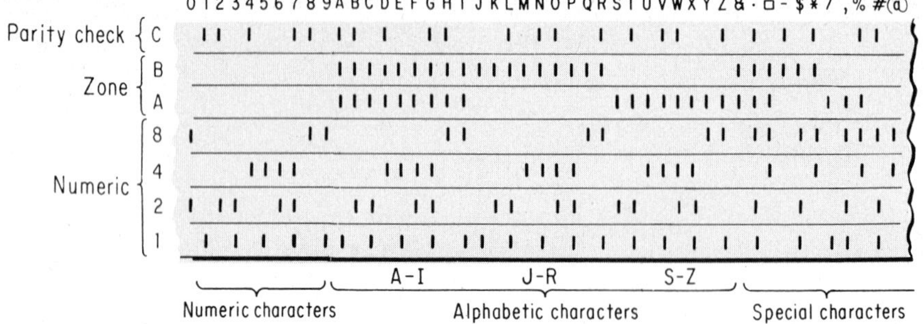

FIGURE 9-16. *Seven-bit alphanumeric code*

Track No.	Equivalent 7-Track Tape Code Position	0	1	2	3	4	A	B	....Z
9	8								I
8	2			I	I			I	
7	added zone	I	I	I	I	I	I	I	I
6	added zone	I	I	I	I	I	I	I	I
5	B	I	I	I	I	I			I
4	check (odd)	I			I				
3	A	I	I	I	I	I			
2	1		I		I		I		I
1	4					I			

FIGURE 9-17. *Nine-channel code*

in Fig. 9-17. The code uses four numeric tracks (1, 2, 4, 8), a parity check, and four (versus two) zone positions. The additional two zone bits are used in coding lowercase alphabetical and other special characters. Note that the arrangement of the tracks is not in sequential order. The most frequently used tracks are clustered toward the center of the tape so as to protect the data they carry from dirt, dust, or physical damage to the outer edges of the tape.

Other computers use a *packed-decimal* design in a 10-track format, which utilizes 8 BCD numeric bits and 2 check bits (Fig. 9-18). In contrast to the seven-track tape, two characters can be recorded in a single column, thus doubling the use of available storage spots.

Parity Check

Six channels are adequate for recording numeric, alphabetic, and/or special characters. However, the seventh channel in a seven-channel code is needed for checking the coding of the other channels. Magnetic spots

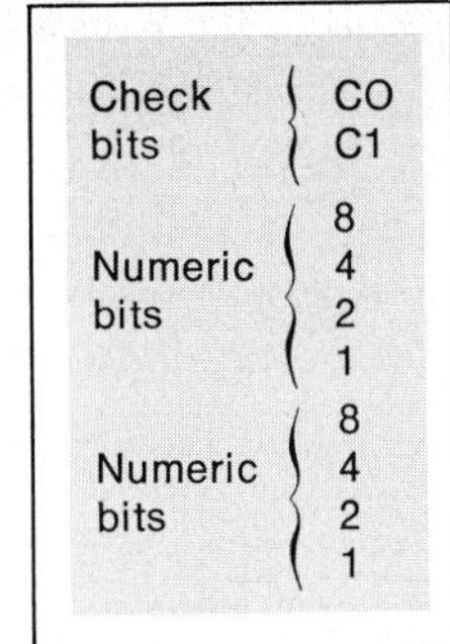

FIGURE 9-18. Ten-track coding-packed format

on tape can be erased accidentally or obscured because of dust, dirt, or cracking of the oxide coating. To ascertain the correctness of data during tape reading or tape writing, the number of magnetized spots, or 1 bits, representing each character are counted. This process is called a *parity check*.

In Fig. 9-16, the magnetized spots, or 1 bits, in positions 1, 2, 4, 8, A, and B are counted vertically. If the total is odd, a magnetic spot is made in the parity check (C) channel on the top. However, if the total number of 1 bits in the six channels is even, nothing is recorded in the C channel. This arrangement is called *even parity check* or *even parity*. Each character is represented on the tape by an even number of 1 bits, because the computer cannot operate if they are odd.

A question commonly raised is what would happen if 2 bits were lost for one character instead of 1 bit, making the count even, so that the computer could not detect the loss by an even parity check. Although such an occurrence is rare, it is avoided by using a horizontal parity check on each record. In this case, the machine counts the number of 1 bits in each of the seven channels. At the end of the record, a check character is added to each channel containing an odd number of 1 bits. Therefore, during readout, parity check is active vertically per column and horizontally per channel.

Instead of even parity check, some machines follow *odd parity check*, as is the case in the nine-channel code (Fig. 9-17). The idea is the same except that a check character is made in the check channel only when the total number of 1 bits representing a given character is even. Here, an even number of bits causes the machine to signal an error and stop the operation.

Packing Density

Packing density refers to the greatest number of columns of data that can be recorded on a unit length of tape, usually 1 inch. Depending on the type of magnetic-tape unit used, data may be recorded at tape speeds ranging from 36 to 200 (commonly 36, 75, or 112.5) inches per second and densities of 200, 556, or 800 characters per inch.[6] The new IBM 370 computer uses a magnetic-tape unit capable of storing 1,600 characters per inch. At this superhigh density, the content of 20 80-column fully punched cards can be stored on 1 inch of tape at approximately one tenth the cost of previous systems. Total storage capacity would be 40 million characters (or the equivalent of 500,000 punched cards) on a 2,400-foot tape. The capacity of single tape reels ranges from 1 million to 43 million characters, depending on both tape speed and density. Steady improvements in effective transmission rate (speed times density) have been made over the years and are likely to continue in the future.

Tape Format

The format of a magnetic-tape run is typically as follows: (1) the load point, (2) the header control label, (3) main information, (4) trailer control label, and (5) the end-of-file indicator (Fig. 9-19).

LOAD POINT. Measuring about 1 by $\frac{3}{16}$ inch, the load point is a reflective spot coated on one side with magnetic material and on the other side with adhesive. Photoelectric cells in the tape unit sense the label and interpret it as the beginning of the usable portion of the tape, where writing or reading is to start. A space of at least 10 feet from the beginning of the tape is recommended for the load-point location. Usually, it is located between 12 and 15 feet from the beginning of the tape.

HEADER CONTROL LABEL. Located between the load-point indicator and the first data record, the header control label identifies the tape contents, specifies the program to be used, and provides other information to prevent accidental erasure of the contents of the tape. When the pro-

[6] Graham Magnetics, Inc., developed a new magnetic particle called "Cobalog," which allows a packing density of up to 8,000 bits per inch. When a new magnetic tape drive is developed to handle this super-high-density tape, it should be a welcome addition for the large-scale computer user.

FIGURE 9-19. Tape format

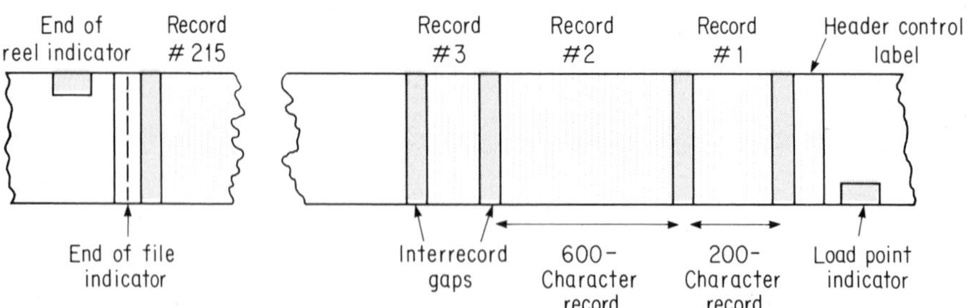

gram is loaded into the computer, the first instruction commands the computer to record the description of the reel of tape, to see if it is the intended application. The tape unit rotates the reel and moves the tape under the read head. If the description read is the same as the one written in the program, the application continues and the data on that tape will be processed. Otherwise, the computer stops and the programmer then diagnoses the nature of the error. If the tape used pertains to a different application, he will have to rewind the tape, take it out of the unit drive, and replace it with the correct tape.

TRAILER CONTROL LABEL. Located between the last data record and the end-of-file indicator, the trailer control label contains the number of blocks in the total file so that a check can be made at the end of processing to make sure that no blocks were overlooked.

END-OF-FILE INDICATOR. Located next to the trailer control label, the end-of-file indicator marks the end of usable tape (Fig. 9-19).

MAIN INFORMATION. The main information can be located anywhere between the header control label and the end-of-file indicator. Records on tape are not restricted to a fixed length, as is the case in a punched card. A record can be of any length within the area of the tape used for writing records.

One record or a block of records is separated from another by a space, referred to as an *interrecord gap* (IRG) (Fig. 9-20). The IRG varies in width from 1/4 to 1 inch, with 6/10 or 3/4 inch being the most common gaps. The gap serves to separate one logical tape record from another, and allows for the waste of tape caused by acceleration and deceleration every time a new record is read. The gap between records is made automatically.

When each logical record on a tape is one block, it is called a *single-record block* (Fig. 9-20). Normally, it is at least 14 characters in size. To illustrate, assume a $\frac{3}{4}$-inch interrecord gap and tape records each averaging

FIGURE 9-20. *Example of interrecord gap and single-record block*

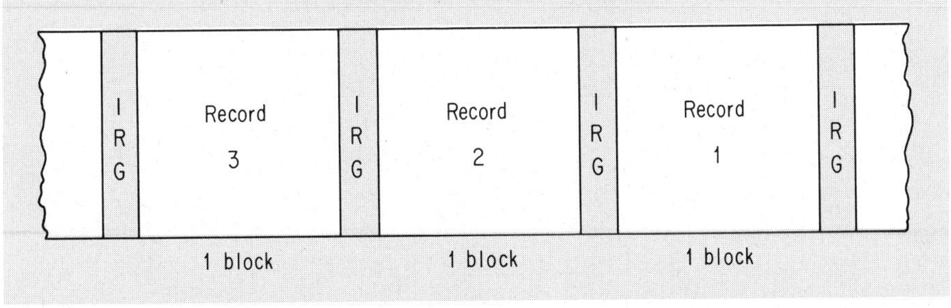

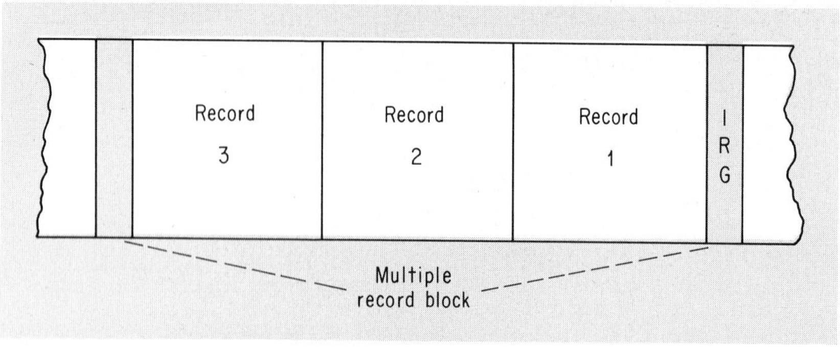

Record 3 | Record 2 | Record 1 | IRG

Multiple record block

FIGURE 9-21. Example of a multiple-record block

55 characters, written at a density of 550 characters per inch. This means that each record is stored on 1/10 inch of tape and is bordered by two interrecord gaps, which occupy $1\frac{1}{2}$ inches of tape. Clearly, much of the tape consists of interrecord gaps or blanks. To solve this problem, a multiple-record block approach is used: a group of logical records is written as one block with an interrecord gap before and after the block (Fig. 9-21). Thus, *blocking* saves tape and speeds data input (especially if the records are short), since the tape unit will accelerate and decelerate less frequently. All the recordings in a given block are read before the machine pauses.

One or more tape reels may be required to record a business application. A tape reel may contain one or more blocks and a tape block may consist of one or more logical records. Figure 9-22 presents a schematic of an accounts receivable application, showing the points just mentioned.

In determining the performance of a tape unit, the following factors must be considered: tape speed, tape density, size of the IRG, rewind speed, start–stop delay time, and the unit's ability to read and write. Although only the first three factors determine the rate of data transfer, all the factors mentioned have some bearing in the final evaluation process and must be geared to both the existing computer system and the size and volume of applications at hand.

Magnetic Tape Unit

The magnetic tape unit operates as both an input and output device. It transports tape from one reel to another as the tape passes the read–write head(s) while actually reading or writing information (Fig. 9-23).

In preparing the reading or writing operation, the data tape or file tape reel is mounted (loaded) on the left side and an empty reel, called the *take-up* or machine reel, is mounted on the right side. The tape from

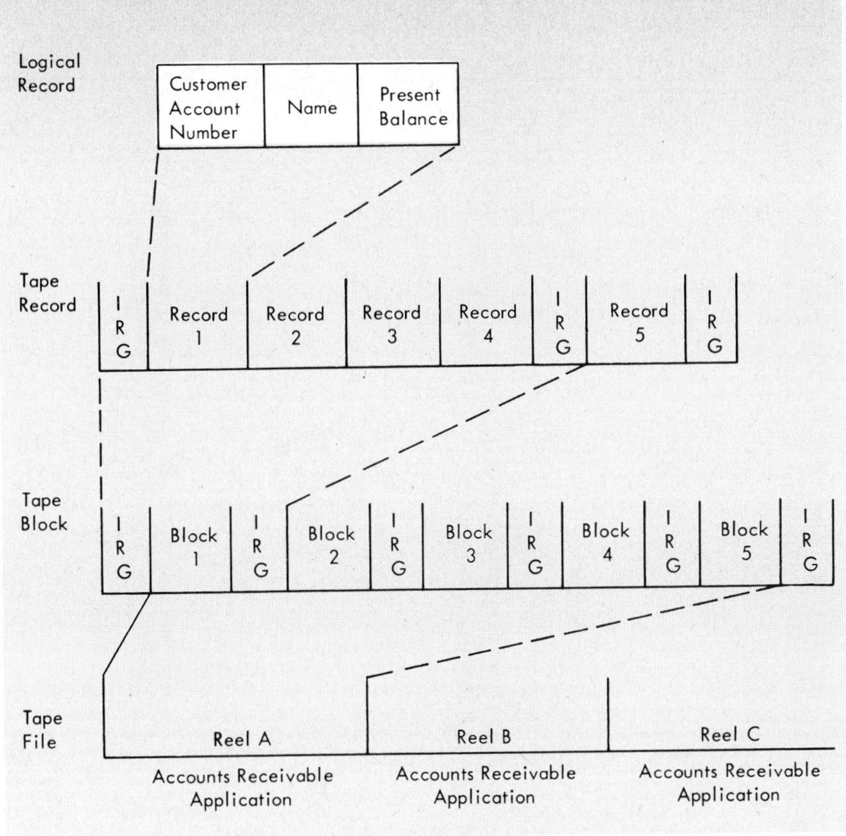

FIGURE 9-22. *Magnetic tape format of an accounts-receivable application*

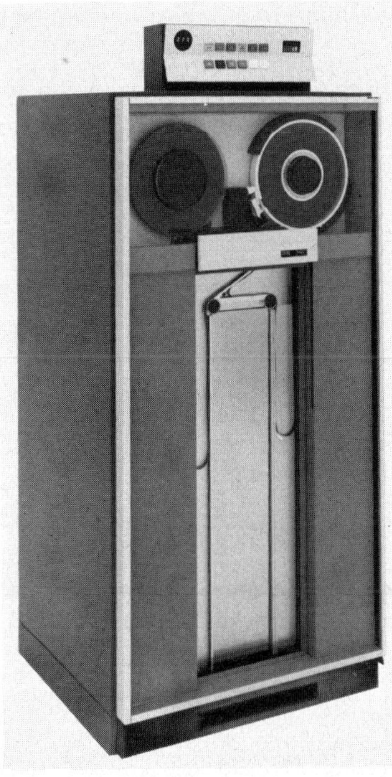

FIGURE 9-23. *IBM 3420 magnetic tape unit (Courtesy IBM)*

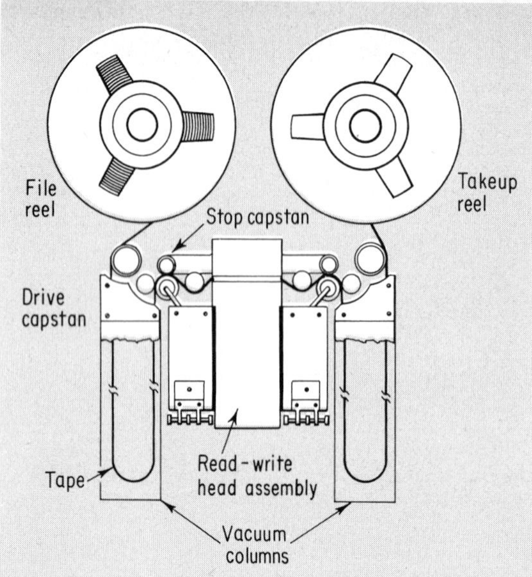

FIGURE 9-24

the left reel is threaded past the read–write heads[7] to the take-up reel. Because of the high speed involved in starting and stopping, a loop in the tape drops (floats) into each vacuum tube acting as a buffer against tape breakage. The resulting slack absorbs tape tension during the sudden burst of speed generated by a read instruction from the computer. When the tape loop in the right vacuum tube begins to reach the bottom, an electronic eye actuates the take-up reel to absorb the slack automatically. As the tape in the left vacuum tube is drawn by the take-up reel, it is replenished by the file reel immediately above it (Fig. 9-24).

When a reading or writing operation has been completed, the data tape is wound around the take-up reel. The operator must rewind the tape and store it on the original reel, leaving the take-up reel empty for the next application. The IBM 7340 hypertape drive, model 3, is a high-performance tape unit, capable of providing data at the rate of 340,000 characters per second. Among its unique features is an automatic cartridge loader designed to automatically unload a processed reel and load the next reel in less than 45 seconds under program control (Fig. 9-25).

Processing Magnetic Tape Files

Magnetic tape file processing is characterized by collecting a suitable batch of transactions and sequencing the batch in the same order as the

[7] Read–write heads are either single-gap or dual-gap. In the more popular dual-gap read–write head, the read gap reads the data that have been written by the write gap for verification—a distinct advantage over the single-gap read–write head, which lacks this feature.

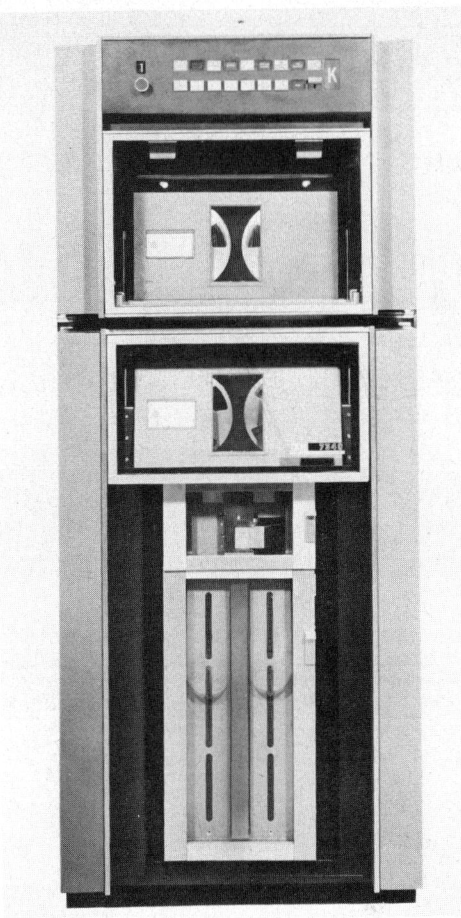

FIGURE 9-25. IBM 7340 hypertape drive unit with automatic cartridge loader (Courtesy of IBM)

master file before processing. Master records are processed against transaction records by a series of comparisons: the computer compares a master record with a transaction record for equality. Master records having the same identification number as the transaction records are processed (updated) and are rewritten on a new tape; unaffected master records are merely copied. Any out-of-sequence records are individually handled before further processing is made. The old master file and transaction tapes are kept until the processing cycle is accurately completed. During the next processing cycle, the updated master file is used as input with a new batch of transactions, as shown in Fig. 9-26.

To illustrate a typical magnetic tape processing run, assume that the master-record tape consists of four logical records identified as M(01), M(02), M(03), and M(04), and the transaction-record tape consists of four logical records identified as T(01), T(03), T(04), and T(04) (Fig. 9-27). Processing these records requires the preparation of a computer program similar in general form to the one shown in Fig. 9-28.

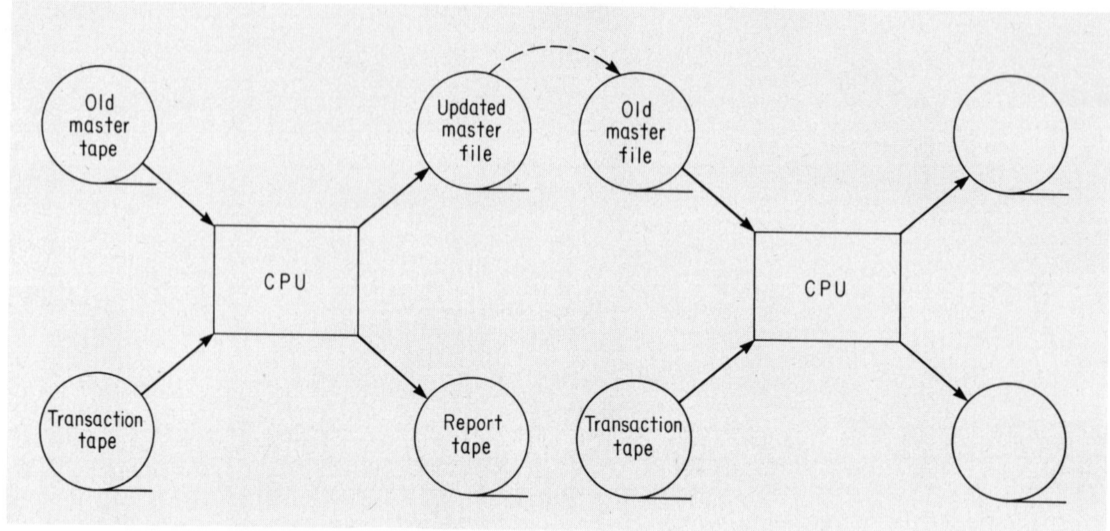

FIGURE 9-26. Processing magnetic tape files

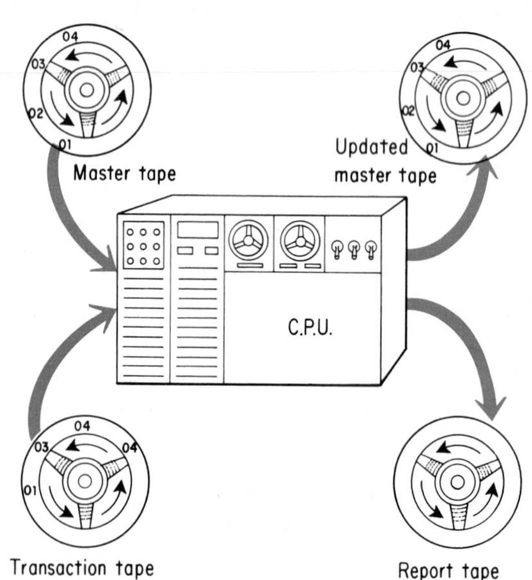

FIGURE 9-27 Processing magnetic tape files—an example

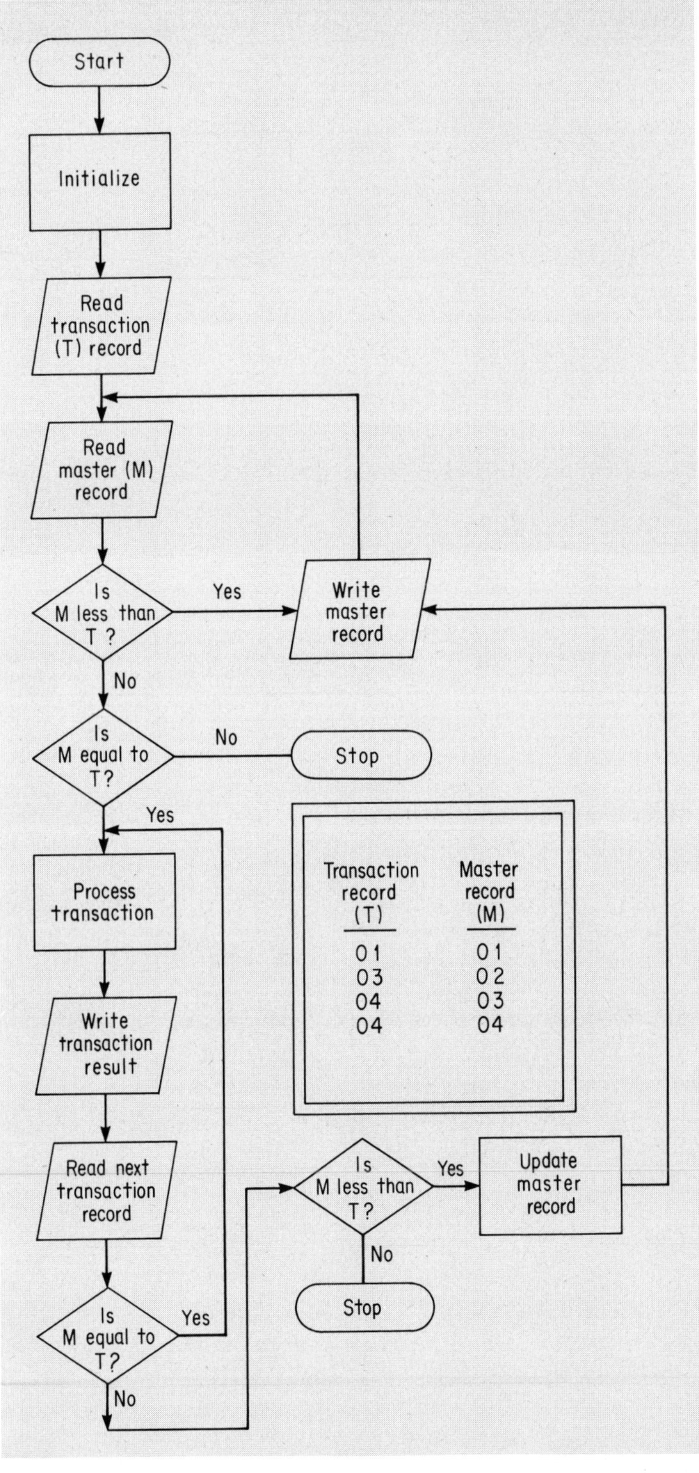

FIGURE 9-28. *General flowchart of a tape processing run*

When the program is loaded and the processing cycle begins, the following steps take place:

1. T(01) and M(01) are read and their identification numbers are compared for equality. Since they are equal, the transaction is processed and an output record of it is written.
2. T(03) is read and, having an identification number greater than M(01), causes M(01) to be updated, and master record M(01) to be written on the output tape.
3. M(02) is read and T(03) is compared with M(02). M(02), having a smaller identification number than T(03), is copied on the output tape, and M(03) is read next.
4. T(03) is equal to M(03). Therefore, the transaction is processed and an output record of it is written.
5. T(04) is read and, having an identification number greater than M(03), causes M(03) to be updated, and master record M(03) to be copied on the output tape.
6. M(04) is read and T(04) is compared with M(04). Since they are equal, the transaction is processed and an output record is written.
7. The last T(04) is read; T(04) and M(04) are again equal, so the transaction is processed and an output record of it is written. Since it is the last transaction and the end of the operation, M(04) is updated, and master record M(04) is written on the output tape.

Today's output tape becomes tomorrow's input tape for file processing. Today's input tape is filed away for future reference.

Sorting Magnetic Tape Files

As mentioned earlier, a magnetic tape file must be in sequence before processing. Because tape records cannot be physically sorted, the computer is used for that purpose. Records written on magnetic tape are sorted by interfiling blocks of sequential records into longer blocks until one large block or sequence of logical records is achieved. To illustrate this method, suppose that we have a magnetic tape containing 20 records. The identification number of each record is shown in Fig. 9-29. Sequencing the 20 records involves the following passes:

Pass 1: Break input tape A into two tapes (B and C), as shown in Fig. 30. Note that the first five records, the next six records, and the remaining nine records are in sequence. The procedure involves writing the first batch of five sequential records on tape B and then switching to tape C for writing the next batch of six sequential records. The next nine sequential records are switched to tape B, thus completing the first pass. In an operation involving many batches of sequential records, switching from one tape to another continues until the last batch has been written.

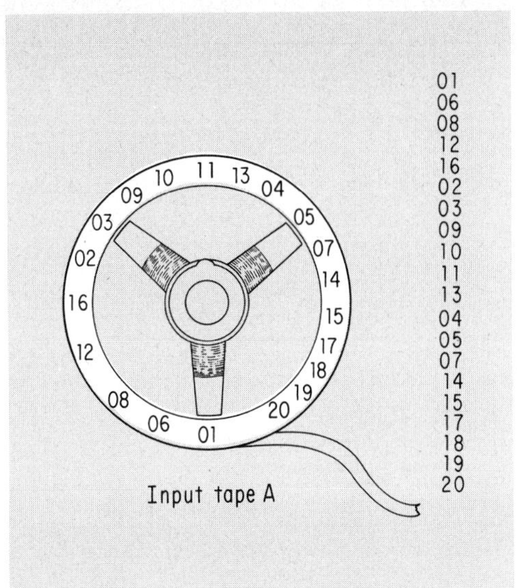

FIGURE 9-29. Block of 20 records on tape A, before interfiling

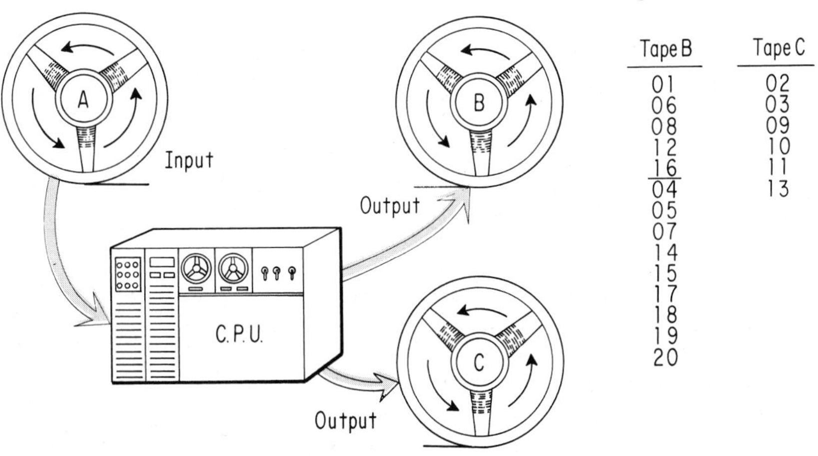

FIGURE 9-30. Sorting tape records—pass 1

Pass 2: Before pass 2 begins, tape A is removed and stored for future reference. A new tape (referred to as tape D) replaces tape A, and an additioanl tape (tape E) is also mounted. In this pass, tapes B and C are the input tapes and tapes D and E are the output tapes (Fig. 9-31). The first batch of 11 sequential records on tapes B and C is merged and written on tape D, followed by writing on tape E the second batch of nine merged sequential records. In other words, the first batch of tapes B and C (01, 06, 08, 12, and 16 of tape B and 02, 03, 09, 10, 11, and 13 of tape C) is merged in ascending sequence and written on tape D (Fig. 9-31). The second batch (in this example, the remaining nine records of tape B in Fig. 9-30) is copied on tape E.

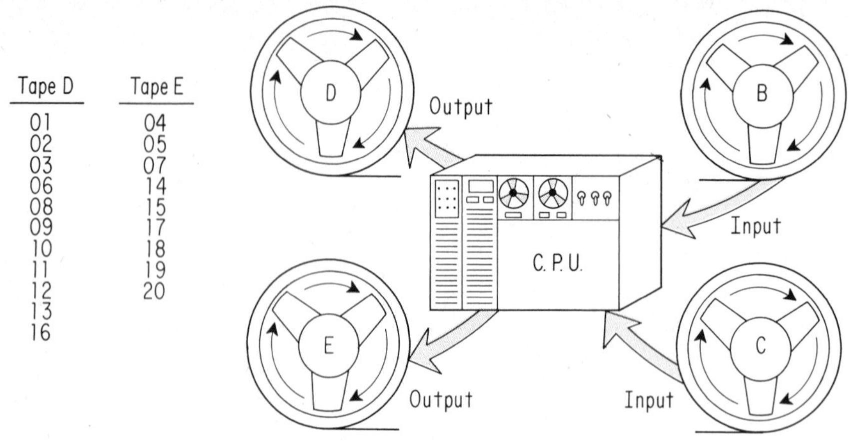

FIGURE 9-31. *Sorting tape records—pass 2*

Pass 3: A third pass is needed to merge the two sets of records on tapes D and E into one sequence. Tapes D and E now become the input tapes, and a new tape (tape F) becomes the output tape. Since there is only one batch of sequenced records on each tape, it is merged in one final pass and is written on tape F (Fig. 9-32).

Advantages of Magnetic Tape

COMPACT STORAGE. The compactness of magnetic tape permits data to be written at a density of 1,600 characters per inch or the equivalent of the contents of 20 fully punched cards. A 2,400-foot reel of tape can store up to 40,000,000 characters and can be filed in one drawer.

FIGURE 9-32. *Sorting tape records—pass 3*

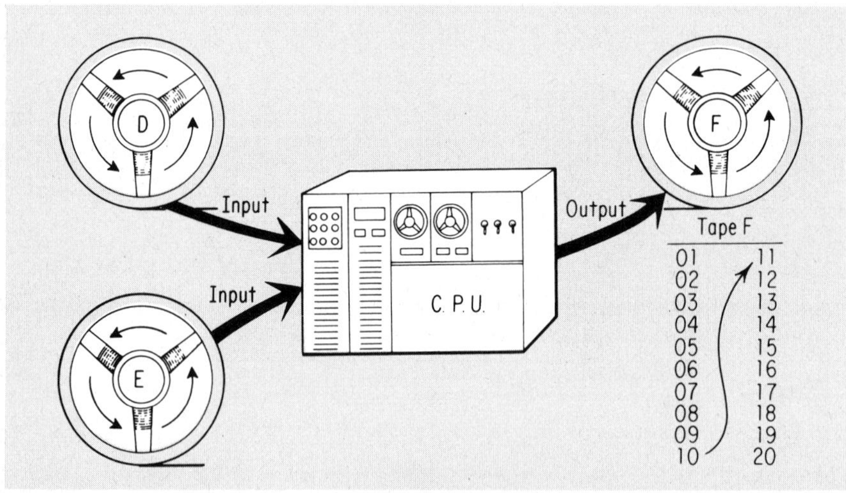

If these data were permanently stored on 80-column punch cards, 500,000 cards would be required. Several file cabinets and much floor space would be needed.

Ease of Handling. Cards, although of convenient size, are bulkier than tape. It is much more convenient to handle a reel of tape than thousands of cards. Recording on tape also is much easier than recording on cards, since each card must be handled separately by the machine or by a human operator.

More Efficient Unit Record. Punched cards are limited to 80 or 96 columns of data storage. The use of magnetic tape as a unit record is more flexible; more freedom is gained because each record can be as long or as short as desired. The only limiting factor is the length of the tape itself.

Saving in Recording Data for Storage. Once punched with certain data, a card cannot be used again for recording different data. By contrast, magnetic tape can be erased and used over and over again for recording any kind of data, which means considerable saving in the cost of recording data for storage.

Correction of Errors. In keypunching, a mispunched hole in a card cannot be removed. To make corrections the card is destroyed and a new one is punched with the correct data. On magnetic tape, a mistake can easily be erased and replaced with the correct data. No other data in the record in which the mistake occurred need to be rewritten or duplicated, as would be the case in the punched card.

Reduced Cost. The character density of tape makes it a low-cost storage medium. Storing equivalent amounts of data on any other storage medium requires a substantially larger investment. For instance, a $35 reel of tape would store the same amount of data as punched cards costing approximately $325.00. Because of its low cost and high capacity for data storage, the use of magnetic tape has been steadily on the increase. It has been estimated that over 30 million reels of tape were used in 1972, with some users holding as many as 30,000 reels in their tape libraries.

High Speed. Magnetic tape is the fastest form of direct input and output medium available to computer users. Magnetic-tape units make up the chief secondary storage components of medium- and large-scale computer systems. High speed is attained despite limitations imposed on all forms of input and output equipment because of the mechanical parts used in their construction.

SLOW ACCESS TIME. A magnetic tape is often described as a very long, thin memory. That is, to find specific data on the tape, read–write heads must start scanning the tape from the beginning. This takes time, since the only data immediately available to the computer are those located under the heads. Naturally, if read–write heads could be used so that each set could read a separate section of the reel tape, the time taken to locate wanted data would be considerably reduced.

PHYSICAL AND ENVIRONMENTAL WEAKNESSES. Dust is one of the great enemies of magnetic tape and can cause reading or writing errors. Heat and humidity can cause separation of the oxide coating from the plastic base of the tape, destroying the data completely. For this reason, a computer department in which magnetic tape is used for input and output must install air conditioning in the computer room to maintain constant control over humidity, temperature, and dust or any other foreign particles that might damage the data stored on tape. A "No Smoking" sign is used in most computer departments, although it is often conveniently ignored.

TAPE BREAKAGE. When tape breaks, some data will be destroyed regardless of how neatly and carefully the tape is spliced, because of the density at which data are recorded.

Tape Handling and Storage

A business firm converting from punched-card or other systems to a tape system frequently retains its present employees to operate the new equipment. Because of the special characteristics of tape, the company must train its personnel in handling the equipment, and include instructions in the proper handling, control, and storage of tape. Some points to consider in tape storage and handling are

1. Accidental dropping or careless handling of a tape reel often causes nicks or kinks and, in time, will affect the recording or reading quality of the data. A damaged tape is as inferior as a chipped or broken phonograph disk.
2. When not in use, a magnetic tape reel should be supported at the hub, especially when it is in storage. Otherwise, it may warp and lose its efficiency.
3. While the tape unit is in operation, its door must always remain closed to prevent any foreign particles from entering and interfering with the processing of vital data. Even when the tape is mounted on the machine, the plastic tape container must remain closed to prevent dust or dirt from accumulating in it.
4. The top of the tape unit must not be used for a working area, as objects left on it might interfere with the efficiency of the cooling system or block the heat discharged by the unit's blowers.

5. In tape control, some form of visual identification must be made. A typical computer department might have hundreds of tape reels related to its applications. Since one reel of tape on file looks the same as any other reel, an external label is used to describe the data recorded on the tape. It shows the tape serial number, reel number, date of application, type of application (payroll, accounts receivable, accounts payable, etc.), number of times the tape has been passed through the machine, and the name of the programmer who made up the stored program. An index also can be made (by serial number or by type of application) of all the reels available. When a processing run becomes necessary, the librarian or the programmer merely looks for the label for proper identification of the correct reel.
6. Accidental destruction of recorded data is avoided by placing a plastic "ring" in the groove of the reel. The saying, "No ring—no write," among console operators simply means that the tape unit always reads data from the reel of tape unless a plastic ring is inserted in its groove, permitting the tape unit to write data on tape (Fig. 9-33).

When the program is loaded into the computer, the first instruction commands the computer to record the description of the reel of tape, to see if it is the intended application. The tape unit rotates the reel and moves the tape under the read heads. If the description read is the same as the one written in the program, the application continues and the data on that tape will be processed. Otherwise, the computer stops and the operator then diagnoses the nature of the error. If the tape used pertains to a different application, he will have to rewind the tape, take it out of the unit drive, and replace it with the correct tape.

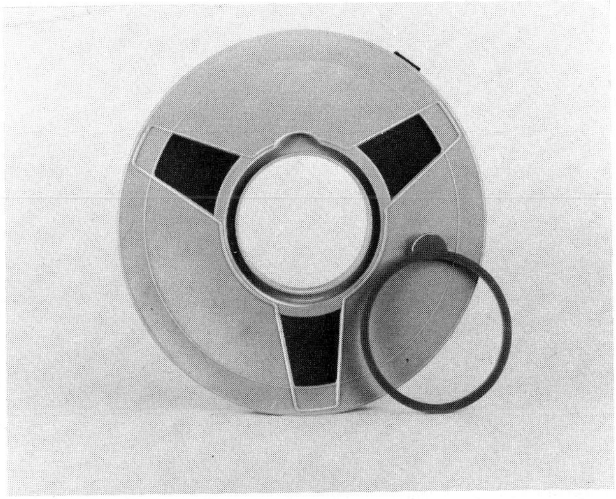

FIGURE 9-33. IBM protective file ring (Courtesy IBM)

Are Magnetic Tapes Vulnerable to Magnets?[8]

For over a decade, various data-processing journals have published articles related to the vulnerability of magnetic tape files to magnets. Here are some of the claims made:

1. Entire tape library erased by a dime-store magnet.
2. Tape inside a metal file cabinet erased by a magnetic flashlight placed on the side of the cabinet.
3. Thousands of tapes destroyed within minutes with magnets the size of a quarter.
4. A thousand tapes destroyed with a small hand magnet.
5. Data tapes endangered by metal detectors at airline gates.

The Stanford Research Institute began to look into the foregoing claims by testing various versions and sizes and magnets against data files stored on tape. Some of the results of their experiments show that

1. Even a high-strength, heavy magnet poses little threat to tapes properly stored in double-walled, fire-resistant, tape filing cabinets.
2. The airline's present metal detectors by themselves do not disrupt the validity of the stored data on tape.
3. Computer malfunction can take place if small magnets are brought into direct contact with data throughout the length of the tape. Thus, in a 9,000-tape library, the time it would take to alter existing data would be substantial.
4. A large magnet in excess of 20 pounds and with a magnetic intensity of about 3,000 gauss at the poles could alter recorded tape data if it could be moved along tape reels in an open file rack.

Among the steps recommended to protect data from possible damage are (1) a thorough investigation of the background of the data-processing personnel, (2) the maintenance of copies of the active tapes in a separate, security proof and fireproof cabinet, and (3) development of an effective computer-room-access control system so that it is always known who is using what tape, when, and for how long. Depending on the particular installation, both management and outside consultants should work together on designing and implementing the plan that would best provide maximum security for the critical and other tape files of the system.

MAGNETIC DISK INPUT–OUTPUT

Magnetic disk units are normally used as input–output auxiliary devices in medium- to large-sized installations or for those applications requiring

[8] The details included in this section have been adapted from W. D. Tiffany, "Are Computer Files Vulnerable to Magnets?", *The Office,* Sept. 1972, pp. 51–54ff.

large-volume master-data records with immediate accessibility. As the disks spin, the unit can be instructed by the computer program to read from (input) or write on (output) any disk when necessary. Unlike magnetic tape, which is used in sequential-access processing, magnetic disk is ideally suited for random-access processing. Random-access processing is characterized by skipping around within the file and reading or writing specific data with no particular regard to their sequence. As with magnetic tape recording, there is no limit to the number of times data can be recorded on disk. Old data are automatically replaced by the data being recorded. Once recorded, they can be used as often as necessary.

Types of Magnetic Disks

A magnetic disk is a very popular on-line secondary storage medium. It is a thin circular plate coated on both sides of its flat surfaces with a ferrous oxide recording material. This material is much the same as that used on magnetic tapes. Data are represented by a 6-bit (1, 2, 4, 8, A, B) code and are stored along circular tracks on either side by magnetic spots caused by a read–write head(s). Each disk is separated from the disks above and below it by small read–write heads, which read information from or write it on the disk's two surfaces. A selected-access arm, which controls the read–write head(s), is directed by the program to manipulate data on a specific section of the disk. Earlier disk models had one large access arm that served a stack of 25 or 50 stationary files. Since it required some time for the arm to reach its destination, designers later introduced the two-access-arm model: one arm processes a specific transaction at a given storage position, while the other arm moves toward the next record.

Many of the latest magnetic disk files include a comb-shaped access mechanism that moves in and out among the disks. Enough movable read–write heads are attached to allow each disk its own read–write head, thus reducing average access time to a fraction of a second (Fig. 9-34). Burroughs has developed a unique head-per-track disk system that couples the recording economies of magnetic disks with the programming simplicity of magnetic core storage. With no moving read–write heads or access arms, there is no time requirement for their positioning over the disk tracks containing the needed data. Instead, individual read–write heads are permanently positioned over each information track on each disk surface. The disks spin at a constant speed under the read–write heads. Heads are air-flown to within a few millionths of an inch of the vertical disk surface, and they store or extract information at rates ranging from 100,000 to over 500,000 characters per second (Fig. 9-35).

The IBM 2305, Model 2, disk storage file is a key direct-access secondary storage component of the new IBM 370 computer system. Presented in terms of modules, each storage module contains six non-removable disks with fixed read–write heads positioned to access each of the 64 recording and 8 spare tracks on the 12 disk surfaces. The spare

FIGURE 9-34. *IBM head-per-disk magnetic disk file (Courtesy IBM)*

FIGURE 9-35. *Burroughs head-per-track disk de (Courtesy Burroughs)*

FIGURE 9-36. *Access mechanism and tracks of the IBM 2305 disk surface*

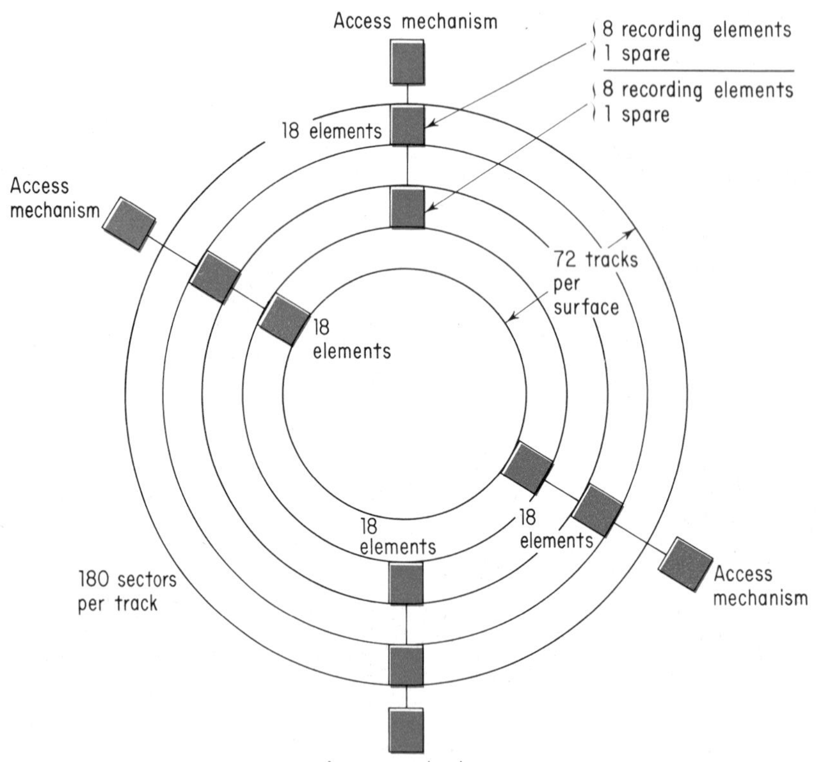

64 recording tracks/surface x 12 = 768 recording tracks/module
8 spare tracks/surface x 12 = 96 spare tracks/module
216 recording elements (read/write heads)/access mechanism x 4 = 864 recording elements

(or alternate) tracks are positioned as every ninth track on the surface. In the event that a permanent track error occurs during processing, the system automatically accesses the spare track without interruption.

The IBM 2305 (Fig. 9-36) is designed with four fixed access mechanisms positioned around the rotating disks. Each access mechanism contains two sets of nine read–write heads (16 recording and two spare) and accesses one fourth the tracks on each disk surface. Note that each set accesses every other track. For example, the outermost set of eight read–write heads at the top of the figure accesses data tracks 1, 3, 5, 7, . . . , 15, while the outermost set of eight read–write heads at the bottom of the figure accesses data tracks, 2, 4, 6, 8, . . . , 16.

Disk packs have been widely used for many years. A disk pack is a compact device that weighs between 8 and 20 pounds and contains a stack of magnetic disks handled as a unit, with an average capacity of 1 million bytes (Fig. 9-37).

To illustrate, an IBM 3336 disk pack assembly that weighs about 20 pounds goes into the IBM 3330 disk-drive unit, which accommodates a total of eight disk packs (Fig. 9-38). The disk pack is composed of 10 recording disks, each 14 inches in diameter. The disks provide 19 surfaces on which data can be recorded. The entire assembly rotates at a speed of 3,600 revolutions per minute in the IBM 3330 disk unit, which stores up to 800 million bytes of data. Disk packs have an edge over original disk files; if the computer breaks down or the user wishes to process the stored data on a computer system located elsewhere, the disk pack can be easily removed from one drive unit and inserted in the drive unit of another system. Furthermore, replacement of one disk pack with another in the same system takes less than a minute.

An important point to consider pertains to the efficient use of disk packs. The user is often confronted with applications or files containing information that exceed the disk-pack capacity. A popular solution is to

FIGURE 9-37. *IBM 3336 disk pack (Courtesy IBM)*

Specifications
No. of recording disks: 10
No. of recording surfaces: 19
No. of tracks/pack: 7,676
Maximum Capacity (Megabytes): 100

FIGURE 9-38. IBM 3330 disk-drive unit (Courtesy IBM)

organize the data by priority and store them in as many removable disk packs as needed. Active data used daily can be stored on one disk pack; the remaining, relatively inactive data can be stored in separate disk packs. Although access time may not be so fast as having the entire file in the unit, substantial cost saving can be realized. The final choice depends largely on the access requirements of the data involved, the overall characteristics of the existing computer system, and the deadlines imposed by management in obtaining the results.

Disk Layout and Data Transfer

Data are addressed on magnetic disk by disk number, track number, and sector number. A sector is normally fixed in length and accommodates one or more records. The number of sectors per track and the number of tracks per disk surface differ with different manufacturers and models. Generally, however, one can figure the maximum capacity of a given disk pack by multiplying the *number of disk surfaces* in the pack by the *number of tracks* per surface by the *number of sectors per track* by the *number of bytes* per sector.

Some disks do not have sectors, which means that data are addressed by disk face and disk track only. A physical record may occupy an entire track, but since a disk track is usually much too large for one record, several records are normally stored on it with each record assigned a sequential address for future access. Also, each record is preceded by a gap and a count area, which contains the record number and the number of bytes making up the data field. The count area is separated from the record data by a gap, as shown in Fig. 9-39.

Four factors have direct bearing on the speed with which data is transferred from disk to primary storage.

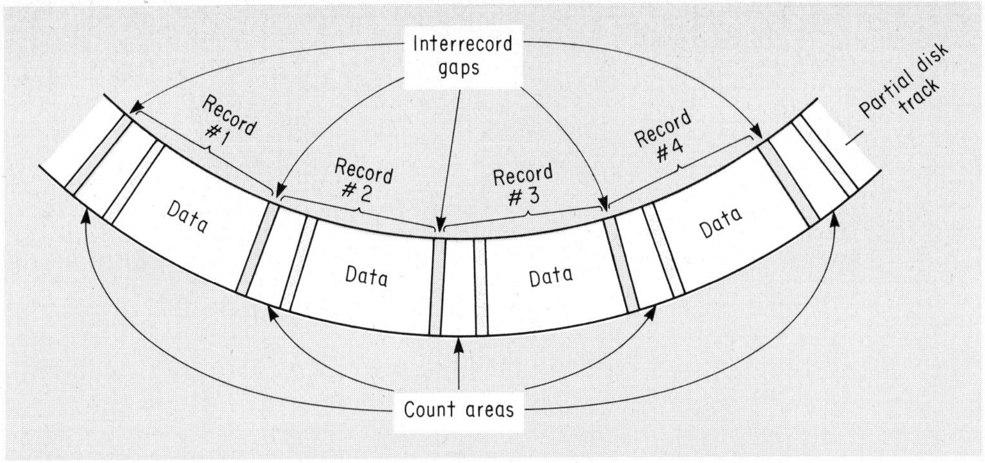

FIGURE 9-39. Layout of variable-length records on a partial disk track

1. **Access-motion (seek) time.** The time it takes to position the read–write head over the track containing the record. If the head is fixed, the access-motion time is zero.
2. **Head-activation time.** The time required to electronically select the proper read–write head of the access mechanism. It is generally considered to be negligible.
3. **Rotational delay.** The time required for the desired data to reach the read–write head so that actual reading or writing may begin. Rotational delay ranges from none to one complete revolution of the disk. Rotational delay depends upon how fast the disk is rotating and the location of the data in relation to the read–write head.
4. **Data-transfer time.** The amount of time required to transfer the data from the storage device to the primary storage (memory) of the computer. It is a function of the rotational speed and the density of the recorded data, and is usually expressed in thousands of characters (or bytes) per second.

In designing a disk-file system, identification of each record on disk is necessary for random-access processing. Given a record identification (ID) number, a disk address is obtained in a number of ways: (1) assigning a record ID number the same as its disk address; (2) randomizing—dividing the record ID number by a value equal to that of the number of locations in the disk file (the remainder can be used in determining the disk-file address of the record); (3) indexing—a record ID number leads to the track where an index is stored, which, in turn, identifies the sector of the track where the record is located. The first method is not used as often as the other two methods because of the problems of assigning new record numbers or reassigning new numbers to replace the records that are no longer carried in the file.

Uses and Limitations of Magnetic Disks

Some applications (e.g., various billing systems) require processing of a relatively limited number of input transactions against a very large master file. The use of random-access devices allows retrieval of any single record without extensive searching for or examining of other records in storage. Disk storage is equally effective in high-activity applications (e.g., a payroll of 5,000 employees) involving a comparatively small number of records updated frequently. The random-access approach allows direct access to all types of tables and other relevant data without the need for batching or extensive searching through the data files.

In deciding whether to use magnetic disk rather than magnetic tape, a data-processing manager needs to consider the following factors: (1) the applications involved, (2) the required data-access speed, (3) storage-size requirement, and (4) budget constraints.

Random-access applications are best handled by magnetic disk files, whereas sequential processing is best handled by magnetic tape. In disk-file processing, a computer system is programmed to locate and process a specific record stored in a predetermined disk-file address. The record is located immediately and read into core memory almost immediately. Although the speed factor depends on the particular disk model, hypothetically it takes about 42 milliseconds for the read–write mechanism to go into action and access a record. By comparison, it takes about 5 minutes to access a similar record on tape.

The storage-size requirements should also be considered. Disk storage is quite durable but is not as popular a medium for bulk data storage as is magnetic tape.[9] Furthermore, in a tape-updating routine, a new tape is created, leaving the old tape (unaltered) for reference. In magnetic disk processing, the record is read, updated, and written back on the disk, erasing most, if not all, of the original record data.

Finally, the price factor can be crucial. Magnetic disk files are more expensive than magnetic tape. A removable disk pack, for example, might be up to 20 times as expensive as a reel of tape of the same storage capacity. The trade-off here is that the more expensive disk file offers faster access speeds, which, in turn, are likely to cut processing cost when one needs to send data from one processing site to another. This situation is quite evident in a decentralized data-processing structure.

Since 1970, magnetic disks have become more and more the medium for external storage. Except for minicomputers, most digital computers

[9] Tape mobility is also an important benefit, especially to users who regularly transfer large volumes of data from one location to another, or who want to run a job on one computer but print it on another computer.

FIGURE 9-40. Magnetic drum unit (Courtesy IBM)

can now be obtained with magnetic disks. Although the total number of devices ordered still favors tapes, the sales figures for reels of tape and disks have shown a more rapid growth rate for disks.

Magnetic disk storage devices are potentially powerful and efficient devices for a great many applications. However, in some applications it is necessary or desirable to access a smaller volume of data very quickly. In this situation, magnetic drum storage would probably be used.

MAGNETIC DRUM STORAGE

The magnetic drum (Fig. 9-40) is a high-quality metal drum coated with magnetically sensitive material on its outer surface. The surface is divided into a number of tracks. Each track has single or multiple read–write heads, depending on whether data transfer is serial (bit by bit) or parallel (multiple bits at a time).

The presence of one or more read–write heads for each track eliminates any access-motion time associated with the access of data stored on a magnetic drum. Since the only timing factors pertinent to drum operation are head-selection time (which is negligible), rotational delay, and data transfer, the use of the magnetic drum as a storage device provides faster and more efficient operation than other direct-access storage devices.

Most current magnetic drums are high-speed, low-capacity devices with a rotational delay to specific track areas ranging from 0 to 17.5 milliseconds and storage capacities from 125,000 to 12 million characters. They are generally used as on-line storage devices in systems requiring fast access and fast transfer speeds. One particular magnetic drum transfers data at over 1 million bytes per second—a rate unmatched by any other similar device to date.

One advantage of the magnetic drum is the absence of acceleration problems, since it rotates at constant speed. By contrast, acceleration problems often occur in magnetic tape during reading and/or writing operations and, unless periodically checked, could have some bearing on the efficiency of data transfer. On the other hand, magnetic drums pose some limitations. They cannot be removed from one unit and used elsewhere and do not come in "drum packs" as do magnetic disks.

MAGNETIC CARD STORAGE

Another random-access storage device is the Mylar magnetic card. It is a flexible plastic strip with a magnetized coating. The cards are grouped in random order in a cartridge. They are capable of storing a large volume of randomly accessible information, which can be removed with the same flexibility as from magnetic tape or magnetic disks (Fig. 9-41).

Like magnetic tapes, magnetic cards represent data in the form of magnetic spots on their seven individually addressable tracks. A randomly selected record is obtained by releasing the proper card from a cartridge onto a rotating drum. The drum, in turn, moves the card past a set of read–write heads to perform the routine. Once accomplished, the card is released and restacked in its original location for future processing.

Some of the good features of magnetic cards are their relatively low storage cost per digit, the availability of a large number of records at any given time, and ease of removal, storage, or replacement as a pack. However, when compared to magnetic disks or magnetic drums, one major problem is slow access time. The mechanical process of accessing the data-bearing cards takes time. Access time ranges from 125 to 600 milliseconds, with drum devices often at the lower end of the scale.

MAGNETIC STRIP STORAGE

A magnetic strip file is a unique type of temporary secondary storage designed to supply the computer with the required facts for an immediate up-to-date report on a given account. A direct, rather permanent hookup (on-line) to the computer system is required. Insurance companies utilize this system, usually through a direct-access device, to satisfy customers' inquiries regarding policy billing information. This service can be provided manually, but because of the thousands of policyholders and hundreds of daily inquiries, it would be both costly and inefficient.

A magnetic strip file is similar to a library card catalog. When someone wishes to know about a particular book, he searches in the card file, which normally is arranged alphabetically by subject or author. New book information may be added to the file with little difficulty. The cards for lost books may be removed from the file with relative ease. Such flexibility and convenience are also desired in a computer mass-storage device. It must be large enough to accommodate new data, as well as being capable of dropping or altering old data. The magnetic strip meets these requirements, and, although storage is slower than on magnetic disk, the strip is inexpensive, has large storage capacity per holder, and allows direct access during processing.

Magnetic strip storage is known under such names as the IBM Data Cell and the NCR CRAM (Card Random-Access Memory) (Figs. 9-41 and 9-42). The IBM 2321 data cell is made up of an array of cells divided

FIGURE 9-41. CRAM unit—NCR (Courtesy NCR)

FIGURE 9-42. Magnetic strip file—IBM data cell (Courtesy IBM)

into 20 subcells. A subcell contains 10 magnetic strips with a magnetically sensitive (oxide) coating on one side. When a magnetic strip has been selected, the pickup arm withdraws the strip from the subcell and wraps it around the drum. As the strip revolves, it passes a set of 20 read–write heads. Each head services 5 of the 100 "tracks" on the strip. The strips are returned to the subcell by reversing the rotation of the drums. The total storage capacity of a data-cell drive with 10 data cells and 200 strips may be up to 400 million 8-bit bytes or 800 million digits.

EXTENDED CORE STORAGE

For some time, large-scale computer users have found it necessary to extend the capacity of the system's core storage. As a secondary-storage device, each extended-core-storage unit is designed to store approximately 20 million characters at an average access time of 5 milliseconds. Such an extension is ideal in dealing with a large volume of input–output data or many small applications.

Bulk core storage provides the advantage of fast direct access, owing to the absence of moving parts. However, the primary limitation on its use is cost. Today, core storage is primarily restricted to CPU memory. When bulk core-storage prices are reduced and its use increases, there will be a significant impact in various areas. Information retrieval becomes easier, commercial time sharing will be more economically manageable, and system reliability will improve. Until then, bulk core storage is limited in use to large-scale computer systems requiring very high speed secondary storage.

In summary, we note that direct-access devices are useful in terms of their ability to hold large amounts of data at reasonable cost and in the necessary forms for processing. A business firm integrating direct-access devices into its system must maintain an efficient balance between storage volume and unit cost of storage. Compared to magnetic tape, however, direct-access devices have certain disadvantages in the way of control and are comparatively higher in cost. As cost is reduced, direct-access devices are likely to be the most popular form of secondary storage in the future.

With the foregoing random-access devices in mind, it can be safely generalized that the choice of the type of auxiliary device depends on some trade-off among storage capacity, speed, and price. Extended core storage, which can be shared by two or more computer systems, offers large computer systems the accessibility characteristics of primary core storage (fast access time and transfer rate) at a fraction of the cost. As far as hardware costs are concerned, magnetic tape storage is the least expensive, but it is not as efficient as other auxiliary random-access memories. For random processing of large-sized files, data cell units and removable disk packs can be acquired at a relatively reasonable cost. For smaller files, drum memory or the conventional disk memory unit might be the best choice.

SUMMARY

Input–output devices are required components of a computer system. Input devices transfer input data into the central processing unit for processing from such media as punched cards, magnetic tape, or magnetic disk. Output devices, on the other hand, deliver output information via the on-line printer to the user for action or store it on a secondary storage medium for future processing. Input–output devices are manipulated by a control unit, which decodes program instructions and initiates the operation of the designated devices.

Differences in speed and efficiency between the central processing unit and the input–output devices make it necessary to have overlapping input–output operations for maximum processing speed and efficiency of the system.

The punched-card reader is a popular input device in small- to medium-sized installations. Its job is to read and transfer the data punched in the card to the central processing unit when needed. The card punch of the reader is activated when a program instruction calls for punching output information into a set of blank cards. A paper-tape reader performs a similar function, except for reading punched data on paper tape.

Compared to the punched card, paper tape offers the advantages of easy and compact storage and easy handling. It is also cheaper to use and to mail. Compared to more advanced media, however, paper tape is as slow and as impractical as the punched card. It breaks easily and cannot be visually read by the average operator when necessary.

A line printer is strictly an output device. Character-at-a-time printers include the console typewriter, the matrix printer, and the teletype printer. Among the line-at-a-time printers are the wheel printer and the chain printer. Xerographic and electrostatic printers are available, but are not as popular as the chain printers.

Magnetic tape and magnetic disk are the most popular secondary storage media used in computer processing. Magnetic tape offers the unique advantage of high-data-density recording. Hundreds of characters can be stored on 1 inch of tape. As file storage, it is ideally used for regular updating of sequential accounts.

The primary advantages of magnetic tape are compact storage, ease of handling, a more efficient unit-record medium, low-cost storage, and data transmission at high speed. Among its drawbacks are slow access time and its vulnerability to dirt, dust, heat, humidity, and tape breakage. Consequently, it is essential for the operator to follow basic guidelines for proper tape handling.

Random-access media, such as magnetic disks, are appropriately used in updating accounts quickly without having to have them in sequence. A disk file is used most commonly in business applications if the incoming data enter the system in a random manner and require an immediate response. Updating and/or obtaining information on certain accounts in the file is faster, because access to these accounts is made easier when they are available on a stack of individual disks. If, for instance, the same accounts were stored on magnetic tape, updating specific accounts somewhere in the middle of the tape would mean that the tape had to be read and unwound until the desired location was reached. Therefore, tape processing is an efficient operation only when each and every account in the file needs to be read and worked upon sequentially. When certain accounts in random locations must be read, the disk medium is the better system. One can go to any record in the disk file at any time, because each record is individually and directly addressable; that is, it has a separate location number.

Other secondary storage devices include the magnetic drum, magnetic card, magnetic strip, and extended core storage. The general idea behind these devices is to supplement primary storage by holding related data until needed for processing.

TERMS TO LEARN

Blocking
Chain printer
CRAM
Dual-gap read–write head
Electrostatic printer
End-of-file indicator
Interrecord gap
Load point
Magnetic drum
Magnetic strip file
Magnetic tape
On-line input
Packing density
Parity check
Random access
Record
Sequential data processing

QUESTIONS

1. What role do input and output devices play in a computer system?
2. Distinguish between the two types of punched card readers.
3. What are the primary media used for storing input data? output data?
4. Explain briefly the difference between impact and nonimpact printers.
5. Explain why secondary storage is needed in business data processing.
6. What is magnetic tape? Why is it called sequential file storage? Mention some of its physical characteristics.
7. Assume that 25 customer records are stored on magnetic tape. If only record 25 (the last record) is needed for processing, how does the machine have immediate access to it? Explain.
8. Explain the 7-bit, nine-track, and ten-track codes.
9. Assuming the use of even parity check, determine the status (0 bit or 1 bit) of the parity-check core in the representation of the following characters: 3, 4, 5, 6, A, C, J, L, S, T, V, X, Z.
10. What is meant by packing density?
11. Define the following terms:
    a. Load point
    b. End-of-file indicator
    c. Interrecord gap
    d. Single-record block
    e. Multiple-record block
    f. Count area
    g. Header control label

12. List and discuss briefly the advantages and disadvantages of magnetic tape.
13. What physical and environmental factors should be considered in tape handling?
14. Do you believe magnetic tape is vulnerable to magnets? Substantiate your answer by three sources from journals available in your school library.
15. List and explain briefly the steps to be taken in tape handling and storage.
16. What are the three different ways of distinguishing a data reel? Explain.
17. When and why is a plastic ring used in the tape-recording unit?
18. What is a magnetic disk? What advantages does a random-access file have over magnetic tape? Explain.
19. What is a magnetic drum? What is it ideally used for?
20. Explain briefly the features and uses of magnetic strip storage. How are they different from extended core storage?

pattern recognition and computer-output-microfilm devices

10

A steady increase in the cost of input preparation has prompted many business firms to move away from punched-card input preparation. The introduction of direct data-entry devices (discussed in Chapter 8) is a step forward in providing a more efficient alternative for input-data preparation at low cost. The computer's ability to recognize the presence and absence of a magnetic flux and to evaluate a printed character represented by a light pattern on special paper has also led to the development of pattern recognition devices such as magnetic-ink character-recognition (MICR) and optical character-recognition (OCR) devices. Depending on the particular model, data are entered directly into the computer for processing or are stored in secondary storage (e.g., on magnetic tape) in a machine-processable format for later processing.

MAGNETIC-INK CHARACTER RECOGNITION

Magnetic-ink character recognition (MICR) was pioneered by the banking industry to automate check processing through the computer. Over the years, the use of checks has increased at a fantastic rate; today over 25 billion checks are processed each year. The task of processing this voluminous amount of data manually staggers the imagination. In 1955, the American Bankers Association (ABA) recognized the need for a way to automate banking paperwork. Either the check or some new document had to be further developed as direct input to an automated system.

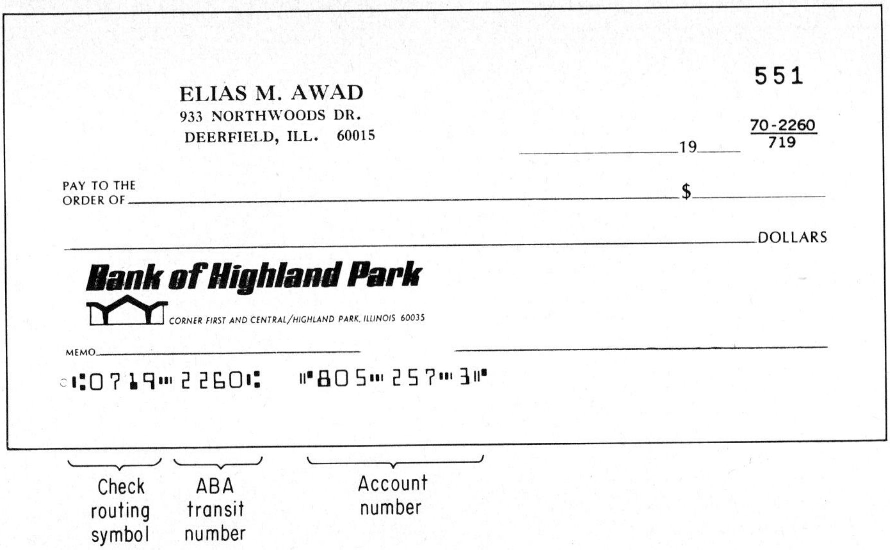

551

ELIAS M. AWAD
933 NORTHWOODS DR.
DEERFIELD, ILL. 60015

19____

70-2260
719

PAY TO THE ORDER OF _____ $_____

_____ DOLLARS

Bank of Highland Park

CORNER FIRST AND CENTRAL/HIGHLAND PARK, ILLINOIS 60035

MEMO _____

Check routing symbol | ABA transit number | Account number

FIGURE 10-1. Blank check showing the magnetic-ink character (bottom)

Under pressure from larger banks and after consideration of the various sizes, shapes, and thicknesses of the printed checks issued, the Association agreed in 1959 to adopt a standard type font to be used by the banking industry in coding all checks, since a check may be processed by as many as four banks before it is received by the originating bank. In 1960, the encoding of checks with magnetic ink was finally standardized throughout the banking industry.[1] Magnetic ink solves three major problems: (1) the check as an original document can be used directly as input to the computer for processing, (2) the necessary information can be coded on checks of any reasonable size, and (3) the information is easily readable by man. Check encoding represents a positive step toward developing a universal language understandable by man and machine. Now MICR devices can read all checks and process them quickly and accurately (Fig. 10-1).

Check processing begins with the blank check. When a customer opens a general checking account, the bank prints his name and address on the top of a set of checks precoded on the bottom in the special E-13B font with the bank number, bank branch (if any), account number, and check number, respectively (Fig. 10-2).

During the processing phase, each of the stacked checks is fed automatically into the MICR reader–sorter, where the special ink is magnetized by generating a flux pattern on each character (Fig. 10-3).

[1] The wide acceptance and success of MICR was illustrated in September 1967, when Federal Reserve banks stopped handling through regular channels checks not encoded with magnetic ink.

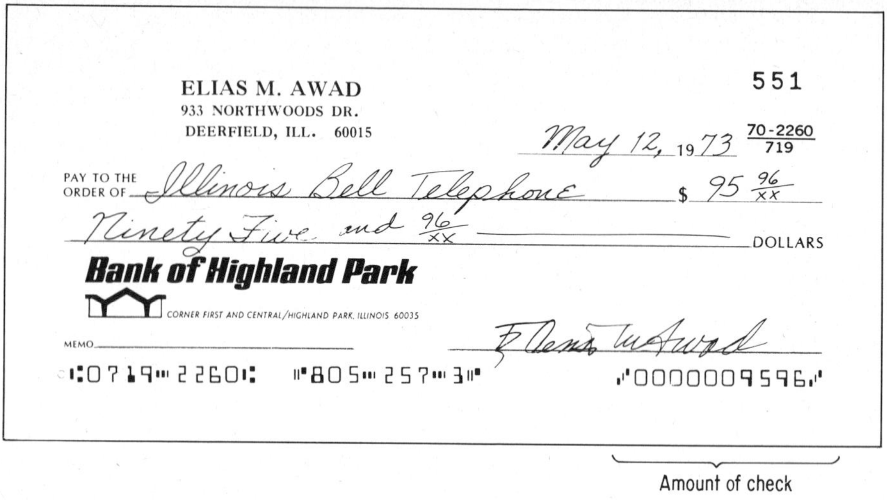

ELIAS M. AWAD
933 NORTHWOODS DR.
DEERFIELD, ILL. 60015

551

May 12, 1973 70-2260/719

PAY TO THE ORDER OF Illinois Bell Telephone $ 95 96/xx

Ninety Five and 96/xx DOLLARS

Bank of Highland Park

CORNER FIRST AND CENTRAL/HIGHLAND PARK, ILLINOIS 60035

MEMO

Elias M. Awad

⑆0719⑉2260⑆ ⑈805⑉257⑉3⑈ ⑇0000009596⑇

Amount of check

FIGURE 10-2. Canceled check showing amount imprinted in the lower right corner with MICR character inscriber (left)

FIGURE 10-3. IBM 1419 magnetic-ink character reader-sorter (Courtesy IBM)

Once detected, the pattern is converted into electronic signals to be used by the computer for updating the customer's account.

The MICR reader–sorter's primary function is to read checks of various sizes and thicknesses and transfer the information to the computer. It is also designed to physically sort checks [2] by account number and

[2] The reader–sorter is the final judge of the proper coding of documents. Unreadable data go to a separate reject pocket for manual handling.

arrange their return to their respective owners. In an on-line system, the MICR device is hooked to the computer system for direct processing. Otherwise (off-line), the data are stored on magnetic tape for later processing.

The use of MICR offers several advantages:

1. High reading accuracy of checks, including those that might be folded, stamped, or roughly handled.
2. The type font is easily readable by the user.
3. The data on the check can be fed directly to the computer for processing.
4. Encoding checks with the customer's account number and the bank's own coded number minimizes chances of error.

In addition to the need for manual handling of damaged and improperly encoded checks, another limitation of MICR is the reader–sorter's inability to read alphabetic characters or characters other than those printed with the special type font, since only certain characters can be clearly set up in magnetic flux. The present E-13B font system consists of 10 numeric digits (0 to 9), an "Amount" symbol, an "On Us" symbol, a "Transit Number" symbol, and a "Dash" symbol (Fig. 10-4). Furthermore, although magnetic ink retains its ability to be magnetized indefinitely, most of the magnetism imprinted in the characters vanishes soon after imprinting is finished. This limitation makes magnetic character reading unreliable for source documents that must be processed several times in different applications.

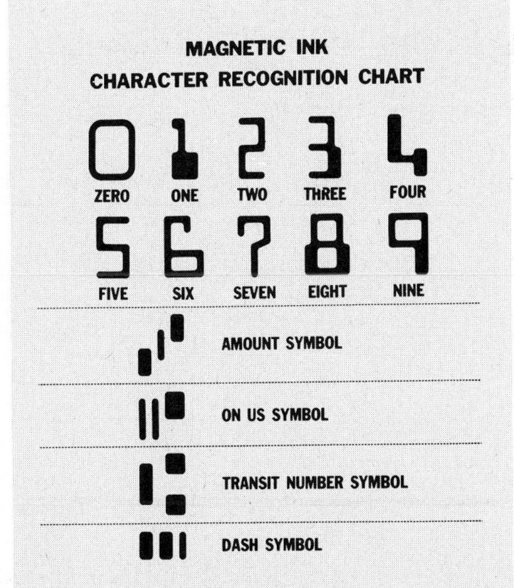

FIGURE 10-4. Magnetic ink character identification chart

Like other direct-input devices, the primary objective of optical character-recognition (OCR) devices is to reduce the cost of capturing source data. Their use also eliminates the need for keypunching and makes it possible for data to be prepared in the conventional human communication medium. Thus, since people need not adjust to the machine by converting human-readable information into machine code, OCR data can be easily read at any phase of the data-processing cycle. During the past few years, this relatively new technology has produced a number of new devices, ranging from large-scale units capable of reading almost any machine-printed and hand-printed information at high speed to relatively slower, small-scale terminals that read information at remote locations when needed.

OCR readers have a history dating back to the early 1800s, when similar devices were used to help the blind. In 1870, an image transmission unit was developed that used photocells. Around 1890, a sequential scanning device was built to analyze the image one line at a time. In 1912, a machine was invented to read a printed set of characters and convert it into telegraph code.

No practical commercial OCR devices were developed until 1951, when the Intelligent Machine Research Corporation (IMR) developed the first commercial optical reader for handling typewritten data. Since then, other machines have been introduced on the market; but it is only during the past decade that OCR devices have begun to have a significant impact on business data processing. Today, among the major OCR users are credit-card organizations, airlines, banks, and government organizations. In oil company credit-card operations, for instance, OCR devices are widely used to read carbon imprints of customer card numbers and the amount charged for billing purposes. The OCR system proved to be the answer to the "input bottleneck."

Optical Character Readers

Optical character readers identify each character by comparing its features with features stored in memory. They offer the most efficient direct reading and translating of typed, printed, or handwritten letters, numbers, or special symbols into machine language. The reader, called an optical character-recognition (OCR) reader, consists of (1) a transport unit, (2) a scanning unit, and (3) a recognition unit (Fig. 10-5). It converts the characters into a "picture" through the use of a photoelectric eye. The circuitry is designed to break up this image into pulses that identify the specific characters. Internally stored reference patterns guide the recognition unit to verify (match) the patterns held by the scanning unit. Generally, the *matching process* is made on the basis of either the line formation of each character (referred to as stroke analysis) or, in the case

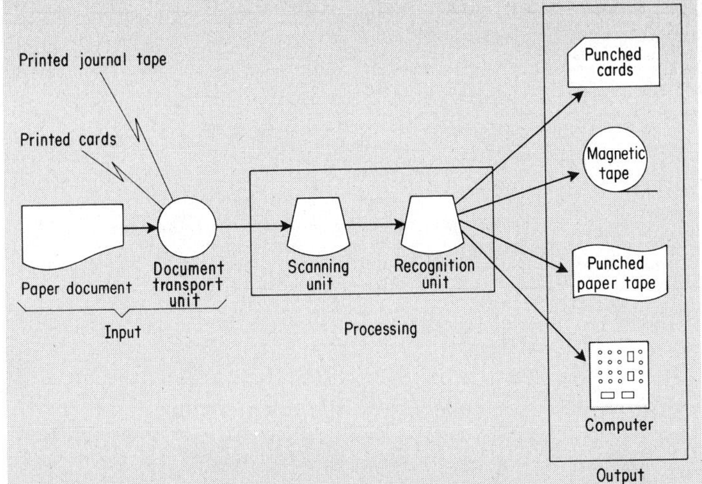

FIGURE 10-5. The primary elements of an optical character reader

of handwritten characters, the outline of the character (called curve tracing). Unmatched character patterns cause the document to be rejected. The reject rate runs around 5 percent of the total documents scanned.

Some difficulty is still encountered in optical reading. Diversity in hand-printed characters and in the type and quality of printed styles is continuously being adjusted. Today, fewer documents are rejected, indicating reduction in error rate and improvement in optical scanning techniques.

Classification of Optical Character-Recognition Devices

Pure OCR equipment has been in commercial use since the early 1950s. Although its use has not grown by leaps and bounds, all indications point to increasing future growth. OCR readers can be used on-line (simultaneously as sorters and as input device) or off-line (as sorters) for input only. They are generally categorized on the basis of the physical size of the documents they process and the classes and complexity of type fonts they will read.

CLASSIFICATION BY SIZE OF DOCUMENT. Three generalized classes of document-handling mechanisms are available:

1. **Journal-tape readers** are designed to read paper tapes such as those used in cash registers or adding machines. Journal-tape readers were developed in response to the retailer's need for a faster and

more efficient method of processing daily sales information. The use of cash registers capable of recording data in the proper font allows these organizations to obtain machine-ready input as a by-product of a normal retail merchandising function, thus realizing substantial savings in keypunching and other data-preparation costs.

2. **Small-document readers** scan documents the size of a punched card or smaller, which may include turnaround documents (such as utility bills or credit-card preprinted stubs) used later for re-entry to and processing by a computer system. Most document readers handle an average of 400 documents per minute, a throughput (performance) rate of 160,000 to 200,000 documents per day.
3. **Page readers** are capable of reading multiple lines of typed or printed material from a normal page layout. The minimum document size is usually 6 by 8 inches and the maximum 12 by 14 inches. Reject rate depends on the print quality and condition of the typed material; a 0.1 percent reject rate is considered average for good-quality input, but it can go as high as 0.5 percent.

CLASSIFICATION BY FONT CAPABILITY. Four classes of OCR font capability are

1. **Mark readers.** Mark sensing is the machine reading of pencil marks placed in predetermined positions on predetermined forms. In its early use, a special "electrostatic" pencil was required so that the marks would be electrically conductive. The advent of sensing mechanisms based on optical techniques led to the use of light sources to detect character presence, diminishing the need for special pencils.

   Mark representation is determined by the position of the mark on the document. Each position is preassigned a value, which remains fixed for that type of document. The preassigned value of any of the characters must be acceptable to the equipment being used. Mark sensing has been widely used in inventory control and in the administration and scoring of exams. However, the necessity of coding preassigned values limits its application in other areas of information processing.
2. **Single-font readers** are capable of reading a single style of type only. Some readers have limited character sets (i.e., the font may be restricted to numbers only or to uppercase letters only); other readers are capable of reading uppercase, lowercase, and certain symbols.
3. **Multifont readers** are designed to read a minimum of several standard typewritten or printed fonts (both upper and lowercase).
4. **Hand-print readers.** Some OCR devices have recently been designed to read hand-printed characters. For the device to do an acceptable job, each character must be clearly block-printed with no open loops, disconnected lines, or linked characters. Examples are shown in Fig. 10-6.

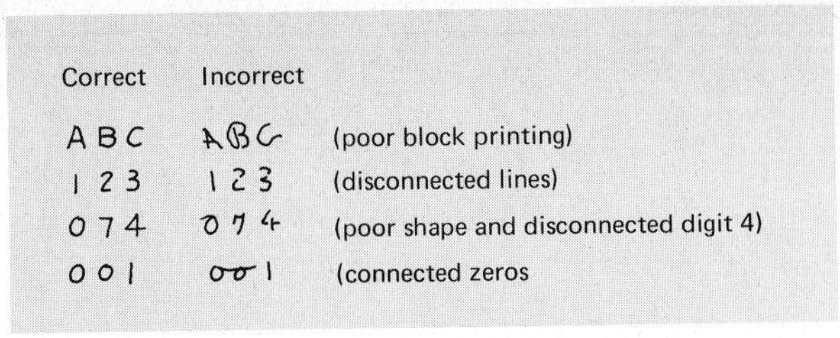

Correct	Incorrect	
A B C	A B C	(poor block printing)
1 2 3	1 2 3	(disconnected lines)
0 7 4	0 7 4	(poor shape and disconnected digit 4)
0 0 1	0 0 1	(connected zeros

FIGURE 10-6

A popular hand-print reader is the IBM 1287 document reader. Using a circular scan, it traces the outline of the hand-printed character. The reader identifies a given character if the trace formed by the character fits within the tolerance configuration for it. Otherwise, the traced character is rejected.

Hand-printed numeric input to OCR systems is used ideally in cases involving high-volume source documents with limited formats. Staff members who have to hand print numbers must be trained in advance. Proper training takes as long as 3 days. Rejection rates for hand-print form among new users can be as high as 10 percent; established users can drop this rate to as low as 0.75 percent.

The bulk of the OCR equipment used today may operate either on-line or off-line. On-line OCR units are *computer-compatible* and are connected to a channel for direct data input. The off-line units include control logic and output devices, and have a magnetic tape drive that produces computer-compatible tape for processing.

Although OCR is a significant step toward source-data automation, it is not as yet a perfect solution to all input problems. On the one hand, low-priced OCR units generally have a low reject rate, but their reading vocabulary is limited to one font or to numbers. On the other hand, OCR units with almost unlimited font-reading capability and high reading rates are so expensive that some units cost up to $1 million. Furthermore, the high reading speed and the complexity of the reading process often result in a high reject rate because of the unit's sensitivity to document condition (smudges, grease, poor-quality paper, etc.).

In evaluating the purchase price and the characteristics and capabilities of OCR readers, it is apparent that the more flexible the OCR reader and the larger the scanning area it covers, the higher the purchase price. Most page readers are in the $150,000 to $400,000 range, with the most expensive reader exceeding $1 million. Document readers range from $100,000 to $225,000. Journal-tape readers carry a price tag from $85,000 to $125,000. Lower-priced equipment, such as the mark reader, ranges from $7,000 to $50,000. The high price of the multifont page reader is explained by the flexibility required of the unit in handling loose formats of various pages and the delicate movement of its paper-handling system. Document, journal-tape, and mark readers are lower in price since they scan smaller areas and have simpler transports.

OCR readers are widely used by companies with large-volume billing requirements. These include insurance companies, utilities, department stores, petroleum companies, mail-order houses, airlines, and publishing firms. The oil industry was the first major industry to adopt OCR on a large scale. A typical installation handles approximately 80,000 documents per hour, contributing to rapid billing and more available cash flow.

The *utility* industry uses optical mark readers to process turnaround documents returned (with payment) by customers. Information handwritten by meter readers is read by an OCR device and written directly on magnetic tape, which is later used as input for processing. This system simplifies the chores in billing and accounts receivable.

Large *mail-order houses* use OCR systems to process tens of thousands of turnaround documents returned by customers every day. A mail-order house in Chicago, for example, uses a large OCR system to process over 85,000 customer account statements every day.

The Social Security Administration in Baltimore, Maryland, uses the IBM 1975 optical page reader, which scans the name, Social Security number, and quarterly earnings of 70 million reported wage earners. Punching the data in cards for conventional reading takes over 3 months. The OCR system is reported to have saved the bureau over $1,250,000 to date.

Airlines also find much use for the OCR system. United Airlines, for example, operates a Recognition Electronic Computing Reader, which processes over 2 million coupons per month by scanning each coupon's 14-digit ticket and coupon number at an effective throughput rate of 590 documents per minute with a document reject rate of 11 percent. Nonscanable items, such as special coupons, constitute around 8 percent of the rejected documents; rejects resulting from agents' errors are estimated at 1.5 percent. Print quality and the reader's scanning errors account for the remaining 1.5 percent of the rejected documents.

Other industries using OCR include insurance companies, industries using credit cards, the food industry for controlling inventory, breweries, telephone companies, banks, and the postal system. In each case, justification for the use of OCR is based on the economic benefits derived from processing large volumes of data at a speed unmatched by alternative data-entry methods.

Status of Optical Character Recognition

The input bottleneck has plagued most computer users,[3] especially with the increasing adoption of larger, newer, and faster computer systems. With efficiency and cost effectiveness in mind, the solution is not more

[3] A survey conducted by *Computer World* (August 26, 1970) of 1,647 data-processing managers showed revealing results. Forty-five percent of the respondents were experiencing serious input bottlenecks, and two thirds of the managers agreed that input preparation is a greater problem than output. The majority of managers

key punches, but more direct and faster input devices, such as OCR scanners.

OCR dates back to January 1956, when it was first used for commercial purposes. Its performance in the 1960s has been disappointing. In 1969 around 700,000 key-punch machines were in use, but only 1,000 OCR installations were in operation. There will be an accelerated increase in the 1970s in the rate and number of OCR installations if the problems of the 1960s can be acted upon. Some of these problems are (1) the indifference of administrative officials and distrust of data-processing managers for the OCR field, (2) the cost factor, (3) the lack of font standardization, and (4) the tolerance factor regarding imperfectly printed characters.

One unfortunate factor that has deterred wide use of OCR systems is not lack of performance, but lack of acceptance and suspicion by administrative officials of the capabilities of OCR in general. Most computer systems were initially installed with the punched card as a primary source of data input, and many users have been reluctant to introduce a change of such a major nature. Furthermore, some users have had bad experience with OCR readers because they failed to realign their ongoing system to facilitate proper performance of the readers. Consequently, OCR manufacturers have been in favor of selling a total OCR system rather than an OCR device that merely replaces the key punch.

The cost factor is the key to a growing OCR market, and it plays a major role in the degree of OCR acceptance. In 1967, only five companies [4] were actively engaged in manufacturing or marketing OCR readers. In 1973, many more manufacturers entered the field, with over one half the recently introduced scanners manufactured by smaller firms.

Today, new devices are available at a more reasonable cost, owing primarily to improved techniques in the production of the electronic circuitry for OCR's recognition logic. Furthermore, the development of hand-print readers opened a new application area, in that data can now be processed directly from the source. Optically reading original input data at its source bypasses keypunching entirely and holds the key to the future of OCR devices. When the overall manufacturing cost is further reduced and the OCR unit's price/performance ratio begins to match or surpass other direct-input devices, there should be no doubt of its con-

---

blamed this on human error. For solutions, 23 percent suggested source data capture; 21 percent preferred on-line operation; 1.5 percent offered OCR devices; 13 percent indicated better hardware; 9 percent suggested a better systems approach; 6 percent were in favor of standardized operation; 6 percent suggested better training programs; only 4 percent were for more key-to-tape devices; and only 3 percent believed in the direct voice-input approach.

The largest input-preparation expenses were in banking, communications, and utilities; the lowest were in hospitals, publishing, and manufacturing organizations. These expenses were said to be on the rise by over half the managers interviewed. Although one third of the respondents were planning to begin a data capture program, over one half of those surveyed had no such plan at present. The conclusion arrived at by most managers was that non-key-punch devices are more efficient, faster, more accurate, and less costly than key-punch equipment.

[4] Control Data, Farrington, IBM, Optical Scanning, and Recognition Equipment.

tinued acceptance and growth. In 1966, the value of total OCR shipments was less than $20 million. In 1970, it was around $150 million. In 1973, it increased to $275 million. This growth trend is expected to reach the $500 million mark by 1975.

With regard to font standardization, the American standard font OCR-A is now accepted throughout the country. Constraining the form of input to one or two highly readable fonts leads to the production of less complex devices and, consequently, lower prices.

Finally, research in the 1970s should produce new techniques of processing imperfectly printed or formed (especially handwritten) characters. If such perfected techniques at high processing speeds can be achieved at a competitive cost, there is no doubt that the OCR concept will eventually take over most, if not all, of the input preparation work done by the key punch and even the key-to-tape machines. In the meantime, for an OCR system to operate successfully, effective follow-up procedures must be established to correct any weakness in the system, to keep management's attention during conversion, and to bring documents, forms, and character style within the tolerances of the system in operation.

COMPUTER OUTPUT MICROFILM

In producing computer output information a bottleneck often develops due to poor match between the electromechanical speed of the line printer and, the electronic speed of the central processor. This problem can be solved, especially in installations producing high-volume output, by the adoption of nonimpact printers and computer-output-microfilm (COM).

The concept of microfilm is not new. It found its first application in the military. When the Prussian Army laid siege to Paris in 1870, a man by the name of Dagron used carrier pigeons to fly microfilmed messages over enemy lines into Paris. The year 1920 marked the beginning of the microfilm industry, when a clerk in a New York City bank developed a device for photographing canceled checks. It gained immediate acceptance. Finally, V-mail during World War II relied on microfilm to handle correspondence to U.S. troops abroad. Letters were first microfilmed to reduce their weight and bulk before they were flown overseas. Upon arrival, they were enlarged to size, printed out, and delivered.

Today, both government and business find full-time use for microfilm. The Social Security Administration, for example, distributes yearly on the average of 3 million *microfiche* (sheets of microfilm) to hundreds of its offices across the country to provide a quick scan of any beneficiary record. During the Apollo 7 Mission, more than 2 million "pages" of vital data were microfilmed, which served to offer quick, reliable data on demand. The Bank of America is one of the world's largest microfilm users, taking over 2 billion photographs of checks and documents in 1973. Other examples of COM utilization are listed in Fig. 10-7.

Industry	Application Area	Distribution
Banking	Demand deposit accounting	Branch offices
Automotive	Parts lists	Suppliers and dealers
Airlines	Fare information	Agents
Libraries	Book inventories	Reading rooms
Specialty steel	Item inventories	Warehouses
Mail order	Catalogue information	Order takers
Publishing	Micropublishing	Customers
Engineering	Scientific graphs, engineering drawings, schematics	Engineers and technicians
Financial and investment	Charts, graphs, tables, general printing	Personnel, clients and governmental agencies
General commerce and industry	Customer accounts, office records, trial balances, balance sheets, payroll, other records	Personnel, customers and other company divisions
Insurance	Agent commission statements, agent digest system, customer statements, check copies retrieval, payroll statements, physician records, vendor records	Agents, personnel, supervisors and branch offices
Animated movie making and scientific sequencing	Advertising, engineering, science	TV stations, theaters, laboratories, universities
Education	Education and training	Classrooms and auditoriums

FIGURE 10-7. Representative COM application areas.
Source: Modern Data, *Dec. 1972, p. 36*

Advantages

COM offers several advantages, among which are the following:

1. Smaller storage space. Business firms pay between $35 and $100 rent for space occupied by each file cabinet. Microfilmed computer output occupies 2 percent of the space required for an equivalent paper printout. One hundred pounds of computer printout, for example, can be stored on only 60 microfiches. A recent study reported that 100,000 pages of computer printout weighing 750 pounds, occupying 15 cubic feet of filing space, and costing $250 to produce can be produced on microfilm weighing 13 pounds, occupying 27/100 of a cubic foot of filing space, and costing only $100. The savings in cost and storage space is obvious.
2. Quick retrieval of records by simple and inexpensive methods. The average microfilmed record can be retrieved in about one ninth the time it takes to retrieve the same data on paper.

3. Lower material cost. As indicated in the study mentioned it costs, on the average, about $0.001 per page to microfilm, or less than one half the cost of paper printout for an equivalent page.
4. Up to six readable carbon copies can be produced by an impact printer, but an unlimited number of high-quality copies can be made from a master film.
5. Recording at high operating speed. COM recorder units operate at 40,000 lines per minute; the fastest commercial line printer operates around 2,100 lines per minute.
6. Microfilm records are lightweight, making them easy to carry and store.
7. Labor-saving. Airlines, railroads, and some large rent-a-car agencies employ a microfilm retrieval system at their computerized reservation centers that stores thousands of pages of information on various tours, daily and special schedules, destinations, and special services. Eastern Airlines' microfilm system, for example, is reported to save over 500 agent-hours of telephone time each day.

Disadvantages

1. Probably the most serious limitation of COM systems is the negative reaction of many people who are unfamiliar with film. To some extent, the reaction is justified. Data stored on microfilm is not easy to search and read especially when such data must be readily available for decision making. Furthermore, access to COM readers is often limited in many systems.
2. If data are constantly changing, it is impractical to use a COM system, especially when the user requires frequent interaction with the data.
3. Initial and total costs of a COM system are quite high and can only be justified in business firms handling high-volume documents on a regular basis.
4. Filming and film developing are new skills that require special training. Many users have experienced problems in training their personnel in the proper operation of a COM system.
5. A COM system is a poor choice for applications that require hard-copy output.
6. Unlike hard-copy output, a microfilm cannot be written on and provides no room for notes, which are often helpful in evaluating output.

System Storage and Technologies

In a computer system using COM, output information is produced in human-readable form by a microfilm process using a COM recorder. COM storage may be on roll film, microfiche, cartridge, or cassette. *Roll film*

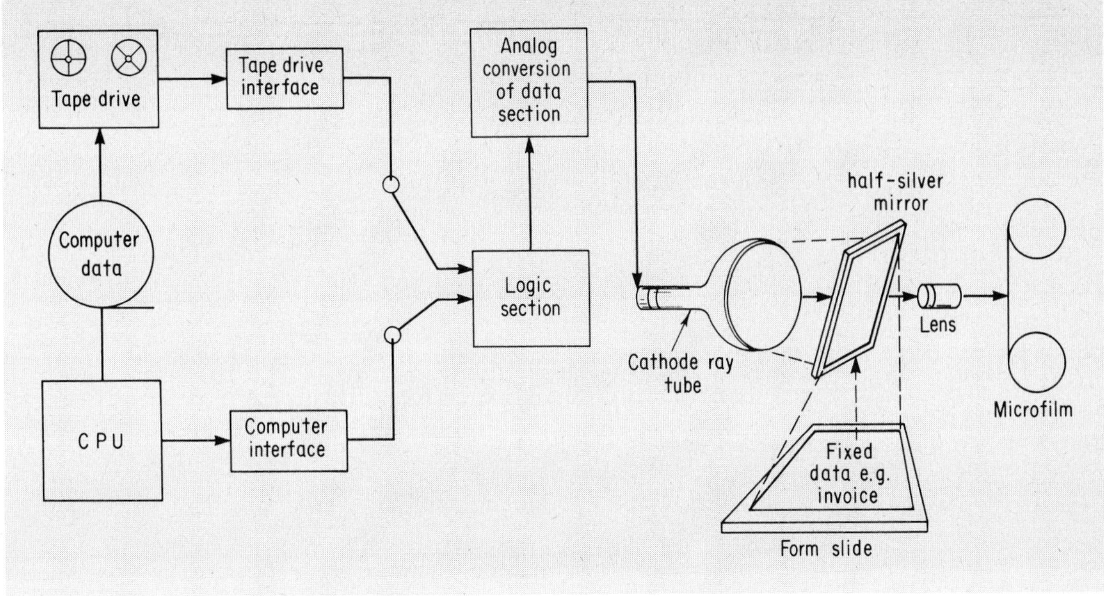

FIGURE 10-8. CRT recording on microfilm

is normally a 100-foot reel of either 16- or 35-millimeter film. Compared to other types, roll film is relatively slow to use as it must be manually mounted and taken off by the operator. Furthermore, data are accessed sequentially—a time-consuming task when searching for a specific record.

Film also may be inserted in strips into a clear plastic carrier (sometimes called a jacket) or made into a number of rows of images on a sheet of film, known as *microfiche.* Some 35-millimeter films are cut into individual frames and placed in a cut out area of a punched card (called *aperture*-card microfilm) for a specialized retrieval system.

A COM recorder generally consists of an input section, a logic and conversion section, a display section, and a microfilm-handling section (Fig. 10-8). Computer output data are first transmitted to the logic section in the form of electronic signals for logical conversion. The logic section routes the data received to the conversion section, which, in turn, converts the electronic signals to voltages applied to a cathode-ray tube (CRT). The image from the CRT screen passes through a semi-reflective mirror and a microfilm lens onto an unexposed film. Once exposed, the film is advanced, and the next page is displayed on the face of the CRT screen.

As shown in Fig. 10-8, a COM recorder can operate on-line from the host computer or off-line from magnetic tape drives. The interface used in either operation mode is designed primarily to interpret the codes of incoming signals. On-line COM systems produce data 10 times faster than printing and are less costly to run than off-line systems.

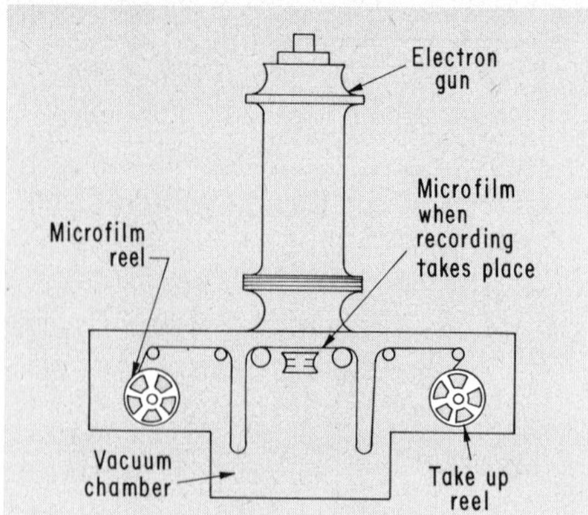

FIGURE 10-9

The CRT technique is the most common method. Other COM imaging technologies include the following:

1. **Electron-beam recording** (EBR) was developed by the 3M Company; it employs an electron beam, which writes a latent image of the data directly onto a dry silver film transported through an evacuated chamber. The film is later developed by applying heat to its surface. It is then advanced for writing the next page in sequence (Fig. 10-9).
2. **Fiber-optics recording** forms alphanumeric characters by using a translation matrix, a set of light-emitting diodes (LED), and a luminous fiber-optics character assembly. The process leads to the display of characters on fiber optics, which are then recorded on microfilm through a film transport and a special-purpose lens.
3. **Laser-beam recording** uses laser beams to record directly on film, in a manner similar to that of electron-beam recording.

A major advantage of CRT recording is its excellent image resolution and use in generating graphics. Fiber-optics recording, however, is more economical, more reliable in certain respects, and easier to operate than CRT recording. Advances in CRT recording are expected to improve its reliability and simplify its operation.

In selecting a COM system, the user must decide on (1) the type of microfilm storage (i.e., reel film, microfiche, cassette, etc.) he will use, (2) whether to operate on-line or off-line, and (3) whether to use an in-house or an outside system. Then he may contact COM manufacturers for descriptive details of the systems that meet his specifications. The system chosen should also be evaluated in terms of the quality of its output, hardware integrity, reliability, and price. If an outright purchase cannot be justified, rental arrangements might be negotiated, or a service center might be considered a satisfactory compromise.

Compared to the impact printer, COM is gaining acceptance and, according to a leading authority, is threatening to replace everything except the central processor. In the near future, several improvements are expected in COM technology. For example, some manufacturers are working on a terminal display/microfilm-photography hybrid that will make it possible for the user to edit data on film from his terminal. A new concept under development employs a light pen with which the user adds or changes information directly on microfilm. Some new COM units even produce hard copy from the display screen simply by pushing a button. Finally, research is being done on the possibility of allowing the user to sort or merge directly from microfilm to produce specialized reports.

The foregoing examples illustrate the increased growth of COM. Microfilm sales were under 0.25 percent of the sales of printing paper in 1970, but are expected to increase to 1 percent by 1985. COM systems sales and rental, which represented 30 percent of micrographic equipment sales in 1970, are expected to increase to 70 percent by 1985. The major uses will be to record computer-generated output data and reduce the weight and bulk of hard copy.

SUMMARY

In this chapter we discussed the characteristics and operation of magnetic-ink character recognition (MICR), optical character recognition (OCR), and computer-output-microfilm (COM) devices. MICR was developed primarily to automate banking paperwork. The process involves encoding checks with magnetic ink, which is magnetized by generating a flux pattern on each encoded character. During processing, a MICR reader–sorter reads checks by converting the magnetic ink pattern into electronic signals to be used by the computer for updating the customer's account.

Check encoding represents a positive step toward developing a universal language understandable by man and machine. It makes possible the use of checks as direct input to the computer for processing.

Optical character recognition is another direct-input device designed to reduce the cost of capturing source data, to eliminate the need for keypunching, and to make it possible to prepare data in a conventional human communication medium. OCR readers identify each character by comparing its features (pattern) with features stored in memory. Their circuitry is designed to break up the character image into pulses for proper identification. Internally stored reference patterns guide the reader's recognition unit to match the pattern held by the scanning unit. The matching process is made on the basis of stroke analysis or curve tracing. Unmatched character patterns cause the document to be rejected.

OCR devices are classified either by size of document, which includes journal-tape, small documents, and/or page readers, or by the class of font read, such as mark, single-font, multifont, and hand-print readers. The hand-print reader identifies a handwritten character if its trace fits within the tolerance configuration set for it. Extra care and special training are needed for the effective preparation of hand-printed numeric input, which is ideally suited to cases involving high-volume source documents with limited formats.

A unique approach to combating output bottlenecks is computer output microfilm (COM). It offers the advantages of smaller storage space requirements, quick record retrieval, lower cost of supplies, high recording speed, and unlimited copies of original data with reproduction quality that cannot be matched by the impact printer. Among its limitations are slow acceptance of COM as a substitute for the traditional hard copy, high costs except in handling high-volume documents, and its impracticality in situations requiring hard copy or frequent interaction with output data. COM imaging techniques vary from the more popular CRT system, which offers excellent image resolution, to electron-beam, fiber-optics, and laser-beam recording. Awareness of the differences among these techniques and alternative storage media (i.e., roll film, microfiche, cartridge, etc.) is essential in evaluating a COM system to best meet the needs of a particular user.

TERMS TO LEARN

COM
Data recorder
Magnetic-ink character recognition
Microfiche
On-line
Optical character recognition
Optical scanning

QUESTIONS

1. What is MICR? How does it help process information? Explain.
2. Distinguish the primary characteristics of recognition devices.
3. Explain OCR's operation and use in business data processing.
4. What are the characteristics of document and page readers?
5. State and explain an application area of your own where an OCR reader can be used.
6. Summarize the advantages and limitations of COM.
7. Describe the basic components and operation of a CRT-oriented COM system.
8. What imaging techniques are available for computer output?

SUGGESTED READING

AVEDON, D. M. "The Fundamentals of a Micrographic System," *The Office,* April 1973, pp. 57–59ff.

CARPENTER, J. W. "The Personal Microfiche Reader," *The Office,* April 1973, pp. 52–54ff.

CHU, A. L. C. "COM Takes on an Active Image," *Business Automation,* April 1972, pp. 30–35ff.

CONNERS, RICHARD. "Microfilm: Past, Present, and Future," *Infosystems,* March 1973, pp. 39–41.

FEIDELMAN, L. A. "The Application-Oriented OCR System," *Modern Data,* Feb. 1973, p. 20.

———. "A New Voice in Data Entry," *Modern Data,* April 1973, p. 28.

FLOMENHOFT, MARK. "Computer Output Microfilm," *Modern Data,* Dec. 1972, pp. 32–33ff.

LEE, JACK. "A Penetrating Look at Today's Micrographics," *The Office,* April 1973, pp. 18–21.

LUNDELL, E. D., JR. "OCR Use Requires Concentrated, Constructive Effort," *Computerworld,* June 21, 1972, p. 3.

MACHOVER, C. "Interactive CRT," *Society for Information Display Journal,* Nov./Dec. 1972, pp. 10–17.

MCGRATH, J. D. "Does COM Eliminate the Output Bottleneck?", *Data Management,* May 1971, pp. 14–20.

MENKHAUS, E. J. "Microfilm: New Power for Information Systems," *Business Automation,* May 1971, pp. 38–42.

"OCR's Cost, Capabilities Scare Some Users Away," *Computerworld,* Sept. 27, 1972, Supplement, p. 21.

TIERNEY, D. F. "Traditional OCR Problems Passé in Today's Market," *Computerworld,* Nov. 8, 1972, p. 9.

telecommunications and the computer

11

WHAT IS TELECOMMUNICATIONS?

FEATURES OF A TELECOMMUNICATIONS SYSTEM

APPLICATION AREAS

Computer Time Sharing

Inquiry Processing

Message Switching

Data Collection

PRIMARY ELEMENTS OF A DATA-TRANSMISSION SYSTEM

Data Transmission

TELECOMMUNICATIONS FACILITIES

Modes of Communication

Classes of Service

Telecommunications Codes

CENTRAL SWITCHING SYSTEMS SERVICES

DATA-TRANSMISSION TERMINALS

Audio Terminals

Visual Display Terminals

Facsimile Terminals

PLANNING AND DESIGN OF A TELECOMMUNICATIONS SYSTEM

Design Criteria

Network Control

THE COMMON CARRIERS

In this chapter we cover the concepts and technological developments in telecommunications when combined with the capabilities of the computer. Although either of these established fields can perform independently and make headway in handling information, combining their complementary features increases the power and performance of both in a manner previously unknown to man. Telecommunications links the capabilities of the computer in processing transmitted data to thousands of business organizations in dispersed locations. Computers, on the other hand, not only process the transmitted data, but also direct the inflow of demands from various centers into an organized set of communication channels.

Historically, communication channels were first implemented through oral, written, or symbolic types of devices. Smoke signals were used by the Indians to cover the distance between camps, and seagoing ships used flags for day communication and lights for transmitting night messages. With the advent of electricity, electrical impulses flowing in the form of radio wave, microwave, or similar processes could be used for communicating information between two points at high speed. This giant step was instrumental in the creation of the sophisticated communications systems of space exploration and rocketry. Information flow transmitted by a spaceship hundreds of thousands of miles away can be received in a matter of seconds.

The key channel used in telecommunications is the telephone line. In 1918, the *carrier* concept was implemented when 12 voice channels were carried over one wire pair. By the mid-1940s, a large number of voice channels could be carried over coaxial cables, and 10 years later microwave chains were developed to carry many more channels. Today's telephone cables and microwave chains carry up to 21,000 voice channels. In the 1970s, we shall see the use of cross-country helical wave-guide channels, with a 100,000-or-more voice-channel system designed to accommodate virtually any request for commercial data transmission.

Such steady growth in the types and capacities of telecommunications systems was made to keep pace with man's accelerated information growth. Acceptance of telecommunications is due in part to the birth of more conglomerates and the expansion and diversification of many corporations and government agencies. The need to quickly process data between the headquarters and various field offices becomes paramount. The earlier conventional batch processing of vital information can now be accomplished on-line, thus providing management with up-to-the-minute reports on request. Commercial on-line control of many operations means savings in the form of better customer service, increased efficiency, and more effective use of facilities.

Since the role of telecommunications is vital, we shall explore its key elements and structure. As this area can be quite technical, we shall avoid the pitfall of overemphasizing the technical details, and present, instead, an overview of telecommunications and supportive devices.

WHAT IS TELECOMMUNICATIONS?

Communication is the act of exchange or transmission of information orally or in writing. The communication essentially involves *a set of functional units designed to transfer digital data in machine-processable form between two or more terminals by using private or public networks.* The objective is to shorten the time it takes to transfer data from its source to the computer and back to the user. Transmission must be over a distance of 50 feet or more before it can be classified as data communication. It can be either off-line (where data are read from an input medium, transmitted to another location, and written on some machine-processable form) or on-line (from a reading device directly into a computer, from a computer to some remote output device, or even from one computer directly to another).

FEATURES OF A TELECOMMUNICATIONS SYSTEM

Viewing data-communication facilities as a part of a computer system to transmit data from remote locations or from another computer, a modern telecommunications system offers several features:

1. **System modification.** More applications can be handled by the central processing unit simply by adding one or more modules as needed. In this respect, the original system design and its peripheral devices remain undisturbed.
2. **Space flexibility.** Incoming messages can be temporarily allocated to specific segments in core storage for processing. When they are no longer needed, another incoming message is stored instead. Thus, the *storage-segment* feature eliminates the need for reserving an entire area for incoming data.
3. **Maintenance of low-cost transmission.** Systems that use multiple channels are monitored by a transmission control device which allows simultaneous transmission from as many as 40 lines (and, in some larger systems, 275 lines), and requires no particular stored-program unit. The lines link terminals, inquiry displays, and audio-response units to the system.
4. **A fast, efficient, built-in interrupt subsystem.** The computer system is designed to handle any interrupt, whether it stems from an incoming message or a processing error. A switching center performs like a traffic policeman, funneling the many interrupts continuously without trouble.
5. **Low operating costs.** An electronic data-transmission system is ideal in high-speed data transmission and requires only a nominal operating expense for the physical handling of transmitted data. By contrast, physical data transmission, which may involve the use of the U.S. mails or a private messenger service, is ideal in situations involving (1) a short distance between the sender and the receiver, (2) data that must be regularly received in a specific medium, and (3) data that can be reproduced in the event of loss during their transfer.
6. **Channel input–output operations.** Incoming data are channeled directly into computer memory at predetermined locations. Once the desired amount of data are available, the processing resumes automatically. Since input–output devices operate in a different capacity and at a slower speed than the computer itself, programming is carried out independently of these devices, as long as a minimum amount of input data is available for processing.

In terms of the specific contributions of each technology to the other, computers offer communications technology several benefits:

1. **Automatic error handling.** Computers can be programmed to halt the transmission of input messages once an error has been detected.
2. **Message buffering.** The buffering feature in computers means that the sender can send his message at all times. During peak periods or if the receiver's line is busy, the message is temporarily stored and is transmitted later as lines become available.
3. **Multiple-transmission capability.** When the sender wishes to transmit a message to several receivers, all he need do is provide

the message with a list of the receivers. The computer transmits the message to each station as its line becomes available.

4. **Flexibility in routines.** With a computer, rates, sequence of message transmission, and other routines can be made with minimum delay.

Communications, on the other hand, offers computers two important benefits:

1. **Implementation of time-sharing systems.** Users from various locations are allowed to have direct access to the computer.
2. **Remote data acquisition.** Through remote terminals, hundreds of users can inquire about and receive certain data stored in a centralized location. Data can also be fed into a centralized computer system from such points as warehouses and distribution centers.

To bring computer power and the data it can handle to the maximum number of users, serious attention should be given to the man–computer interface. Since interface differs from one man to another and from one computer to another, a wide variety of data-transmission systems have been designed, each system differing in the way it functions. Some systems are on-line; others are off-line. Some are interactive; others are noninteractive.

In an *on-line system,* telecommunications data go directly to the computer from some point of origination and/or output data are transmitted directly to the user. Most human transmission from terminals is interactive, since a response is generally received from the computer. Some on-line systems, however, are noninteractive, such as when the computer merely receives a batch transmission requiring no response.

An *off-line system,* on the other hand, is one in which input data are first written on magnetic tape or disk or punched into cards or paper tape for later processing. Off-line systems are noninteractive, since no direct linkage is made between the computer and the input data source to provide data response to the source.

APPLICATION AREAS

Data communication is used in a wide range of computer processing routines, among which are computer time sharing, inquiry processing, switching, and data collection.

Computer Time Sharing

Computer time sharing typically involves communication links between a central computer facility and a number of remote input–output terminals. In some cases, two or more computers may be linked together for sharing the overall work load. Time sharing is explained in more detail in Chapter 12.

Inquiry Processing

In inquiry processing, remote devices are linked to central data files for direct access. If the setup is in real time, inquiries and other transactions are processed immediately, thus keeping the files up to date at all times. Among users of real-time inquiry-processing systems are airline and hotel reservation systems, and those brokerage firms involved in the handling of hundreds of transactions each day.

Message Switching

Some organizations use a message-switching technique for handling large volumes of messages among their geographically distributed locations and a central computer facility. By two-way communication, a message-switching center receives messages from and transmits them to designated receiving terminals, and stores them in between if ncessary.

Data Collection

A data-collection system refers to the transmission of data from remote (batch) terminals directly to a central computer facility. A *remote-batch terminal* is generally an input–output device or similar peripheral unit that provides the input and output information; the computer facility provides the processing and most of the storage. Although the terminals do not offer every type of computing capability, they do offer to a remote user the convenience of computer access without the need for an on-site installation. Furthermore, direct transmission of data decreases the frequency of data handling, and this, in turn, cuts down on manual processing and errors. In business applications, remote-batch processing can be applied in handling payroll, inventory control, production control, market and sales analysis, labor cost distribution, and information retrieval.

Communications networks accommodate three key remote-batch-terminal modes of operation: (1) point-to-point with a central computer system, (2) point-to-point with another remote-batch terminal, and (3) a multipoint structure involving some combination of other terminals and/or computer systems.

PRIMARY ELEMENTS OF A DATA-TRANSMISSION SYSTEM

Understanding data-processing systems involves a study of the elements responsible for data flow or communications. Communications is the central phenomenon in information processing. Information is of no value

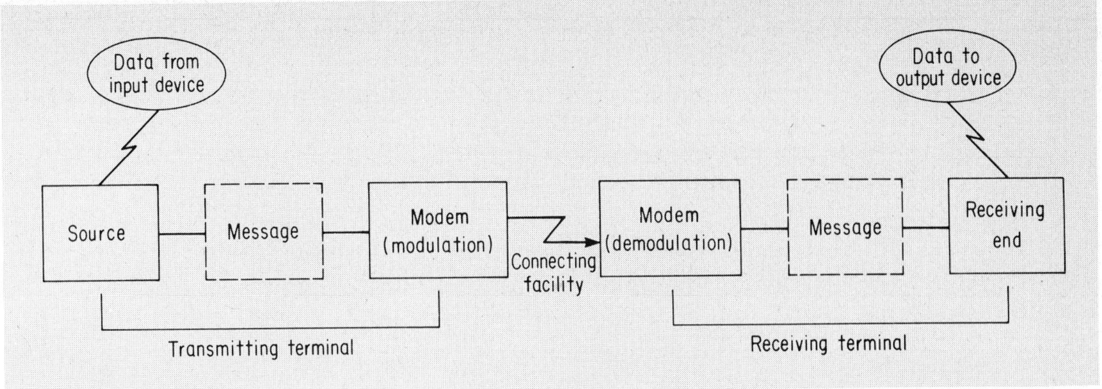

FIGURE 11-1. General telecommunications system—data flow

unless it is fully communicated to its proper destination. To accomplish this task, source data must be transmitted and received through effective and fast channels without distortion or alteration. This means that the type and strength of the receiving and transmitting devices must be carefully selected, especially when they are employed in long-distance data communication.

In a general communications system, source data are converted into an organized set of symbols, dashes, or electrical impulses in the form of a coded message. This encoded message is next handled by a transmitter, which uses a communication facility such as the telephone line to relay the message to its destination. Before reaching its destination, the message is intercepted by a receiver, which converts it into an understandable language. The validity of the decoded message is error-checked before it is finally released to its proper destination.

A data-transmission system is similar to a general communications system. As illustrated in Fig. 11-1, it consists of the following elements:

1. **Data source.** The point from which data are generated by a person or a device to be transmitted through known channels, such as the telephone and telegraph. More recently, industry has been using a television channel especially designed for data-transmission systems. The data being transmitted are later relayed to another person or device located elsewhere.
2. **Message.** A set of symbols that represents the information being transmitted. The message can be expressed orally, in written form, or as a digital signal. Like a business letter, which begins with the address of the sender and is followed by the address of the receiver, a message, and an end-of-message phrase, message elements must be formated in the proper sequence and in a manner prescribed by a set of related rules. Furthermore, the text of the message should be relayed in such a way as to give a true and clear interpretation to the sender.

3. **Channel.** A transmission channel facilitates the communication of source data between two or more transmission points.
4. **Receiver–transmitter.** A person, device, or center capable of receiving, retaining, and, if necessary, transmitting the message to a predetermined person, device, or destination.
5. **Terminal.** An area in a data-transmission system where messages can enter or exit.
6. **Switching centers.** Much like traffic policemen, switching centers funnel incoming messages from the line to an outgoing channel.

Data Transmission

Data transmission is carried out in various forms. It may take place between two computers, between man and a computer, or between a computer and input–output devices. For example, a computer may be connected to another computer by a telephone line and programmed to transmit data to the other computer as though it were an output device. Some computers are even assigned coded (telephone) numbers that other computers can dial for data acquisition or transmission. Man also can "talk" to computers through special telecommunications devices. However, the more common data-transmission approach is between input–output machines and a computer center connected remotely by a private telephone line or by a dial system much like that of the ordinary telephone.

Data may be transmitted electrically over direct-wire hookup using telephone or telegraph lines or by electronic wave form (signal), which is referred to as microwave transmission. *Microwave* channels rely on a network of relay stations posted about 50 miles apart to amplify the radio signal they receive so that the transmitted message reaches its destination clearly, accurately, and in the shortest time possible.

The electrical signal or wave form employed in transmitting data is defined by its *amplitude* (strength), *phase* (duration), and *frequency* (the number of times the signal recurs over a period of time). Changing any of these characteristics will produce a different signal to represent a 1-bit or a 0-bit state.

MODEMS. Terminals transmit signals in digital form, whereas telephone lines use analog transmission. A transmission medium accommodates several independent data paths called *bands*. When bands are used, a device called a *modem* (short for *modulator–demodulator*) or data set serves as the interface between remote terminals and the central computer facility. It is designed to convert constant-level direct-current pulses or digital signals into analog or wave-like signals suitable for transmission over a voice line (modulation). At the receiving end, another modem converts the signal back into digital pulses for processing and printout (demodulation) (Fig. 11-1).

Modems, then, are used to modify data signals so that they can be properly transmitted and, later, processed. They use four methods of modification:

1. **Amplitude modulation** involves changing the waves' amplitude. Transmission is accomplished by a sequence of tone bursts when used with a device like the DATA-PHONE. Amplitude modulation, then, varies the tone bursts. A tone of one amplitude would represent a 1 bit; another tone would represent a 0 bit.
2. **Frequency modulation** is similar to amplitude modulation. A change in frequency of the signal represents a 1 bit to be transmitted; another frequency represents a 0 bit.
3. **Phase modulation,** in effect, is jumping along the carrier wave, past a point, to a fixed reference point. Phase modulation is used only with digital transmission systems, since phase-change detectors can detect only large, abrupt changes, such as those produced by digital signals.
4. **Pulse modulation.** In this technique, as the signals occur, they are sampled at regular intervals and then converted into a signal pulse of one of three types: pulse amplitude modulation (PAM), pulse width modulation (PWM), or pulse position modulation (PPM). In each case, the signal is converted, and the amplitude, width, or position is allowed to vary while the other characteristics remain constant. That is, in PAM, the amplitude varies; in PWM, the width varies; and in PPM, the position varies. After the signals have been converted, they are transmitted to their destination.

ASYNCHRONOUS AND SYNCHRONOUS TRANSMISSION. The types of modems available to telecommunications users include (1) hard-wired modems (capable of speeds of up to 1,000,000 bits per second) used mostly for short-range transmission (such as found in in-plant systems); (2) wide-band modems (capable of speeds ranging from 19,000 to over 200,000 bits per second) used primarily for computer-to-computer communications or large-volume multiplexing applications; and (3) the broad category of devices used for transmission over the Bell System's voice-grade telephone circuits. Modems designed for use on these lines (either dial-up or leased from the telephone company for one user's exclusive use) fall into two broad categories: those handling asynchronous data, and those handling synchronous data.

Asynchronous modems are generally low-speed devices capable of handling up to 1,200 bits per second over dial-up telephone facilities, or up to 1,800 bits per second using a conditioned leased line. Asynchronous data come over the transmission line one character at a time and are typically produced by low-speed terminals such as teletypes. In asynchronous systems, the transmission link is in a mark (binary 1) condition. As each character is transmitted, it is preceded by a start bit or transition from mark to space (binary 0), which indicates to the receiving terminal that a character is being transmitted. The receiving device repeats the mark and space transitions originated by the transmitter, thereby recreating the character. At the end of the character transmission, the line is returned to a mark condition by a stop bit, and is ready for the beginning of the next character. This process is repeated, character by character, until the entire message has been sent.

Synchronous transmission, on the other hand, makes use of an internal clocking source within the modem. Once the start bits have been sensed by the receiving terminal, the system put into "synch," and the clock started, data transmission proceeds character by character in a continuous stream without the intervening start and stop bits. The incoming stream of data bits is interpreted on the basis of the clocking signals and decoded character by character by the terminal until the final stop bits are received, indicating that the message is over.

Asynchronous transmission is superior when transmission is irregular, and is also cheaper because of the simpler terminal interface logic and circuitry. Synchronous transmission, on the other hand, makes far better use of the transmission facility (elimination of start and stop bits on every character speeds throughput), and allows higher transmission speeds; however, the cost is greater because of the more complex circuitry needed for the operation.

Medium-speed modems are almost entirely synchronous, and operate between 2,000 and 3,600 bits per second over dial-up or leased lines. High-speed synchronous units operate at speeds ranging from 4,800 bits per second on voice-grade lines to 9,600 bits per second on leased circuits. Such high speed is maintained either by conditioning or by equalization. *Conditioning* refers to the process the telephone company follows in maintaining the quality of a privately leased line to a predetermined standard of performance and clarity. In this context, *equalization* refers to the process by which the modem itself accomplishes this task. Lower-speed modems attached to a leased line do not normally require equalization, since minimum line conditioning is adequate. However, conditioning and equalization are required when higher-speed modems are attached. Modems used for high-speed transmission over the dial-up net require equalization because it is never known in advance which unconditioned telephone line will be used. Modems in these categories are typically used for multiplexing applications.

MULTIPLEXING. Because of increasing need for data communication and rising telecommunications charges, many computer users with multiple locations can realize substantial savings and greater operating efficiency through multiplexing. Multiplexing expands the capacity of the line by concentrating the signals from several terminals on to a single line for transmission to a distant computer. At the other end, a similar unit separates the discrete data inputs. By definition, *multiplexing is the simultaneous transmission of several messages over a single channel through the use of predetermined frequencies within the full bandwidth.*[1]

Basically, a multiplexor queries each input line (device) in some predetermined sequence to check the device's readiness to transmit. When a device is found ready to transmit, the multiplexor connects it to the device until it completes transmission of its message. Then the multiplexor proceeds to examine the remaining lines in sequence and without delay. In such a system, if a second device is ready to transmit while the first one is transmitting, it must wait until the first device has completed its message. If several activities occur simultaneously, the last one in line could be forced to wait for an extended period of time, which makes this type of multiplexing satisfactory mostly for connecting manual-entry devices to a computer.

TELECOMMUNICATIONS FACILITIES

Telecommunications is generally accomplished by transmitting over telephone and telegraph lines, radio, or microwave. The Bell Telephone System and Western Union provide the most widely used lines. Details on the types of services they offer are covered later.

Modes of Communication

There are three modes of communication facilities: simplex, half-duplex, and full-duplex.

1. **Simplex** channel transmits in one direction only. The sender may transmit messages to the receiver, but not vice versa.

   A ——————→ B

2. **Half-duplex** channel transmits in either direction, but in one direction at a time; that is, the sender transmits information to the receiver, and vice versa, but not simultaneously.

   A ⇄ B

3. **Full-duplex** line transmits in both directions simultaneously and is equivalent to two simplex lines or to one half-duplex line used in opposite directions. A full-duplex line is used for voice and data transmission or for data transmission only; that is, communication devices may use the conventional two-way voice transmission or the data-only mode for data transmission.

   A ←——————→ B

[1] There are two types of multiplexing: the older frequency-division multiplexing (FDM) and the later time-division multiplexing (TDM). An FDM multiplexor combines the signals it receives by slicing the bandwidth of a voice-grade channel and assigning each signal its own portion of the frequency band. A TDM multiplexor, on the other hand, is more flexible. It slices up the available transmitting capability according to time elements.

Transmission rate depends on the bandwidth of the transmission medium, which, in turn, determines maximum capacity or transmission speed (measured in bauds).[2] Thus, the wider the band, the higher the frequency and, consequently, the faster the transmission rate. A bandwidth is categorized into four classes of service:

1. **Telegraph.** The narrowest or the lowest-grade channel; it transmits up to 150 bits per second.
2. **Narrow band.** It is more commonly used with low-speed terminals such as the teletypewriter and can transmit up to 300 bits per second, depending on the services used.
3. **Voice band.** Used for communicating by human voice or data over public or leased lines. Maximum speed is up to 4,000 bits per second, depending on the modem used.
4. **Broad band.** A channel with a band greater than 4,000 bits per second is considered a *broad-band* channel. It uses coaxial or microwave cable in transmitting data at up to 50,000 bits per second over switched connections and over 225,000 bits per second over private-line channel offering; in some late-model terminals, over 1 million bits per second are transmitted.

Modern technology is contributing to the steady increase in the capacity of the existing bands. American Telephone and Telegraph (AT&T), for example, plans to increase its data facilities by utilizing portions of present voice microwave links. This effort will make use of baseband frequencies in the existing microwave systems by adding a 1.5 million bit data-stream capacity without reducing existing voice-channel traffic.

Telecommunications Codes

A telecommunications system may use several different codes. The five most commonly used codes are

1. Baudot five-level code, which uses 5 bits to represent each character; since its coding structure allows for only 32 characters and, consequently, cannot account for the 26 alphabetic and 10 decimal characters, the Baudot code assigns two characters to a few of the 5-bit codes.
2. ASCII seven-level code, with provision for a compatible eight-level code. The 8-bit code contains 128 characters: 94 graphic characters, and 34 control symbols.

[2] Some books use the term "bauds" to indicate the signaling speed (not line capacity) of a data-transmission line. For lines using two-state signaling, bauds are synonymous with bits per second. However, it is more generally the case that bauds is used when referring to lines that do not use two-state signaling. Therefore, the term "bits per second" will be used instead in this section.

3. BCD six-level code.
4. Teletypesetter six-level code.
5. Field data seven-level code, with provision for a compatible eight-level code.

Of the foregoing, the Baudot and the ASCII codes are the most important. Other codes used include the data interchange, four-of-eight, Hollerith, and extended binary-coded decimal interchange (EBCDIC) codes.

CENTRAL SWITCHING SYSTEMS SERVICES

Connections between a sending and a receiving terminal may be established permanently or on a temporary basis. In a permanent or *direct-line* system, a sender has a direct line to each location to which he transmits data. Such arrangements can be quite uneconomical, especially in situations when the transmission process does not make constant use of the linkup.

A more practical alternative is to provide upon request a temporary connection between a sending station and any receiving station. This switching approach means that all sending lines funnel into a switching center, which links with the desired receiving station until the entire message has been transmitted. Line switching of this type is a one-to-one relationship; that is, only one connecting line is required for each receiving station. In direct-line switching, however, more core connecting lines are required than the number of stations involved and an *arithmetic increase of one location in the communications network results in a geometric increase in the number of connections required*—equal to $n(n-1)/2$.

In Fig. 11-2, a few points are worth noting:

1. The number of connections in a direct-line system increases by more than one for each additional location. With three locations, three direct lines are needed; with a fourth location, another three lines (a total of six) are required, and so on.
2. In line switching, only one connection is required for every location in the communications network. The net saving becomes more significant as more locations are included in the network.
3. With a line-switching system, then, there are fewer connecting lines and, therefore, a less costly system is realized than would be the case in a direct-line system.

Some switching systems are designed to store messages temporarily for later transmission to their proper destination. This type of switching makes better use of the communications network, since it does not require

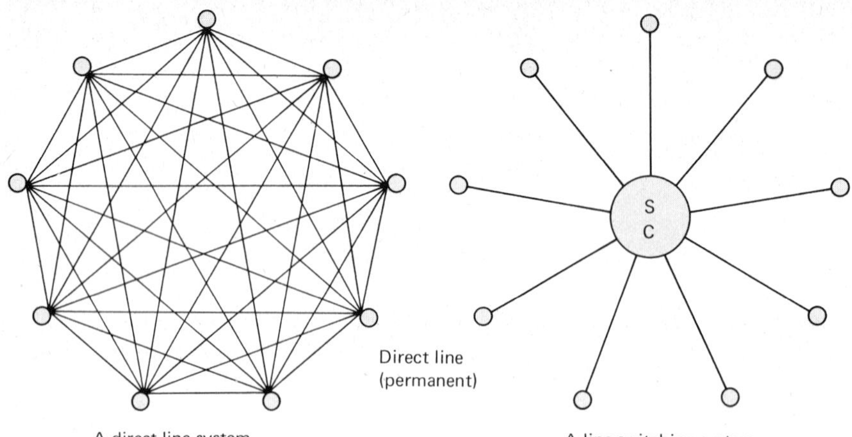

No. of Locations	Total Number of Connections: Direct-Line n(n—1)/2	Total Number of Connections: Line Switched	No. of Lines Saved with Line Switching
3	3	3	0
4	6	4	2
5	10	5	5
6	15	6	9
7	21	7	14
8	28	8	20
9	36	9	27
10	45	10	35

FIGURE 11-2. *Direct-line and line-switching systems*

the sender or receiver to stay on the line until the message has been transmitted.

For many years, engineers have been searching for ways to apply computer techniques to the control of switching systems. Now being mass-produced is the Bell Telephone No. 1 ESS (Electronic Switching System), which is capable of handling 65,000 channels with up to 100,000 messages in a busy hour. When set up as a PBX (private branch exchange) for large firms, it can effectively handle up to 200 extensions. This system is one of 32 other systems under the control of a large centrally located computer.

The electronic switching system provides many benefits. In addition to an increase in switching capacity, callers can now arrange for conference calls with several parties in remote locations, dial an extension in the same office complex, dial certain selected seven-digit numbers through two-digit codes, and arrange for automatic call transfer, if necessary. For example, a person can dial a special code and then the number of the party where he plans to spend the evening. During that period, all incoming calls will be switched automatically to that number. A recent service allows the computer to dial a busy number. If a party's line is busy and the caller wishes to make a connection when it is free, he dials a code which instructs the computer to redial that number automatically.

DATA-TRANSMISSION TERMINALS

As explained earlier, a transmission terminal is an area or a location in a data-transmission system where messages can enter and/or exit. With this in mind, there are human-input as well as human-output terminals [3] and two-ways transmission devices such as audio, visual display, and facsimile terminals.

Audio Terminals

The use of voice transmission of data to and from a computer is becoming more widely accepted. Most computer systems currently under design provide facilities for voice-communication channels, as compatibility between data processing and data communication is becoming more complete each year.

One of the latest breakthroughs in computer technology has been the development of the computer's ability to "talk" with the user, called *voice response.* Early uses of this technique are now well developed and involve the user's transmitting a coded message to a central processing unit and in return receiving a voice reply. For this to happen, the computer must have access to a prerecorded vocabulary, which is used in giving out a certain answer. In some systems, a sizable number of human-voice words in recital form can be stored on active files.

Voice-response systems are commonly used in many business activities. A bank teller, for example, uses a special terminal to dial in a coded message to the computer to ask if it is all right to cash a check. The communication exchange goes something like the following:

Computer: This is the EZ system. Who are you?
Teller: 201 (teller's number).
15 (branch number).
Computer: Enter transaction code.
Teller: 03 (checking account inquiry).
Computer: Enter checking account number.

[3] Document-transmission terminals are also used in dealing with large-volume input–output data. They were included in Chapter 10 under optical document readers. Such terminals are primarily magnetic tape units, paper-tape readers/punches, card readers/punches, optical document readers, and magnetic-ink character readers. Facsimile devices that can be used as document and human-input terminals are included in this chapter.

Teller: 805-257-0.
Computer: Balance on checking account number eight zero five dash two five seven dash zero is one zero seven dollars and zero five cents. Repeat, one zero seven dollars and zero five cents.

A major department store in Chicago has a voice-response system that employs more than 1,000 touch-tone phones at the main store and its 12 branches. When a charge card is presented for a purchase, the clerk dials a special number to the computer. If the account is in good standing, the computer authorizes the sale and issues a special number to the audio-response unit. A "voice" then gives the approval number to the clerk by telephone to authorize the sale. In the meantime, the computer automatically subtracts the amount from the customer's credit limit. The balance is ready to be used for checking on future credit purchases.

TOUCH-TONE DEVICES. The touch-tone telephone has been effectively used in various data-transmission applications. Unlike the ordinary telephone, the touch-tone allows both voice and data transmission, is easy to move around, if necessary, and can be used with any electronic data-processing system that is linked by telecommunications channels (Fig. 11-3).

The touch-tone system consists of 12 standard keys—10 numeric keys and 2 special-character keys for data transmission. The special characters can be used to indicate end of transmission or end of message to control carriage return, or for other predetermined control codes. When depressed, each key generates a unique transmittable tone that is recognized by a receiving unit. Transmitting coded messages is as easy as keying in a telephone number. See Fig. 11-4 for a summary of touch-tone devices and a photograph of the card dialer.

FIGURE 11-3. Telephone data set (Courtesy of Bell Systems)

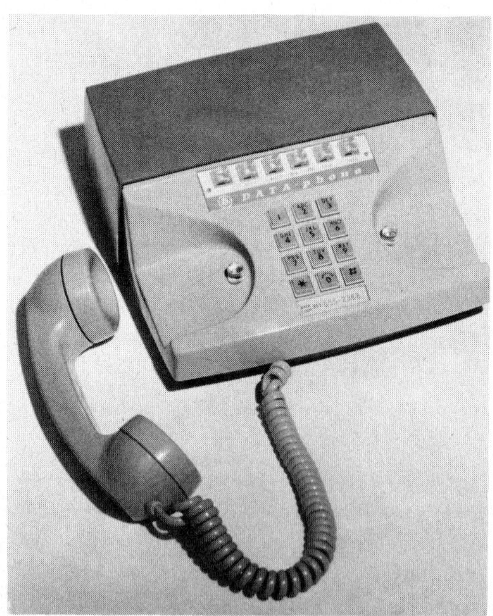

Equipment	Primary Functions	Application Areas	MEDIA Input	MEDIA Output	Data Volume	Primary Advantages	Limitations
Touch-Tone Devices	Translating and recording data received from a touch-tone telephone	Retail sales Dispatching Stock transactions Credit card sales	Plastic card Manual Cash register Punched paper tape	Direct to computer Machine readable magnetic tape or paper tape	Limited to 3,000 bits per second	Real-time applications Use of common carrier facilities Good low-speed data transmission	Special optional equipment limited throughout

FIGURE 11-4. *Summary of touch-tone devices*

Command	Coded entry
Multiply	4✱
Divide	7✱
Clear	+✱
Decimal point	1✱
Repeat answer	8✱✱✱
End of entry	✱✱

1	2	3
4	5	6
7	8	9
✱	0	+

FIGURE 11-5. Touch-tone keyboard and selected commands

One type of touch-tone device, called the *card dialer,* reads prepunched holes in a plastic card at eight to nine characters per second. This combination of the card and dialer is ideally used in information retrieval and in applications requiring entry of fixed information, such as the account number punched in a gasoline credit card.

The *Call-A-Matic* is an on-line touch-tone device that stores several hundred entries on a magnetic belt by the telephone dial. To read the information into the telephone network, the user depresses a button after verifying the entry, which is displayed at a window beside the dial.

Many educational institutions now use touch-tone telecommunications systems to help students do their homework. Coded instructions fed into a 12-key touch-tone telephone keyboard tell a remote computer to calculate various types of complex problems. The answers come back in audible voice. The keyboard and selected coded commands are presented in Fig. 11-5. Figure 11-6 shows two examples.

PORTABLE AUDIO TERMINALS. Recently, portable audio terminals have been used to allow entry of alphabetic and numerical data into a computer system from any standard touch-tone telephone (Fig. 11-7). Ideal users include salesmen, industrial and insurance agents, and other

FIGURE 11-6

Example 1. Problem: 2.07 × 1.06

Multiply
decimal point
End of message

Coded entry: 2 1*07 4* 1 1*06 **

Computer response: Your Answer: Two. Point. One. Nine. Four. Two.

Example 2. Problem: 448 ÷ 14

Coded entry: 448 7* 14 **

Computer response: Your Answer: Three. Two.

To repeat the answer, the coded entry is: 8***

The computer response is: Your Answer: Three. Two.

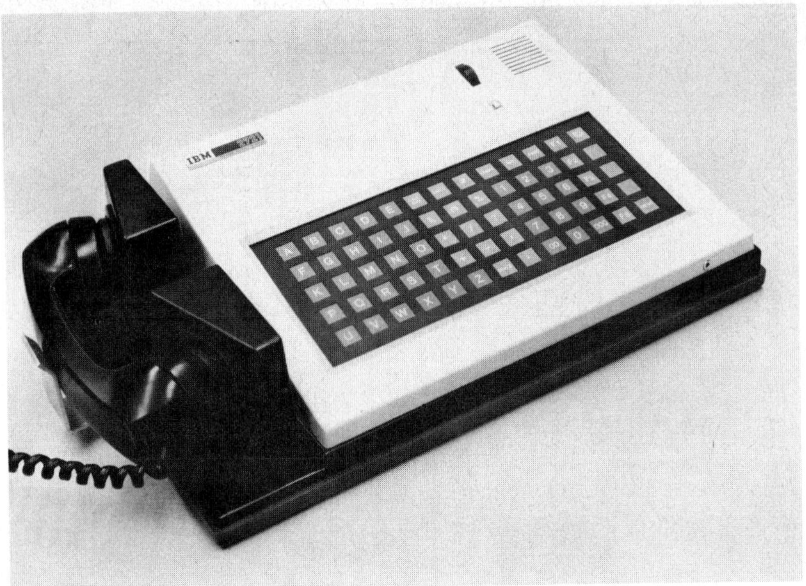

FIGURE 11-7. IBM 2721 portable audio terminal (Courtesy IBM)

business representatives with the need to feed data from the field directly to their company's computer facility for on-the-spot response.

PICTUREPHONE SERVICE. Picturephone is a recently developed service that permits the calling party to see as well as to hear the person with whom he is talking on the telephone and vice versa. A long-distance "booth-to-booth" service was established in 1964 on a trial basis between New York, Washington, and Chicago. "See-while-you-talk" calls were on an appointment basis. Early in 1970, regular service was established between these cities, with a high probability of extending the same operation to other large cities within the next 2 to 5 years.

Although today only a head-and-shoulders image of a person is transmitted, the future holds many interesting possibilities. Someday we may be able to transmit finely detailed printed material with clarity. Although a great deal of development work must be completed before this service is acceptable for any type of data transmission, its potential is evident.

Visual Display Terminals

NEED FOR VISUAL DISPLAY TERMINALS. The first real-time computer systems used the keyboard and printer as the universal means of feeding input data to the computer and recording the output data from it. Many applications automated by a real-time computer system were dynamic applications with no requirement for preserving output data once they

Equipment	Primary Functions	Application Areas	MEDIA Input	MEDIA Output	Data Volume	Primary Advantages	Limitations
CRT Devices	Displaying (via CRT) data received from remote computer or keyboard entry; transmitting to computer for storage or other media output	Text editing Computer input File maintenance Stock quotations Air traffic control	Computer Keyboard Punched tape	Video display Punched paper tape Direct to computer	Limited by message length and transmission facilities	Real-time file Minimal training Response time	Common carrier facility costs Limited character set and display capacity

FIGURE 11-8. *Summary of CRT devices*

were interpreted by the human operator. The need to automate dynamic applications, which becomes increasingly important each year, caused the search for a substitute for the conventional keyboard and printer, which, in addition to being slow, was not a very satisfactory man–machine interface.

The logical substitute is a visual display device, which can interact with the operator by means of the keyboard and display. Like a television screen, the display device (sometimes called a plotter) is a *cathode-ray tube* (CRT) that flashes graphs, numbers, or messages on the screen. A new-product concept, visual display devices *extend man's cognition* and are useful for those applications which require direct operator interaction with a centralized computer system. Information generated by the operator is displayed on the device prior to its transmission to the computer, so that any required changes or editing can be made where necessary. Furthermore, data transmitted from the computer are displayed to the operator for interpretation and understanding. Figure 11-8 is a summary of CRT devices.

TYPES OF VISUAL DISPLAYS. Digital data displays fall into one of three categories: alphanumeric, graphic, or large-screen. The *alphanumeric* display unit (commonly used on telephone lines) has a 5- to 10-inch screen and a typewriter-like keyboard[4] with which the user can operate the system, modify existing data, or key in new data. An input message interrogating the system is often very short, but the response could be a screenful of meaningful data provided in 4 seconds at a reasonable cost. (Fig. 11-9).

[4] A visual display unit without a keyboard functions as an output terminal with incoming data displayed on its screen. These units can be commonly found in bus and air terminals where up-to-date information on arrivals and departures is displayed.

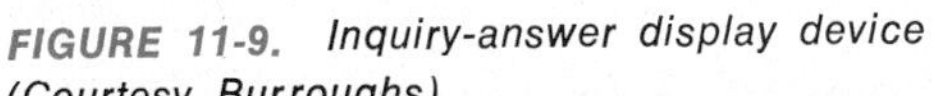

FIGURE 11-9. Inquiry-answer display device (Courtesy Burroughs)

FIGURE 11-10. Alphanumeric display unit

Alphanumeric display terminals are either buffered or unbuffered. *Buffered* displays include a memory for storing the binary-coded characters of a message. They perform whatever editing and other necessary operations are required on the message before it is relayed to or received from the computer. *Unbuffered* displays have no such memory, and keyed messages are sent directly to the computer for further work.

Graphic display devices display graphs and line drawings, as well as alphanumeric data output, on an 8- to 20-inch screen. Displays with graphic capability require high-capacity transmission lines to fill the screen quickly. Using the telephone line, it would take over 4 minutes to fill the screen, compared to 4½ seconds for alphanumeric display units (Fig. 11-10). Computer support of graphic displays is required in controlling the light pen, keyboard, and data tablet.

Large-screen display units are usually custom-built to accommodate six or more viewers. This type is likely to be in greater demand by industry in the future. The computerized management control room of the future could feasibly include a wall-sized display screen and a number of individual consoles where each executive could communicate directly with the computer.

There are four special kinds of visual display units:

1. The **CRT** display device is as commonly used as the television picture tube. Basically, it consists of a cathode, an electronic unit, a processing structure, deflection electrodes, and a phosphor coat-

ing on the screen surface. The cathode emits a stream of electrons, which are focused into a beam by an electronic gun at the center of the tube. The beam reaches the phosphor-coated screen surface, forming a spot of light.

2. The **Charactron** display unit is a special type of CRT unit. The beam forms characters (not spots) on the screen through a stencil designed for that purpose.
3. In a **video** display unit (similar to a television tube) a picture is generated by constant variation of the intensity of the beam, which scans the whole face of the tube. The degree of variation depends on the brilliance of the image to be shown.
4. A **storage-tube** display unit combines scanning and video features with a memory unit that controls the intensity of the beam during scanning.

APPLICATIONS. Applications for display devices all imply necessity, speed, and human intervention. The belief exists that operations and profits could be better if the quality and timeliness of the available information were better. These applications are dynamic.

Since the applications are so varied, cover so many industries, and include a myriad of functions, it is impossible to describe them in detail and difficult to put them into categories. A discussion of two categories, however, will provide an adequate breakdown for examination of the broad ideas involved in applying display devices. These categories are *information retrieval* and *direct data input*. If any particular installation were to be examined, we would probably find that these categories overlapped or that both were being covered. *Applications for visual communication terminals or CRT displays are becoming universal.*

A corporation can benefit immensely by using visual display devices in a telecommunications system for *information retrieval* (Fig. 11-11). Before the information can be retrieved, it must be streamlined, concise, and to the point. This means that the data-gathering function must be standardized, selected input data must be reduced, and the controlling program must make the clearest possible presentation.

Applications where information retrieval can be gainfully used with respect to management problems, services, and file inquiry are as follows:

1. **Management problems.** Information retrieval presents an up-to-the-minute picture of financial reports, competitive position, program milestones, inventory status, deliveries, and product development.
2. **Services.** Information retrieval can be used in banking, insurance, and information industries to answer customers' requests, to centralize records, to monitor and simplify work flow, and to deploy personnel.
3. **File inquiry.** Information retrieval provides immediate presentation of retail credit or inventory status, medical case histories and references, and library applications.

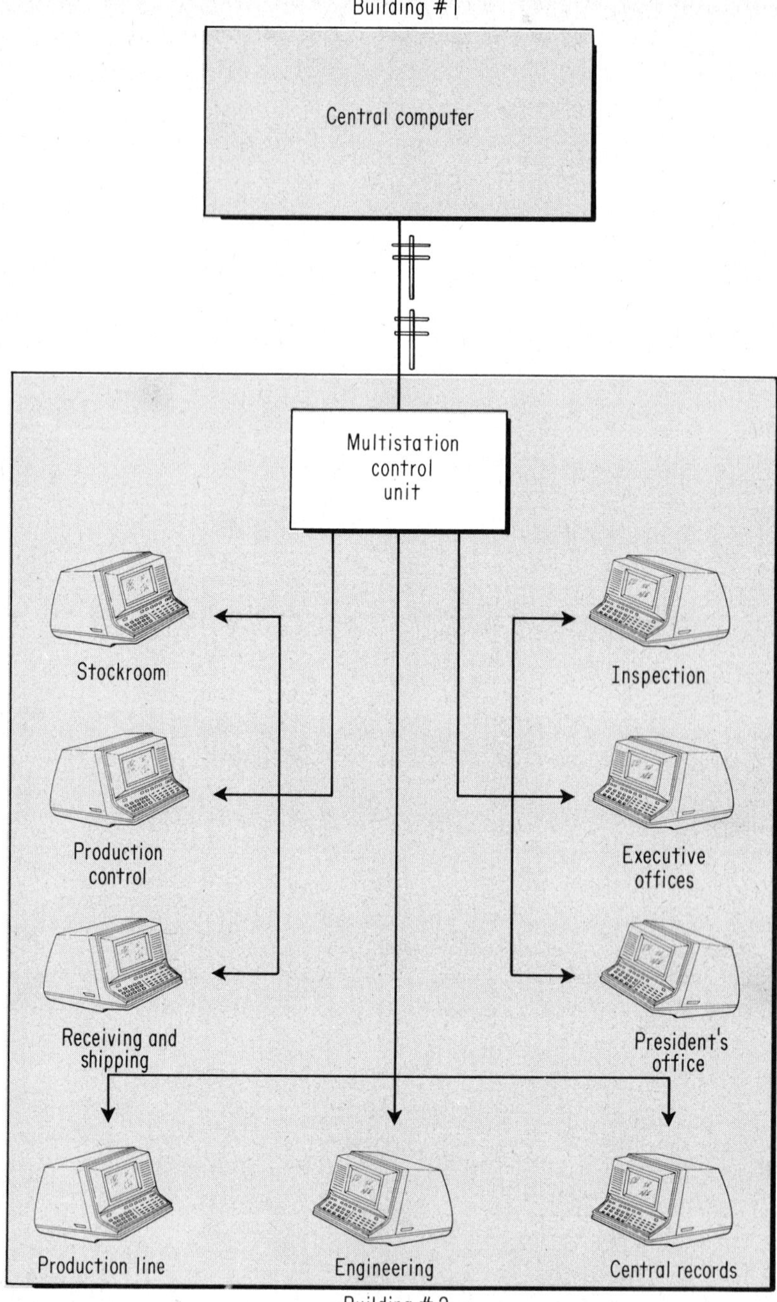

***FIGURE 11-11.** Network of single control points within one building*

Direct data input has been covered in Chapter 8. Today, access to mass storage and computer power can be accomplished through multi-access communications systems. Because of the direct interface with computer power, human errors are minimized by immediate computer validation. Ease of direct data input, then, can provide (1) simplified file maintenance, because a data base can be updated in real time so that subsequent inquiries can be made immediately, and (2) simplified new-data entry, because new input data can be taken directly from the source, thus eliminating several entry steps and thereby avoiding the possibility of human error, the necessity for intermediate storage of bulky source material, or the need for expensive off-line data-manipulating machines.

SELECTING A DISPLAY SYSTEM. In shopping for a visual display system, the prospective user should first evaluate his display requirements and distinguish among the routines that are display-dependent, those that are computer-dependent, and other processes with questionable dependence. Display requirements generally relate to the type (alphanumeric, graphic, etc.) and quantity of data to be displayed, the communication capabilities needed for proper display interaction, and the type and extent of operator interaction expected.

Once the user's display requirements have been determined, the next phase is to consider the capabilities, data-handling capacity, and data-processing capacity of the available displays. Display capabilities can be determined from the display manufacturer's manuals or literature. Like any flexible item, displays offer auxiliary devices such as joysticks and light pens at extra cost. Acquisition of these devices must be based on need and not on glamor, as they can be quite costly. Special-purpose devices are sometimes available and can be ordered directly from the manufacturer.

Display capacity, on the other hand, has to do with the amount of data that can be displayed and processed. Storage-tube displays have a high display capacity but a smaller processing capacity, because of the relatively long time it takes to fully display a new screen. Alphanumeric display units' memory units determine their data-handling capacity; the amount of processing they are capable of performing depends on the type of data to be processed and is inversely related to the rate at which data are transferred from the computer system and the display device.

Determining the capacity of graphic displays is probably the most difficult task; it depends on hard-to-figure factors such as the average time it takes to access data stored in memory and the total time required to process all details related to a given operation.

FACSIMILE TERMINALS. Facsimile terminals are devices capable of transmitting and reproducing handwritten or typewritten documents. A document at the sending station is scanned and converted into electrical impulses or signals. These signals are transmitted to a receiving station, where they are decoded and a copy of the original document is printed.

Many facsimile terminals use digital coding and code a document as though it were in black and white, or in shades of gray if sending halftone pictures. In black-and-white transmission, scanning divides the document into small squares, which are transmitted as on or off impulses. In halftone transmission, each point is transmitted as a group of bits. Facsimile transmission speeds for a standard 8½ by 11-inch page vary from 1 to 15 pages per minute, depending on the capacity of the telecommunication channels used.

PLANNING AND DESIGN OF A TELECOMMUNICATIONS SYSTEM

Design Criteria

In view of the many devices available in the telecommunications field, prospective users are often confused and find it difficult to decide on a proper system. Since each user has his own set of requirements and applications, no selection procedure can be acceptable to all users. However, certain design criteria can be suggested as a general guideline:

1. **Function.** Function refers to the capabilities of the communications system. The decision as to what system to use depends on the type of information to be transmitted or the specific operation to be carried out. Some systems are designed to collect, process, and/or distribute information. The more functions that are to be carried out by a communications system, the more expensive are the components necessary to do the job. Other factors to be considered include accuracy, reliability, volume, and speed of transmission.

   For large volumes of data to be transmitted among geographically dispersed locations, communications systems equipped with message-switching centers are desirable. As the message is received by the center, it is transmitted to its destination or stored temporarily until the channel for that destination becomes available.
2. **Distribution.** Distribution refers to the number of locations involved in the transmission of information. Data may be transmitted from one point to another, from one point to a few other points, from one point to many points, or from many points to many other points. An increase in the number of locations requires more sophisticated devices and a better quality data-transmission channel. For example, the public telephone line might be more economical to use for transmitting a small volume of data to many distant locations, whereas two-way transmission of a large volume of data might be more effectively carried out through private lines.

3. **Volume.** Volume refers to the total amount of information that must be transmitted over a given period of time. This is determined by the average length and number of messages involved. As the volume of data increases, it becomes necessary to resort to faster data terminals to do the job. In this regard, several data-transmission facilities are available with various bandwidths—the broader the bandwidth, the greater the data transfer rate and, therefore, the cost.

Among common-user-exchange services are the Teletypewriter Exchange Network (TWX) for narrow-band transmission; the direct-distance-dialing (DDD) network, Public Exchange Service (PBX), Broadband Exchange Service (BEX), and Wide Area Telephone Service (WATS) for voice-grade data transmission; and DATA-PHONE 50 for wide-band transmission. TWX is most appropriate for users with low-volume requirements. The service is set up by the telephone companies using leased telephone wires. Each user has his own wire and the wires can be addressed by other TWX outlets. Also available is a directory listing the users of these wires and their access numbers.

The DDD network facilitates data transmission through DATA-PHONE, which includes a data set that converts the electrical output of the terminal into a signal suitable for transmission. At the receiving end, the data set converts the transmission signal into electrical signals acceptable to the terminal. Data sets differ in transmission speeds and in the modulation techniques used to transmit the data over telephone lines.

PBX is a telephone system offered by the various telephone companies; BEX is offered by Western Union. Wide area telephone service (WATS) is a dial-up service that provides selected access to the DDD network. The continental United States is divided into six regions, or bands. The first band consists of the states that border on the one in which you are contracting for service. The second band consists of those states which border on the first band, and so on. The WATS service equipped with telephone channels is ideal for transmitting a large volume of outgoing data.

With the foregoing services, it can be summarized that for short or in-house distances it is more practical for a company to own its own telecommunication lines. However, when there is a sufficient volume of communications between two or more locations, it is practical to obtain leased (nonswitched) lines connecting the locations. The lines are permanently connected to the user's terminals for direct service. No dialing is required. The lines may be leased for any period of the day and may be used for any mixture of voice communication, written communication, and data transmission. Rental charges depend on the quality of the line and the distance covered. On a contract, long-term basis, the monthly charge for a leased telephone line is approximately $3.75 per mile.

In cases where the volume of transmission between any two points is too small to justify leased lines, it is possible to use dial-up facilities; data are routed and transmitted over the normal telephone switching network, and the connection is dialed and paid for as is a long-distance call. A continuous data path is established for only the period of time during which transmission is to take place. Although the leased line is more expensive than the switched line, it is available at any moment, and its transmission quality is superior to that of the switched line, which must be connected for each dial-up.

4. **Message urgency** involves the time factor in message delivery and the consequences of delay. In planning a communications system, delivery requirements must be carefully assessed to determine the speed requirements of the system. In other words, the cost of speed must be weighed against the consequences of delay.

   Generally, low-speed transmission equipment would be suitable for a small to average volume of data with a flexible delivery time. The demand for faster transmission devices increases as large volumes of data need to be transmitted and as faster delivery times are required.

5. **Specific language requirements of the user.** Language refers to the form in which transmitted data are received and the medium on which they are transmitted. Messages are transmitted in typewritten, oral, pictorial, or handwritten form, and are transcribed on punched paper tape, punched cards, magnetic tape, and other appropriate media. Message forms and media are largely determined by the user's delivery requirements. For example, intraoffice messages might be oral, whereas interoffice and other messages must be in some other form.

   For efficient operation of a data-communications system, an effort must be made to establish a common data-transmission language. Certain terminals might require conversion from one language to another more frequently than other terminals, which causes delays and increases costs. Thus the communications system requiring minimum conversion and providing a language understandable to both man and machine would be the ideal system to adopt.

6. **Accuracy.** One hundred percent accuracy of data transmission is rare and too costly in most systems. The higher the requirements for error-free data transmission, the costlier the system will be to the user. For most applications, however, using a data-communications system that transmits data at close to 100 percent accuracy is quite satisfactory.

   During data transmission, errors are caused by man-made noise, natural disturbances, thermal noise, and equipment malfunction. For most applications, transmission errors can be handled either by (1) ignoring them, (2) retransmitting the data once errors are detected (called automatic request for correction, ARQ), or (3) employing forward error correction (FEC). Ignoring errors is an acceptable procedure in cases involving a substantial volume of narrative text. However, the more popular approach is to retransmit the data through a "read-after-write" routine. Data are read back a few milliseconds after they are written, and if an error is detected, an automatic request for repetition of the garbled portion is made. In the forward error-correction approach, an adequate amount of redundancy is incorporated into a code to make possible automatic checking at the receiver. This technique is generally feasible only at high-speed transmission.

The time of the day might be a critical factor in determining the error rate. In a recent study, it was shown that the error-transmission rate in one 12-hour period was almost twice that of another 12-hour period. Furthermore, the worst error rate took place during the peak telephone traffic hours from 10:00 to 11:00 A.M. and from 3:00 to 4:00 P.M. This possibility should be at least a consideration in the designing phase of a data-communications system.

7. **Security.** When data can be read in or changed by operators at terminals, it is important to build into a telecommunications system special steps to prevent unauthorized access to stored information. Security of this kind can add up to 5 percent of the overall system cost, which might be justified in certain highly sensitive systems. Details on the issue of privacy are explained in Chapter 12.
8. **Cost.** The cost factor is invariably dependent on the other factors in one form or another, and is directly proportional to them. For instance, increasing the volume of messages that a communication system can handle generally results in a corresponding increase in its cost. Ideally, cost factor enters the picture after the system has been designed and is ready for implementation.

The overall success of the system depends greatly on the designer's ability to consider all factors that affect the system's makeup and structure. The task facing the designer is challenging and complex. He must choose among some 30 basic types of service, each characterized by such factors as transmission rate, termination requirements, duplex versus half-duplex operation, and whether the proposed terminals are to be connected directly to the computer facility, or by multiplexing, or by WATS. Furthermore, the designer needs to balance the expected data network costs against anticipated service through a continual evaluation of communication channel requirements, message routings, and rates.

Calculating the cost of alternative ways of designing a data-communications network is a challenge even to the best-qualified designer, and software packages have recently been developed to help tackle this problem. Among others, there are programs capable of pricing private lines and listing communication services based on mileage and the type of channels and terminals to be used. Other programs handle major segments of the design problem by determining the least-cost paths between rate centers and by providing response times and line loadings for specific types of communication services offered by the common carriers. With this service, the designer can customize the solution to certain systems requirements by evaluating the options and constraints available to him without much difficulty. Such design aids save many weeks in planning large networks.

Network Control

Another major consideration in planning a data-communications system is the problem of determining which devices will control the communications network. The objectives of network control are to (1) ensure the orderly exchange of information, (2) synchronize the flow of data into and out of the computer facility, and (3) define the system checkpoints for automatic restart in the event of disruption.

Control on a *point-to-point* system is relatively simple. Two ordinary terminals are able to dial each other either manually or automatically. The sender requests permission to transmit (which readies the receiver); upon receiving the request symbol, the receiver must react with its own acknowledgment of the request. The sender, then, begins with a "start-of-message" signal and proceeds at this point to send the message. When finished, the sender notifies the receiver with an "end-of-message" signal. It is an automatic request for the receiver to acknowledge the fact. Once it is acknowledged, both terminals revert to idling again.

Control on the *multipoint-line* system is more complicated, since a message reaches all terminals, including the CPU. If the terminals transmit at the same time, the pulses they emit are mixed; thus some procedure is required to prevent this from taking place. This could include the following steps:

1. A signal at the beginning of each message identifies the terminal to which the message is transmitted.
2. A signal indicates the beginning of the message and the "protocol" for acknowledgment by the receiver. Once this is performed, other terminals can ignore the message transmission.
3. A signal indicates the end of transmission, and also notifies other terminals that they should become "alert" again.

Other methods of network control are used. In the *relay* method, which applies to a multipoint leased line, an operation involves the computer's initiating a transmit request to the "slave" devices in the order of their priority or numerical sequence. The first device with available data receives the relayed transmit request and responds accordingly.

A second network control method, called *contention,* is one by which the computer senses a bid and authorizes the terminal to begin transmission. The computer has preestablished queuing procedures and priorities designed to handle the request. The contention method offers the advantage of involving the computer only during the stage when data are ready to be transmitted from a terminal or from some other "slave" device.

The most popular method of network control, called *polling,* emphasizes the computer's constant control over the overall system. It is designed to allow the computer to determine the order in which each terminal is allowed to transmit data, based either on a predetermined priority or on some formal access list. To implement this method, however, it is necessary to provide complex addressing and status tables within the computer facility, thereby creating overhead processing requirements.

Two types of polling are used: (1) *roll-call* polling and (2) *hub polling.* In roll-call polling, the computer makes inquiries from a list of all the existing terminals to check on their send status. Hub polling entails passing an inquiry from the computer to the farthest terminal. If it is not found in a sending mode, the terminal relays the inquiry to the next farthest terminal, and so on, until all available terminals are polled. The purpose of this procedure is to do away with the turnaround time between the computer and its terminals.

Minicomputers are excellent devices to perform the various functions of a communications network at a relatively low cost. They can be set up to interface several input terminals to a single communications facility, check data for errors, reformat data to delete unnecessary information, convert one code to another code, and coordinate communications input devices for larger computers. Furthermore, minicomputers are capable of interfacing an existing communications system with a larger, on-line system for smooth interaction, a function called *front-end processing.* In this role, the computer is more of a peripheral device ready to receive and send data as requested by the choice of an appropriate grade (low speed, voice grade, or broad band) of transmission service, which is also important. The decision concerning an acceptable quality at the lowest cost is complicated by details of related time and frequency multiplexing. For example, while broadband service is considered the most costly service, it could turn out to be a relatively low-cost service. When time- and frequency-division multiplexing are taken into consideration, the line's capacity is divided into several low-speed subchannels with a lower effective cost per channel than separate low-speed channels.

THE COMMON CARRIERS

Data communication dates back to the days of the early computer. In 1940, Bell Laboratories demonstrated a data-communication capability through a link between a computer located in New Jersey and a terminal in Hanover, New Hampshire. Twelve years later, the first two business-oriented data-communication systems were used by American Airlines and the Toronto Stock Exchange. In 1958, American Telephone and Telegraph (AT&T) began installing its DATA-PHONE sets—the first data-communication equipment capable of handling transmission over a public carrier's line.

Common carriers such as AT&T provide communication lines to geographically linked data-communication terminals and compete with various data-processing service organizations in offering a full range of data-communication services. Common carriers also enjoy a competitive advantage in offering time-sharing service to customers over their owned and operated lines. This competitive advantage by a regulated monopoly prompted a Federal Communications Commission (FCC) inquiry in 1966 into the adequacy of the common carriers' services and the reasonableness of the related traffic rules and charges. Before the inquiry was initiated, common carriers had a tariff rule against allowing the hookup of customer-owned devices to the carrier's switched network.

A test case developed when Carter Electronics brought suit against AT&T. The suit attacked the sweeping generality of AT&T's attachment prohibition. Carter had developed Carterfone (a coupling device), which allowed the telephone receiver to be coupled with a private radio system. In effect, it extended the communication service by a simple private attachment. The concept was technically and commercially feasible, but AT&T brought pressure to have the product stopped by threatening service disconnection under the provision of the attachment tariffs. Carter responded by bringing an antitrust action against AT&T in the Federal courts. The court referred the action to the FCC, which ruled in favor of Carter and ordered AT&T to modify its tariffs to allow for the use of the device. The ruling was specific and pertained only to the Carterfone device; this led General Telephone and Electronics Corporation to join AT&T in an appeal to the FCC. The FCC upheld the previous ruling and even broadened it to make invalid the prohibition against the use of independently manufactured attachments.

Since the Carterfone decision was made, the availability of non-Bell, buyer-oriented modems or data sets has steadily increased. The non-Bell modem buyer can now exercise more control over more of his system. This is particularly useful when using modems in the speed class of 2,400 bits per second and lower, because modems at such speeds are usually built into the terminal; this means that the user can have his modem serviced on a card-exchange basis by the terminal service personnel.

Major attempts to offer a choice of carrier service have been made during the past decade. In 1963, Microwave Communications, Inc., (MCI) applied to the FCC for a license to transmit data by microwave from Chicago to St. Louis. When the license was approved in 1969, the door was opened, and by March 1971, 33 additional applicants had filed for approval of 1,877 microwave stations. The MCI network, now serving a limited number of users, is expected to eventually serve 41 states, with rates estimated at about 50 percent less than those of the Bell system.

Datran, a subsidiary of University Computing, has embarked on the most ambitious plan to date—to operate a switched digital network linking 35 major cities. In April 1972, Datran received 63 initial construction permits, which involve a $300 million investment through 1975. Although Datran's network is not planned to be operational until mid-1974, these developments can be viewed as threatening the hold that AT&T once had on the data-communication market. Datran's complete success, however, is believed doubtful by many industry experts. But regardless of the final outcome, the communications user stands to benefit from competition in this field.

SUMMARY

Data communication is a natural extension of a management information system. Any automated information system reflects a state of urgency. Otherwise, there would be little reason, if any, to automate the response capabilities of the system.

To assume that a sense of urgency exists only in the central office of an organization seems illogical. As more and more companies and government agencies find their component organizations geographically dispersed, they discover the limitations in their ability to exchange timely information throughout the organization. Traditionally, the data-processing facility is designed to quickly handle volumes of data only when they are physically entered into the "headquarters" computer system. Getting data from far-flung field offices to headquarters and back again is generally left to antiquated, physical delivery methods. There is little use in discussing data-processing speeds in terms of microseconds and milliseconds if it takes days for eventual delivery of the urgent data. Today, the importance of data communication as a means of improving the total response time of an automated data-processing system is becoming better appreciated.

A data-transmission system consists of a data source, a transmission channel, two or more terminals, modems, and a switching center. Data may be transmitted over direct-line hookup using telephone lines or by microwave channels.

Modems act as interface between remote terminals and the central computer facility. They modify data signals so that they can be properly transmitted for processing. The four methods of modification are amplitude, frequency, phase, and pulse modulation. Modems designed for use on dial-up or leased circuits handle either asynchronous data or synchronous data. Asynchronous transmission is superior to synchronous transmission when transmission is irregular, and is cheaper due to the simpler terminal interface logic and circuitry. Synchronous transmission, on the other hand, makes better use of the transmission facility and allows higher transmission speed. Companies with multiple locations resort to multiplexing for a more efficient and economical transmission link with the central computer.

Modes of communication are simplex, half-duplex, or full-duplex, with four classes of service: telegraph, narrow band, voice band, and broad band. A telecommunications system may also use several different codes, with the Baudot and the ASCII codes being the most important.

Data-transmission terminals include keyboard-oriented, voice-response, visual (CRT) display, remote-batch, and intelligent terminals. Each terminal generally acts as an interface between man and the transmission line for effecting a data-processing cycle.

Finally, in planning a telecommunications system, design considerations pertaining to system function, message distribution, volume of transmission, message urgency, language requirements, accuracy, and cost are worth noting. In addition, any system chosen must incorporate a central structure designed to ensure orderly exchange of information and synchronize data flow into and out of the computer facility.

TERMS TO LEARN

Amplitude	Half-duplex channel
Asynchronous	Modem
Baud	Modulation
Cathode-ray tube	Multiplexing
Channel	PBX
Clock	Phase
Data communication	Plotter
DATA-PHONE	Polling
Demodulation	Redundancy
Equalization	Simplex channel
Facsimile	Synchronous system
Frequency	Terminal
Full-duplex channel	Time-division multiplexing

QUESTIONS

1. What is data communication? What are its primary elements?
2. What are the differences among narrow-band, voice-band, and wide-band transmission?
3. Explain the Baudot code. What other codes are used in data communication?
4. Distinguish among simplex, half-duplex, and full-duplex modes of transmission.

5. What is a modem? How does it contribute to the processing of data?
6. Briefly explain the difference among amplitude, frequency, phase, and pulse modulation.
7. How do asynchronous and synchronous modems differ in handling data?
8. What is the difference between conditioning and equalization? Explain each briefly.
9. Explain briefly the uses and characteristics of keyboard and visual display devices.
10. How does a touch-tone system facilitate problem solving?
11. What design criteria must be considered in planning a data-communication system? Explain.
12. Explain the various ways of handling transmission errors.
13. What are the primary objectives of network control? What is involved in control on a point-to-point versus multipoint line system?
14. Distinguish between roll-call polling and hub polling.

SUGGESTED READING

DAVENPORT, WILLIAM. *Modern Data Communications.* New York: Hayden Book Company, Inc., 1971.

DEAL, R. L. "Programmable Communications Processors—Applications Advantages," *Modern Data,* July 1972, pp. 30ff.

FIELDMAN, LAWRENCE. "A New Voice in Data Entry," *Modern Data,* April 1973, p. 28.

HORNSBY, T. G., JR. "Voice Response Systems," *Modern Data,* Nov. 1972, pp. 46–50.

KRAFT, ROBERT, and THOMAS HORNSBY. "360/370-Compatible Peripherals—Part II—Data Communications Terminals," *Modern Data,* Sept. 1972, pp. 38–43ff.

MACHOVER, C. "Interactive CRT," *Society for Information Display Journal,* Nov./Dec. 1972, pp. 10–17.

MARTIN, JAMES. *Future Developments in Telecommunications.* Englewood Cliffs, N.J.: Prentice-Hall, Inc., 1972.

———. *Systems Analysis for Data Transmission.* Englewood Cliffs, N.J.: Prentice-Hall, Inc., 1972, Chapters 1–3.

MATHISON, S. L., and P. M. WOLKER. *Computers and Telecommunications.* Englewood Cliffs, N.J.: Prentice-Hall, Inc., 1972.

WEBSTER, EDWARD. *Data Communications and Business Systems.* Arlington, Va.: International Business Forms Industries, 1972.

ZAKARIAN, Z. V. "The Mad Mad Mad World of Data Communications," *Infosystems,* Aug. 1972, pp. 18–21.

real-time, time-shared, and data-base systems

12

Virtual Time-Sharing Operation

DATA SHARING— THE CORPORATE DATA BASE

Advantages of Data Base

Data-Base Structure

storage requirements
access methods

Data-Base Design and Management

Data Integrity and Security

THE COMPUTER UTILITY AND THE PRIVACY ISSUE

JUSTIFICATION FOR REAL-TIME SYSTEMS

Prior to the development of on-line communications to a central computer, most computer operations were performed by batch processing; data were grouped into batches and accumulated until a sufficient volume was collected to justify computer time. Data were forwarded for processing in the form of original documents punched into cards or tape, or were added as supplementary data to prepunched cards as they were received. Further off-line handling was also required to sort and sequence the file data in the proper order for processing. The cumulative process associated with establishing each batch resulted in peak load requirements, often necessitating around-the-clock operations to obtain the desired reports. These peak processing periods frequently led to the establishment of oversized systems to absorb the peak volume at costs far in excess of the overall productivity realized.

As the use of data processing was expanded for multiplant or multi-office operations, data-collection problems grew more complex. This led to the multisystem approach, which involves systems of different sizes located in the various departments, divisions, and offices. Data from these systems were then sent to the main site for organization-wide processing and analysis. This method worked in some instances, but serious problems of data collection persisted.

At this stage, the physical transfer of data and documents by mail, messenger, or similar means slowed down computer operations. Attention logically turned to public telephone and teletypewriter facilities. Teletypewriter facilities, which offered the advantage of printed copies of each communication, were rented from common carriers such as American Telephone and Telegraph Company and the Western Union Telegraph Company.

The combination of semiautomatic electrical data communication and the multisystem approach yielded a partial solution to the problem of data collection and processing. However, the actual processing of data was still being performed on a batch basis, which meant that transactions were transmitted only periodically. As a result of this processing time lag, data for management were historic rather than current. What was lacking was the ability to operate upon a transaction as it took place.

To understand this problem more fully, assume that a sales office at a remote location receives a customer order. Inventory listings are consulted, and if the listings indicate that the required items are available, an order is placed and the customer informed of when delivery will be made. There is, however, one flaw in this arrangement. The inventory listings used by the sales office may not reflect the true status of the inventory at the time the order is placed. This situation results from the fact that the inventory listings are updated at the computer site only on a periodic basis and are, therefore, correct only on the date on which they are processed. Between updatings, orders may be placed for items that are not actually available, with the result that these items will later have to be back ordered, and the customer will not receive them on the date promised.

REAL-TIME PROCESSING

From the foregoing, it can be concluded that, although batch processing makes more efficient use of computer systems and permits economies of scale through accumulating enough transactions for large-volume processing, it has certain inherent drawbacks. The requirement of arranging batched transactions in sequential order is expensive and time consuming. Furthermore, the time required to accumulate data into batches destroys much of the value or timeliness of the data. To close the time gap between actual transactions and updating of the master file, real-time processing was developed. This unique approach combines data processing with communication; it involves direct (on-line) communication of transaction data between remote offices and the central computer, and allows the data to be processed almost simultaneously with transmission.

To explain more fully the capabilities and implications of a real-time system, let us refer to the previously mentioned sales application. The remotely located sales office would be supplied with an inquiry–answer device capable of communicating directly with the computer (Fig. 12-1). To place an order, the required information is entered into the system

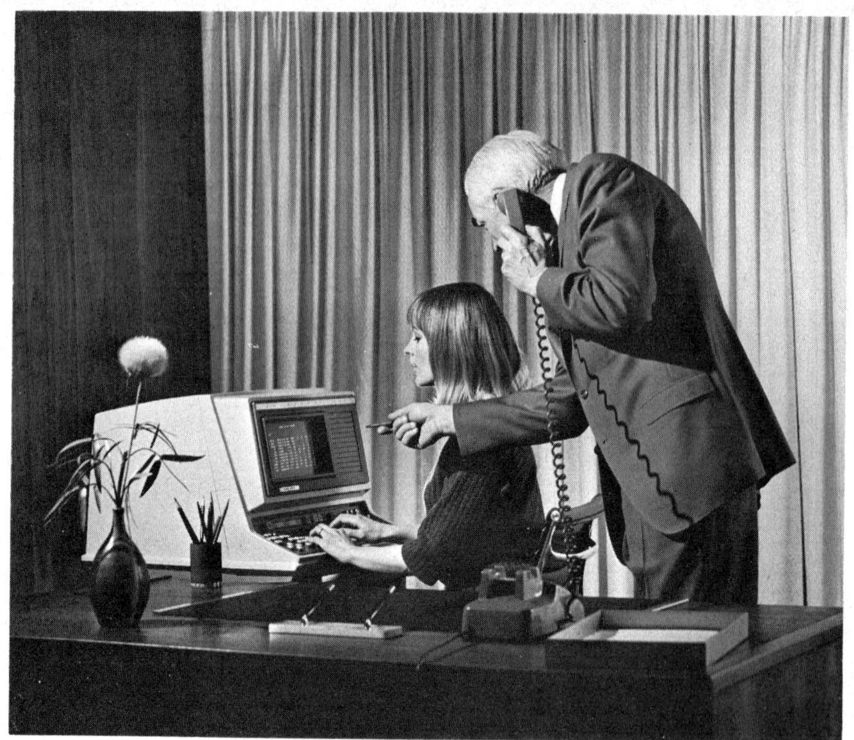

FIGURE 12-1. Inquiry-answer device (UNIVAC)

by the input device. Since the device is connected directly to the computer, complete information, including the availability and status of the item ordered, is provided in seconds. If the items are available, the invoice is printed automatically, along with associated shipping information, at the sales office, indicating to the salesman that the order has been filled as requested. If any particular item on the order has depleted the inventory to the reorder point, the computer automatically sends a message to the reorder source, which is connected directly to the computer, to request updating of inventory. All these operations are accomplished in a matter of seconds (Fig. 12-2).

By integrating computer hardware, transmission devices, and communication lines, all required data can be instantly available to the computer system. Direct-access devices linked to the computer by telecommunication lines allow management, many miles away, to transmit and receive data at high speed and maintain minute-by-minute control over various key operations. Live interaction between the thought processes of users and the data-manipulation capabilities of the computer produces results more effective and more powerful than either of these elements functioning separately.

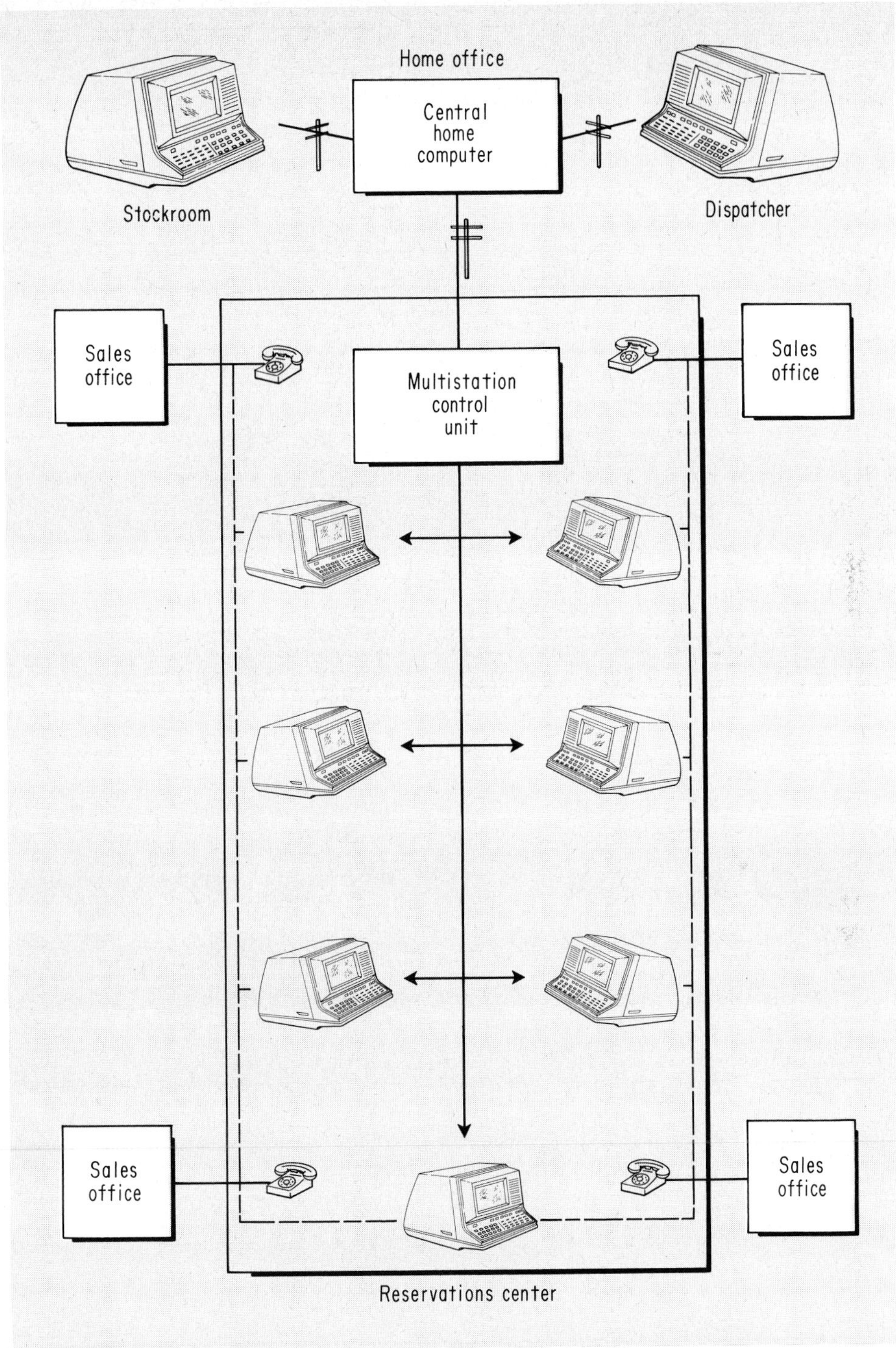

FIGURE 12-2. Typical real-time system

Characteristics of Real-Time Systems

A real-time system is considered here as having the on-line features of (1) direct connection between input–output devices (regardless of location) and the central processor, and (2) fairly fast response time, permitting two-way communication between the user and the system. Unlike on-line processing, however, real-time processing requires more severe time constraints so that processing can be carried out and the results transmitted fast enough to control an ongoing activity.

The factor of "immediacy" is measured in *response time* (throughput), or the time interval between the availability of input information and the computer's response to that information. The quicker the results become available, the greater the real-time capability of the system. Response times range from 0.1 microsecond to over 20 minutes, depending on the requirements of the application. For example, in a military defense real-time system for radar scanning, a response time measured in microseconds is required. By contrast, a commercial airline reservation system requires response time between 3 and 5 seconds, and a production-control real-time system may find response time of 4 minutes quite adequate.

Unlike other systems that require different programs for new situations, programs used in controlling real-time operations must be stable and detailed enough to handle every conceivable problem that may arise during the operation. This is necessary so that users can depend completely on the real-time system, leaving only rare and exceptional matters for human manipulation. An exceptional, nonrecurring transaction, such as overstocking a given item as a result of a huge one-time order placed by a local wholesaler, or allowing a given merchandise to go below the reorder point while awaiting a new model, is checked immediately and does not justify a change in the overall program for proper handling.

Primary Types of Real-Time Systems

BASIC AND TIME-SHARED SYSTEMS. For a computer to meet the requirements of a real-time system, it must be directly connected by communication lines to appropriate terminal devices and direct-access files. In Fig. 12-3, two alternative real-time systems are illustrated. The *one-user-at-a-time* system (shown by thin lines) allows only one terminal to be linked to the central processor, leaving all other terminals inoperative. The *multiuser system* (heavy lines) employs a *multiplexing* device that provides each existing on-line terminal a "time share" such that each user gets direct access to the system independent of the simultaneous demands of other terminal users. This system is discussed in a later section. It provides a great deal of flexibility and boosts the efficiency of the central processor.

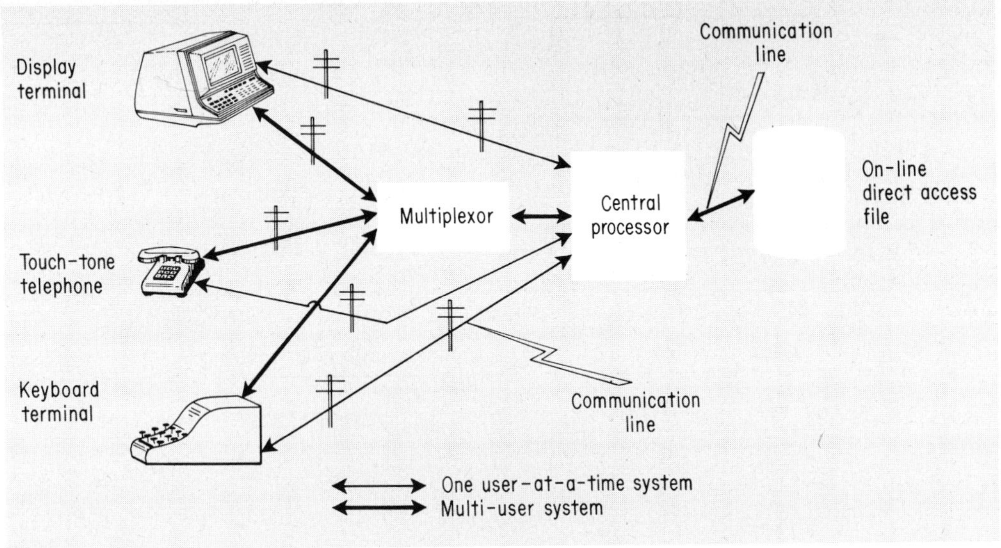

FIGURE 12-3. Single and multiuser real-time systems

MULTIPROGRAMMING SYSTEMS. In a *multiprogramming* real-time system, two or more programs are manipulated within the same time period by one central processor. The advantage of this capability is the increased utilization of the total computer system. Some programs require substantial input–output time, but relatively limited computational time; others require little input–output time, but considerable computational time. The availability of both types of programs for simultaneous execution makes feasible the maximum utilization of the central processor and its existing input–output devices throughout a given time period. The central processor no longer remains idle because of the slower speed of the input–output devices.

In multiprogramming systems, a supervisory program is used to control the central processor's switching from one program to another and to make sure that each processing phase is fully executed and handled in proper order (Fig. 12-4). A multiprogramming system has three types of programs located in primary storage:

1. The *supervisor* program, held in storage throughout processing, manipulates program switching. Main storage is divided into partitions for controlling the order of executing the programs and for protection against partial destruction of a program by another program. Thus, the supervisor program ensures against loss of transactions during switchover. It also notifies the terminal operator as to how long the system may be unavailable as a result of the switch-

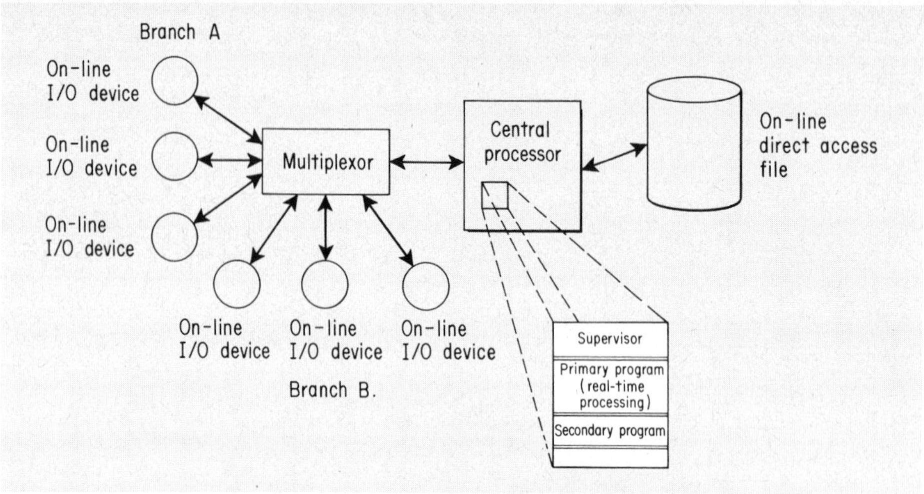

FIGURE 12-4. Multiprogramming system, showing contents of main storage

over phase, and communicates information about matters related to manipulating switches, changing file cartridges, and so on.

2. The primary program, often called the *foreground program*(s), has priority over all other programs in storage and controls the computer system whenever data are received from an on-line input–output device.
3. The secondary or *background* program becomes operative when input–output devices are not in operation, or while the system is not engaged in a real-time transaction. Once input–output devices begin handling data, the processed results from the background program are stored; the foreground program is then reloaded for real-time operation. This switching back and forth between programs continues until the whole operation is completed.

Multiprocessing Systems

A multiprocessing real-time system uses two or more computers linked together for coordinated functioning and leads to computer-to-computer communication, since any computer may access the main storage of other computers in the system. It is designed around a functional principle. The smaller computers that are integrated into the system handle "housekeeping" routines such as file maintenance and input–output processing; this leaves the larger computer to perform computational tasks. Thus, the larger computer becomes the master and the smaller computer (or computers) the slave. Figure 12-5 illustrates a basic multiprocessing real-time system in which all existing terminals are interfaced with the smaller (peripheral) computer, which, in turn, is directly linked to the larger

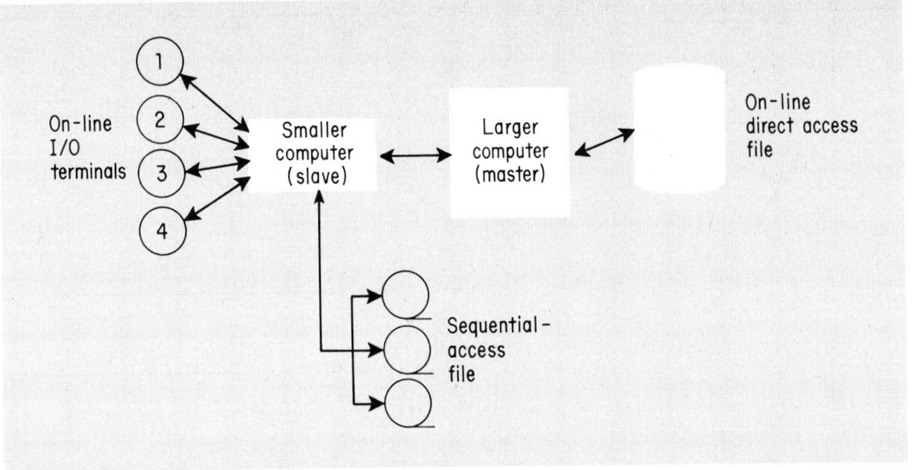

FIGURE 12-5. Basic multiprocessing real-time system

(master) computer. Storage devices may be linked to the smaller computer for retrieving data, if they are needed. The real-time nature of this system depends on the attachment of an on-line direct-access file to the system's master computer.

The foregoing system has a relatively high probability of failure, since the malfunctioning of any component beyond the terminal will cause the whole system to fail. The reliability of a multiprocessing system can be increased by using two peripheral computers; each computer interfaces with one half the existing terminals. In this configuration, if either peripheral computer malfunctions, only one half the system will fail (Fig. 12-6). Total system failure resulting from the malfunctioning of the main computer, however, is still a factor to consider, especially in applications requiring perfect real-time-system operation.

For applications requiring highly reliable, perfect computer system operation, a second master computer is added with both processors directly accessible to either peripheral computer. In this case, no more than one half the existing terminals will become inoperative as a result of one master computer failure. Furthermore, during peak processing, either peripheral computer can alternate its tasks between master computers (Fig. 12-7).

From the foregoing variations of real-time system development, it can be concluded that an increase in the number of computers (master and peripheral) results in a positive increase in the system's reliability, and, especially, in its throughput, since it reduces the amount of time it takes to process incoming data from input–output devices or terminals. It should be noted, however, that as system reliability and throughput increase, so does the cost of the system. In designing a real-time system, an organization should carefully plan the size and requirements of its

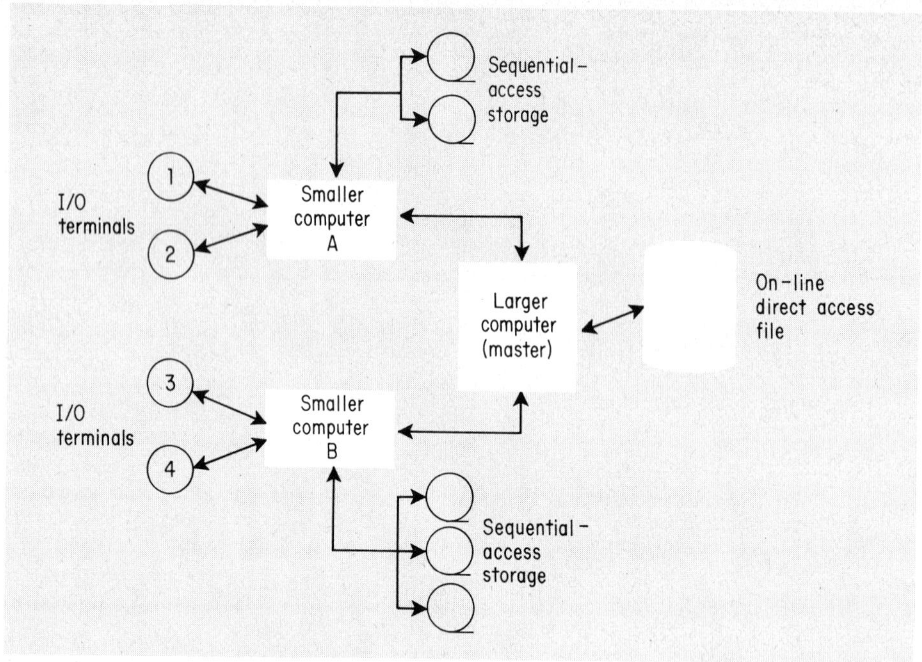

FIGURE 12-6. Multiprocessing system, using two peripheral computers

FIGURE 12-7. Multicomputer real-time system

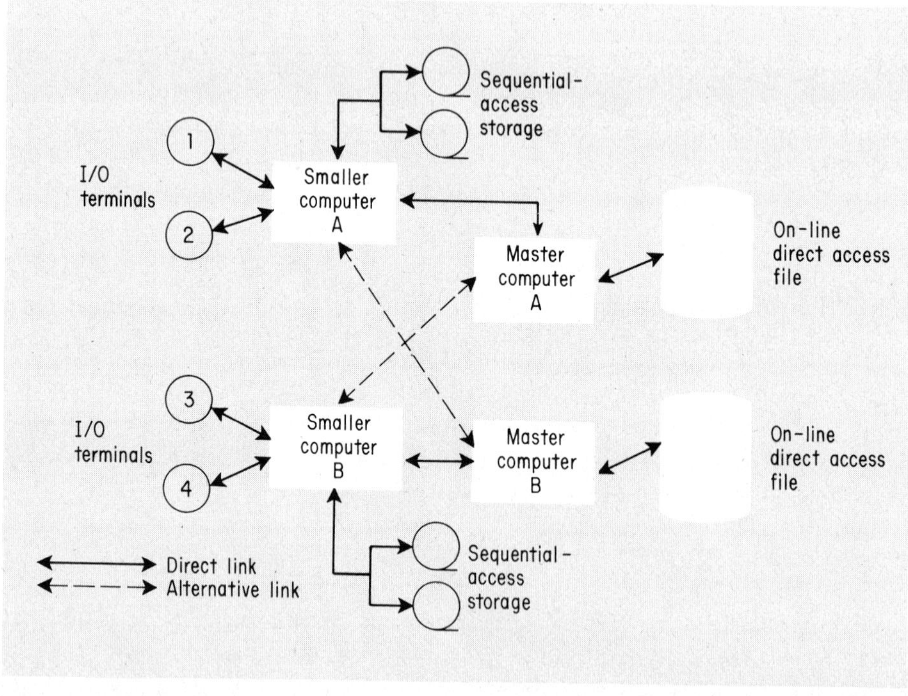

proposed system at a cost figure within its budget. A poorly implemented system-acquisition plan could easily result in a system costing as much as 10 to 15 times the figure agreed upon in the initial proposal.

Justifying Real-Time Systems

A real-time system involves equipment, programming, and system design costs that are generally greater than the cost of a traditional batch system. Hardware costs cover terminals, communication lines, large-capacity direct-access devices, special components such as modems for facilitating transmission of data between the terminals and the computer, and components for controlling the order of data entry from and transmission to the system's terminals. Real-time programming is more complicated, often involving many hundreds of instructions, and requires a high-level and well-trained staff. Likewise, real-time system design demands top talent and thousands of man-hours in determining the type and number of terminals needed, the types of communication lines that should be used, the size of direct-access devices that must be installed to accommodate the proposed system, and whether to purchase or lease needed components.

Real-time system construction is a developing art. The issue of its usefulness in solving business problems is highly controversial. Overwhelming errors, which stem from a lack of top talent and the need for standard operating procedures for design and implementation, have been made in its design and development. In the final analysis, and assuming the availability of talent and resources, hardware, programming, and design costs must be measured against the benefits of a real-time system—improved and quicker customer service, better control of operations, and more timely management information. It might be months, and in some cases years, before actual savings resulting from a real-time system operation can be realized.

TIME SHARING

The time-sharing technique—a development rather than a discovery—was introduced to provide more computer power to more users. Since its inception in the early 1960s, it has changed the way people view data processing and computers, and has had a significant impact on the software requirements for manipulating computer systems.

In a conventional batch-processing system, managers, when requiring a service, communicated their needs to the programmer who, in turn, had to write, debug, and test a program before it became available for processing. Since programs are run serially (one program at a time), it often took hours and sometimes days before the results were available to the user. Thus, an inherent problem with this type of processing is *turnaround time,* or the inefficient use of the system's resources.

Because of the foregoing complexities and demands, a new line of thinking was developed. Since an ongoing computer system is capable of handling any given instruction in a very short time, it also is capable of handling a number of tasks concurrently by switching back and forth among those tasks without obvious delay. With this in mind, when developing a program, the programmer can feed his program instructions one at a time through a remote terminal and get a status report on their validity without delay. Also, many terminals can be attached to a given real-time system, and a number of users are thus able to have independent direct access to the same installation.

Time-Sharing Growth

Time sharing was initially developed through research papers and experimentation in the late 1950s. In 1959, Christopher Strachey, a British mathematician, made public a paper on time sharing at a UNESCO Congress. During the same year, John McCarthy circulated a paper of his own on time sharing at the Massachusetts Institute of Technology (MIT). In addition to these pioneers, much early work on time sharing is attributed to J. C. R. Licklider, often called the father of time sharing. He viewed the symbolic relationship between man and machine as "an unexpected development in cooperative interaction between men and computers." Through his efforts, and with the involvement of F. J. Corbato of MIT, adequate funds were secured from the Department of Defense, which led in 1962 to the development of project MAC (an acronym for multiple-access computer or machine-aided cognition), the world's largest and perhaps best-known general-purpose time-sharing system.

Since the development of MAC, the idea of time sharing has spread to other colleges and universities where additional contributions have been made toward advancing the use of time sharing. The first time-sharing demonstration was held at MIT's computer center in November 1961. The system consisted of an IBM 709 vacuum-tube computer and four remote consoles located in the same room. In September 1962, Cambridge University put into operation a time-sharing system that used a Digital Equipment Corporation PDP-1. In 1964, Dartmouth joined the time-sharing group. Under the direction of John Kemeny (now president of Dartmouth) and Thomas Kurtz, General Electric's BASIC system was developed. During the same year, IBM made its debut in the business time-sharing field with its QUIKTRAN system. Unlike Project MAC, which offers the user a variety of languages, both QUIKTRAN and BASIC restrict the user to one or a limited number of languages. Their unique contribution is in providing the user with an interactive system capability for solving arithmetic problems. Later that year, American Airlines installed its SABRE system, a *special-purpose* time-sharing system. The first commercial, general-purpose time-sharing system was introduced by General Electric in 1965.

Since 1965, when total time-sharing revenues were close to $10 million, the time-sharing market has grown quite rapidly. In 1969, there were about 200 firms producing time-sharing equipment, with $180 million in revenue. By 1975, competition is expected to leave no more than 15 companies in control of about 80 percent of the total market, which is expected to exceed the $1.5 billion mark.

Definition

Time sharing is defined in one of three ways: (1) a computer service bureau that offers a variety of application programs or specialized problem-solving languages to scientists to do on-line problem solving independent of other users; (2) an internal scheduling algorithm through which a "time slice" is offered by the central processor—once the allotted time expires, control is switched to the next job; and (3) a computer system to which several on-line terminals are linked and through which many users communicate for solving various problems.

Relying primarily on the third definition, a time-sharing system is used here to refer to *an orderly organization of computer and communication equipment and specialized programming that permit almost simultaneous utilization of the system by several users working at remote, on-line terminals.*

Users employ the system to solve or to create a problem, feed or retrieve data, interact directly with stored files, process a nonconversation program, or for a combination of these uses. A time-shared computer can

FIGURE 12-8. *Typical time-sharing system*

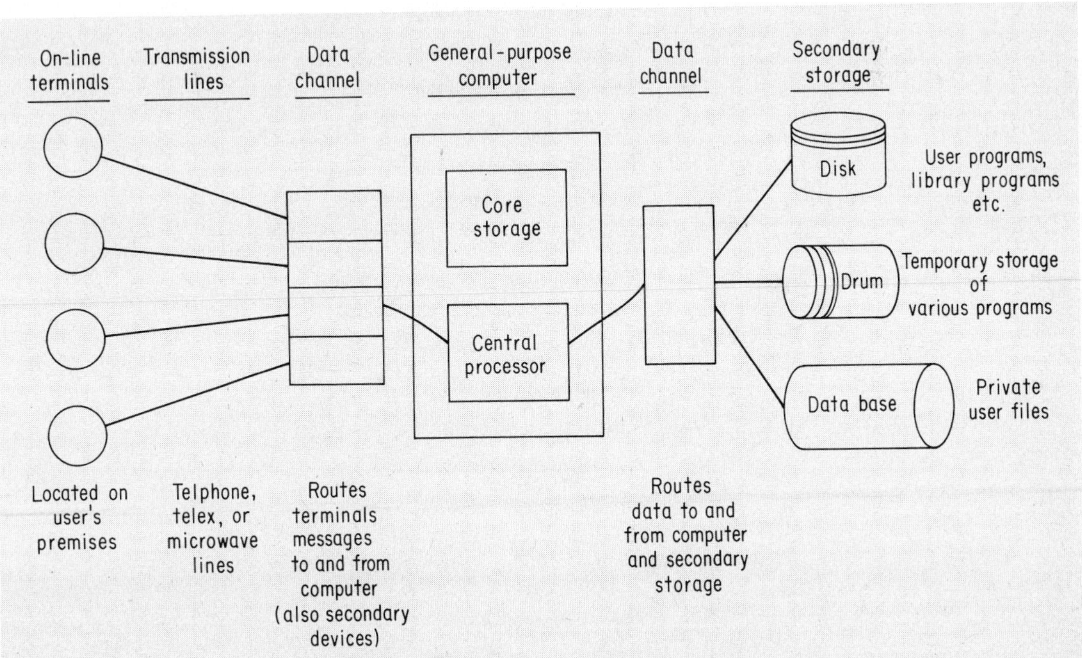

be used in conversational mode or for remote batch processing. The *conversational* approach involves using a data-transmission terminal and dialing the system through a touch-tone telephone for on-line conversation. *Remote batch processing* is basically the processing of accumulated data from a remote terminal. Figure 12-8 illustrates a typical time-sharing system.

Major Characteristics

A typical time-shared system has the following characteristics:

1. **On-line operation.** A time-sharing system must be capable of receiving data from and sending responses to a remote input–output device or terminal.
2. **Real-time processing.** The system must be ready to handle all users' needs at a speed within the requirements of the applications being processed. That is, the system must offer rapid response to users' inquiries.
3. **Almost-simultaneous access.** The system must be capable of handling many users at almost the same time. One common method, called *queuing*, involves lining up waiting input instructions or messages from various terminals and processing them on a first-come, first-served basis, or according to a priority system controlled by a multiplexor-programmed routine.
4. **Multiprogramming ability.** Since it is an extension of the multi-programming concept, a time-sharing system must be capable of handling a variety of programs to meet various users' informational needs. Because of the speed of the CPU, the system can produce output to the user almost immediately, although it is engaged in handling other programs at the same time.
5. **Supervisory program control.** As will be explained in a later section, a time-sharing system employs a supervisory program to schedule the handling of problems received through various terminals and allocates working storage space and computer time for processing.
6. **Integrity.** The time-sharing system must provide privacy and protection against access to data and programs by unauthorized individuals. The system must behave as though it were exclusively dedicated to each user's requirements. The user's data files and/or programs are maintained on-line by the system and are available by special codes or instructions.
7. **Independence of operation.** Each on-line terminal must function independently of all other terminals and as though it were the computer console. In this way, each user can test and carry out programming details without any interference from other users.
8. **Flexibility.** A time-sharing system is generally designed to handle a variety of applications. Major applications include mathematical

calculations, simulation, and operations research. Other applications are forecasting, data-bank use, sales analysis, portfolio analysis, personnel scheduling, queuing studies, linear programming, inventory control, quality control, and production scheduling.

There are systems, however, in which the user neither programs the system at his terminal nor expects complete independence and private use of available data. For example, in an airline reservation system, each reservation clerk has equal access to stored data regarding seat availability, which is handled by a single, fixed program. Thus, functionally, time-sharing systems are divided into three major categories, which differ by the degree of independence of the user:

1. **Unlimited** (or nearly unlimited) **systems.** General-purpose systems that accept a variety of programming languages and allow the user to create and write his own programs. A truly unlimited system does not exist, although the IBM T50 (Time-sharing Option S360/370) approaches this concept. It is designed to run any program concurrently, in a batch or multiprocessing environment.
2. Systems with **multiple-application** programs in which the user can choose a program but cannot alter the program he decides to use.
3. **Limited-application systems.** Systems offering the user only one fixed application program, as is the case in airline reservation systems.

The first two categories, in effect, divide the computer system into a number of time slices, and allot each programmer his time share in which to do whatever he wants.

Advantages

Time sharing offers users who cannot justify the investment in a system of their own a time share in an already operational system. Several other advantages are offered, most of which relate to cost savings:

1. **More efficient utilization of the system.** In a conventional batch-processing system, the central processor's utilization (percentage of total time spent on computations) is generally low, since it has to remain idle during the operation of the system's input–output devices. Furthermore, organizations with in-house systems have many components idle when small applications are run, since the system has been installed to handle peak loads. By comparison, in a time-sharing system, the processor's productivity is increased by overlapping or interweaving several applications. The result is data processed at a lower unit cost.
2. **Lower processing cost.** A time-share user pays only for the computer time he uses, plus related expenses. His total costs consist of

charges for the use of (a) an on-line terminal, (b) communication lines, and (c) central processor time. In return he gets a high level of service from a system much larger and more sophisticated than a normal in-house system, at a lower cost. Lower costs are also related to the fact that an arithmetic increase in hardware cost leads to a geometric decrease in the amount of time it takes the central processor to process a given task.

3. **Elimination of overhead costs.** The use of time-sharing systems means minimizing the fixed costs related to full-time management, system installation, and program development incurred by organizations with in-house systems. The amount of saving is often as much as the monthly charges for time-sharing use.
4. **On-line programming.** On-line access to a time-sharing system allows program writing and debugging. A beginning programmer can have his work edited and diagnosed for errors quickly enough to allow him to analyze his work as he progresses. An experienced programmer can use the facility to test more complex programs without unnecessary waiting. Program writing and debugging can thus be improved by as much as 900 percent. Some creative programmers have increased their productivity by well over 1,000 percent.
5. **Program availability.** A primary advantage of using a time-sharing system is the availability of fully developed program libraries to the user, representing significant savings in time and development costs and offering the user a wider choice of powerful programming languages.
6. **Minimization of data conversion.** The use of remote terminals in a time-sharing system reduces the need for recording data on such media as punched cards or magnetic tape. This advantage not only saves recording time, but also simplifies and automates the data-recording process. Furthermore, using terminals for direct input is generally faster and cheaper than conventional input recording devices, such as the key punch.
7. **Conversational mode of processing data.** The availability of on-line remote terminals permits the user to establish relatively fast two-way communication with the system. This feature is especially helpful in program debugging and testing. The programmer can get on-the-spot response from parts of his program without having to wait for a complete program run.
8. **Easier programming.** The relatively simpler programming demands of a time-sharing system make it possible for users with limited programming background to learn how to program their applications without any difficulty. This benefit cuts down on the programming expense and time normally encountered in a conventional batch-processing computer system.
9. **Fast response time.** Implicit in the foregoing benefits is the factor of *immediacy* or *turnaround time.* Although not necessary in all applications, a fast response time increases the productivity of programmers, reduces idle time, improves man–machine com-

munications, and offers the user greater insight into his particular problems by giving immediate on-line results. On-line applications such as airline reservation systems simply could not exist without the utilization of time-sharing systems.

10. **Greater management control.** With time sharing, a management information system now can be effectively implemented. Through remote terminals, managers and other administrative officials can have direct, immediate access to computer-created files related to inventories, personnel, production, and other records. Instead of hours, it now takes minutes or even seconds to obtain the data necessary for prompt decision making.

Drawbacks

1. Time sharing is not a panacea. To the owner of a time-sharing system, the major drawback is *acquisition cost.* A full-fledged system requires large capital investment, which often results in relatively slow returns. Computational time sharing generally is not a profitable business; at best it is only marginally profitable, unless a large number of users can efficiently utilize available computer time.

   A moderate-sized time-sharing installation consists of a large computer with high-speed memory. A major expense item in itself, this high-speed memory must be supported by a number of direct-access storage devices and special multiplexors to maintain proper interface between multiple terminals and the computer. The cost of on-line terminals and communication facilities also must be considered. Remote terminals range in complexity from the Teletype to the graphic display or to the high-speed line printer. The complexity of some terminals labels them as satellite computers. With respect to communication facilities, selection must be based on the balance of utilization and productivity of the communication facility and the terminals that will maintain the best user–computer interface.

2. From the user's viewpoint, a private, in-house computer installation often provides several distinct advantages over a time-sharing system. First, it generally offers more independence of operation and greater program and file security than a time-sharing installation. Second, a private installation is unlikely to be as complex or to affect as many users as a typical time-sharing system. In the event of a temporary breakdown, fewer users are inconvenienced under the former system than under the latter one. Third, as an organization grows in size, it usually considers conducting its computations in-house. Even if it requires limited computer use, a small minicomputer system is often more beneficial. In this case, the user has complete access to the system at all times.

   Users needing a small computer system can purchase one or more minicomputers, link their small system to an outside time-sharing system, or install their own mini-time-sharing system. In-house time sharing can be a complex and costly endeavor. There are many hidden costs, such as hardware and software maintenance, telephone and communication network costs, personnel turnover and training, and the cost for computer overcapacity. The prospective user must assess such factors as his computation workload, the proposed system's reliability and extendability, and compatible program sizes and languages. Any of the three alternatives, however, has unique advantages over the conventional large time-sharing system. Final choice must be based on both short-term and long-range needs and on the factors that the user considers critical for effective handling of his particular problems.

3. Time sharing can become an *executive toy*, rather than a tool. A time-sharing system, especially during the first few months of its use, offers a type of "sex appeal" to some executives who have a compulsion to feed in unnecessary problems or to show off their competence in manipulating the remote terminal. Also, such convenient access could lead executives to use the system as a crutch. During the planning stage, management should consider the *personal* as well as the *personnel* impact of the new system, with the hope of avoiding any unnecessary post-installation and implementation problems.
4. **Security.** Many users are concerned about the possibility of someone else, especially competitors, gaining access to their files. The use of passwords to identify each file does not seem to provide adequate security, since they can be leaked by the system's staff to the wrong party. Data leakage, however, is equally likely by staff members of an in-house facility. It is perhaps the idea of storing one's personal files in a remotely located system that gives the feeling of vulnerability.

With the foregoing pros and cons, an organization can evaluate the appropriateness of using a time-sharing system by finding answers to certain key questions. For example,

1. What type of projects can be efficiently handled through a time-sharing system?
2. How critical are these projects?
3. How costly is the proposed time-sharing system?
4. Would the time-sharing costs justify the type of projects planned for the system?
5. Can management plan adequately for the system to avoid major operating and other problems?
6. Can management cope with changes in personnel, working methods, and company reorganization as a result of the proposed time-sharing system?
7. How reliable are the existing data files for satisfactory operation of the proposed system?
8. How well documented are the existing data for a backup system in the event of emergencies?

Engulfed in the glamor and publicity of time-sharing systems, companies often overlook the seriousness of these questions. Unless they are carefully answered and all associated factors are considered, the adoption of a time-sharing system can turn out to be a costly experience.

Software

Like any other computer system, a time-sharing system performs useful tasks through a functional set of program instructions that gives it direction. The software package generally consists of (1) supervisory programs stored permanently in the system's memory and serving all operations, and (2) user programs prepared by or available to the user for solving specific problems. Each program carries out certain functions and has a variety of operating requirements.

SUPERVISORY PROGRAMS. The supervisory program, sometimes referred to as the *executive program,* is a monitor on the time-sharing system, and performs a strategic role in the operation of the system. It supervises the speed and capability of the computer and determines when and where the computer should be available. The program's complexity depends on the type and size of the time-sharing system, and may range from a few to many thousands of words in length. It is a separate entity from user programs and is mandatory in each operative system.

Among the primary responsibilities assumed by the supervisory program are the following:

1. **Space allocation and supervision.** For efficient utilization of the system's main memory and auxiliary storage space, the supervisory program allocates the exact physical memory location of certain data for processing, and supervises the relocation of the user program during queuing and other operations. A set of constantly maintained tables is used for keeping track of data location and protecting transactions against accidental or intentional loss.

   Memory protection is necessary in all time-sharing systems. In general-purpose systems accessed by many users, some users may demand that information related to their files be kept confidential. The supervisory program has the responsibility of blocking off the loaded memory areas to prevent them from being used by unauthorized persons. One common technique is to incorporate a code within the user's number that specifies the memory areas containing his file. Other codes can also be used to allow the user to read but not change the data in the file, or vice versa.
2. **Computer time allocation.** In handling user demands made through their respective remote terminals, the supervisory program determines and assigns a specific slice of computer time (quanta) to each user. The length of computer time depends on the number of users and the response time they require. The problem is compounded by the diversity of users and their computational needs.

"Conversational" or interactive users, for example, require relatively smaller quanta for their smaller computational problems than do "production" users, whose programs are more lengthy. The supervisory program's role here is to swap programs into and out of the computer's main memory in order to efficiently serve all users with minimum delay.

One way of handling interactive and production users is to assign high-priority interrupt to interactive users, while assigning low-priority (stack) status to production users. When a production job becomes available in the main computer's memory, it is processed without interruption, except when an interactive user requests computer time. In this case, the latter's job is promptly handled, with the former program shelved in the interim. Another method is to assign specific computing quanta to each user (e.g., 30 milliseconds). After the program uses its allotted number of consecutive quanta (say, five) without reaching an output, it is interrupted in response to another job in queue (e.g., a production user) in sequence. After the latter job uses its computer time, the once-interrupted program is allowed to continue processing.

Thus the supervisory program not only allocates computer time for various jobs, but also handles *priorities, program swapping,* and *response to interrupts* from system devices and programs. This overall scheduling function is a complex and involved task; the supervisory program is constantly determining what transaction should be processed next (priority factor) and monitoring the computer time allotted to it.

3. **Polling terminals.** The time-sharing system takes action on data transmitted from one terminal at a time. When several terminal users wish to transmit at the same time, only one user can do so, based on his predetermined priority, or if he happens to be the first one on the waiting list. Other users have to wait their turn.[1] The supervisory program handles input from these terminals by *polling* (scanning) them. Normally, the time-sharing computer has in memory a polling list that gives the sequence in which to poll the existing terminals. Certain terminals are high on the polling list and therefore have high priority. Others might be listed more than once on the same list so that they are polled twice as often as other terminals.

   Briefly, the supervisory program polls each terminal for input. If there are input data, it gives control to the user program for processing. Otherwise, it moves on to poll the next terminal on the list, and so on, until all terminals are polled and served. The supervisory program keeps track of which terminal is related to which user program.

4. **Input–output processing.** In time-sharing systems with multiprogramming capability, the supervisory program controls the processing of two or more programs within quanta allotted in advance.

[1] Since waiting time is a matter of seconds, or sometimes a fraction of a second (depending on the number and usage of available terminals), each user feels as though he has a direct connection, independent of other users.

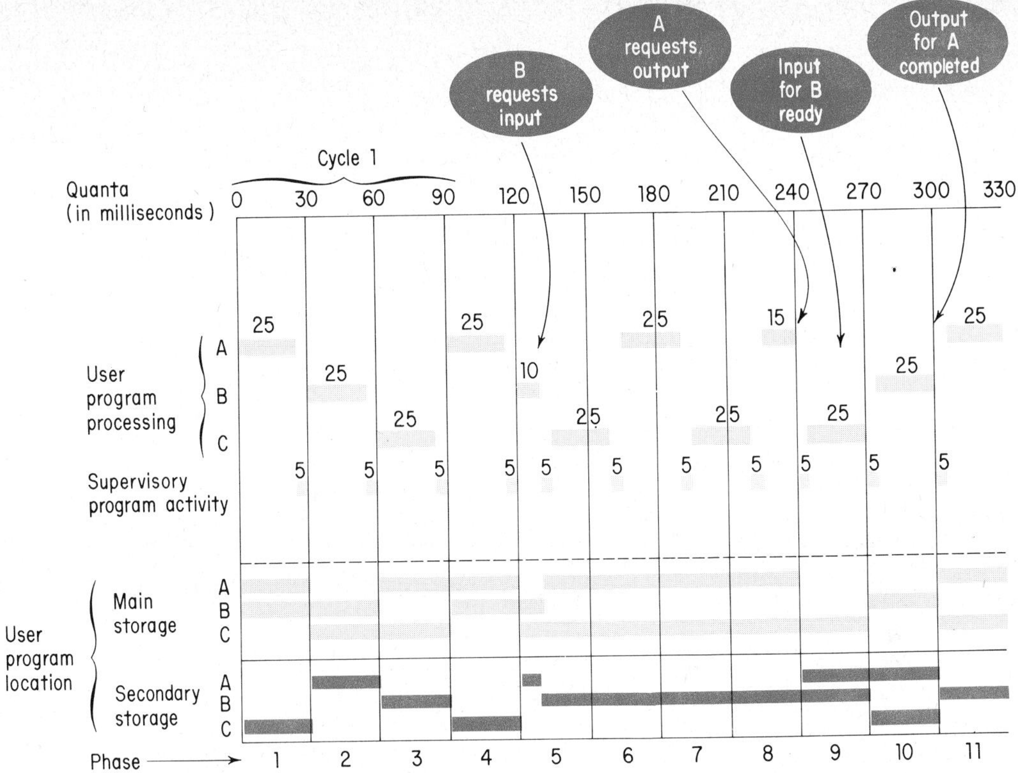

FIGURE 12-9. Program swapping

To illustrate this key function, assume the availability of three user programs with each program allotted 25 milliseconds of computation time. Assume further that the supervisory program requires 5 milliseconds to do such routines as polling terminals and swapping user programs. Figure 12-9 shows the procedure as follows:

Phase 1: For the first 25 milliseconds, program A is performing calculations while program B is waiting in the computer's main memory for processing. Program C is held in secondary storage. Once the 25-millisecond quanta is used by program A, the supervisory program uses 5 milliseconds to transfer program A to secondary storage, move program C to main memory, and release program B to perform calculations.

Phase 2: Program B is executed for the next 25 milliseconds, after which the supervisory program transfers it to secondary storage, moves program A to wait its turn in main memory, and releases program C to perform calculations.

Phase 3: Program C goes through 25 milliseconds of calculations, followed by the supervisory program's 5-millisecond routine of bringing program C to secondary storage, moving program B to main memory, and releasing program A for computation. Thus, the first 90 milliseconds constitutes a total cycle, since each of the three user programs has gone through its slice of computing time, or quanta.

Phase 4: At 90 milliseconds the cycle starts all over, with program A computing while program B is waiting its turn, and program C is in secondary storage. At 115 milliseconds, the supervisory program interrupts program A, transfers it to secondary storage, and releases program B for computation.

Phase 5: In phase 5, program B runs for 10 milliseconds only, requesting more input data. The supervisory program moves it to secondary storage where it remains until input data are ready. Program A is brought into main memory, and program C (already in main memory) is allowed to run.

Phase 6: At the end of the 25-millisecond limit, program C is interrupted, giving control to program A.

Phase 7: The supervisory program bypasses program B and gives control to program C, since program B is still in storage waiting for input data.

Phase 8: Control again is transferred back to program A.

Phase 9: At 240 milliseconds, after only 15 milliseconds of processing, program A requests output. The supervisory program transfers it to secondary storage and, since program B is still without input, it allows program C to run. However, at 260 milliseconds, input for program B becomes available. The supervisory program waits until program C completes its quanta before it takes action.

Phase 10: Program C is moved to secondary storage, and program B is allowed to run. Program A is still in the output phase.

Phase 11: At 300 milliseconds, program A's output is completed. The supervisory program moves it to main memory and allows it to run.

The overall multiprocessing routine of processing input and output data continues until the whole operation is completed. The operation becomes more complex in time-sharing systems handling a large number of user programs with different levels of priority.

User Programs. A user program is the set of program instructions designed to direct the system in solving a problem or performing a given routine. Since the user is more concerned with getting the job done than with the techniques the system uses in handling the details, special time-sharing languages have been developed for that purpose.

A widely used language in time-sharing is called BASIC. An acronym of *beginners all-purpose symbolic instruction code,* BASIC [2] was developed at Dartmouth College by John Kemeny and Thomas Kurtz; it has a structure similar to that of FORTRAN.[3] Although BASIC offers a limited number of instructions, it is quite adequate for solving a wide

[2] Other time-sharing languages include ALGOL, QUIKTRAN, FORTRAN, STRESS, COBOL, and PL/1. BASIC is explained in Chapter 19.

[3] FORTRAN is discussed in Chapter 18.

variety of business problems. The procedure generally involves the following steps:

1. The user dials the number of the time-sharing facility, and when a high-pitched tone is heard, the handset is placed in an acoustic coupler attached to the terminal, which, in turn, types basic information such as the name of the time-sharing facility, the time of the service, and the ID number of the terminal used.
2. The terminal then types on a separate line USER NUMBER and pauses. The user keys in his number and depresses the RETURN button to start a new line.
3. The terminal types the word PASSWORD and pauses at the next line. The user enters his password, which is stored (not typed) by the system. The RETURN button is depressed to go to another line.
4. The system asks TYPE OLD OR NEW. The user enters his response and depresses the RETURN button. In the sample program in Fig. 12-10, the response is NEW.
5. The system next asks PROBLEM NAME. The user types his response (in the example, SUM) and depresses the RETURN button.
6. The system types READY, indicating to the user that the time-sharing system is ready to accept his program. The user then depresses the RETURN button and proceeds to key in his BASIC program (Fig. 12-10).
7. Once entered, the user types RUN and depresses the RETURN button. The system responds by typing identifying information

FIGURE 12-10. BASIC program entry and format

Key Entries		***Response***
ØN AT—12:19 PØRT:07		
USER NUMBER		0471
PASSWØRD		
TYPE ØLD ØR NEW:		NEW
PRØBLEM NAME:		SUM
READY		
10 READ A, B, C		
20 DATA 8, 9, 5		
30 LET S = (8*8) + (9*9)/5		
40 PRINT "VALUE IS" S		
50 END		
RUN		
SUM	12:21 TSS 09/20.74 TUES.	
VALUE IS 80.2		
RUNNING TIME 02.0 SECS.		
READY		
BYE		
ØFF AT 12:23		

such as the name of the program, time, name of service, date, and day of service.

8. Assuming an error-free program, the program is executed and the answer printed out, followed by the running time.
9. The system prints READY, signaling a new operation. Since the program has been executed, the user types the command word BYE, which disconnects the terminal from the system. Upon depression of the RETURN button, sign-off time is typed.

Virtual Time-Sharing Operation

An advanced technique in some larger time-sharing systems employs a virtual control program that offers the user an expanded functional capability of the computer through a combination of main storage and direct-access devices. The user treats secondary storage as an extension of main storage, giving the illusion of a very large core memory. Thus virtual memory can be larger than real computer storage. For example, the IBM 360/67 time-sharing system (TSS/360) has 512,000 to 2,048,000 bytes of real (actual) storage, but it gives each user virtual memory of approximately 16 million bytes.[4]

Each user's virtual memory, then, is partitioned into a combination of main storage and auxiliary storage volume. Virtual memory and real and auxiliary storage are managed on a *paging* basis. A paging process involves moving pages (in the case of the TSS/360 system, each page is 4,096 bytes) between main and secondary storage. For example, when a user references a page in virtual memory, the control program checks on its availability in main storage. If available, processing proceeds. Otherwise, interrupt occurs, allowing the supervisor program to bring, or "page in," the needed page into main storage.

While a page is being brought into main storage, the job needing a page is put in a "page wait," allowing the CPU to work on another job. When the page becomes available, the supervisor puts the waiting job in a ready state so that it can complete its time slice the next time it is given control of the CPU.

Virtual-memory-storage hierarchy is sketched in Fig. 12-11; we see that

1. A large virtual memory is viewed by the user for preparing and executing his programs.
2. Main storage contains only needed pages for different programs being multiprogrammed.
3. Additional pages are "paged in" on demand (called *demand*

[4] Main computer storage is partitioned by the supervisor program in units of 4,096 bytes, called pages. In the TSS/360 system, there are 256 pages to a segment, giving around 1 million bytes per segment. With 24-bit addressing, there is a maximum virtual memory of 16 segments or 16 million bytes for each user (or $2^{24} - 1$). A 32-bit addressing gives a virtual memory of 4 billion bytes (or $2^{32} - 1$).

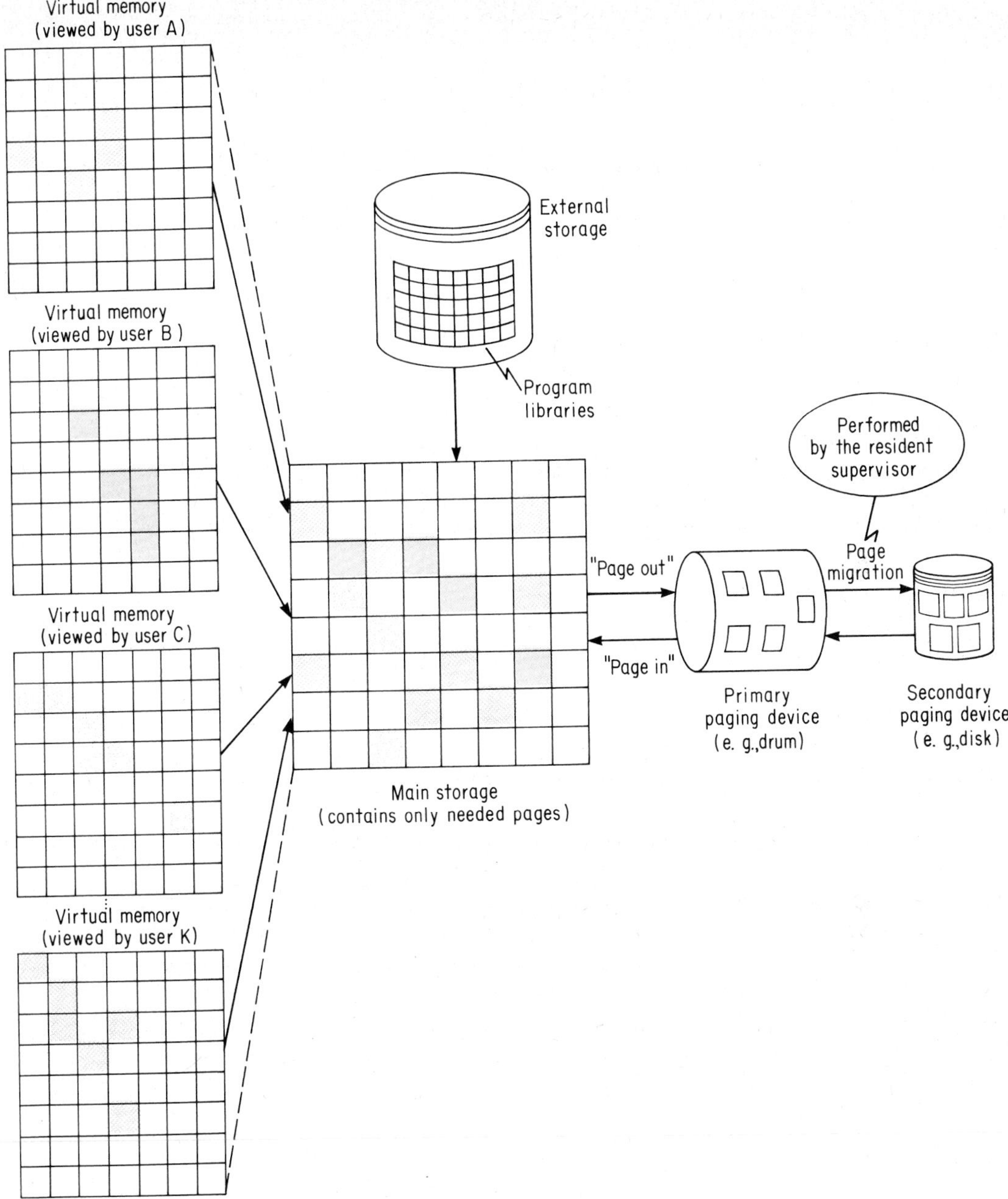

FIGURE 12-11. Virtual-memory-storage hierarchy

paging). Unneeded pages are "paged out" to a primary paging device, usually a magnetic drum.

4. Since the primary paging device has limited storage capacity, infrequently used pages migrate to a backup, secondary paging device for storage until needed.

Several major information-handling problems face business organizations and managers each day. The huge volume of information generated by various departments or divisions tests the manager's ability to cope with the complexity of his dynamic environment. The fact that many managers are often far removed from the source of activities and information, coupled with the rapid obsolescence of most information, makes these problems all the more difficult. Although time-shared computers cannot be expected to solve these problems, they have the capability of acting as personal reference libraries for the user through the tapping of a corporate data base. A data base can also be independent of a time-shared environment, per se. That is, an organization can have a data-base structure with a quickly responding computer that shares data with corporate users and even other peripheral computers.

A corporate data base is developed in an attempt to make better use of files and to achieve user-oriented, organization-wide access to data. A data base permits more effective computer utilization and on-line, real-time processing, thus making it possible to have available the current status of the "real world" for organizational functioning (Fig. 12-12).

Data base is one "buzz" phrase that has been overworked and seems to be very much in vogue in the literature. It is used either by itself or, frequently, with other words in combinations such as *corporate data base*, *data-base management*, *data-base management system*, *common data base*,

FIGURE 12-12. Computer data base

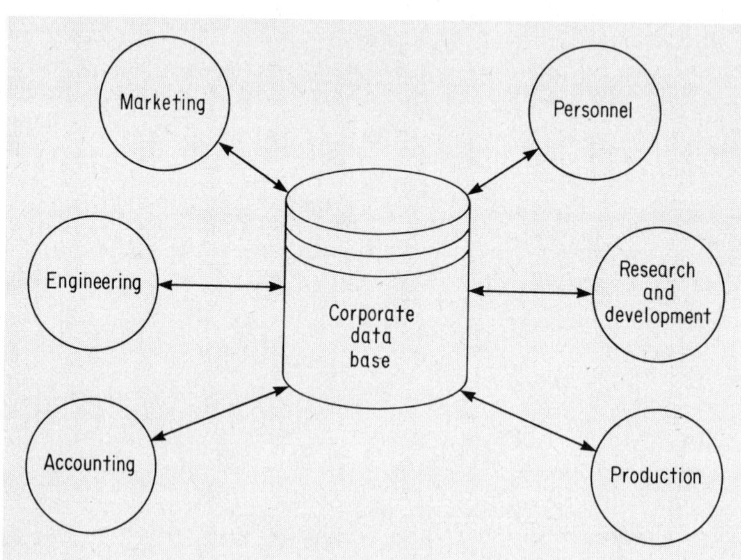

data-base file management, data-base language, and so on. Whichever phrase is used, it very likely refers to interrelated data items common to several data records, stored only once, and linked to many related records. To make use of the data, data from one or several records in the data-base files must be integrated or pulled together. Thus the sharing of common data refers to the fact that many programs can use the same files and records.

In theory, an ideal corporate data base encompasses all the information that the user or the organization would ever require; each record would contain sufficient room for future expansion of the data base and would also be on a direct-access device accessible in such a way that a minimum search would be needed in order to obtain any record. In practice, however, this ideal is unattainable, since it is extremely difficult for management to determine the organization's long-range development and, consequently, the information it will require. Even if it were technically feasible, it would be relatively uneconomical for all but a few data-processing departments.

Advantages of Data Base

The data-base concept is one answer to management-information requirements regarding such matters as short lead time for the preparation of new reports, requests for information from different files, and predictions of future needs. The main advantages of a corporate data-base system are

1. Reduced computer processing time.
2. Centralized files for all applications.
3. Reduced sorting of records.
4. Reduced number of programs to be written.
5. Elimination of duplicate space and effort.
6. A single source of information for complete, accurate data processing and information retrieval.

Once data are stored in the system, they are easily accessible when needed, and there is extensive two-way communication among the various files. These files are also shared among all the application programs that have need for the data.

Data-Base Structure

The structure of a data base is determined by the logical arrangement of the records and the means provided for their access. The logical structure is one of the more important factors in ultimately determining the usefulness of the data base. By contrast, the physical structure of the data base is secondary in importance, because random accessing permits records to be located at any convenient spot in the data base.

Storage Requirements. With a view to potential growth, sufficient space should be included in each record format to allow for future expansion. The extent of such allowance depends on the value of the data and the accuracy of the projection of future information needs.

The storage requirements of a data base can become extremely troublesome in terms of configuration and throughput. If the requirements should exceed the capacity of available high-speed devices (such as magnetic drums and disks), slower devices with greater capacity might be necessary. However, limiting the data-base storage size has the advantage of containing it on a high-speed device. If this is not possible, segmentation can be implemented. In the segmentation approach, only certain segments of the data base are on-line at the same time. Although it is the least expensive method, it is unworkable for data that must be on-line, as in teleprocessing.

Access Methods. Data may be accessed through indexing or linking.

Indexing. Data-base records are usually concerned with business applications (inventory control, payroll, production control, machine-load planning, etc.) that can be formated according to strict rules and have readily apparent relationships. A technique often used in retrieving a record from a data base is to first address an index containing the identification and the data-base address of that record. With an index, data base records may be in any sequence, which permits the utilization of the whole available capacity of the device. Several different indexes (and, therefore, several different sequences of accessing) can be used in conjunction with the same data base.

The use of indexes creates a need for additional programming and processing, because it is necessary to update the indexes as well as the data base when records are added, deleted, or moved to different data-base addresses. If space is available in the records, the index reference can be included in the record, so that later changes to the index make it unnecessary to search the index itself for locating the index entry that needs to be altered.

Linking. When a record is retrieved from the data base, linking is used as an alternative method of accessing related records. A reference to a related record can be included in the data-base record and, by addressing the referenced location, a related record can be read into the core in a nonrandom, nonsequential manner. Links to related records differ from indexes, since indexes exist only as means of accessing related records, whereas links are additional data elements and are valid and usable data records.

Data-Base Design and Management

In designing a corporate data-base system, the following questions are important:

1. Does the data base satisfy existing application, or are additional files required?
2. Is the data base verified?
3. How accurate are the data files in the system?
4. How long does it take to get the data required for updating or for running a given report on a regular basis?
5. How satisfactory is the system for future growth?

That is, for a corporate data base to function effectively, it must be as complete, unified, accurate, accessible, and timely as possible.

Data base management involves file creation, file organization, and file maintenance. *File maintenance* consists of all the programs that are required to maintain and update the data base. In *file creation,* some files are created by combining previously separate application files into one new file to serve the same function as the old files. A given data field in two files, for instance, may be found to have different ranges of parameter values, different field size, and so on. The emerging function often results in discrepancies or loss of key data. To eliminate such a problem, one-time-only programs are written to compare old files with the newly created files. Any unintended difference between the files can then be corrected. Since creating the new data base is likely to be time consuming, management must allow adequate time for both the cleanup of data and the creation of files of interrelated records.

Regarding *file organization,* several new powerful software systems are available for performing the data-handling functions of a data base. One such package is IBM's Data Base Organization and Maintenance Processor (DBOMP), which rents for $100 a month. When using this package, a manufacturing organization separates its files into two types: master files and chain files. Master files are accessed through an index, either the index sequential access method (ISAM) for high-volume, volatile files, or the controlled sequential access method (CSAM). In a manufacturing data base, several master files may be used for storing nonrepeating data. Each master file has a key. The key for the part-number master file may be *part number,* while the key for the station master file is *station number.* Each master file also has chain files associated with it. The tool master file can be chained to a tool-usage file, which, in turn, is chained to the part-number master file. The tool-usage file shows what tools are used to make designated parts. The chains are also bidirectional, so one could search in both directions. For example, one could start with a tool number or a part number to get at either the parts made with a particular tool or the tools used to make a certain part.

Data Integrity and Security

Data integrity has to do with keeping data-based information accurate and up to date. Data security refers to protecting specific data from unauthorized use. It is divided into (1) information that may be damaging or harassing to an individual when improperly disseminated through a data base, and (2) proprietary information that would give competitors an unfair advantage if released to them.

Automatic protection of proprietary information in a data base is generally handled via a security key or data scrambling. The *security key* may be a simple password or a more complex key derived from a combination of factors. IBM has a package that assigns a key to the operator, the terminal, and the module used in accessing data. The keys are combined and compared to the file security key with a Boolean AND. The data may be accessed only if the AND yields a value of "true."

To extend protection techniques below the file at data-set level means examining the field of each record involved. Two factors are basic to this examination: (1) A field or data element by itself is not sensitive unless it is related to some identifier. For example, "salary" is not a sensitive data element without "employee name" as identifier. Even then, protection against exposures resulting from association or inference is still required when the user has authorized access to various files. (2) Individual fields need separate definition only when the form of protection differs from that of the adjacent fields that are already defined.

Data scrambling is especially useful to discourage unauthorized users outside the company. A key is normally added to each character at the central computer and subtracted at the receiving terminal. This is usually done with software or, in the case of a nonprogrammable terminal, by a designated sequester device on the telephone line.

THE COMPUTER UTILITY AND THE PRIVACY ISSUE

The emphasis on on-line, general-purpose, multiuser systems has aroused interest in establishing a computer public utility. As with any other utility, this system would make available to many geographically separated users a wide range of data-processing services on an on-line basis with the overhead shared among the users, depending on the actual time and extent of the facilities they use. Thus, the term "utility" bears a connotation similar to that of the electric power and telephone utilities, where each user has full benefits but bears a small fraction of the total cost. In such an ideal system, the user sits at a console in his home or office in a man–machine interactive mode—the machine becoming his intellectual partner in the way it answers his inquiries, checks his errors, extends his mental capabilities, and stores his private data.

The latter element—storing private data—has become an issue in today's general-purpose time-sharing systems. It is unlikely for a businessman to allow his private records or company files to be entrusted to a system accessible by many other users (including competitors) without some reasonable safeguards against indiscriminate access. Regardless of the many uses of the computer utility, whether it provides computerized shopping, electronic legal and medical libraries, or other interactive forms of processing, there are certain dangers that might face the user if certain utility system capabilities were misdirected or left uncontrolled. These dangers could be anything from industrial espionage to various forms of blackmail and political repression. In the final analysis, the computers that our nation's leading computer manufacturers have built could turn us into a nation of "slaves."

These fears are not without foundation. Today massive banks of personal data are held by the state and federal governments, insurance companies, banks, and credit bureaus; these pose a direct threat to man's civil liberties. Here are some examples of incidents that have already taken place:

The California Department of Motor Vehicles sells information submitted by applicants for a driver's license to junk mailers. The information is later combined with census data so that computerized "personal" junk mail can be tailored to each individual by class level, car model owned, and the like. This author averages 5 minutes a day sorting out and disposing of unsolicited junk mail.

The following excerpt from an article written by Phil Hirsch serves to illustrate a breach of individual privacy:

> I received one of those [personalized promotion] letters last fall. It came from Jerome P. DuFore, Sr., a complete stranger. He began by saying, "I'm amazed at the number of my friends who have dramatically increased their incomes in just the past few months." Then Mr. DuFore identified three people in my area who had allegedly increased their incomes by going into businesses of their own. . . .
>
> Most people who grow rich "started out with no more money than the few hundred dollars you have in the bank right now," the letter continued. "Few of them had two cars like the Hirsches do. Usually, they had a car less desirable than your '65. . . . After making a careful household-by-household study of Washington residents with incomes in the critical $12,500–$19,500 range, I have selected you and Mrs. Hirsch as possibly being among the few who will take positive action if given the opportunity." [5]

Further investigation by Hirsch revealed that this information was a combination of census data sold by the Bureau of the Census, automobile registrations sold by the Department of Motor Vehicles, and a private data base maintained by R. H. Donnelley Company.

Several suits have been filed against the federal government in attempts to remove information from data banks on individuals who participated in rallies or other similar activities. For example, one suit

[5] Phil Hirsch, "The World's Biggest Data Bank," *Datamation*, May 1, 1971, pp. 70–71.

alleged that a New York bank allowed the FBI to search a Peace Parade committee's checking account. Another suit charged that confidential bank records of individuals opposed to the war in Indochina were entered into FBI computer data banks.

A man with no criminal record who was arrested and later released without being charged is fighting to purge his arrest record from the FBI files. The District Court refused to hear his case, but the decision was later reversed by the Court of Appeals on the premise that arrest records can be harmful and that the problem was to "balance the need for the information by the FBI against the harm that would be done by disseminating the data."

Questions that need to be answered are, does a man have the right not to have data concerning him included in a data bank and does the government have the right to collect information about a citizen even if that individual has done no wrong, especially if such information might be potentially damaging to him? The traditional policy has been to collect data and then offer it to anyone with "a need to know." Many experts feel that this policy is inadequate, considering the potential harm that could be inflicted if such data were improperly disseminated. For example, by statute, FBI records are available to authorized federal, state, and city government officials. However, under regulations issued by the Attorney General, authorized recipients include (in addition to government agencies) most banks and insurance companies.

Ways to breach man's rights to the privacy guaranteed by the Fourth Amendment existed long before the computer. The computer, however, was a factor in accelerating the invasion of privacy on an unprecedented scale. In a speech reprinted in the *Congressional Record,*[6] Senator Sam Ervin, more recently known as the Chairman of the Senate Committee for investigating the Watergate bugging, concluded that the threat to individual privacy comes not from the computer but from man.

A constructive solution to computerized invasion of privacy appears to lie in devising formal procedures and controls for data-bank supervision. Congressman Cornelius Gallagher, a leading foe of the computerized invasion of privacy, has drafted a bill that would clamp down on the providing of name lists for junk mail. Ralph Nader, the consumer crusader, suggested an "information Bill of Rights" to protect an individual's privacy and allow him to examine his own file and challenge any inaccuracy through a hearing. Government, industry, and business administrators should protect the individual's right to privacy by assuring that only relevant data necessary for management goals be collected and filed. The computer industry must have a strict code of ethics, with the government taking the lead by defining the threats to privacy for public and private management. If a National Data Bank, as called for by the

[6] Sam J. Ervin, Jr. "The Computer and Individual Privacy," *Congressional Records Senate,* March 8, 1967, pp. 83369–83372.

Bureau of the Budget, is established, Congress must consider controls to protect privacy.

Considering the benefits as well as the problems that could result from the computer utility, the first and foremost goal of man is to control the power of this electronic marvel. Time-sharing systems can be directed to serve man in several constructive ways. They can provide informational details regarding new and existing products; help in determining the quality and efficiency of various competitive items; help the consumer in assessing the details of his insurance policy, mortgage loan contract, and other banking documents; and otherwise provide whatever service he requires that he cannot do himself because of time and background limitations. However, if proper measures are not taken in time to steer the computer toward preserving the privacy and serving the interest of its users, the computer, by virtue of its powers and capabilities, can ultimately become the master, rather than the slave. We may wish to believe that this is tomorrow's problem, but it is already here.

SUMMARY

Real-time processing was developed in an attempt to close the gap between actual transmission and updating of data, thus allowing immediate processing. Management can now transmit and receive information at high speed and maintain minute-by-minute control over various key operations.

The key characteristics of a real-time system are direct connection between input–output devices and the central processor and fairly quick response time. Real-time systems may be one-user or multiuser systems (providing each user a computer time share). Multiprogramming systems are capable of manipulating two or more programs with one central processor within the same time period. Systems with multiprocessing capability use two or more computers linked together for coordinated functioning. Since a real-time system involves a high cost in hardware, programming, and design, top talent must be employed to justify a binding commitment.

Time sharing involves the use of computers, communication equipment, and programming to allow many users almost simultaneous utilization of a system. The system is fast enough to give each user the feeling of having independent use of the facility. Among the major characteristics of a time-sharing system are on-line, real-time processing, almost simultaneous access, multiprogramming capability, flexibility, and independence of operation.

A time-shared system offers the advantages of lower processing cost, on-line programming, access to developed programs, and fast response time. From the viewpoint of the owner of a time-sharing system, the major drawback is acquisition cost. Profitability depends on regular use of the facility by a large number of users. From the user's viewpoint, the possibility of system failure and data security are factors to consider.

Time-sharing software includes primarily supervisory programs that monitor and coordinate the operation of the total system in terms of computer space and time allocation, polling terminals, and processing routines. User programs are written in special time-sharing languages such as BASIC.

A corporate data base is a centralized pool of user-oriented, organization-wide data available to management for more effective decision making. In designing a corporate data base, the factors of data integrity and data security are of major importance. An effective system must use automatic protection techniques to prevent sensitive information or information that might be damaging or harassing to individuals from leaking into the hands of unauthorized persons. The concept of a computer utility potentially offers thousands of users low-cost computer time for processing. However, the possibility of data leakage and, therefore, invasion of privacy threaten its implementation unless government and other agencies enforce protective measures.

TERMS TO LEARN

Basic	Polling
Data base	Quanta
Multiplexing	Queuing
Multiprocessing	Supervisory program
Multiprogramming	Throughput
On-line, real-time	Time sharing

QUESTIONS

1. Explain the factors that contributed to the development of real-time systems.
2. What is real-time processing? Explain its essential requirements.
3. Distinguish the difference(s) among basic, time-shared, multiprogramming, and multiprocessing real-time systems.
4. Explain and illustrate the uses and capabilities of a basic multiprocessing real-time system.
5. What factors must an organization consider in designing a real-time system?
6. What is time sharing? Explain briefly its main characteristics, advantages, and drawbacks.
7. Summarize the leading events that contributed to the growth of time-sharing.

8. Explain briefly the primary categories of time-sharing systems.
9. Discuss the elements making up a time-sharing software package.
10. What are the primary functions of a supervisory program?
11. What is a data base? What are the key advantages?
12. Explain briefly data-base access methods.
13. What is involved in data-base management?
14. Distinguish between data integrity and data security. How is data integrity maintained in a data-base system?
15. Discuss briefly the concept of computer utility and how it relates to the privacy issue. What steps can you suggest for better control of private records?

SUGGESTED READING

BRIGGS, P. L. "Time-Sharing Can Be a Company Tool or Toy," *Computerworld,* March 25, 1970, p. 4.

"Considerations of Data Security in a Computer Environment," IBM 520-2169-0. IBM Corporation, White Plains, N.Y.

DALY, DIANA. "How to Choose a Time-Sharing Service," *Computer Decision,* March 1970, pp. 12–16.

DONOVAN, S. F. "Time-Sharing Techniques," *Data Management,* Sept. 1971, pp. 80–83.

FEENEY, GEORGE. "A Three-Stage Theory of Evolution for the Sharing of Computer Power," *Data Processing Digest,* Feb. 1972, pp. 26–27.

HIRSCH, PHIL. "The World's Biggest Data Bank," *Datamation,* May 1970, pp. 70–71.

LIPP, M. F. "The Language Basic and Its Role in Time-Sharing," *Computers and Automation,* Oct. 1969, pp. 42–43.

MARTIN, JAMES, and A. R. D. NORMAN. *The Computerized Society.* Englewood Cliffs, N.J.: Prentice-Hall, Inc., 1970, pp. 3–19, 267–325.

PARKER, D. B. "Profile of a Computer Criminal," *Data Management,* July 1973, pp. 32–34.

POPELL, S. D., et al. *Computer Time-Sharing.* Englewood Cliffs, N.J.: Prentice-Hall, Inc., 1966, pp. 3–28, 109–147.

VAN TASSEL, DENNIS. *Computer Security Management.* Englewood Cliffs, N.J.: Prentice-Hall, Inc., 1972, pp. 13–27, 139–160.

———. "Information Security in a Computer Environment," *Computers and Automation,* July 1969.

WESTIN, A. F., and MICHAEL BAKER. *Databanks in a Free Society.* Chicago: Quadrangle Books, Inc., 1972.

YOURDON, EDWARD. *Design of On-Line Computer Systems.* Englewood Cliffs, N.J.: Prentice-Hall, Inc., 1972, pp. 26–48.

computer system configurations

13

MINICOMPUTER SYSTEMS

Minicomputer Uses

Key Characteristics

Advantages

Limitations

Types of Hardware

Basic Structure

Selection Criteria

Minicomputer Makers

Minicomputer Market Potential

SMALL COMPUTER SYSTEMS

Burroughs B1700 Systems

IBM System/3, Models 6 and 10

System 3/15

MEDIUM-SIZED COMPUTER SYSTEMS

Burroughs B2500 and B3500

LARGE-SCALE COMPUTERS— THE MILLION-BYTE CLUB

IBM 370 System

IBM 370, Model 165

Burroughs 700 Computer Series

SUPER COMPUTERS

MINICOMPUTER SYSTEMS

Between the field of full-scale computer systems and the conventional series of office machines, a small group of aggressive technocrats and businessmen have created a totally new industry—minicomputers. Most of these newcomers are smaller in physical size, sleeker, and more economical than other computers. Although they cannot do the same job as larger computers, they have consistently proved their worth in handling various types of jobs that are either too complex for the calculator or too basic for the larger computer.

A technological extension of on-line, real-time computers, the minicomputer was made commercially available in the mid-1960s for a purchase price of $18,000 to $50,000. Since then, increased demand has attracted over 50 manufacturers and an unknown number of independent suppliers of software and peripheral services. There are also consultants, analysts, and software package specialists, all ready to make one's entry into the minicomputer processing world as easy and as convenient as possible.

Minicomputer Uses

Minicomputers, the "blue-collar" computers in business, are everywhere. They are used in areas such as data acquisition, accounts payable, sales statistics, freight billing, stock and commodity trading, production, quality control, and telecommunications.

Production and Quality Control. In production, a plant-floor minicomputer may be designed to retain data for later analysis, compare data with production schedules to determine if specific action is needed, recognize events as they happen (real-time status), and provide periodic "exception" reports and answers to various inquiries.

In quality-control testing, the operator reads the quality-control program into the system's memory via a tape reader. The system is interfaced to the testing devices, and the operator feeds in the required testing parameters to initiate the testing process. When the testing data for a given sample are received, the minicomputer processes them. If the data are within the parameters, the whole lot is accepted. Otherwise, the computer tests the entire lot and accepts only the items that pass the test. Statistical data pertaining to the testing operation are later presented in the form of a report to management for further action.

Telecommunications. Minicomputer control of telecommunications is a most promising application area. Four broad areas are considered:

1. **Remote concentrators.** A remote concentrator takes the data communication low-speed terminals and concentrates them onto one telephone line by a special multiplexing arrangement. The mini's function is to convert the transmissions into such a format as to make the multiplexed transmission appear to the computer as the input from one high-speed device. Among its other functions are editing, code conversion, error checking, and temporary buffer storage.
2. **Front-end communications processors.** A front-end processor is a programmable device that serves as a CPU interface to the telecommunication system. Minicomputers in front-end processors convert codes, check for errors, maintain records of message traffic, and poll and address terminals.
3. **Message switching.** In a telecommunication system using remote concentrators or front-end processors, a terminal can talk only to the computer. A message-switching system makes it possible for a terminal to address several other terminals singly by sending the message once to the message switcher.
4. **Intelligent terminals.** Minicomputers also have brought processing power to remote-batch, data-entry, buffered, and CRT terminals. In remote batch-terminals, for example, they handle input–output peripherals for high-speed telecommunications with a remote computer.

Other Areas. A minicomputer's great versatility, blended with its relatively low price, makes its use ideal in areas not previously handled by computers. Many time-sharing service centers use them as a liaison or a concentrator between their remote users and the central processing center.

Furthermore, minicomputers have been used in previously unautomated activities, such as training employees to run various machines and handle complex jobs. For example, a minicomputer is used to run simulators for training railroad conductors. By providing the environment and conditions of a "live" train, the simulator responds to the trainee's action in the same way as a real train would. If errors are made, the computer can rerun the operation as often as necessary with no chance of damaging the equipment. Such an approach is not only safer and faster, but was found to be much more economical than tying up a track, a train, and a qualified conductor for on-the-job training. Simulation and other new uses for minicomputers will be discussed in a later section.

Minicomputers are expected to eventually flood the market. Mass production has brought a continued drop in price, so that a typical system runs under $10,000. Digital Equipment, a leading manufacturer, has already introduced a minicomputer processor for as low as $800.

In the first section of this chapter we present an overview of the characteristics, basic structure, and future prospects of minicomputers; this is followed by a discussion of small, medium-sized, and large-scale computers. The coverage is brief, the objective being to expose the student to a general understanding of the field with no particular emphasis on specific systems or computer manufacturers.

Key Characteristics

A minicomputer is characterized by the fact that it is a *low-cost, physically small, general-purpose, word-oriented, digital computer, with a 4,096 (4K) basic word memory and a price ranging between $800 and $15,000.* Word-length varies from 8 to 24 bits—most commonly 12 and 16 bits. Although minicomputers share many characteristics, each system offers its own unique features. Figure 13-1 shows three popular systems.

Advantages

1. **Flexibility.** Compared to a desk calculator, a minicomputer can be altered by simply reading in a new program.
2. **Adaptability.** The minicomputer is easily upgraded into a powerful system, since many compatible peripheral and memory-extension devices are available.
3. **Low cost and ease of use.** Relatively low cost is a major attraction, and ease of use makes an in-house time-shared system ideal for a company with multiple users. Because of these features, it is readily accessible to each user and offers many programming languages to suit the particular user. Additional advantages include:
   a. Increased use at a relatively fixed cost.
   b. Low-cost access with protection of key, sensitive data.
   c. Availability of common programs to all in-house users.
4. It excels in applications calling for special software and communication capabilities.

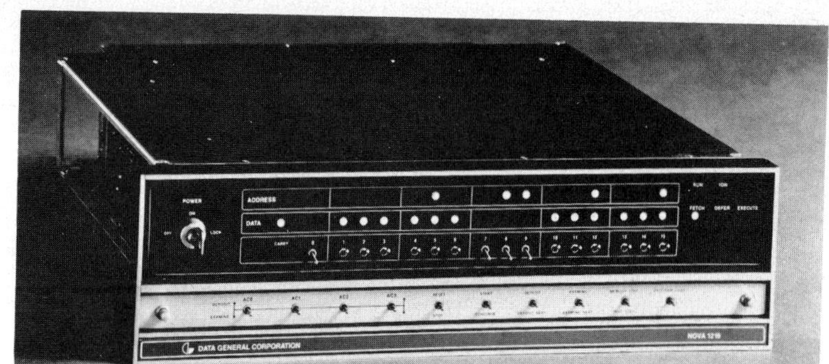

NOVA 1210 (Courtesy of Data General Corporation)

VARIAN 73 (Courtesy of Varian Data Machines)

PDP-8/model I

FIGURE 13-1. *Representative minicomputer systems*

Limitations

1. There are many complex jobs (e.g., mathematical simulation) that cannot be handled by a minicomputer.
2. Core size is more limited than in larger systems.
3. Execution times are slower than in larger systems.
4. On an industry-wide basis, minicomputer manufacturers have not quite established themselves as known and responsible companies, as have the large computer makers.
5. The minicomputer's cost may well be less than the cost of its peripheral devices, which means that the total cost of the system is likely to be much higher than the basic computer.

Types of Hardware

In considering a minicomputer, the user faces a choice among three types of hardware:

1. **Single processor, single access,** which handles only small programs effectively, with limited simultaneous-user capability.
2. **Dual processor, single access.** One processor handles communications, freeing the other processor to act as the monitor control and to handle compilations and program executions. That is, it is generally a "one-language" processor system.
3. **Dual processor, dual access.** One processor handles communications and monitor control, while the other processor handles program execution and compilations. Among its advantages are
   a. Multilanguage capability.
   b. Ability to handle many simultaneous users.
   c. Ability to handle many programs effectively.

Basic Structure

Minicomputers, like large systems, consist of a central processing unit and a number of input–output devices for various operations. The CPU includes (1) a core storage memory with an operating speed between 0.5 and 1 microsecond per cycle, (2) a set of registers generally designed to hold one word of data, (3) an arithmetic unit for performing arithmetic and logical operations, and (4) one or more data buses for facilitating data transfer to the various CPU components (Fig. 13-2).

MAIN MEMORY. Minicomputer memory size starts at a minimum of 4,000 words, with word lengths ranging from 8 to 24 bits per word. Core storage is organized so that a specific number of bits are combined to represent a word size. For example, a 16-bit machine is one that treats 16 bits of data as a separate addressing unit.

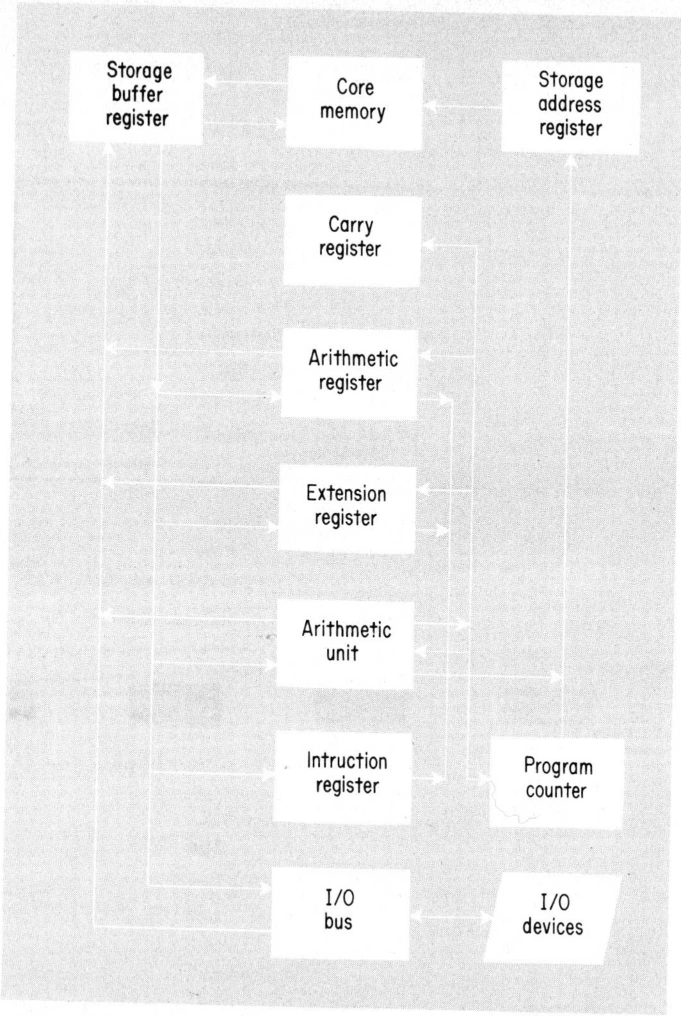

FIGURE 13-2.

REGISTERS. The primary registers are (1) the carry register, (2) the arithmetic register, (3) the extension register, (4) the storage address register, and (5) the storage buffer register. The *carry register* stores the carry bits resulting from an arithmetic operation. The *arithmetic register* stores data that are used for arithmetic and logical routines. For example, in an ADD instruction, a specific value stored in memory is added to the value stored in the arithmetic register. The sum is automatically placed in the arithmetic register. The *extension register* is used as secondary storage for the arithmetic register or for storing the second half of a double precision product specified by a MULTIPLY instruction.

The storage address and storage buffer registers are programmer-addressable, in that they hold the address or location of any word as specified by the programmer's instructions. The function of the *storage address register* is to store the *location* of a given word that is being read from or written into the main storage unit. The *storage buffer register,* on the other hand, stores the *content* of a word that has been read or the data to be written into a word. The data it stores are channeled through data buses to the arithmetic unit, input and output devices, and other components of the system.

As shown in Fig. 13-2, an *instruction* address is channeled to the storage address register from either the arithmetic unit or the program counter. Once received, the instruction is moved to the storage buffer register; it is later sent to the instruction register for execution. In the meantime, the program counter is incremented by 1, which represents the next sequential instruction.

INPUT–OUTPUT DEVICES. Input–output and other peripheral devices are connected to the central processor by an input–output bus, which makes available appropriate data paths for processing. Several devices can be linked to function simultaneously on one input–output bus. When the program provides the data channel with a given data address and size in memory for storage, the program first activates the input–output device and then the data channel to handle the transfer. Once completed, the program proceeds with other calculations as planned.

PERIPHERAL DEVICES. Among the peripheral devices available, *Teletype* devices are used most frequently. They are both economical and functional to operate, and provide printed output at 10 characters per second. Teletype can be used either on-line at the same rate of speed or off-line in cases involving program or data-input preparation. Higher-speed *paper-tape* readers, operating at 300 characters per second, are used in handling substantial amounts of program or data-input preparation. Other peripheral devices, including magnetic tape drives, cassettes, tape cartridges, and "mini"-tape, are also used, depending on the size of the minicomputer system and the needs of the user.

AUTOMATIC INTERRUPTS. An automatic-interrupt feature is incorporated in most minicomputers to permit their use with attached system components. It alerts the central processor to nonrecurring events and synchronizes the inflow and outflow of data. When an interrupt service routine is activated, the central processor saves the next sequential instruction to be executed and proceeds to determine the nature of the interrupt, taking appropriate action and then returning to the original program at the point of interruption.

The basic type of interrupt is called a *single-level interrupt.* In this case, a storage location is reserved to hold the address of the interrupt service routine. The central processor transfers to that location for action. Interrupts from any other devices are ignored until work on the first interrupt has been completed. Such a single-level scheme has pitfalls. It requires a search for the device that caused the interrupt, and a decision on the appropriate interrupt service routine to be executed. To eliminate "search waste," an interrupt program can be developed that gives frequently needed peripheral devices higher priority than other devices connected to the system.

High-level sophistication is reached through the use of the *multilevel priority interrupt* scheme, which reserves several storage locations for handling interrupt service routines. Each location (ranked by priority) can handle one or more peripheral devices. In operation, the occurrence of a high-level interrupt takes priority and "cuts in" for prompt execution.

The foregoing description of the basic minicomputer structure does not take into consideration the total range of peripheral devices and expanded core power utilized in many higher-priced systems. Peripheral devices go beyond the teletypewriter, typewriter, or card-reader level. They include magnetic tape units, paper tape readers, cassettes, plotters, CRT devices, disks, line printers, and drums. Likewise, the basic system's minimum 1,024- to 4,096-word memory can be expanded in most minicomputers to 32,000 words. Naturally, purchase price increases with an expanded configuration and often reaches a $65,000 limit.

Selection Criteria

In selecting a minicomputer, basic knowledge of the following key related areas is important.

1. **Accumulators** are registers that hold an operand, and are where arithmetic and logical operations are performed; therefore, the larger the number of accumulators, the greater the power of the minicomputer.
2. **Power-failure protection** is significant in real-time processing, so that the minicomputer shuts down without destroying the data in memory.
3. **Input–output word size** relates to the number of bits transferred in parallel in an input–output routine. This area has much to do with determining the data-transfer rate.
4. **Direct memory access** refers to a minicomputer that allows an input–output operation to proceed to or from memory without tying up a CPU register, which means a faster data-transfer rate than in computers without this feature.
5. **Program interrupt** is a critical feature in real-time applications; it signals the processor to stop program execution to consider the condition represented by the signal. The condition may be a parity error, a power failure, an invalid instruction, or an input–output device signaling its readiness to be read again.

6. **Compilers** make it possible for programmers to write in higher-level languages such as FORTRAN or BASIC. Although this feature may be important for certain operations, compilers generally take up much memory space.
7. **Operating systems** are normally designed to ease time-sharing or multiprogramming operations and for more effective handling of the various peripherals that might be available to the minicomputer.

Given the foregoing knowledge, the user proceeds by considering the execution speed for typical classes of instructions, and then tries to examine both internal and external factors. Regarding the internal factors, the following questions are critical:

1. How much can a given instruction perform in the specified execution time?
2. How many cycles does it take to execute an instruction?
3. How many instructions does it take to perform a specific required task?
4. What is the system's direct and indirect addressing capability?

The external factors relate primarily to (1) the proposed system's input–output capabilities in terms of speed and flexibility in handling the user's particular requirements; (2) the ease of interfacing special-purpose devices with the main system; (3) the power and quality of the minicomputer manufacturer's software with regard to its ability to meet the user's requirements; and (4) the service and support capability of the manufacturer.

In selecting a time-shared minicomputer, however, the following capabilities should be explored:

1. The system's backup and reliability.
2. Available computers and assemblers.
3. Ability to transfer data to and from the system.
4. File security for each program.
5. Ability to store programs in a common library.
6. The system's ability to access other users' programs.

Minicomputer Makers

Since its inception in the early 1960s, the minicomputer has shown continued promise and has proved its worth in handling areas previously ignored by computer manufacturers. The steady demand for its use has attracted a number of computer and noncomputer firms in search of profits. A few large diversified firms, such as Lockheed, Motorola, Scientific Control, and Litton, are also involved. Calculator makers such as

Burroughs, Wang Laboratories, and Victor Comptometer have also expressed interest in this field.

The "big five" minicomputer makers are Digital Equipment Corporation, Honeywell, Varian Associates, Hewlett-Packard, and Data-General. The first entrant in the minicomputer field was Digital Equipment Corporation, which introduced its basic PDP-1 in 1959 at a cost of $120,000 —an expensive system by the standards of that time. Today, the stripped version of its PDP-8 system sells for less than $10,000 (Fig. 13-1), and its PDP-11/03 minicomputer sells for $3,995. Computer Automation, Inc., sells a $1,700 minicomputer (in quantities of 200) with a 4K-memory parallel processor assembled into a 15- by 15-inch module. The price refers to a system stripped of its power supply, console, and metal chassis.

Like its counterpart (IBM) in the large-computer market, Digital Equipment Corporation accounts for approximately 80 percent of the total minicomputer market. Its dominance of the market is explained mainly by its ability to provide not only a minicomputer but also the necessary peripherals and software to solve the problems of the users. These benefits are not so easily accomplished by other manufacturers, especially if their objective is to just sell the system for quick returns.

Several advantages have enticed other firms to enter the minicomputer market. Entry costs into the field are low, technical know-how for designing the basic system is common, and software and service requirements are minimal. In most cases, a manufacturer acquires the required integrated circuits from one of many suppliers and can assemble these and other parts into a system without much difficulty. The amount of capital needed for such an endeavor is not as great as that needed for building larger computers. Furthermore, financing a computer company is relatively easy because of the psychological benefits that the word "computer" adds to a manufacturer's loan application.

Of all the foregoing factors, the development of the minicomputer was made easiest (physically and financially) by the perfection in the mid-1960s, of integrated circuits, which are tiny silicon chips vital to the minicomputer structure. First, their miniature size accounts for the small size of the basic system; second, the engraving of the circuitry on a single piece of silicon offers a high degree of reliability and durability; and third, although quite complex in operation, they are cheaper to manufacture than the transistor or the conventional vacuum tube. Thus, because of integrated circuits, the minicomputer manufacturer is less concerned with the problems of servicing the system he sells than is often the case with larger computer systems.

Minicomputer Market Potential

For some time small business firms have been ambivalent about the use of computers. The advent of the minicomputer now makes it feasible for practically every business concern to justify computer use, with the cost

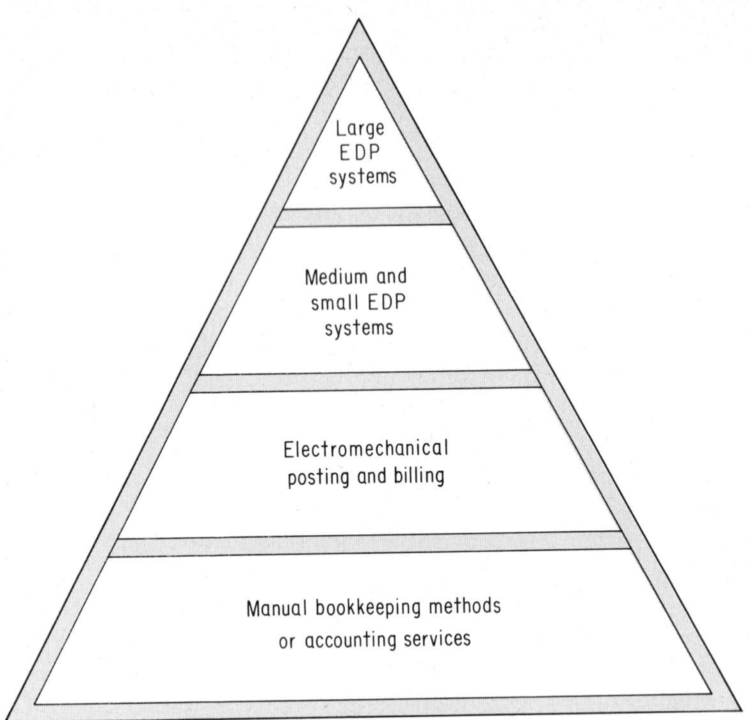

FIGURE 13-3. Potential area of minicomputer use

to be amortized in a few years. The technical reality has established a trend, probably never to be reversed.

Potential minicomputer users are generally divided into four areas. The largest percentage encompasses users who currently handle their data through manual bookkeeping methods, by an accounting service bureau, or through another similar system. The second largest potential user includes those using electromechanical posting and billing devices. The third area includes users of small and medium computers who might find the minicomputer, especially the sophisticated configuration, quite competitive with their present system. The fourth area includes large-scale computer users for which the minicomputer performs the role of a satellite or a "terminal" for the large system (Fig. 13-3). Here the minicomputer performs such perfunctory tasks as doing preliminary computing, keeping track of incoming and outgoing data, and formating certain information for immediate use by the larger system.

The first two potential areas mentioned are especially worth noting. Noncomputer data processing requires frequent human intervention—the more frequent the intervention, the greater the errors. Furthermore, with increased volume, business firms using electromechanical or manual processing systems often find it necessary to invest more money in additional equipment and labor for handling various records and accounts.

Thus, both system vulnerability and increased cost leave the minicomputer as a better choice. Once the basic system is installed, it can be expanded later to meet the user's expanding operation. Not only is it more economical in the long run, but it is also more efficient and accurate and offers flexibility unavailable in either manual or electromechanical systems.

Minicomputers promise to help thousands of business firms combat the high cost of labor and the growing complexity of business operations. By the end of 1969, 5,000 systems had been sold. In 1970, 12,000 systems were in operation. With a probable annual price decline of 18 percent, fierce competition among minicomputer manufacturers, and changing technology, the market potential could easily exceed 500,000 units, with industrial control applications predicted as the largest growth area.

Some experts have already put into operation a hierarchy of minicomputers, consisting of blue-collar, supervisor, management, and corporate computer systems. The *blue-collar* (worker) computer controls inventory, the supply of raw materials, and shipping details and distribution, and even monitors the production process, giving instructions when necessary. The *supervisor* computer instructs the worker computer to do various tasks; supervises production schedules, raw materials, and semifinished products; and prepares production reports for the management computer. The *management* computer uses the data received from the supervisor computer to project the market, decide on the production rate, correct one-time problems, and act upon any reported malfunctions. The *corporate* computer is designed to plan the total organization, including mortgage loans and financing, computing the corporate income and profits, paying stockholder dividends, and deciding on possible future expansion in physical facilities and production.

All indications point to the fact that minicomputers are here to stay, and that they will appear in staggering numbers. In the next two decades, they will become a part of everyday life. Children will grow with them to adulthood and will use them in the same way we use the telephone today. They will be acknowledged as a special tool for working out general problems. When future microcomputers—the $1,000 to $3,000 models—become available, man will find it as necessary to purchase or have access to one as it is now to purchase or lease an automobile. By then, there will be no limit to the uses of these computers in our daily endeavors. They will test our products, project our sales, control the atmosphere of our home, operate our car, act as our secretary, and even prepare our meals; in general, they will serve as our alter ego.

SMALL COMPUTER SYSTEMS

Small computers are usually general-purpose, word-oriented digital computers with a memory capacity of up to 65,000 characters. They have a number of index registers, multiple accumulators, and direct-access memory (DAM) channels [1]; some offer multiplexor channels and one or more memory buses for improved efficiency. Among the available small computers are the IBM System/3 Models 6, 7, and 10, NCR Century 100, UNIVAC 9200 and 9300, Honeywell 115, and Burroughs 1700 series.

Small computer installations are justified on the basis of their ability to offer the management of small businessses better control over various operations; in the case of first-time users, such a system is justified on the basis of employee labor displacement. Larger business firms install small computer systems as terminals to a larger system and in situations requiring decentralized processing capability.

Burroughs B1700 Systems

A recent addition to the small-scale computer field is Burroughs B1700 series. First introduced in June 1972, the B1700 system is designed for small business management and first-time users with emphasis on ease of operation, system responsiveness (expanding the system without reprogramming or recompiling), immediate productivity through ready-to-use applications, and processor and control-system flexibility.

The B1700 series consists of the B1712, B1714, and B1726 systems. All have the large-scale integrated (LSI) circuit memory and accommodate the programming of several high-level languages (e.g., COBOL, FORTRAN, etc.). The B1712 system has a memory capacity between 16,384 to 40,960 bytes and an operating speed of 2 million cycles per second. The B1714 system offers a memory capacity between 16,384 to 65,536 bytes and an operating speed of 4 million cycles per second. The B1726 is the largest of the series with a memory capacity between 24,574 and 98,304 bytes and an operating speed of 6 million cycles per second. A typical system rents from $1,600 per month and includes a 16,384-byte memory, an 80- or 96-column reader–punch, a line printer, a dual disk cartridge file, and a console printer (Fig. 13-4).

A unique contribution of the B1700 systems is the series of ready-to-use programs, called *business management systems* (BMS). The BMS library covers all major areas of business operations. Packages currently available are for applications in manufacturing management, wholesale management, bank management, and hospital management. Their use reduces the user's programming costs to a fraction of the costs otherwise incurred in a traditional programming operation. Additional benefits include multiprogramming capability, use of virtual memory, which enables large programs to be run without regard to the size of main memory, and data communications capability through the system's interface with a variety of data entry and display terminals.

[1] A DAM channel is available to an input–output device for transferring data to the central processor. It consists of a storage address and a storage content register for handling data addresses and contents from the input–output device.

FIGURE 13-4. Burroughs B1712 system (Courtesy Burroughs)

IBM System/3 Models 6 and 10

The basic IBM System/3, first introduced in 1969, is specifically designed for marginal computer users whose volume and/or financial resources are not sufficient to support a full-scale computer installation, but who otherwise can benefit from computer processing techniques. Model 6, an extension of the 96-column minicard System/3, is a low-cost direct-entry disk system designed to handle business applications such as accounts receivable, inventory control, billing, sales analysis, payroll, and general ledger. A typical system consists of an 8,192-character core memory, a two 45-million-character disk file, and an 85-character-per-second matrix printer (Fig. 13-5). The disk capacity is up to 9.8 million bytes with a dual drive. A typical model rents for approximately $1,025 per month. Purchase price is around $48,250. Model 15 is a more recent version of System/3.

CENTRAL PROCESSING UNIT. The main processing component uses monolithic systems technology (MST)—an integrated circuit that allows a maximum of five circuits in a module and switching speeds of 8 to 12 nanoseconds. The CPU consists of primary core storage with 8,192- to 32,768-byte capacity, arithmetic and logic units, a control system (including registers for sequencing instructions and initiating communication between memory and input–output devices), an inquiry and control console, and an optional *dual-program* feature.

The dual-program feature (used with disk versions of System/3) allows the concurrent loading and running of two independent programs. That is, when one program is undergoing an input or output function, the CPU is processing details for the other program, thus putting the CPU to more efficient use. The internal machine code is EBCDIC with a memory cycle (the time it takes to access and store 1 byte) of 1.52 microseconds.

INPUT–OUTPUT DEVICES. Input–output devices include multifunction card units (MFCU), printers, and disk-storage units. The MFCU, a single machine, is capable of multiple functions. It is designed to read, punch, collate, sort, and print cards in a single path without intermediate operator handling.

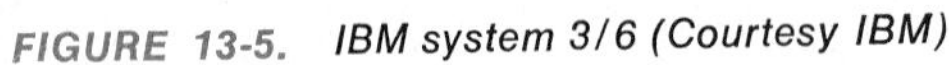

FIGURE 13-5. IBM system 3/6 (Courtesy IBM)

The line printer operates at 100 or 200 lines per minute, depending on the model. Similar to the Selectric-type typewriter and capable of both input and output functions, the system's printer-keyboard is available for supporting inquiry, data-entry, or operator-communications applications, or may be used as a second printer.

DISK-STORAGE UNITS. The basic disk-storage unit of System/3 consists of one fixed and one removable disk cartridge on a single drive. Other disk-storage configurations are (1) single drive with two 14-inch disks, having 2.45 million characters of storage and an average access time of 153 milliseconds; (2) single drive with two disks, having 4.90 million characters of available storage and an average access time of 269 milliseconds; (3) dual drive with three disks (one fixed and two removable), having 7.35 million characters of available storage and an average access time of 269 milliseconds; and (4) dual drive with four disks (two fixed and two removable), having 9.80 million characters of storage and 269 milliseconds access time.

OFF-LINE DEVICES. In an auxiliary role, sorters using photoelectric sensing elements are available for off-line use, and are capable of handling 1,000 or 1,500 cards per minute, with special features for sorting numeric and alphabetic data at a reduced number of passes. A magnetic character reader (IBM 1255) designed to process up to 500 checks and other related bank documents per minute also can be acquired.

PROGRAMMING. The programming language for System/3 is called RPG II, a modified version of System/360 RPG (Report Program Generator). Programs are written on special specification sheets in English-like statements that describe information such as the format of the input data, the functions and ways in which the computer is expected to perform, and the format of the desired output. Once the data on the specification sheets are punched into cards, the source program is ready to be entered into the computer. Other programs available for the IBM System/3 include a sort program, a utility program, and a system-control program.

System 3/15

The recurring question of where the user will go once he outgrows his System/3 prompted IBM to introduce in 1974 a more powerful, *no longer small* system, called System/3, Model 15 (Fig. 13-6). Unlike previous System/3 models, the new system is larger in size and has the ability to multiprogram and handle data communication activities. It also has almost three times the memory size (49,000 to 131,000 bytes) and 78 percent more disk-storage capacity than previous models.

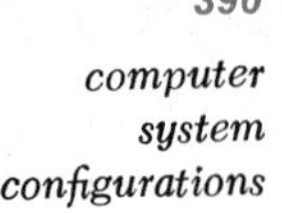

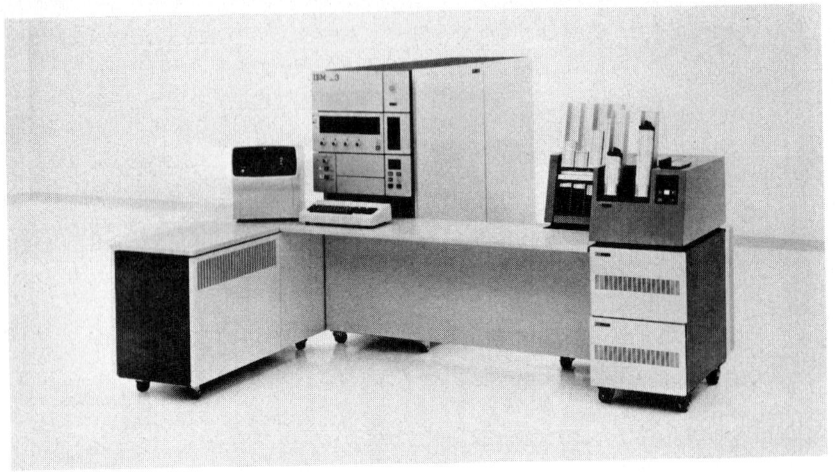

FIGURE 13-6. System/3 model 15 (Courtesy IBM)

The communication capabilities use a binary synchronous communications adapter (BSCA), which makes it possible for Model 15 to become a central processor in a communications terminal network or to function as a satellite processor in a larger network. For instance, a user can use Model 15 to control inventory from various remote warehouses by getting input data from and to their terminals over telephone lines. Once the data are received, Model 15 can perform some processing and transfer the data to a 370 system for final processing. The central processing includes main memory, which makes use of metal oxide semiconductor field-effect transistors (MOSFET) capable of handling fast input–output devices, and storage protection to prevent interference of user programs with one another or with the supervisory program.

Finally, an optional software program, called Data/3, can be used to provide conversational interaction between the central system and a remote terminal, and makes it convenient for the operator to interact data files during data .entry or inquiry.

MEDIUM-SIZED COMPUTER SYSTEMS

Medium-sized computer systems surpass small computers in providing greater operating speed, larger memory capacity, and high-speed input–output devices for efficient data handling. Among their unique features are high-level language compilers, personnel training by and support from the manufacturer, software operating systems, utility routines, and documentation. Prices vary, and rental ranges between $10,000 and $75,000 per month.

The Burroughs B2500 and B3500 computer systems are designed for a wide range of business and data-communications applications. They offer a totally integrated hardware–software design that incorporates monolithic, solid-state circuitry, and high-speed disk capabilities. The basic differences between the two systems are internal speed, peripheral component capacity, and memory capacity. Since they both fall in the medium-sized classification, the following description applies to both systems (Fig. 13-7).

The Burroughs system offers the following services:

1. **Fast hardware speeds,** some measured in nanoseconds.
2. **Multiprogramming** for increased productivity, easier handling of scheduling problems, and automatic manipulation of priority changes related to unscheduled tasks.
3. **Multiple read–write** compute capability on single programs.
4. **Operating system (supervisory program) control,** which synchronizes the system's operations for optimizing available processing power, operating procedures, and programming efforts.
5. **Modularity,** which permits the user to expand the existing system to meet increased processing demands or to handle new applications.
6. **Language versatility,** which allows programming in COBOL, FORTRAN, Assembler, or Generator languages to fit the job at hand.

FIGURE 13-7. Burroughs 3500 system (Courtesy Burroughs)

7. **Design flexibility,** which meets the requirements of various-sized organizations and services, and of batch and random-access processing as well as on-line applications. The average monthly rental of the B3500 system is approximately $20,000, with an average purchase price of $960,000.

INTERNAL ORGANIZATION. The Burroughs system is organized around a set of input–output channels, a main memory, a central control, an address memory, base and limit registers, and a processor. The basic mode of the operation is such that all input–output channels can transfer data simultaneously without disruption of processing. Data transfer is achieved at rates of up to 2 million bytes (4 million digits) per second (Fig. 13-8).

The *main (core) expandable memory* is time-shared among the individual channels and the central processor.

FIGURE 13-8. Internal organization of Burroughs B2500, B3500, and B4500 systems

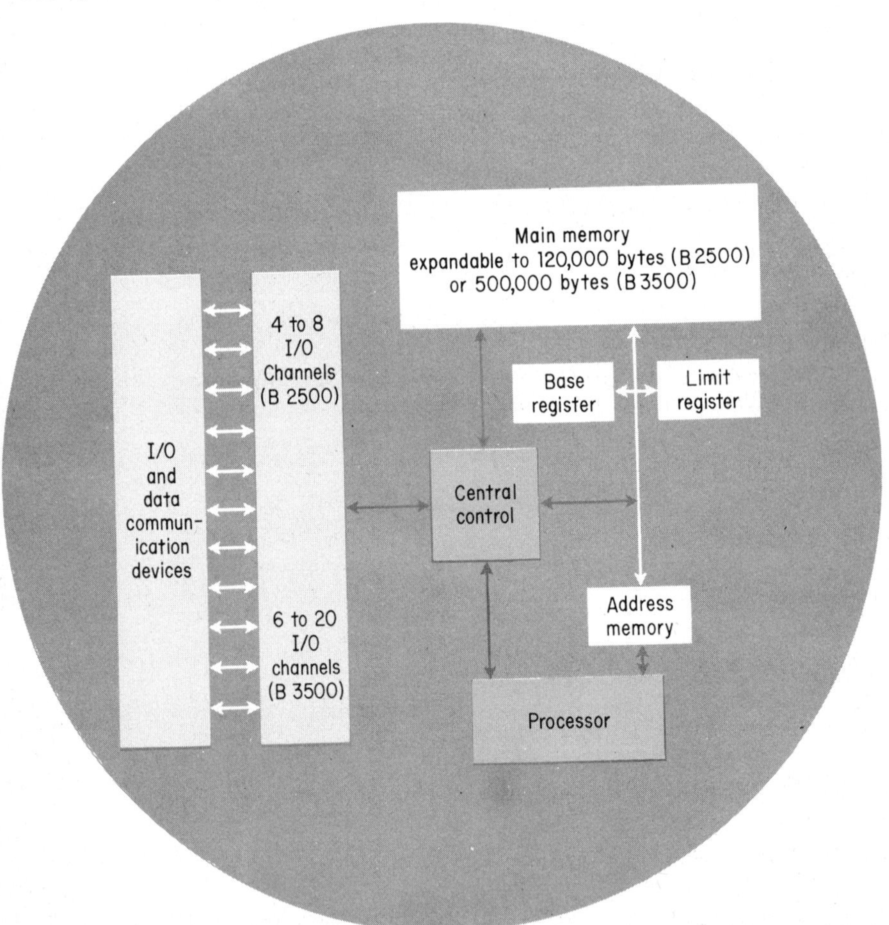

The *central control* is designed to allocate main memory access to individual input–output channels and the processor on a priority basis. Each peripheral device, along with the processor, competes with all other peripherals for access to core memory. To handle such multiple demands, each device makes an access request to central control, which grants the request as soon as all requests from higher-priority devices have been satisfied.

The function of the *address memory* is to designate core memory addresses for input, output, and processing. *Base* and *limit registers* specify the block of main memory reserved for the program by the operating (supervisory) system. Throughout a given operation, each active memory address is compared to the base and limit registers, thus allowing multiprogramming and time sharing without the danger of interference between two jobs.

The *processor* contains the arithmetic units and the logical controls to execute all instructions. Object programs are floated in memory through a base register, thus allowing several programs to be available at the same time. To activate a specific program, a *master-control program* (MCP) sets the base register to the location to which the program is assigned, retrieves the data, and turns control for processing. A program limit register protects memory from programs attempting to access areas outside of their boundaries.

INPUT–OUTPUT DEVICES. Special-purpose devices can be incorporated into the basic system, depending on the user's requirements and the type of operation to be handled. Among the key devices are card reader, card punch, paper tape reader, line printer, document reader, disk file, and magnetic tape units.

SOFTWARE. The Burroughs system's operating system, the master control program, handles many activities. It allocates memory, loads and schedules various programs, initiates input and output, maintains a data and program library, communicates with the console operator, and distributes processing and input–output device time to multiprogramming jobs. COBOL and FORTRAN are the two primary programming languages used.

LARGE-SCALE COMPUTERS— THE MILLION-BYTE CLUB

Compared to smaller-sized systems, large-scale computers are the ultimate in system sophistication, flexibility, and speed. To be considered large-scale, their main memory must have 1.5 million bytes or more and operating speeds in the nanosecond range. Their features and capabilities are exemplified in two new computers, commonly labeled as "computers

FIGURE 13-9. IBM 370, model 165, system (top) and Burroughs 7712 system (right)

for the seventies." They are the IBM 370 and the Burroughs 700 systems series (Fig. 13-9).

IBM 370 System

On June 30, 1970, IBM announced the availability of a new 370 system, which was labeled by the firm as "the landmark of the seventies," in contrast to the 360 system, which dominated the 1960s. Unlike past announcements, when the introduction of a new system rendered former systems obsolete, the evolutionary approach incorporated in the 370 system makes it compatible with its predecessors. All the software and most peripherals used in the 360 system can be used in the new 370 system. Thus the 370 system is more an extension of the 360 architecture than a fourth-generation computer, and provides users with dramatically higher performance and greater data storage capacity than past medium- and large-scale systems.

When first announced, the IBM 370 series consisted of three models: Models 145, 155, and 165; the 165 was considered the large-scale computer. Later, in 1972, smaller-scale Models 125 and 135 were added. In February 1973, Model 115—an entry-level machine to the 370 line—was unveiled, with deliveries made early in 1974. The most recent additions are Models 158 and 168, with first shipments delivered in May 1974. The two systems have a multiprocessing capability and operate in a *virtual-storage* environment. The user's program is segmented with fixed-length pages by the virtual-storage supervisor, which transfers to main storage, as space becomes available, as many pages as needed.

A typical Model 158 system with 512,000 characters of main storage rents from about $50,000 per month, or for approximately $85,000 per month for a model with 2,000,000 characters of main storage. Purchase price ranges from $1.6 to $2.3 million. The Model 168 system typically rents for $93,000 per month for a model with 1 million characters of main storage to about $170,000 per month for a model with 4 million characters of main storage. Purchase prices range from about $4.2 million to $7.3 million.

The 370 system has stirred controversy as to its benefits over a comparable 360 system. In a study[2] conducted in November 1972 and covering 350 major corporations, 30 percent voted against upgrading the 360 line. Among the reasons given were

1. Limited need for the 370's expanded capability.
2. Non-IBM users indicated that the 370 lacks direct compatibility with their system.
3. Present 360 system users were able to arrive at cost–performance advantages equal to the 370 line.
4. Since the 370 lacks new software advances (e.g., improved operating system), there is no point in considering change.

[2] *Computerworld,* Jan. 31, 1973, pp. 5, 18, 20.

Furthermore, one environmental drawback of a 370 over a 360 system is the heat problem.[3] Unit for unit, the 370 generates more heat than the 360. For example, a 360 Model 50, with 256,000 characters of main storage generates 22,000 BTU's per hour of operation; its 370 replacement, Model 145, generates 54,600 BTU's. The 1,100-line-per-minute 1403 printer for the 360 generates 4,500 BTU's of heat; the 3211 printer, which operates at twice the speed, generates 13,800 BTU's. These factors are important when considering air conditioning requirements for the computer center.

IBM 370, Model 165

Labeled as "bigger" and "faster," the IBM 370, Model 165, is a high-speed, large-scale digital computer designed for handling both commercial and scientific applications. Its primary features are

1. Upward compatibility with its predecessors in terms of architecture and programming requirements.
2. A free-standing system console that features an alphanumeric keyboard and a cathode-ray tube for operator–system communication (Fig. 13-10).

[3] *Computerworld,* April 26, 1972, p. 1.

FIGURE 13-10. *IBM 370/165 system console (Courtesy IBM)*

3. Multiplexor and block multiplexor channels to permit more data to enter and leave the system, thus increasing total throughput.
4. The central processing unit—a two-level memory system made up of a large-sized processor that functions as a backing storage for smaller, monolithic buffer storage. The processor is capable of requesting 8 bytes from the buffer every 80 nanoseconds. Memory capacity is up to 3,072,000 characters (Fig. 13-11).

   The addition of more processor storage offers the advantages of (a) processing several jobs concurrently; (b) adding or expanding teleprocessing, time sharing, remote data entry, and other applications with large storage requirements; (c) using higher-level language translators for faster program execution; and (d) using

FIGURE 13-11. *IBM 370/165 central-processing-unit elements (Courtesy IBM)*

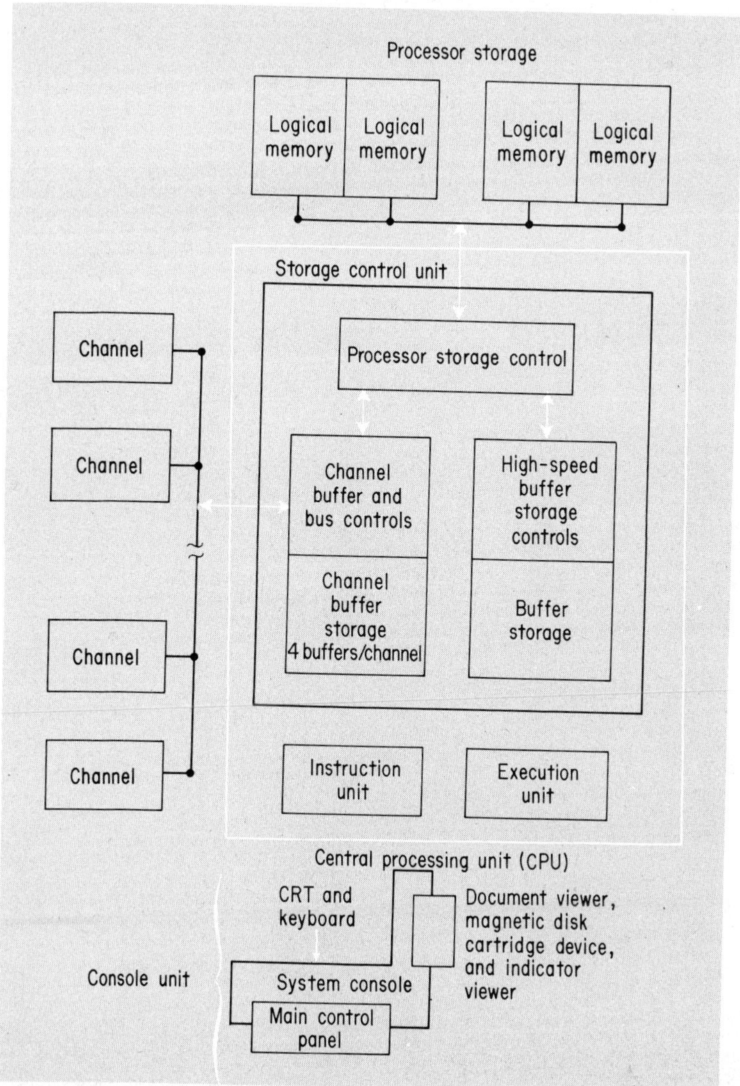

FIGURE 13-12. IBM 3330 disk storage, showing the 3336 removable disk pack (Courtesy IBM)

FIGURE 13-13. IBM 3211 printer (Courtesy IBM)

more and larger input–output buffers for increasing the overall speed of input–output operations.

INPUT–OUTPUT DEVICES. The unique input–output devices used with the Model 165 system are as follows:

1. **The 3330 disk storage and 3830 storage control.** This direct-access external storage subsystem consists of a storage control unit and from one to four, 3330 disk storage modules, which use removable 3336 disk packs. Each module has a storage capacity of 200 million bytes (Fig. 13-12).
2. **The 3211 printer.** This is a new, high-speed printer with a tapeless carriage and an alphanumeric print speed of 2,000 lines per minute. The tapeless-carriage concept decreases operator intervention by eliminating the carriage tape loading and unloading required on other printers (Fig. 13-13).

Other peripheral devices include

1. **The 2420 magnetic tape unit,** which uses a nine-track recording format and a 1,600-bit-per-inch recording density, maintains a recording speed of 160,000 or 320,000 bytes per second, depending on the model.
2. **A card read–punch,** with reading and punching speeds of 1,000 and 300 cards per minute, respectively.
3. **An on-line optical page reader** that reads printed alphabetic and numeric characters and specified symbols from documents ranging in size from 3 × 6.5 inches to 9 × 14 inches.
4. **An on-line tape-cartridge reader.** This reader reads tape cartridges inscribed on the IBM50 magnetic data inscriber or the IBM magnetic tape Selectric typewriter. It loads, reads, rewinds, and unloads each of the 12 cartridges automatically at the rate of one cartridge per minute.
5. **The 7770 audio-response unit,** which provides a composed audio response to a digital inquiry from a data-transmission terminal. Once the inquiry reaches the processing unit, it is processed, and the result—a coded response message—is transmitted back to the audio-response unit. The unit interprets the response message, elects the desired words in proper order from a prerecorded analog vocabulary, and transmits them to the inquiry terminal.
6. **The 2250 display unit** is a 21-inch CRT that projects alphanumeric information or images in the form of a series of dots or straight lines.
7. **The 2740 on-line communication terminal** consists of a printer and a keyboard for printing hard copy transmitted from the computer or for entering data into the computer via the keyboard.

FIGURE 13-14. Representative Burroughs 1700 system (Courtesy Burroughs)

Burroughs 700 Computer Series

Like IBM, Burroughs Corporation announced in October 1970 the availability of a unique 700 systems series designed to meet intermediate and large prospective users' needs for the 1970s. The series consists of the B5700 (two models), the B6700 (five models), and the B7700 (three models) (Fig. 13-14). The B6714 and the B7712 computers are believed to be highly competitive with IBM's 370, Models 155 and 165, respectively.

Among the B7712 system's general features are

1. Multiple (one to six) independent processors sharing a single operating system. Each processor is capable of handling 32 input–output channels at data transfer rates of up to 8 million bytes per second.
2. Data-communication processing. Data-communication processors are designed to relieve the central processors of handling line discipline routines and to provide the capability of handling large complex work efficiently.
3. A central exchange device that is employed to allow independent communication between memory modules, central processors, and input–output processors. The input–output processor controls data flow to disk subsystems, data-communication subsystems, and all peripheral units, and is capable of transferring data at rates up to 8 million bytes per second. It multiplexes up to four disk controls, 20 peripheral controls, and four data-communication processors.
4. An ultrahigh-speed main memory stores either 786,432 or 1,572,864 bytes of data, depending on the memory model. Maximum main-memory-system capacity is 6,291,456 bytes.

5. Optimized-access memory bank systems.
6. System software for continuous multiprogramming and multiprocessing.
7. Head-per-track disk-file memory-bank systems. The new memories offer basic file sizes of 450 million and 600 million bytes and may be expanded into 112 billion bytes of random access.
8. Use of front-end data communication processors instead of a second full-scale system for handling data communications.

SUPER COMPUTERS

IBM has recently introduced a super computer—the System 360, Model 195—with an internal processing speed twice as fast as the 360, Model 85, and with a more powerful rating than the earlier Model 95. Its immense size can be adequately used only in such operations as a central control for nationwide time-sharing systems or manipulating the complex operations of a large airline's reservation system.

The super 195's central processor is made of monolithic integrated circuits, with a main core storage capacity of from 1 million to 4 million bytes of data. Machine cycle time is rated at 54 nanoseconds.

The internal organization of this new computer is designed for handling many tasks in parallel; it can process up to 15 different jobs concurrently. Monthly rental ranges from $165,000 to $300,000, with the purchase price from $7 million to $12 million, depending on the peripheral and other devices involved (Fig. 13-15).

FIGURE 13-15. *IBM system 360, model 195 computer system (Courtesy IBM)*

SUMMARY

A minicomputer is defined as a low-cost, physically small, general-purpose, word-oriented, digital computer with a 4,096 basic word memory and a price under $15,000. Minicomputers are aimed primarily at first-time users or others who need a "slave" computer to do preliminary work for an established system. They are widely used in areas such as data acquisition, production, quality control, and in telecommunication as remote concentrators, front-end communication processors, intelligent terminals, and in message-switching systems.

The key advantages of minicomputers are flexibility of operation, adaptability to the changing needs of the business, low cost, and ease of use. Among their chief drawbacks are limited computational capability and memory size for handling complex jobs, the questionable reliability of some minicomputer firms, and the potentially high cost of the total system when peripheral and other devices are included.

Minicomputers are structured around a central processing unit (CPU) and input–output devices. The CPU consists of main memory, a set of registers, an arithmetic unit, and one or more data buses for transferring data to and from the CPU. In selecting a minicomputer, a prospective user needs to have basic knowledge of (1) internal factors related to the system's instruction execution time, the number of instructions needed for specific tasks, and direct and indirect addressing capability, and (2) external factors, which relate to the system's capabilities, the power and quality of available software, and the services and support of the manufacturer.

Steady demand for minicomputers has attracted a number of computer and noncomputer firms in search of profits. Low entry costs, common technical know-how, and minimal software, service, and financial requirements made it possible to produce minicomputers. The first entrant and leading manufacturer is Digital Equipment Corporation. Others include Honeywell, Varian Associates, Hewlett-Packard, and Data-General.

Small computers offer faster processing, larger memory capacity, and greater flexibility than minicomputers. They are justified on the basis of their ability to offer management better control over various operations. Larger firms install them as terminals to larger systems and in situations requiring decentralized processing capability. Examples of small computers are IBM System 3, models 6, 7, and 10, and Burroughs new 1700 series.

Medium-sized computers surpass small computers in providing greater operating speed, larger memory capacity, and high-speed input–output devices. They also offer high-level language compilers, training of personnel and support by the manufacturer, software operating systems, and utility routines. Examples of medium-sized systems are UNIVAC 9480, Burroughs 2500/3500, and IBM 370/145 systems.

Large-scale computers are the ultimate in sophistication, speed, and flexibility, offering memory capacity in the millions of bytes and operating speed in the nanosecond range. Typical large-scale computers are IBM's 370, Model 165 and the 168 virtual system, and Burroughs 700 series.

TERMS TO LEARN

Front-end processor	Modularity
Interrupt	MOSFET
Minicomputer	Operating system

QUESTIONS

1. Explain the role of the minicomputer in large computer systems and in ongoing operations. Explain briefly three application areas where minicomputers are ideally used.
2. What are the primary components of a minicomputer? Explain each component.
3. Explain briefly the various registers used in minicomputers.
4. What types of peripheral devices can be integrated into a minicomputer system?
5. Distinguish between single-level and multilevel priority interrupt.
6. Discuss the minicomputer market potential.
7. How practical do you feel is the possible development of a hierarchy of minicomputers to process data at various organizational levels?
8. What advantages do small computers have over minicomputers? Explain.
9. Is the IBM System/3 a small computer? Why?
10. What applications can be processed on the IBM System/3? Elaborate.
11. Summarize the primary components of the IBM System/3.
12. In what respect do medium-sized computers surpass small computers?
13. Give an example of a medium-sized computer. Explain its features.
14. Contrast and summarize the essential features of the Burroughs 700 and the IBM 370 series.

SUGGESTED READING

ALOSI, ALVIN. "Objectivity Must Rule Any Vendor Evaluation Method," *Computerworld,* June 27, 1973, p. 22.

BLAKE, NEIL. "Minis: What to Look For," *Data Systems,* June 1971, pp. 22–23.

CARTER, WOODWARD. "Getting to Know Your Mini," *Computer Decisions,* Nov. 1970, pp. 17–21.

FORD, M. A. "Buying the New Minicomputer," *Modern Data,* Sept. 1972, pp. 52–54.

"The Mighty Minicomputer: A Special Report," *Computerworld,* Aug. 30, 1972, supplement, pp. 1–15.

ZACK, R. A. "Minicomputer Application—Do They Imply Something for Everybody?", *Computers and Automation,* Dec. 1969, pp. 6–40.

COMPUTER APPLICATION DEVELOPMENT AND PROGRAMMING

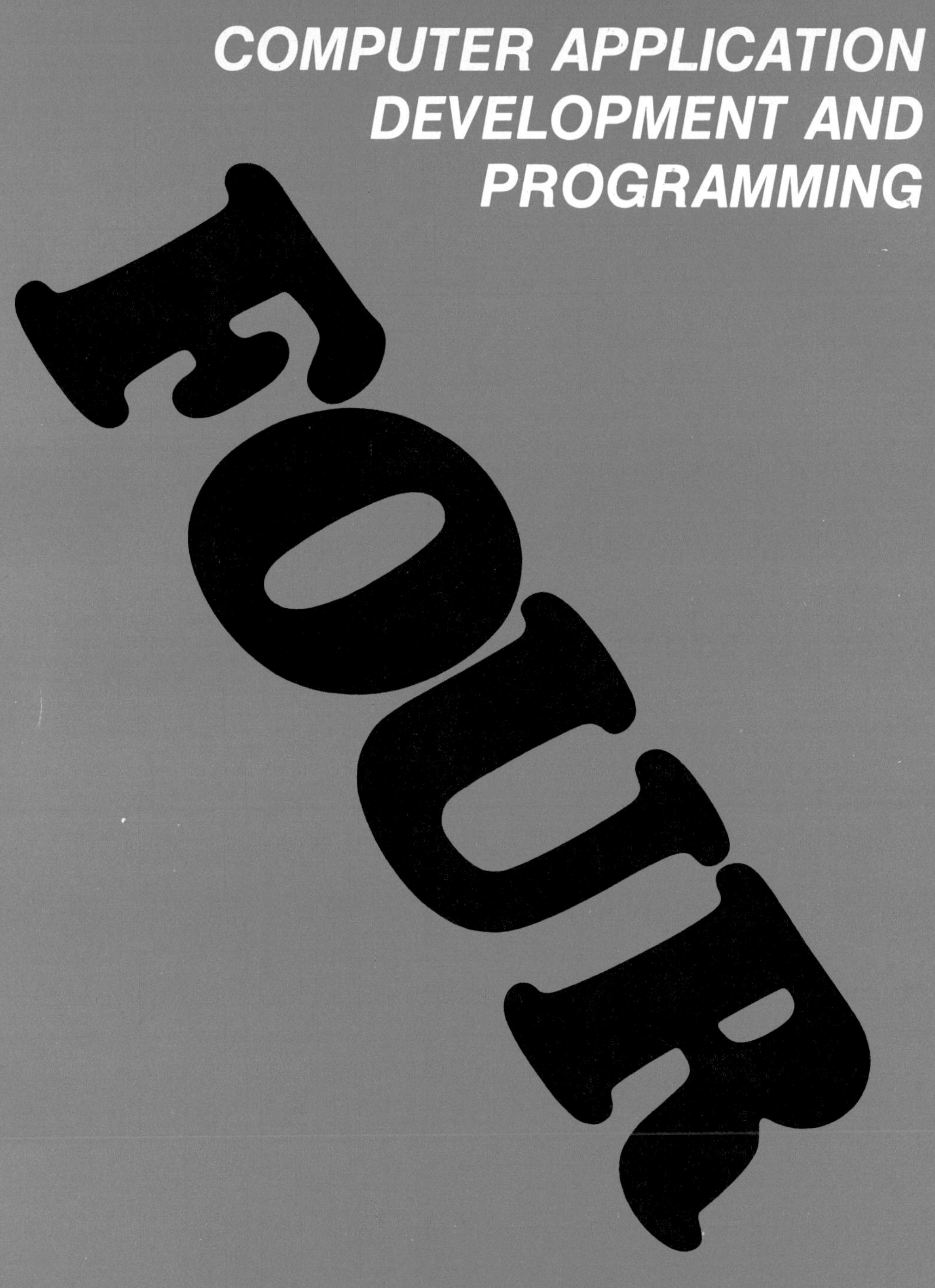

computer application development life cycle

14

THE MEANING OF SYSTEM

THE NEED FOR A DATA-PROCESSING SYSTEM

PRIMARY FUNCTIONS OF A DATA-PROCESSING SYSTEM

Creation of Data Files

File Maintenance

THE MEANING OF SYSTEM PROCEDURE

COMPUTER APPLICATION DEVELOPMENT LIFE CYCLE

Origination

identifying the objectives (output) of the system

data collection

determining and defining the system's requirements

designing the new system

Procedure and Program Development

Implementation

DOCUMENTATION

Project Initiation and Development

system documentation

program documentation

operations documentation

project summary and feedback

non-data-processing personal aids

OCCUPATIONAL SPECIFICATIONS OF THE SYSTEMS ANALYST

Occupational Definition

Education, Training, and Experience

Special Characteristics

aptitudes

interests

temperament

physical activities and environmental conditions

THE MEANING OF SYSTEM

The term *system* is defined as the result of dovetailing all operations, one with another, to make a firm a productive business organization. The terms *systems design* or *systems study,* as commonly used, rarely refer to this meaning, however, but are, instead, used to refer to any *disciplined framework of reference which requires proceeding in an orderly fashion to accomplish the work demanded by an activity and to ensure that the objectives of the activity will support the objectives of the firm in the best possible way.* Hence, *systems* is used in this chapter in a broad sense and describes the firm's activities in terms of a system made up of subsystems.

The basic activities, or functions, that characterize business firms are (1) production, (2) marketing, (3) accounting, (4) finance, and (5) management of men, money, materials, and equipment. The first two are sometimes referred to as *principal activities,* and the latter three as *supportive activities.* Branching off from these broad basic classifications are activities that reinforce the work of each specialized class or function. Hence, a shipping and receiving department reinforces the work of the marketing activity as well as the work of the production activity and the accounting activity; an employment office reinforces the work of the personnel activity as well as the work of all other activities; and so forth. If an activity is described as a system making up an integral part of the firm, then the reinforcing activities may be described as *subsystems.* Subsystems, thus, make up the system—and a system is simply the sum of its subsystems.

THE NEED FOR A DATA-PROCESSING SYSTEM

As we saw in Chapter 2, a subsystem is the organization of the required manual and machine-related procedures for generating the results of data in connection with a given project. Any application must be worked out in a systematic form if the data produced are to be meaningful. Although one may logically assume that the amount of data to be processed is dependent upon the size of the organization, companies of all sizes find themselves faced with the necessity of processing data at regular intervals. A large department store, for example, processes data involving thousands of customer accounts daily. A small shoe repair shop checks the quantity and the sale price of each item on hand at least once a week. Regardless of the frequency with which it is done and the volume involved, however, manipulation of data in an orderly and logical manner requires the development of a disciplined framework to guide men in reaching a desired objective.

PRIMARY FUNCTIONS OF A DATA-PROCESSING SYSTEM

A data-processing system serves two primary functions: first, it creates data files with respect to a specific organizational activity; and second, it allows for extraction, manipulation, and reporting of any part of a file of data requested—that is, file maintenance.

Creation of Data Files

In a manual system, hand-posted cards constitute a file. In an electromechanical system (such as the window-posting machine used by bank tellers), machine-posted standard-sized documents—for example, savings books—constitute a *data file*.[1] In a punched-card system, a deck of punched cards containing specific account information makes up a data file; in an electronic system, a set of magnetic tape reels storing specific data is referred to as a data file.

File Maintenance

The second function served by a system is purposive extraction, manipulation, and reporting of any part of the data in a file, when necessary. This is referred to as *file maintenance*. File maintenance is necessary because of the day-to-day changes that take place in the records of an organization.

[1] A *file* is defined as a collection of data records, each consisting of information regarding a specific activity (e.g., accounts receivable).

A department store, for instance, in handling its accounts receivable, has to update the accounts of all customers to allow for (1) payments against their outstanding balances, or (2) increases in the amounts owed because of additional purchases on credit. Likewise, the data in the file of a payroll system must be updated to account for changes in the status of current employees and to provide details on new employees. File maintenance requires updating routine data because the information is used to produce significant output data, such as payroll checks.

THE MEANING OF SYSTEM PROCEDURE

To produce the desired output, procedural routines must be set up. For the purpose of this discussion, a *procedure* is defined as an orderly way of handling a task. It comprises all steps required to accomplish a particular job. To illustrate systems procedures, assume that 2 weeks after the beginning of the school quarter (or semester) you have decided to drop a course from your schedule. Upon making this decision, you are likely to be instructed by your advisor or handed a written outline prepared by the registrar describing the steps you must take to drop the course. The *system* set up by the registrar might be made up of the following *procedure:*

1. Pick up a drop slip form from the registrar.
2. Fill out the details (such as course number, department number offering the course, course title, number of credit hours, etc.).
3. Have your advisor sign the card.
4. Withdraw the course card from the instructor teaching the course.
5. Submit the drop slip and the course card to the registrar.
6. Pay a fee (if required).

COMPUTER APPLICATION DEVELOPMENT LIFE CYCLE

An information processing system consists of many individual systems or applications. In designing and putting into operation computer applications, the systems analyst must define and keep in mind the objectives of the entire system, specify its inputs and boundaries, and determine how each proposed application fits in with the overall scheme. A computer application goes through a life cycle or a planned process involving the phases of *origination, procedure and program development,* and *implementation.* Each phase is equally important, in that deemphasizing one phase could adversely affect the validity and usefulness of the end result.

The first step leading to the preparation of a computer application is a decision made by a company official (referred to as a user) that new or improved information (e.g., more prompt reports, improved record-keeping procedure) is needed. Once the request for information is formally received, the systems analyst proceeds to (1) identify the objectives of the proposed system, (2) determine and define the system's requirements, and (3) design a new system that best meets the needs of the user. Stated somewhat differently, the role of the systems analyst is a combination of determining the information needed (data collection), showing how it is to be handled (data analysis), and creating the routine pattern to be used in pursuing and attaining the overall objective (system design).

System analysis and design is a team effort, requiring cooperative efforts between the systems analyst(s) and those who need the data. The analyst is the key figure in the systems concept. He is directly involved in and directs those in charge of developing the procedures for achieving desired results, designates which of the management techniques are to be used in informing management of the status of the information system, and explores new techniques for designing a more effective system. Through feasibility analysis, the systems analyst must justify the need for developing proposed applications, eliminate any unnecessary procedures, and switch people from routine to creative roles wherever this is possible.

IDENTIFYING THE OBJECTIVES (OUTPUT) OF THE SYSTEM. Systems or application objectives (e.g., more prompt reports or improved record-keeping procedure) are usually identified through examining the

1. Type of information expected from the system.
2. Reportorial format in which the information should be presented.
3. Time between the collection of raw data and the date on which the results of their processing are to be reported.

Identifying the objectives of a system is synonymous with defining a problem. In studying a given problem, the analyst must distinguish between "problems" and "symptoms" as he gathers data from various departments. For example, a "bottleneck" *problem* of the shipping and accounting departments in handling a large number of orders during the last few days of each month might turn out to be a *symptom* of the *real problem,* which is salesmen withholding orders because they feel that it is better to place them all at once instead of as received. An analyst must discover, therefore, what the actual problem is through detailed evaluation of each activity before he makes a decision as to why the present system is not satisfactorily accomplishing its objectives. In the example given, the system functioned imperfectly because the procedure followed by the salesmen interfered with the objective of smoothing out operations so that customers could receive efficient service on their orders. To accomplish all the system's objectives, the salesmen must be instructed to change their procedures in handling orders.

DATA COLLECTION. Data collection is done by means of *written documents* or *interviews*. In carrying out this phase, the systems analyst must determine the sources in the organization that make the data available, since the sources of data vary depending on the type of information demanded. The personnel department creates data on employees, such as their qualifications, academic and practical backgrounds, ages, aptitudes, and the like. The accounting department builds up data in connection with material costs, taxes, packing and shipping costs, and operating expenses. The sales department creates information regarding the volume of sales, behavior and attitude of clients, and so forth. The production department is the source of information on production planning and procedures, material handling, and quality control. The systems analyst is, of course, dependent on the departments involved for the information he needs in any specific case.

Data collection through interviews is a specialized field. Unlike when responding to written documents, people are generally sensitive and respond differently to different types of direct questioning. The analyst can obtain desired information from members of the organization only when an atmosphere of mutual trust prevails. He must avoid all appearances of being a "snooper" by making clear what he must know and why he must have the information. He must be detached and objective about what he is doing, and not become emotionally involved over any difficulties he may face in doing it.

In interviewing, the interviewer faces the possibility that interviewees will give answers which they feel would please him. For this reason, the interviewer should be able to differentiate between *opinion* and *fact*. If the employee who is being interviewed is resentful toward the current system, the interview, to him, may be an opportunity to air the reasons for his hostility. In this case, the interviewer should encourage the interviewee to suggest improvements rather than to voice only adverse criticism.

Structural information. To summarize the first phase of systems analysis, a systems analyst's first function is to understand thoroughly the problem to which he must find a solution. He also must understand the attitudes and philosophies that dominate management in realizing its objectives, as well as details connected with the current system. This would include gathering structural information describing the interaction between an organization's environment and its resources. Figure 14-1 emphasizes the three basic elements connected with structural information: (1) the company's outputs, in terms of its products and markets; (2) its inputs, in terms of materials and supplies; and (3) its resources (finances, personnel, facilities, and information). Structural information

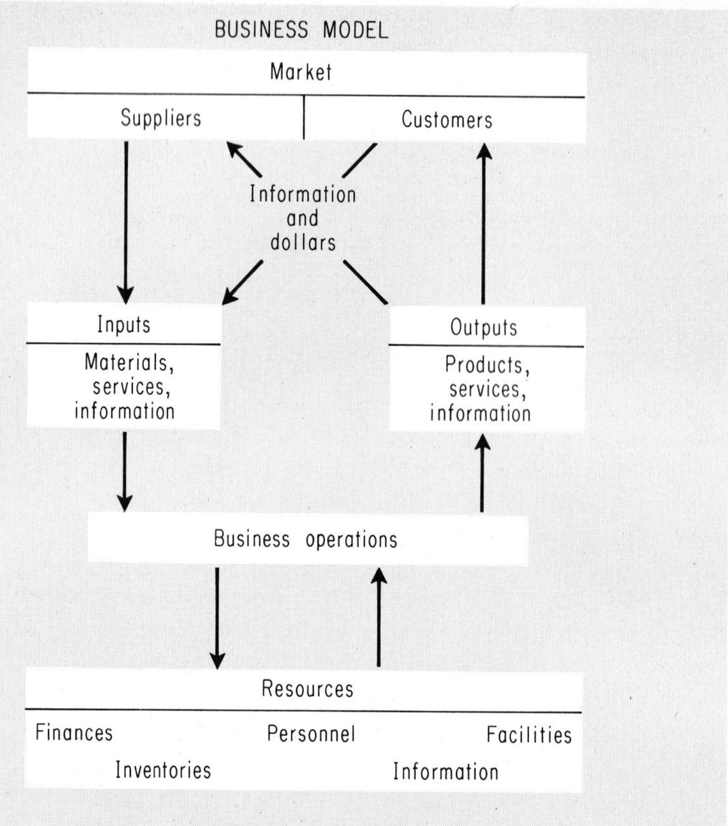

FIGURE 14-1. Basic elements of structural information (IBM F20-81-50, Basic System Study Guide)

helps the systems analyst acquire a broader understanding of the organization involved, which in turn helps him in performing the systems design work ahead.

In addition to the foregoing, it should be stressed that the systems analyst does not set, but rather defines, for the user a set of meaningful goals on which agreement can be reached. When the goals are defined to everyone's satisfaction, the analyst is free to proceed in developing the application.

DETERMINING AND DEFINING THE SYSTEM'S REQUIREMENTS. Once the objectives (output) of the system have been determined, the next step is to determine what the system is required to do, via a study geared to finding out *how* (procedure) and *what* current work is being done and *who* is doing it. The study examines the input data at hand, the data files and the type of information necessary for their up-to-date maintenance, the output data being produced by the present system, and the physical and informational resources the system must use.

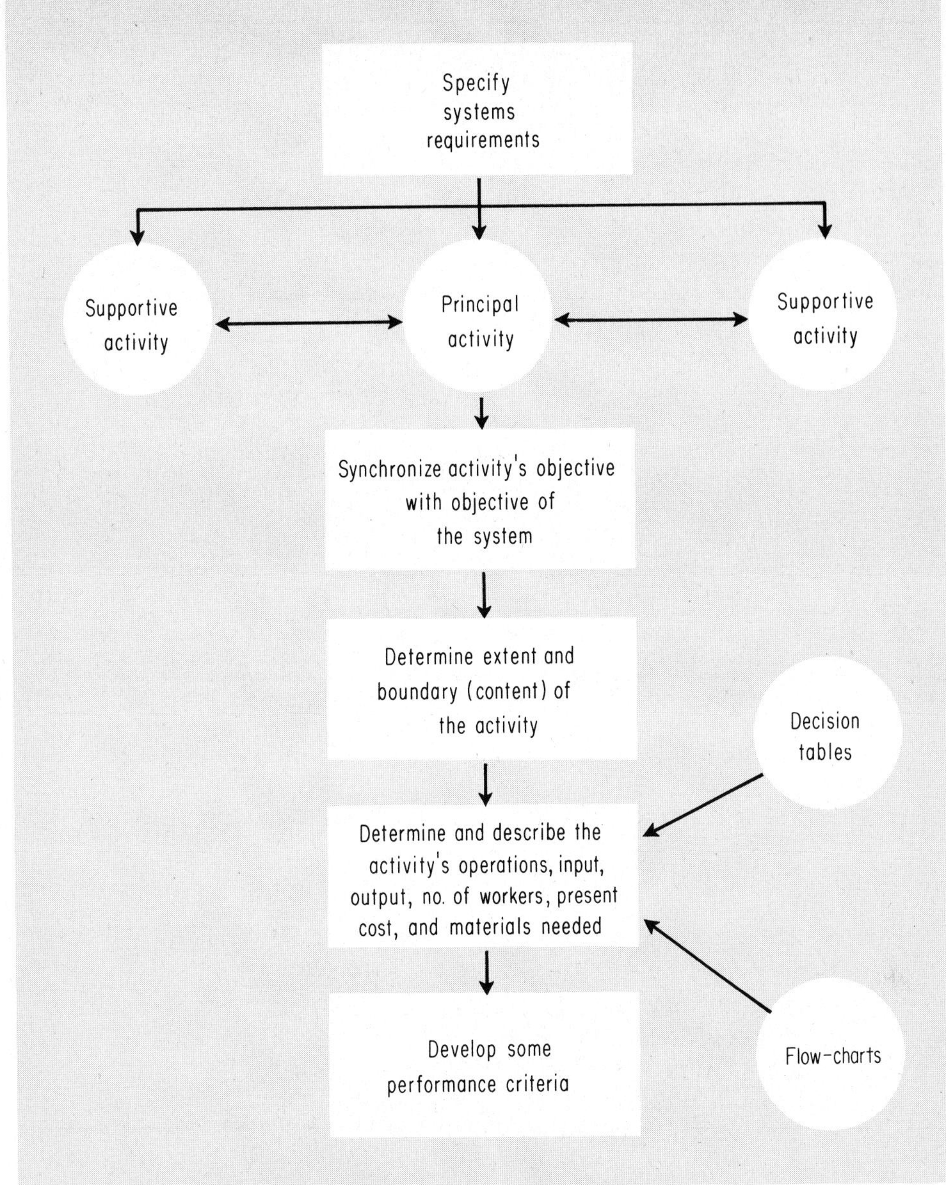

FIGURE 14-2. Elements involved in determining the system's requirements

This phase results in a plan (1) specifying the primary characteristics of the proposed new system, (2) specifying all related supportive or reinforcing activities, and (3) indicating the inputs, outputs, and human, financial, and physical resources of the principal activities needed to better the present system or replace it with a new one (Fig. 14-2). It is highly recommended, then, that keen evaluation and, if necessary, modification of the present *goals* be made before modifications of the procedures making up the activities, or the development of new ones, are executed. In other words, do not "change for the sake of change," but change only for the sake of meeting the overall objectives of the firm.

Before concluding the second step, we should remember that *no system design is considered adequate without prior specification of some performance criteria which the new system is expected to achieve, followed by specification of ways of measuring these criteria.* Once the performance criteria are specified, the systems designer should be in a position to design a system that best satisfies the demands and operates within the constraints of the facilities, personnel, and costs which can be justified by the usefulness of the expected results.

DESIGNING THE NEW SYSTEM. System design is creative in approach and orientation. Like a tailor-made suit, each system is designed to meet the requirements of the user and the problem involved. Although there is no standard approach to systems design, certain basic steps are commonly taken in its development.

1. The systems analyst selects the key, or the most crucial, activities (e.g., input steps), and analyzes each activity separately, listing it in the order of its importance or of the role it plays in the performance of the application under study. He examines the characteristics and requirements of input data. How should they be presented to the system? How important is the accuracy phase of input data? What time constraints are to be considered? Likewise, output data have their own characteristics. In terms of the format, which printout is called for, how many copies are required, and how much is allowed to produce the output? Other data (primary or secondary) may be involved. What is the volume of the data? At what rate do data grow? In what manner should data be filed (direct access versus sequential)? Finally, the relationship between input and output must be examined in terms of combining minor operations or splitting major ones for maximizing efficiency.
2. Alternative machine methods that may be used to meet the objectives of the system are established, helped by the results of the first step. The term *method* refers to how a given data-processing operation is performed. Any manual, electromechanical, or computer technique can be employed as a method of performing an operation. With the system's objectives in mind, the systems analyst proceeds to array the methods in terms of their effectiveness and performance, and then applies the available hardware *that best achieves the system's objectives* while meeting any constraints set by management.
3. For each application the analyst must develop all necessary routine and special operational procedures, including machine runs, that will govern the manner in which certain data files must be organized. Once these are selected, all necessary procedures with respect to designing the flow of required manual and machine

operations must be developed. These procedures include the type, content, and format of input and output data.

4. A detailed report on the proposed system is prepared for management, linking its advantages, limitations, characteristics, and capabilities, the type and degree of effectiveness the system generates, the kind of changes in organizational and other areas it is likely to cause, the factors to be considered in its implementation (e.g., programming, personnel, installation, and conversion problems), and a comparative cost analysis of the new and the present system. After the report is presented, management must take action to authorize the implementation of the new system.

Tools used in systems design. Among the tools used in systems design are (1) layout charts showing the form and location of data files, data records, data reports, and the like, and (2) system flowcharts,[2] which present in a logical sequence the procedures or flow of activities that make up the application under consideration and the manual, noncomputer, and computer operations affecting the processing of the application.

In addition to layout of data items and system flowcharts, the system analyst prepares other specifications for the computer application and its program runs. They include

1. Preparation of manual routines required for the system.
2. Narrative description of the function of each application.
3. A plan for file conversion.
4. A plan for system testing and implementation program.
5. An operational plan for developing the necessary manpower within the time and cost constraints.

The foregoing phase of system analysis and design culminates in a set of specifications and other key information for the computer application program(s), and makes available the plans for testing and operationalizing the new system.

Procedure and Program Development

The second phase in computer application development pertains to writing and debugging programs and procedures for the operation of the system. Writing a program usually begins with flowcharting the steps to be processed. Although decision tables are occasionally used as an alternative, program flowcharting is more commonly used and presents more readily the overall flow of program steps.

Preparation of procedures generally includes detailed, easy-to-follow instructions and manuals required for the system. Once the procedures

[2] System flowcharts and flowcharting techniques are explained in detail in Chapter 15.

and program(s) are written and tested, the system is ready for the final phase—implementation.

Implementation

The implementation phase includes *final testing, conversion* into the new system, *operation* of the new system, and program *maintenance.* Final testing and conversion require that all programs and components of the system run together smoothly. Although programs have been debugged (using test data), it is not uncommon to expect other errors when the system is run for the first time. Instructions may not have been followed or exceptions not considered. Thus, the system encounters considerable strain during its initial phases of operation until all problems have been corrected and the system is fully tested.

When the system finally becomes operational, the old system is discarded. From this point on, any future changes become a part of program maintenance, which is controlled by documenting all approved changes on a special change request form.

DOCUMENTATION

Documentation is a method of communicating and refers to a written record of a phase of a particular project. It describes a system at various steps and establishes design and performance criteria to be met at future stages of the project. Thus better control of the project becomes possible.

Documentation serves the following purposes of special significance:

1. Minimizes distortion or ambiguity regarding the elements involved in a given project.
2. Guards against loss of key information in the event that the staff member in charge of the project decides to leave the organization.
3. Evaluates progress made on a project and acts as a source of reference for system modification.
4. Communicates between data-processing specialists and users. Often, the user needs instruction on the proper application of his system. By providing this instruction, the specialists can see to it that good electronic data processing–user relations are maintained.

In discussing documentation techniques, there are no uniform standards that are applicable to all computer systems. Although general documentation systems are adopted, each installation ultimately develops its own documentation routines, within given constraints. Some of these constraints include (1) management's attitude toward documentation, in general; (2) the number, complexity, and level of documentation; (3) the level of sophistication of the hardware and software systems; and (4) the structural makeup of the organization. Let us elaborate briefly on each of these factors.

When we speak of management, we mean to emphasize the persons in charge and in a position to command others to perform certain functions or to carry out specific instructions. Those in a managerial capacity must be sold on the need for good documentation before they will be willing to make a commitment to support and authorize the expenditure of adequate funds for this purpose.

The level of rigidity and complexity of documentation often depends on the type of project involved, the amount of time it takes to develop it, the number of system analysts assigned to it, and the number of users affected. For maintaining adequate control, *lengthy, complex projects requiring more system analysts demand more documentation than do short straightforward projects.* Furthermore, *the greater the number of users having access to the system, the greater the need for complete documentation.*

Rigidity of documentation also has much to do with the frequency of use of a system. A one-time system, for example, that is intended for temporary or short-term use would require less rigid documentation than a system intended for permanent use, thus having a long life-span.

In terms of volume of documentation, it is generally the case that larger computer installations (especially those with extensive transmission and peripheral links) demand more documentation than do smaller computer installations. Although the size of the hardware system is not, in itself, a mandatory criterion for documentation, it tends to generate over time the need for more and more documentation (in terms of quantity rather than types). Likewise, the software system influences, to some extent, the type of documentation required. Here we find an inverse relationship between the level of software languages and the form of documentation required. High-level languages require technical documentation that is less rigorous than that required by low-level languages.

Finally, the structural makeup of the organization is a contributing factor in determining whether documentation is necessary. In a classical sense, a large organization with a rigid chain of command would normally require detailed and complete documentation of its operations, which, in turn, imposes the same requirements on its data-processing documentation. The converse is the case in smaller, less rigidly structured organizations.

The primary forms of documentation are explained next; they include project initiation, systems, program, and operations documentation (Fig. 14-3).

Project Initiation and Development

The initial phase of a project encompasses the preparation of a formal, written statement of the nature, objectives, and analysis of the work requested by the user. The primary related documents in this phase are

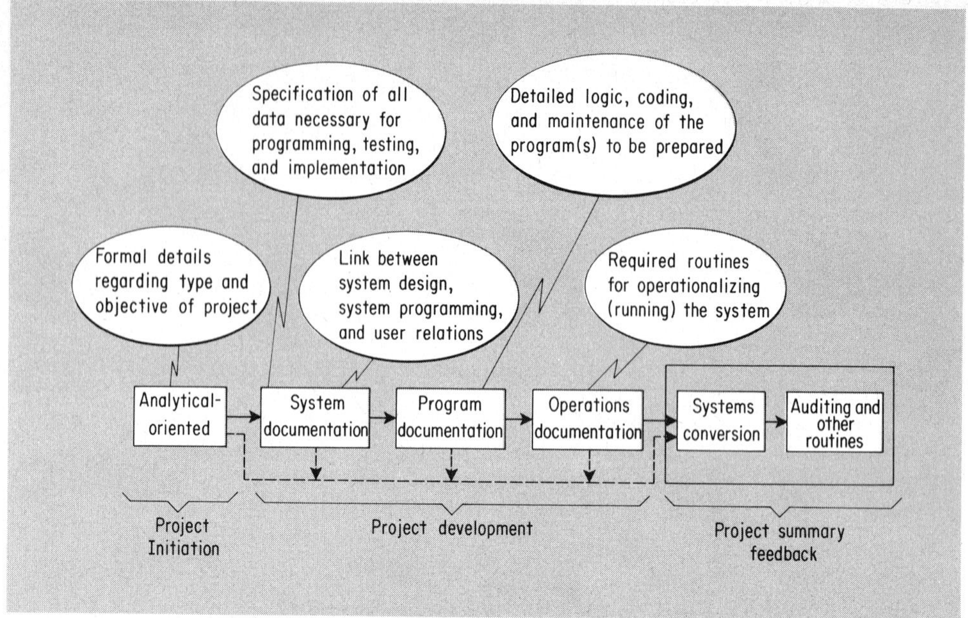

FIGURE 14-3. Primary forms of data-processing documentation

(1) the user request, (2) a system study of the problem, (3) a detailed description of the proposed project, and (4) a detailed statement of the system's objectives (Fig. 14-4).

The *user's request* defines the problem in outline form and briefly describes its nature. Generally, it provides such information as the name and official title of the user, a clear statement of what the project is expected to produce and whom it will accommodate, the source of input data, the desired output information, and the anticipated deadline. Once received, a system analyst drafts a proposal describing the user's problem, the variables to be considered, and a tentative approach to solution. The user's request and the system proposal establish a rapport between the user and the data-processing staff.

The document representing a detailed description of the proposed project is analytic in orientation and can be used either as a supplement to or a substitute for a system study. It clearly states functions, areas of responsibility, project scheduling, and determination of resource requirements. When tagged to the user's report, it often portrays adequate details of the project initiation phase.

Finally, the detailed description of the system's objectives specifies the anticipated results of the project. The more poorly drafted the user's request, the greater the need for this document.

SYSTEM DOCUMENTATION. System documentation generates key information for programming, testing, and project implementation in the form of a report, called *system specification*. It indicates the fulfillment of the system analysis and design functions and serves as a communication

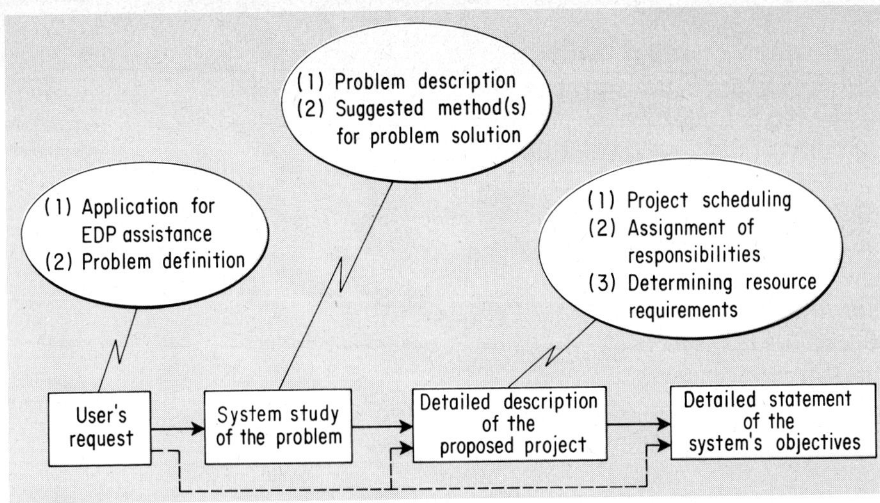

FIGURE 14-4. *Project initiation*

link between the user, the programmer, and the system designer for later programming and operations work.

Although the complexity and size of the system specification is a function of the demands of the project under consideration, it is generally an involved and lengthy form of documentation, requiring much care and detailed planning. Thus, it contains several "subdocumentations" (Fig. 14-5).

FIGURE 14-5. *Schematic system-documentation diagram*

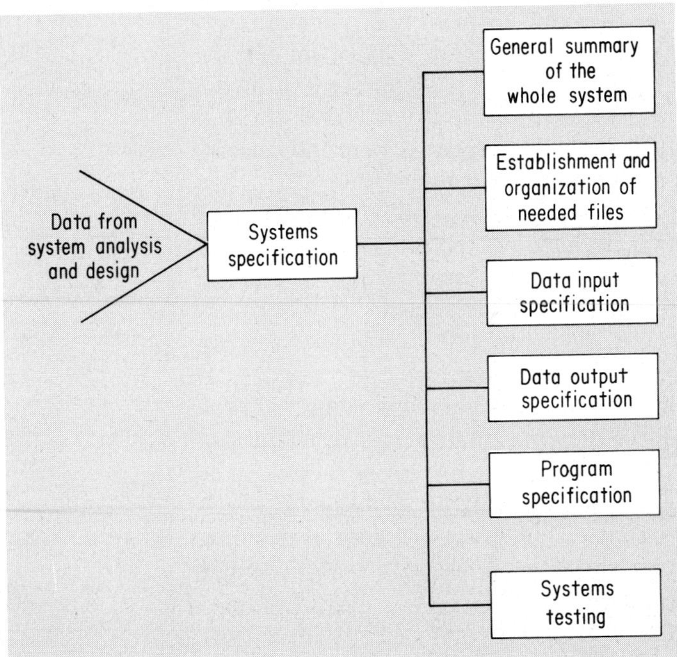

General summary. A general summary of the system orients the user and the line executive to the nature, objectives, and details of the project. It also explains the relationships between the input and output data and their sources, the files containing related data records, and the required steps later taken for processing purposes. To illustrate a part or parts of these relationships, a *system flowchart* is often prepared to show the logic pattern of the overall system and to pinpoint each operational step to be taken.

Establishment and organization of needed files. All *files* related to data sources, storage media, and so on, are *identified* and *coded.* Descriptions of the format and content (including name, type, length, and sequence) of each file record are also made. By the establishment and organization of such files, programmers and systems staff members can at any time refer to the files for future modification or for updating the system. The user also finds it a useful source of information whenever a review of the system becomes necessary.

Data-input specification. A key aspect of systems specification is the preparation and description of all data inputs related to the proposed system. A *data-input specification* describes in proper order the required data inputs in a computer-acceptable form. Specifically, it begins with the identification of the system and the system designer in charge of its preparation; summarizes the features and acceptable values of the input data and the media on which they are recorded; and indicates the files involved in or affected by the input data, the volume and frequency of entry of input data, and its originating source. Special forms are used to describe these details.

Data-output specification. Similar to the data-input specification in format, the *data-output specification* describes in detail the proposed system's output. It identifies the expected output in a predetermined sequence and the person in charge of its preparation; summarizes the features, purpose, and content of the data output; specifies the media on which they will be recorded; and defines the volume, format, and number of copies needed and their destination. Special preprinted forms are used to describe the details entailed in this phase.

Program specifications. One function of the system designer is to help the programmer develop program logic for the proposed system. To formalize this phase, he prepares a *program-specifications* document, which lists the information requirements of the system, with emphasis on the input and output specifications, the existing files, and the processing details. The program-specifications document includes (1) input and output information; (2) the rules, logic, and regulations to be followed in the process; (3) specific ways of handling, modifying, or evaluating such key information as inputs in the program; (4) clarification of the primary functions performed; (5) establishment of a linkage between the proposed program and other available programs for ascertaining maximum results; (6) decisions on particular routines to be followed in handling exceptions or in correcting errors; and (7) whatever charts, formulas, or tables are required for carrying out the processing details.

System testing. A final stage in system documentation results in the preparation of a system-testing document, which determines the required steps that would put the system into operation. It specifies the purpose and lays out the procedure to be followed in testing the system, and defines the inputs involved and the expected outputs. The document also includes details concerning the persons responsible for carrying out the system's tests and those who would synchronize the required elements prior to testing. Furthermore, a quality-control approach is emphasized throughout. Procedures related to the handling of errors, exceptions, and space constraints are carefully shown.

Once the foregoing stages have been laid out, the system-testing document indicates the sequence in which the proposed system can be completely tested. Each operation is numbered and sequenced. Input information and files are referenced by names or numbers.

PROGRAM DOCUMENTATION. Unlike project initiation or systems documentation, the clearly defined functions of the programming phase explain the relatively straightforward routine in the preparation of program documentation. Designing, coding, and testing a program generally follow the availability of system specification. These substeps lead to the preparation of a program document, which makes up a program manual, and to final implementation.

Like other documentation components, program documentation entails certain required functions, such as analysis of program logic, coding, checking out the data involved, program assembly and compilation, final documentation, and the means of putting the program into operation. Although open for modification and overlapping, these tasks require documentation so that delay resulting from reassignment of programming personnel will be minimum, owing to direct and immediate access to the details by management. Thus both technical and nontechnical personnel are likely to find use for the availability of program documentation.

Program manual. For several years, program documentation has been presented in a manual that basically

1. Describes the functions and procedures of a given program.
2. Indicates the input and output data and files involved.
3. Presents the flow diagrams that show the sequential steps taken by the program.
4. Specifies coding and testing details, as well as operating and other instructions.

A program manual is typically identified with a particular system (by name and/or by a special number) and indicates the serial number of the program, the programmer who developed it, and his title. It begins

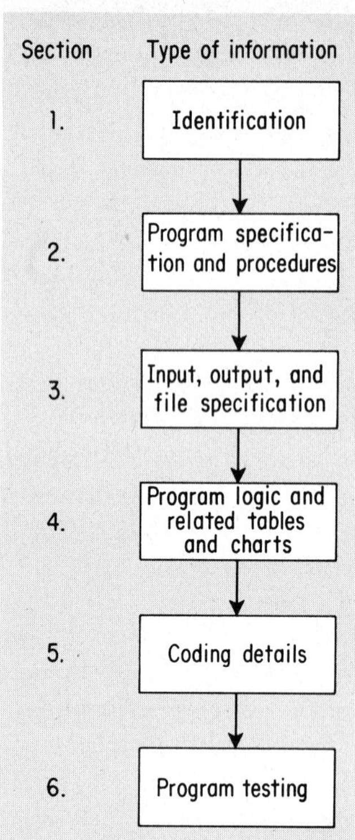

FIGURE 14-6. Basic components of a program manual

with the program specifications (described earlier) and a narrative prepared by the programmer regarding the programming logic followed, formulas or other special-purpose routines, and any other data related to the overall program (Fig. 14-6).

In addition, a program manual includes a copy of the input, output, and file specifications (described earlier) and illustrative details. This section is followed by a subsection consisting of the tables and charts (optional) related to the program logic used in the project. Depending on their nature and complexity, some description is commonly made of items such as complex tables and special search techniques.

The final section of the program manual lays out the coding details of the program, followed by a carefully worked out plan for program testing. In preparing the program for testing, the programmer normally checks for clerical and logical errors. Once these are checked out, artificial test data are used to test the various aspects of the program and the overall logic. It is assumed that the artificial data are valid and reliable. Testing can be extended to handle more complex artificial data until a point is reached when the obtained results are comparable to what is expected in a "live-data" program run. The methods followed and a list of the artificial data used in testing the program must be documented and incorporated in the program manual for reference.

Operations Documentation. Once the computer program becomes available for the actual production run, instructions to the operator on how to run a program test and a properly sequenced list of processing steps specifying the necessary operating requirements are prepared. Thus, in operations documentation emphasis is on the need for developing (1) instructions for program testing, and (2) a processing routine for operating the system.

Although the instructions for program testing are normally prepared by the programmer in charge of the system, instructions for operating the system are prepared jointly by the programmer running the system and the systems staff. In terms of content, however, it is not uncommon for the user, for example, to provide instructions related to ways of preparing and collecting the source data and the handling of input and output, while the data-processing staff provides instructions and/or details related to job assembly (data and program availability requirements) and the overall work flow of the proposed system. In any case, it is expected that the user will provide the required source data on schedule and in a usable form, while the data-processing staff assumes the responsibility of handling all matters regarding processing details.

Development of instructions for operating the system is commonly made in a descriptive manner. However, a more formal, structural approach is often used for greater effect. Many installations use various special-purpose, preprinted forms. Among these are (1) forms for data preparation (in the case of keypunching, details regarding format, codes, destination, etc.), (2) computer operating instructions (supported by the program manual), and (3) a process flowchart related to each operating instruction form.

Project Summary and Feedback. The purpose of this final phase is to analyze and decide on the appropriateness of current documentation for systems conversion. Actual results from a major test run are compared with a predetermined result. Discrepancies are detected, and modification of the documentation involved is made in order to produce a workable, accurate, and completely debugged system.

The foregoing remarks point out the need for some form of control of the proposed system at various stages. Upon the termination of each stage in the project, key checkpoints are established at which the rate of progress of the system is monitored and the quality of the documentation is evaluated. Thus, during the project-initiation phase, a check is made (against prescribed standards) regarding (1) the clarity of the user's definition of the project and its objectives, (2) the assignment and availability of the needed staff, and (3) the amount of time allotted to the project. This last step is necessary for arriving at an estimation of the cost of the project.

During the project-development phase, a check is made on the workability, accuracy, and completeness of the systems study and analysis, the pertinent documentation, the systems summary, coding details, logic flow, and program testing.

NON-DATA-PROCESSING PERSONNEL AIDS. In our discussion of the project-initiation phase it was mentioned that a proposed system is initiated when the user formally requests the assistance of the data-processing department. It was assumed throughout this discussion that the user's request was made with management's approval and support. In developing and implementing a system it is necessary not only to carry out the details that lead to an operational program, but also to inform and instruct both the user and management in a nontechnical manner on the capabilities and limitations of the system. Thus, formal documents are prepared for both parties for that purpose.

User-oriented documentation (procedure manual) serves the purpose of allowing the user to understand and participate in running the system. Once the system is implemented, he ultimately takes charge of its routine operation. The user's understanding of the system is vital, in that it makes him more cognizant of its components and how well it satisfies his needs. A procedure manual helps him to better prepare the source data and interpret the output information.

Management-oriented documentation (economic analysis) is designed to help management evaluate the impact of the system on the project involved and justify the investment committed to its development. One document management receives is a nontechnical summary of the current application or system in each division or area of responsibility. Other documents include reference manuals, which vary depending on the type and the function they perform. Written in simple language, each manual begins with a section indicating its title, purpose, function, and how it should be used and updated.

Some of the reference manuals available to users and management are (1) coding manuals illustrating the contents and sequence of the codes used in the project-implementation phase, and (2) instructional manuals aimed at educating the system user. Such manuals explain the system and provide related background information for user participation. Each type of manual can be supplemented by a systems-conversion guide, which presents detailed conversion steps from manual to computer system.

OCCUPATIONAL SPECIFICATIONS OF THE SYSTEMS ANALYST

Occupational Definition

The systems analyst analyzes a business problem, such as the development of an integrated production, inventory control, and cost analysis system, to refine its formulation and convert it to a programmable form for application to an electronic data-processing system. He confers with the project director, business data-processing department heads, and department heads of the units involved to ascertain specific output requirements, such as types of breakouts, degree of data summarization, and format for management reports. He confers with personnel of operating units to devise plans for obtaining and standardizing input data. He studies the current system or develops new systems and procedures to devise a work-flow sequence. He analyzes alternative means of deriving input data to select the most feasible and economical method. He develops process flowcharts or diagrams in outlined and then detailed form for programming, indicating external verification points, such as audit trial printouts. He may work as a member of a team, applying his specialized knowledge to one phase of project development. He may coordinate the activities of the team members and direct the preparation of programs.

Education, Training, and Experience

A college degree with emphasis on business administration and accounting is usually required for entrants without prior experience in data processing. Some employers, while requiring a college degree, do not require a specific major or course content. A successful college record is regarded as proof of the ability to reason logically, which is considered more important for successful performance than knowledge of techniques acquired in any specific area. Many employers waive the formal educational requirements for those employed in their establishments who have had several years' manual and machine systems experience prior to computer conversion. Business programmers without a college degree can, through experience, acquire a background in business systems and procedures and may thereby advance into systems analysis. Currently, the trend is to require knowledge of advanced mathematics because of the rapidly increasing sophistication of business systems. Continuing education, through specialized courses, self-study, and participation in activities of professional associations, is the rule rather than the exception in this occupation, as in all high-level occupations related to the computer. A section dealing with the professional orientation of the systems analyst is presented in Chapter 22.

Special Characteristics

APTITUDES. The systems analyst is expected to have the following aptitudes:

1. Verbal ability to discuss problems and progress, prepare reports, and make annotations for graphic representations of work.
2. Numeric ability to select from alternatives to develop the optimal system, procedures, and methods. Mathematical investigation of

such factors as variation in volume of input data and the frequency of appearance of exceptions to normal work flow in processing is often necessary. The level of mathematics varies from business arithmetic and algebra to differential equations.

3. Spatial ability to visualize, prepare, and review two-dimensional graphic representations of work flow.
4. Form perception to identify nonverbal symbols on records such as block diagrams and flowcharts.
5. Clerical perception to avoid perceptual errors and to recognize pertinent detail in recording and identifying letters and numbers that often occur in abbreviated or acronymic combinations.

INTERESTS. The systems analyst who would devise new or modify standardized computer-oriented systems to meet the specific needs of an organization should have a preference for activities that are technical, analytical, abstract, and creative in nature.

TEMPERAMENT. The analyst should have the ability to confer with personnel from other departments, develop flowcharts, devise work-flow sequences, and prepare reports. He is required to deal with people in conference and interview situations, to make judgmental decisions, and to select from alternatives when devising the optimal system. To design a system within machine capability, he also is required to make decisions on the basis of factual data.

PHYSICAL ACTIVITIES AND ENVIRONMENTAL CONDITIONS. The work is sedentary, with occasional standing and walking. There is occasional handling of source documents, books, charts, and other records that seldom exceed 10 pounds. Talking and hearing are involved in discussing and conferring with management and technical personnel to devise suitable business systems. The analyst should have nearly perfect visual acuity to prepare and review work-flow charts and diagrams.

SUMMARY

The development of computer applications takes into consideration the idea of and the need for a system—an orderly structuring of interdependent activities designed to accomplish a predetermined objective. Application development life cycle involves the phases of origination, procedure and program development, and implementation. Data origination is represented by a user's request for developing or improving a particular system. Once received, a systems analyst proceeds to identify the proposed system's objectives, to determine and define the system's requirements, and to design a new system that best meets the user's needs.

Program and procedure development pertains to writing and debugging programs and procedures for the operation of the system. System implementation covers final testing, conversion into and operation of the new system, and program maintenance.

Documentation is important in application development. It is the means of communicating in writing between the user and the system staff and allows better control of the project. The primary forms of documentation are user's request and system, program, and operations documentation. Operations documentation includes the program run manual and user-oriented and management-oriented documentation. Most of these details are prepared by the systems analyst—a key electronic data-processing staff member with specialized education, training, and experience.

TERMS TO LEARN

Documentation
Feasibility study
File
Operations documentation
Program documentation
Program specifications
System
System analysis
System specifications
User's request

QUESTIONS

1. How is a subsystem related to a system? Give an example.
2. Explain why a data-processing system is needed.
3. What are the primary functions of a data-processing system? Give an example of each function.
4. Distinguish between systems analysis and systems procedure.
5. Explain the life cycle of computer application development.
6. How does a systems analyst collect data? Which source or method is superior?
7. What steps are involved in determining the system's requirements? Explain each step briefly.
8. What tools does a systems analyst use in outlining the flow of data or operation?
9. List and describe the key steps in systems design.
10. What activities are included in the implementation stage?

11. Why is documentation necessary?
12. For what reason do we find lack of uniform documentation standards? Explain.
13. Explain the primary components of data-processing documentation.
14. What is system documentation? What are its primary elements?
15. Distinguish between program and systems specifications.
16. What is the difference between systems and program documentation?
17. What purpose does a program manual serve? What information does it contain?
18. Distinguish between program and operations documentation.
19. Explain briefly the uses of non-data-processing personnel aids.

SUGGESTED READING

ACKOFF, R. L. "Towards a System of Systems Concepts," *Management Science*, Nov. 1971, pp. 661–671.

DANIELS, ALAN, and DONALD YEATES. *Systems Analysis*. Chicago: Science Research Associates, Inc., 1971.

GLANS, T. B., et al. *Management Systems*. New York: Holt, Rinehart and Winston, Inc., 1968.

RUBIN, M. *Introduction to the System Life Cycle*. Princeton, N.J.: Auerbach Publishers, Inc., 1970.

———. *System Life Cycle Standards*. Princeton, N.J.: Auerbach Publishers, Inc., 1970.

tools for program planning

15

LAYOUT CHARTS

GRID CHARTS

FLOWCHARTS

Types

Symbol Standardization

PROGRAM FLOWCHARTS

Use of Templates

Basic Symbols

Specialized Input–Output Symbols

Specialized Process Symbols

Other Symbols

SUBROUTINES

CROSS REFERENCING A PROGRAM FLOWCHART

USE OF NOTATIONS

GENERAL PROGRAM FLOWCHARTING HINTS

DECISION TABLES

Elements of a Decision Table

Application of Decision Table to a Problem

Types of Decision Tables

limited-entry tables
extended-entry tables
mixed-entry tables

The ELSE Rule

Logic Flow and Construction of Decision Tables

Program planning represents a key step in program preparation. Very few programs are properly coded without some preparatory routines. Systems analysts and computer programmers apply special-purpose tools in analyzing and planning a system project or a computer program. The tools are layout charts, grid charts, flowcharts, and decision tables. They help the systems analysts and the programmer organize the details affecting the project to be processed. The charts used represent a written record and documentation for future reference.

LAYOUT CHARTS

Layout charts are preprinted forms depicting input–output data records and/or the location of key information in storage. Among these are card layout, tape and disk layout, and printer layout. A card layout is designed to help the user plan the location of various data (alphabetic and numeric) within the constraints of the card. Using this, the processing staff can be more certain that the information is processed properly and fully (Fig. 15-1).

Tape and disk layouts indicate the manner in which data are written on a magnetic tape or a magnetic disk. Unlike the card layout, which is limited to 80 columns, tape and disk layouts are bound only by the length of the tape and dimensions of the disk, which accommodate the contents of hundreds of punched cards (Fig. 15-2).

The printer layout is used to design the exact location of processed data for a printed output. The layout also provides an area for designat-

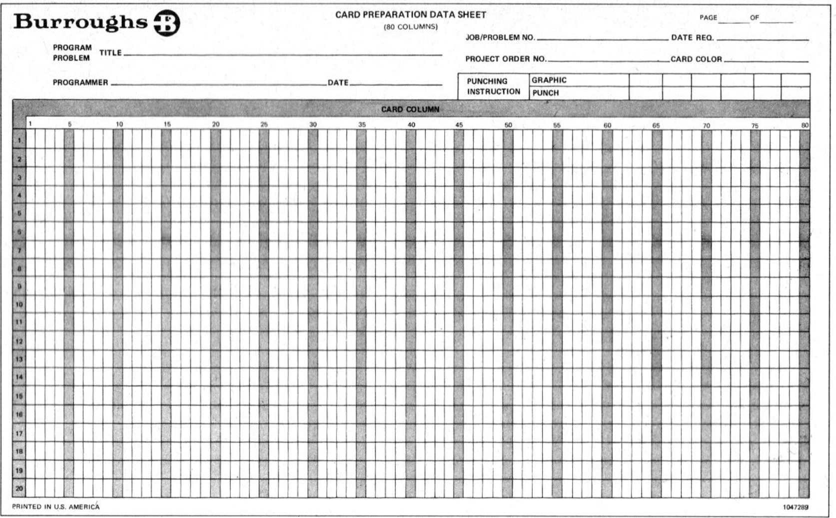

Burroughs

CARD PREPARATION DATA SHEET
(80 COLUMNS)

PAGE ____ OF ____

PROGRAM PROBLEM TITLE ____

JOB/PROBLEM NO. ____ DATE REQ. ____

PROJECT ORDER NO. ____ CARD COLOR ____

PROGRAMMER ____ DATE ____

PUNCHING INSTRUCTION | GRAPHIC | PUNCH

CARD COLUMN

1 5 10 15 20 25 30 35 40 45 50 55 60 65 70 75 80

1 2 3 4 5 6 7 8 9 10 11 12 13 14 15 16 17 18 19 20

PRINTED IN U.S. AMERICA

1047289

FIGURE 15-1. *Card layout*

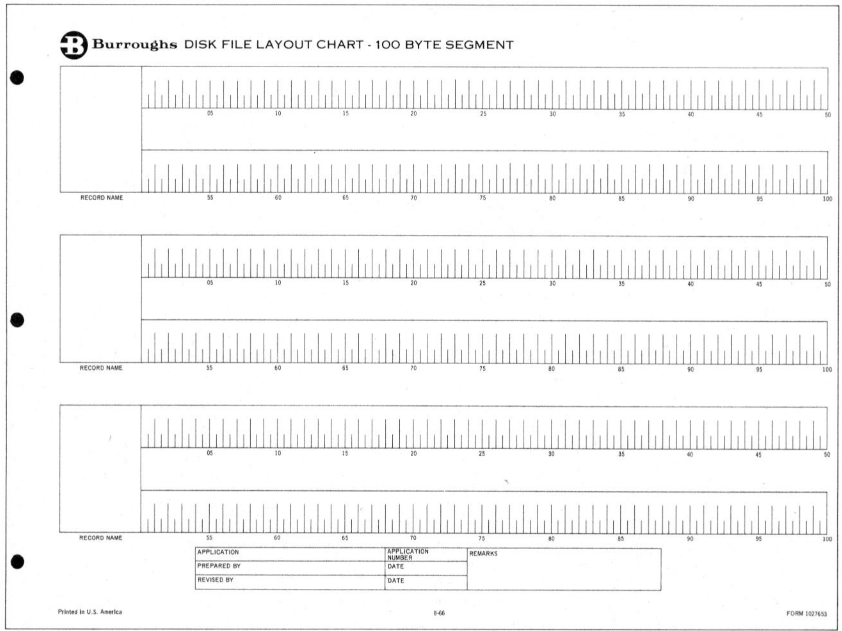

Burroughs DISK FILE LAYOUT CHART - 100 BYTE SEGMENT

05 10 15 20 25 30 35 40 45 50

RECORD NAME 55 60 65 70 75 80 85 90 95 100

05 10 15 20 25 30 35 40 45 50

RECORD NAME 55 60 65 70 75 80 85 90 95 100

05 10 15 20 25 30 35 40 45 50

RECORD NAME 55 60 65 70 75 80 85 90 95 100

APPLICATION	APPLICATION NUMBER	REMARKS
PREPARED BY	DATE	
REVISED BY	DATE	

Printed in U.S. America 8-66 FORM 1027653

FIGURE 15-2. *Tape layout*

ing the location of holes to be punched later in a carriage control tape, which controls the vertical spacing of the printer (Fig. 15-3).

GRID CHARTS

A grid chart is another tool for summarizing the relationship between two key variables. It is useful in situations where duplicate information

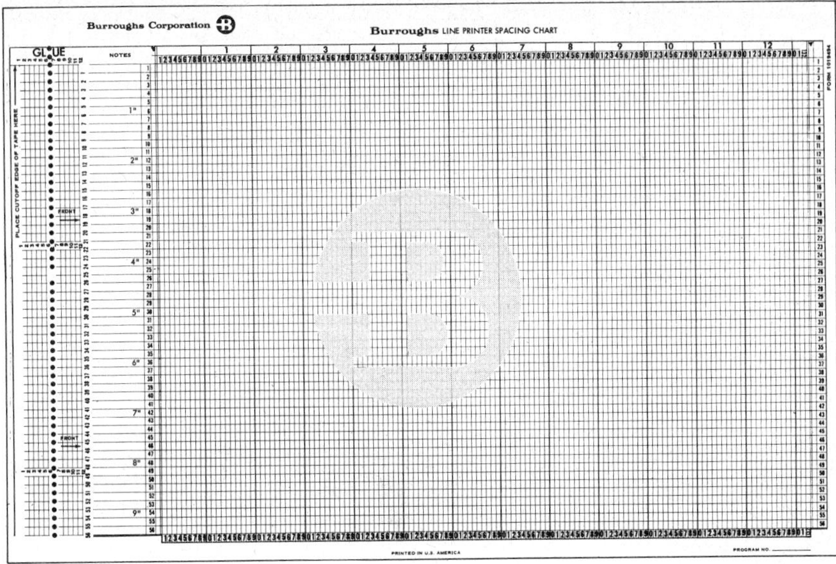

FIGURE 15-3. *Printer layout*

Item \ Report	Sales Report	Salesman Performance	Delinquency Report
Cust. Number			
Cust. Name			
Cust. Address			
Cust. Rating			

FIGURE 15-4. *Grid chart*

is present in various reports. The systems analyst can refer to the chart and take steps to discard unnecessary reports, or to simplify the ones in current use (Fig. 15-4).

FLOWCHARTS

Types

The two most common types of flowcharts are *system* flowcharts and *program* flowcharts. The distinction between the two types is important, for each serves a unique role. The *system* flowchart (also referred to as a procedure chart, run diagram, and flowchart) is a diagram of the design of the run that focuses on the broad data flow and operations in a data-processing system. It specifies the inputs (programs and raw data), the stages through which they will be processed, and the outputs produced by using a wide variety of symbols. Thus symbols representing input, processing, and output are frequently used in system flowchart construction. Specialized symbols are also used instead of the basic input–output symbol to emphasize a particular device or operation. These and other symbols are shown in Fig. 15-7.

The *program* flowchart (also called a block diagram, process chart, and flowchart), on the other hand, emphasizes the *how* (versus the system flowchart—the *what*). It focuses on the sequence of data transformations from the input- to the output-data structure. It is usually an expansion of what is indicated by a simple process symbol in a system flowchart. Thus, it is more logically complex than the system flowchart.

Flowcharts, in general, are frequently used by many computer staff members in various phases related to the preparation of the computer: that is, problem definition, system analysis, system design, programming, debugging, conversion, documentation, system operations, and maintenance.

Symbol Standardization

Systematic use of graphic arts dates back to John von Neumann, the intellectual father of flowcharting, who, with his associates at the Institute for Advanced Study at Princeton, were the first to use and publish information about the use of flowcharts. Although the symbols have changed over time, the philosophy and rationale of flowcharting remain the same.

National and international cooperation have resulted in the development of a number of national and international standards for computer processing. During the 1960s, the first formal U.S. attempt to develop a flowcharting standard was made. A committee worked with the Business Equipment Manufacturing Association (BEMA) and the American Standards Association (ASA).[1] The latter association's members include representatives from computer manufacturers and a few computer users. The result was the drafting of a standard, which was approved in 1963 and published as the ASA X3.5. This American effort toward flowcharting standardization was matched by similar efforts made for the International Standards Organization (ISO).

[1] In 1965 the name of the American Standards Association was changed to the United States of America Standards Institute (USASI), and ASA X3.5 became USASI X3.5 Standard. When the name was again changed in 1969 to the American National Standards Institute (ANSI), the flowchart standard also changed to ANSI X3.5 Standard.

The X3.5 standard was later revised in 1965, 1966, 1968, and 1970. The 1970 revision brought the X3.5 standard closer to the ISO standard.

PROGRAM FLOWCHARTS

A program flowchart is a *graphic representation* of the operations and decision logic and the order in which they are to be handled. In effect, it is a detailed outline giving the sequential steps that must be performed by the computer for the processing of business data. As a graphic representation, the flowchart improves communication between one person and another and aids the programmer in visualizing the sequence of the necessary operations. Once "debugged," it becomes a part of program documentation, serving as a primary source for future reference.

The relatively high attrition rate in computer processing and the frequent requirement for modifying programs to satisfy existing situations account for the need to document program flowcharts and their respective coding. Many computer installations suffer from inefficient program documentation and face the frustrating task of rewriting programs or analyzing their makeup. Inadequate program documentation becomes more critical when a new computer system is installed. Programs that were run on the former installation almost always require rewriting to meet the requirements of the new installation. Such rewriting is extremely difficult without adequate program documentation.

A program flowchart, then, is a means of outlining a given problem. The author recalls how his speech instructor outlined on the blackboard the steps involved in delivering a speech: (1) "stand up," (2) "speak up," and (3) "shut up." Each of these steps can be expanded to show other detailed substeps leading to a complete speech. A term paper follows a similar basic set of steps: the introduction, the main body, and the conclusions. Many ideas can be presented under each of these three headings, particularly the middle one. The three headings constitute a *general flow diagram.* When the details are included, the diagram is called a *detailed flow diagram* or *program flowchart.* Figure 15-5 presents an example of a program flowchart of "How to get to school in the morning." It illustrates that plans of action for our daily routines are really flowcharts which are repeated so often that they are "written" in our memory. The box at the bottom of Fig. 15-5 is a general flow diagram of the procedure.

Use of Templates

Flowcharting is an art in which competence is developed with experience. No two individuals draw flowcharts exactly alike. The important factors to consider are the clarity of presentation and the validity of the

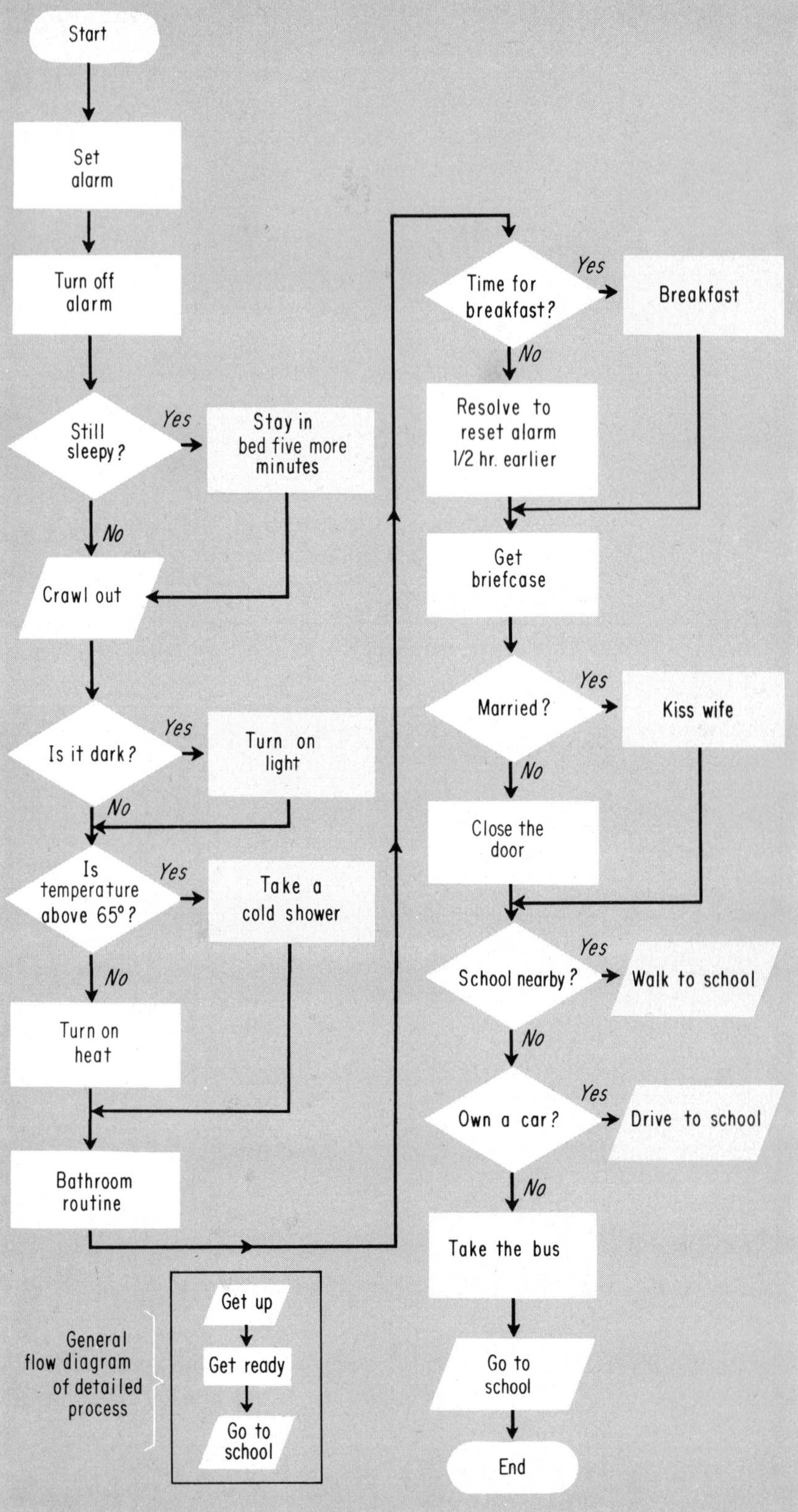

FIGURE 15-5. Detailed block diagram and a general diagram of "How to get to school in the morning"

FIGURE 15-6. IBM flowcharting template X20-8020-1

symbols used. Other than the freehand drawing of symbols on a chalkboard or on paper using pencil, flowcharts are more precisely and neatly prepared by using templates provided by computer manufacturers or manufacturers of plastic drawing aids. A good flowchart template should be flexible and transparent, with clearly visible registration lines to help in aligning the symbols when they are drawn (Fig. 15-6).

The following section introduces the basic international and American national symbols used in developing system and program flowcharts for data processing. Although various steps are used by different manufacturers for representing instructions in a flowchart, each has as its purpose the representation of a specific action. A survey of the flowcharting symbols is presented in Fig. 15-7.

Basic Symbols

Two flowchart symbols are used in describing computer program operations. They are the input–output symbol and the process symbol. The other basic symbols are the flowline and the annotation symbols.

INPUT–OUTPUT SYMBOL. The input–output symbol (parallelogram) stands for an instruction to either an input or an output device The input device transfers input data to the computer for processing. The output device prepares the result of the processed information for the user. These symbols are usually shown on both ends of a complete flowchart. At times, other symbols are shown before the input symbol to instruct the computer in what is referred to in programming as "housekeeping," or preparing the system for a new application.

In Fig. 15-8, the "read a card" instruction simply tells the card reader to read the first card in a sequence, thus causing the transfer of the card's contents to the central processing unit. Without this step, it would be impossible for the computer to do any work, unless other means were used to move the data into primary storage.

The "punch the results" instruction is an output instruction and is usually the last step before the computer stops or loops (branches) back

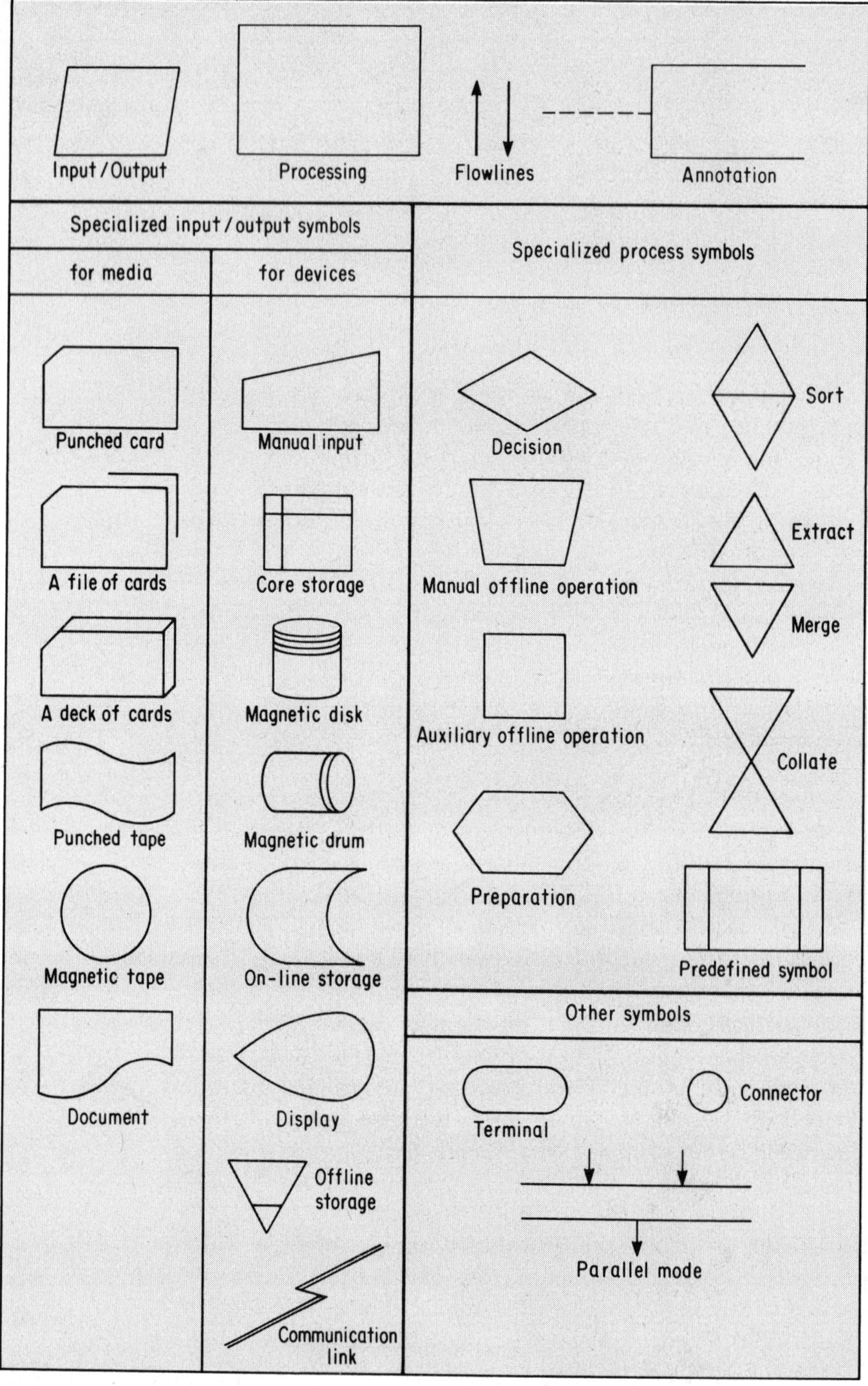

FIGURE 15-7. *International and American national symbols for data processing*

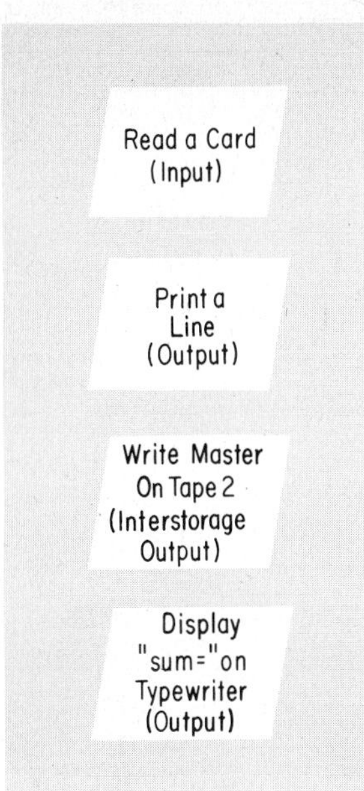

FIGURE 15-8. Input-output operation symbols

to the beginning of the program to repeat the steps on another account. This instruction causes the punch unit of an output device—that is, an auxiliary machine connected by a cable to the computer—to punch in a card the results of the processing phase.

The "print a line" instruction is another output step. The printer receives the output data from the computer and prints them on a form. Output can be presented to the user either in printed or in punched form. The former method is used when management wants the results immediately; the latter, when the data are to be sorted for future processing. Both punching in a card and printing the same data on a line can be done simultaneously in the machine run if desired. However, the printer has preference (in terms of timing) over the punching unit.

The "write master on tape 2" instruction tells the computer to transfer master-record data from core storage to magnetic tape unit 2.

The "sum =" instruction requires the computer to type the message "sum =" on a typewriter connected to it.

PROCESS SYMBOL. The process symbol denotes an operation involved in the actual processing of data. It is used in manipulating data within the computer (e.g., moving data from one field to another) and in arithmetic operations. The process operation is shown in Fig. 15-9. Since these operations are carried out in the central processing unit, the process symbol is often called the *stored program* symbol.

FLOWLINE SYMBOL. The flowline (direction-of-flow) symbol is a

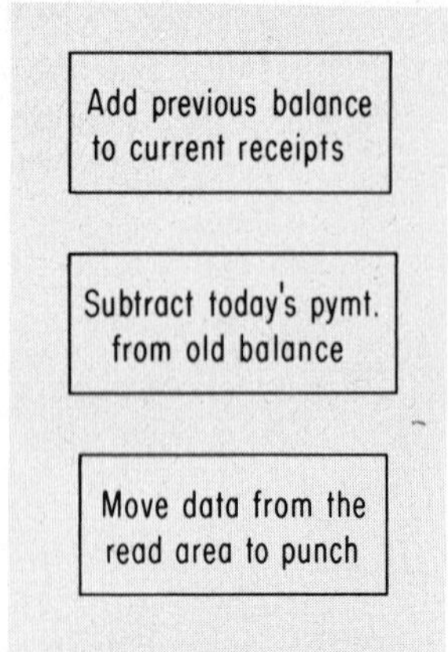

FIGURE 15-9. Process operation symbols

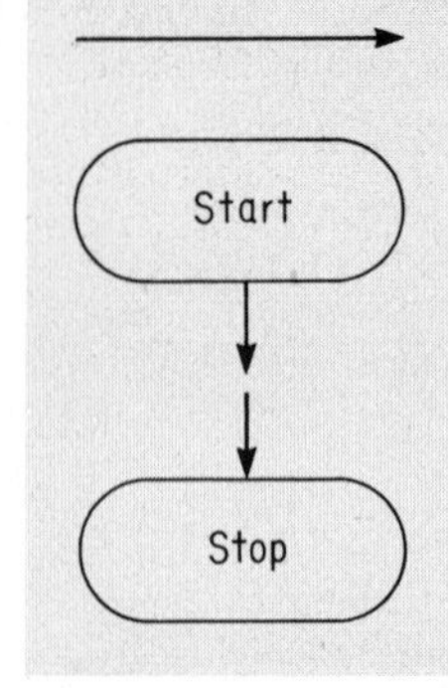

FIGURE 15-10. Flowline (direction-of-flow) symbols

line or arrow of any length. It is used to link symbols and to indicate the sequence of operations (Fig. 15-10). Flowlines may cross, form junctions, or connect any two symbols so that program flowchart symbols follow in a logical, meaningful relationship. Occasionally, broken arrows are used to specify a possible flow change in the computer during the program run, depending on the conditions dictated in the process.

The flowchart is constructed so that the normal direction of flow is from top to bottom and from left to right to conform to the manner in which English is read or written. During its development, if the flowchart is to be longer than one column, the programmer begins at the top left area of the sheet. As he reaches the bottom, he goes to the top of the next column, and so on until the flowchart is completed. However, if the flowchart is completed in one column of symbols, the middle area of the sheet is used. Because the top-to-bottom rule is familiar, the use of the direction-of-flow arrow at the end of a flowline is optional. The main factors to keep in mind are neatness and consistency. Flowchart construction is a work of art. Creativity pays dividends as long as the overall approach used is consistent throughout.

Annotation Symbol. Also called an assertion flag, the annotation symbol is an open rectangle with a broken line connecting the symbol to another flowchart symbol. It does not signify any action in the program, but is used to give descriptive comments or explanatory notes for clarification (Fig. 15-11).

Terminal Symbol. Although it is not considered a basic symbol, a terminal (flat oval) symbol is included here to emphasize its use in designating the beginning and the end of a program. It can also be used

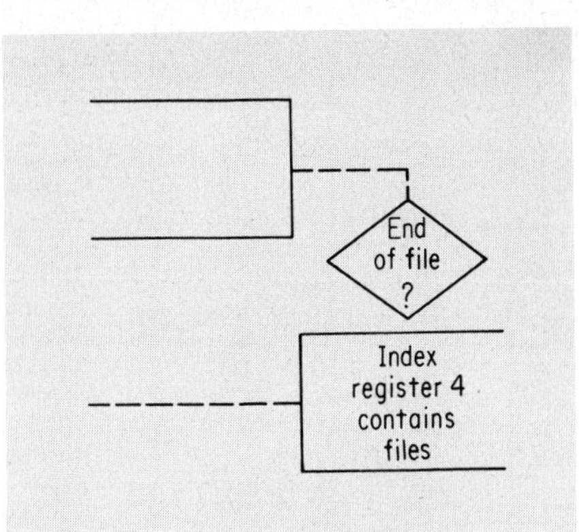

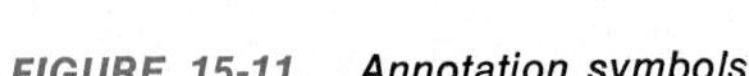

FIGURE 15-11. *Annotation symbols*

FIGURE 15-12. *Uses of terminal symbols*

elsewhere in the flowchart for specifying error conditions, such as parity error checks or detection of invalid characters. In this case, manual intervention is required (Fig. 15-12).

Specialized Input–Output Symbols

Several specialized symbols have been developed that, in addition to representing the input–output function, indicate the medium in which the information is recorded and/or the method of handling the information (Fig. 15-7). In the absence of any suitable specialized symbol, the basic symbol is normally used.

PUNCHED-CARD SYMBOL. This symbol is used to represent an input–output function using any type of punched card, including mark-sense cards, stub cards, deck of cards, and the like. Additional specialized versions of the punched-card symbol represent a deck (collection) of punched cards or a file of punched cards (a collection of related punched-card records).

PUNCHED-TAPE SYMBOL. This symbol represents a punched-tape routine.

MAGNETIC-TAPE SYMBOL. This symbol represents a magnetic-tape routine.

MANUAL-INPUT SYMBOL. This symbol represents an *input* function in which information is entered manually at the time of processing by means of keyboards, switches, buttons, or the like.

Display Symbol. This symbol represents an input–output function in which the information is displayed for human use at the time of processing by means of video devices, console printers, plotters, or the like.

Document Symbol. This symbol represents a printed-document format.

Communication-Link Symbol. This symbol represents data transmitted automatically from one source to another.

On-Line Storage Symbol. This symbol represents an input–output function using any type of storage, such as magnetic tape, drum, or disk.

Off-Line Storage Symbol. This symbol refers to any storage not directly accessible by the computer system.

Specialized Process Symbols

Specialized process symbols (Fig. 15-7) indicate, in addition to the processing function, the specific type of operation to be performed on the information.

Decision Symbol—Looping and Decision Making. A computer executes program instructions one by one, unless it is directed to alter the sequence. Altering the sequence of instruction execution is called *looping*. Other terms used are *jumping, transfer of control, branching,* and *program modification.*

To illustrate the use of looping, we use the balancing of accounts receivable in a card-oriented computer system. Given the input card shown in Fig. 15-13, the steps followed in solving the problem are:

a/c No.	Previous balance	Cash received	Sales on account

FIGURE 15-13. Card input of accounts-receivable problem

Previous balance − cash received + additional sales on account = present balance.

The construction of a program flowchart follows the same reasoning, obviously, as if the application were to be performed manually. Because

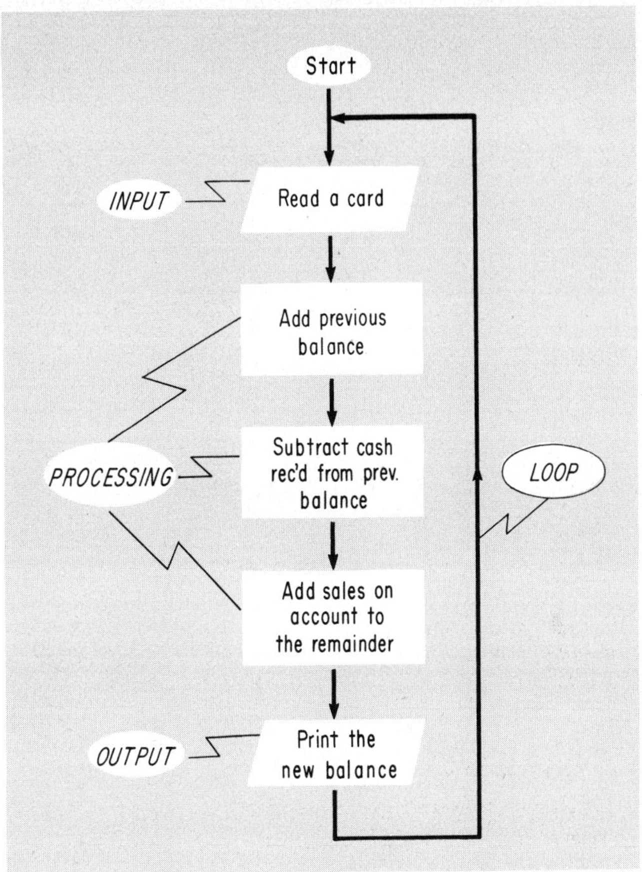

FIGURE 15-14. Looping routine

a number of accounts (all following the same repetitive procedure) will be processed, the program must be designed in such a way as to allow the computer to go through the same necessary procedures for each account without stopping. To do this, *looping* is used. In Fig. 15-14, after the computer executes the last instruction of the program, which is to "print the new balance" on the first account card, it loops to the first instruction, "read a card," which causes the second account card to be read and the same procedure applied to it. Only one program is necessary for the whole file of accounts receivable cards. If the computer were unable to loop, the only alternative would be to store as many complete programs as there were accounts to be processed. This approach would not be practical in updating the accounts because the programs might occupy a substantial part of primary storage unnecessarily.

Looping is also used to control arithmetic operations and the number of records to be processed. Suppose, for example, that we wish to process

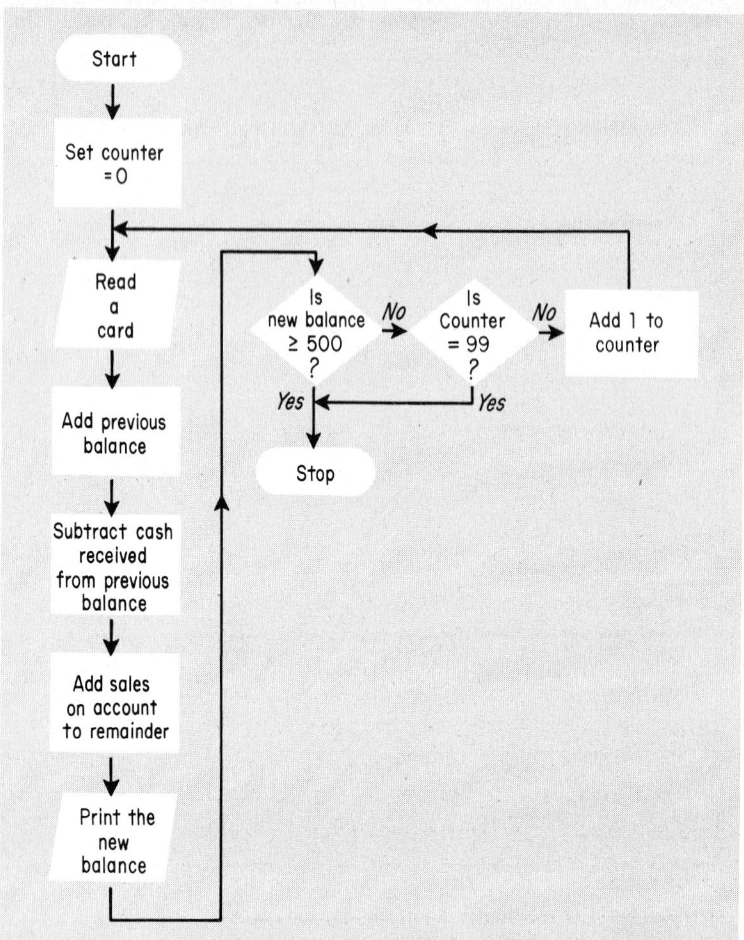

FIGURE 15-15. *Modified routine*

a set of 100 customer accounts and to instruct the computer to stop the operation if a customer's new debit balance equals to or exceeds $500. The flowchart in Fig. 15-14 can be modified to look like the one shown in Fig. 15-15. Briefly, a counter is set to zero, and the first record is read. Cash received is subtracted from the previous record, and any sales purchased on account are added to the remainder. Next, the computer is required to test whether the new balance is equal to or greater than $500. If the answer is yes, it is instructed to stop. Otherwise, it is instructed to further test whether the record just processed is the hundredth record. If it is, it must stop. Otherwise, one number is added to a counter reserved to keep track of the number of records processed, and the next sequential record is read as indicated by the conditional loop.

The loop in Fig. 15-14 is called an *endless* or *unconditional* loop,

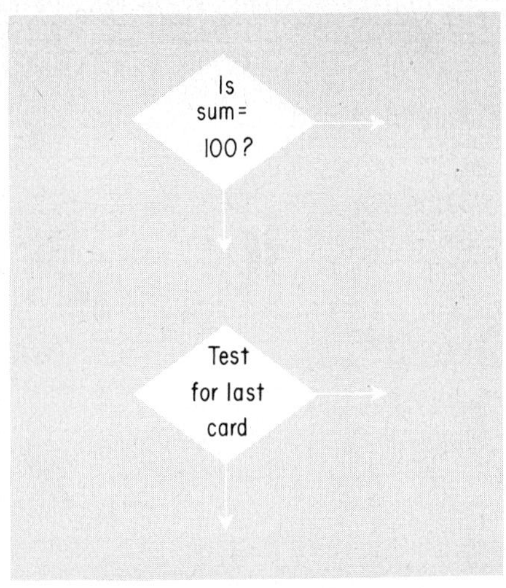

FIGURE 15-16. Decision symbols

because the program does not provide for conditions to be tested by the computer. Most functional programs, however, include one or more loops to test various conditions or to decide on a particular course of action based on the test. This decision-making ability is symbolized by the process decision or logic operation symbols, as shown (with examples) in Fig. 15-16.

The decision symbol, then, represents the "thinking" part of a computer and relates to algebraic notations used to test a given relationship. These tests, also called relational expressions, are in three forms:

Expression	*Arithmetic Form*	*Coded Form*
A is equal to **B**	$A = B$	A.EQ.B
A is not equal to **B**	$A \neq B$	A.NE.B
A is greater than **B**	$A > B$	A.GT.B
A is greater than or equal to **B**	$A \geqq B$	A.GE.B
A is less than **B**	$A < B$	A.LT.B
A is less than or equal to **B**	$A \leqq B$	A.LE.B

In a card-oriented computer system, although the card reader stops the operation automatically at the end of the program, the computer checks to see if the card being processed is the last card. Two alternatives exist: If it is the last card, the operation will stop. Otherwise, it loops back and starts from the beginning in order to process the next card in sequence. When this decision symbol is added to the example in Fig. 15-14, the diagram looks like the one in Fig. 15-17. The loop here is called a *conditional loop*.

A decision symbol does not have to be in any specific location in the flowchart. In Fig. 15-17, it is located toward the end, because its

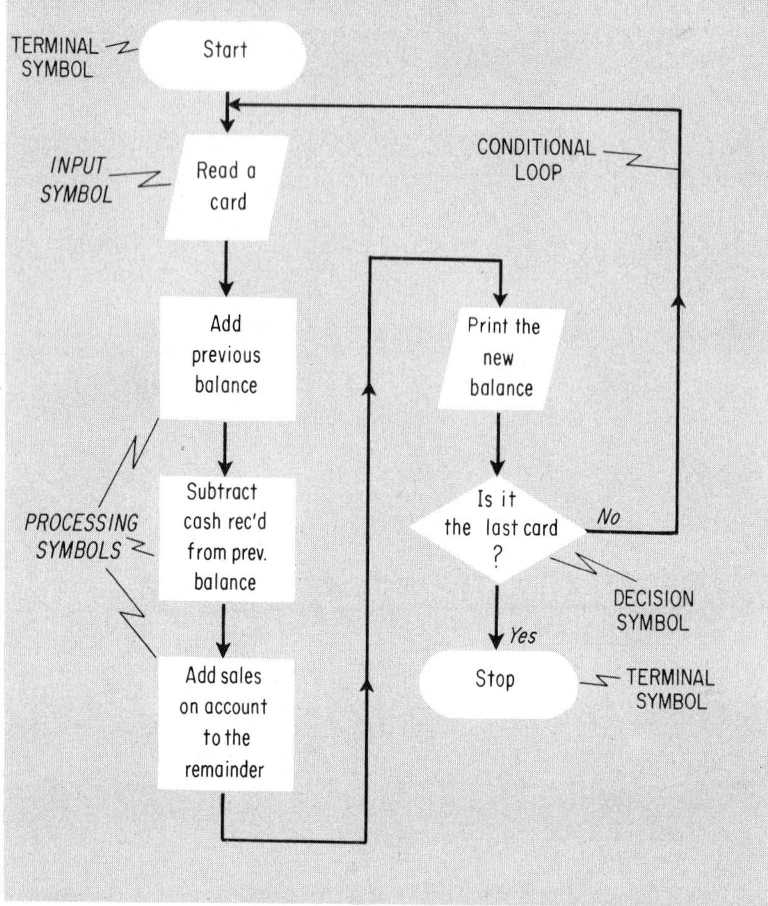

FIGURE 15-17. ***Block diagram showing the use of a decision symbol***

purpose is to check for a last card and to cause the system to stop if it is the last card. A decision symbol is usually located somewhere between the input and the output symbols, depending on the type of decision that must be made. It is also very likely that a program flowchart will include more than one decision symbol. The number of decision symbols depends on the number of alternative courses of action requested by the program.

To illustrate the use of decision logic (other than testing for a last card), assume the following situation:

A group of cards in a file representing both employees and their supervisors is to be processed. Fifty dollars is to be added to each employee's current pay. In the event that the card represents a supervisor, an additional $40 is to be added. The output is to be printed. To distinguish an employee's card from that of a supervisor, an × punch is made

Employee clock no.	Employee name	Employee's net earnings	Blank
1-4	5-36	37-43	44-80

FIGURE 15-18. *Input card*

in column 76 of the supervisor's card. The input card is divided into the fields shown in Fig. 15-18.

The flowchart is designed to instruct the computer to read the first card in sequence. Next, it is instructed to add $50 to the earnings field. In this case, it makes no difference whether the earnings field is that of the employee or the supervisor, since either individual is entitled to the initial $50. The third symbol tells the computer to identify the card to which $50 has just been added. Identification in this case is done by the detection of an X punch in column 76. Only a supervisor's card contains an X punch in that column. When an X punch is detected, the computer interprets it as a supervisor's card and takes the next instruction in sequence, which is "Add $40 to earnings." However, if no X punch is detected, the card is an employee's card, which causes the computer to "branch" to block 5 of the program and move the data in the card to the print area, where the results are printed (Fig. 15-19).

Looping, then, is similar to a road detour. It bypasses the regular route for a logical reason. In Fig. 15-19 the computer loops, by passing block 4, only when the card is an employee card. Otherwise, it follows the program from top to bottom as presented, one instruction at a time. The last decision symbol tests for a last card. If the answer is "No," it loops the program back to the beginning for processing of the remaining cards in the hopper. If the answer is "Yes," it halts.

PREDEFINED SYMBOL. The predefined symbol is a specialized process symbol that represents a named operation or programmed step not explicitly detailed in the program flowchart (Fig. 15-20). As a subroutine symbol, the details included in the predefined process are laid out separately and do not appear in the main flowchart.

PREPARATION SYMBOL. The preparation symbol is a specialized process symbol used to specify operations, such as control, initiation, determining an index register, and the like, that will alter the program's

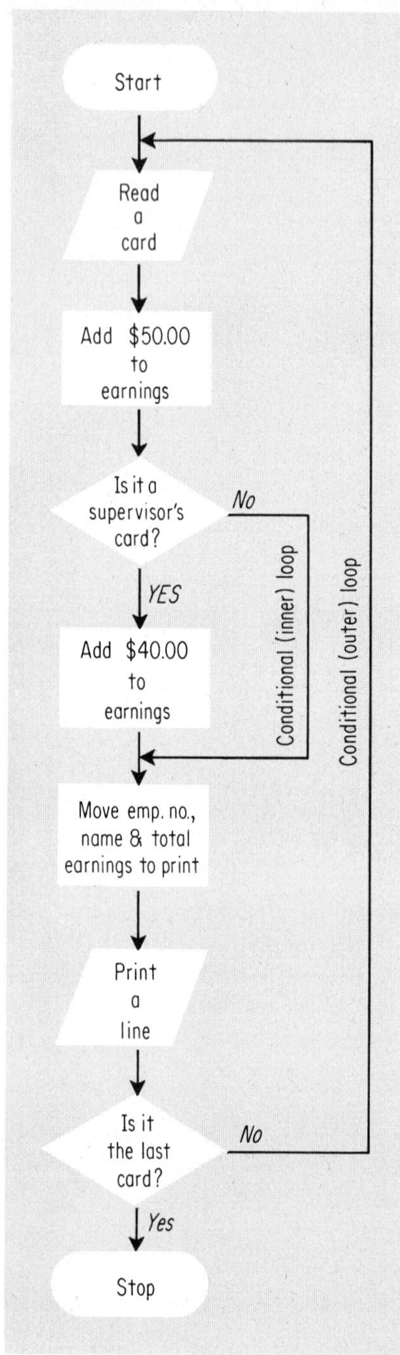

FIGURE 15-19. Use of decision in a program flowchart

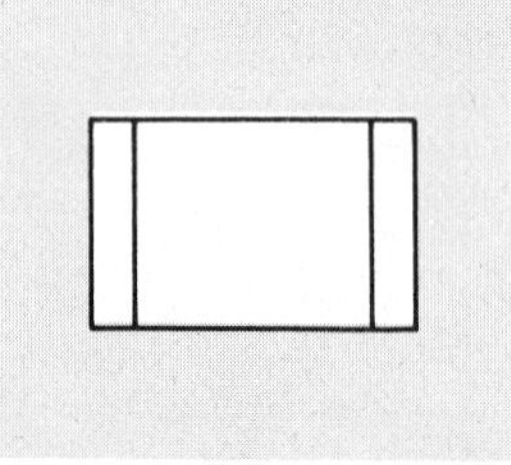

FIGURE 15-20. Predefined symbol

FIGURE 15-21. Instruction modification symbol

course of execution. In addition, some programmers use this symbol for various housekeeping routines (Fig. 15-21).

Other Symbols

PARALLEL-MODE SYMBOL. The parallel-mode symbol is two parallel lines of any equal length. It represents the beginning or the end of two or more simultaneous operations (Fig. 15-7).

FIXED AND INTERPAGE CONNECTOR SYMBOLS. A fixed connector symbol is a nonprocessing symbol used to connect one part of a flowchart to another without drawing flowlines. It denotes an entry from or an exit to another part of the flowchart. When used, it conserves space by keeping related blocks near one another, reduces the number of flowlines in complex programs, and eliminates cross lines from taking place (compare Figs. 15-22 and 15-23). Thus, the fixed connector symbol aids in developing a clearer, better organized, and more simplified flowchart.

Figure 15-23 illustrates the use of fixed connector symbols in a hypothetical flowchart consisting of blocks A to I. The cross line going from the output symbol "Write C" to the initiate routine has been eliminated. Also, space is conserved and the related blocks stand out more clearly, yet they are conveniently accessible to the program for processing.

Complex problems often require a detailed flowchart extending over several pages for complete logic. A nonprocessing symbol, called an interpage (or off-page) connector, is used to indicate an exit from one page to another. In Fig. 15-24, the left symbol is the last symbol on the first page, indicating continuation of the flowchart on the second page. The first symbol on the second page should be the same symbol, which refers to the continuation of the flowcharting from the first page.

SUBROUTINES

In an effort to reduce programming and compiling costs, programmers often develop a set of instructions, called *subroutines,* that are kept in a "library" and made available to the main program when needed. When it is in operation, the subroutine derives its information from the main program, performs the necessary routine, and relays the results back to the main program.[2]

In Fig. 15-23, a subroutine headed by connector symbol 2 is initiated from two separate decision points in the main flowchart. After execution, control will return to the instruction following the decision point that initiated the entry. For example, if entry is made from the decision point

[2] Entrance to and exit from a subroutine are often called *entrance parameters* and *exit parameters,* respectively.

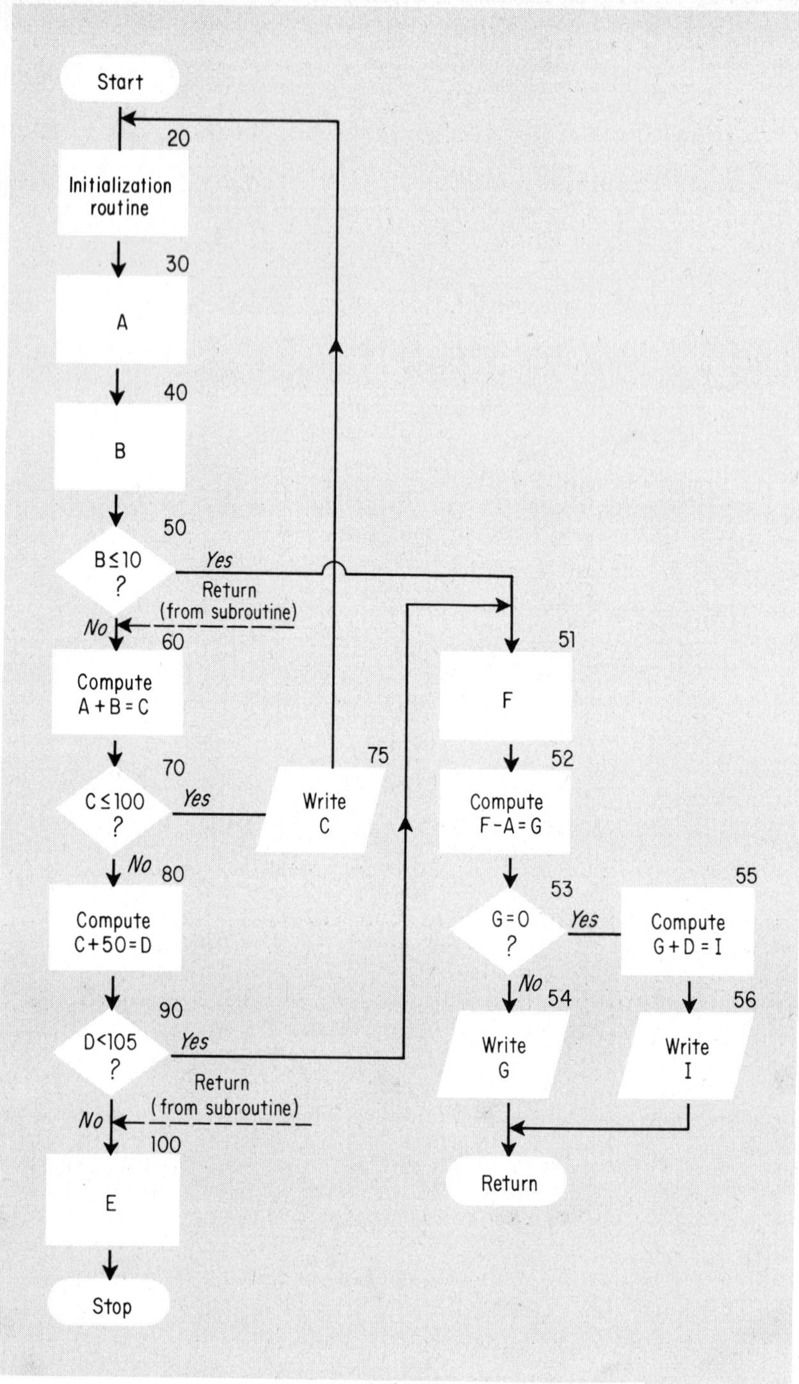

FIGURE 15-22. *Hypothetical program flowchart*

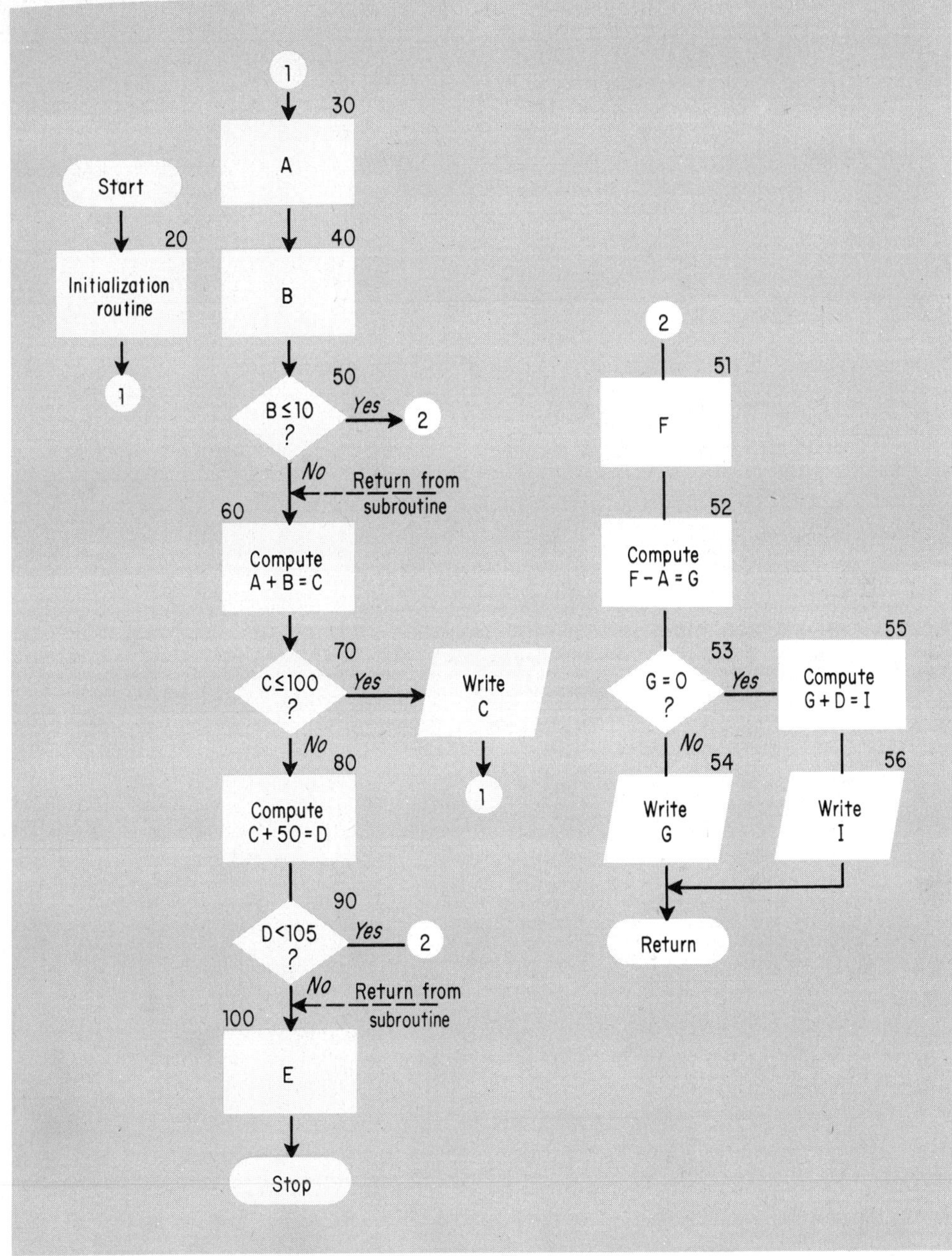

FIGURE 15-23. Hypothetical program flowchart using connector symbols

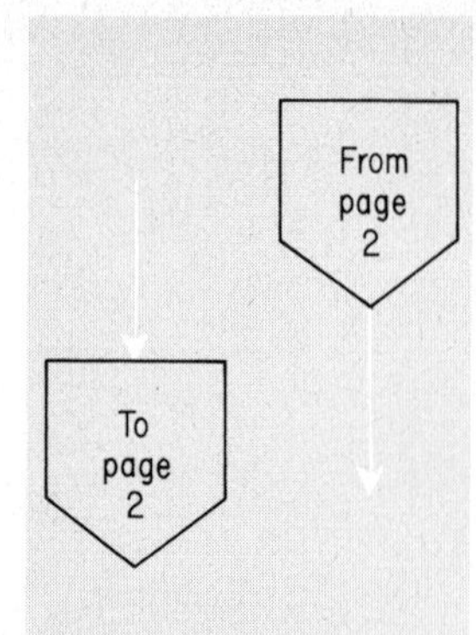

FIGURE 15-24. Interpage connector symbols

"B $<$ 10?", control will return to the instruction "Compute A + B = C". However, if entry is made from the decision point "D $<$ 105?", control will return to the instruction "E". Since a subroutine can be initiated from several places in the main program, care must be provided to return control to the proper instruction.

Although subroutines use relatively more core storage and object time, their repetitive use saves prime storage space throughout the operation.

CROSS REFERENCING A PROGRAM FLOWCHART

Once a program flowchart has been completed, many programmers give each block a number based on its sequence in the flowchart. This optional step is called cross referencing the program, and can be used later as a statement number in the coding phase of program preparation. In Fig. 15-22, for example, the functional blocks constituting the main instruction flow are arbitrarily numbered from 20 to 100, by increments of 10. The numbers within an increment are used to label up to nine blocks that might be derived from any given block. A case in point is the decision symbol, labeled 50. A "Yes" alternative leads to the execution of six instructions. These instructions are given cross references 51 to 56. Thus the increment between any two blocks in the main program should be constant and sufficient for labeling secondary instructions.

USE OF NOTATIONS

The use of ordinary English is often too verbose for specifying operations or naming data within flowcharting symbols. Although the American National Standards Institute (ANSI) does not specify any special language, some compact set of notations would seem desirable. Figure 15-25 lists

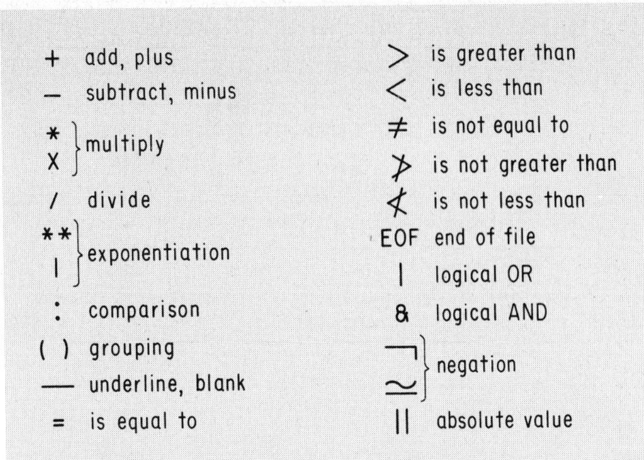

+ add, plus
− subtract, minus
* X multiply
/ divide
** ↑ exponentiation
: comparison
( ) grouping
— underline, blank
= is equal to
> is greater than
< is less than
≠ is not equal to
≯ is not greater than
≮ is not less than
EOF end of file
| logical OR
& logical AND
¬ ≃ negation
|| absolute value

FIGURE 15-25. Primary notations used in flowcharting

some of the more commonly used notations in flowcharting. Notations summarize within flowcharting symbols greater amounts of information than ordinary English, improving the flowchart's communication value.

GENERAL PROGRAM FLOWCHARTING HINTS

Some points considered helpful in constructing a program flowchart are

1. The flowchart should be legible, clean, and simple. Use a standardized template with clearly recognizable symbols; the diagram will look neater and more presentable than a hand-drawn flowchart.
2. Where possible, only one entrance and exit flowline should be drawn for each symbol. Also, the flowline should be drawn so that it enters or exits at the visual midpoint of the symbol(s). Symbols that may require more than one exit flowline are decision and input–output symbols.
3. The flowchart should maintain a consistent, general flow pattern—from top to bottom and from left to right. When this is done, arrowheads are not needed.
4. Each page should be numbered sequentially, and enough space should be allowed for the title of the application, the name of the programmer, and the data on which the flowchart was constructed. The title should be short and clear.
5. The language used in describing each step in the flowchart should be English or common notations, not machine language. This is desirable because it contributes to a better understanding of the instructions by people other than the programmer who may not be familiar with the system used.
6. In each instruction the wording should be clearly written within the symbol and consistent with the level of detail in the flowchart.

7. Intersecting lines should be avoided as much as possible.
8. In a complex program, connectors and cross references should be used in a consistent manner to minimize the presence of crossing flowlines. Entry and exit connectors are most effective when they are positioned in a consistent manner.

Several drawbacks can be mentioned regarding flowcharts:

1. Flowcharting is time consuming and, in cases involving complex programs, requires substantial revisions before the flowchart can become operational. Tight deadlines often cause the preparation of messy flowcharts or the ignoring of the flowcharting phase completely. In either case, trouble lies ahead when it comes to the coding or debugging phase of program preparation. To ease this chore, junior programmers or electronic data-processing clerks are assigned the task of preparing program flowcharts from rough data they receive from the programmers in charge of the problem at hand.
2. Lack of a standard method of construction. During flowchart preparation, a programmer often finds himself under strain, with a long list of ideas and relevant data. The drawback is further compounded by the fact that flowcharting involves other personnel in the department. Communication problems and the lack of speed and accuracy of data acquisition could be significant.
3. The flowchart generally tells *what* and *how* but rarely *why* a given set of operations is made.
4. Other than its documentation value, a flowchart is often viewed by programmers and analysts as a waste of time, especially since neither member thinks in terms of flowcharts.
5. Subjectivity in condensing details. Summarizing the wrong details can render the flowchart useless.

For complex problems, some installations use a special computer program designed to write program flowcharts. Once it is fed the data for each symbol and the squares in which the data go, the program utilizes the printer to draw flowchart symbols on paper marked with numbered squares and to connect them to one another. This technique is quite efficient, especially in complex programs, and makes it convenient for the programmer to look over the results and make changes where necessary.

DECISION TABLES

A *decision table* (sometimes referred to as a *decision logic table*) is an effective tabular approach used in (1) planning programs, (2) showing cause–effect relationships, and (3) handling situations that involve complex decision logic. It presents the original conditions and the course of action to be taken if the conditions are met.

	excellent	good	average	poor	fail
90–100	✓				
80–89		✓			
70–79			✓		
60–69				✓	
below 60					✓

FIGURE 15-26. *Decision table*

For many years tabular representation of data has been an effective means of communicating data clearly and concisely. A typical table is one that gives the status of various term test grades. In Fig. 15-26 the table has a one-to-one relationship and reads as follows: IF the test grade is between 90 and 100, THEN it is "excellent"; IF the test grade is between 80 and 89, THEN it is "good"; . . . ; IF the test grade is below 60, THEN it is "fail." Or, the table can be turned around by stating that IF the test is excellent, THEN the grade is between 90 and 100, and so on. Thus, a decision table explains a situation involving more than one if–then relationship.

Decision tables are of some use to everyone—programmers, analysts, supervisors, and managers:

1. As a documentation tool, they provide a more concise and simpler form of data analysis than either the narrative or the flowchart form.
2. They can be an effective tool for extracting details pertinent to a given problem and in formulating questions.
3. Unlike flowcharts, which are developed around the programmer's logical thinking and are arbitrarily made simple or complex, decision tables bind the one preparing them to be concise and to consider all sets of conditions.
4. When completed, they serve as an easy-to-follow communication device between technical and nontechnical personnel. They are verbally oriented for managers and logically prepared for programmers and analysts.
5. They are easy to learn and to update, and continue to function once the logic is developed.

Elements of a Decision Table

In limited-entry form, a decision table is divided into an upper left quadrant (called the *condition stub*), which sets forth in question form the conditions that may exist, and a lower left quadrant (called the *action stub*), which outlines in narrative form the action to be taken to meet each condition (Fig. 15-27).

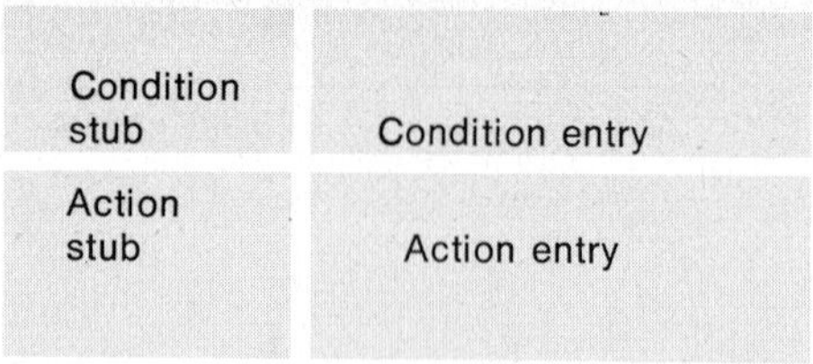

Condition stub	Condition entry
Action stub	Action entry

FIGURE 15-27. *Elements of a decision table*

The right part of a decision table is also divided into an upper section, called the *condition entry,* and a lower section, called the *action entry.* The condition entry provides the answers to the questions asked in the condition-stub quadrant. Answers are represented by a Y to signify "yes," an N to signify "no," or a blank to show that the condition involved has not been tested. The action entry, on the other hand, indicates by a check mark or by an × the appropriate action resulting from the answers to the conditions entered in the condition-entry quadrant. A number of columns are also available in the condition-entry section, each representing a condition (an alternative plan), and a number of rows are available in the condition stub, each representing a logical question answerable by Y or N. The same logic applies to the columns and rows of the action entry and action stub—that is, the action entry shows completion of the action statement, and the action stub presents an indication of where to go next for each instruction or rule (Fig. 15-28).

Application of Decision Table to a Problem

To illustrate the application of decision tables, suppose that early on September 28, 1974, a college student, because of a change in either the weather forecast or the weather itself, is faced with the problem of determining what to wear to school. Figure 15-29 presents, in flowchart

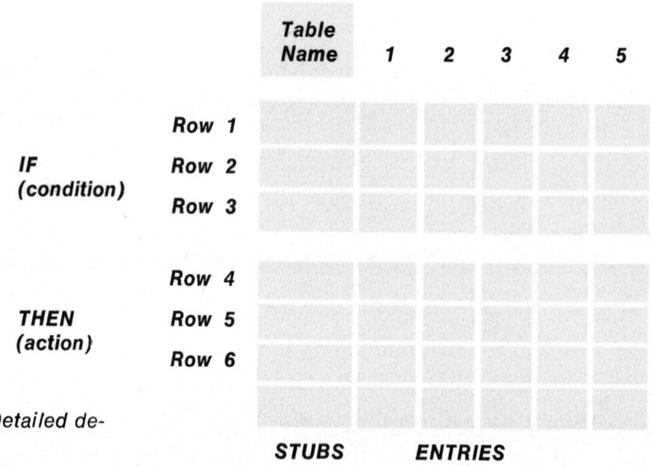

		Table Name	1	2	3	4	5
	Row 1						
IF (condition)	Row 2						
	Row 3						
	Row 4						
THEN (action)	Row 5						
	Row 6						
		STUBS	ENTRIES				

FIGURE 15-28. *Detailed decision table*

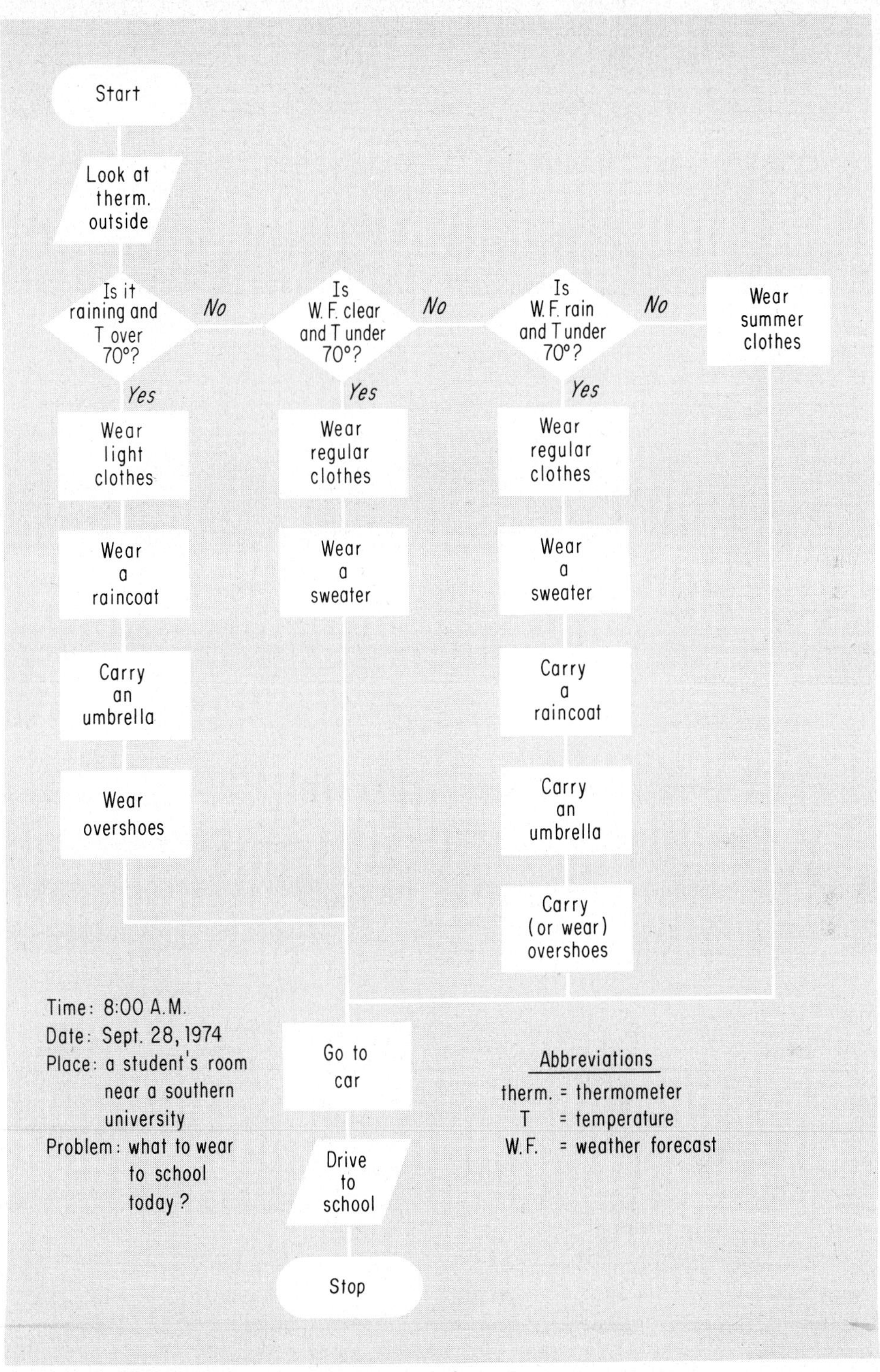

FIGURE 15-29. ***Systems and procedures flowchart to determine what to wear to school***

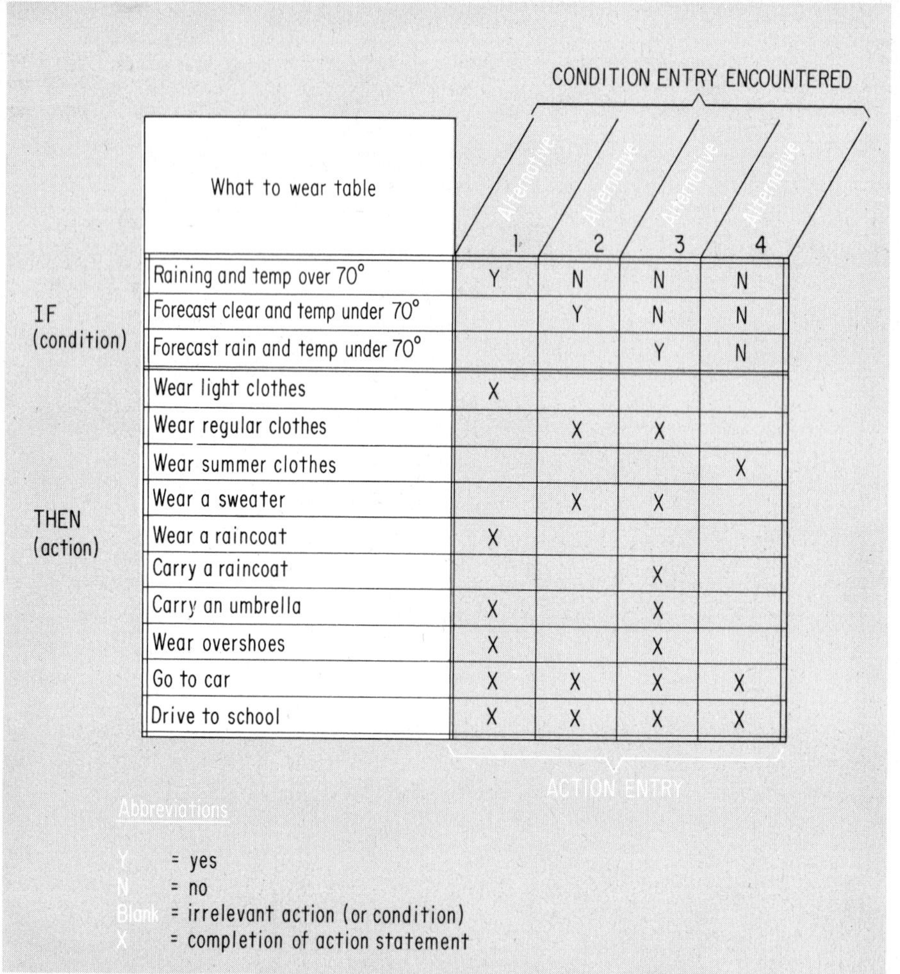

CONDITION ENTRY ENCOUNTERED

	What to wear table	Alternative 1	Alternative 2	Alternative 3	Alternative 4
IF (condition)	Raining and temp over 70°	Y	N	N	N
	Forecast clear and temp under 70°		Y	N	N
	Forecast rain and temp under 70°			Y	N
THEN (action)	Wear light clothes	X			
	Wear regular clothes		X	X	
	Wear summer clothes				X
	Wear a sweater		X	X	
	Wear a raincoat	X			
	Carry a raincoat			X	
	Carry an umbrella	X		X	
	Wear overshoes	X		X	
	Go to car	X	X	X	X
	Drive to school	X	X	X	X

ACTION ENTRY

Abbreviations

Y = yes
N = no
Blank = irrelevant action (or condition)
X = completion of action statement

FIGURE 15-30. ***Decision table to determine what to wear to school***

form, the decisions he would make regarding the procedure to be followed. His usual routine would have to be changed in favor of another. The problem is what system to choose. A look at either a flowchart or a decision table would give the answer immediately. The illustration shows the details that go into the construction of a simplified flowchart and a decision table. In the decision table, the condition constitutes the input, while the action is the output (Fig. 15-30).

The student looks outside at the thermometer, and if it is raining and the temperature is over 70 degrees with a forecast that these conditions will continue, reference to the flowchart tells him that he should wear his light clothes and a raincoat, carry an umbrella, wear overshoes, go to the car, and drive to school. However, if the weather is clear and the forecast indicates clear skies and a temperature under 70 degrees, the flowchart tells him to wear regular-weight clothes and a sweater, go to the car, and drive to school. If the weather forecast calls for rain and temperatures under 70 degrees, the flowchart shows that he should wear regular clothes and a sweater, carry a raincoat and umbrella, wear overshoes, go to the car, and drive to school. If the weather is clear and the forecast is for a continuation of clear weather, with no change in temperature, the student does not have to make any decision because no problem exists. He simply follows his usual routine by proceeding to wear summer clothes, go to his car, and drive to school.

Of course, the construction of a flowchart for an actual business application is likely to involve more detailed logical and processing steps as well as several data computations. Once these are prepared, a programmer converts the steps into a language understandable to the computer, and, finally, debugs the program through testing it against actual (live) data. The decision table in Fig. 15-30 presents the same information as the flowchart in Fig. 15-29 in a form more easily read. The first column reads as follows: IF it is raining and the temperature is over 70 degrees, THEN wear light clothes and a raincoat, carry an umbrella, wear overshoes, go to the car, and drive to school. The remaining columns are read in the same manner.

To summarize, decision tables stand out as excellent communication aids to both programmers and other personnel of the organization; in situations involving complex relationships between key variables, they can be very effective, although relatively simple to construct and follow. The main rules to follow are

1. Each table should be given a name, shown in the table header.
2. Development of a table begins from the top.
3. Although the logic of the decision table is independent of the sequence in which condition rules are written, the action takes place in the order in which the events occur.
4. Use standardized language as much as possible.
5. Eliminate duplication, redundancy, and contradiction.

Types of Decision Tables

Decision tables are normally classified by the type of information recorded. Generally, decision tables are one of three types: limited entry, extended entry, or mixed entry.

LIMITED-ENTRY TABLES. Probably the most widely used type, the limited-entry approach requires a fixed form of information in each quadrant and limits condition entries to Y, N, or a blank. Action entries are also limited to × or a blank. The condition stub must be written so

Mortgage Loan Table	1	2	3	4
Credit record excellent?	Y	N	N	N
Annual salary over $30,000?		Y	N	N
Net worth over $50,000?			Y	N
Approve loan for 20 yrs.	X			
Approve Collateral loan for 10 yrs.		X		
Approve Conditional loan for 8 yrs.			X	
Reject Application				X

FIGURE 15-31. Limited-entry decision table

that it is either true or false, and the action stub must completely describe the action to be taken.

Figure 15-31 is a typical example of a limited-entry decision table. The problem here is to determine whether or not to extend a real estate mortgage loan against a table of key values. Note that the statements in the condition stub are written in question form, and require either a yes or no response. The response to each statement is written in the condition entry, accordingly. Likewise, the action is written in a narrative form in the action stub, with X's in the action entry responding to each Y in the condition entry.

Since they are limited to a yes or no alternative, as is the case in binary logic, limited-entry tables are ideally suited for computer-oriented applications.

EXTENDED-ENTRY TABLES. In extended-entry decision tables, the the statements written in the stub section are extended into the entry section. The condition stub identifies the elements to be tested; the condition entry states those elements or defines the value in absolute or relative form. Similarly, the action stub states the action, and the action entry specifies the stated action. Figure 15-32 presents an extended-entry table of the information provided in Fig. 15-31. Extended-entry tables offer the advantage of reducing the number of items listed in the condition and action stubs, while providing essentially the same information.

Extended-entry decision tables resemble conventional data tables and are ideally suited to problems that have few variables, with each variable having many values.

MIXED-ENTRY TABLES. As the name implies, a mixed-entry table is a combination of rows with extended entries and rows with limited entries. One rule to remember is that, although the rows may be mixed, each row must be either entirely extended or entirely limited. In Fig. 15-33, rows 2 and 3 have an extended-entry format, while the remaining rows have a limited-entry format. Conversion from either extended entry or mixed entry is done by writing the value of each element as an independent condition or action and assigning Y's, N's, or X's where applicable.

Mortgage Loan Table	1	2	3	4
Credit rating?	Excellent	Good	Fair	Poor
Salary (in thousands)		>30	<30	<30
Net worth (in thousands)			>50	<50
Decision	A	B	C	D
A. Approve loan for 20 yrs.				
B. Approve Collateral loan for 10 yrs.				
C. Approve Conditional loan for 8 yrs.				
D. Reject Application				

FIGURE 15-32. Extended-entry decision table

Mortgage Loan Table	1	2	3	4
Credit record excellent?	Y	N	N	N
Salary (in 1000's)		>30	<30	<30
Net worth (in 1000's)			>50	<50
Approve loan for 20 yrs.	X			
Approve Collateral loan for 10 yrs.		X		
Approve Conditional loan for 8 yrs.			X	
Reject Application				X

FIGURE 15-33. Mixed-entry decision table

In comparing limited- and extended-entry decision tables, we find that each type has certain advantages. In a limited-entry table, for example, the status of each condition, as either true or false, and each action, as applied or not applied, makes it more precise than either the extended-entry or the mixed-entry table. On the other hand, the extended-entry table is best suited for problem solving, and offers the possibility of having two or more responses to a given condition.

The Else Rule

A catchall convention occasionally applied in decision tables is the ELSE rule. It represents any condition (or rules) not mentioned in the decision table. In Fig. 15-34 the four rules mentioned are

1. If less than 400 units are sold, then the salesman's commission is 1 percent of total sales.
2. If between 400 and 499 units are sold, then the salesman's commission is 2 percent of total sales.
3. If between 500 and 599 units are sold and if the salesman has been with the company more than 1 year, then the salesman's commission is 3½ percent of total sales.

Salesman's Commission Table	1	2	3	4	5
units sold <400?	Y	N	N	N	ELSE
units sold 400 – 499?		Y	N	N	
units sold 500 – 599?			Y	Y	
with firm more than 1 yr?			Y	N	
1% commission of total sale	X				
2% commission of total sale		X			
3½ % commission of total sale			X		
3% commission of total sale				X	
Investigate					X

FIGURE 15-34. Decision table using the ELSE rule

4. If between 500 and 599 units are sold, and the salesman has been employed by the firm for 1 year or less, then his commission is 3 percent of total sales.

The ELSE rule (written in the extreme right column of a decision table with an X in the action-entry section) simply calls for investigating the situation in the event that none of the first four rules or conditions applies. Its frequent use is discouraged, because it does not offer a clear-cut statement of the action to be taken and is likely to hide both logic and redundancy errors.

Logic Flow and Construction of Decision Tables

As indicated earlier, a primary objective of a decision table is to present the logic patterns of a basic problem in a clear, concise, and easy-to-follow sequence. However, major problems, especially those involving complex decision logic and relationships, often cannot be effectively written in one table. Thus, several tables encompassing the necessary details of logic groups must be constructed and linked together in a sequential order similar to the order applied in program flowchart construction.

In constructing a set of tables, the main logic flow is written in what is called *open-end tables;* the set of actions and conditions common to these tables is written separately in *closed* tables. Linkage of these tables is accomplished by two control instructions:

1. A GO TO instruction (GO TO, followed by a table number or a table name)[3] directs logic flow to another open-end table, which will then take control. After the appropriate rule has been acted on,

[3] In a limited-entry table, the name or number of the table to which control is transferred is written as a part of the GO TO instruction (Fig. 15-35, the Begin Table and Table 2); in an extended-entry table the table name or number appears in the entry part of the table (Fig. 15-34, Table 1).

a GO TO instruction in the latter table directs the user to the next open-end table for processing.

2. A DO instruction (DO, followed by a table number or a table name), on the other hand, directs logic flow from an open-end table to a closed table.

After execution, the closed table transfers control back to the point of reference in the open-end table.

Figure 15-35 depicts seven logic flow steps involving four open-end tables and three closed tables. The steps are as follows:

1. The "GO TO Table 1" instruction in the Begin Table takes us to Table 1 and, following the execution of the appropriate rule, the last instruction in the action section leads to Table 2—an open-end table.
2. Table 2 takes control throughout the execution of the appropriate rule or rules. Then the next action is "DO Table 4"—a closed table. Table 4 takes temporary control and then returns to the next sequential instruction in Table 2—"GO TO Table 3."
3. This instruction transfers control to Table 3 (open-end table), which takes control throughout the execution of the appropriate rule or rules.
4. Next, the "DO Table 5" instruction in the action section of Table 3 is picked up, transferring temporary control to Table 5 (closed table); when the appropriate rule or rules have been executed, control is transferred back to the next sequential instruction in Table 3, which is "DO Table 6."
5. The "DO Table 6" instruction transfers control to Table 6, the appropriate rule is executed, and control is transferred back to the next instruction in Table 3, which is "DO Table 4."
6. This instruction uses Table 4 again and later returns to the next instruction in Table 3, which is "GO TO Begin Table."
7. The "GO TO Begin Table" instruction sends the user back to the Begin Table to continue this operation.

Several observations can be made from the foregoing illustration:

1. A closed table does not end with a special instruction on where to go next. Return of control to the table that originally caused the transfer is indicated by the word *Closed* in the table header, or, sometimes, a return or exit entry is made instead.
2. When both DO and GO TO control instructions are written in the action section of an open-end table, the DO instruction is written first, followed by the GO TO instruction.
3. More than one open-end table can reference a given closed table. In. Fig. 15-35, closed Table 4 was referenced by open-end Tables 2 and 3.

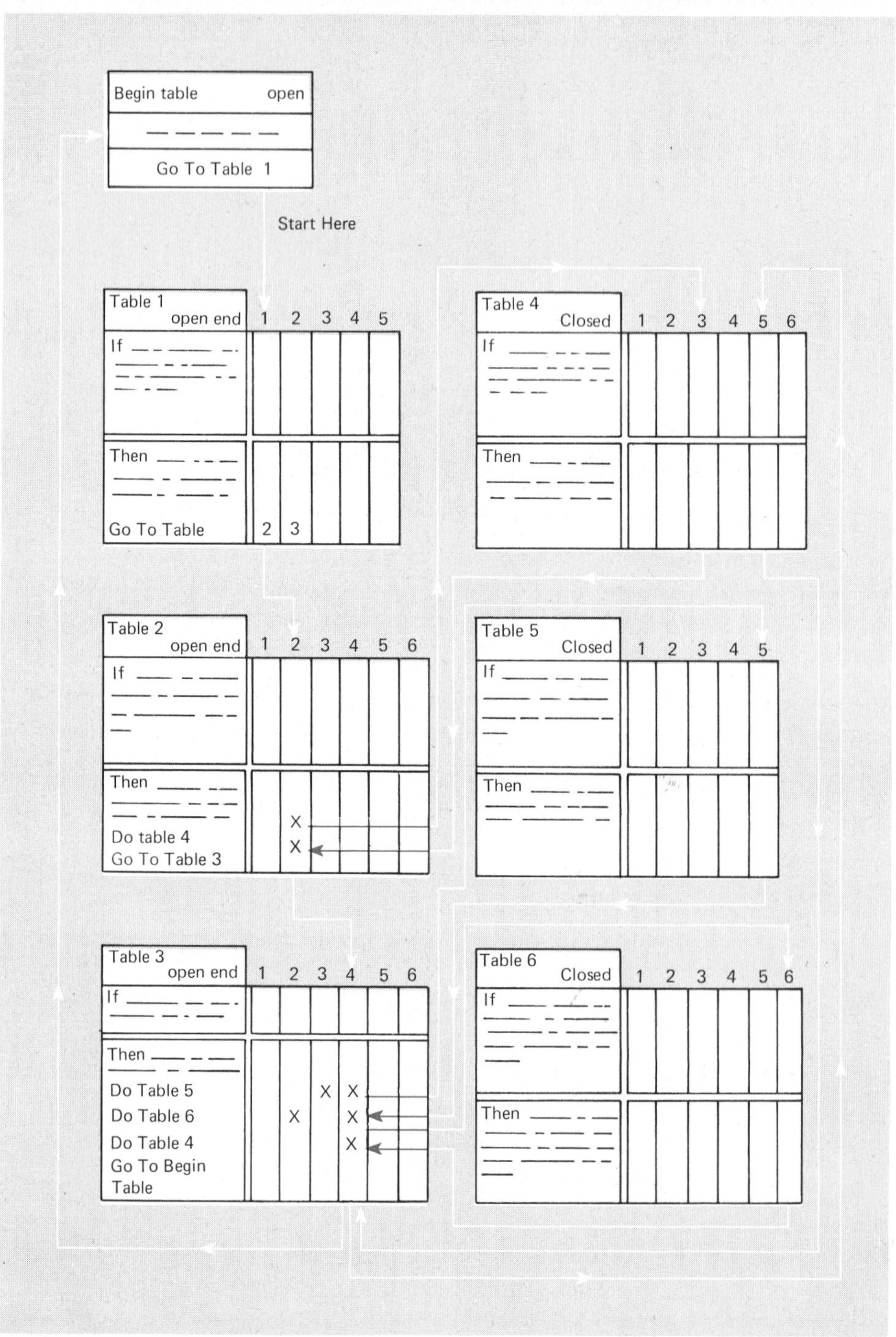

FIGURE 15-35. *Flow of logic decision tables*

	COMBINATION (RULE)							
	1	2	3	4	5	6	7	8
1	Y	Y	Y	Y	N	N	N	N
2	Y	Y	N	N	Y	Y	N	N
3	Y	N	N	Y	N	Y	Y	N

FIGURE 15-36

In constructing a decision table, every possible useful combination or rule must be taken into consideration. The total number of combinations of Y and N in a given table is computed by raising 2 to a power equal to the number of rows involved. For example, in a three-row table, the total number of combinations of Y and N is 2^3 or 8. The combinations are shown in Fig. 15-36.

Thus, each combination is covered by a separate rule in the table. Tables that do not have all required combinations but include an ELSE rule in the right column are considered complete tables, since the ELSE rule covers all missing combinations. However, its use, especially in computer-oriented projects, is not recommended, as it covers up inconsistencies and redundancies. In the absence of the ELSE rule, inconsistency occurs in a table when a number of its rules have comparable overall conditions but result in different actions or results. Redundancy also occurs when two or more rules in a table display or stress the same combination. Thus, to minimize redundancy, calculation of the required combinations should be made and no two rules should have the same combination.

Finally, regardless of the complexity of the problem at hand, the decision table should be of manageable size. Smaller tables are easier to read and comprehend and are relatively more complete and lacking in redundancy than the often unwieldy and data-loaded larger tables. Proper judgment as to size should be made as the details of the problems are gathered and the variables determined. Common sense, in this case, should lead to determining the size and number of tables that would best solve the problem.

SUMMARY

In preparing a computer program, special-purpose tools such as layout charts, grid charts, flowcharts, and decision tables are used by systems analysts and programmers to organize the details of the proposed project. The charts represent a written record and provide documentation for future reference.

Flowcharts are either system or program flowcharts. System flowcharts present the broad data flow and operations of the system; program flowcharts focus on the sequence of data transformation from the input- to the output-data structure. Basic and specialized symbols are used for developing both types of flowcharts. The symbols used are standardized through national and international efforts represented by the American National Standards Institute (ANSI) and the International Standards Organization (ISA).

The basic symbols used in describing or specifying computer program operations are input–output, processing, flowline, annotation, and terminal symbols. Looping and branching operations are represented by the decision (logic) symbol. Specialized input–output and process symbols for media or devices are often used for emphasizing a specific operation. A terminal symbol designates the beginning or end of a program. A connector symbol connects parts of a program together without drawing flowlines.

Flowcharting is an art and is time consuming. In preparing flowcharts, the important factors to consider are neatness, consistency, and clarity of details.

Compared to the flowchart, decision tables offer a more concise documentation tool and a simpler form of data analysis. They are designed around the programmer's logical thinking and are verbally oriented for managers. They are easy to learn and continue to function once the logic is developed.

Decision tables are classified by the type of information recorded in their entries. They are limited entry, extended entry, or mixed entry. Limited-entry tables are the most widely used and are ideally suited for computer-oriented applications. Extended-entry tables resemble conventional data tables and are best suited for problem solving. A mixed-entry table is a combination of rows with extended entries and rows with limited entries.

In constructing decision tables, every possible useful combination must be considered and covered by a separate rule in the table. The ELSE rule can be used to cover all missing combinations. In computer-oriented projects, however, its use is not recommended, since it may cover up inconsistencies and redundancies.

TERMS TO LEARN

Action entry
Action stub
Closed tables
Condition entry
Condition stub
Decision table
ELSE rule
Extended-entry table
Limited-entry table
Looping
Mixed-entry table
Open-end table
Program flowchart
Redundancy
System flowchart

QUESTIONS

1. What is the difference between a system flowchart and a program flowchart?
2. Prepare a program flowchart to instruct an out-of-town visitor to drive from the center of town to your school.
3. Explain briefly the following flowcharting symbols:
   a. Process
   b. Annotation
   c. Logic operation
   d. Interpage connector
   e. Terminal
4. Explain the advantage(s) of cross referencing a program flowchart.
5. What are the elements of a decision table?
6. Explain and illustrate the difference between limited-entry and extended-entry tables.
7. Show (by an example) how a mixed-entry table is constructed.
8. What is the difference between open-end and closed tables?
9. What rules should be followed in constructing decision tables?

SUGGESTED READING

ANSI, *Standard Flowchart Symbols and Their Use in Information Processing (X3.5)*. New York: American National Standards Institute, 1971.

BOHL, MARILYN. *Flowcharting Techniques*. Chicago: Science Research Associates, Inc., 1971.

CHAPIN, NED. "An Introduction to Decision Tables," *DPMA Quarterly*, III, April 1967, 2–23.

FARINA, M. V. *Flowcharting*. Englewood Cliffs, N.J.: Prentice-Hall, Inc., 1970.

GLEIM, G. A. *Program Flowcharting*. New York: Holt, Rinehart and Winston, Inc., 1970.

GOLDSTINE, H. H., and JOHN VON NEUMANN. *Planning and Coding Problems for an Electronic Computing Instrument*. New York: Van Nostrand Reinhold Company, 1947, Vols. I, II, and III.

HAIN, G., and K. HAIN. "Automatic Flowchart Design," *Proceedings of the Association of Computer Manufacturers 20th National Conference, 1965*. The Association, 1965, pp. 513–525.

KNUTH, D. F. "Computer-Drawn Flowcharts," *Communications of the Association of Computer Manufacturers*, VI, Sept. 1963, pp. 555–563.

LEWIS, F. D. "Evolution of Automatic Flowcharting Techniques." Unpublished IBM Internal Memorandum, March 5, 1969.

McInerney, T. F., and A. J. Volla. *A Student's Guide to Flowcharting*. Englewood Cliffs, N.J.: Prentice-Hall, Inc., 1973.

Sherman, P. M. "Flowtrace, a Computer Program for Flowcharting Programs," *Communications of the ACM,* IX, Dec. 1966, pp. 845–854.

Sidney, B. S. "Logic Flow Tables," *Journal of Data Management,* V, Dec. 1967, pp. 30–36.

program preparation

16

WHAT IS A COMPUTER PROGRAM?

STEPS IN PROGRAM PREPARATION

Problem Definition

Program Planning

Program Coding

machine-language coding

symbolic-language coding

higher-level language coding

Debugging and Testing

Documentation and Maintenance

PROGRAMMING SYSTEM AIDS

Utility Programs

Library Routines

Application Programs

Conversion Programs

Criteria for Evaluating Software Packages

An electronic computer is dependent on man. Although it simplifies his tasks and solves many of his problems, it cannot replace him. The extent of its aid, moreover, is limited to the experience and level of knowledge of the human programmer. To follow an old adage, "The stream can be no greater than its source." On that basis, this chapter provides an overall understanding of the problem-solving process and explains the steps involved in preparing and putting in operation computer programs. Like the links in a bicycle chain, each step is a link that, if weakened or detached, can hamper the effectiveness of the other links.

WHAT IS A COMPUTER PROGRAM?

The key to manipulating a computer system is the specialized field of programming and the programmers who perform this function. The term *program* is neither new nor applicable solely to computers. Any formal social, political, or economic activity is carried out within a preplanned program. A pertinent example is a commencement program listing the activities or steps to be taken during the commencement. The main activities include the following:

1. Processional.
2. National anthem.
3. Opening remarks.
4. Main speaker.

5. Speeches of those awarded honors.
6. Awarding of diplomas.
7. Recessional.

Like a commencement program, a *computer program* consists of a *set of detailed, sequential, and clearly phrased instructions that direct the computer to perform predetermined tasks.* It must offer complete instructions in the proper order, but must also be brief enough to be considered efficient. The brevity of the program depends on the type of application. The term *sequential* means that the instructions are to be followed in the exact order in which they are presented. In the example of the commencement program, the diplomas could not have been awarded without the speeches of the honor graduates. Their speeches, in turn, could not be delivered before that of the main speaker. The main speaker could not deliver his speech until after the national anthem and the opening remarks had been completed. None of these things could be done until the completion of the processional, which set the stage for their occurrence. In this example the program began with the processional and ended with the awarding of the diplomas. The seniors to be graduated can be thought of as "input," and the awarding of the diplomas as "output." The processional can be considered the "input device." The activities in between "input" and "output" represent the "processing" steps that lead the audience and the speakers (the "computer") through the exercises ("operation") in an orderly manner, so that a successful commencement is conducted.

It should be kept in mind that an accurately produced program depends on the way a computer functions and the job it is directed to process. By analogy, a vacationing motorist would need to know where he wanted to go before a local resident could give him accurate directions as to how to get there. Also, since computers differ from one another, the preparation of accurate instructions is more easily accomplished when the programmer has a basic understanding and sound knowledge of the computer to be programmed. Using a similar analogy, the directions given to a vacationing motorist are likely to be different from those given to a truck driver, even though both are heading for the same destination.

Once the computer has been provided with a valid program, it becomes self-operative and should require no human intervention during processing. The computer executes one instruction at a time in a single path or, in the case of alternative instructions designed to handle a special subroutine, it handles that alternative path for proper execution. When the last instruction is executed, the computer stops automatically unless it is directed to branch back to a specific area in the program. In the latter case, the program is used again for processing additional data.

Computer programming demands skill and knowledge of the subject matter. The amount of skill is related to the aptitude level and experience of the human programmer. The more experince and the higher the aptitude a programmer possesses, the more likely it is that he will succeed in presenting a factual, informative, clear, and otherwise well-prepared program. Although academic background in the fundamental fields of finance, production, accounting, marketing, and management is highly desirable, it is not absolutely necessary. Many successful programmers do not have a college education, but have gained knowledge in those fields by experience. However, knowledge of the principles of management and experience in dealing with people will brighten the programmer's prospects for becoming the manager of his department.

STEPS IN PROGRAM PREPARATION

Preparing a program for processing a given application requires a series of key steps. The overall steps considered here are (1) problem definition, (2) program planning and coding, (3) assembly or compilation, (4) debugging and testing, and (5) documentation and maintenance (Fig. 16-1).

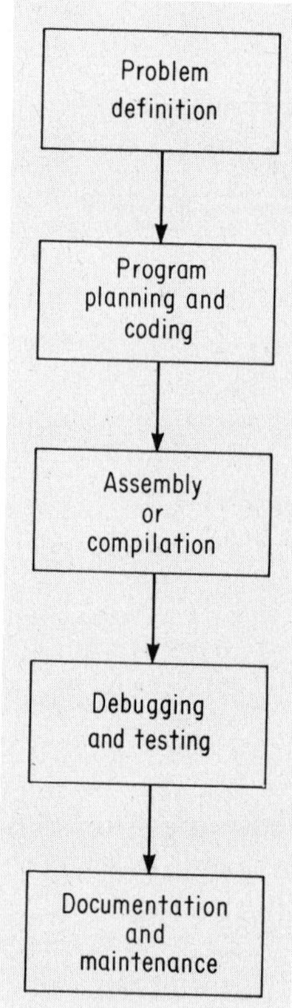

FIGURE 16-1. Steps in program preparation

Management expects from a computer system the production of useful output information for decision making and guidance. Problem definition, a subject of systems analysis and design,[1] involves the advance determination of what is needed as input for obtaining the desired information as output. In formulating a statement of the problem, the systems analyst or programmer analyst[2] must be familiar with the requirements of the application and how the data are expected to pass from one stage to the next. He takes into consideration key factors such as the following:

1. The form of input data available (handwritten, typed, etc.).
2. The specific input medium to be used and its format.
3. Ways of structuring input documents for efficient processing.
4. Ways of transcribing source data into machine-oriented form.
5. The arithmetic and logical choices to be considered within the rules and guidelines of the business problem.
6. The manner of handling normal situations and exceptions in the program.
7. The final form of the output data—that is, whether or not it must be produced in report form or stored in a secondary-storage device for reference.

As a first step in program preparation, then, it is important to produce a clear, detailed definition of the type of information needed and to determine the objective of each step in the program. The following quotation from *Alice in Wonderland* brings out the basic idea that the objective must be set before effective action can be taken:

> "Cheshire Puss . . . would you tell me, please, which way I ought to go from here?"
> "That depends a good deal on where you want to get to," said the Cat.
> "I don't much care where—" said Alice.
> "Then it doesn't matter which way you go," said the Cat.

Such aimless wandering cannot be condoned in problem solving because it is costly and time consuming. A sufficient amount of time must

[1] The other steps in systems analysis and design include designing a system for data collection, processing, and dissemination, and specifying required computer runs and procedures. Details on systems analysis and design have been presented in Chapter 14.

[2] Depending on the specific computer installation, problem definition either is under the jurisdiction of a systems analyst, who designs the entire process and also does the programming portion, or is assigned to a programmer who has basic knowledge about systems design and who is called a programmer analyst. Rather than have one person do both systems design and programming, many installations assign these functions separately to two people, on the basis of their qualifications and experience.

be allowed for defining the specific problem, as well as for gathering together the specific information to be used in its solution. If the objective is not clearly defined, or if the goal is determined too hurriedly, the steps followed will lead to meaningless results. The errors made in this phase usually result from failure to account for all possible exceptions, rather than from a poor method of handling one step. Thus, an exception that is inadvertently skipped can be costly to rectify in a later stage of program development.

When the goal has been determined, the staff responsible for its achievement should keep in mind the capabilities and limitations of the particular computer system, since the type of output information desired must be within the capabilities of the system. Through experience and observation on the job, one can determine the details of what the computer installation can and cannot do. If such an installation is the wrong type or size or was acquired by the firm without regard for the value of the computer in helping to do repetitive work, the firm will have an expensive layout that cannot be justified. It becomes entirely purposeless when management does not receive the hoped-for information. The computer is not to blame, because this is the result of bad human judgment. In such a case, the computer is the "victim," not the "villain."

Systems design, the degree of experience of the programmers, and other factors involved in problem definition are all closely related to the success or failure of a computer data-processing system. The failure of the system to produce effective results is due either to the inability of humans to define precisely the organization's need for it, or the failure of those in charge to fully utilize its capabilities.

Program Planning

Having defined the problem, the programmer uses various preprinted layouts to record information dealing with the number and type of records of input files and the manner in which data are to appear at various processing stages. With these layouts as a program guideline, the programmer proceeds to describe the processing sequence of the operation by *program flowcharts, decision tables,* or both, by several stages. Although the programmer's job is to write down precise instructions for each processing step, flowcharting generally begins at a broad (macro) level of "general logic," followed by detailed (micro) flowcharts of portions of the program.

Program planning often involves dividing the program into a number of modules or subroutines and determining the manner in which they should be tested. A *subroutine* is a set of instructions that varies in size, ranging from a few to several hundred instructions. When in operation, the subroutine derives its information from the main routine, performs the required steps within its capacity, and then sends the results back to the program.

Thus, subroutines are programs within a program that determine the specific order of the subroutine execution. This arrangement offers several advantages:

1. Makes possible the standardization of common functions, which can then be used in any program when needed.
2. Reduces programming cost by eliminating duplication of common instructions in each program.
3. Cuts down on debugging cost and time, since it is easier to locate and correct errors by subroutine than by program.
4. Improves program maintenance, since only subroutines that are subject to modification need to be altered or updated.

Program Coding

MACHINE-LANGUAGE CODING. Writing a set of computer instructions in a language that will cause the execution of certain steps is called coding. Coding can be performed in several languages, ranging from the absolute machine language, to symbolic assembly language, to higher-level (procedure- or problem-oriented) languages. Writing a program in machine language is complicated and often tedious. In early computers the programmer had to work with a string of numbers that represented each instruction's operation code and operand. Furthermore, he had to remember a relatively long list of code numbers representing operation codes, and keep track of the storage location of both data and instructions. This type of procedure was time consuming, expensive, and subject to error.

SYMBOLIC-LANGUAGE CODING. Since the early 1950s, programmers have been working on easier ways of transcribing source programs into machine-language programs. This has led to the development of various programming aids, often referred to as *processor* or *translating programs.* The general idea is that the processor program translates the recorded coding of the programmer's English-like (symbolic) program into a machine-readable language, culminating in the *object* program, which is later used for actual processing. Symbolic names are codes that aid the programmer's memory about certain referenced data or program instructions.

The first level of language described for a class of processor programs is called the symbolic (mnemonic) assembly, or one-for-one language. As the latter term implies, the characteristic of this language is that there is one line of coding for each machine instruction as it finally appears in the output program. Examples of symbolic language are AUTOCODER (IBM), SPS (Symbolic Programming System), and S-4 (UNIVAC).

The use of a symbolic language eases the chore of program coding and improves program preparation, since letter symbols can now be substituted for numeric machine-language codes, and the task of assigning and keeping track of instruction address is turned over to the computer. Figure 16-2 presents a summary list of symbolic and machine operation codes used in the IBM 360 and 370 computer series.

Assembly and production runs. A symbolic-language (source) program is converted into a machine-language (object) program by a proc-

Command Name	Symbolic Code	Operation Code
Input–output		
Halt input–output	HIO	9E
Start input–output	SIO	9C
Test input–output	TIO	9D
Data movement and manipulation		
Convert to binary	CVB	4F
Convert to decimal	CVD	4E
Edit	ED	DE
Execute	EX	44
Load	L	58
Load	LR	18
Load address	LA	41
Load and test	LTR	12
Load complement	LCR	13
Move	MVI	92
Move characters	MVC	D2
Move numerics	MVN	D1
Move zones	MVZ	D3
Store	ST	50
Store character	STC	42
Translate	TR	DC
Translate and test	TRT	DD
Arithmetic		
Add	A	5A
Add	AR	1A
Divide	D	5D
Divide	DR	1D
Multiply	M	5C
Multiply	MR	1C
Subtract	S	5B
Subtract	SR	1B
Logic		
Compare	C	59
Compare	CR	19
Compare logical	CL	55
Transfer of control		
Branch on condition	BC	47
Branch on condition	BCR	07
Supervisor call	SVC	0A

FIGURE 16-2. Selected names and codes for the IBM 360 and 370 computer systems

essor package called an *assembly program.* The assembly program (provided by the computer manufacturer) is coded in such a way that it instructs the computer in detail about the appropriate translation routine. The steps followed in the assembly routine are illustrated in Figure 16-3 and summarized as follows:

1–2. Each instruction on the coding sheet is punched in a separate card. Data are punched into the card in specific locations as they appear on the coding sheet. Next, the punched source program is fed through the computer to produce a listing. The programmer checks the listing for clerical and logical errors.

3. The assembly program (stored on disk, tape, or cards) is first read into the computer.
4. During the assembly run, the assembly program takes control and reads the source program, one instruction at a time.
5. The object program (output) begins to develop in the form of a punched deck, a paper tape, a magnetic tape, a printed listing, or a combination thereof. It should be remembered that up to this point no problem data are processed.
6. The object program is read into the computer, thus initiating the production run.
7. Input data recorded on an input medium (punched cards, magnetic tape, etc.) are read into the computer under the control of the object program. This step makes up the production run. When processing is completed, the object program is filed for future reference.

HIGHER-LEVEL LANGUAGE CODING. Symbolic language, although a step ahead of machine language, has several limitations: (1) it is time consuming and tedious to handle; (2) it is machine oriented, in that it is designed for use on a specific computer make and model, which means that recoding is necessary when a new computer is introduced; and (3) detailed knowledge of the computer's processor is necessary for a programmer to successfully use its symbolic language.

The introduction of *macroinstruction* (each instruction produces several lines of machine language instructions), has relieved the programmer from having to write an instruction for each operation. Also, *input–output control systems* (IOCS) using macroinstruction routines are used to provide greater efficiency in (1) reading and writing records, (2) scheduling the demands on the input–output devices for maximum use, and (3) identifying and correcting errors within the minimum time limit.

The trend in computer programming has been more in the direction of higher-level (procedure- and problem-oriented) languages than of symbolic (machine-oriented assembly) languages. In a procedure-oriented language such as COBOL, FORTRAN, and PL/1, the program-

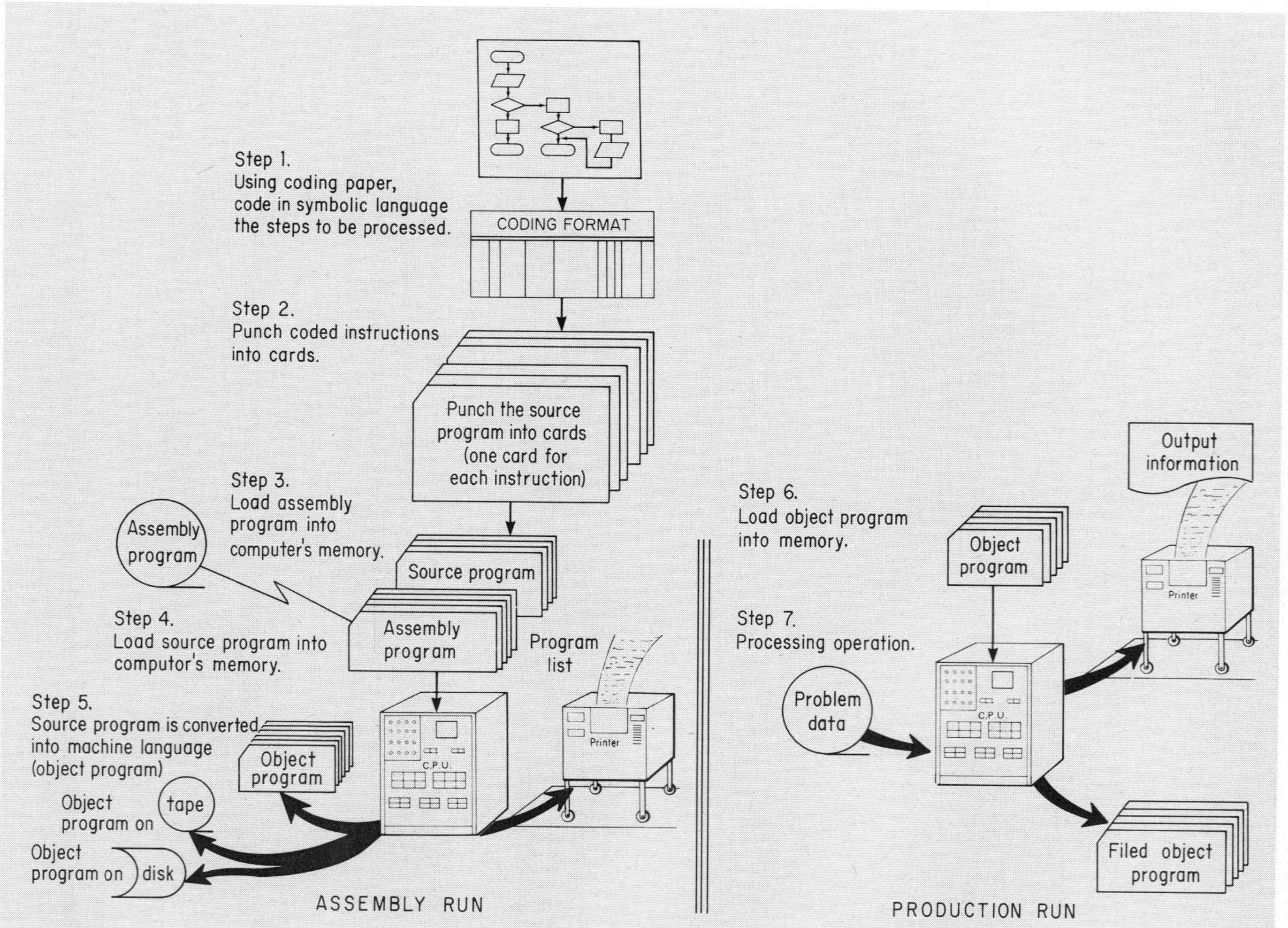
Step 1.
Using coding paper, code in symbolic language the steps to be processed.
CODING FORMAT
Step 2.
Punch coded instructions into cards.
Punch the source program into cards (one card for each instruction)
Step 3.
Load assembly program into computer's memory.
Assembly program
Source program
Step 4.
Load source program into computor's memory.
Assembly program
Program list
Printer
Step 5.
Source program is converted into machine language (object program)
Object program
C.P.U.
Object program on
tape
Object program on
disk
ASSEMBLY RUN
Step 6.
Load object program into memory.
Object program
Output information
Printer
Step 7.
Processing operation.
Problem data
C.P.U.
Filed object program
PRODUCTION RUN

FIGURE 16-3. *Steps in the symbolic assembly and production runs*

mer uses the language to describe the routines required to solve the problem.[3] Unlike assembly languages, which require the programmer to adapt his thinking to the particular computer, higher-level languages help the programmer by adapting the computer to his thinking. In writing a program the programmer is not concerned about the particular computer on which the project will be run. Thus the language he uses is machine independent, and, although each computer has a separate compiler, a program written in compiler language can be run on different computer systems without much difficulty.

Evaluation of higher-level languages relates to programming, maintenance, and computer-running-time cost. Compared to symbolic language, the use of a higher-level language means relatively less time (therefore, lower cost) spent on program coding, debugging, documentation, and maintenance, coupled with the efficiency of the compiler in producing an object program ready for processing. Furthermore, the higher-level language is easier to learn than a machine-oriented language, and is adaptable to other computers with minor coding changes. This means that machine-oriented and symbolic assembly languages are used primarily in (1) second-generation computers with inadequate compilers, (2) small computers with limited primary storage or with primary storage too costly to accommodate a compiler, and (3) those problems which require special coding for proper handling. With the advent of fourth-generation computers, advances in hardware storage, and improvements in compiler efficiency, it seems very likely that more and more programs will be written in higher-level languages.

Compiling and production runs. A higher-level language carries with it certain rules and specifications. Each instruction is written in a predetermined form and structure, and the terms it contains are also predefined. Precompiling preparation requires punching each of the procedure-oriented program instructions (in the coding sheet) into a separate card. Once they are fed through the computer, a listing of the source program is produced for error checking and verification.

Next a compiler (translator) is provided for reading and translating the source program into an object program. Once it has been generated, the object program is combined with certain prewritten compiler library routines and is loaded in memory for the processing of "live" input data. Figure 16-4 illustrates the steps taken in a compiler language routine for developing a compiling and a production run.

Debugging and Testing

To *debug* means to locate and correct any errors (bugs) that have been made in preparing a program. Human errors in programming are not

[3] By contrast, a problem-oriented language describes the problem itself, in that the language used approximates the language of the problem to be solved by the computer. An example of a problem-oriented language is RPG, which will be discussed in Chapter 21.

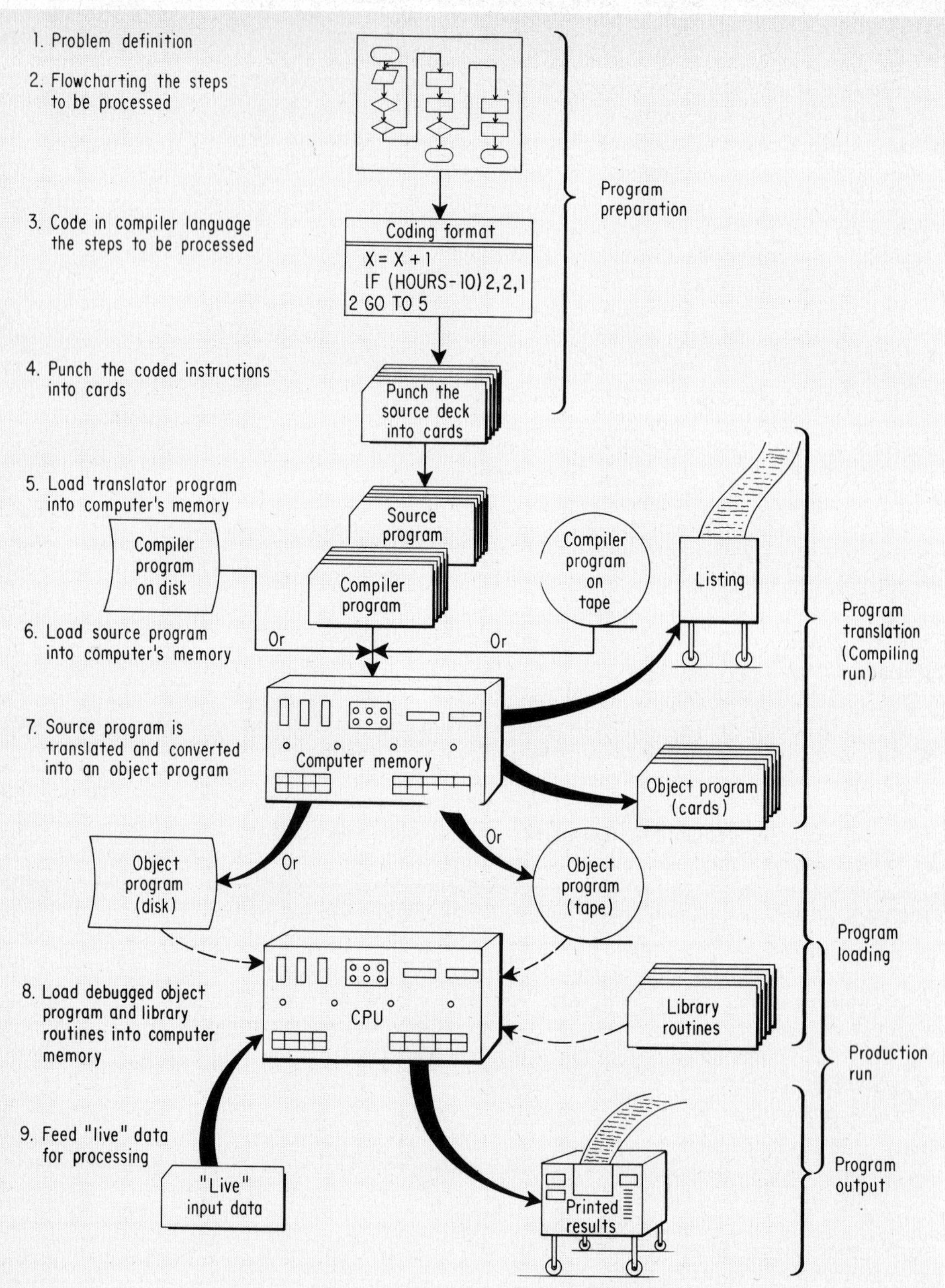
1. Problem definition
2. Flowcharting the steps to be processed
3. Code in compiler language the steps to be processed
Coding format
X = X + 1
IF (HOURS-10) 2,2,1
2 GO TO 5
4. Punch the coded instructions into cards
Punch the source deck into cards
Program preparation
5. Load translator program into computer's memory
Source program
Compiler program on disk
Compiler program
Compiler program on tape
Listing
6. Load source program into computer's memory
Or
Or
Program translation (Compiling run)
7. Source program is translated and converted into an object program
Computer memory
Object program (cards)
Or
Or
Object program (disk)
Object program (tape)
Program loading
8. Load debugged object program and library routines into computer memory
CPU
Library routines
Production run
9. Feed "live" data for processing
"Live" input data
Printed results
Program output

FIGURE 16-4. Steps in a compiler language routine

rare and increase with the complexity of the program. In some cases, a complex program takes days or even weeks to debug thoroughly. Thus, minimum delay in processing can be maintained and valuable time and money saved if the program has been written accurately and debugged systematically throughout the various stages of program preparation.

In debugging, two major types of errors may be detected: (1) logical errors and (2) clerical errors. A *logical error* occurs as a result of either poor interpretation of a problem area or lack of knowledge of some part of the data-processing setup. For example, failure to take into consideration the overtime rate requirement is considered a logical error. In the absence of instructions to control this element in the program, the computer computes gross pay by multiplying an employee's reported 65 hours for the week by the regular hourly rate. The result of this calculation is obviously inaccurate and is caused by an oversight on the part of the programmer to take overtime rates and hours into account.

A *clerical error* often occurs in programming, especially in the coding stage. A programmer, for instance, may inadvertently assign two unrelated values to the same memory location, or the wrong address of the data involved in processing a certain application. An example of the latter case would be assigning address 7128 instead of 7218. Automatic programming reduces the error of assigning more than one character to a given address. When the assignment of addresses to data is made manually, use of the debugging technique to locate and correct all types of errors within the shortest time possible is especially important. Again, in this case, the cost factor is of importance. If debugging causes too great a delay before the program can be made ready for processing, the results obtained may not be delivered in time to be used effectively by management.

To simplify the debugging routine, most assembly and compiler programs are designed to detect and analyze errors through printout messages describing the nature of the error and its location in the source program. Among the more common errors detected in compilation are invalid characters or statements punched in the source deck, undefined symbols, incorrect operation codes, illegal names, improperly sequenced statements, spelling errors, and labels omitted in the program. *Postcompilation* listing of the program can also be produced; this reflects the status of the program in core storage and any errors that might have been detected. The programmer uses this listing to modify the program in whatever manner is necessary for eliminating all errors.

Once the program has been debugged and errors eliminated, the next logical step is to test its accuracy and effectiveness. The program is loaded into the computer; then test data (normally made up of representative data, unusual exceptions, and inappropriate data to check on the capability of the program to handle errors) are loaded in the input device. The computer is started and the program begins to process the data. Answers to data being processed for testing purposes must have been worked out in advance by the programmer or his supervisor so that they can be compared with those arrived at by the computer. If the results match, the program is considered clear of errors. "Live" input data can then be processed with confidence. However, if the answers differ, the program must be analyzed and worked on further. Overlooking one factor, however minor it may be, at any program preparation stage will greatly amplify the error at the testing stage. In a complex program that includes hundreds of instructions, the search for an error or errors is as difficult and time consuming as searching for a needle in a haystack. Great patience, experience, and technical know-how are necessary before a program of large size can be put to use in a reasonable length of time. The programmer should review the program for the correction of logical, as well as clerical, errors. Often, a *storage dump* (a "snapshot" of the computer's internal storage) is ordered to search for any logical errors that might be causing invalid output. Other methods used include tracing the program through the computer console, one instruction at a time, or calling for a printout of the contents of the computer's registers after each operation. Both alternatives are expensive, in that much computer time is taken in tracing errors.

When the program is completed, it is stored for future use. If future input data pose exceptions for which the program is unprepared, it should be modified or changed sufficiently to handle the "new" input data.

Documentation and Maintenance

Once a program becomes operational, some form of program documentation should be kept on file. A documentation record is essentially a "carbon copy" of the work performed on the program. The life of the program is independent of the time committed by the programmer to his employer. In the event that the programmer involved is transferred or later resigns, good documentation puts someone else in a position to answer questions and to modify or otherwise service the program. Thus, documentation simplifies program revision, provides key information for answering various inquiries about the status and operation of the program, contributes to educating incoming personnel, and guides the console operator by providing pertinent operating instructions.

Some specific details included in a program-documentation package are

1. Preflowcharting data.
2. A problem definition statement and the methodology used in program preparation.
3. A copy of the master program flowchart and decision tables (if used).
4. A detailed description of input data preparation.

5. A master list of details in connection with the record layout and code forms used in writing the program.
6. An adequate program-run manual, listing the instructions the console operator must follow in running the program.
7. A sample of tested data and their output.
8. Storage dumps and diagnostic messages, if any.

With the availability of the foregoing details, the data-processing manager can easily assign periodic modifications to a qualified programmer, thus minimizing the need for a major program overhaul. Program maintenance can affect any or all steps of program development. It can be so involved that some programmers have a full-time commitment to this area.

From the foregoing stages it can be concluded that no meaningful result can be realized without the creative and ingenious efforts of human beings. Although an indispensable tool, the computer cannot perform the many chores it is programmed to do without the advance preparation of a valid, well-debugged program. In this respect, man remains the "master" and the computer the "slave."

PROGRAMMING SYSTEM AIDS

In addition to the software available from the computer manufacturer, a broad range of software is also available from software concerns. Most computer users belong to one of several computer users' organizations that maintain and share whole libraries of programs written by the users themselves. Other than symbolic assembly systems and compilers, programming aids available to the user include utility programs, library routines, applications, and conversion programs.

Utility Programs

Many common jobs recur frequently. These are serviced by a set of general-purpose programs called utility programs or *utilities.* Their function is to aid in the production of programs for the computer system. Some of these include:

1. **Memory dump:** used to write out complete areas of primary storage, up to and including the entire memory capacity.
2. **Program loader:** introduces a new program into memory.
3. **File-conversion routines:** the use of large-capacity random-access files requires the user to copy the information from these files onto magnetic tapes with some regularity for protection purposes. With so much of a firm's active data in these files, it is necessary to be

sure that the files can be reconstructed if a major stoppage occurs. Three common file-conversion routines are tape duplicate, card-to-tape, and tape-to-disk.

4. **A program to trace the step-by-step operation** of a program.
5. **Sort and merge programs.**
6. **Simulators:** routines that run on one computer, imitating the operation of another computer.
7. **Housekeeping routines:** designed to set storage to a certain condition or to initiate placing of data into or out of storage. Clear storage, punch storage, and print storage are examples of the more common housekeeping routines.

Naturally, there are many other utilities; however, the foregoing list should give the reader an idea as to the kind of work they do. Almost all these utilities take a common form: each is supplied as an assembled program, ready to run. The user puts it to work through either a well-defined console operation or a combination of the console and a control card that contains initiating data. For example, the memory-dump program usually requires the programmer to specify the locations in storage that are the boundaries of the area to be written. These are punched into specific columns of a control card. After the memory-dump program is loaded, the card is read, the program is initiated, and the printout takes place.

Library Routines

Library routines are program segments or a standard sequence of instructions that directs the computer to carry out a specific calculation. The routine is normally a mathematical or statistical computation (e.g., calculating the standard deviation of a set of numbers) provided by the computer manufacturer or developed by the user. When that specialized program segment is inserted in a specific area(s) of the user's source program and assembled along with the rest of the program, it is called an *open subroutine* (Fig. 16-5). However, when it is attached to the user's main routine, but remains a separate program, it is referred to as a *closed subroutine* (Fig. 16-6).

It should be noted that a closed subroutine requires programming only once, since it can be entered several times during processing. Furthermore, since control can be transferred to the closed subroutine from various places in the main program as needed, some return instruction must be included for returning to the main program every time the subroutine is used (Fig. 16-6).

Application Programs

Application programs are ready-to-use programs, many of which are written by computer manufacturers in the form of program libraries and made available to the user. They are designed to solve specific problems

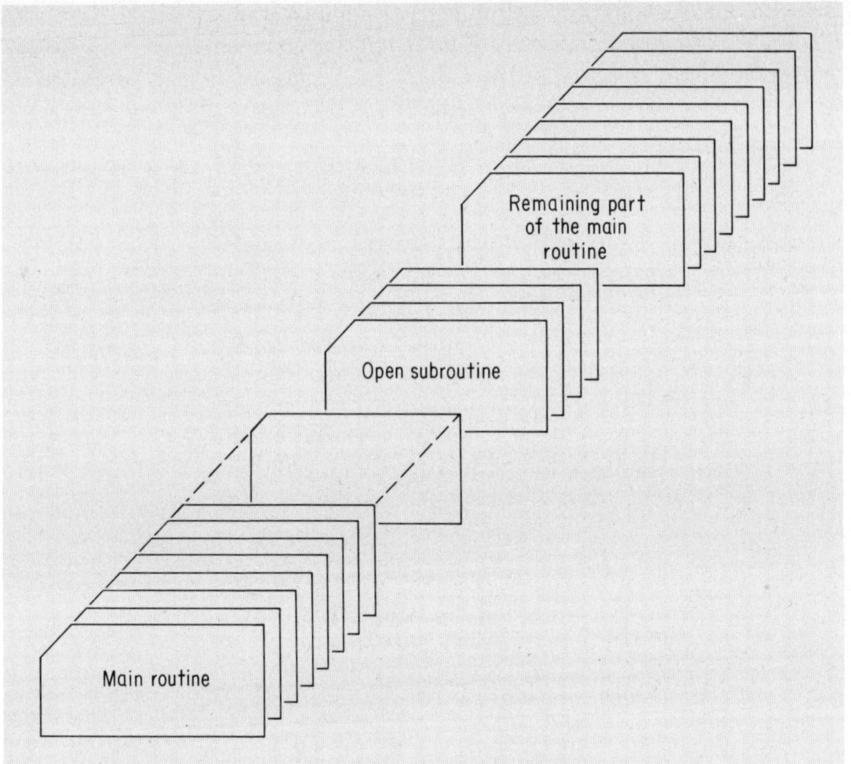

FIGURE 16-5. Computer program using an open subroutine

FIGURE 16-6. Computer program using a closed subroutine

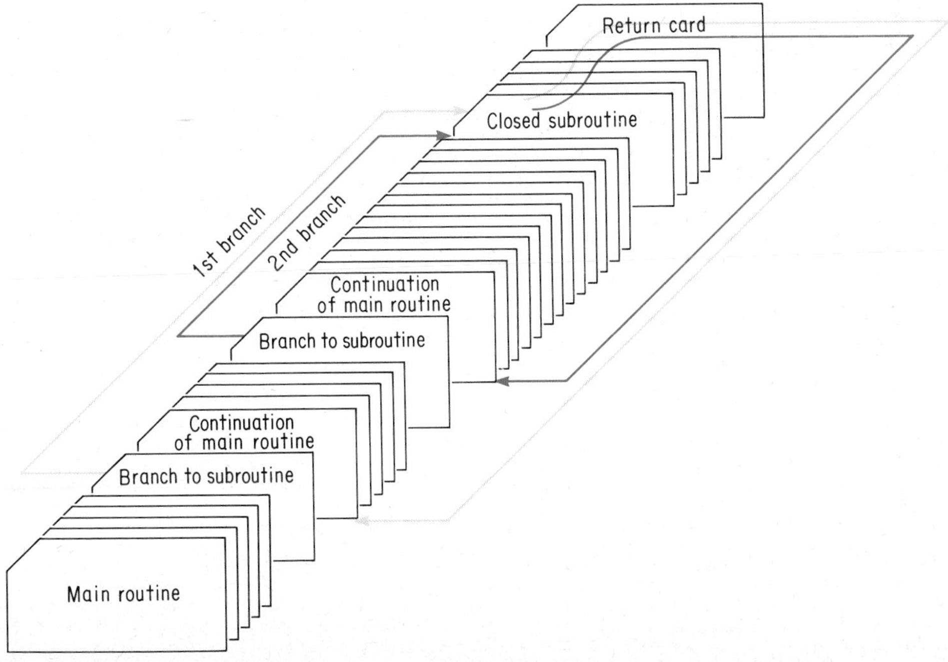

common to many users, such as linear programming, sales analysis, and so on. A new trend initiated by various software houses and independent agencies is geared to developing application programs encompassing a whole industry.

Conversion Programs

Computer manufacturers offer new computer users programs designed to assist in converting the programs used by the existing system into the new system. Some conversion programs code instructions for the new computer from the machine-level coding of the old computer. Other programs designed for the new computer accept programs for the old computer by interpreting the old instructions and causing the computer to produce an equivalent set of instructions through a stored microprogram designed to do the conversion. Although no conversion programs relieve the programmer completely from the conversion routine, they are, no doubt, time-saving devices that cannot be overlooked.

Criteria for Evaluating Software Packages

The user is often faced with the decision of whether to develop his own software package or to buy it from outside. Either alternative carries with it certain costs and constraints. In developing one's own package, the programming staff needs a complete layout of what is to be done; that is,

1. Layout of input and output records for storage media such as magnetic tape or disks.
2. Flowcharts showing the input and output equipment to be used.
3. Specifications explaining how the various types of records are to be handled.
4. Miscellaneous information related to equipment capacities and operating system standards.

Of a programmer's time, approximately 33 percent is devoted to designing program logic, 20 percent to coding in mnemonic language, 33 percent to debugging and testing, and the remaining time to documentation. Thus designing one's own package can be very costly, especially if the department is already committed to ongoing projects.

In considering a ready-made package, on the other hand, several factors should be evaluated. Among others are the following:

1. **Package cost.** There is a wide range in package costs, depending on the quality, reliability, and expandability of the package. The purchase price should be weighed against the approximate cost of in-house package development and the availability of qualified

talent for the job. When the need for the package is critical, it is often the case that purchasing a ready-to-use error-free package is the best decision under the circumstances. In purchasing a package, the user should check on what the seller is including in the quoted price. Some sellers, for example, do not include personnel training, modifications, installation, and/or supplying technical and operating staff in the initial price. These items can be costly and have to be carefully looked into before a final commitment is made.

2. **System configuration requirements.** The user should also determine the minimum equipment configuration and the type and speed of the input–output devices needed to efficiently operate the package. A major change in the system to accommodate the package can cause prohibitive costs and unnecessary delays.
3. **Expandability.** For a software package to be effective in serving the user's needs, it should be designed to adapt to a particular installation and to be expandable so that it can meet the system's projected needs. One way of verifying the performance of the package is to talk to actual users or, if this is not possible, to have the supplier conduct a demonstration at the user's own site, using existing system configuration and sample data. Although most on-site, trial installations require a fee, it is a secondary expense considering the benefits derived from such an exposure.
4. **Technical support.** In evaluating a package, the user should find out how much support (in the way of on-site training, maintenance, etc.) is included in the package. For most commercially available packages, basic technical support is offered to the user at no additional cost.

In the final analysis, the user chooses the supplier whose reputation stands behind a quality package offered at a competitive price and backed by all the necessary services and technical support. No alternative can be more attractive.

SUMMARY

In this chapter we have explained the key steps in preparing a computer program. They are problem definition, program planning, program coding, assembling or compiling, debugging and testing, and, finally, documenting the results.

The programmer begins with a clear definition of the type of information needed, followed by the preparation of program flowcharts and, if necessary, decision tables. In addition, he looks into the feasibility of dividing the program into modules and proceeds to code the program in an assembly or a higher-level language. When the source program is completed, it is assembled or compiled to produce an object program for processing the application at hand. Assemblers and compilers are special translating programs designed to convert symbolic language into machine language.

Before "live" processing takes place, it is normally expected that the object program be subjected to a debugging and testing phase so that all errors (logical and clerical) be eliminated. To do so means checking manually through the program, checking the validity and accuracy of the program by processing test data, and finally running it in parallel with "live" data. Finally, all the key information pertaining to the preparation of the program must be documented for future reference.

There are two major levels of symbolic coding. The lower-level symbolic assembly language is more oriented to machine language. Each symbolic instruction is equivalent to a machine instruction after compilation. The higher-level language is designed to help the programmer concentrate on describing the problem to be solved. In addition to being machine independent, higher-level coded instructions after compilation generate many more machine instructions.

The trend in coding is toward greater use of higher-level languages, which are easier to use, are more efficient in terms of reduced programming time, and provide for better documentation than lower-level symbolic languages. The primary advantage of lower-level languages is in storage utilization and machine running time.

A number of program system aids are available to the user from computer manufacturers, software houses, and independent agencies. Among others are utility programs, library subroutines, applications, and conversion programs. The purpose behind these aids is to avoid programming duplication and to make it easier for the programmer to handle the more complex aspects of his job.

TERMS TO LEARN

Assembler	Library routine
Coding	Problem-oriented language
Compiler	Procedure-oriented language
Debugging	Storage dump
Documentation	Subroutine
Flowchart	Utility program

QUESTIONS

1. Why is problem definition essential in preparing a computer program?
2. Explain the difference between machine language and symbolic assembly language. What advantages does one language have over the other?

3. What steps are involved in assembly and production runs? How do they differ from compilation and production runs?
4. Distinguish between a procedure-oriented language and symbolic language. What advantage(s) does each language offer?
5. Explain the debugging and testing routine in program preparation.
6. How are errors handled? Explain.
7. Why should debugged programs be documented?
8. What specific items are normally included in a program-documentation file?

SUGGESTED READING

GLASS, R. L. "An Elementary Discussion of Compiler/Interpreter Writing," *Computing Surveys,* March 1969, pp. 55–60.

GRAY, M., and K. R. LONDON. *Documentation Standards.* Princeton, N.J.: Auerbach Publishers, Inc., 1969.

HARRISON, W. L. "Program Testing," *Journal of Data Management,* Dec. 1969, pp. 30–33.

HEAD, R. V. *A Guide to Packaged Systems.* New York: John Wiley & Sons, Inc., 1971.

JUDD, D. R. "Program Testing and Validation," *Computer Bulletin,* March 1967, pp. 28–32.

LEE, J. A. N. *The Anatomy of a Compiler.* New York: Van Nostrand Reinhold Company, 1967.

NAFTOLZ, S. M. "How to Pick a Programming Language," *Data Processing Digest,* Nov. 1966, pp. 1–14.

RIGGS, ROBERT. "Computer Systems Maintenance," *Datamation,* Nov. 1969, pp. 227ff.

COBOL concepts

17

LANGUAGE ELEMENTS

Symbols

Reserved Words

Level Numbers

Programmer-Defined Words

Literals

Pictures

PROGRAM STRUCTURE

Divisions

Sections

Paragraphs

Entries

PROGRAM-CODING SHEET AND ENTRY-RECORDING SPECIFICATIONS

PROGRAM CONTENTS

Identification Division

Environment Division

Input–Output Control

Data Division

file section

working-storage section

Procedure Division

program comments—note

input–output

data movement—move

arithmetic

program instruction execution control

COBOL is an acronym for *common business-oriented language* —a high-level procedure-oriented application.[1] The title explains the general purpose of this unique language. It is "common" in that it provides one common language for all computers by using standard language elements in standard entry sheets. Although there are various versions to suit specific computers, the similarities of COBOL systems far exceed the dissimilarities.

COBOL is "business-oriented" in the following ways:

1. It allows program instructions to be constructed in paragraph- and sentence-like form, using words encountered in business situations.
2. Programs are written in English to communicate data-processing procedures to businessmen as well as to serve as source programs for computers. For example, the COBOL sentence MULTIPLY QUANTITY BY PRICE GIVING TOTAL PRICE is self-explanatory and easy to understand.
3. It is particularly applicable to business (rather than scientific) data-processing problems.

Since it is a machine-independent language, the programmer is more concerned with the layout of data records and the media used in their recording than in specifying operation codes and the handling of registers.

No single company can claim full credit for the creation of the COBOL language. Several users and computer manufacturers (including IBM) contributed to its development. Unlike other languages, which are

[1] COBOL is pronounced *ko-ball.*

dated to a particular computer system or generation, COBOL's machine-independent nature has permitted updating by new developments in the computer field. The Conference on Data Systems Languages (CODASYL) regularly revises and updates COBOL specifications.

Finally, a COBOL program's English-language feature means a relatively limited need for documentation. A program written in a machine or symbolic language often requires a time-consuming supplementary writeup or documentation of what it does and how it does certain routines. The documentation needed in COBOL only involves occasional remarks or notes added to the overall program.

LANGUAGE ELEMENTS

The COBOL language makes use of six elements: (1) symbols, (2) reserved words, (3) level numbers, (4) programmer-defined words, (5) literals, and (6) pictures. The first three elements are predefined in fixed sets and must be used without alteration. The last three elements may be defined by the programmer within specified rules.

Symbols

Symbols are selected characters that have a special meaning for the COBOL compiler. Some symbols are used in testing data conditions; others become a part of arithmetic formulas; others are used in punctuating program entries. These symbols are as follows:

Symbol	Meaning
=	Is equal to
>	Is greater than
<	Is less than
( )	Left and right parentheses

Condition Symbols

Punctuation Symbols

Symbol	Meaning	Operation
.	Period	Terminates entries
,	Comma	Separates clauses or operands
;	Semicolon	Separates clauses
'	Apostrophe	Encloses nonnumeric literals
( )	Left and right parentheses	Enclose subscripts

Symbol	Meaning	Operation
+	Plus	Addition
—	Minus	Subtraction
*	Times	Multiplication
/	Divided by	Division
* *	Raise to the power of	Exponentiation
=	Makes equal to	Used in an arithmetic formula
( )	Left and right parentheses	Used in enclosing expressions or variables

Arithmetic Symbols

Reserved Words

A reserved word represents a particular meaning and is used for a specified purpose. The programmers can choose the appropriate words for his program from a list of over 250 words. No change in either their meaning, spelling, or definition is allowed. Also, a word must not be duplicated in any programmer-defined names. Examples of some reserved words and their special purposes are

Reserved Words	Purpose
ADD	Specifies action to be taken
COMPUTATIONAL-3[2]	Denotes a specific function
ENVIRONMENT	Specifies a program unit
PICTURE	Identifies a part or parts of an entry
ZERO	Represents a data value (zero)

Level Numbers

Level numbers [3] are used to indicate the level of various data items in relation to others in the program. The numbers used and their functions are

[2] Note that a reserved word may be alphabetic or numeric and may have a hyphen. That is, COMPUTATIONAL 3 is not a reserved word, but COMPUTATIONAL-3 is. All reserved words as well as statements are written in capital letters, since lowercase alphabetic characters are not produced by the key punch.

[3] A level number is optional; when used, it is written as the first element of an entry and is followed either by the reserved word FILLER or by a programmer-defined name.

Level-Number	Function
01	Always assigned to represent the data record as a whole
01–49	Used for indicating the level of data items making up the record
77	Designates the data item or items that are not a part of the data record; that is, independent data items
88	Written in entries that represent names to predetermined values to be assumed by data items

```
       01  DATA-RECORD.
           02  RECORD-IDENTIFICATION.
               03  RECORD-CODE, PICTURE XX.
                   88  EXPECTING, VALUE 'D'.
               03  CUSTOMER-NUMBER, PICTURE 9999.
           02  CUSTOMER-ADDRESS.
```

FIGURE 17-1. *Language elements*

An example of level numbers and other elements is given in Fig. 17-1.

Programmer-Defined Words

Programmer-defined words or *data names* are supplied by the programmer to represent data items or data procedures involved in the problem. A data name may contain alphabetic and numeric characters, as well as hyphens. Hyphens may be anywhere in the name, but not at the beginning or end of it. Other rules are (1) that there can be no blanks within the data name, (2) that no data name can be exactly the same as a reserved name, and (3) that a data name may not exceed 30 characters (Fig. 17-2).

Literals

A *literal* is a true value (a number) defined by a programmer. The two main types are numeric and nonnumeric literals. A *numeric literal* is a string of numeric characters (0 to 9) which consists of up to 18 digits.

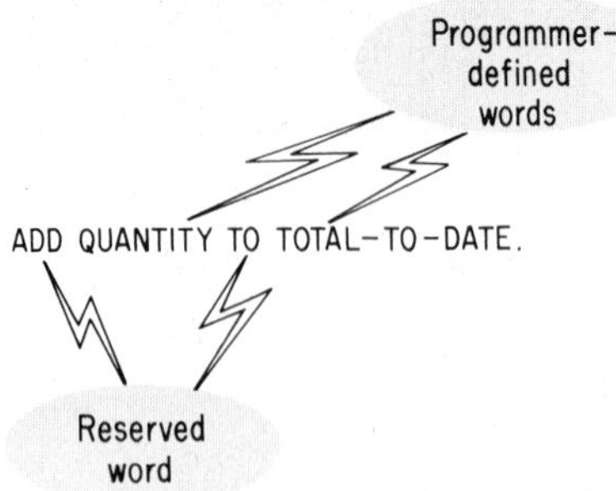

FIGURE 17-2. Programmer-defined words

There may be a decimal point anywhere in the literal except in its rightmost position. It may also contain a sign or may have a sign as its leftmost character. The absence of a sign means that the literal is positive.

A *nonnumeric literal* is a string of up to 120 characters enclosed by single quotation marks. It may contain any characters except a quotation mark. The quotation marks are not a part of the literal. An example of numeric and nonnumeric literals is shown in Fig. 17-3.

Pictures

A *picture* is a string of specific alphabetic, numeric, or alphanumeric characters that gives certain characteristics of data items. It may describe the number (size) and type (alphabetic, numeric, or alphanumeric) of characters in a data item, the location of a decimal point, if any, and the extent of editing needed to form a data item. This information is often necessary before the computer is able to process certain files.

The specific characters that constitute a picture are

A B CR DB E K P S V X Z 0 9
\+ − , . $ * ( )

FIGURE 17-3. Numeric and non-numeric literals

The numbers 143, 30, and 400 are numeric literals	COMPUTE TAX = RATE * AMOUNT + 143 MULTIPLY PRICE BY 30 GIVING AMOUNT-DUE. ADD SALES TO 400 GIVING TOTAL.
characters enclosed by quotation marks are non-numeric literals	77 LOWER-LIMIT, PICTURE XXX.X, VALUE '81'. DISPLAY 'GUEST NAME JIM BOYD'.

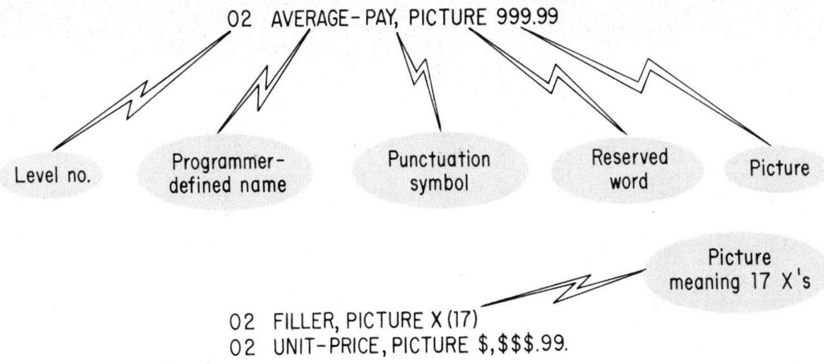

FIGURE 17-4. Picture entries

Some of these characters are explained in a later section. A picture may also use an unsigned numeric literal enclosed in parentheses to indicate a repetition of picture characteristics. In any case, each picture entry must be preceded by the word PICTURE. Some examples are shown in Fig. 17-4.

PROGRAM STRUCTURE

The basic structure of a COBOL program is a hierarchy of entries arranged in divisions (highest levels), sections, paragraphs, and entries (lowest level). Generally, a division is made up of sections, a section, of paragraphs, and a paragraph, of entries.

Divisions

Each COBOL program is divided into four sequential divisions. They are *identification, environment, data,* and *procedure.* Deciding on the set of entries related to each division simplifies somewhat the programming effort, compared to the traditional approach in which the programmer handles the whole program at once. Furthermore, a program divided into a fixed number of divisions presented in the same order allows others to better locate the sought-for program entries. Thus, standardizing a program structure is helpful to both programmers and program readers.

Each division is entered on a separate line. It is identified by a division header that contains the name of the division and the word DIVISION, followed immediately by a period. The four required division header entries are

```
IDENTIFICATION DIVISION.
ENVIRONMENT DIVISION.
DATA DIVISION.
PROCEDURE DIVISION.
```

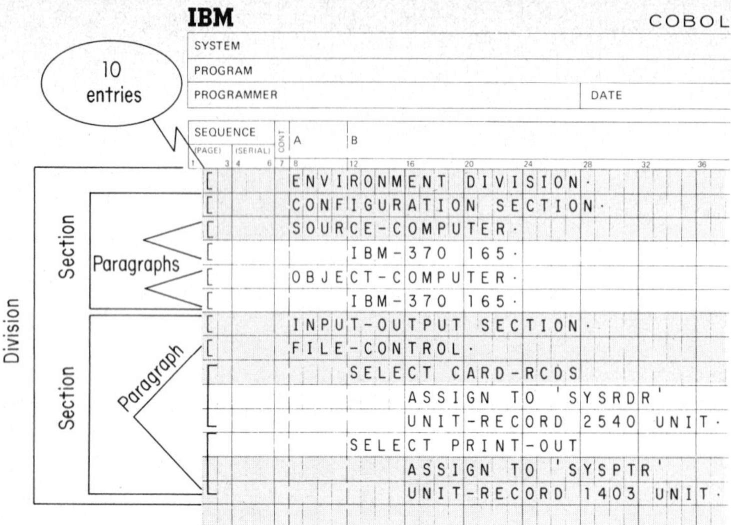

FIGURE 17-5. Structural makeup of the environment division

Sections

Like a division header, a section is entered on a separate line and is identified by a header entry that contains the name of the section, the word SECTION, and a terminal period. No sections are permitted in the identification division, whereas they are required in the environment and data divisions, and are optional in the procedure division (Fig. 17-5).

Paragraphs

For proper control of a COBOL program flow, paragraph names are used for identifying certain positions in the flow. A paragraph is identified by a header entry that consists of a name followed by a period. For example,

```
100.
         MULTIPLY A BY B GIVING C.
COMPUTATION.
         ADD NET-PAY TO 50 GIVING PAY.
```

The words 100 and COMPUTATION are paragraph names. Each must start in column 8, followed immediately by a period. Note that a paragraph name may be a string of alphabetic or numeric characters. With the exception of the data division, each division consists of one or more paragraphs. Paragraph names are fixed in the identification and environment divisions; they are programmer-defined in the procedure division.

Entries

An entry is a string of two or more language elements sequenced according to specified rules and followed by a period. A paragraph header is an example of a simple entry; most other entries are more detailed and more complex. The structural makeup of the environment division is shown in Fig. 17-5.

PROGRAM-CODING SHEET AND ENTRY-RECORDING SPECIFICATIONS

The COBOL coding sheet is designed for entering source program entries, which are later keypunched into COBOL program cards. It is divided into 25 lines; each provides room for 80 columns of data to correspond to the standard 80-column card (Fig. 17-6).

Columns 1 to 3 are reserved for a three-digit page number. Page 1 is numbered *010;* page 2, *020;* and so on.

Columns 4 to 6 indicate the line or statement number. The first line is numbered *010;* the second, *020;* and so on. Thus, when using columns 1 to 6, *010080* would mean page 1 and line 8.

Column 7 is reserved for indicating the continuation of nonnumeric literals. For example, if a nonnumeric literal requires three lines, a hyphen is entered in column 7 of the second and third lines.

Columns 8 to 72 [4] are reserved for program entries. They are divided into margin A (columns 8 to 11) and margin B (columns 12 to 72). The entries that must begin in column 8 are

1. Division headers.
2. Section headers.
3. Paragraph headers.
4. Declaratives and end declaratives in the procedure division.
5. File-description entries in the data division. A file-description entry begins with the reserved word FD (file description). It is written in columns 8 and 9. The remaining part of the entry is entered beginning in column 12.

Level numbers may be written in margin A, but this is not mandatory. All other entries must be written in margin B, beginning in column 12 or indented to a column number which is a multiple of 4—that is, to column 16, 20, 24, and so on.

Other entry-recording specifications include

1. An entry that must begin in margin A is written on a new line. The next entry, consequently, is also written on a new line.
2. Although it is common that each entry begin on a new line, an entry not required to start on a new line may be written on the same line as the preceding entry, separated by one or more spaces.
3. An entry that can be written on one line may be arbitrarily written on two or more lines.

[4] Columns 73 to 80 are reserved for program identification. The use of this field, however, is optional.

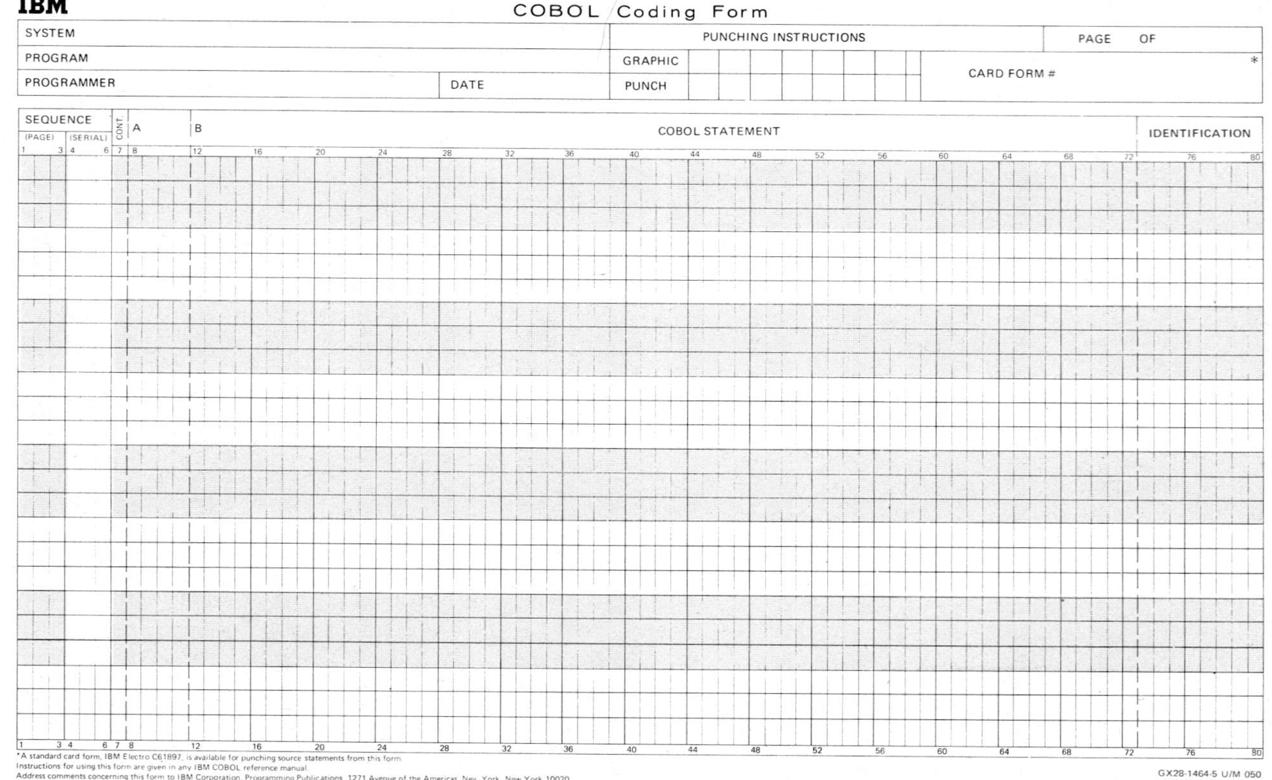

IBM COBOL Coding Form

SYSTEM		PUNCHING INSTRUCTIONS	PAGE OF
PROGRAM		GRAPHIC	CARD FORM # *
PROGRAMMER	DATE	PUNCH	

SEQUENCE (PAGE) 1–3	SEQUENCE (SERIAL) 4–6	CONT. 7	A 8	B 12	COBOL STATEMENT 16 20 24 28 32 36 40 44 48 52 56 60 64 68 72	IDENTIFICATION 76 80

*A standard card form, IBM Electro C61897, is available for punching source statements from this form.
Instructions for using this form are given in any IBM COBOL reference manual.
Address comments concerning this form to IBM Corporation, Programming Publications, 1271 Avenue of the Americas, Nev. York, New York 10020.

GX28-1464-5 U/M 050
Printed in U.S.A.

FIGURE 17-6. *COBOL coding sheet*

SEQUENCE (PAGE) (SERIAL)	CONT	A	B	COBOL STATEMENT
			DISPLAY	'THIS PROGRAM IS NOT VALID. MORE ENTRIES ARE REQUIRED
	-			'BEFORE COMPUTER RUN.'

FIGURE 17-7. A continuation line

4. In addition to writing a hyphen in column 7 for every continuation line, a quotation mark is also written in margin B, followed by the remaining characters of the literal (Fig. 17-7).
5. No space is allowed immediately after a left parenthesis or a beginning quotation mark.
6. No space is allowed immediately preceding a right parenthesis, an ending quotation mark, a comma or a semicolon used to punctuate a program entry, or a period written at the end of an entry.

PROGRAM CONTENTS

A COBOL program consists of four divisions presented in the following sequence:

1. Identification division
2. Environment division
3. Data division
4. Procedure division

Identification Division

The identification division provides key information for identifying the program. It states primarily the name of the program, followed by optional details such as the name of the programmer, the date it was written, and remarks related to the job for which the program was written.

Three entries are required in the identification division. They are: IDENTIFICATION DIVISION (division header), PROGRAM-ID (paragraph header), and a *program name* enclosed in single quotation marks.[5] Up to six optional paragraphs can also be added. Represented by reserved words, these paragraphs are entered in the sequence shown in Fig. 17-8.

Any number of entries can be added to each paragraph at the discretion of the programmer. An example of the identification division is presented in Fig. 17-9.

[5] A program name must not exceed eight characters. The first character must be a letter. The remaining characters may be letters or digits, but not special characters. The program name may be written on a separate line or on the same line as the paragraph header.

```
IDENTIFICATION DIVISION.

PROGRAM-ID.
    'program name'.

[AUTHOR.
    entry . . . .]

[INSTALLATION.
    entry . . . .]

[DATE-WRITTEN.
    entry . . . .]

[DATE-COMPILED.
    entry . . . .]

[SECURITY.
    entry . . . .]

[REMARKS.
    entry . . . .]
```

LEGEND: A line under a word is used to refer to a required reserve word. Brackets are used to refer to optional paragraphs or portions of the format.

***FIGURE 17-8.** Identification division format*

***FIGURE 17-9.** Identification division*

```
SEQUENCE          CONT. A   B                                  COBOL STATEMENT
(PAGE) (SERIAL)
1    3 4     6    7     8   12

                        IDENTIFICATION DIVISION.
                        PROGRAM-ID.
                                'PAYROLL'.
                        AUTHOR.
                            SANDY TREMAINE.
                        INSTALLATION.
                            ACCOUNTING DEPARTMENT.
                        DATE-WRITTEN.
                            DECEMBER 11, 1971.
                        DATE-COMPILED.
                            DECEMBER 18, 1971.
                        REMARKS.
                            THIS PROGRAM PROCESSES THE PAYROLL OF THE
                            STAFF OF THE ACCOUNTING DEPARTMENT. IT IS
                            DUE BY THE 30TH DAY OF EACH MONTH.
```

Environment Division

The second division of a COBOL program is the environment division. It provides information about the computers to be used in compiling and executing the object program and, using problem-oriented names, assigns

```
ENVIRONMENT DIVISION.
CONFIGURATION - SECTION.
[SOURCE - COMPUTER.
        computer's name  [model - number]  . ]
[OBJECT - COMPUTER.
        computer's name  [model - number]  . ]

INPUT-OUTPUT SECTION.
[FILE-CONTROL.
        SELECT-entry . . . . ]

[I-O-CONTROL.
        APPLY-entry . . . . ]
```

FIGURE 17-10. Environment division format

data files to input–output devices. Thus, this division is primarily computer-dependent, since it is directly involved with specifications of the computers to be used. The general format is shown in Fig. 17-10.

The primary entries and sections of the environment division are illustrated in Fig. 17-11. Line 01 indicates the first required entry—ENVIRONMENT DIVISION, followed by the division's two main sections: the configuration section and the input–output section. The *configuration section* identifies the source computer (the computer in which the program is compiled) and the object computer (the computer in which the computed program will be executed). Normally, the source and object computers are the same machine. Thus, the two required paragraph headers in the configuration section are SOURCE-COMPUTER and OBJECT-COMPUTER. Each header is followed by the computer's name and model number (Fig. 17-11).

The *input–output* section assigns data files to input–output devices and specifies certain input–output conditions. File assignment is carried

FIGURE 17-11. Environment division

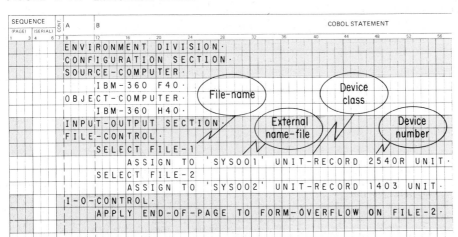

```
SEQUENCE        CONT. A   B                                    COBOL STATEMENT
(PAGE) (SERIAL)
1    3 4    6   7     8   12      16      20      24      28      32      36      40      44      48      52      56

      ENVIRONMENT DIVISION.
      CONFIGURATION SECTION.
      SOURCE-COMPUTER.
          IBM-360 F40.
      OBJECT-COMPUTER.
          IBM-360 H40.
      INPUT-OUTPUT SECTION.
      FILE-CONTROL.
          SELECT FILE-1
                ASSIGN TO 'SYS001' UNIT-RECORD 2540R UNIT.
          SELECT FILE-2
                ASSIGN TO 'SYS002' UNIT-RECORD 1403 UNIT.
      I-O-CONTROL.
          APPLY END-OF-PAGE TO FORM-OVERFLOW ON FILE-2.
```

out by a file-control paragraph, FILE-CONTROL, followed by an entry that *selects* the file by a programmer-defined name and *assigns* it to an "external" file name [6] and an input–output device. The key words SELECT and ASSIGN are reserved words and must be written exactly as they appear (Fig. 17-11, lines 08 to 12).

Three *device types* are used with an ASSIGN entry. They can be UNIT-RECORD, UTILITY, or DIRECT-ACCESS. The UNIT-RECORD class refers to card read–punch and printer machines; the UTILITY class refers to input–output devices capable of reading and writing data sequentially. Examples are magnetic tape, magnetic disk, and magnetic drum devices. The DIRECT-ACCESS class includes devices that can read and write data in a random manner. Examples are magnetic disk and magnetic drum machines. When one of these device classes is used, it should be entered with its model number. For example, lines 10 and 12 assign FILE-1 to a 2540R card reader and FILE-2 to a 1403 printer, respectively. Both of these units are UNIT-RECORD devices.

Input–Output Control

In addition to file assignment, the input–output section also defines certain input–output conditions or techniques for files. For example, to test for the end of a page, an input–output control paragraph is written following the file-control paragraph, as follows:

```
I-O-CONTROL.
  APPLY END-OF-PAGE TO FORM-OVERFLOW ON FILE-2.
        (overflow-name)                 (file-name)
```

The words APPLY and TO FORM-OVERFLOW are reserved words; END-OF-PAGE and FILE-2 are programmer-defined words of the file being printed. FILE-2 is the file name of the output file being used. It must also appear in a SELECT entry in the file-control paragraph.

An APPLY entry is written only for an output file that is to be printed and that overflows from page to page. A program involving more than one output file will require a separate entry for each printed file when an overflow test is required.

Data Division

The primary function of the data division is to describe (1) the data files and the records they contain, and (2) the items in working storage. The two most frequently used sections are the *file section,* which describes the data files (stored externally) and their records, and the *working-storage section,* which describes records and elementary data items that

[6] An external file name must begin with an alphabetic character, followed by no more than seven alphabetic and/or numeric characters. Special characters are not allowed. The file name is enclosed by single quotation marks.

FIGURE 17-12. Data division format

```
DATA DIVISION.
[FILE SECTION.
[file-description . . . .
 record-description . . . . ] ]

[WORKING-STORAGE SECTION.
[independent-item-description . . . . ]
[record-description . . . . ] ]
```

FIGURE 17-13. File description (top) and an example

```
                        FORMAT

FD   (file-name)
     RECORDING MODE IS (mode)
     BLOCK CONTAINS (integer) RECORDS
(or) BLOCK CONTAINS (integer) CHARACTERS
     RECORD CONTAINS (integer) TO (integer) CHARACTERS
     LABEL RECORD IS       { STANDARD
(or) LABEL RECORDS ARE     {   (or)
                           { OMITTED
                           {   (or)
                           { data-name
     DATA RECORD IS          (record-name)
(or) DATA RECORDS ARE        (record-name)
```

```
A   B                              COBOL STATEMENT
8   12  16  20  24  28  32  36  40  44
FD  FILE-1
    RECORDING MODE IS F
    BLOCK CONTAINS 40 TO 125 RECORDS
    LABEL RECORDS ARE OMITTED
    DATA RECORD IS RECEIVABLE-RECORD.
```

are not a part of the data files in the file section, but are generated and processed internally. The general format of the data division is shown in Fig. 17-12.

FILE SECTION. The file section is mandatory in every program that processes input or output data files. It consists of a *file-description* entry for every file named in a SELECT entry in the environment division. Each file description must be followed by two or more *record descriptions* or one record description for each record in the file.

File-description entry. The FD (file-description) entry specifies a given input or output file's *mode,* the number of data *records* (or characters) *per block,* the number of *characters per record, label records* (if any), and *names of each data record.* These details must be entered in the sequence shown in Fig. 17-13. The example below the format is explained as follows:

> On line 01, *level indicator* FD is a special two-letter reserved word entered in columns 8 and 9 of area A. It identifies the beginning of the file description. FD is followed by a programmer-defined *file name,* FILE-1 (beginning in column 12). It is the same file name specified in the SELECT entry in the environment division (Fig. 17-11). The remaining clauses are entered on separate lines, beginning in column 12.

On line 02, the RECORDING MODE IS clause indicates whether the length of the data file recording mode[7] is V (variable), F (fixed), or U (unspecified). In the example, recording mode F means that all the records in the file are of equal length. When the recording mode is U, the records may be either fixed or variable in length.

On line 03, the BLOCK CONTAINS clause specifies the number of records transferred at one time to and from main storage by an input–output device. This clause can be omitted when there is only one record per block.

On line 04, the RECORD CONTAINS clause specifies the range of record sizes. However, if we had RECORD CONTAINS 105 CHARACTERS, the integer 105 would refer to the number of characters of the longest record in the data file.

On line 05, the required LABEL RECORDS ARE clause indicates that the file has no label. It could also be used to mean that the file has "nonstandard" labels. If the clause uses the word STANDARD, it means that the labels conform to the label format specified by the computer system in use. However, if a name is used, it indicates the inclusion of user names in addition to standard labels.

On line 06, the required DATA RECORD IS clause gives the name of the record (RECEIVABLE-RECORD) in the file. This clause appears in every FD entry and must have below it 01-level numbers that describe the items in the record or records.

Record-description entries. After a given data file has been described, each record it contains must also be described. In the example given in Fig. 17-13, the data record clause gives the name of the record, RECEIVABLE-RECORD, which must appear as level 01 as follows:

```
01  RECEIVABLE-RECORD.
```

This initial entry is then followed by item-description entries that describe the items in that record. Each item-description entry also takes an appropriate level number, depending on its *level* in the record structure.

To illustrate, suppose that we wish to describe the items of an accounts receivable record, as shown in Fig. 17-14. It can be seen that the receivable record is divided into three smaller items, with the customer and invoice items further divided into still smaller items.[8] In subdividing a record, the record name (in this example, RECEIVABLE-RECORD) or the most inclusive record is assigned the highest level number, 01, with each succeeding level given a larger number. In this

[7] The term *file recording mode* may appear as RECORDING MODE IS (mode), RECORDING MODE (mode) or just RECORDING (mode).

[8] The digits between parentheses represent the number of positions the item occupies or the size of the item.

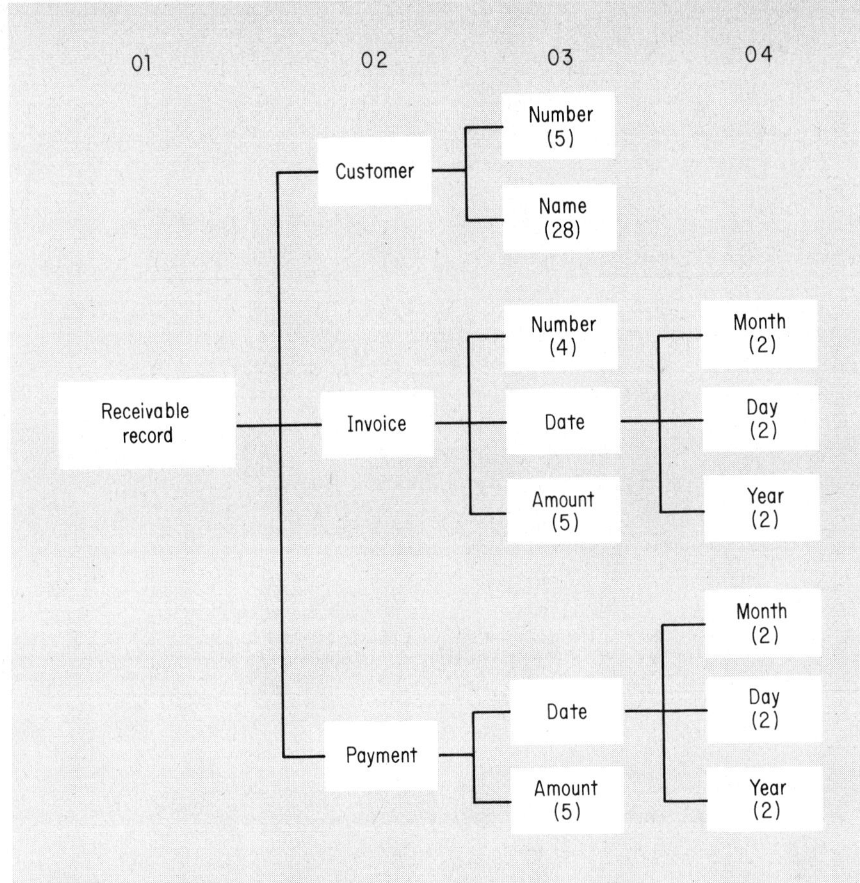

FIGURE 17-14. Record structure

example there is a hierarchy of four levels[9]: 01 to 04. Note that an item that is further subdivided is called a *group item;* an item that is not further subdivided is called an *elementary item.* Thus the date item is a group item, whereas the month, day, and year items are elementary items. The record-description entries are shown in Fig. 17-15.

Item-description entries. A separate entry is made for each item included in the record involved. The entry specifies the characteristics of the data it contains, using a format that begins with a *level number,* followed by a *data name* or the word FILLER, and normally a descriptive clause, which begins with a word such as PICTURE, USAGE, or VALUE.

A *level number* must be the first element of an item description

[9] Level numbers need not be in consecutive order. For example, the form levels may be numbered 01, 03, 05, and 07, or 01, 05, 10, and 15. The important point is that the level numbers should be assigned in consecutive order in line with the order in which the hierarchy is subdivided.

```
01  RECEIVABLE-RECORD.           Picture clause
    02  CUSTOMER.
        03  NUMBER               PICTURE X(5).
        03  NAME                 PICTURE X(28).
    02  INVOICE.
        03  NUMBER               PICTURE 9(4).
        03  DATE.
            04  MONTH            PICTURE 99.
            04  DAY              PICTURE 99.
            04  YEAR             PICTURE 99.
        03  AMOUNT               PICTURE 9(3)V99.
    02  PAYMENT.
        03  DATE.
            04  MONTH            PICTURE 99.
            04  DAY              PICTURE 99.
            04  YEAR             PICTURE 99.
        03  AMOUNT               PICTURE 9(3)V99.
```

FIGURE 17-15. Record description entries

entry. As we see in Fig. 17-15. The number 01 indicates that the item is the most inclusive record, 02 is for group items, 03 for smaller items, and so on. Level numbers 02 to 49 are usually used for items that are subdivisions of a whole record.

A name is called a data name if it follows the level number and supplies the names of the data being described. For example, on lines 02 to 14 of Fig. 17-15, data names PAYMENT, DATE, and MONTH follow level numbers 02, 03, and 04, respectively.

FILLER is not a name but is used instead of a data name to specify the unused part of a logical record or that the information will not be processed. For example, if columns 40 to 46 of each card are always blank, the word FILLER can be used to identify this unused field.

A PICTURE clause is used only in describing an elementary item. It specifies item size, class, sign, assumed decimal point, and certain other editing requirements. Three classes of data items can be described. They are alphabetic, numeric, and alphanumeric. A picture clause defines an *alphabetic item* by the letter A for each alphabetic character or space. For example,

Item	Picture Clause	Picture Size
ABC	PICTURE IS AAA. (or) PICTURE IS A(3).	3
CREDIT FILE	PICTURE IS AAAAAAAAAAA. (or) PICTURE IS A(11).	11

A PICTURE clause defines a *numeric item* if its character strings consist of the digit 9 or the letters V, S, or P. The functions of these characters are as follows (see Fig. 17-16 for examples):

Actual Value of item in storage	PICTURE is	Item Value treated as
1294	9999	1294
1294	9 (4)	1294
1294	99V99	12.94
129	S99V9	+ 12.9
25	99PP	2500
25	PP99	0.0025
25	P (3) 99	0.00025
3795	9 (4) PPV	379500
3795	V9 (4)	0.3795

FIGURE 17-16. Numeric examples defined by PICTURE clauses

9—Represents a character position that contains a numeral only.

V—Indicates the location of an assumed decimal point. It may appear once only in a character string. Since it does not represent a character position in memory, it does not count in the size of the item. The absence of V in the character string means that the decimal point is to the right of the item involved.

S—Indicates the presence of an operational sign (plus or minus) and must be entered as the leftmost character in the character string. It is not counted in determining the size of the item.

P—Indicates that the assumed decimal point is not within the number that appears in the data item. That is, it positions the assumed decimal point away from the actual number. Each P represents an assumed zero.

A PICTURE clause describes an *alphanumeric item* if its character strings contain a combination of the characters X, A, or 9. However, the data item is treated as though it contained all X's. Characters A and 9 have already been described. The letter X stands for a character of any kind—that is, a letter, a digit, a special character, or a space. For example, if the actual value of the item in storage is BD20, it will be treated the same if its PICTURE is XXXX or X(4).

A PICTURE clause can also be used in *editing* a data item. Editing involves preparing certain data for printing. For example, the dollar amount might be stored in computer memory as 12345, with an assumed decimal point between the digits 3 and 4. Although the dollar sign and the decimal point are not required for processing, they are necessary for the printout to appear as $123.45. In this case, an editing picture of $999.99 will accomplish the result. The period is used here to represent the decimal point for alignment purposes.

Some of the common symbols used in the character strings of an edited picture are 9, Z, $, +, and —. Character 9 has already been discussed. The functions of the remaining characters are as follows:

Z Represents the leftmost positions that are to be *zero-suppressed;* that is, a leading zero is replaced by a space for each Z included in the character string. For example, if the actual value of the item is 004, it will be treated as 4 if its editing picture is ZZ9.

\$, −, + Each of these symbols occupies the same character position in the actual result as the editing picture character string and is counted in the size of the item (Fig. 17-17).

A USAGE clause is used in data division entries at all levels. It specifies the form in which an item is represented in computer storage. For a more efficient program, it is necessary to determine how a given item will be used most frequently and to specify the appropriate usage. This clause has the following general format:

```
USAGE        COMPUTATIONAL
                 (or)
                DISPLAY
```

USAGE DISPLAY tells the computer to store a particular data item in character form, one character per byte. The word DISPLAY is optional, since the usage of an elementary item is assumed to be *display* in the absence of specification of some other usage for it. Also, the word USAGE or USAGE IS is optional. For example, if an item's usage is computational, the usage clause may consist of a single word, COMPUTATIONAL, although stating it as USAGE COMPUTATIONAL or USAGE IS COMPUTATIONAL is also correct.

A data item can have display or computational usage, depending on whether it is alphabetic, numeric, or alphanumeric. Alphabetic items, as well as those that store special characters and/or spaces, cannot be com-

Actual value of item in storage*	"PICTURE IS"	Edited result
123	\$999	\$123
123	+\$999	+\$123
$12\bar{3}$	−ZZ999	− 123
0014	\$ZZZZZ	\$ 14
0001	\$ZZ99	\$ 01

* A dash above the unit's position indicates a negative sign

FIGURE 17-17. Edited PICTURE clauses

putational, but can only have display usage. Likewise, alphanumeric items can only have display usage. For example, the following entry is a display entry:

```
03  SHIPPING-CODE  PICTURE XXXX.
```

Numeric items, however, can have display or computational usage, since they can be stored in any data code. Conversely, a display item can have any type of picture, and nondisplay items (e.g., numeric items) can have only a numeric picture. Examples are shown in Fig. 17-18.

WORKING-STORAGE SECTION. The working-storage section describes independent data items and/or logical records. An independent data item is not a member of a larger group and is not further subdivided. It is defined in a separate data-description entry with level number 77. Level 77 begins in column 8 of the COBOL coding line; the data name following begins in column 12.

In addition to the use of PICTURE and USAGE clauses, the VALUE clause is commonly used in an item-description entry, but only in the working-storage section. A VALUE clause is used in instances when it is necessary to specify the initial value of an item, to set up a constant, or

FIGURE 17-18. *Examples of usage clauses*

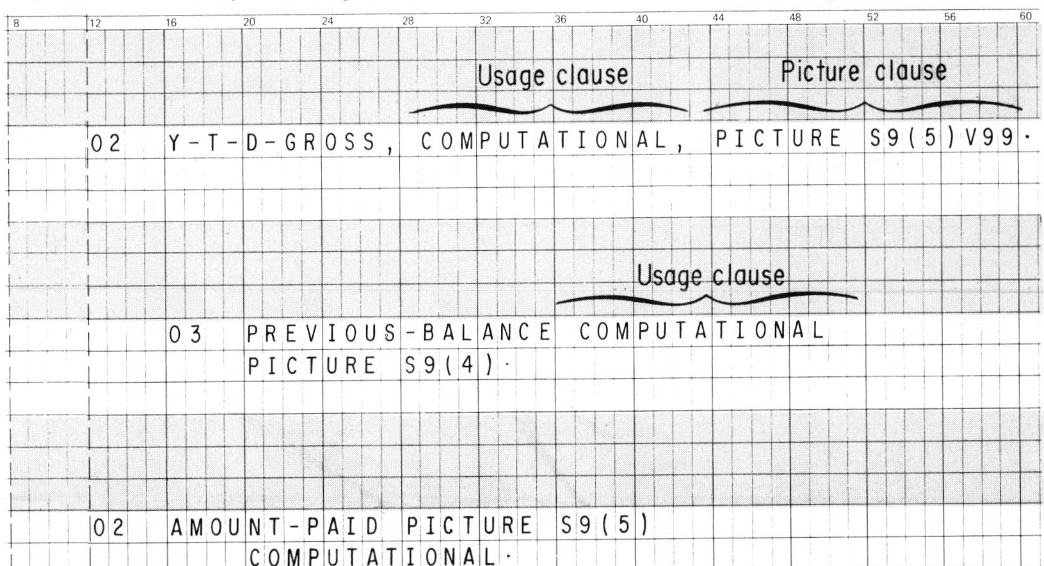

to have a certain value in a working area prior to program execution. The value assigned to an item remains unchanged throughout the execution of the program. The general format of the VALUE clause is

```
77 (data name) VALUE (literal)
```

For example, to define a constant named LOWER-LIMIT having a value of 800, the entry is as shown in Fig. 17-19.

```
77  LOWER-LIMIT, PICTURE S999, VALUE 800,
           COMPUTATIONAL.
```

FIGURE 17-19

A nonnumeric literal can also be used in the VALUE clause of alphabetic or alphanumeric items. For example, an alphabetic constant, called RECEIVABLE SCHEDULE, is used in a VALUE clause of an item-description entry having a 25-alphabetic-character size called REPORT as shown in Fig. 17-20.

```
77  REPORT, PICTURE A(25),
        VALUE 'RECEIVABLE SCHEDULE'
```

FIGURE 17-20

Several rules apply to the use of the VALUE clause:

1. The value of the literal must be the same class as the item. That is, for a numeric item, the value of the literal must be numeric. Likewise, for an alphabetic item, the value of the literal must be alphabetic.
2. The size of the literal used in the VALUE clause must not exceed the size of the item.
3. The value of a numeric literal must be within the range of values defined by the picture clause. For example, if the picture clause is PICTURE P999, the literal must be within the range 0.0000 to 0.0999.

Procedure Division

The procedure division is programmer-defined and consists of one or more *paragraphs* that determine the required processing steps for solving a given problem. Each paragraph consists of a heading entry and one or more *sentences*. Each sentence, in turn, may be one or more *statements* constructed within the constraints of a preestablished format. Most procedural statements begin with a *reserved verb,* which specifies actions to be taken, such as data movement, input–output, and arithmetic. The general format of a procedure division is as follows:

```
PROCEDURE DIVISION.
paragraph-name-1.
                    processing steps
paragraph-name-2.
                    processing steps
paragraph-name-n.
                    processing steps
```

The most commonly used procedural statements are explained under five headings: *program comments, input–output, data movement, arithmetic,* and *sequence control.* Students who wish to go beyond the scope of this presentation may refer to any COBOL text for additional information.

PROGRAM COMMENTS—NOTE. A NOTE sentence allows the programmer to write explanatory remarks that will be produced on the compiler listing, but will not be included in the object program. It can be of any length and may include any words or characters. If a paragraph's first word is NOTE, the entire paragraph is treated as notes. If the word is in a sentence other than the first one, the note terminates with the first detection of a period, followed by a space. The general format and an example of the NOTE sentence are shown in Fig. 17-21.

INPUT–OUTPUT. The input–output procedural statements allow efficient processing of data into and out of the computer. The four statements briefly explained here are the OPEN, CLOSE, READ, and WRITE statements.

Open. The OPEN statement conditions one or more data files for reading or writing. Although it does not retrieve or release the first data

Format:

NOTE: character string

Example:

```
   NOTE--  THIS ROUTINE COMPUTES THE
           TOTAL AMOUNT OF STATE TAX
           WITHHELD FOR THE THIRD PERIOD
           OF 1970.
```

FIGURE 17-21. The NOTE format and an example

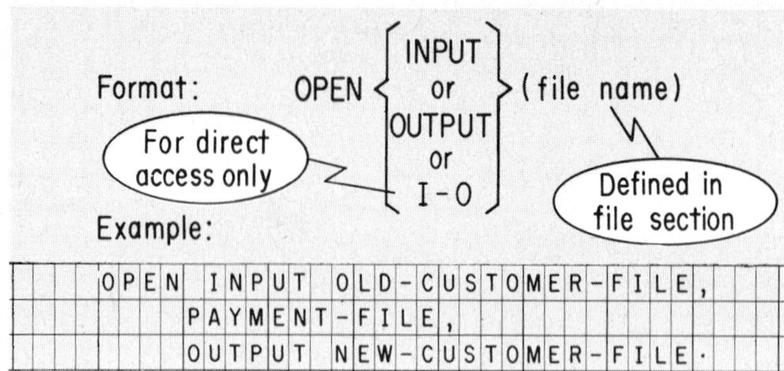

FIGURE 17-22.

```
CLOSE OLD-CUSTOMER-FILE.
CLOSE NEW-CUSTOMER-FILE.
```

FIGURE 17-23

```
READ INVENTORY-FILE,
     AT END, GO TO CLOSE-FILE.
```

FIGURE 17-24

record for processing, it performs the required step of opening a file before any records can be read or written. When a file is opened, checking and/or writing beginning-of-file labels and other necessary preparatory steps are also performed. The OPEN statement must precede the first READ or WRITE statement for that file. The general format and an example are shown in Fig. 17-22.

Close. The CLOSE statement is used to terminate the processing of input and output files that were opened; only a single file may appear in each CLOSE statement (see Fig. 17-23).

Read. The READ statement makes the next logical file record available for processing and, in sequential files, causes specified action to be taken after the last file record has been processed (see Fig. 17-24). When the last record has been processed, control switches to the close file for further processing.

Write. The WRITE statement releases a logical record for an opened output file. When the record is to be printed or punched, it consists of the following format:

```
                          { BEFORE }
WRITE record-name         {  (or)  }   ADVANCING integer LINES.
                          { AFTER  }
```

FIGURE 17-25

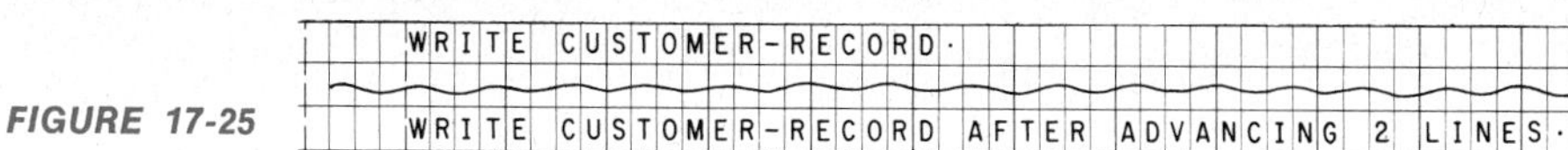

WRITE CUSTOMER-RECORD.
WRITE CUSTOMER-RECORD AFTER ADVANCING 2 LINES.

The *record name* must be the same as the one described in the file section of the data division. The use of the ADVANCING clause is optional. It allows manipulation of the vertical positioning of each printed line on the page. The *integer* part represents the number of lines the page is to be advanced (see Fig. 17-25).

DATA MOVEMENT—MOVE. A key operation in programming is transferring selected data from one area in computer storage to another. The MOVE statement executes such transfer based on the data description established in the data division. The general format is

```
         { area-name-1 }   TO area-name-2
MOVE     {    (or)     }
         {   literal   }
```

Area-name-1 is the sending or FROM area. Area-name-2 is the receiving or TO area. When the statement is executed, the contents of area-name-1 are moved to the area-name-2 referred to in the statement. If a literal is used instead of area-name-1, the characters specified by the literal will be moved to the proper receiving area (see Fig. 17-26).

In using a MOVE statement, several points should be noted.

1. An alphabetic item must not be moved to a numeric item (as described in the PICTURE clause), or vice versa.
2. A numeric item whose decimal is not directly to the right of its low-order position cannot be moved to an alphanumeric item.
3. Data transferred from a sending area to a *numeric* receiving area are

FIGURE 17-26

```
MOVE BALANCE-OUTSTANDING TO AMOUNT-DUE
    IN CUSTOMER-BILL.

MOVE 104 TO TOTAL.

MOVE SALE TO TOTAL.
```

positioned according to the decimal point in the latter area, with excess characters truncated. If no decimal point is specified, the data received will be right-justified.

4. Data transferred from a sending area to a *nonnumeric* receiving area will be left-justified and any excess characters truncated. If the data received are smaller than the size of the receiving area, any unused character positions are left as spaces instead of zeros.

ARITHMETIC. The four arithmetic statements presented in this section are ADD, SUBTRACT, MULTIPLY, and DIVIDE. Although each statement has its own unique format and rules, the following rules are applicable to all of them:

1. Literals used in an arithmetic statement must be numeric.
2. A data name used in an arithmetic statement must be numeric and defined in data division as an elementary data item.
3. A data name or a numeric literal must not exceed 18 digits in length.

Add. An ADD statement adds two or more numbers and stores the sum according to the following format:

```
        ( literal-1     )  ( literal-2     )          TO
ADD     {   (or)        }  {   (or)        }  . . .  (or)    data-name-n
        ( data-name-1   )  ( data-name-2   )        GIVING   ROUNDED.
```

TO or GIVING are two options available to the programmer. When TO is used, it must be preceded by at least one data name or literal. The values are added to the value of data-name-*n* and the sum is stored in data-name-*n*. (see Fig. 17-27).

When the word GIVING is used, it must be preceded by at least two data names or literals. They are added and their value becomes the new value of data-name-*n* (see Fig. 17-28).

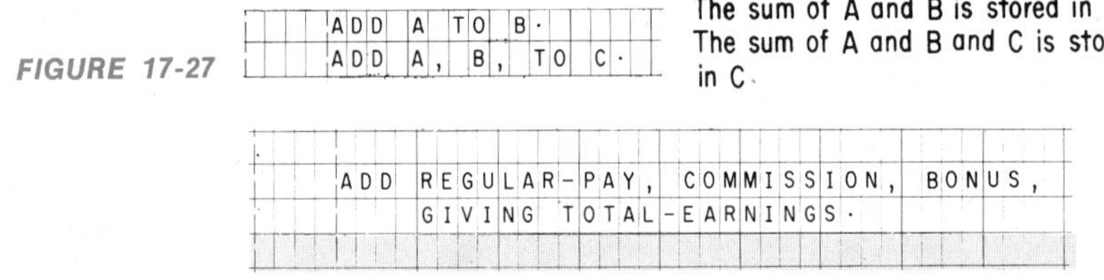
ADD A TO B.
ADD A, B, TO C.
ADD REGULAR-PAY, COMMISSION, BONUS,
GIVING TOTAL-EARNINGS.

Explanation

The sum of A and B is stored in B
The sum of A and B and C is stored in C.

FIGURE 17-27

FIGURE 17-28

Explanation

The contents of regular pay, commission, and bonus are added. The sum is stored in total-earnings.

	Explanation
SUBTRACT A FROM B	Difference placed in B.
SUBTRACT TAXES, PREMIUMS, FROM EARNINGS.	Sum of taxes and premiums subtracted from earnings. Difference placed in earnings.
SUBTRACT DEDUCTIONS FROM GROSS, GIVING NET-PAY.	Deductions subtracted from gross. Difference placed in net pay.
SUBTRACT A FROM 90, GIVING C, ROUNDED.	A subtracted from 90. Difference is rounded and then placed in C.

FIGURE 17-29

The use of the word ROUNDED is optional. Its function is to round the result before it is stored in data-name-*n*. It can be used with each of the four arithmetic statements by entering it following data-name-*n*.

Subtract. The SUBTRACT statement subtracts one or more numbers from another number and places the difference into a data-name-*n* or a literal *n* following the word FROM, unless there is an optional GIVING clause. If a GIVING clause is defined in the statement, the difference is placed in the data name after the word GIVING and is edited according to the item's picture (see Fig. 17-29).

Multiply. The MULTIPLY statement multiplies one number by another and places the product into the second item or the data name after the word BY, unless there is an optional GIVING clause. If a GIVING clause is defined in the statement, the product is placed into the data name after the word GIVING and is edited according to the item's picture (see Fig. 17-30).

Divide. The DIVIDE statement divides one number into another, and the quotient replaces the original value of the second number, unless there is an optional GIVING clause. If a GIVING clause is defined in the statement, the clause places the quotient into the data name after the word GIVING and is edited according to the item's picture (see Fig. 17-31).

Statement	Explanation
MULTIPLY A BY B.	A multiplied by B. Product stored in B.
MULTIPLY A BY B, GIVING C.	A multiplied by B. Product stored in C.
MULTIPLY AMOUNT BY RATE, GIVING TOTAL, ROUNDED.	Amount multiplied by rate; product rounded and stored in a location called total.

FIGURE 17-30

	Explanation
DIVIDE A INTO B.	A divided into B. Quotient placed in B.
DIVIDE A INTO B, GIVING C.	A divided into B. Quotient placed in C.
DIVIDE A INTO B, GIVING C, ROUNDED.	A divided into B. Quotient is rounded and then placed in C.

FIGURE 17-31

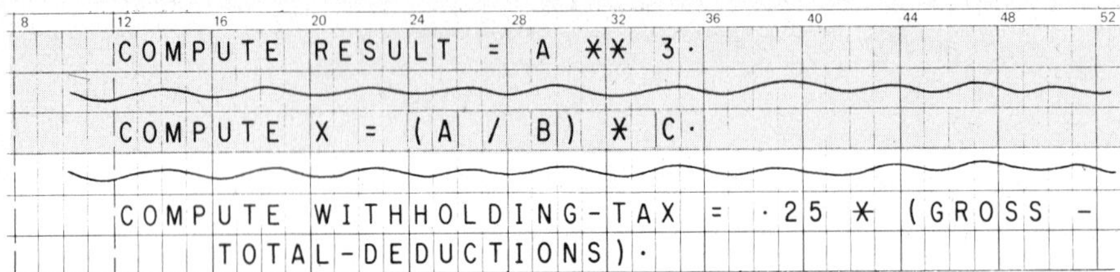

FIGURE 17-32

Compute. In addition to the four arithmetic statements, COBOL also allows calculations to be made using a COMPUTE statement. Suppose that we wish to calculate the interest rate of 8 percent for a principal amount defined as PRINCIPAL in the data division. The COMPUTE statement in the procedure division would be

```
COMPUTE CHARGE = .08 * PRINCIPAL
```

This means that the expression (the calculation to the right of the equal sign) is to be performed and the result is to be stored in a computer location named CHARGE. The COMPUTE statement can be used to add, subtract, multiply, divide, or exponentiate numbers (see Fig. 17-32).

PROGRAM INSTRUCTION EXECUTION CONTROL. Control flows automatically from one statement to the next in the order in which they are written except when (1) a GO TO statement causes the program to branch to a procedure in the program, (2) an IF statement causes the program control to skip over certain statements, (3) a PERFORM statement allows temporary control to another procedure, or (4) a STOP statement delays or terminates program execution. These statements are explained next.

Go To. The GO TO statement causes transfer of program control from one part of the procedure to another, either unconditionally or conditionally. The general format of the unconditional GO TO statement is

```
        { paragraph-name. }
GO TO   {      (or)       }
        {  section-name.  }
```

For example, the GO TO statement, GO TO TAX-FILE., simply directs the computer to branch unconditionally to that part of the procedure division identified by the procedure name TAX-FILE.

The general format of the conditional GO TO statement is

```
GO TO  procedure-name-1  procedure-name-2 . . . procedure-name-n
        DEPENDING on data-name.
```

For example,

GO TO ROUTINE-A, ROUTINE-B, ROUTINE-C DEPENDING ON ROUTINE-CODE.

In executing this statement, the computer branches to ROUTINE-A, ROUTINE-B, or ROUTINE-C, depending on the current value of the ROUTINE-CODE (defined in the data division). If the ROUTINE-CODE contains integer value 1, the computer will branch to ROUTINE-A; if integer value 2, the computer will branch to ROUTINE-B; and if integer value 3, the computer will branch to ROUTINE-C. However, if the ROUTINE-CODE contains a zero, a negative value, a value that is not an integer, or a value greater than the number of ROUTINES listed (i.e., 3), then the GO TO DEPENDING statement is ignored and the next sequential instruction is handled instead.

If. The IF statement evaluates the data and causes one or more statements to be executed if a certain condition exists. The reserved word IF is followed by a description of the data condition and the action to be taken if the data condition is true. Then the optional reserved word ELSE or OTHERWISE is written, followed by the action to be taken if the data condition is false. Such groupings of words make up what is called a *conditional* statement. The general format is

IF	Test-Condition	Statement-1	{ ELSE (or) OTHERWISE }	Statement-2.
IF	TEST	TRUE ACTION		FALSE ACTION

A *test-condition* may specify a relation condition, class condition, sign condition, or overflow condition. The first two conditions are explained later.

Statement-1 and *statement-2* represent imperative statements. Any number of statements may follow the test condition. If the test condition is true, the statements following it (represented by statement-1 in the general format) are executed. However, if the test condition is false, the next sequential statement in the program is executed, or if an ELSE or OTHERWISE clause is included, the statement following ELSE or OTHERWISE is executed.

Two basic test conditions, relational tests and class tests are shown in conditional statements. In a *relational test,* one data item is compared with another data item (each of which may be a data name or a literal) and some action is indicated based on the relation that exists. One data item is called the *subject operand* and the other the *object operand.* The general format is

```
{ data-name-1 }                          { data-name-2 }
{    (or)     }   relational operator    {    (or)     }
{   literal   }                          {   literal   }
```

Data-name-1 (or literal 1) and data-name-2 (or literal 2) represent the the two operands. *Both operands cannot be literals,* as it makes little sense to compare two literals to each other. For example, a test such as IF 5 IS GREATER THAN 4 does not require a computer to determine the result; therefore, it is illegal.

The *relational operator* (preceded and followed by a space) specifies the type of comparison to be made. It may be one of the following (for examples, see Fig. 17-33):

```
IS EQUAL TO (or =)
IS GREATER THAN (or >)
IS LESS THAN (or <)
IS NOT EQUAL TO
IS NOT GREATER THAN
IS NOT LESS THAN
```

Examples:

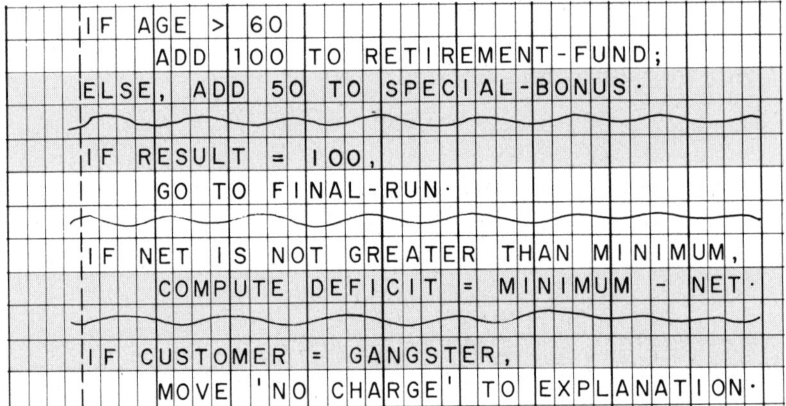

IF AGE > 60
ADD 100 TO RETIREMENT-FUND;
ELSE, ADD 50 TO SPECIAL-BONUS.
IF RESULT = 100,
GO TO FINAL-RUN.
IF NET IS NOT GREATER THAN MINIMUM,
COMPUTE DEFICIT = MINIMUM - NET.
IF CUSTOMER = GANGSTER,
MOVE 'NO CHARGE' TO EXPLANATION.

FIGURE 17-33

A *class test* determines whether the contents of one operand are *all* numeric (characters 0 to 9) or *all* alphabetic (A to Z, space). The use of this test can be helpful in verifying incoming data. The general format is

```
                IS        NUMERIC
IF data-name   (or)        (or)
               IS NOT    ALPHABETIC
```

Perform. The PERFORM statement is similar to a subroutine in that it causes a branch to one or more procedures in the program and, following their execution, returns control to the statement after the PERFORM statement. The general format is

```
PERFORM  procedure-name
```

An example is

```
PERFORM NET-PAY-ROUTINE.
```

A procedure name can be the name of a paragraph or a section in the procedure division. It must not be the name of the procedure that includes the PERFORM statement.

There can be practically any number of procedures in the series. In this case, the PERFORM statement would perform the first procedure (called procedure name 1) THRU the last procedure (called procedure name 2) with an optional TIMES clause that tells the computer the number of times a procedure should be executed before control returns to the normal program sequence (see Fig. 17-34).

```
PERFORM NET-PAY CALCULATION 4 TIMES.

PERFORM TAX-CALCULATION X TIMES.

PERFORM CALCULATION-1
     THRU CALCULATION-2.
```

FIGURE 17-34

Stop. The STOP statement causes either a temporary or a permanent halt in the execution of the object program. The general format is

```
         ⎧ literal ⎫
STOP     ⎨   or    ⎬
         ⎩  RUN    ⎭
```

If the RUN option is used, execution of the program will be permanently halted. If the literal option is used, the literal will be communicated to the operator and a temporary halt will occur. Continuation begins with execution of the next sequential statement. Examples are

```
STOP RUN.
STOP 'ERROR'.
```

SUMMARY

COBOL is a business-oriented language that allows instructions to be constructed in paragraph- and sentence-like form, using English words encountered in business situations. COBOL language makes use of symbols, reserved words, level numbers, programmer-defined words, literals, and pictures. *Symbols* represent a special meaning to the compiler. There are condition (e.g., $=$, $<$, $>$), arithmetic (e.g., $+$, $-$, $/$), and punctuation (e.g., . , ;) symbols.

A *reserved word* has a particular meaning and is used by the programmer for a specific purpose. *Level numbers* are used to indicate the level of various data items in relation to others in the program. *Programmer-defined* words or data names are supplied by the programmer to represent data items or data procedures involved in the problem. They may contain alphabetic or numeric characters as well as hyphens. Hyphens may be anywhere in the data name but not at the beginning or end of it.

A *literal* is a number defined by the programmer. It may be numeric or nonnumeric. A numeric literal is a string of characters (0 to 9); a decimal point is allowed anywhere except in the rightmost position. A nonnumeric literal is a string of up to 120 characters enclosed by single quotation marks.

A *picture* is a string of special alphabetic, numeric, or alphanumeric characters that gives certain characteristics of data items. Each picture entry must be preceded by the word PICTURE.

A COBOL program is a structured hierarchy arranged in divisions, sections, paragraphs, and entries. A division is made up of paragraphs, and a paragraph is made up of entries. The four main divisions are identification, environment, data, and procedure. Each division is entered on a separate line in the coding sheet and is identified by a division header, which consists of the name of the division and the word DIVISION, followed by a period.

The *identification division* provides information for identifying the program (e.g., program name, date, and name of the programmer). The *environment division* provides information about the computer to be used in computing and executing the object program, and (using problem-oriented names) assigns data file to input–output devices. The *data division* describes the data files and records and the items in working storage. The *procedure division* is programmer-defined and consists of one or more paragraphs, each paragraph consisting of a heading entry and one or more sentences. Each sentence, in turn, may be one or more statements constructed within the constraints of a preestablished format.

Input–output procedural statements allow the processing of data into and out of the computer. Among the more commonly used are OPEN, CLOSE, READ, and WRITE statements. Arithmetic, compute, and move statements are also used in handling the details of a program. Program control flows automatically from one statement to another, except in situations requiring special attention, which involve the use of GO TO, IF, PERFORM, or STOP statements. These and other statements perform a vital role in effective processing of business problems in COBOL.

TERMS TO LEARN

COBOL
Data division
Environment division
Identification division
Literal
Picture
Procedure division
Program-defined word
Relational test
Reserved word

QUESTIONS

1. Explain the general purpose of COBOL.
2. List and describe COBOL's primary language elements.
3. What types of symbols are used in COBOL programming? Illustrate.
4. Define and give an example of each of the following terms. a. reserved word; b. level number; c. data name; d. literal; and e. picture.

5. Describe briefly the primary structure of a COBOL program.
6. List and explain COBOL's required divisions.
7. Briefly explain the primary entries and sections of the environment division.
8. What is the primary function(s) of the data division? Distinguish between its file section and working-storage section.
9. Describe and illustrate the use(s) of each of the following: a. FILLER; b. picture clause; c. usage clause; d. note sentence; e. OPEN; f. WRITE; g. MOVE; h. COMPUTE; i. GO TO; j. IF; k. PERFORM.
10. Flowchart and code a program to compare *A* to *B*. If *A* is greater than *B*, the program is to go to ALPHA-1. Otherwise, it should go to ALPHA-2.
11. Flowchart and code a program based on the following information:
    IF *A* is greater than *B* and *A* is greater than *C*, THEN add *B* to *C* and go to ALPHA-1.
    IF *B* is greater than *A* and *B* is greater than *C*, THEN add *A* to *C* and go to ALPHA-2.
    IF *B* is greater than *A* but less than *C*, THEN subtract *A* from *B* and go to ALPHA-1.
12. Simplify the following statement:
    IF $A > 10$ and if $A < 14$, subtract $A - X$. If $A < 10$ and if $A > 14$, go to WORK-ROUTINE.

SUGGESTED READING

DRUMMOND, MARSHALL, et al. *American National Standard Cobol for the IBM System 360–370.* Belmont, Calif.: Wadsworth Publishing Company, Inc., 1973.

SEIDEL, K. P. *Cobol.* Pacific Palisades, Calif.: Goodyear Publishing Company, 1971.

FORTRAN IV concepts

18

arithmetic "if" statement

logical "if" statement

relational "if" statement

Imperative Statements

"do" statement

"continue" statement

"stop" and "end" statements

SAMPLE FORTRAN PROGRAM

In this chapter we examine one of the more popular high-level programming languages, FORTRAN IV. In general, high-level programming languages are oriented more toward problem solution or procedure development than toward a particular computer. Thus FORTRAN is machine-independent. It is specifically oriented to the solution of mathematical types of problems. The language consists of a set of symbols and words and specific rules for writing procedural instructions.

FORTRAN, an acronym for *FORmula TRANslator,* was originally developed in 1957 by a group of 13 men from IBM to simplify the work of scientists and engineers in stating their problems for machine solution. Since then it has progressed through several versions (where "version" is taken to mean an improvement over the previous state rather than a major modification in concept). The current version is FORTRAN IV, which has stabilized sufficiently to lead the American National Standards Institute (ANSI) to develop a standard FORTRAN IV. For brevity, it will be referred to in this chapter as FORTRAN.

FORTRAN PROGRAM CARD

In preparing a FORTRAN program, statements (the equivalent of natural-language sentences) are written on a FORTRAN coding sheet with a format in line with that of the program card (Fig. 18-1). Each line of the coding sheet represents an instruction and is punched in a separate 80-column card. Unlike data cards in which data can be punched in any of the 80 columns, a FORTRAN program card is divided into areas reserved for specific types of information.

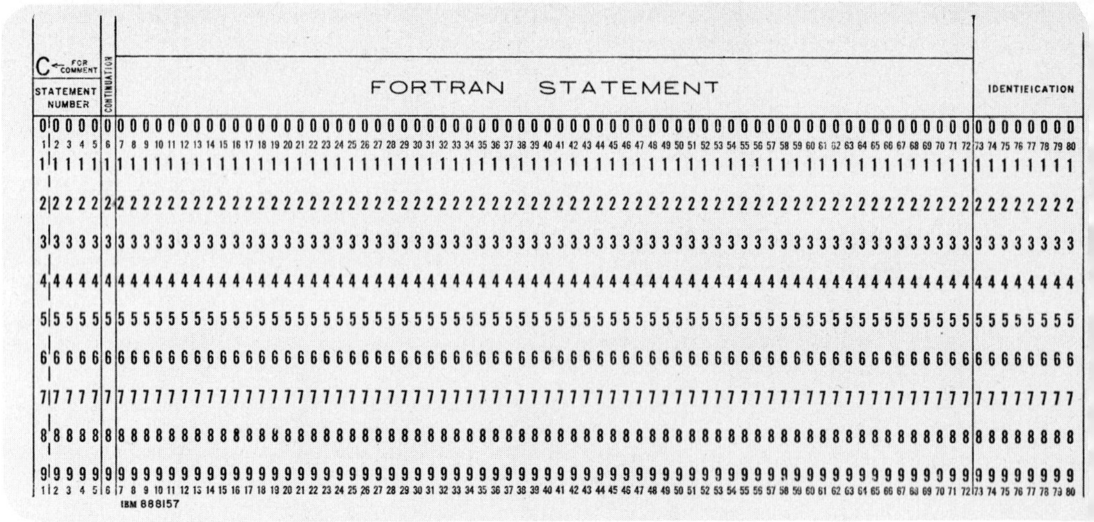

FIGURE 18-1. FORTRAN program card

Briefly, column 1 is punched with the letter c (meaning *comment*) when the card contains explanatory (versus instructional) information and is not a part of the operating program. The computer ignores the contents when the object program is executed. In most FORTRAN statements, however, column 1 is used with columns 2 to 5 to store a statement number for later reference. A statement number identifies the statement so that it can be used later in the program in a branching or other out-of-sequence situation. Although any numeric value may be used as a statement number, no two statement numbers within a given routine may be the same.

Column 6 is usually left blank, unless a program instruction requires additional cards. In this case, a punch (other than zero) is made to tell the computer that the remaining part of the instruction is punched in the succeeding card.

Columns 7 to 72 are reserved for punching a program instruction. An instruction requiring more than one card is continued (beginning in column 7) in each succeeding card.

Columns 73 to 80 are reserved for punching such information as the sequence numbers of the cards of the program or other legal characters. This field is ignored by the computer during processing.

BASIC ELEMENTS OF FORTRAN

Like any other language, FORTRAN is composed of key elements that serve to define its formal structure. They are

1. Character set
2. Constants
3. Variables
   Array variables and subscripts
4. Dimension statements
5. Arithmetic statements
   Arithmetic assignment statement
6. Input–output statements
7. Format statements
   I specifications
   F specifications
   A specifications
   H specifications
8. Control statements
   Unconditional GO TO statement
   Conditional GO TO statement
   Arithmetic IF statement
   Logical IF statement
   Relational IF statement
9. Imperative statements
   DO statement
   CONTINUE statement
   STOP and END statements

Character Set

The FORTRAN character set consists of decimal digits 0 to 9, letters A to Z (uppercase), the period, comma, parentheses, apostrophe, and arithmetic operators +, —, *, and /.

Constants

A constant is any specific value (e.g., 27) or number that does not change during the execution of the program. Two valid types of numeric constants are used: (1) integer or (2) real. An *integer* (or fixed-point) constant consists of one or more decimal digits containing no decimal point and may be preceded by a plus or a minus sign. In the absence of either sign, the constant is assumed to be positive. Examples of valid constants are

341, +101, —40 (not —4.0), 10211 (not 102.11)

A *real* (or floating-point) constant is a number (0 to 9) written with a decimal point. The decimal point can be placed between any two digits, or can precede or follow the string of digits. For example,

0.   1.   .020   3.02141

represent the *fixed* format of a real constant. The *floating-point* format is an adaptation of "scientific notation" and is represented as a real constant followed by the letter E and a one- or two-digit integer constant. The letter E and the integer constant comprise the exponent that represents the power of 10 by which the real constant is to be multiplied. For example,

7.0E3 means 7.0×10^3, or 7,000

The maximum value of the exponent is determined by the specific computer used. Other examples of valid real constants are

56.58, −.0061, +5., 35.1E20, 7.E + 10, 3.24E − 9, −18.E − 8

Examples of invalid real constants are

4E10 (no decimal point present)
2,100.7 (no comma allowed)
11.0E674 (no more than two digits allowed in the exponent)
.18E1.1 (exponent not an integer)

Variables

Variables are symbolic of different value representations. For example, in the formula $Y = 7X^3 + 4X^2 + 2X + 3$, the digits 7, 4, 2, and 3 are constants, while Y and X are variables. It is common for programmers to use variables that clearly indicate the represented quantities. For example,

```
VALUE = UNITS * PRICE
```

Thus variables can be considered as names of memory locations. They remain unchanged throughout the program, even though the contents of the memory locations they represent change frequently.

A variable name must begin with a letter and is composed of a fixed number of alphanumeric characters, depending on the machine. For example, 7C14 is not a valid variable name because it begins with a digit.

Value representation can be either integer or real depending on whether the value represented is integer or real. An *integer variable* is a series of alphanumeric characters with the first letter being I, J, K, L, M, or N. Some examples are

IMAX, JOLT, KLARK, LEM10, MR121, NSUM
↓ ↓ ↓ ↓ ↓ ↓
I J K L M N

A *real variable*, on the other hand, is a series of alphanumeric characters with the first letter being any letter other than I to N. Some examples are

XMIN, SUM, PAY1, A9999

Although the programmer exercises freedom in deciding on the variable names to be used, there are certain predefined names (processes) that are reserved and must be avoided. For example, SQRT (abbreviation of

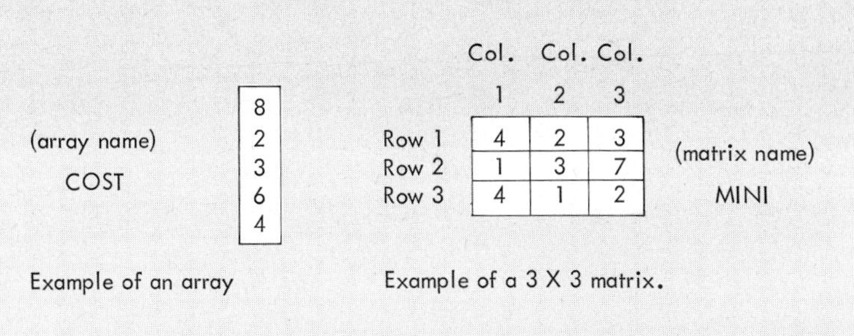

FIGURE 18-2. Arrays and matrices

square root) is a reserved word for the generalized square root subroutine and is incorporated in the FORTRAN compiler for the programmer's convenience.

ARRAY VARIABLES AND SUBSCRIPTS. It was mentioned earlier that a real or an integer variable name may be used as the name of a memory location. The term *array* is used in this section to refer to any *dimensioned* (or array) variable. A dimensioned variable represents one or more memory cells specified in a dimensioned statement, and appears as the first statement in the program. Arrays are either lists of values or matrices (Fig. 18-2).

In Fig. 18-2 we have an array, arbitrarily named COST. If we wish to refer to the third value, we would write the FORTRAN notation COST(3), 3 being the *subscript,* which must be enclosed in parentheses and follow the variable name. Reference to any element of the array requires the use of subscript I [e.g., COST(I)], where I defines the position in the array.

Figure 18-2 also shows a 3 by 3 matrix (3 by 3 being the dimensions of the matrix), arbitrarily called MINI. If we wish to refer to the value 1 in row 3 and column 2 (the elements of the intersection), we write the notation MINI(3,2), where 3 and 2 are the subscripts. The first digit always refers to the row number and the second digit to the column number. The two digits are separated by a comma and enclosed in parentheses following the variable name. Reference to the nine values of the matrix is written as follows:

Row No. ↓ Col. No. ↓	Value
MINI(1,1)	4
MINI(1,2)	2
MINI(1,3)	3
MINI(2,1)	1
MINI(2,2)	3
MINI(2,3)	7
MINI(3,1)	4
MINI(3,2)	1
MINI(3,3)	2

In FORTRAN, any element of a given two-dimensional matrix is represented by the subscripts I and J. Thus, in the matrix named MINI, the FORTRAN notation is written as MINI(I, J), where I represents values in rows 1, 2, and 3, and J represents values in columns 1, 2, and 3.

Dimension Statements

In FORTRAN programming, when a series of memory locations is reserved for array variables, a dimension statement (first statement of the program) is used to specify the dimensions of the variables involved.[1] Referring to Fig. 18-2, the dimension statement for the array and another for the matrix are written as follows:

```
DIMENSION COST(5)
DIMENSION MINI(3,3)²
```

DIMENSION COSTS(5) tells the computer that the array, named COST, consists of five elements. DIMENSION MINI(3,3) tells the computer that the matrix, named MINI, consists of three rows and three columns, respectively.

Arithmetic Statements

In constructing a FORTRAN program, various elements of the language (i.e., constants, variables, subscripts, or operation symbols) are combined in some predefined manner to form statements or expressions. One of the more commonly used statements is the arithmetic statement. It ranges from the simple form of a single operand (i.e., a real or integer variable or constant) to a relatively complex mathematical expression. In cases where more than one operand is present, arithmetic operators are used to "tie" the operands together into a valid arithmetic expression. The operands and operators are used in the same way as when building a normal mathematical equation. The operation symbols are

```
 +  addition
 -  subtraction
 *  multiplication
 /  division
 ** exponentiation
```

There is a predetermined priority for the performance of arithmetic operations. A statement is scanned from left to right and executed as follows:

[1] If no array variables are used, then no dimension statement is necessary.

[2] The two statements can be written on one line with a comma separating them:
DIMENSION COSTS(5), MINI(3,3)

1. All exponentiations are performed first.
2. All multiplications and divisions are performed next.
3. All additions and subtractions are performed last.

For example, the statement

$$\frac{A}{B^2} + C \times D + E^3$$

is expressed as A/B**2 + C*D + E**3 and is treated as

```
(A/(B**2)) + (C*D) + (E**3)
```

The innermost parenthetical expressions are evaluated first, leading to the evaluation of the outermost expressions. All equal levels of groupings are evaluated before moving to the next higher level.

In the case of multiple operations of equal priority,[3] operations are performed in order from left to right. For example, A + B + C is treated as (A + B) + C. One exception to this rule is the case of exponentiation. In an expression consisting entirely of exponentiations, the operations are performed from right to left. For example, the expression E**F**G would be equivalent to E** (F**G). It is important to note that parentheses may be used to override the implied priority of the operators. When parentheses are used, the expressions within the parentheses are first evaluated from innermost to outermost. Thus, parentheses are useful in clarifying an expression to avoid any probability of misinterpretation or ambiguity.

Other rules that are followed are:

1. All FORTRAN expressions must be clearly stated. For example, if we wish to multiply A by B, the statement is written as A*B. Any other expression (e.g., AB) is interpreted as a variable name.
2. Only one operator is permitted between two valid characters. Two or more consecutive operators require the use of parentheses; for example, the expression ISUM + —5 is not valid because of the presence of two consecutive operators between ISUM and 5. It must be rewritten as ISUM + (—5) or ISUM—5.
3. Operands in any arithmetic expression must be of the same type—integer or real constants. While some compilers allow mixed mode arithmetic, performing mixed mode arithmetic is considered poor programming practice.

Arithmetic Assignment Statement. This statement has the general form VARIABLE = EXPRESSION and, in effect, replaces the value

[3] It should be kept in mind that multiplication and division have the same priority. Addition and subtraction also have the same priority.

of the single variable on the left by the computed value of the expression on the right. Although arithmetic assignment is represented by an equal sign, the sign does not have the same connotation in FORTRAN as it does in mathematics. In mathematics, the equal sign means "is identical to" or "has the same magnitude as." In FORTRAN, however, the equal sign is interpreted as "is replaced by." In other words, the expression A = B + C actually means that the sum of the values of the variables B and C must be computed and the sum placed in the storage location assigned to the variable A. Thus, we see that in FORTRAN the expression I = I + 1 is completely legitimate and means "take the contents of the storage location assigned to the variable I, add 1 to that content, and place the sum in the storage location assigned to the variable I." Thus, if the value of I were 3 prior to execution of the arithmetic assignment, it would be 4 after execution. It should be obvious, then, why the left side of the statement can only be a single variable.

Generally, both sides of the statement are of the same type—that is, either integer or real. However, there is no rule against mixing types for the two sides. In the case when an expression (expressed in floating-point) is assigned to an integer variable, it is converted to a real result (with a fractional part of zero) before the assignment. Then, the fractional part of the real result will be dropped before final assignment. On the other hand, if an integer expression is assigned to a real variable, the expression is converted to a real configuration in its final assignment. For example, assume the assignment I = X/Y, where X = 5.0 and Y = 2.0; the real result of the division would be 2.5 but the value assigned to I would be 2 (fraction dropped).

Input–Output Statements

Input–output statements instruct the computer on the steps to be taken (read a card, print a line, punch a card, etc.); how to arrange data for input–output (i.e., what format is to be used); and what data (reference to variable name) to manipulate. Thus, input–output statements manipulate the transfer of data between the computer's primary storage and external (input and output) devices.

Each input–output word (READ, WRITE) is followed by an input–output device number, a format statement number (separated by a comma), and a list of variable names. READ statements initiate the transfer of input data from the punched cards to the computer's primary storage for processing. The READ format specifies the conversion from character to internal representation. The WRITE statement specifies conversion to external (character) form and actuates the printer to print out the result of certain computations (output data).

The READ statement takes the form

```
READ (integer, integer) LIST
```

Using the array in Fig. 18-2, the READ statement would be written

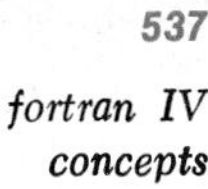

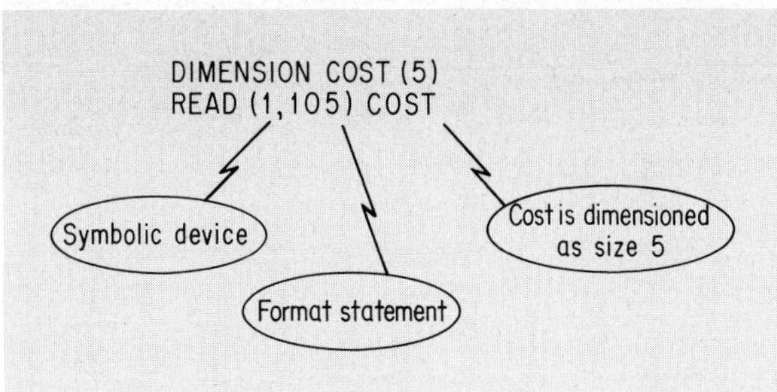

The statement instructs the computer to read from input device number 1, five elements into a storage location named COST according to a format specified in a statement having reference number 105. Thus, the first integer of the READ instruction refers to the input device number and the second integer refers to the format statement number. The LIST specifies the variable name and the quantities to be transferred into computer memory. Any number of quantities may be included in the LIST.

The WRITE statement takes the form:

```
WRITE (integer, integer) LIST
```

For example,

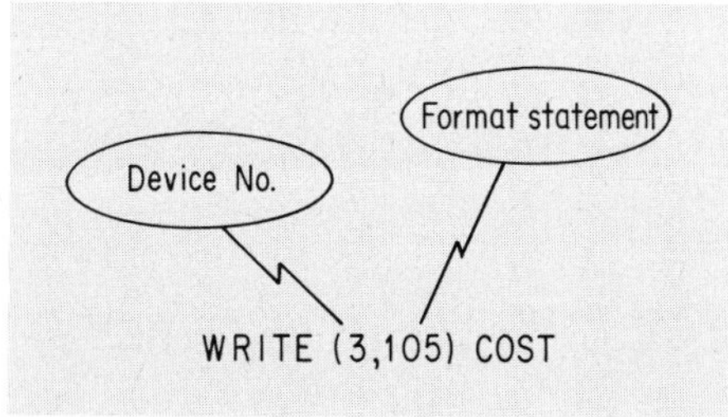

Like other input–output statements, execution of the WRITE statement is based on the FORMAT statement specifications. It should be noted that up to 120 or 132 characters (depending on the printer used) can be printed on one line.[4]

Format Statements

FORMAT statements are nonexecutable and serve input–output statements to specify the arrangement of data in an external medium (such as punched cards, magnetic tapes, or printed paper). Its form is:

```
FORMAT (specifications)
```

[4] See page 543 on H specifications for carriage control.

The list of specifications must be enclosed in parentheses and separated by commas.

In this section, two broad classes of data and the way they are specified are discussed. They are numeric and alphanumeric data. Numeric data may be (1) integer data, (2) real data in fixed-point form, or (3) real data in floating-point form.

I SPECIFICATIONS. The FORMAT specification for integer data is called *I FORMAT specification* [5] and is given in the form IW, where I signifies that the number to be read is an integer and W denotes the field or the number of character positions to be assigned (including a + or a − sign and any required blanks).

Several rules must be followed:

1. Leading zeros are replaced by blanks on output.
2. Blank card columns are interpreted as zeros on input (a zero value is not affected).
3. Available data are right-justified.
4. Output data exceeding W positions are lost and an asterisk is printed. However, if the data are less than the specified W position, unfilled positions are indicated by blanks.

For example, assume that the following data are punched in columns 1 to 11:

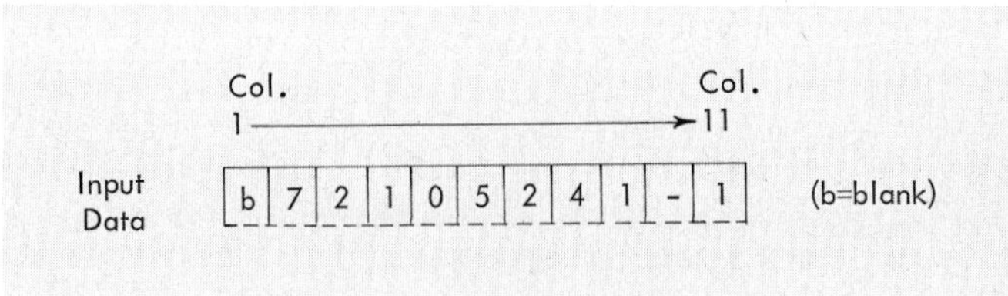

The input I specifications (4I1, I2, I3, I2)[6] show the values in seven memory locations as

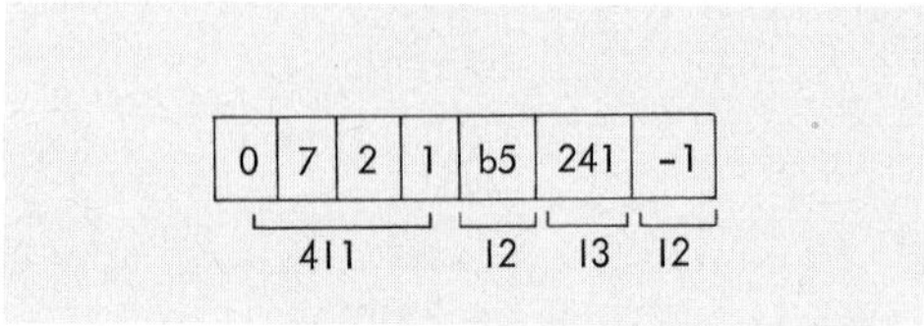

[5] I stands for integer.

[6] 4I1 means four fields, each consisting of one integer character. I2 means one field consisting of two integer characters. I3 means one field consisting of three integer characters.

Given the output I specifications

(313, 215, 13, 14)

the output would be punched in columns 1 to 26 as follows:

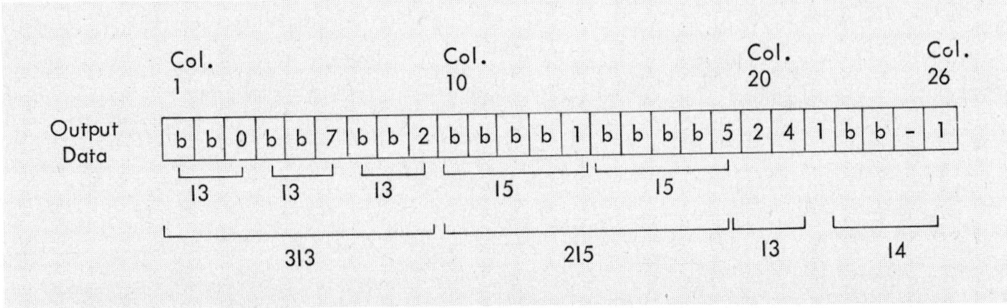

F SPECIFICATIONS. The F (meaning floating-point) specifications statement takes a given field read from an input medium as a real value and stores it in computer memory, the location of which is specified by the input statement. When output is desired, values stored in each memory cell involved are interpreted as real values (numbers) and placed in designated fields in an output medium. The F statement should also specify the length of the field and the number of decimal places required.

The F specification statement takes the general format

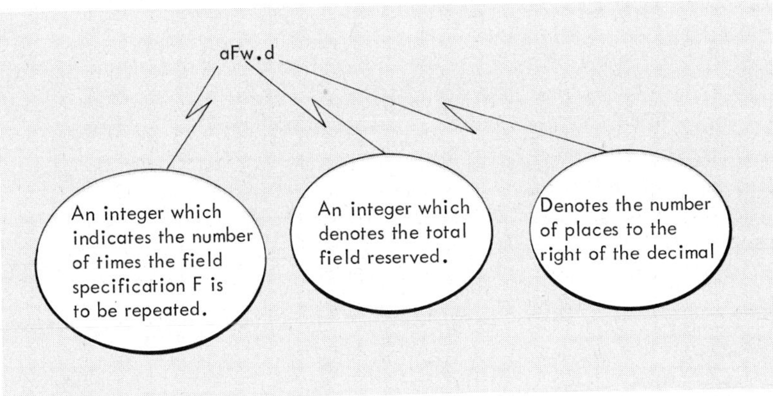

It should be noted that a period between the w and d in the F specification format is mandatory. For input data no decimal point is required, since its position is implied in the F format specifications. If a point is punched, it overrules the specifications in the format.

In determining the total field length for real values, character positions should be reserved for signs that precede the first significant digit in input and output data fields.

To further illustrate the F format specifications, assume that the following input data are punched in columns 1 to 15:

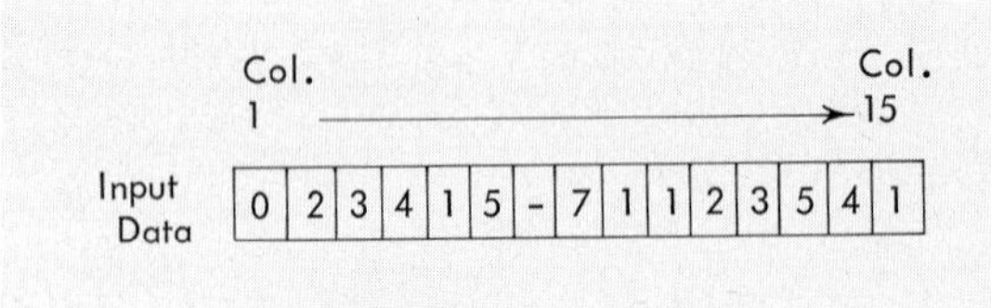

The input F specifications

```
(2F2.2, 2F2.0, F3.2, F4.0)⁷
```

show the values in six memory storage locations as follows:

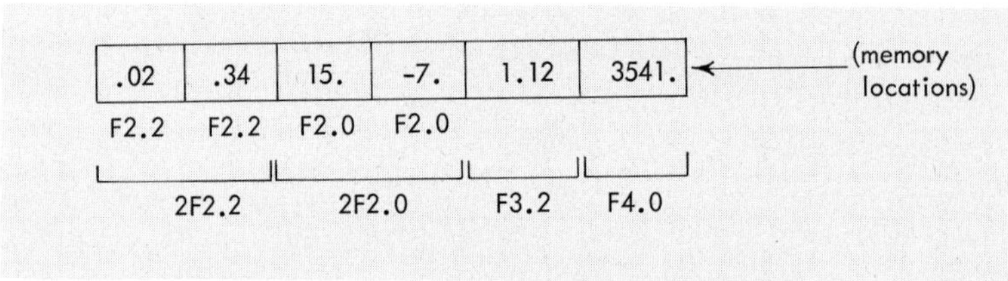

Given the output F specification

```
(5F5.2, F5.0)
```

the output would be punched in columns 1 to 30 as follows:

	Col. 1					Col. 6					Col. 11					Col. 16					Col. 21					Col. 26				Col. 30
Output Data	b	0	.	0	2	b	0	.	3	4	1	5	.	0	0	-	7	.	0	0	b	1	.	1	2	3	5	4	1	.
	F5.2					F5.2					F5.2					F5.2					F5.2					F5.0				

[7] 2F2.2 means two fields, each consisting of two characters with two digits to the right of the decimal point.

2F2.0 means two fields, each consisting of two characters with no digits to the right of the decimal point.

F3.2 means one field consisting of three characters with two digits to the right of the decimal point.

F4.0 means one field consisting of four characters with no digit to the right of the decimal point.

A SPECIFICATIONS. The A (meaning alphanumeric) specifications take alphabetic, numeric, and special characters in the form of input data and store them in computer memory in the form of words. Each computer varies in the manner of representing data in its memory and in the number of characters per word of storage.

The A specification statement takes the form

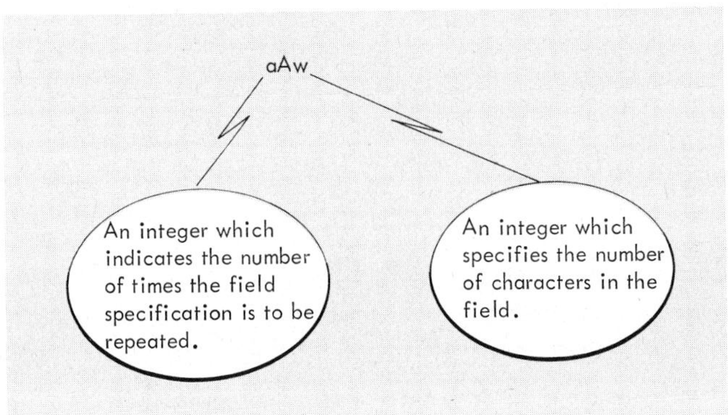

Thus, each w is read into one word of storage and left-justified. Any unused positions are interpreted as blanks. On input, if the characters read exceed the field length, all excess leading characters are left out. On output, any unfilled character positions of a given word of storage are filled with trailing blanks.

Assuming that the following alphanumeric data are punched in columns 1 to 15,

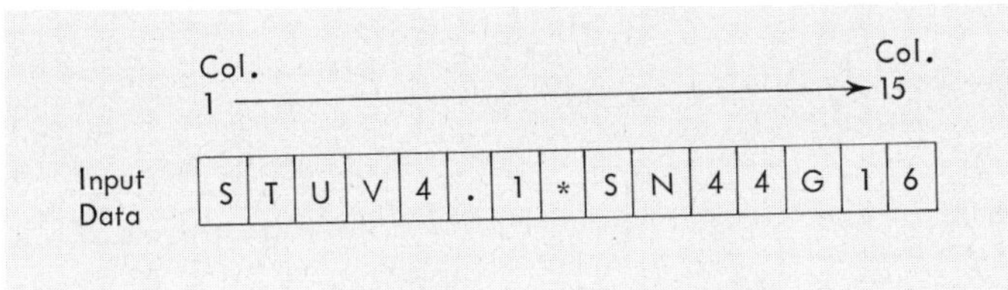

specifying six characters per word of storage, the input A specifications statement

```
(3A2, 3A3)
```

shows the values in six memory locations as follows:

STbbbb	UVbbbb	4.bbbb	1*Sbbb	N44bbb	G16bbb
A2	A2	A2	A3	A3	A3
3A2			3A3		

Given the output A specifications

```
(A3, 3A2, A4, A3)
```

the output would be punched in columns 1 to 20 as follows:

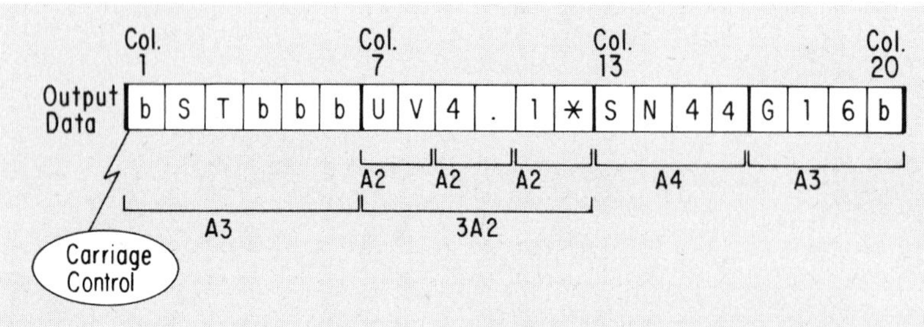

H SPECIFICATIONS. The H (meaning Hollerith) specifications statement is used in cases when certain alphanumeric constants are desired in the data output. Any such constants are included in the statement. The general format statement takes the following form:

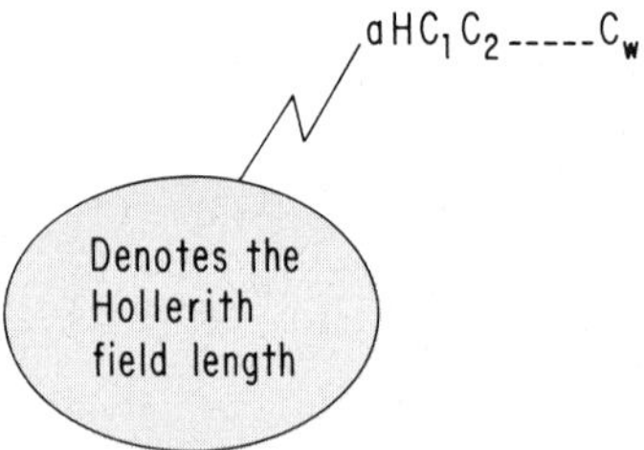

The spacing of values within a given line is signified by X specifications. For example, the H specification statement

```
(4X,14HRECTANGLEbBCD.)
```

results in 18 consecutive card columns, 1 to 18, as follows:

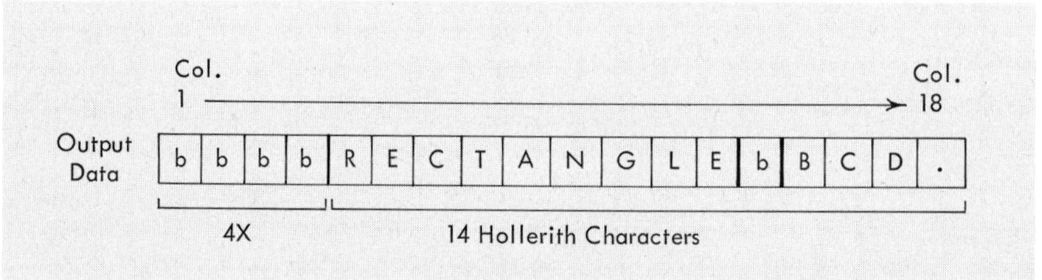

A carriage control character is used to control the printer. It is not relevant for punched output but it is a necessary part of the WRITE OUTPUT statement. The first character of an output line is interpreted as a carriage control character. The primary control characters are

b	(blank)	single space before printing
0		double space before printing
1		skip to a new page
+		no paper motion

The carriage control character is most commonly provided by incorporating it in an H specification of the type 1HX (where X is the carriage control character) as the first entry in the FORMAT list. For single spacing, the alternative 1X may be used. The following example illustrates the FORMAT statement in conjunction with a WRITE statement.

Assume the following requirements:

1. To print on the top of a new page the answers to three problems. The answer to problem 1 consists of three alphabetic characters. The answer to problem 2 consists of five-digit integer numeric characters, and the answer to problem 3 consists of nine-digit real numeric characters (five of the digits to follow the decimal point).
2. To print the statement THE ANSWERS ARE followed by five blanks and the three answers, respectively.
3. Each of the three answers is to be separated by three blanks.

Given the digit 6 to denote the output device and variable names ALPHA, IANSR, and RANSR, we would have

```
   WRITE(6, 10) ALPHA, IANSR, RANSR
10 FORMAT(1H1, 15HTHEbANSWERSbARE, 5X, A3, 3X, I5, 3X, F10.5)
```

Control Statements

FORTRAN statements are executed according to their sequence in the program deck, unless a control statement clearly interrupts sequential execution by transferring control to a statement elsewhere in the program. Transfers may be either conditional or unconditional, depending on the type of operation and evaluation desired.

UNCONDITIONAL "GO TO" STATEMENT. The unconditional GO TO statement causes unconditional transfer of control. Its general form is GO TO W, where W specifies the statement number that will be executed next. For example,

Statement No.	Instruction
12	GO TO 20
6	X = 3.*Y
	Y = 4.*B
20	STOP

This GO TO statement tells the computer to alter the next two sequential instructions to execute the STOP statement, causing termination of the program.

CONDITIONAL "GO TO" STATEMENT. This type of GO TO statement causes optional transfer of control to any of the series of statements (enclosed in parentheses), depending on the value of i in the general form

```
GO TO (n1, n2, . . . , nm), i
```

This means that if the value of i is 1, control is transferred to execute statement number n_1; $i = 2$, n_2; . . . ; if $i = m$, n_m. For example, in the statement

```
J = 4
 .
 .
 .
GO TO (5, 6, 7, 9, 11), J
```

the program transfers to the statement numbered 9 (fourth value between parentheses).

ARITHMETIC "IF" STATEMENT. The IF statement is a conditional transfer of the control statement, in that control is transferred to a given statement number only IF a particular condition is met. The general form is

```
IF (expression) n1, n2, n3
```

where n_1, n_2, and n_3 are executable statement numbers.

The execution of the arithmetic IF statement follows three key rules:

1. If the expression is negative, control is transferred to n_1.
2. If the expression is zero, control is transferred to n_2.
3. If the expression is positive, control is transferred to n_3.

For example, in the following IF statement

```
IF(A*3.0—40.0)1,2,3
```

if A = 4, control goes to statement 1, since the result is —28.

An IF statement is quite powerful in operations that require routine, repetitive computations. To further illustrate its use, assume a banking routine where 500 customer accounts must be updated on Monday of each week. The basic operation requires subtraction of payments from the balance outstanding. After the subtraction is performed, the balance outstanding takes on the new value.

In preparing the partial program, we need to set up an index to count the number of accounts updated and, when it contains 500, to branch the program to a specific statement that would proceed in executing the remaining parts of the program.

Given an index K, PREB (for previous balance), and PAYM (for payments), the partial program would be as shown in Fig. 18-3.

LOGICAL "IF" STATEMENT. A logical IF statement causes transfer of control based on whether a specific expression is *true* or *false*. If the expression is found to be true, control is transferred to the statement number following the parentheses in the IF statement. Otherwise, the next sequential statement is executed.

The general form of the logical IF statement is

```
IF(expression) statement a
statement b
```

RELATIONAL "IF" STATEMENT. An expression is evaluated not only by logical operands, but also by relational operators. The operators may be expressions, variables, or constants. FORTRAN's six relational operators are

Relational Operator	Description
.GE.	Greater than or equal to
.GT.	Greater than
.EQ.	Equal to
.NE.	Not equal to
.LE.	Less than or equal to
.LT.	Less than

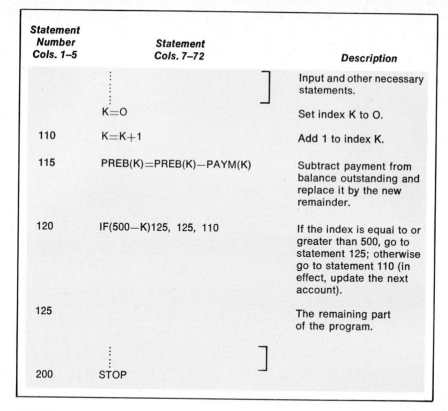

Statement Number Cols. 1–5	Statement Cols. 7–72	Description
	⋮	Input and other necessary statements.
	K=O	Set index K to O.
110	K=K+1	Add 1 to index K.
115	PREB(K)=PREB(K)−PAYM(K)	Subtract payment from balance outstanding and replace it by the new remainder.
120	IF(500−K)125, 125, 110	If the index is equal to or greater than 500, go to statement 125; otherwise go to statement 110 (in effect, update the next account).
125		The remaining part of the program.
	⋮	
200	STOP	

FIGURE 18-3. *A partial program*

Note that a period before and after each relational operator is mandatory.

Examples of relational expressions and their evaluation are

Relational Expression	Evaluation
100.EQ.100	True
400.GE.399	True
941.LT.940	False

Thus the expressions are logical as well as relational.

Relational expressions can be linked within a given logical IF statement by the logical operators .AND. and .OR.

The general form is

n_1.AND.n_2 n_1.OR.n_2

Using the logical operator .AND., the relational expressions n_1 and n_2 are considered as true only when both of them are true. However, with the logical operator .OR. the relational expression is considered as true when either n_1 or n_2 or both are true. Some examples follow:

1. IF(X*4.1.LE.A)J=4
2. IF(X.EQ.10.0)GO TO 100
3. IF(X.LT.3.AND.A.GT.Y)J=10
4. IF(A.LE.0.4.OR.A.GE.6.0)K=40.0/A

It should be kept in mind that precedence of execution takes the following order of priority—arithmetic operators, relational operators, logical operators.

Imperative Statements

"DO" STATEMENT. The Do statement is basically a convenient method of repetitive looping through a series of FORTRAN statements. The general form is

DO *n i* = m_1, m_2, m_3

where *n* is an executable statement number located at some later point in the program, *i* is an integer variable representing a counter to be incremented, and m_1, m_2, and m_3 are unsigned integer constants such that m_1 designates the initial value of the counter, m_2 designates the final value of the counter, and m_3 designates the value by which the counter is to be incremented each time through the loop. If m_3 is not explicitly stated, it is assumed to be 1.

The function of the DO statement is to execute all the statements immediately following it up to *and including* the statement with the number *n*. It will perform the designated series of statements as many times as necessary to increment the counter from its initial value to its final value. For example, if $m_1 = 1$, $m_2 = 5$, and $m_3 = 1$, then the DO loop will be executed five times, each time incrementing the counter by 1. In practice, the counter is initiated and the series of statements is performed. Then control is returned to the DO statement, which increments the counter by the appropriate value and determines if the counter has *exceeded* the final value specified (m_2). If the value of the counter *exceeds* m_2, control is transferred out of the loop. Otherwise, the sequence is repeated. Exit from the loop will occur automatically when the counter exceeds the value of m_2.

It is also possible to exit from the DO loop before completion of the loop by using a conditional-transfer-of-control statement within the range of the DO statement. However, it is not valid to transfer control into the range of a DO statement from an outside point.

Several rules must be observed in constructing a DO statement:

1. The last statement in the range of a DO statement must be an executable statement. It *cannot* be
   a. Any type of transfer of control statement.
   b. Another DO statement.
   c. A logical IF statement.
2. The parameters i, m_1, m_2, and m_3 *cannot* be changed by any other statement within the range of a DO statement. They may be changed outside the loop if transfer is not later made back into the loop.
3. A complete DO loop may be contained within another DO loop. This is commonly referred to as *nested* DO loops. There is no restriction on the extent of nesting that may be done. However, there is a restriction on transfer of control between nested DO loops. Although control may be transferred from an inner DO loop into an outer DO loop without restriction, control must never be transferred from an outer loop into an inner loop.

To illustrate nested DO loops, assume that it is necessary to perform a given major operation 10 times and that for each occurrence we wish to perform a minor operation 20 times. Given that the minor operation increments the counter in steps of 2, the DO statements required would appear as they do in Fig. 18-4.

"CONTINUE" STATEMENT. This is a dummy executable statement that can be placed anywhere in a program. Although executable, it does not perform any logical functions and does not change the sequence of instruction operation. It exists primarily to facilitate termination of a DO loop, which would otherwise terminate on a prohibted statement. For example,

FIGURE 18-4. Nested loops

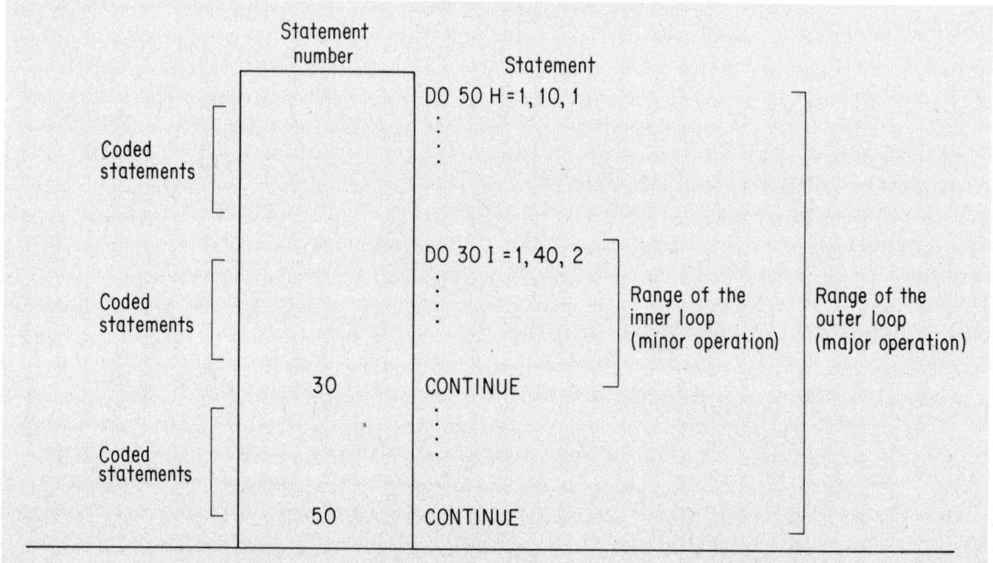

```
      DO 10 I=1, 15, 2
      IF (A(I).EQ.0.0)A(I) = 5.0
10    CONTINUE
```

"STOP" AND "END" STATEMENTS. The STOP statement is executable. It terminates execution of the object program. The END statement is required and is the last statement in a FORTRAN program. It is non-executable and serves to terminate the compiling routine.

The statements described are by no means a complete description of the FORTRAN language. They are, however, the most commonly used subset and are sufficient for a large proportion of applications. If a more extensive understanding of FORTRAN is desired, a text on FORTRAN or manuals provided by those offering FORTRAN compilers should be consulted. As a method of relating the preceding statements to their practical use, the solution of a problem using FORTRAN and the statements discussed previously will be presented next. A flowchart of the sample problem (Fig. 18-5) and a completed program (Fig. 18-6) are also presented by way of illustration.

FIGURE 18-5. *Flowchart for a sample FORTRAN program*

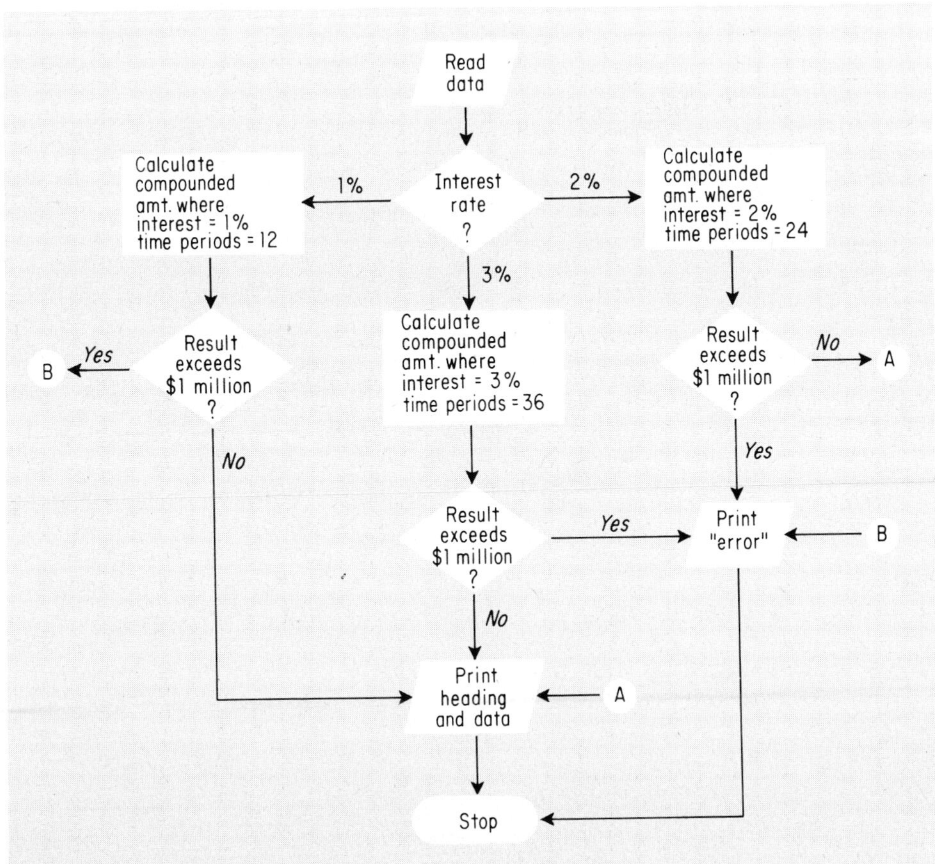

FORTRAN Coding Form

PROGRAM SAMPLE PROGRAM
PROGRAMMER JOHN GUERRA
DATE DEC. 14 ,197X

```
      XM=100.0
      XMAX=1000000.00
      READ(5,10)PRINC,I
   10 FORMAT(F6·2,I1
      RESLT=PRINC
      XI=I
      XI=XI/XM
      GO TO(20,30,40),I
   20 DO 25 J=1,12
      XINT=RESLT*XI
      RESLT=RESLT+XINT
      IF(MAX-RESLT)100,25,25
   25 CONTINUE
      GO TO 50
   30 DO 35 K=1,24
      XINT=RESLT*XI
      RESLT=RESLT+XINT
      IF(MAX-RESLT)100,35,35
   35 CONTINUE
      GO TO 50
   40 DO 45 L=1,36
      XINT=RESLT*X1
      RESLT=RESLT+XINT
      IF(MAX=RESLT)100,45,45
```

FIGURE 18-6. *Program for a sample FORTRAN program*

FORTRAN Coding Form

PROGRAM SAMPLE PROGRAM
PROGRAMMER JOHN GUERRA
DATE DEC 14 ,197X

```
   45 CONTINUE
   50 WRITE(6,60)
   60 FORMAT(1H1,45X,29HCOMPOUNDED AMOUNT CALCULATION,45X)
      WRITE(6,70)PRINC,I,RESLT
   70 FORMAT(1H0,10HPR\NCIPAL=,2X,F6·2,5X,9HINTEREST=,2X,I1,5X,7HRESULT
     1,2X,F10·2)
      GO TO 110
  100 WRITE(6,80)
   80 FORMAT(1H1,57X,5HERROR)
  110 STOP
      END
```

To illustrate the FORTRAN coding of a problem solution, the following sample program executes the routines for compounding a simple sum. Performing the calculations in a stepwise fashion, the basic procedure is: old amount (at beginning of time period) + (old amount × interest rate) = new amount (at end of time period). This new amount becomes the old amount for the next consecutive time period. The assumptions are

1. The principal and interest rate will be constrained variables, their value to be read as input from input device number 5.
2. The allowable interest rates are 1 percent for 12 time periods, 2 percent for 24 time periods, and 3 percent for 36 time periods.
3. The maximum allowable principal is $999.99.
4. If the compounded amount exceeds $1,000,000.00, the program should immediately print ERROR and terminate execution.
5. The output is to be printed on device 6 (assume 120 print positions). An appropriate heading is required, and the sequence of the output data is to be principal, interest rate, and compounded amount.
6. Name assignments: I = interest rate, PRINC = principal, RESLT = compounded amount, and MAX = maximum allowable compounded amount.

SUMMARY

FORTRAN is a popular, high-level programming language. Although it is more specifically designed for solving mathematical problems, it can also be used in solving a variety of business problems. Some of the elements used in FORTRAN are real and integer constants and variables. A real constant is a number written with a decimal point; an integer constant is a number containing no decimal points. A real variable is a series of alphanumeric characters with the first letter being a letter other than I to N. An integer variable is a series of alphanumeric characters, except that the first letter must be I, J, K, L, M, or N.

A real or an integer variable may be used as the name of a memory location. When a list of memory locations is reserved for array (dimensioned) variables, a dimension statement is used to specify the dimensions of the variables involved. Thus, the statement DIMENSION COST (5), tells the computer that the array, named COST, consists of five elements. In the case of a matrix, the dimension statement shows the dimension of the matrix. For example, the dimension statement for a 4 by 4 matrix is DIMENSION (4, 4); the digits between parentheses are called subscripts.

In FORTRAN programming, constants, variables, subscripts, or operation symbols are combined in some predefined manner to form statements. The major statements are arithmetic, input–output, format, control, and imperative statements. The *arithmetic* statement ranges from the simple form of a single operand to a relatively complex expression. *Input–output* statements instruct the computer to read a card, print a line, punch a card, how to arrange input–output data, and what data to manipulate. A *format* statement serves input–output statements to specify the arrangement of data in an external medium.

Control statements may be conditional or unconditional. A conditional GO TO statement causes optional transfer of control to a specific statement, depending on the value of *i* in the GO TO statement. An unconditional GO TO statement, on the other hand, causes unconditional transfer of control.

IF statements, whether they are arithmetic, logical, or relational, are conditional-transfer-of-control statements. The arithmetic IF statement causes transfer of control to a statement number if a particular condition is met; the logical IF statement causes transfer of control depending on whether a specific expression is true or false; the relational IF statement causes transfer of control depending on the relational operator.

Imperative statements refer to the DO, CONTINUE, and the STOP and END statements. A DO statement is basically a convenient method of repetitive looping through a series of statements. A CONTINUE statement is used primarily to allow the termination of a DO loop. The STOP statement simply terminates the execution of the object program, and the END statement terminates the compiling routine.

TERMS TO LEARN

Array variable	FORTRAN
Constant	Imperative statement
Control statement	Integer variable
Format statement	Real constant

QUESTIONS

1. What type of information is punched in columns 1 to 6 of a FORTRAN card?
2. List and briefly explain the primary elements of FORTRAN.
3. What is the difference between an integer and real constant? an integer and real variable? Give an example of each.

4. Give an example of a 3 by 4 matrix.

5. When is a dimension statement used?

6. Explain the order of priority for evaluating an arithmetic statement.

7. Give the format of the following statements:
   a. Arithmetic assignment statement.
   b. Input–output statement.
   c. FORMAT statement.
   d. Logical IF statement.

8. Explain briefly the function of the following specifications:
   a. F specifications.
   b. A specifications.
   c. H specifications.

9. Distinguish between a conditional and an unconditional statement. Give an example of each.

10. Distinguish between a logical and a relational IF statement. Give an example of each.

11. Explain the function of the DO statement.

12. Write the following expressions and statements in FORTRAN notation. Use capital letters for identifiers.
    a. $x + y + c$
    b. $ax + by + cz$
    c. $x = y + z + 2a$
    d. $\frac{x}{a} + \frac{y}{b}$
    e. $a = \text{int}$
    f. $a + b = c - d$

13. Given $J = 3$, $K = 4$, $L = 6$, and $M = 5$, what is the value stored in I after the formula I = (J*K) + (L—M) is executed?

14. Flowchart and code a program to compute net pay.

    Input Data
    G gross pay
    W federal withholding tax
    O other deductions
    Formula: N=G—(W+O)
    Input format: (3F9.2)
    Input device number: 1
    Input FORMAT statement number: 40

    Output Data
    N, G, W, O
    Output format: (4F9.2)
    Output device number: 3
    Output FORMAT statement number: 50

15. Which of the following are valid names for integer variables? real variables? Why? NADER, FAY, ZONA, L678P2, MONEY, COUNTER, TI, IT.

16. Which of the following are valid names for integer constants? real constants? Why? 4567, .456, —4567, —.04567, 100, 0, +210., 01247, 3.4E-10.

17. Given $J = 15$, $K = 4$, $L = 9$, and $M = 19$, determine the truth value of the following expressions.
    a. J.LT.L.OR.K.GE.M-J.
    b. J.GT.L.OR.K.LT.M-J.

SUGGESTED READING

COUGAR, D. J., and L. E. SHANNON. *FORTRAN IV, a Programmed Instruction Approach: Revised Edition.* Homewood, Ill.: Richard D. Irwin, Inc., 1972.

FARINA, M. V. *FORTRAN IV, Self-Taught.* Englewood Cliffs, N.J.: Prentice-Hall, Inc., 1966.

LEE, ROBERT. *A Short Course in Basic FORTRAN IV Programming.* New York: McGraw-Hill Book Company, 1972.

RAUN, D. L. *An Introduction to FORTRAN Computer Programming for Business Analysis.* Encino, Calif.: Dickenson Publishing Company, Inc., 1973.

basic

19

BASIC (Beginners All-Purpose Symbolic Instruction Code) is a higher-level programming language developed at Dartmouth College especially for time-sharing computer users. It is a mixture of plain English and algebra (arithmetic operations and exponentiation) and has a structure similar to that of FORTRAN. Competence in either language makes it easier to learn the other. In addition to being a powerful language, BASIC is easy to use, has few rules to remember, uses ordinary English words and familiar arithmetic symbols, and provides a real-time environment in which the user interacts directly with the computer for problem solving.

SIGN ON AND PROGRAM ENTRY

BASIC is designed for on-line processing in a time-sharing environment. On-line processing involves a conversational dialogue with the computer via a terminal. The dialogue essentially relates to signing on and entering the program into the system as follows [1]

1. Press the ORIG button below the telephone dial and, when a dial tone is heard, dial the computer system's phone number.
2. When a high-pitched tone is heard, the terminal prints a sign-on message consisting of the name of the time-sharing facility, the time of the service, and the ID number of the terminal used. (See Fig. 19-1).

[1] The procedure presented here is general. The exact procedure depends largely on the type of terminal and the size and requirements of the time-sharing facility.

Computer Messages	Typed Response
ØN AT — 12:19 PØRT:07	
USER NUMBER	1471C,BD
PASSWØRD	
TYPE NEW ØR ØLD:	NEW
NEW PRØBLEM NAME:	SUM
READY	
10 READ A,B,C	
20 DATA 8,9,5	
30 LET S=(8*8)+(9*9)/5	
40 PRINT "VALUE IS" S	
50 END	
RUN	
SUM	
	12:21 TSS 09/20.74 TUES.
VALUE IS 80.2	
RUNNING TIME 02.0 SECS.	
READY	
BYE	
ØFF AT 12:23	

FIGURE 19-1. BASIC program entry and format

3. The terminal then types USER NUMBER on a separate line and pauses. The user keys in his number and depresses the RETURN button to start a new line.
4. The terminal types the word PASSWORD and pauses at the next line. The user enters his password, which is stored (not typed) by the system. The RETURN button is depressed to go to another line.
5. The system asks TYPE NEW OR OLD. The user enters his response and depresses the RETURN button. In the sample program in Fig. 19-1, the response is NEW.
6. The system next asks NEW PROBLEM NAME. The user types his response (e.g., SUM)[2] and depresses the RETURN button.
7. The system types READY, indicating to the user that the time-sharing system is ready to accept his program. The user then depresses the RETURN button and proceeds to key in his BASIC program (Fig. 19-1).
8. Once entered, the user types RUN and depresses the RETURN button. The system responds by typing identifying information such as the name of the program, time, name of service, date, and day of service.
9. Assuming an error-free program, the program is executed and the answer printed out, followed by the running time.
10. Once the program is executed, the system prints READY, signaling a new operation.[3] Since the program has been executed, the user

[2] Although the arbitrary program name SUM is three alphabetic characters, actual program names may be up to six alphanumeric characters; the first character must be a letter.

[3] If the user wishes to save his program in the computer's memory, he types SAVE after pressing the RETURN key.

types the command word BYE or GOODBYE, which disconnects the terminal from the system. Upon depression of the RETURN button, sign-off time is typed.

BASIC ELEMENTS

Constants and Variables

A *constant* is a number that is used with or without a decimal point as a part of a statement. It may be positive, negative, or zero, and should be shown in decimal (not fractional) form. If the constant is negative, it must be preceded by a minus sign. If positive, a plus sign is optional.

Very large or very small numbers may be represented by using the letter E. The representation is a number followed by letter E, plus an exponent. Letter E means "10 raised to a power." For example,

1. 17E4 means 17 times $(10)^4$ = 17 times 10,000 = 170,000.
2. .14E—2 means 0.14 times $(10)^{-2}$ = 0.14 times 0.01 = 0.0014.

Thus, the negative exponent indicates the number of places to the left that the decimal point should be located. In the case of the second example, exponent —2 indicates that the decimal point should be moved two places to the left, causing two zeros to be written between digit 1 and the decimal point. The following BASIC examples should clarify this point:

Before		After
1.4E3	interpreted as	1400
1.4E—3	interpreted as	0.0014
.8E—5	interpreted as	0.000008

A *variable* represents (1) a number or a constant, and, in some BASIC systems, (2) a string variable that stands for a word (a combination of letters). A numeric variable must be either a single letter or a single letter followed by a single digit; a string variable consists of a letter followed by a dollar sign.

Examples of numeric variables are

Correct Variable	***Incorrect Variable***
A	10A
D1	ID
Z4	AZ4

Examples of string variables are

```
C$ may stand for COSINE
S$ may stand for SQUARE
Z$ may stand for ZONE
```

Statement Format

As explained in previous chapters, a program is made up of several related statements presented in a logical sequence for computer processing. A very common BASIC command takes the following format:

(statement (or line) number)	(special BASIC command)	(variable name)	=	(a number or an expression)
10	LET	A	=	6

LET is used to define the expression. The statement means: *Generate digit 6 and place it in a computer cell having variable name A.* With this in mind, a program designed to multiply two digits and print their product might require the following set of statements:

```
10 LET A = 5
20 LET B = 6
30 LET C = A*B
40 PRINT A,B,C
50 END
```

Arithmetic Operators

Arithmetic signs in BASIC are called *operators.* They are used in a manner similar to that of ordinary arithmetic. Arithmetic operators are as follows:

Arithmetic Notation	***Operation***	***BASIC Operator***
+	Addition	+
−	Subtraction	−
×	Multiplication	*
÷	Division	/

For example, 265 × 14.5 is written in BASIC as 265*14.5; 116 ÷ 4 is written in BASIC as 116/4.

BASIC arithmetic calculations follow normal mathematical rules. That is,

1. Calculations inside parentheses are performed first. If there are parentheses within the outer parentheses, calculations inside the inner parentheses are performed first. 5 + (5+4*(7*2)) for example, is computed as follows:
   Step 1. 7*2 = 14.
   Step 2. 4*14 = 56.
   Step 3. 5+(5+56) = 66.
2. In the absence of parentheses, the order of calculation takes the following priority:
   a. Exponentiation (represented by ↑ or **).
   b. Division and multiplication.
   c. Addition and subtraction.

It should be noted that when a statement contains two or more computations on the same level of priority, they are handled from left to right. The following examples illustrate these rules.

```
                                  10 LET A = 4+14/2—1*4
step 1: divide                             = 4+7—1*4
step 2: multiply                           = 4+7—4
step 3: add and subtract                   = 7

                                  10 LET A = 4+14/2*7↑3—9
step 1: find exponential value             = 4+14/2*343—9
step 2: divide                             = 4+7*343—9
step 3: multiply                           = 4+2401—9
step 4: add and subtract                   = 2396

                                  10 LET Y = 4+(10↑2/5)*(2↑3—4)
step 1                                     = 4+(100/5)*(8—4)
step 2                                     = 4+(20)*(4)
step 3                                     = 4+80
step 4                                     = 84
```

Built-in Mathematical Functions

The BASIC built-in mathematical functions help the programmer perform special calculations (see Fig. 19-2). The letter X accompanying each function represents an arbitrary value (argument). The argument may be a *variable* or an *expression*. For example, a program to compute the square root of 89,052 (the argument here is a variable) and place the answer in an area called Y consists of the following statements:

```
10 LET X = 89052
20 LET Y = SQR(X)          Can also be written as
                           20 LET Y = SQR(89052)
30 PRINT Y
40 END
```

Built-In Functions	Use	Comments
ABS(X)	Find absolute value of *X*	Gives positive version of some number
ATN(X)	Find arctangent of *X*	Trigonometric function
COS(X)	Compute cosine of *X*	Trigonometric function
EXP(X)	Exponentiate e^X	Compute value of *e* (2.71828 . . .) raised to the *X* power
INT(X)	Extract largest integer portion of *X*	Gives the largest whole number that can be obtained within a given value; also used to round numbers
LOG(X)	Log to base *e*	A log cannot be taken of a negative value
RND(X)	Generate a random number	Gives a different random number between 0 and 1 every time the function is called in the program
SIN(X)	Compute sine of *X*	Trigonometric function
SQR(X)	Take square root of *X*	
TAN(X)	Compute tangent of *X*	Trigonometric function

FIGURE 19-2. *Built-in functions*

When the argument is used as an expression, a program to find the square root of $4X^3 - 1$, where $X = 5$, is

```
10 LET X = 5
20 LET Y = SQR(4*↑3—1)
30 PRINT Y
40 END
```

SYSTEM COMMANDS

A system command is a computer instruction that tells the system what specific action to take. Unlike BASIC statements that begin with a statement number, system commands are written without a statement number. Some of the more frequently used system commands are

RUN — Tells the computer to execute the stored program. It is typed at the beginning of the next line, followed by returning the carriage (depressing the RETURN key).

SAVE — Causes the existing program to be placed in the library for later use.

LIST — Causes printing of a program statement or complete listing of the program, including any changes made.

HELP — Asks for system assistance in resolving certain errors. For example, the statement

```
10 LET A = B*C+5/2)
```

causes the computer to print an arrow below the error as follows:

```
10 LET A = B*↑C + 5/2)
```

In this case, the arrow indicates a missing left parenthesis, which the user has to insert before the program can be run.

NEW Used when one begins writing a new program.

OLD Accesses a saved program.

SCRATCH Used when one wishes to wipe out the instructions of a program being worked on.

INPUT–OUTPUT STATEMENTS

Input and output statements are used to call for data from the typewriter keyboard, or for data included in the program, and to print the results, if required. There are four basic input–output statements:

DATA Specifies the data for use by the program to be accessed by the READ statement; for example,

```
DATA 7, 8, 9, 4, 1
```

READ Precedes a corresponding DATA statement. It lists variable names that take corresponding values from the DATA list; for example,

```
10 READ A, B, C          10 READ A, B, C          10 READ A, B, C
20 DATA 7, 8, 9    or    20 DATA 7          or    20 DATA 7, 8
                         30 DATA 8                30 DATA 9
                         40 DATA 9
```

The READ statement takes the data values 7, 8, 9 and assigns them to A, B, C, respectively. Note that the number of DATA statements does not have to equal the number of READ statements, but the number of constants in the DATA statement(s) must be equal to the number of variables in the READ statement.

INPUT Indicates to the computer that data are to be entered from the user's terminal; for example,

```
INPUT A, B, C
```

During execution, when input is requested by the program, a question mark (?) is printed on the terminal or teletype. At this time, input data called for by the input statement can be entered.

PRINT Tells the computer to print the value of specific variables (e.g., PRINT A), skip a line, or print descriptive information or headings (e.g., PRINT "THE SUM IS").

There are cases when two or more data items must be printed on one line. To do so, a comma is placed between the items in the PRINT statement. For example, 40 PRINT A, B will print the value of A and B in 15 spaces each on one line. To narrow the space to two spaces, a semicolon is used instead of the comma.

Finally, printing the output of two or more PRINT statements in one line is achieved by placing a comma after the last item of the first statement. For example,

```
40 PRINT A, B,
50 PRINT C, D
```

will cause the four values to be printed on the same line. Again, to print the four values closer, semicolons are used instead of commas.

REMARK STATEMENT

It is often desirable to include in the program descriptive information for documentation purposes. This is accomplished by starting the statement with REM (meaning REMark), which is interpreted by the system to mean that the statement is for documentation only. For example,

```
20 REM THIS PROGRAM COMPUTES SICK PAY
```

In some systems, information can be inserted by typing a single quotation mark at the end of any statement, followed by the information; for example,

```
50 LET A = 15' SETS A TO 15
```

CONTROL STATEMENTS

A control statement allows program flexibility by branching (transfer of control) to a different program instruction to handle an exception or to satisfy a condition.

There are two types of control statements:

1. Unconditional transfer of control, with the format

(statement number)	GO TO	(statement number)
40	GO TO	70

A GO TO statement simply tells the computer to jump to the program instruction that carries the statement number indicated in the GO TO statement. In the example, the next instruction to be executed is statement 70.

2. Conditional transfer of control with the format

(statement number)	IF	(condition to be tested)	THEN (or GO TO)	(statement number)
40	IF	A = B	THEN (or GO TO)	80

A conditional statement transfers control to the statement number indicated only if the specified condition is met. In the example, if A (the subject) is equal to (the relation) B (the object), THEN the computer is told to transfer control to (or GO TO) statement 80. Otherwise, it automatically executes the next sequential instruction.

A conditional statement is further illustrated in the following program:

```
10 LET J = 1
20 PRINT J
30 LET J = J+1
40 IF J<101 THEN 20     or     40 IF J<101 GO TO 20
50 END
```

The program is designed to tell the computer to count from 1 to 100. Statement 10 sets the initial value of J to 1. Statement 20 prints the value of J. In this case, it is 1. Statement 30 increments the value in J by 1. Statement 40 is a conditional statement that tests the value of J for 100. *If* the value is less than 100, *then* the computer is told to jump to statement 20 (print the present value of J) and proceed with the rest of the program (in this case, statement 30 only). Otherwise, the computer will take statement 50, which ends the running of the program.

Relational Symbols

Conditional statements use six possible BASIC relational symbols (see Fig. 19-3).

FIGURE 19-3. *BASIC relational symbols*

Relational Symbol	***Meaning***	***BASIC Notation***	***Examples***
$=$	Equal	=	A4 = K7
$\neq$	Not equal	<>	K2 <> 6
$<$	Less than	<	B < 7
$>$	Greater than	>	Y4 > N9
$\leq$	Less than or equal to	<=	A4 <= 2
$\geq$	Greater than or equal to	>=	U4 >= U3

It should be noted that two or more consecutive conditional statements may be used in the program, if necessary. For example, suppose that we wish to compare the values X, Y, and Z to find out which of the three is the largest value. A program similar to the following might be used:

```
10 READ X, Y, Z
15 DATA 14, 12, 17
20 IF X>Y THEN 90
30 IF Y>Z THEN 70
40 LET A = Z
50 PRINT A
60 GO TO 130
70 LET A = Y
80 GO TO 50
90 IF X>Z THEN 110
100 GO TO 40
110 LET A = X
120 GO TO 50
130 END
```

END and STOP Statements

An END statement defines the end of the program. It must have the highest statement number and be placed at the end of the program. The STOP statement is used for terminating the program. The program, however, will stop if it runs out of data. The STOP statement, then, is used most often as a matter of convenience.

ARRAYS AND SUBSCRIPTS

Loops are often connected with subscripted variables. BASIC language offers instructions that make it possible to define these variables and, consequently, perform the necessary looping operation. Assume a single variable J as being subscripted. The first 10 subscripts of J are

Arithmetic Representation	BASIC Representation
J_1	J(0)
J_2	J(1)
J_3	J(2)
J_4	J(3)
•	•
•	•
•	•
J_{10}	J(9)

An *array* is a list of values or entries that are classed as a unit. Each entry is identified by the name of the list and by its position in the list.

For example, assume a list of the following five entries with the name[4] A:

A
1
2
3
4
5

The fourth entry is identified as A_4, or A(3) in BASIC. Arithmetic notations use a lowered number (subscript)[5]; in BASIC, the subscript must be in parentheses. So the entries above are subscripted as follows:

Arithmetic Notation	***BASIC Notation***
A_1	A(0)
A_2	A(1)
A_3	A(2)
A_4	A(3)
A_5	A(4)

Note that in BASIC the subscript for the first entry is generally 0, for the second entry is 1, . . ., and for the fifth entry is 4. When we have a list of subscripted values in a single column, the list is called a *one-dimensional array*.

BASIC provides 11 places in memory for any one-dimensioned array. If more than 11 places are desired, a BASIC *dimension* (abbreviated DIM) statement can be used. The DIM statement format is

(statement number) DIM (array name (size)), (array name (size)) (, . . . , (array name (size))^n

10 DIM A (99), B (55), . . . N (940)

Note that commas are used to separate the arrays listed in the dimension statement. Also, remember that an array in BASIC begins with a *zero*

[4] The name of an array must be a single letter, such as A, P, X. Any other arrangement is illegal.

[5] A subscript may be a whole, positive number such as 6, 8, or 40, or a variable name like *I, J, K, L, M,* or *N*. It must never be larger than the maximum number of entries in an array as specified in the DIM statement.

subscript. In the example, array A(99) reserves 100 cells [A(0), A(1), . . ., A(99)] in computer memory.

To illustrate the use of the DIM statement, suppose that we need a program to add five types of income and print out the sum. The five figures are 1,400, 670, 145, 716, and 801. Using a DIM statement, we have the following program:

Program	Comment
10 DIM A(5)	Reserves five computer locations (5 A's). Technically, there are six locations [A(0), . . ., A(5)].
20 READ A(1), A(2), A(3), A(4), A(5)	
30 LET X=A(1) +A(2) +A(3) +A(4) +A(5)	The five types of income are added together.
40 PRINT X	The sum is printed out.
50 DATA 1400, 670, 145, 716, 801	Each value corresponds to the subscripted values in the READ statement, respectively.
60 END	

Note that the DIM statement can be written anywhere in a BASIC program, provided that it precedes the appearance of any entry of the array to be used in the program.

Looping

In a looping operation, a segment of a program or a sequence of statements is repeated a specific number of times to solve a problem. The effect is to reduce the number of required instructions to run a program. In BASIC programming, the special FOR–TO and NEXT statements are used for this purpose. The FOR–TO format is

(statement number) FOR (legal variable name) = (number) TO (number)

The NEXT format is

NEXT (legal variable name)

Take the following partial program:

```
         (30 FOR A = 1 TO 5
Partial  )40 PRINT A
program  )50 NEXT A
         (60 END
          RUN
            1
            2
            3
            4
            5
          READY
```

Statement 30 initiates the sequence of statements that will be performed five times, with A being successively incremented in value from 1 to 5. Thus, every time the sequence is executed a printout is made of the value of A. The NEXT statement (number 50) merely tells the computer to continue executing the sequence. When A is equal to 5, the next statement (END) is executed, ending the program.

An important point to remember is that a FOR–TO statement is used when a set of statements is to be executed several times. Compare the following programs:

Looping with a GO TO Statement	***Looping with FOR, NEXT Statements***
10 READ B	10 FOR J=1 TO 5
20 LET A=B*5	20 READ B
30 PRINT A, B	30 LET A=B*5
40 GO TO 10	40 PRINT A, B
50 DATA 1.7, 6.9, 17.1, 8.4, 3.8	50 NEXT J
60 END	60 DATA 1.7, 6.9, 17.1, 8.4, 3.8
	70 END

The way the two programs are written produces the same result. However, the operation in each is different. In the program on the left, the computer reads from the DATA statement one value at a time, multiplies it by 5 (statement 20), prints the product along with the value of B, and returns to read another value when the GO TO statement is executed. This looping phase continues as long as there are values in the DATA statement.

In the program on the right, however, the special FOR–TO and NEXT statements are used as a pair to specify the number of times looping is to be made. The FOR–TO statement causes the computer to initiate a counter with the name J as it appears in the statement. It simply means: *Execute all subsequent statements up to and including the NEXT statement with variable name J, five times.* Here, the DATA statement must have five values. On the first round of execution, the computer sets the counter at 1. When it executes the NEXT J statement, the counter is incremented by 1, initiating the second round of execution (statements 20, 30, and 40). Looping continues until the counter registers 5, which means that the computer has executed the set of statements exactly five times. At that time, the computer jumps the loop and takes the statement following the NEXT statement in the program.

Two-Dimensional Arrays

It was mentioned with regard to one-dimensional arrays that, when entries (variables) are to be subscripted, a DIM statement must be written if the number of entries to be dimensioned is equal to or larger than 11. A dimension statement is also used in a two-dimensional array. A two-dimensional array, also called a *matrix*, is one in which individual variables are identified by their row and column numbers. A matrix can be represented by a general double-subscript variable $A\ (I,\ J)$, where I represents the number of rows and J the number of columns. Figure 19-4 is a 3 by 4 matrix consisting of 12 variables. A DIM statement 40

		Columns			
		1	2	3	4
	1	15	71	10	1
Rows	2	2	18	8	15
	3	9	14	4	3

FIGURE 19-4. Two-dimensional array A

DIM A(3,4) reserves an area in computer memory for these variables. It tells the computer that the dimensions of the matrix are three rows and four columns, respectively. Note that items shown between parentheses are subscripts, are separated by a comma, and denote the location of a given constant in the matrix. For example, A(3,2) refers to 14—the intersection of the third row and the second column.

Inner and Outer Loops

BASIC programming allows one or more loops (called inner loops) to be inserted within a major (outer) loop. An example of the general format of loops within loops is shown on the next page.

Here we have one inner loop controlled by counter B within an outer loop controlled by counter A. Execution is carried out by executing the inner loop three times for each execution of the outer loop. This means that the statements within the inner loop will be executed a total of 12 (3×4) times.

Another way of using the loop-within-loop concept is to set the

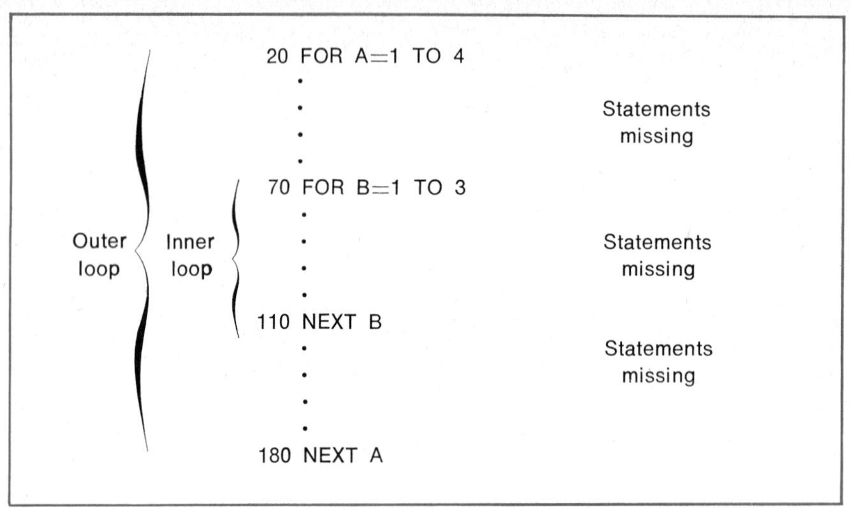
20 FOR A=1 TO 4
Statements missing
70 FOR B=1 TO 3
Outer loop
Inner loop
Statements missing
110 NEXT B
Statements missing
180 NEXT A

elements of a two-dimensional array to a specific digit, depending on the problem. The following is a sample program [6]:

```
10 DIM A(4,3)
   .
   .
   .
40 FOR I=1 TO 4
45 FOR J=1 TO 3
50 LET A(I,J)=7
60 NEXT J
70 NEXT I
   .
   .
   .
   .
```

When execution is initiated, J cycles from 1 to 3 while I remains at 1. Then I advances to 2, followed by J cycling from 1 to 3 for the second time, and so on, until I advances to 4, followed by J cycling from 1 to 3 for the fourth time. At that stage, both loops (I being the outer loop and J the inner loop) will have been completed. The final values of I and J will be 4 and 3, respectively.

SAMPLE PROGRAM—NET PAY CALCULATION

To illustrate the use of the BASIC statements explained in this chapter, suppose that a company pays each of its 13 employees $4.25 per hour.

[6] Elements in a two-dimensional matrix are represented by the subscripts I and J, where I represents values in rows 1, 2, 3, . . . , m of the matrix, and J represents values in columns 1, 2, 3, . . . , n of the same matrix.

No overtime is allowed. Also assume that total taxes withheld are based on the following schedule:

Gross Earnings* *($)	***Tax Withheld***
Under 100	0
100 to 125	15% of amount over $100
Over 125	20% of amount over $125

For example, if gross earnings are $175, the tax withheld is 15 percent of $25 ($3.75) and 20 percent of $50 ($10) or $13.75. The program is designed to print the net pay and tax withheld for each employee.

The Program

```
 10 REM THIS IS A SIMPLIFIED PROGRAM TO CALCULATE
 20 REM NET PAY AND TAX DEDUCTIONS
 30 DIM S(150), H(150), P(150), T(150)
 40 READ N' NUMBER OF EMPLOYEES
 50 DATA 13
 60 FOR I = 1 TO N
 70 READ H(I)' H(I) REFERS TO NUMBER OF HOURS WORKED
 80 LET S(I) = H(I)*4.25' 4.25 IS WAGE RATE PER HOUR
 90 NEXT I
100 DATA 36,40,15,28,40,34,26,38,20,40,31,40,34
110 PRINT "NET PAY AND TAX IN DOLLARS"
120 FOR I = 1 TO N
130 IF S(I) > 100 THEN 160
140 LET T(I) = 0' TAX DEDUCTIONS
150 GO TO 200
160 IF S(I) > 125 THEN 190
170 LET T(I) = .15*(S(I)—100)' TAX DEDUCTIONS
180 GO TO 200
190 LET T(I) = 3.75+.20*(S(I)—125)' TAX DEDUCTIONS
200 LET P(I) = S(I)—T(I)' NET PAY
210 PRINT P(I), T(I)
220 NEXT I
230 END

RUN

NET PAY AND TAX IN DOLLARS
143.65          9.35
157.25         12.75
 63.75          0
116.15          2.85
157.25         12.75
136.85          7.65
108.92          1.58
150.45         11.05
 85             0
157.25         12.75
126.65          5.10
157.25         12.75
136.85          7.65
```

SUMMARY

BASIC is a special, powerful language designed for on-line processing in a time-sharing environment. Using plain English and familiar arithmetic symbols, a user can feed his program via a terminal for processing.

Like FORTRAN, BASIC uses constants, variables, and arithmetic operators to form statements. The order of calculations also follows similar rules. The primary statements used are (1) the REMark statement, which indicates nonexecutable, descriptive information that the user can include in his program; (2) input/output statements, which are primarily the DATA, READ, INPUT, and PRINT statements; (3) control statements designed to allow conditional (IF–THEN) or unconditional (GO TO) transfer of control within the program; and (4) END and STOP statements used to define the end of the program and to terminate the program, respectively.

BASIC also offers instructions that make it possible to define subscripted variables and, consequently, perform looping routines. When more than 11 memory places are needed, a DIMension statement is used to define the necessary computer memory area for processing. It is also used to define a two-dimensional array. A looping routine utilizes the FOR–TO and the NEXT formats to allow repetitive execution of the statements placed between the two formats.

TERMS TO LEARN

- BASIC
- Constant
- DIM
- END
- FOR–TO
- HELP
- LET
- LIST
- NEXT
- READ
- RUN
- SAVE
- SCRATCH
- System command
- Variable

QUESTIONS

1. Explain briefly the characteristics of BASIC language. What similarities and differences are there between BASIC and FORTRAN?
2. List briefly the steps taken in feeding a BASIC program into a time-shared computer facility.
3. Distinguish between
   a. A constant and a variable.
   b. END and RUN.

c. FOR, NEXT, and GO TO.
d. END and STOP.
e. One- and two-dimensional arrays.

4. What sequence of messages and responses is involved in feeding a new program? Give an example.
5. Explain briefly the order of arithmetic calculations in BASIC.
6. What is the primary purpose of built-in mathematical functions?
7. For what purpose are the following input–output statements used?
   a. DATA
   b. INPUT
   c. READ
   d. PRINT
8. Define the terms SAVE and HELP.
9. Explain the difference between a conditional and an unconditional statement. Give an example.
10. What is a DIM statement? Give an example.
11. What special statements are used in a BASIC looping operation?
12. Explain the BASIC procedure involved in inner and outer loops.
13. Which of the following variables are invalid? Why?
    a. 3P
    b. P3
    c. P3A
    d. 7
14. Write a BASIC program to multiply 17 by 8. Enter the appropriate messages to the computer.
15. Find the value of X in each of the following statements:
```
LET X = 19+20/4*3 ↑ 3 – 8
LET X = 4+(10*6 ↑ 2)*3 ↑ 3 – 4
LET X = (3+12)/3*2 ↑ 4 – 1)
```
16. Write the BASIC set of instructions to find the square root of $4X^2 + 5$, where $X = 10$.
17. Write a partial BASIC program to cause the computer to print out digits 1 to 50.
18. Write a partial BASIC statement to print the heading "DAILY VALUE IS".
19. Write a partial program to input five values into A and print them out.
20. What does the following program accomplish?
```
10 READ A
20 LET B=2*3.1416*R
30 PRINT B,A
40 GO TO 10
50 DATA 1.7,2.8,3.9,4.5,7.5
60 END
```
21. Suppose that you know in advance that six data items will always be in DATA statement. Use a special loop statement(s) in the program in Question 20 to do the job.

SUGGESTED READING

DIEHR, GEORGE. *Business Programming with BASIC.* New York: John Wiley & Sons, Inc., 1972.

FARINA, M. V. *Programming in BASIC.* Englewood Cliffs, N.J.: Prentice-Hall, Inc., 1968.

PEGELS, C. C. *BASIC—A Computer Programming Language with Business and Management Applications.* San Francisco: Holden-Day, Inc., 1973.

system/3 programming—RPG II fundamentals

20

CALCULATION SPECIFICATIONS FORM

Operations Area

Numeric Literals

Arithmetic Operations

Branching

OUTPUT-FORMAT SPECIFICATIONS FORM

File Identification (Columns 7 to 31)

Field Description (Columns 23 to 70)

APPLICATIONS

Detail Printing of a Card Deck

Printing Cards of Two Input Files

Computing Gross Pay

Like any computer system, the IBM System/3 requires an appropriate language to prepare programs for processing. A popular language used in programming this system is called RPG II—*Report Program Generator II*. Although it has a set of rules for placing certain information in designated positions in the program, RPG II does not require the programmer to memorize them, since he is provided with coding sheets indicating the exact location of the data to be coded or programmed. Because of this simplified procedure, programming in RPG II consists of the programmer simply "filling in the blanks." (For brevity, this language will be referred to here as RPG.)

PRELIMINARY CONSIDERATIONS

Before discussing various RPG coding forms, consideration must be given to the nature of (1) data files, (2) input and output data, and (3) required calculations. The RPG language is designed to process files of records. A *data file* is a group of related records that are either input to the system or output from it. In RPG terms, *data file* can also refer to the input or output media or devices involved in processing file records. We refer to any of the following as files: a deck of punched cards, a reel of tape, a magnetic disk, and a line printer (this actually refers to the "stored" data on paper).

In addition to input and output files, the system may also have combined files. A *combined file* is made up of both input and output information. For example, a file of customer account cards may have the customer's previous balance and the amount received in each card. It is described as a combined file in a program that subtracts the amount received from the previous balance and punches the new balance in the same card.

With the different types of files involved, it becomes necessary in programming to describe each file to be processed. For input files, the programming must identify each record by the unique name of the input file, specify the length of the record field to be processed, and assign names to each field. Likewise, in describing output files, the programmer must identify each file record by file name, specify the output fields to be printed or punched, and assign names to these fields. He must also specify the sequence in which the information should appear on the output format or medium. With respect to calculations, specifications of the type of calculation (addition, subtraction, etc.) to be performed on input data and the time of such calculations are also required.

In summary, then, planning a given application requires four major sequential steps:

1. Determining the desired end results. This is described on the *output-format specifications* sheet.
2. Presenting the available input data. This is entered on the *input specifications* sheet.
3. Deciding on the calculations required to get the results. This is detailed on the *calculation specifications* sheet.
4. Specifying the input and output devices needed to handle the data. This is described on the *card control and file description* sheet (Fig. 20-1).

Each specification has its format, which later becomes a part of the source statements to be punched into cards. Each line on a specifications sheet is represented by a single punched card. When all the specifications have been punched, the resulting deck, called a *source program,* is later compiled for producing an object program for processing.

THE RPG COMPILER

After the source program has been punched and debugged, it is converted into an object program by an RPG compiler. The compiler must punch the object program into a set of blank cards through the *Multi-Function Card Unit* (*MFCU*) or, using a control card, store it on magnetic disk. Figure 20-2 illustrates the procedure used in converting a source program into an object program. The six-step cycle is as follows [1]:

[1] It is assumed that, prior to proceeding with the six-step cycle, the programmer has evaluated the problem in terms of determining (1) the layout for input and output card formats on a multiple-card layout form, and (2) the appearance of the output report. This includes determining the input record fields to be used, the type of calculations to be performed, the location of data in the output records, and the numbers and types of totals to be computed.

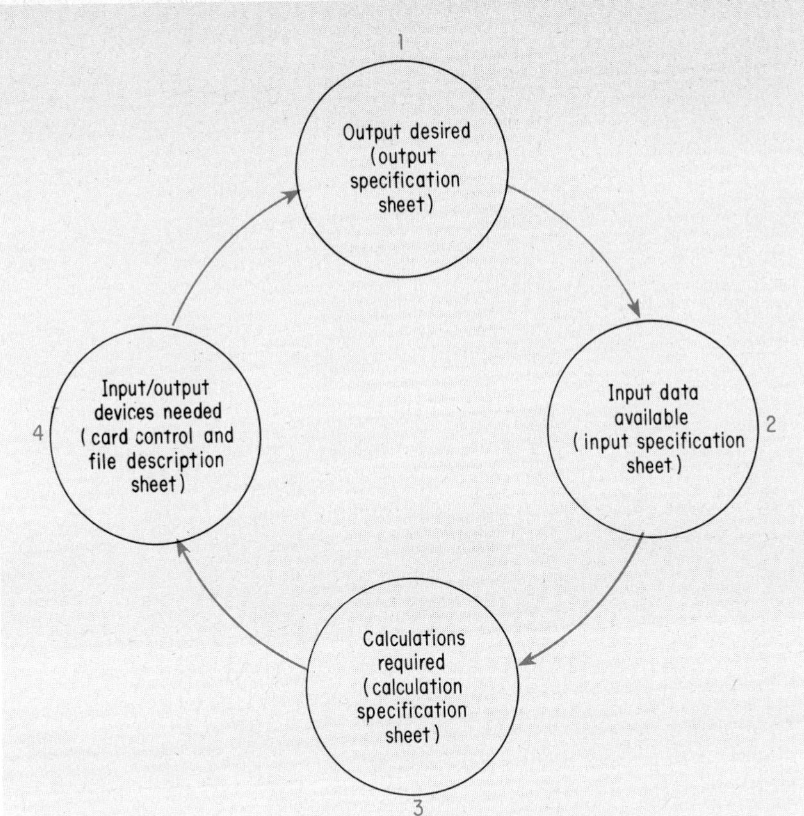

FIGURE 20-1. *Primary steps in application planning*

1. The source program is written on specification sheets.
2. The source program is punched into System/3 (96-column) cards.
3. The source program is read into main storage. The compiler program (on cards or disk) is also read into main storage.
4. The compile phase produces an object program deck stored on disk or in punched cards.
5. The object program is read into main storage. It performs processing on the source data in cards, on disks, or from a printer–keyboard device.
6. Output data are punched in cards, listed through a line printer, stored on disks, or made available through a printer–keyboard.

FILE SPECIFICATIONS FORM

The file specifications form provides additional information about the files needed in performing the job. It provides a file name, identifies the input and output devices to be used, and indicates whether the file is an input, output, or combined file. The form is easy to fill out, since only a few fields must be completed (Fig. 20-3). The essential fields follow.

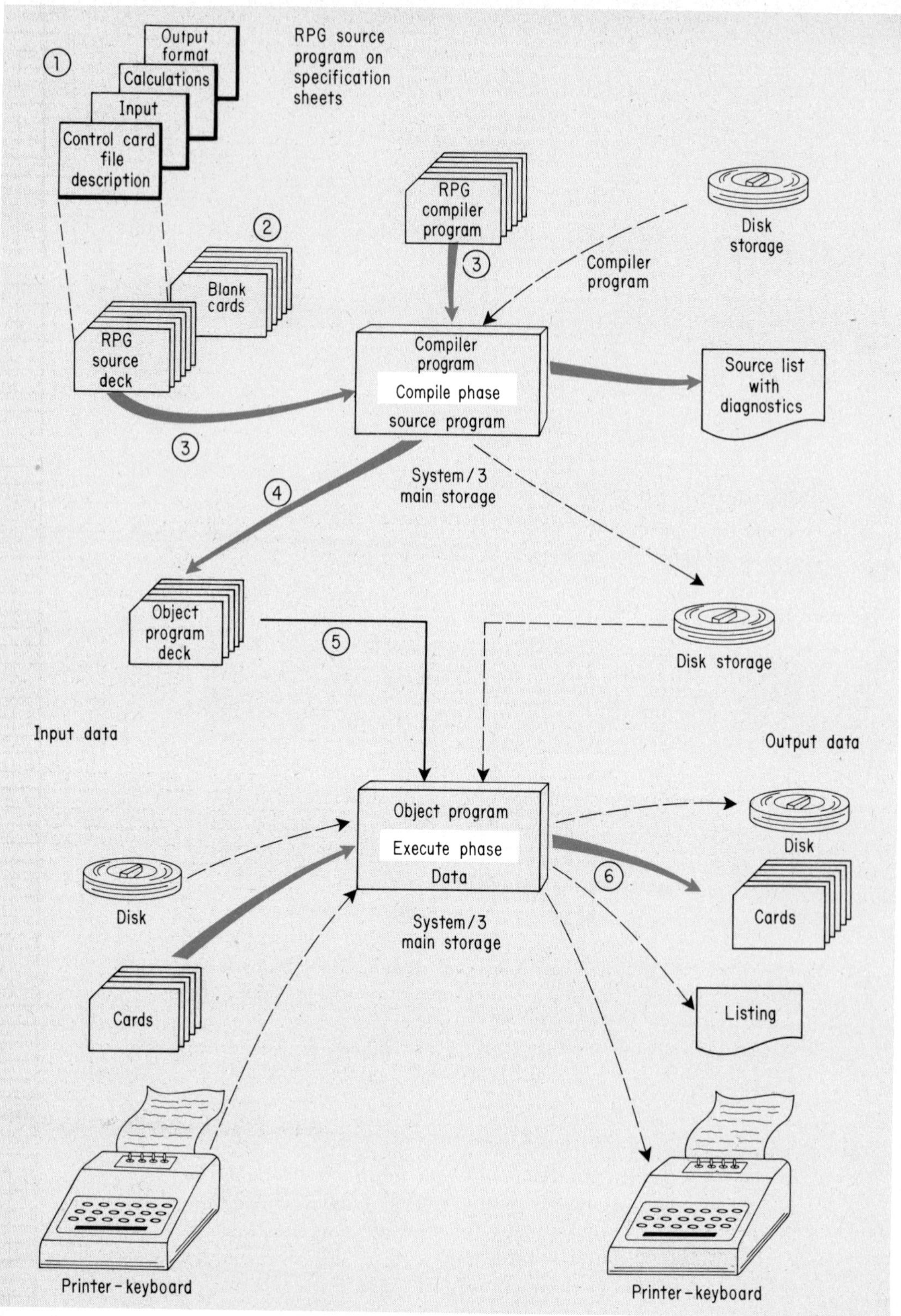

FIGURE 20-2. *Source deck to final output cycle*

IBM

International Business Machines Corporation

GX21-9092-1 U/M050
Printed in U.S.A.

RPG CONTROL CARD AND FILE DESCRIPTION SPECIFICATIONS

Date ______________

Program ______________

Programmer ______________

Punching Instruction	Graphic							
	Punch							

Page (1 2) ☐☐

Program Identification (75 76 77 78 79 80) ☐☐☐☐☐☐

Control Card Specifications

Line	Form Type	Core Size to Compile	Object Output	Listing Options	Core Size to Execute	Debug	MFCM Stacking Sequence	Sterling: Input–Shillings	Sterling: Input–Pence	Sterling: Output–Shillings	Sterling: Output–Pence	Inverted Print	360/20 2501 Buffer	Number Of Print Positions	Alternate Collating Sequence	Refer to the specific System Reference Library manual for actual entries.
3 4 5	6	7 8 9	10	11	12 13 14	15	16	17	18	19	20	21	22	23 24 25	26	27 28 29 30 31 32 33 34 35 36 37 38 39 40 41 42 43 44 45 46 47 48 49 50 51 52 53 54 55 56 57 58 59 60 61 62 63 64 65 66 67 68 69 70 71 72 73 74
0 1	H															

File Description Specifications

Line	Form Type	Filename	File Type (I/O/U/C/D)	File Designation (P/S/C/R/T/D)	End of File (E)	Sequence (A/D)	File Format (F/V)	Block Length	Record Length	Mode of Processing (L/R)	Length of Key Field or of Record Address Field	Record Address Type (A/K/I)	Type of File Organization or Additional Area (I/D/T or 1-9)	Overflow Indicator	Key Field Starting Location	Extension Code E/L	Device	Symbolic Device	Labels (S, N, or E)	Name of Label Exit	Extent Exit for DAM / Core Index	File Addition/Unordered (A/U)	Number of Tracks for Cylinder Overflow	Number of Extents	Tape Rewind (N/U)	File Condition U1-U8	
3 4 5	6	7 8 9 10 11 12 13 14	15	16	17	18	19	20 21 22 23	24 25 26 27	28	29 30	31	32	33 34	35 36 37 38	39	40 41 42 43 44 45 46	47 48 49 50 51 52	53	54 55 56 57 58 59	60 61 62 63 64 65	66	67	68 69	70	71 72	73 74
0 2	F																										
0 3	F																										
0 4	F																										
0 5	F																										
0 6	F																										
0 7	F																										
	F																										
	F																										

FIGURE 20-3. *Control card and file description form*

Columns 1 to 2

Columns 1 to 2 are in the upper right corner and contain a page number for identifying each form. Thus, 01 is written for the control card and file description form, 02 for input, 03 for calculation, and 04 for output format.

Columns 3 to 5

Columns 3 to 4 are preprinted with the first 15 line numbers. Additional instructions can be added at the bottom of the form. Column 5 is used to insert missing instructions between preprinted lines. For example, an instruction to be inserted between lines 02 and 03 is numbered 021 and is written at the bottom of the sheet. When each line is later punched in a single card, the card punched with instruction 021 is inserted behind card 020. Up to nine instructions can be added between any two preprinted lines. Description of this section is common for all RPG specifications forms.

Column 6

Column 6 is preprinted with the letter F to indicate the file description form. Other forms have their respective codes: the letter I for the input specifications form, C for the calculation form, O for the output-format form, and H for the control card.

Columns 7 to 14

Columns 7 to 14 are reserved for a unique file name not to exceed eight positions. The file name is written left-justified. The first position (column 7) must be alphabetic. No special characters or embedded blanks are allowed. Column 7 can have an asterisk to show that the line is exclusively a *comments* line (Fig. 20-4).

Field	Field Name: Correct (columns 7–14)	Field Name: Incorrect (columns 7–14)
Inventory file	I N V E N T R Y	1 _ I N V T R Y
City	C I T Y _ _ _ _	_ _ _ _ C I T Y
Inventory Amount	I N V A M T _ _	_ I N V A M T _
Customer Name	C U S T N A M _	C U S T _ N A M
Invoice Number	I N V N O _ _ _	$ I N V N O _ _

FIGURE 20-4

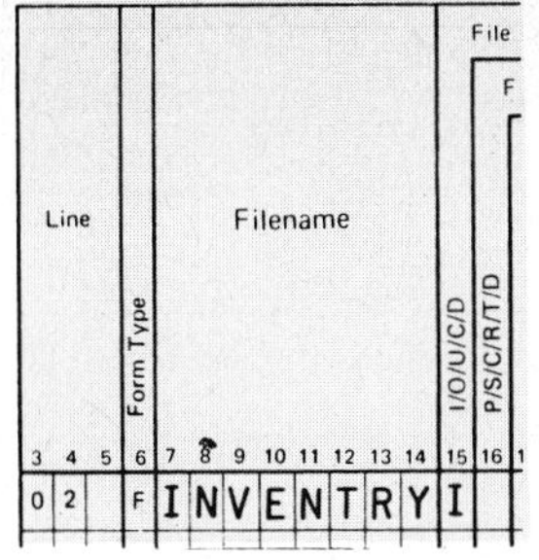

File
F
Line
Filename
Form Type
I/O/U/C/D
P/S/C/R/T/D
3 4 5 6 7 8 9 10 11 12 13 14 15 16
0 2 F INVENTRY I

FIGURE 20-5

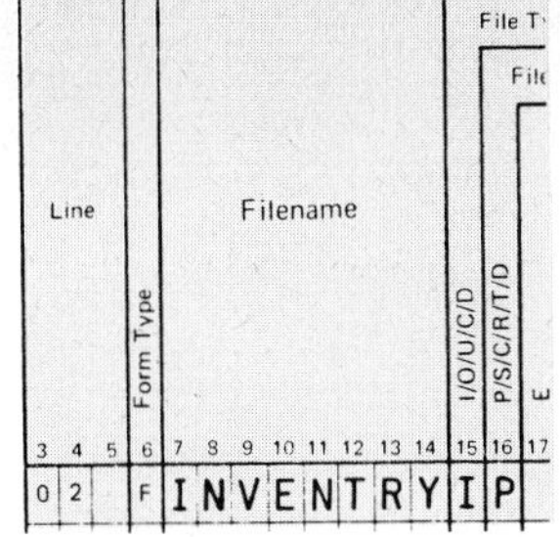

FIGURE 20-6

Column 15

Column 15 tells the computer whether the file is an input (I), output (O), or combined (C) file (Fig. 20-5).

Column 16

Column 16 indicates whether the file is a primary (P) or secondary (S) or combined (C) file. Only one file may be designated as an input file (Fig. 20-6).

Column 17

Column 17 is left blank if there is only one input file. However, the letter E is written if there are two input files; processing is to stop when one of the files has been read.

Column 18

Column 18 is required when matching fields are used. The letter A is written if the input or combined file is in ascending order and the letter D if it is in descending order. The column is left blank for output files or if the input or combined file is without matching fields.

Column 19

Column 19 indicates whether the file is fixed or variable in length. For 96-column card records, the letter F is written in column 19, since the record is fixed in length (Fig. 20-7).

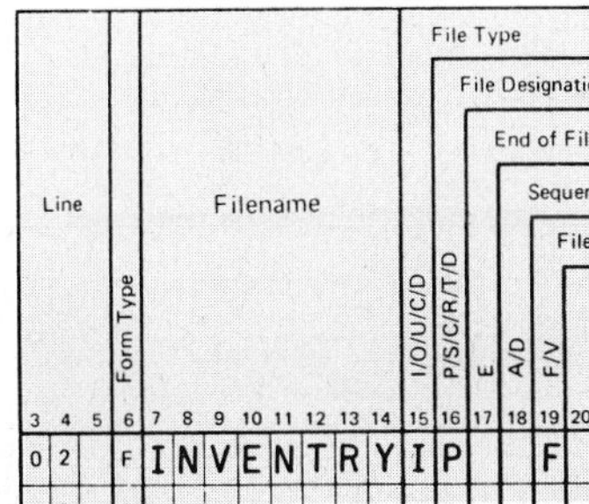

FIGURE 20-7

Line (3–5)	Form Type (6)	Filename (7–14)	File Type I/O/U/C/D (15)	File Designation P/S/C/R/T/D (16)	End of File E (17)	Sequence A/D (18)	File Format F/V (19)	Block Length (20–23)	Record Length (24–27)	L/R (28)
02	F	INVENTRY	I	P			F		96	
03	F	INVAMT	O				F		96	
04	F									

FIGURE 20-8

Line (3–5)	Form Type (6)	Filename (7–14)	File Type I/O/U/C/D (15)	File Designation P/S/C/R/T/D (16)	End of File E (17)	Sequence A/D (18)	File Format F/V (19)	Block Length (20–23)	Record Length (24–27)	L/R (28)	Mode of Processing (29–30)	Length of Key Field or of Record Address Field A/K/I (31)	Record Address Type I/D/T or 1-9 (32)	Type of File Organization or Additional Area / Overflow Indicator (33–34)	Key Field Starting Location (35–38)	Extension Code E/L (39)	Device (40–46)
02	F	INVENTRY	I	P			F		96								MFCU1
03	F	OUTPUT	O				F		96								PRINTER

FIGURE 20-9

Columns 24 to 27

Columns 24 to 27 specify the length of the file record. For input records punched in 96-column cards, 96 is written in columns 26 to 27. If output records are listed on a 96-character line printer, 96 is also written for an output record (Fig. 20-8).

Columns 40 to 46

Columns 40 to 46 identify the input or output device to be used with the file name. The identification must not exceed seven positions and is written left-justified. The input file must be described on one line and the output file on another line (Fig. 20-9).

Columns 66 to 74

Columns 66 to 74 are used for explanatory comments and do not become a part of the object program.

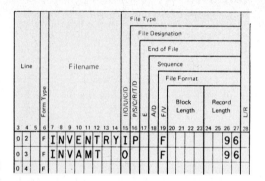

To illustrate the basic entries of a file specifications form, assume that we have two input files: a *primary* file, called the *balance-outstand-*

ing (BALOUT) file, and a *secondary* file, called the *payment* (PAYMT) file. Both files are in 96-column cards in ascending order—the payment file matched against the balance-outstanding file. We wish to (1) print out only if the balance outstanding and payments match, (2) update, and (3) output both files. Processing is to stop when the end of one of the primary files has been reached. The file name for printing is PRTFILE. The entries are shown in Fig. 20-10.

Line (3–5)	Form Type (6)	Filename (7–14)	File Type (15)	File Designation (16)	End of File (17)	Sequence (18)	File Format (19)	Block Length (20–23)	Record Length (24–27)	L/R (28)	Length of Key Field or of Record Address Field (29–30)	Record Address Type (31)	Type of File Organization or Additional Area (32)	Overflow Indicator (33–34)	Key Field Starting Location (35–38)	Extension Code E/L (39)	Device (40–46)
02	F	BALOUT	C	P	E	A	F		96								MFCU1
03	F	PAYMT	C	S		A	F		96								MFCU2
04	F	PRTFILE	O				F		96								PRINTER

FIGURE 20-10. *File specifications sheet—key entries involving two input files*

INPUT SPECIFICATIONS FORM

The primary function of the input specifications form is to identify different types of cards within a given file and to specify their sequence (Fig. 20-11). The form is divided into two major areas: (1) record identification (columns 7 to 42), and (2) record field identification (columns 44 to 74).

Record Identification

Record identification generally consists of a file name (columns 7 to 14), record identification codes (columns 21 to 41), and stacker select (column 42).[2]

File Name (Columns 7 to 14). As with the restrictions mentioned in the file description form, an input file is given a *unique* name and is written left-justified. It must not contain special characters or embedded blanks. The first position (column 7) must be an alphabetic character. Examples are given in Fig. 20-12.

Record Identification Codes (Columns 21 to 41). Record identification codes consist of three identical areas (columns 21 to 27, 28 to

[2] Columns 15 to 20 are explained separately at the end of the record identification section.

IBM International Business Machines Corporation

GX21-9094-1 U/M050
Printed in U.S.A.

RPG INPUT SPECIFICATIONS

Date ____________

Program ____________

Programmer ____________

Punching Instruction	Graphic							
	Punch							

Page (1 2) ☐☐ Program Identification (75 76 77 78 79 80) ☐☐☐☐☐☐

Line	Form Type	Filename	Sequence	Number (1-N)	Option (O)	Record Identifying Indicator or **	Record Identification Codes 1: Position	1: Not (N)	1: C/Z/D	1: Character	2: Position	2: Not (N)	2: C/Z/D	2: Character	3: Position	3: Not (N)	3: C/Z/D	3: Character	Stacker Select	P = Packed/B = Binary	Field Location From	Field Location To	Decimal Positions	Field Name	Control Level (L1-L9)	Matching Fields or Chaining Fields	Field Record Relation	Field Indicators Plus	Field Indicators Minus	Field Indicators Zero or Blank	Sterling Sign Position
3 4 5	6	7 8 9 10 11 12 13 14	15 16	17	18	19 20	21 22 23 24	25	26	27	28 29 30 31	32	33	34	35 36 37 38	39	40	41	42	43	44 45 46 47	48 49 50 51	52	53 54 55 56 57 58	59 60	61 62	63 64	65 66	67 68	69 70	71 72 73 74
0 1	I																														
0 2	I																														
0 3	I																														
0 4	I																														
0 5	I																														
0 6	I																														
0 7	I																														
0 8	I																														
0 9	I																														
1 0	I																														
1 1	I																														
1 2	I																														
1 3	I																														
1 4	I																														
1 5	I																														
	I																														
	I																														
	I																														
	I																														
	I																														

FIGURE 20-11. *Input specifications sheet*

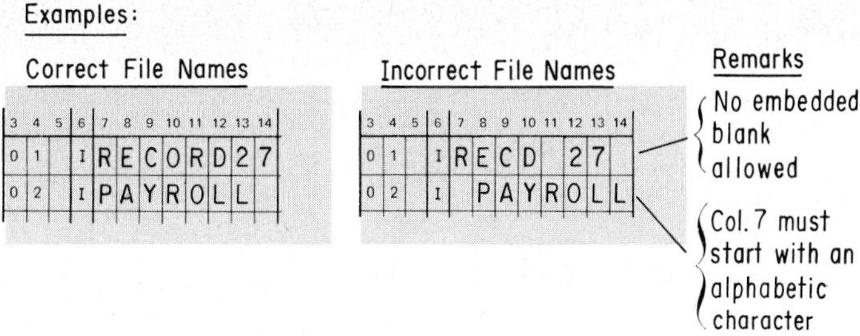

FIGURE 20-12

34, and 35 to 41), each area containing four fields: a four-column position field, a NOT field, a C/Z/D field, and a character field.

The *position* field identifies the location of an identifying code on an input data card. It is written right-justified. No high-order zeros are necessary.

The NOT field (column 25) is left blank unless the program requires the absence of a character described in column 27 and indicated in the position field.

The C/Z/D field (column 26) specifies whether a character, a zone, or a digit is to be checked. The letter C is written to test a character, the letter Z to test a zone punch, and the letter D to test a digit.

The *character* field (column 27) identifies the character to be tested. For example, if we wish to identify the character F in column 1, we have the entry shown in Fig. 20-13.

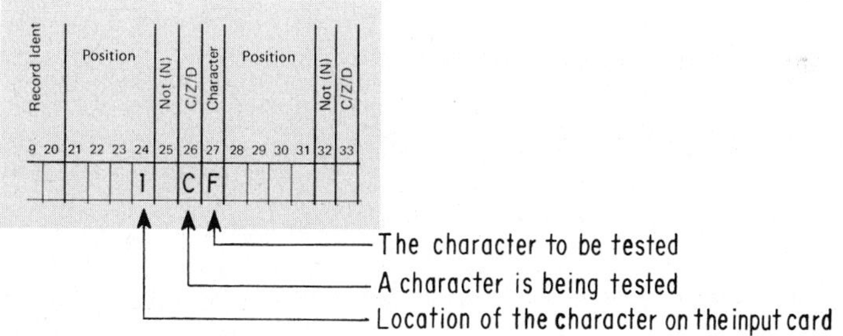

FIGURE 20-13

Stacker Select (Column 42). Stacker select is used to direct certain cards to a particular stacker. The program must be directed to drop such cards into a particular stacker by an identifying code written in columns 21 to 27. The absence of a stacker number in this column causes all cards to fall in the normal pocket after processing.

For example, suppose that we have a deck of employee cards with the cards of both male and female employees. Each female employee's card is identified by the letter F punched in column 1. To cause female employee cards to drop in stacker 2 of the MFCU, the line shown in Fig. 20-14 is written on the input specifications sheet.

Line	Form Type	Filename	Sequence	Number (1-N)	Option (O)	Record Identifying Indicator or **	Record Identification Codes 1: Position	Not (N)	C/Z/D	Character	2: Position	Not (N)	C/Z/D	Character	3: Position	Not (N)	C/Z/D	Character	Stacker Select	P = Packed/B = Binary
3 4 5	6	7 8 9 10 11 12 13 14	15 16	17	18	19 20	21 22 23 24	25	26	27	28 29 30 31	32	33	34	35 36 37 38	39	40	41	42	43
0 1	I	EMPLDECK					1		C	F									2	
0 2	I																			

FIGURE 20-14

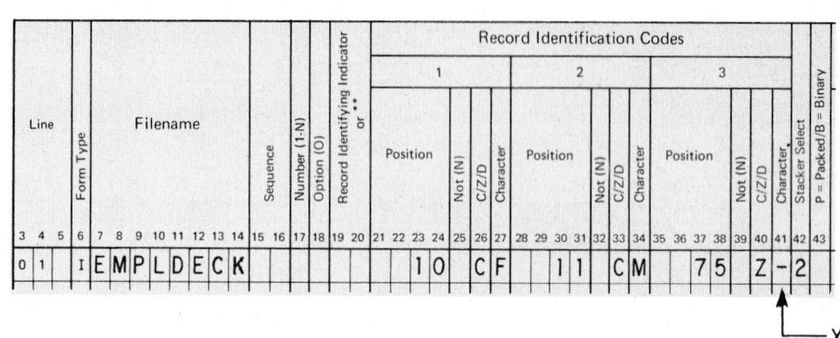

Line	Form Type	Filename	Sequence	Number (1-N)	Option (O)	Record Identifying Indicator or **	Record Identification Codes 1: Position	Not (N)	C/Z/D	Character	2: Position	Not (N)	C/Z/D	Character	3: Position	Not (N)	C/Z/D	Character	Stacker Select	P = Packed/B = Binary
3 4 5	6	7 8 9 10 11 12 13 14	15 16	17	18	19 20	21 22 23 24	25	26	27	28 29 30 31	32	33	34	35 36 37 38	39	40	41	42	43
0 1	I	EMPLDECK					10		C	F	11		C	M	75		Z	-	2	

FIGURE 20-15

As another example, given a deck of employee cards, we wish to separate into stacker 2 of the MFCU the cards of all married female employees over 50 years of age. Assume that such cards have the letter F (female) punched in column 10, the letter M (married) in column 11, and the letter X (for employees over 50 years old) in column 75. The entry for this operation would be as shown in Fig. 20-15.

Record-Sequence Field (Columns 15 to 16). An input deck often consists of a number of multicard sets that must be processed in a predetermined order. The record-sequence field indicates the order in which the cards in each set must be handled. Each card is given a sequence number so that the program can verify the order in which they are placed. If no sequence is required, any two alphabetic characters (e.g., AA, AB, BB) may be entered instead.

To illustrate, consider a simplified accounts receivable deck consisting of 900 customer accounts, each account having three cards: current balance, payments, and name and address cards. The current balance card has the sequence number 01, the payments cards the sequence number 02, and the name and address cards the sequence number 03. Figure 20-16 shows the sequence of the entire deck and the necessary entry in the input specifications form.

Three rules are worth noting:

1. Each different customer card is entered on the input specifications sheet on a separate line.

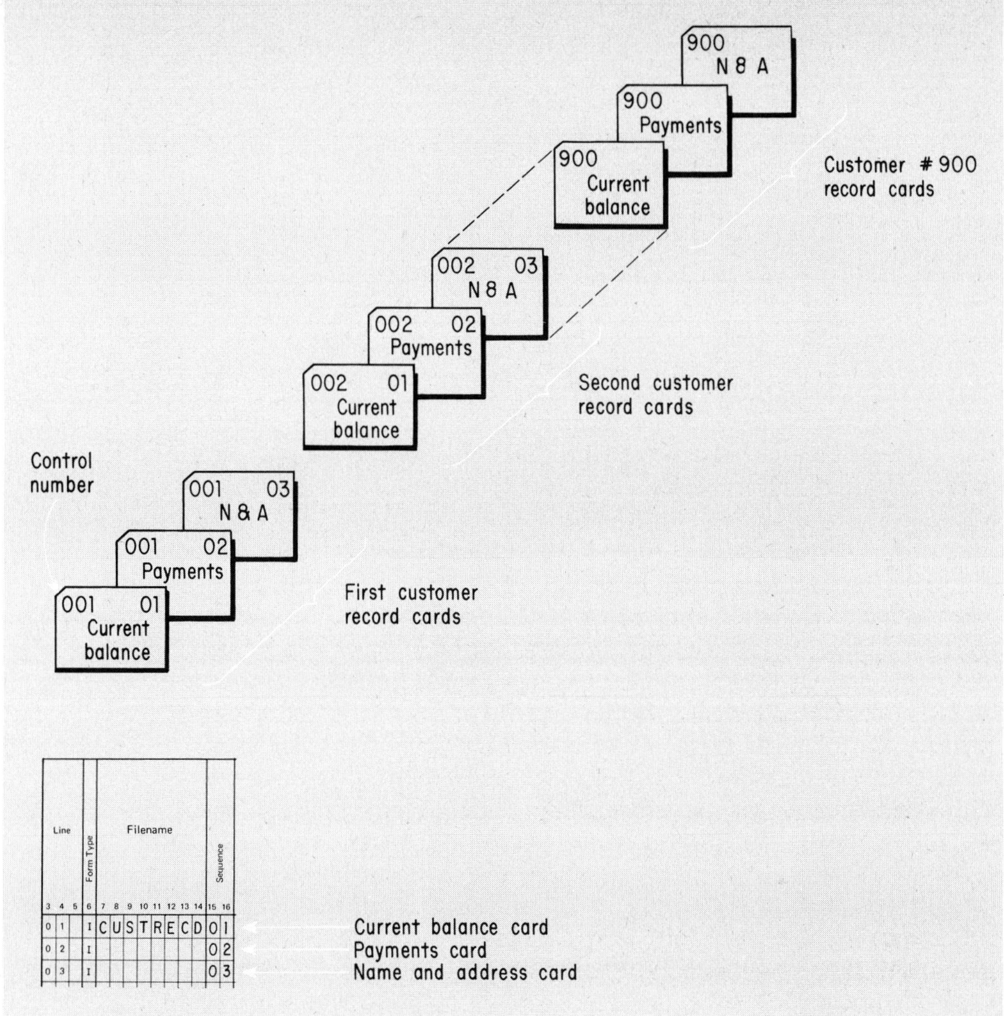

FIGURE 20-16. Record sequence checking

2. Any ascending sequence number may be assigned to the customer card set. For example, the current balance may have the sequence number 01, the payment card sequence number 05, and the name and address card sequence number 09.
3. The sequence field must be filled in for every type of card in the card set.

NUMBER-OF-CARDS FIELD (COLUMN 17). Column 17 is used to indicate the number of cards for each card type. In our accounts receivable example, the digit 1 is entered in column 17 for each of the three single card types. However, the letter N is entered if two or more cards of a particular card type are present. Based on Fig. 20-17, column 17 will

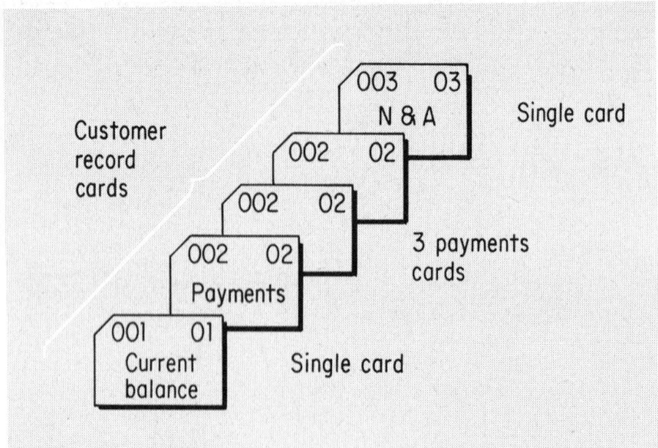

FIGURE 20-17. Source of data for column 17

have a 1 for the current balance card, an N for the payment cards, and a 1 for the name and address card.

OPTION COLUMN (COLUMN 18). It often happens that certain card types are not present in a particular card group or card set. For example, in accounts receivable a current balance card and a name and address card must be present; but the presence of the payment card is optional, since a customer may have missed payment for that particular period. We so indicate by entering the letter O in column 18 of the payments line. For required cards in the card set, column 18 is left blank. Column 18 is also left blank with card sets requiring no particular sequence—that is, when the sequence field (columns 15 to 16) is alphabetic.

RESULT INDICATOR (COLUMNS 19 TO 20). The result indicator is a two-digit numeric code arbitrarily assigned to indicate the type of card to be processed. It acts as a switch. When this code is turned on, all other indicators are turned off; this makes it possible to process one type of card at a time. The field can also be assigned H1 or H2 to halt a program without last-record routines or dependency on a certain condition.

To illustrate the use of columns 15 to 20, assume a payroll card deck consisting of five different types of cards for each employee. The *first* card, called the *name and address card,* includes fixed information, such as the employee's name, address, Social Security number, department number, and so on. It is identified by the digit 3 punched in column 60. The *second* sequential card, called the *detail card,* contains essential data for the payroll process, such as number of dependents, marital status, union dues, and savings plans. It is identified by the letter D in column 17.

The *third* card is optional. When present, it includes changes regarding the employee's marital status, type and number of deductions,

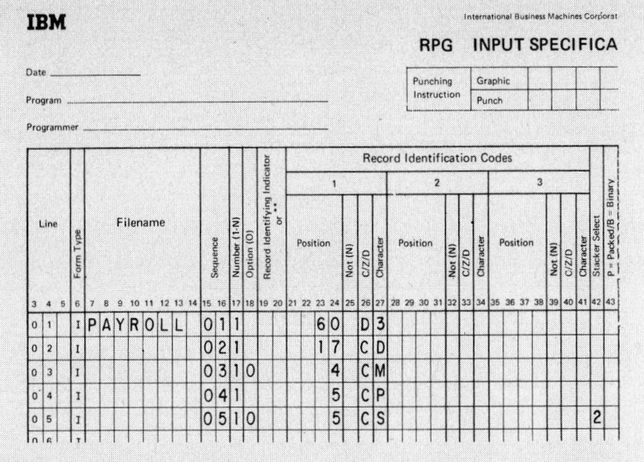

IBM

International Business Machines Corporat

RPG INPUT SPECIFICA

Date ______

Program ______

Programmer ______

Punching Instruction	Graphic				
	Punch				

Line (3–5)	Form Type (6)	Filename (7–14)	Sequence (15–16)	Number (1-N) (17)	Option (O) (18)	Record Identifying Indicator or ** (19–20)	1 Position (21–24)	1 Not (N) (25)	1 C/Z/D (26)	1 Character (27)	2 Position (28–31)	2 Not (N) (32)	2 C/Z/D (33)	2 Character (34)	3 Position (35–38)	3 Not (N) (39)	3 C/Z/D (40)	3 Character (41)	Stacker Select (42)	P = Packed/B = Binary (43)
01	I	PAYROLL	01	1			60		D	3										
02	I		02	1			17		C	D										
03	I		03	1	0		4		C	M										
04	I		04	1			5		C	P										
05	I		05	1	0		5		C	S									2	
06	I																			

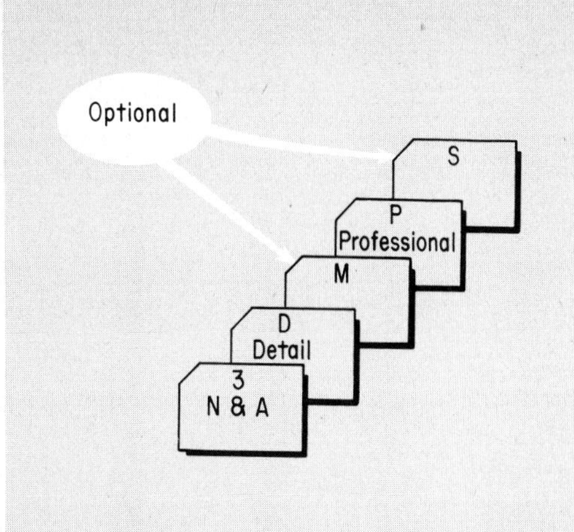

FIGURE 20-18. Record identification codes

and so on, made since the last payroll run. It is identified by the letter M in column 4. The *fourth* card, called the *professional status card,* must be present. It indicates the educational and professional experience of the employee when he was first hired by the company. It is identified by the letter P in column 5. The *last* (fifth) card is optional and shows any changes in the professional status of the employee. It is identified by the letter S in column 5. This card should later be extracted from the file and dropped into stacker 2 for other applications. The card deck and entries are presented in Fig. 20-18.

Field Identification (Columns 44 to 58)

A file record is made up of a number of data fields, each field occupying one or more columns.

Columns 44 to 47 indicate the leftmost location of each data field in the card. The information is entered right-justified, with columns 44 and 45 left blank or filled with zeros.

Columns 48 to 51 indicate the rightmost location of each data field. This information is also entered right-justified, with columns 48 and 49 left blank or filled with zeros. A one-column field number is entered in columns 47 and 51.

Columns 53 to 58 provide the name of each field. The field name should not exceed six alphanumeric characters in length. The first character must be alphabetic. No special characters or embedded blanks are permitted. A field name of less than six characters must be entered left-justified.

To illustrate, suppose that we have a name and address card consisting of the following fields:

Columns	Field Name
1– 5	Account *number*
6–25	*Name*
26–50	Mailing *address*
51–55	*Zip* code
56–58	*Branch*
59	Credit *rating*
60–69	*Phone* number

The necessary entries are shown in Fig. 20-19. Note that field entries begin one line below the file-name entry.

Optional Fields. Columns 59 to 60 are needed in sequencing certain fields or in specifying the order in which calculations for designated fields should occur. Nine control levels ranging from L1 (lowest level) to L9 (highest level) are available for this purpose. When used, they must be listed in ascending sequence.

Columns 61 to 62 are used to indicate whether a single file is to be sequence-checked or if data fields from two input files are to be compared.

CALCULATION SPECIFICATIONS FORM

The calculation specifications form is used to indicate the type of operations that must be performed on input data and the order in which such operations are to be performed. The sheet consists of two primary areas: (1) the operations area (columns 18 to 53), and (2) the indicators area (columns 9 to 17 and 54 to 59) (Fig. 20-20).

FIGURE 20-19. *Field identification*

IBM International Business Machines Corporation GX21-9094-1 U/M050 Printed in U.S.A.

RPG INPUT SPECIFICATIONS

Date 9/17/74

Program PAYROLL

Programmer JOE T HUNT

Punching Instruction: Graphic / Punch

Page 1 2

Program Identification (75–80): J T H 1 2 1

Line (3–5)	Form Type (6)	Filename (7–14)	Sequence (15–16)	Number (1-N) (17)	Option (O) (18)	Record Identifying Indicator or ** (19–20)	Record Identification Codes 1: Position (21–24)	Not (N) (25)	C/Z/D (26)	Character (27)	Field Location From (44–47)	To (48–51)	Decimal Positions (52)	Field Name (53–58)
01	I	CUSTN	01	1			60		D	3				
02	I										1	5		NUMBER
03	I										6	25		NAME
04	I										26	50		ADRESS
05	I										51	55		ZIP
06	I										56	58		BRANCH
07	I										59	59		RATING
08	I										60	69		PHONE
09	I													

Other form columns (all blank): Record Identification Codes 2 (28–34) and 3 (35–41), Stacker Select (42), P = Packed/B = Binary (43), Control Level (L1-L9) (59–60), Matching Fields or Chaining Fields (61–62), Field Record Relation (63–64), Field Indicators Plus (65–66), Minus (67–68), Zero or Blank (69–70), Sterling Sign Position (71–74).

IBM

International Business Machines Corporation

GX21-9093-1

Printed in U.S.A.

RPG CALCULATION SPECIFICATIONS

Date ______

Program ______

Programmer ______

Punching Instruction	Graphic							
	Punch							

Page (1 2) ____

Program Identification (75 76 77 78 79 80) ____

Line (3 4 5)	Form Type (6)	Control Level (L0-L9, LR, SR) (7 8)	Indicators: Not (9)	(10 11)	And: Not (12)	(13 14)	And: Not (15)	(16 17)	Factor 1 (18–27)	Operation (28–32)	Factor 2 (33–42)	Result Field (43–48)	Field Length (49–51)	Decimal Positions (52)	Half Adjust (H) (53)	Resulting Indicators — Arithmetic: Plus; Compare: High 1>2; Lookup Table (Factor 2) is: High (54 55)	Arithmetic: Minus; Compare: Low 1<2; Lookup: Low (56 57)	Arithmetic: Zero; Compare: Equal 1 = 2; Lookup: Equal (58 59)	Comments (60–74)
0 1	C																		
0 2	C																		
0 3	C																		
0 4	C																		
0 5	C																		
0 6	C																		
0 7	C																		
0 8	C																		
0 9	C																		
1 0	C																		
1 1	C																		
1 2	C																		
1 3	C																		
1 4	C																		
1 5	C																		
	C																		
	C																		
	C																		
	C																		
	C																		

FIGURE 20-20

Each calculation consists of an *operation code* (columns 28 to 32) to tell the computer what to do and the two factors involved in the calculation. Some of the operation codes used in RPG are as follows:

Operation Code	Operation
ADD	Addition
SUB	Subtraction
MULT	Multiplication
DIV	Division
Z-ADD	Zero and add
Z-SUB	Zero and subtract
COMP	Compare
MVR	Move remainder

For example, suppose that we wish to add the content of two fields, defined as QUANTA and QUANTB. QUANTA is 18 and QUANTB is 17. In RPG language, 18 and 17 are called *factors*. Thus, 18 may be referred to as factor 1 and 17 as factor 2. In making the proper entry, the name of the fields to be added rather than their values must be entered in factor 1 and factor 2 of the calculation sheet. The entry is shown in Fig. 20-21.

RESULT FIELD (COLUMNS 43 TO 48). The result of an operation, whether it is addition, subtraction, multiplication, or division, must also be specified by a special name for storage until it is printed. This tells the computer where the result is to go. In our example, we might give the sum (35) a name, TOTAL, which is entered in the result field.

FIELD LENGTH (COLUMNS 49 TO 51). Another part of an operation is telling the computer the length of the field where the TOTAL is to be kept. Based on the preceding example, the total (35) is two digits long. Therefore, the digit 2 is entered in column 51.

DECIMAL POSITION (COLUMN 52). The decimal position is used in

FIGURE 20-21. Addition entry

Factor 1 (18–27)	Operation (28–32)	Factor 2 (33–42)	Result Field (43–48)	Field Length (49–51)	Decimal Positions (52)	Half Adjust (H) (53)
QUANTA	ADD	QUANTB	TOTAL	2	0	

arithmetic operations to specify the number of decimal places in the result field. It is left blank in alphanumeric operations.

HALF-ADJUST (COLUMN 53). The letter H is entered in this column when rounding is desired. Otherwise, it is left blank. Half-adjusting adds 5 to the rightmost decimal digit. For example, to half-adjust for two decimal places we get the following results:

Value	*Half-Adjusted*
11.016	11.02
11.096	11.10
11.09	11.09
11.163	11.16
11.166	11.17
11.1666	11.17

Numeric Literals

Often it is necessary to use a numeric literal such as a constant in various arithmetic operations. For example, a company might wish to give each employee a $20 Christmas bonus in addition to his regular pay. To perform this operation, the numeric literal 20.00 is entered as factor 1 (left-justified), the operation code ADD is entered in the operation area, and the arbitrary name PAY is entered as factor 2. The TOTAL (sum) is entered in the result field, with a specified field length and decimal position indicated in columns 49 to 51 and column 52, respectively. If rounding is desired, the letter H is entered in column 53.

Numeric literals may be any combination of numbers, but must not exceed 10 positions in length. If a plus or minus sign is necessary, the sign must precede the literal. Literals without a sign are assumed to be positive. Embedded blanks are not allowed. The first character must not be alphabetic. Some examples are as follows:

Correct Literals	*Incorrect Literals*
−17.01	1.7−
+87	74.0
.87	.87−
− .61	F4.0
9.901	0.1+6

ADDITION (ADD). Numeric addition is carried out by adding the contents of factor 2 to the contents of factor 1 and storing the sum in a specified result field in the same card. The basic rules are

1. When two positive fields are added, the sum is positive. For example, 15 + 20 = +35.
2. When two negative fields are added, the sum is negative. For example, (—5) + (—2) = —7.
3. When a positive and a negative field are added, the sum (actually, the difference between the two fields) carries the sign of the larger field. For example, (+5) + (—2) = +3.

ADDING A LIST OF VALUES. Suppose that instead of adding two numeric fields from the same card, we wish to add a numeric field from several cards and print out the total. In this case, each field must be accumulated in a specific storage location. The accumulated result (TOTAL) is then printed at the end of the report. To illustrate this procedure, suppose that we wish to determine the total sales for the week made by the television sales staff of a local retail store. Each salesman's card consists of an identification number, name, and total sales for the week. The list of data cards is as follows:

	Number	***Name***	***Sales for the Week***
First card	31	Hale, B. J.	$1,299.50
	32	Hays, L. D.	1,705.00
	33	Rehm, E. M.	943.00
	34	Cook, C. L.	1,219.00
Last card	35	Dond, C. M.	1,600.92

The appropriate entries are shown in Fig. 20-22. Note that factor 2 and the result field have the same name (SUM). The SUM field (six columns in length) starts with a blank and accumulates the sales read from each of the five data cards as follows:

Step	***Sales***	***Operation Code***	***Content of Sum***		***Sum***
1	$1,299.50	ADD	0	=	$1,299.50
2	1,705.00	ADD	$1,299.50	=	3,004.50
3	943.00	ADD	3,004.50	=	3,947.50
4	1,219.00	ADD	3,947.50	=	5,166.50
5	1,600.92	ADD	5,166.50	=	6,766.50

Factor 1	Operation	Factor 2	Result Field	Field Length	Decimal Positions	Half Adjust (H)
18–27	28–32	33–42	43–48	49–51	52	53
SALES	ADD	SUM	SUM	6	2	

FIGURE 20-22. Addition

File Description Specifications

Line	Form Type	Filename	File Type (I/O/U/C/D)	File Designation (P/S/C/R/T/D)	End of File (E)	Sequence (A/D)	File Format (F/V)	Block Length	Record Length	Mode of Processing (L/R)	Length of Key Field or of Record Address Field	Record Address Type (A/K/I)	Type of File Organization or Additional Area (I/D/T or 1-9)	Overflow Indicator	Key Field Starting Location	Extension Code E/L	Device
3 4 5	6	7–14	15	16	17	18	19	20–23	24–27	28	29–30	31	32	33–34	35–38	39	40–46
02	F	SALESVOL	I	P					96								MFCU1
03	F	ADDECK	O						96								PRINTER

IBM International Business Machines Corporation

RPG INPUT SPECIFICATIONS

Date ______

Program ______

Programmer ______

Punching Instruction	Graphic	
	Punch	

Page 1

Line	Form Type	Filename	Sequence	Number (1-N)	Option (O)	Record Identifying Indicator or **	Record Identification Codes 1: Position	Not (N)	C/Z/D	Character	2: Position	Not (N)	C/Z/D	Character	3: Position	Not (N)	C/Z/D	Character	Stacker Select	P = Packed/B = Binary	Field Location From	Field Location To	Decimal Positions	Field Name
3 4 5	6	7–14	15 16	17	18	19 20	21–24	25	26	27	28–31	32	33	34	35–38	39	40	41	42	43	44–47	48–51	52	53–58
01	I	SALESVOL	AA			01																		
02	I																				1	2		EMPNO
03	I																				3	25		NAME
04	I																				26	31		SALES
05	I																							

FIGURE 20-23

The final amount, \$6,766.50, is printed out as specified by the output specifications sheet. The file description and input specifications forms provide data as shown in Fig. 20-23.

Adding Positive and Negative Values. Adding a negative value is the same as subtracting a positive value. That is, the sum resulting from —10 added to +15 is the same as the sum resulting from subtracting +10 from +15, or +5. In preparing negative data for computer processing, negative values are specified by punching a negative sign in the B-zone area of the low-order column of the card field. For example, —34 is represented in card column 72 to 73 having a B-zone (negative) punch in column 73:

		3	4			—3	4
	B				B		•
	A				A		
	8				8		
	4		•		4		•
	2	•			2	•	
	1	•			1	•	
Col. No. ⟶		72	73			72	73

Subtraction (SUB). In subtraction, the value stored in factor 2 is *subtracted from* the value stored in factor 1; the difference is stored in a specified result field in the same card. The basic rules are similar to the rules of addition, except that the sign of the subtrahend is first reversed and then added to the minuend:

	Before		After	Before		After	Before		After
Minuend	+8		+8	+5		+5	+5		+5
	—	=		—	=		—	=	
Subtrahend	+5		—5	+8		—8	—8		+8
Difference			+3			—3			+13

Like addition, each subtraction requires an entry in the calculation sheet. In Fig. 20-24, QTY2 is subtracted from QTY1. The five-digit result field stores the difference (DIFF).

FIGURE 20-24. Subtraction entry

Factor 1 (18–27)	Operation (28–32)	Factor 2 (33–42)	Result Field (43–48)	Field Length (49–51)	Decimal Positions (52)	Half Adjust (H) (53)	54
QTY1	SUB	QTY2	DIFF	5	0		

Factor 1	Operation	Factor 2	Result Field	Field Length	Decimal Positions
18 19 20 21 22 23 24 25 26 27	28 29 30 31 32	33 34 35 36 37 38 39 40 41 42	43 44 45 46 47 48	49 50 51	52
QTY1	MULT	QTY2	PRODCT	6	0

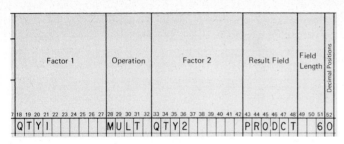

FIGURE 20-25. Multiplication entry

ZERO-ADD (Z-ADD). The Z-ADD code sets the result field to zero and then adds algebraically the contents of factor 2 to it. Factor 1 is not used and must be blank for this operation.

ZERO-SUBTRACT (Z-SUB). The Z-SUB code reverses the sign of the numeric value stored in factor 2 and then adds it to the result field. The factor 1 field is not used and must be blank during this operation.

The Z-ADD and Z-SUB operation codes are used to make sure that the result field is set to zeros (versus blanks) prior to adding or subtracting a quantity from it.

MULTIPLICATION (MULT). Multiplication causes the contents of factor 1 to be multiplied by the contents of factor 2. The product is placed in a specified result field. In making an entry on the calculation sheet, each factor is given a name. For example, in multiplying 110 by 400, 110 can be referred to as QTY1 and 400 as QTY2. The product 44,000 is also given an arbitrary name, PRODCT.[3] The entry is shown in Fig. 20-25.

Note that the digit 6 in column 51 indicates the length of the result field. Any pair of three-digit numbers results in a six-digit product. Thus, the length of the result field is equal to the sum of the digits of the multiplicand and multiplier. If there are decimals, they are also added to determine the number of decimal places required. Here are some examples:

	Factor 1	Factor 2	Result Field
1.	XXX (3)	XXX (3)	XXXXXX ((6))
2.	XXX.XX (3) (2)	XXX.XX (3) (2)	XXXXXX.XXXX (6) (4)
3.	XX.X (2) (1)	X.XX (1) (2)	XXX.XXX (3) (3)

[3] A constant can be entered in either factor.

DIVISION. In division, the value in factor 2 is divided into the value stored in factor 1. The quotient is stored in a specified result field. Several points are worth noting:

1. Factor 2 may not be zero.
2. If the factor 1 (dividend) is zero, the quotient will be zero.
3. Division of values with like signs results in a positive quotient.
4. Division of values with unlike signs results in a negative quotient.
5. The remainder of a division is lost unless the next sequential instruction is a *move remainder* (MVR) instruction. Only the operation code MVR and a specified result field are written on a separate line, causing the remainder to be moved to the specified result field.

To illustrate the use of the four arithmetic operations, suppose that a retail store has a deck of accounts receivable cards, each card containing the following information:

1. Columns 1 to 5: customer account number.
2. Columns 6 to 11: previous balance.
3. Columns 12 to 17: payments made by the customer for the period.
4. The previous balance and payment fields are six-column fields with two decimal digits.

Required are

1. Balance outstanding (previous balance — payments) of each account.
2. Determination of the total previous balance and payments for the whole deck.
3. Percentage decrease in receivables to date (total payments ÷ total previous balance × 100).

The entries made in the file description, input, and calculation specifications sheets are presented in Fig. 20-26. The entries in the calculation specifications sheet read as follows:

Line 01: Subtract *payments* (PYMT) from *previous balance* (PREVBL) to arrive at *balance outstanding* (BALOUT).

Line 02: Accumulate previous balance of each customer account under the name *total previous balance* (TOTPBL).

Line 03: Accumulate payments of each customer card under the name *total payments* (TOTPMT).

Lines 04 to 05: Divide total payments by total previous balance and multiply the quotient (half-adjusted to two decimal places) by 100 to arrive at the percentage decrease in receivables.

File Description Specifications

Line	Form Type	Filename	File Type (I/O/U/C/D)	File Designation (P/S/C/R/T/D)	End of File (E)	Sequence (A/D)	File Format (F/V)	Block Length	Record Length	Mode of Processing (L/R)	Length of Key Field or of Record Address Field	Record Address Type (A/K/I)	Type of File Organization or Additional Area (I/D/T or 1-9)	Overflow Indicator	Key Field Starting Location	Extension Code E/L	Device
02	F	CUSFILE	I	P					96								MFCU1

IBM

RPG INPUT SPECIFICATIONS

Date ______
Program ______
Programmer ______

Punching Instruction	Graphic							
	Punch							

Page 02

Line	Form Type	Filename	Sequence	Number (1-N)	Option (O)	Record Identifying Indicator or **	Record Identification Codes 1: Position	Not (N)	C/Z/D	Character	2: Position	Not (N)	C/Z/D	Character	3: Position	Not (N)	C/Z/D	Character	Stacker Select	P = Packed/B = Binary	Field Location From	Field Location To	Decimal Positions	Field Name	Control Level (L1-L9)
01	I	CUSFILE				01																			
02	I																				1	5		CUSNUM	
03	I																				6	11	2	PREVBL	
04	I																				12	17	2	PYMT	

RPG CALCULATION SPECIFICATIONS

Date ______
Program ______
Programmer ______

Punching Instruction	Graphic							
	Punch							

Page 03

Line	Form Type	Control Level (L0-L9, LR, SR)	Indicators	And	And	Factor 1	Operation	Factor 2	Result Field	Field Length	Decimal Positions	Half Adjust (H)	Resulting Indicators: Plus / High 1>2 / High	Minus / Low 1<2 / Low	Zero / Equal 1=2 / Equal
01	C		01			PREVBL	SUB	PYMT	BALOUT	6	2				
02	C		01			PREVBL	ADD	TOTPBL	TOTPBL	9	2				
03	C		01			PYMT	ADD	TOTPMT	TOTPMT	9	2				
04	C	LR				TOTPMT	DIV	TOTPBL	PART	5	2	H			
05	C	LR				PART	MULT	100	PERCNT	5	0				
06	C														

FIGURE 20-26. Partial problem illustrating arithmetic functions

	Factor 2	Result Field Before	Result Field After
a.	5 6 4	_ _ _ _ _ _	_ _ _ 5 6 4
b.	5 6 4	5 4 8 6 4 7	5 4 8 5 6 4
c.	1 2 3 4 5 6 7	_ _ _ _ _	3 4 5 6 7
d.	A B C D E F G	F G A B Y	C D E F G

FIGURE 20-27

MOVE. This operation is used when it is desired to move the contents of factor 2 to a specified result field. The move is performed right-justified and does not involve factor 1. Any unused leftmost positions in the result field are left undisturbed. Also, in the event that factor 2 is longer than the result field, the excess leftmost digits in factor 2 are not moved. For examples, see Fig. 20-27.

The contents of factor 2 can be moved left-justified by a *move-left-justified* (MOVEL) code. This operation code is similar to the MOVE code except that the leftmost operation digits are moved. Any unused rightmost digits are lost. Also, if the factor 2 field is longer than the result field, the excess rightmost digits in factor 2 are not moved. Examples are shown in Fig. 20-28.

CONTROL-LEVEL INDICATORS (COLUMNS 7 TO 8). In Fig. 20-26 a last record (LR) indicator was entered to signal when calculations were to be performed on the *totals* in the operations area. The control-level field is left blank if all calculations are to be done on the input records.

Other indicators used are L1 through L9. Their function is to control

	Factor 2	Result Field Before	Result Field After
a.	5 6 4	_ _ _ _ _ _	5 6 4 _ _ _
b.	5 6 4	5 4 8 6 7 4	5 6 4 6 7 4
c.	1 2 3 4 5 6 7	_ _ _ _ _	1 2 3 4 5
d.	A B C D E F G	_ _ _ _ _	A B C D E

FIGURE 20-28

designated fields during calculations—L1 is the lowest control and is listed first.

INDICATORS (COLUMNS 9 TO 17). The indicator fields (columns 9 to 11, 12 to 14, and 15 to 17) are used to signal the conditions that control the calculations entered in the operations area of the calculation sheet. If these fields are left blank, the computer will perform specified calculations on each input record. Up to three indicators can be used for any given calculation and are handled as an AND relationship. This means that all the specified indicators must be turned on to execute the calculation. If a specified indicator is not to be turned on, the letter N is entered in the first column of that field—that is, column 9, 12, or 15.

Several indicators can be used individually or in some mixed form:

1. The *record-identifying indicator* calculates records that are defined on the input sheet. Any two-digit indicator from 01 through 99 can be used to control calculations. In Fig. 20-26, indicator 01 is entered in columns 10 and 11 to perform calculations on the input records that have a 01 record-identifying indicator (columns 19 to 20) on the input specifications sheet.
2. An OF (overflow) in columns 10 and 11 means "calculate after overflow."
3. An MR (matching record) code in columns 10 and 11 tells the computer to calculate only if a matching record is detected in another input file.
4. A *record-identifying indicator* can be entered in columns 9 to 11 and a *control-level indicator* (L1 to L9) in columns 12 to 14 to perform calculations on the first sequential record with the specified control level. In the example in Fig. 20-29, calculations are carried out on the record on control level 1 when the indicator 01 is turned on.
5. The *halt indicator* is entered as H1 or H2 if it is necessary to halt a calculation because of an error in a previous calculation. In Fig. 20-30, the calculation is halted when indicator 01 is turned on.

FIGURE 20-29

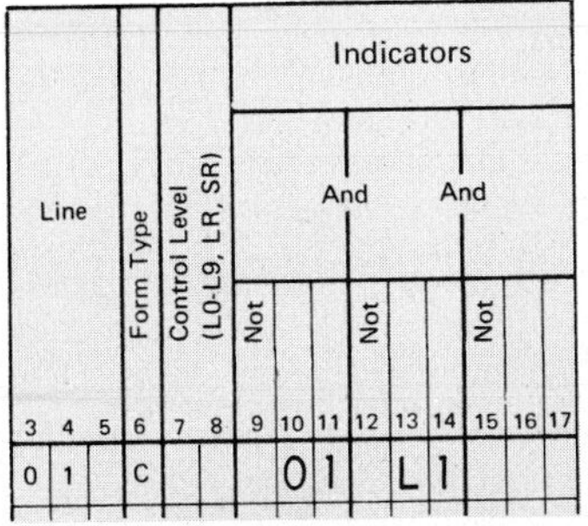

FIGURE 20-30

Line			Form Type	Control Level (L0-L9, LR, SR)		Indicators: Not			And: Not			And: Not		
3	4	5	6	7	8	9	10	11	12	13	14	15	16	17
0	1		C				0	1	N	H	1			

International Business Machines Corporation

GX21-9093-1

Printed in U.S.A.

RPG CALCULATION SPECIFICATIONS

Punching Instruction	Graphic		Page (1 2)		Program Identification (75 76 77 78 79 80)
	Punch				

Factor 1 (18–27)	Operation (28–32)	Factor 2 (33–42)	Result Field (43–48)	Field Length (49–51)	Decimal Positions (52)	Half Adjust (H) (53)	Resulting Indicators — Arithmetic: Plus; Compare: High 1>2; Lookup Table (Factor 2) is: High (54–55)	Arithmetic: Minus; Compare: Low 1< 2; Lookup: Low (56–57)	Arithmetic: Zero; Compare: Equal 1 = 2; Lookup: Equal (58–59)	Comments (60–74)
QUANTA	ADD	QUANTB	TOTAL	7	2	H		H1	H2	COMPUTE TOTAL

FIGURE 20-31. Use of resulting indicators

RESULTING INDICATORS (COLUMNS 54 TO 59). The final section of the calculations sheet consists of the *resulting-indicator* fields, which can be used to test the result fields after a given operation has been completed, and to modify subsequent calculations based on a comparison of the contents of factors 1 and 2.

To illustrate the use of resulting indicators, suppose that we wish to add QUANTA to QUANTB and place the sum in TOTAL—the length of the field is seven positions with two decimal places, rounded. The program is to stop if the result of the addition (i.e., TOTAL) indicates that it is negative or zero. Figure 20-31 shows the appropriate entry.

In a compare (COMP) operation, the value of factor 1 is compared with the value of factor 2. Certain indicators are turned on, depending on whether factor 1 is equal to, greater than, or less than factor 2. The high indicator turns on if factor 1 is greater than factor 2. The low indicator turns on if factor 1 is less than factor 2. The equal indicator turns on if the two factors are equal. Examples are as follows:

	Content of Factor 1	Content of Factor 2	Outcome	Comment
1.	9 8 7 6	9 8 7 6	=	
2.	H A L T	H O P E	<	Letter A precedes letter O in the alphabet, making factor 1 less than factor 2.
3.	9 H 8 P 7	9 H 8 E 7	>	Letter P is higher than letter E, making factor 1 greater than factor 2.

Factor 1	Operation	Factor 2	Result Field	Field Length	Decimal Positions	Half Adjust (H)	High 1>2	Low 1<2	Equal 1=2
QUANTA	COMP	QUANTB	FINAL	7	2		10	15	5

FIGURE 20-32. *A compare entry*

A compare entry generally specifies the indicators that are to be turned on under each of the three alternatives mentioned. For example, suppose that we wish to compare QUANTA with QUANTB and (1) turn on indicator 5 if the two fields are equal, (2) turn on indicator 10 if QUANTA is greater than QUANTB, and (3) turn on indicator 15 if QUANTA is less than QUANTB. The entry is shown in Fig. 20-32.

Branching

With compare and other operations, a program is often made to jump from its normal routine to perform operations elsewhere in the calculation sheet. A GO TO instruction makes branching possible. This consists of a GO TO operation code and a reference name in factor 2 to tell the computer to what instruction to branch. For example, the partial program in Fig. 20-33 illustrates the following branching operations.

FIGURE 20-33. *Branching*

Line	Form Type	Control Level (L0-L9, LR, SR)	Indicators	Factor 1	Operation	Factor 2	Result Field	Field Length	Decimal Positions	Half Adjust (H)
01	C			QUANTA	ADD	QUANTB	SUM	8	2	
02	C			SUM	ADD	OLDBAL	TOTAMT	9	2	
03	C				GOTO	OLDVAL				
04	C			RERUN						
05	C									
06	C									
07	C		Sequential							
08	C		instructions							
09	C									
10	C									
11	C			OLDVAL						
12	C		Sequential							
13	C		instructions							
14	C		17N21NMR		GOTO	RERUN				
15	C									

1. Line 03 contains an *unconditional* GO TO instruction. The reference name is OLDVAL (old value) on line 11. Note that in an unconditional GO TO statement columns 7 to 17 are left blank.
2. Line 14 provides a *conditional* GO TO instruction. It reads: GO TO RERUN (line 04) if indicator 17 is turned on, *AND* if indicator 21 is not turned on, *AND* if a matching record is not present.

OUTPUT-FORMAT SPECIFICATIONS FORM

The output-format form is used to specify the information desired on the report and details regarding the data fields used in the output files (Fig. 20-34). It can generally be divided into two areas: the *file-identification* area (columns 7 to 31) for identifying output files, and the *field-description* area (columns 23 to 70) for describing the data fields pertaining to each file.

FIGURE 20-34. *Output format specifications form*

IBM
International Business Machines Corporation
GX21-9090-1 U/M 050
Printed in U.S.A.
Reprinted 3/70

RPG OUTPUT - FORMAT SPECIFICATIONS

Date
Program
Programmer

Punching Instruction: Graphic, Punch
Page 1 2
Program Identification 75 76 77 78 79 80

Line | Form Type | Filename | Type (H/D/T/E) | Stacker Select/Fetch Overflow (F) | Space: Before, After | Skip: Before, After | Output Indicators: Not, And Not, And Not | Field Name | Edit Codes | Blank After (B) | End Positon in Output Record | P = Packed/B = Binary | Constant or Edit Word | Sterling Sign Position

Edit Codes	Commas	Zero Balances to Print	No Sign	CR	-
	Yes	Yes	1	A	J
	Yes	No	2	B	K
	No	Yes	3	C	L
	No	No	4	D	M

X = Remove Plus Sign
Y = Date Field Edit
Z = Zero Suppress

Lines 01–15, Form Type O

(Output file identification)

(Output field description)

Columns 7 to 14 are reserved for entering the output file name, which must be identical to the output file name mentioned in the file specifications form (columns 7 to 14). As with the input form, a description of the necessary data fields for a given output file begins on another line below the output file name.

TYPE (COLUMN 15). Column 15 is used to specify the time when computer output should occur. The letter D indicates printout during *detail* processing. The letter H is synonymous with the letter D and may be used for a heading line. The letter T indicates printout during *total* processing.

STACKER SELECT (COLUMN 16). Stacker select is used in card files when certain cards must eject into a stacker other than the normal stacker. This is done by entering the stacker number in column 16 and a specific output indicator in columns 23 to 31. For example, suppose that we wish to eject into stacker 2 all output cards (call them CRDOUT) when indicator 10 is turned on *and* when indicator 17 is not on. Figure 20-35 shows the proper entry.

SPACE (COLUMNS 17 TO 18). A digit entered in column 17 tells the computer the number of spaces (zero, one, two, or three) to skip before printing a line; a digit entered in column 18 specifies the number of spaces (zero, one, two, or three) to skip after printing a line. The digits in these columns must be identical to those entered in columns 19 to 20 on the input specifications sheet. They act as indicators for establishing an accurate relationship between the input record and the printed line.

SKIP (COLUMNS 19 TO 22). These two two-digit fields are used for skipping designated lines before and after a line is printed, respectively. An entry (01 through 12) in columns 19 to 20 actuates the printer carriage to skip to the specified channel *before* a line is printed. An entry (01 through 12) in columns 21 to 22 also actuates the printer carriage to skip to the specified channel *after* a line is printed. For example, if the letter H (heading) is entered in column 15, then 06 entered in col-

Line	Form Type	Filename	Type (H/D/T/E)	Stacker Select/Fetch Overflow (F)	Space Before	Space After	Skip Before	Skip After	Output Indicators Not		And Not		And Not		Fie
3 4 5	6	7 8 9 10 11 12 13 14	15	16	17	18	19 20	21 22	23	24 25	26	27 28	29	30 31	32 33
0 1	O	CRDOUT	D	2						1 0	N	I 7			

FIGURE 20-35. Stacker select

umns 19 and 20 tells *where* to print the heading. That is, the printer will skip to line 06 of the next page *before* printing a line.

OUTPUT INDICATORS (COLUMNS 23 TO 31). Output indicators determine whether or not a given output routine is to be performed on a specific output file or field. The absence of output indicators results automatically in carrying out the designated output routine. In addition to the indicators reported in previous forms, first page (1P) and overflow (OF) indicators are exclusively used for preparing written reports.

An OR relationship is often used when either of two indicators initiates a given operation. For example, when certain headings must be printed on every page, output indicators 1P and OF are stated in an OR relationship on two consecutive lines so that the occurrence of either indicator will cause the headings to be printed. An OR is entered in columns 14 and 15 of the second line.

To illustrate, suppose that we wish to print two consecutive headings:

'FINAL INVOICE'
'ITEM QUANTITY SHIPPED NET AMOUNT'

The headings are to be printed if a first page (1P) *or* an overflow (OF) is encountered. The printer is to skip no spaces before printing a line and one space after printing each heading. The printer is also to skip six lines before printing the first heading. The appropriate entries are shown in Fig. 20-36.

FIGURE 20-36. OR relationship

IBM International Business Machines Corporation GX21-9090-1 U/M 050 Printed in U.S.A. Reprinted 3/70

RPG OUTPUT - FORMAT SPECIFICATIONS

Date ____ Program ____ Programmer ____ Punching Instruction: Graphic / Punch. Page 1 2. Program Identification 75 76 77 78 79 80

Line (3–5)	Form Type (6)	Filename (7–14)	Type (H/D/T/E) (15)	Stacker Select/Fetch Overflow (F) (16)	Space Before (17)	Space After (18)	Skip Before (19–20)	Skip After (21–22)	Output Indicators (23–31)	Field Name (32–37)	Edit Codes (38)	Blank After (B) (39)	End Position in Output Record (40–43)	P = Packed/B = Binary (44)	Constant or Edit Word (45–70)
01	O		H		0	1	06		1P						
02	O	O	R						OF						
03	O												13		'FINAL INVOICE'
04	O		H		0	1			1P						
05	O	O	R						OF						
06	O												4		'ITEM'
07	O												24		'QUANTITY SHIPPED'
08	O												22		'NET AMOUNT'

Edit Codes:

Commas	Zero Balances to Print	No Sign	CR	-	
Yes	Yes	1	A	J	X = Remove Plus Sign
Yes	No	2	B	K	Y = Date Field Edit
No	Yes	3	C	L	Z = Zero Suppress
No	No	4	D	M	

Sterling Sign Position (71–74)

The second area of an output-format form specifies the fields and constants related to an output file. Output indicators (columns 23 to 31) are as much a part of this area as they are of the file-description area.

FIELD NAME (COLUMNS 32 TO 37). Columns 32 to 37 indicate (left-adjusted) the name of the specified output field that can be controlled through the output indicators. It should be remembered that the field name must be exactly the same as the one on the input sheet.

EDIT CODES (COLUMN 38). Several digits and letters can be used to edit output data or to punctuate the numeric field specified on the line where the edit code is entered. All codes include zero suppression. The code used depends on the punctuation desired. Some key edit codes are

1. **Edit code 1.** Suppresses leading zeros and inserts a decimal point and commas where necessary. For example, the output number 00745163 would become 7,451.63.
2. **Edit code 3.** Suppresses leading zeros and inserts a decimal point, but no commas. For example, the output number 000142160 would become 1421.60.
3. **Zero suppress (Z).** Eliminates leading zeros in an output number. Examples are

Before	*After*
0017	17
1000	1000
2014	2014
061	61
00123	123

4. **Edit code Y.** Provides slashes (//) in a given number. For example, 121174 will be printed in the form 12/11/74.

Other edit codes are shown in Fig. 20-34.

BLANK AFTER (COLUMN 39). The letter B entered in column 39 causes an alphanumeric field to be cleared to blanks and a numeric field to be set to zeros before new totals can be accumulated for the next set of data cards.

END POSITION IN OUTPUT RECORD (COLUMNS 40 TO 43). Columns 40 to 43 indicate the low-order position of the print field as shown in the printer spacing chart. For example, the end position of print field 51 to 74 is 74. The 74 is entered right-justified—that is, in columns 42 and 43.

CONSTANT OR EDIT WORD (COLUMNS 45 TO 70). Columns 45 to 70 are used for entering an edit word when a field name is specified or a constant if the field name is blank. The maximum size of a constant is 24 positions. Constants with more than 24 positions are entered on two or more consecutive lines with the characters on each line enclosed in single quotes (').

In Fig. 20-36, the second heading consists of three constants: the 'ITEM' subheading consisting of four positions, the 'QUANTITY SHIPPED' subheading consisting of 24 positions (17 character positions plus 7 blank positions to separate it from the 'ITEM' subheading), and the 'NET AMOUNT' subheading, consisting of 22 positions (10 character and 12 blank positions). Note that each subheading is enclosed in single quotation marks.

APPLICATIONS

Thus far we have explained the function and the various operations each RPG specifications sheet is designed to do. For clearer integration of these operations, we shall illustrate some applications performed in RPG II.

Detail Printing of a Card Deck

1. The research and development department of an automobile manufacturer stores on 96-column cards selected information related to its engineers. Each engineer is represented by only one card. Suppose that a printout of the engineers' data deck is required. The appropriate forms and entries are presented in Fig. 20-37.
2. To modify this basic routine, suppose that the research and development department wishes to print out only the identification number (columns 1 to 10), name (columns 11 to 35), and address (columns 36 to 76) of each engineer. What forms and entries would be required? The entries in the control card and file description form remain the same. The entries in the input and output forms are shown in Fig. 20-38.
3. The research and development engineers use a special chemical to test the strength of various metals. This chemical comes in 1-pint bottles and is available upon request. Suppose that the director of the department wishes to have (in addition to the information in item 2) the total number of bottles used by his staff.

   To perform this routine, the input sheet will have on line 05 the name of the new field (KEM) and its location (columns 77 to 79). The calculation sheet is now included to accumulate the

IBM International Business Machines Corporation GX21-9092-1 U/M050 Printed in U.S.A.

RPG CONTROL CARD AND FILE DESCRIPTION SPECIFICATIONS

Date 10/1/74

Program

Programmer RITA PUTKO

Punching Instruction: Graphic / Punch

Page 01 Program Identification

Control Card Specifications

Line	Form Type	Core Size to Compile	Object Output	Listing Options	Core Size to Execute	Debug	MFCM Stacking Sequence	Sterling: Input-Shillings	Input-Pence	Output-Shillings	Output-Pence	Inverted Print	360/20 2501 Buffer	Number Of Print Positions	Alternate Collating Sequence	Refer to the specific System Reference Library manual for actual entries.
3 4 5	6	7 8 9	10	11	12 13 14	15	16	17	18	19	20	21	22	23 24 25	26	27–74
01	H	008			008											

File Description Specifications

Line	Form Type	Filename	File Type (I/O/U/C/D)	File Designation (P/S/C/R/T/D)	End of File (E)	Sequence (A/D)	File Format (F/V)	Block Length	Record Length	L/R	Mode of Processing	Length of Key Field or of Record Address Field	Record Address Type (A/K/I)	Type of File Organization or Additional Area (I/D/T or 1-9)	Overflow Indicator	Key Field Starting Location	Extension Code E/L	Device	Symbolic Device	Labels (S, N, or E)	Name of Label Exit	Extent Exit for DAM / Core Index	A/U	File Addition/Unordered	Number of Tracks for Cylinder Overflow	Number of Extents	Tape Rewind	File Condition U1-U8
3 4 5	6	7–14	15	16	17	18	19	20–23	24–27	28	29–30		31	32	33–34	35–38	39	40–46	47–52	53	54–59	60–65	66	67	68–69	70	71	72–74
02	F	ENGFILE	I	P					96									MFCU1										
03	F	OUTPUT	O						96									PRINTER										
04	F																											
05																												

IBM International Business Machines Corporation GX21-9094-1 U/M050 Printed in U.S.A.

RPG INPUT SPECIFICATIONS

Date 10/1/74

Program

Programmer RITA PUTKO

Punching Instruction: Graphic / Punch

Page 02 Program Identification

Line	Form Type	Filename	Sequence	Number (1-N)	Option (O)	Record Identifying Indicator or **	Record Identification Codes 1: Position / Not (N) / C/Z/D / Character	2: Position / Not (N) / C/Z/D / Character	3: Position / Not (N) / C/Z/D / Character	Stacker Select	P = Packed/B = Binary	Field Location From	To	Decimal Positions	Field Name	Control Level (L1-L9)	Matching Fields or Chaining Fields	Field Record Relation	Field Indicators Plus / Minus / Zero or Blank	Sterling Sign Position
3 4 5	6	7–14	15 16	17	18	19 20	21–27	28–34	35–41	42	43	44–47	48–51	52	53–58	59 60	61 62	63 64	65–70	71–74
01	I	ENGFILE	AA			01														
02	I											1	96		CARD					
03	I																			
04	I																			

IBM International Business Machines Corporation GX21-9090-1 U/M 050 Printed in U.S.A. Reprinted 3/70

RPG OUTPUT - FORMAT SPECIFICATIONS

Date 10/1/74

Program

Programmer RITA PUTKO

Punching Instruction: Graphic / Punch

Page 03 Program Identification

Line	Form Type	Filename	Type (H/D/T/E)	Stacker Select/Fetch Overflow (F)	Space Before	Space After	Skip Before	Skip After	Output Indicators: Not		And: Not		And: Not		Field Name	Edit Codes	Blank After (B)	End Position in Output Record	P = Packed/B = Binary	Constant or Edit Word	Sterling Sign Position
3 4 5	6	7–14	15	16	17	18	19 20	21 22	23	24 25	26	27 28	29	30 31	32–37	38	39	40–43	44	45–70	71–74
01	O	OUTPUT	D			1				01											
02	O														CARD			96			
03	O																				
04	O																				

Edit Codes:

Commas	Zero Balances to Print	No Sign	CR	-
Yes	Yes	1	A	J
Yes	No	2	B	K
No	Yes	3	C	L
No	No	4	D	M

X = Remove Plus Sign
Y = Date Field Edit
Z = Zero Suppress

FIGURE 20-37. *Detail printing*

IBM International Business Machines Corporation

GX21-9094-1 U/M050
Printed in U.S.A.

RPG INPUT SPECIFICATIONS

Date 10/1/74

Program

Programmer RITA PUTKO

Page 02

Line	Form Type	Filename	Sequence	Record Identifying Indicator	Field Location From	Field Location To	Field Name
01	I	ENGFILE	AA	01			
02	I				1	10	IDNUM
03	I				11	35	NAME
04	I				36	76	ADRESS

RPG OUTPUT - FORMAT SPE[C]

Date 10/1/74

Program

Programmer RITA PUTKO

Line	Form Type	Filename	Type (H/D/T/E)	Space Before	Output Indicators	Field Name	End Position in Output Record
01	O	OUTPUT	D	01	01		
02	O					IDNUM	10
03	O					NAME	35
04	O					ADRESS	76
05	O						

FIGURE 20-38. Detail printing of selected card fields

number of bottles used by the research and development staff. In the output sheet, line 05 indicates the name and its printing position; line 06 specifies the type of line and the number of spaces to allow before and after the TOTAL line is printed out. The LR in columns 24 to 25 of line 06 refers to *last record.* Line 07 specifies the printing position of the TOTKEM—the total number of bottles used (Fig. 20-39).

Printing Cards of Two Input Files

In a retail store operation, there are two input decks of cards. The first deck is a primary file, each card containing a department number and department name as follows:

Columns 1 to 4: Department number
Columns 5 to 25: Department name

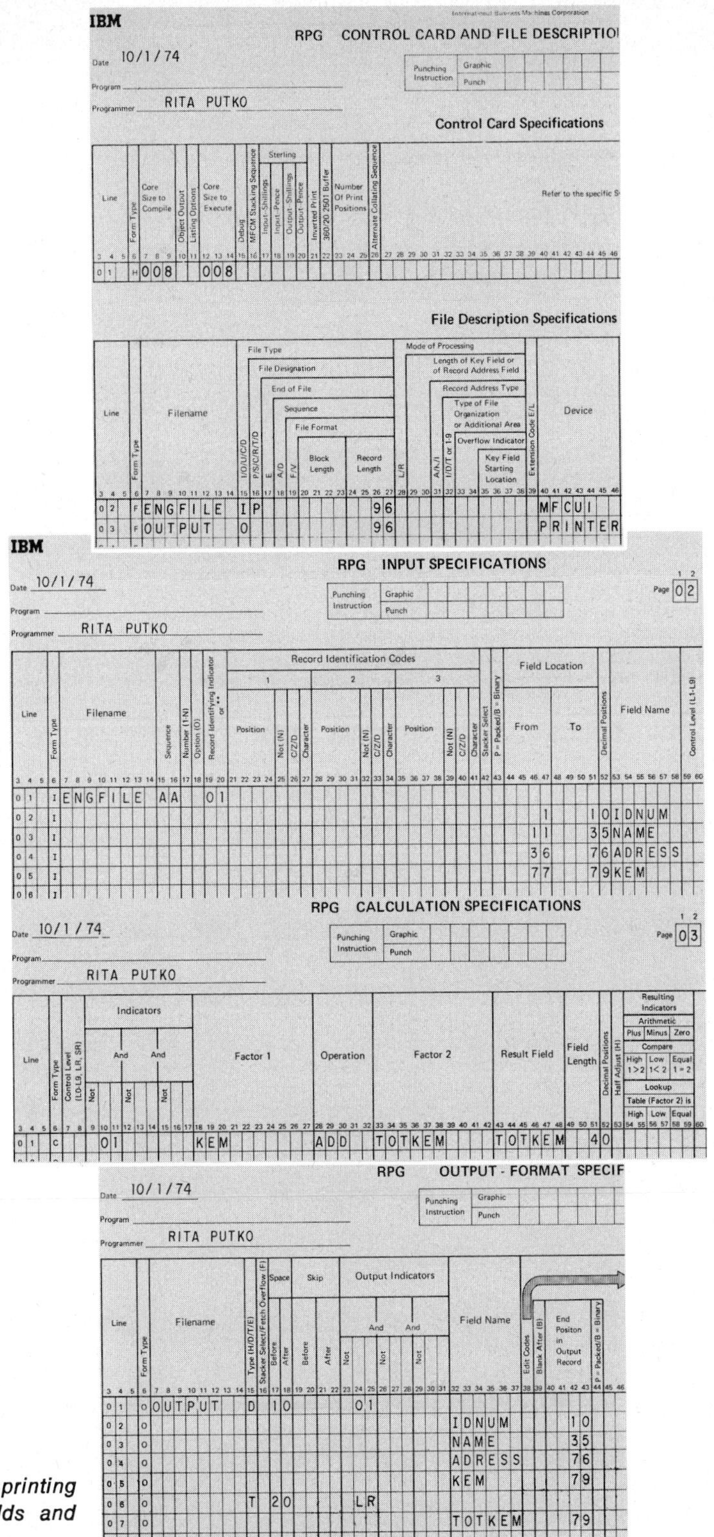

IBM

International Business Machines Corporation

RPG CONTROL CARD AND FILE DESCRIPTIO[N]

Date 10/1/74

Program

Programmer RITA PUTKO

Control Card Specifications

Line	Form Type	Core Size to Compile	Object Output	Listing Options	Core Size to Execute
01	H	008			008

File Description Specifications

Line	Form Type	Filename	File Type	File Designation	Record Length	Device
02	F	ENGFILE	I	P	96	MFCU1
03	F	OUTPUT	O		96	PRINTER

IBM

RPG INPUT SPECIFICATIONS

Date 10/1/74

Program

Programmer RITA PUTKO

Page 02

Line	Form Type	Filename	Sequence	Record Identifying Indicator	Field Location From	Field Location To	Decimal Positions	Field Name
01	I	ENGFILE	AA	01				
02	I				1	10		IDNUM
03	I				11	35		NAME
04	I				36	76		ADRESS
05	I				77	79		KEM
06	I							

RPG CALCULATION SPECIFICATIONS

Date 10/1/74

Program

Programmer RITA PUTKO

Page 03

Line	Form Type	Indicators	Factor 1	Operation	Factor 2	Result Field	Field Length	Decimal Positions
01	C	01	KEM	ADD	TOTKEM	TOTKEM	4	0

RPG OUTPUT - FORMAT SPECIF[ICATIONS]

Date 10/1/74

Program

Programmer RITA PUTKO

Line	Form Type	Filename	Type (H/D/T/E)	Space After	Output Indicators	Field Name	End Position in Output Record
01	O	OUTPUT	D	1	01		
02	O					IDNUM	10
03	O					NAME	35
04	O					ADRESS	76
05	O					KEM	79
06	O		T	2	LR		
07	O					TOTKEM	79
08	O						

***FIGURE 20-39.** Detail printing with selected card fields and totals*

The second deck is a secondary file of the sales staff. Each card has the following information:

Columns 1 to 4: Department number
Columns 5 to 9: Salesman's number
Columns 10 to 35: Salesman's name

Required is a listing of the files such that the first line represents a card from the primary file, followed by all salesmen's (secondary) cards belonging to that department. The listing should be in the following format:

Item	*No. of Positions on the Line*
A heading 'DEPT'	4
Department number	8
Department name	30
Salesman's number	10
Salesman's name	40

Figure 20-40 shows the necessary forms and entries. The file description specifications form lists two input files and one output file. Note that the primary file is listed first, followed by the secondary file and the output file, respectively. The input form lists the two input files and the field location of the data fields. The entry M1 in columns 61 to 62 signifies that the field on that line is a matching field. The output-format form lists the output file (DEPTLIST) as a detail (D) file with three spaces to be allowed after printing a line for output indicator 01 and two spaces for output indicator 02. Note that an arbitrary four-digit heading is specified on line 02.

Computing Gross Pay

An input file consists of cards, each containing an employee's number, name, rate of pay per hour, and number of hours worked. Suppose that we wish to determine gross pay (RATE $\times$ HRS) for each employee and the total number of hours worked.

The RATE field is designated as a four-digit field with two decimal positions. The HRS field is a three-digit field (no decimal positions). The locations of these fields are as follows:

Columns 1 to 5: Employee number (EMPNUM)
Columns 6 to 35: Employee name (EMPNAM)
Columns 36 to 39: Rate per hour (RATE)
Columns 40 to 42: Number of hours worked (HRS)

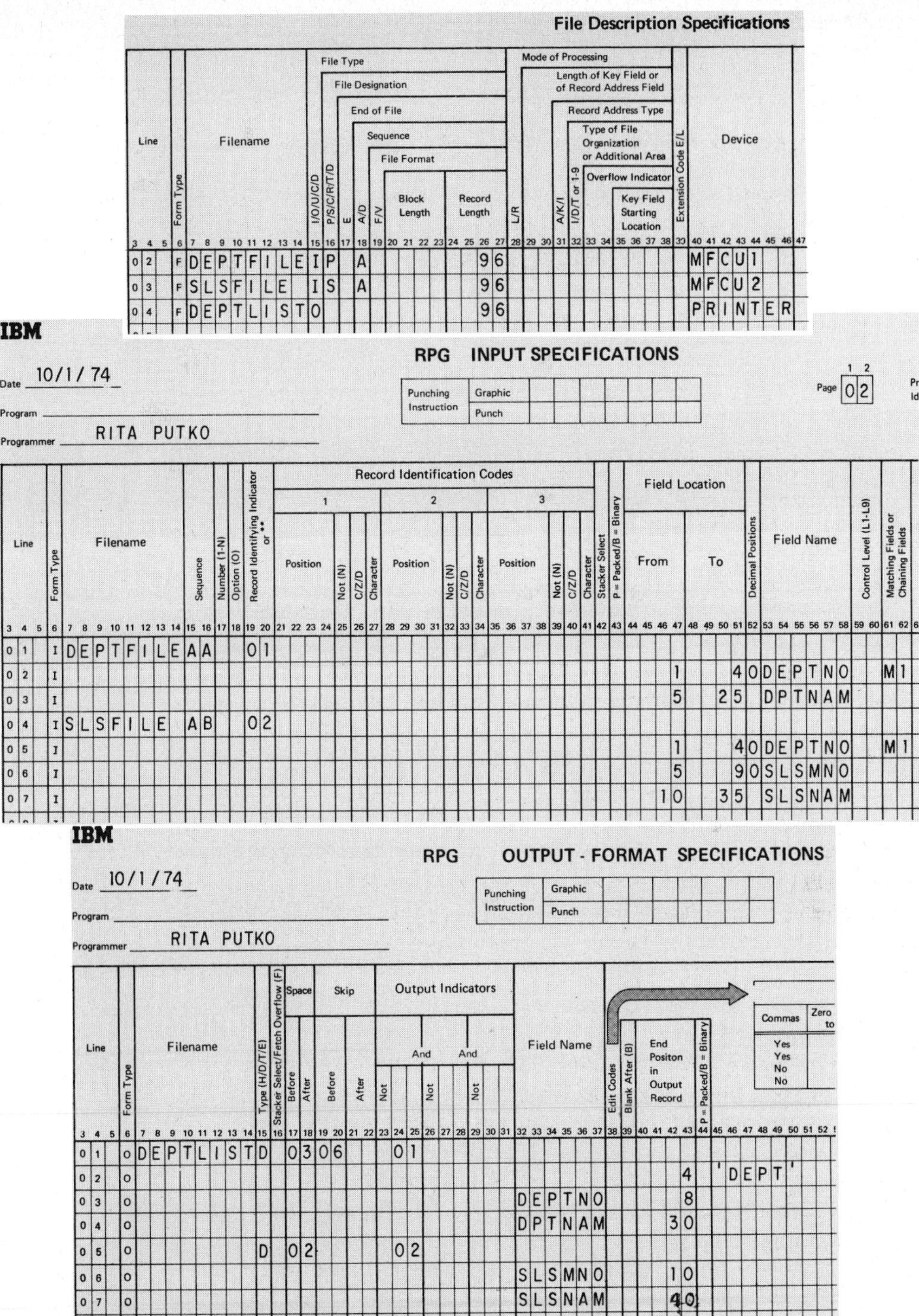

File Description Specifications

Line	Form Type	Filename	File Type (I/O/U/C/D)	File Designation (P/S/C/R/T/D)	End of File (E)	Sequence (A/D)	File Format (F/V)	Block Length	Record Length	Device
02	F	DEPTFILE	I	P		A			96	MFCU1
03	F	SLSFILE	I	S		A			96	MFCU2
04	F	DEPTLIST	O						96	PRINTER

IBM

RPG INPUT SPECIFICATIONS

Date 10/1/74

Program

Programmer RITA PUTKO

Page 02

Line	Form Type	Filename	Sequence	Record Identifying Indicator	Field Location From	Field Location To	Decimal Positions	Field Name	Matching Fields or Chaining Fields
01	I	DEPTFILE	AA	01					
02	I				1	4	0	DEPTNO	M1
03	I				5	25		DPTNAM	
04	I	SLSFILE	AB	02					
05	I				1	4	0	DEPTNO	M1
06	I				5	9	0	SLSMNO	
07	I				10	35		SLSNAM	

IBM

RPG OUTPUT - FORMAT SPECIFICATIONS

Date 10/1/74

Program

Programmer RITA PUTKO

Line	Form Type	Filename	Type (H/D/T/E)	Space Before	Space After	Skip Before	Skip After	Output Indicators	Field Name	End Position in Output Record	Constant or Edit Word
01	O	DEPTLIST	D	0	3	06		01			
02	O									4	'DEPT'
03	O								DEPTNO	8	
04	O								DPTNAM	30	
05	O		D	0	2			02			
06	O								SLSMNO	10	
07	O								SLSNAM	40	

FIGURE 20-40. Printing two input card files

The output layout should be as follows:

Item	Number of Positions
EMPNUM	5
EMPNAM	29
RATE	26
HRS	25
GROSS	35
TOTHRS	28

The result is shown in Fig. 20-41.

SUMMARY

RPG II is a popular language used in processing files of records on the IBM System/3. In planning an application, a programmer must (1) determine the expected end results, (2) present available input data, (3) decide on the required calculations, and (4) specify input–output devices necessary for doing the job. Each step requires a special form for proper handling.

The desired end results are described on the output-format specifications sheet. The sheet is divided into a file-identification area for identifying output files and a field-description area for describing the data fields pertaining to each file.

Presenting the available input data is done on the input specifications sheet. The primary function of this form is to identify different types of cards within a given file and to specify their sequence.

Decisions on the required calculations are detailed on the calculation specifications sheet. The form is used to indicate the type of arithmetic operations to be performed on input data and the order in which they must be performed.

Finally, specifications for the input and output devices needed to handle the data are made on the card control and file description sheet. The file specifications form provides additional information about the files needed in performing the job. It is easy to fill out, since only a few fields must be completed.

Each line on a specifications form is punched into a single card. When all the specifications have been punched, the resulting deck (source program) is later compiled for producing an object program for processing.

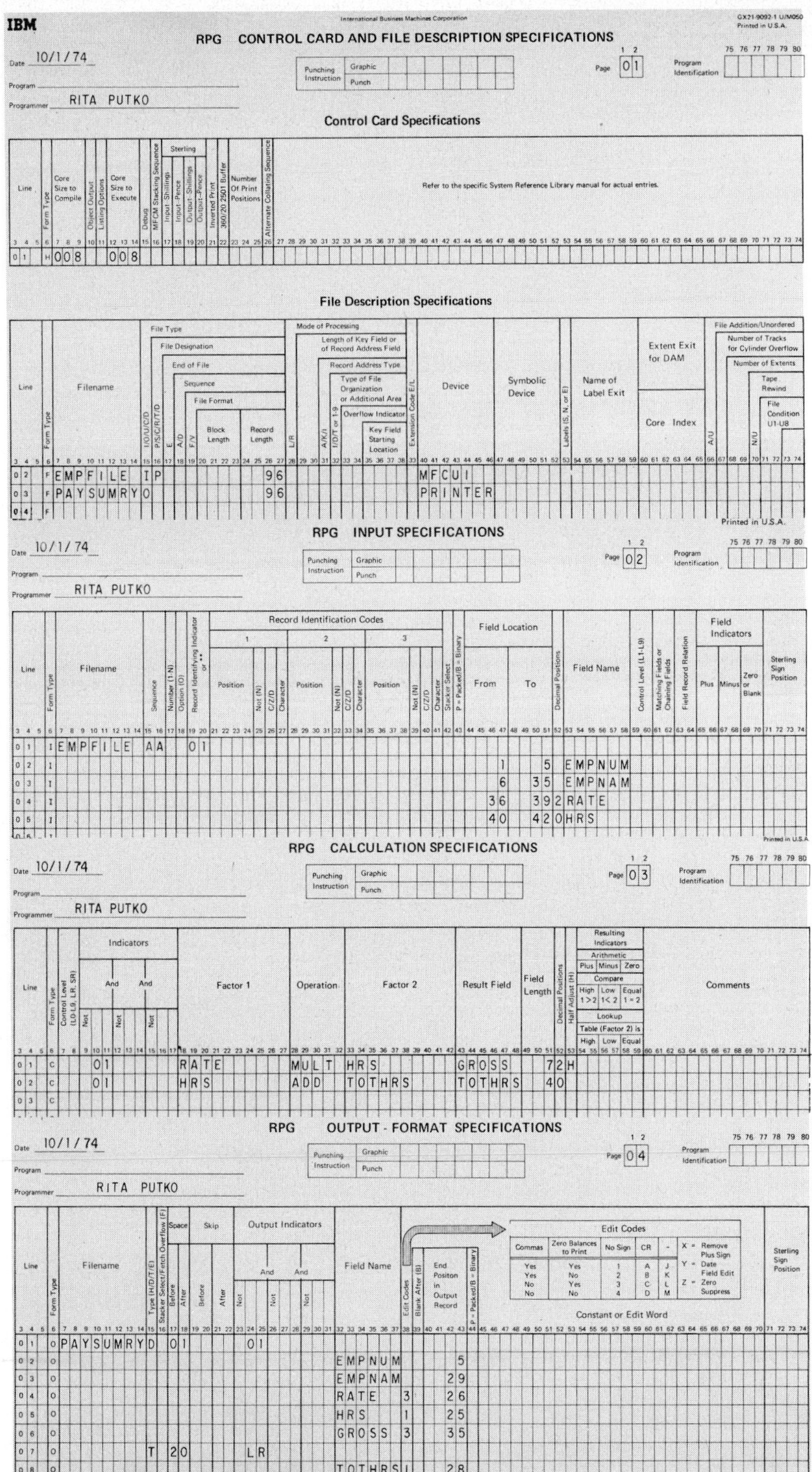

IBM — International Business Machines Corporation — GX21-9092-1 U/M050 Printed in U.S.A.

RPG CONTROL CARD AND FILE DESCRIPTION SPECIFICATIONS

Date 10/1/74 — Page 01 — Programmer RITA PUTKO

Control Card Specifications

Line	Form Type	Core Size to Compile	Core Size to Execute
01	H	008	008

File Description Specifications

Line	Form Type	Filename	File Type	File Designation	Record Length	Device
02	F	EMPFILE	I	P	96	MFCU1
03	F	PAYSUMRY	O		96	PRINTER
04	F					

RPG INPUT SPECIFICATIONS

Date 10/1/74 — Page 02 — Programmer RITA PUTKO

Line	Form Type	Filename	Sequence	Record Identifying Indicator	From	To	Decimal Positions	Field Name
01	I	EMPFILE	AA	01				
02	I				1	5		EMPNUM
03	I				6	35		EMPNAM
04	I				36	39	2	RATE
05	I				40	42	0	HRS

RPG CALCULATION SPECIFICATIONS

Date 10/1/74 — Page 03 — Programmer RITA PUTKO

Line	Form Type	Indicators	Factor 1	Operation	Factor 2	Result Field	Field Length	Decimal Positions	Half Adjust (H)
01	C	01	RATE	MULT	HRS	GROSS	7	2	H
02	C	01	HRS	ADD	TOTHRS	TOTHRS	4	0	
03	C								

RPG OUTPUT - FORMAT SPECIFICATIONS

Date 10/1/74 — Page 04 — Programmer RITA PUTKO

Line	Form Type	Filename	Type (H/D/T/E)	Space After	Skip Before	Output Indicators	Field Name	Edit Codes	End Position in Output Record
01	O	PAYSUMRY	D	01		01			
02	O						EMPNUM		5
03	O						EMPNAM		29
04	O						RATE	3	26
05	O						HRS	1	25
06	O						GROSS	3	35
07	O		T	2	0	LR			
08	O						TOTHRS	1	28

FIGURE 20-41. *Computing gross pay*

TERMS TO LEARN

Calculation specifications form
Card control and file description specifications form
Input specifications form
Output-format specifications form
RPG II

QUESTIONS

1. What coding forms are involved in RPG programming?
2. Describe the procedure used in producing an object program.
3. Explain and illustrate the primary function(s) of the file specifications form.
4. Define the function of the following identification fields:
   a. position field; b. NOT field; c. C/Z/D field; d. record-sequence field; e. result-indicator field.
5. Explain and illustrate the use of the calculation specifications form in RPG programming.
6. Define the function of the following terms:
   a. move left-justified; b. record-identifying indicator; c. resulting indicator; d. branching.
7. What is the primary function of the output-format specifications form? Give an example.
8. For each of the following statements, write an appropriate RPG entry, and indicate the form where the entry is recorded and the location of the entry on that form:
   a. Add SUMA to SUMB. SUMA represents a value of 104 and SUMB represents a value of 107. The result of the addition is to be called TOTAL.
   b. Subtract SUMB from SUMA. SUMB represents a value of 14 and SUMA represents a value of 20.
   c. Multiply QUANTA by QUANTB. QUANTA represents a value of 218 and QUANTB represents a value of 714.
9. Which of the following literals is(are) incorrect?
   a. —.84; b. .84+1; c. D71; d. 7.1098+4; e. 7.0—.
10. Suppose that we have a set of data cards, and each card contains the following information:

Column	*Description*
1– 4	Account number
5–12	Previous balance
13–20	Payments

    Use the proper specification form and record the entries necessary for computing the balance outstanding and the sum of previous balance and payments.

System/3 programming—RPG II fundamentals

BERNARD, S. M. *System/3 Programming—RPG Fundamentals.* Englewood Cliffs, N.J.: Prentice-Hall, Inc., 1972, pp. 57–163.

BRIGHTMAN, R. W., and J. R. CLARK. *RPG I and RPG II Programming.* New York: Macmillan Publishing Co., Inc., 1970, Chaps. 2–6.

MURRAY, J. T. *Programming in RPG II: IBM System/3.* New York: McGraw-Hill Book Company, 1971, Chaps. 3 and 5.

DATA-PROCESSING MANAGEMENT

management planning for computer processing

21

Design of a Proposed System

New Hardware and Cost Determination

purchase versus lease
cost analysis

Evaluation of Study Findings

Preparation of Final Recommendations to Management

ELECTRONIC DATA PROCESSING VERSUS EMPLOYEES OF THE FIRM

CONVERSION PHASE

DURATION OF A FEASIBILITY STUDY

Certain business firms (large and small) seem to be hypnotized by the glamour and prestige of an electronic data-processing installation. They hear about and believe in stories told of the fantastic potential of computers in business. Some envision a system that can solve all their problems, meet their needs and expectations, make decisions in major areas, and eliminate all the worries, pressures, and frustrations often encountered by management. Such firms are said to have "computeritis."

Whereas advances in computer technology place the computer within the reach of virtually every business firm, its use is not in itself a solution to all problems. Investigation of past and existing installations has indicated that most applications handled by computers could adequately and as economically be processed by nonelectronic systems, and that most of the new applications, although necessary, were not critical enough to justify the additional expense and personnel training needed to operate a new computer installation.

Furthermore, many firms fall into the trap of failing to systematically "trim-up" their data-processing system with changes in their operational or organizational strategy. As a firm grows in size and continues to expand profitably, it reaches a stage when it is suddenly realized that existing methods of processing data are no longer adequate. Some firms panic and hurriedly conduct a "feasibility study," resulting in a computer installation. Experience shows that most firms who awaken a bit too late and then haphazardly install a new system soon realize disappointing results. They either have to readjust the system through additional peripheral components (which means a more costly operation) or reluctantly revert to activating their former system.

Deciding on a computer installation is not an easy task. Risks are involved; some factors cannot be accurately determined. These facts, coupled with future uncertainties, cause many firms to feel helpless, especially those with inadequate staff to carry out business forecasting or to conduct system study. Given the need for a computer system, it is extremely important to make sure that the system is capable of handling present as well as future needs.

The question then is: How should an organization proceed to explore its need for an electronic data-processing system? Can it afford to install a system based on the experience of other firms, or should it initiate a study of its own? The former alternative is ill-advised, since no two firms fit the same specifications or share the same problems. Furthermore, it is unlikely that a firm would divulge information that might compromise its competitive standing. The second alternative promises results if a feasibility study is properly carried out and enough time is allowed for selecting the best available system for the job.

Before management can take advantage of the advances in computer technology, it must consider

1. Examining company procedures to determine exactly what they are and where they need correction.
2. The feasibility of using a computer installation in its operation.
3. Acceptance of such an installation by operative members of the firm, including employees and stockholders.
4. The willingness of all concerned to cooperate in using the new system once it is installed.
5. The problem of retraining or transferring employees affected by the installation.

The procedure should be flowcharted so that no important details are overlooked. If each phase is worked out carefully and painstakingly, much time will be saved in the long run, as many of the problems incident to the installation of a computer system will have been foreseen and allowances made accordingly.

JUSTIFICATION FOR AND PRIMARY BENEFITS OF A COMPUTER INSTALLATION

Prior to 1960, most computer systems were designed with the larger corporation in mind. They were extremely expensive and, because of their large size, were best suited for handling complex, lengthy applications. During the 1960s and early 1970s, the computer market changed drastically. First, minicomputers and small- and medium-sized computers began to appear. This means that firms of all sizes and types could select a computer tailored to their needs. Whereas only a few large firms might have acquired a computer system in the past, now even smaller firms could be enticed to join the computer rush.

Second, as computer technology advanced and mass-production techniques improved, the cost of computation steadily decreased. This breakthrough meant the availability of virtually any size of computer at a competitive price. Prices now range from as low as $2,000 for a mini-computer to as high as $7,000,000 for the supercomputer, depending on such factors as speed, memory size, and type and number of peripheral devices.

Now that computers are within the reach of virtually any business firm, each prospective user faces the critical task of choosing from among many manufacturers the computer that will best do the job. This is where a feasibility study becomes necessary.

Given justification for the installation, firms in general can realize several benefits from a computer system:

1. **Savings in processing cost.** Cost savings are an obvious advantage in most operations; a computer can be used to process progressively increasing volumes of data that are not efficiently handled by the existing system. Savings can also be realized through reduction of clerical costs. A computer system operated by a staff of 10, for example, could conceivably process applications once handled by 100 clerks. It should be noted, however, that in practice a computer system often requires a considerable number of supportive staff for effective processing, and in case of emergency. With such overhead costs added to the fixed direct cost, substantial savings in cost might not be realized except by replacement of the many clerks assigned to handling perfunctory operations of a mechanical nature.
2. **Processing complex problems at high speed.** The computer's greater computational power, coupled with its ability to follow instructions for long arithmetic computations at high speed, means that business files which once took clerks weeks to update can now be updated in a matter of hours. This response is especially helpful in such areas as sales forecasting—giving deeper and more thorough analyses of sales volume, trends, and future consumer demand. Considering the dynamic and ever-changing conditions in the business environment, it is exceedingly difficult to expect reasonably accurate and meaningful long-term forecasts without some aid from the computer.
3. **Programmed decision making.** A computer system can be programmed to take over various functions that were once performed manually. For example, in inventory control a computer is much like an automatic pilot. It examines the entire inventory, keeps track of any shortages in stock, correlates the shortages between the items in question and, in some sophisticated systems, lists the name and address of the supplier, the company's account number,

the number of units needed, the unit price of each item, and total cost—all on a standard form for ordering. This entire process, if done manually, would be quite expensive.

WHAT IS A FEASIBILITY STUDY?

A feasibility study is an in-depth study of the company's clerical and management information routines, the operations that can be converted to computer processing, the areas that can benefit most from a computer system, and the overall costs involved. That is, in deciding whether a computer system should be installed, the character of a firm's operations, its present operational procedures, and its general objectives should be carefully reviewed in the light of the purposes that the new system is designed to serve. Management must formulate a sharply defined picture of its data-processing needs and determine how a computer can fit into the organization and effectively serve existing departments. *It should be plainly understood that a computer is intended to aid, not replace, man.* Without this understanding, the whole character of the system is likely to be misconstrued, and frustrations easily develop when the system fails to live up to false expectations.

The steps involved in conducting a feasibility study are often similar to those used in solving many of our personal daily problems. An illustration follows:

> After graduating from college, Ralph Bender, a business management major, accepted a position with a manufacturing concern. Considering the limited income of a management trainee, his new job, and the need to have a mode of transportation, Ralph purchased a used car for $295.00. Ralph advanced within the firm and gained recognition and promotions steadily. A year and a half later he married and, during the same month, was promoted to head a department in the manufacturing division of the main plant.
>
> With a substantial increase in salary and a relocation to a suburban area, Ralph felt that the old "jalopy" was a poor match with his new status. The upkeep proved prohibitive because repairs had to be made frequently. The car was *unreliable,* in that mechanical failure happened at inopportune times, often resulting in his late arrival at the plant. It was also *inefficient* with respect to the excessive gasoline and oil it consumed. It had a shabby appearance, and also was *hazardous* to drive at high speeds.
>
> Knowing that his present car no longer met his needs, Ralph conducted a "study." He spent his free evenings shopping for a new automobile. He contacted dealers who sold various makes and models. He drove a few demonstration cars and obtained literature about the various models. To supplement his general knowledge about the new models, he contacted friends and associates to learn

what their experience had been with the cars they had purchased. Meanwhile, he read articles in independent magazines of test results made on various makes.

After 2 weeks of survey and evaluation, Ralph considered his present position and his chances for further advancement with the firm. The chances looked good. He also considered the expenses involved with regard to his home mortgage, his living and other expenses, the amount of cash he had available, and the amount he needed to borrow to pay for a new car. He weighed the price of the car against the savings in gasoline and oil and the car's known reliability, efficiency, and speed. When his analysis was complete, to his wife's very apparent pleasure, he placed an order for the purchase of a specific make, size, power rating, and price range. He selected the dealer to whom he gave the order because of his reputation for guaranteed prompt delivery, courteous service, and extension of reasonable credit terms.

A business firm conducts a feasibility study in ways similar to the foregoing example. In the remainder of this chapter we discuss the steps involved and the factors to be considered in installing a computer system.

Impetus for a Feasibilty Study

For a feasibility study to succeed, the survey and evaluation phase must be made by competent, qualified personnel. The study must guarantee savings in clerical and other related costs, and, most importantly, it must be approved by top management, even when the need for it is recognized and supported by members of lower management. When top management authorizes a feasibility study, its motive is generally a desire for experimentation, with less emphasis upon the cost or the need to obtain funds. Top management's aim is to use a computer for producing useful information, such as sales analyses or business forecasting, that is unobtainable under the present system. When interest is generated at the top level, the project gets under way fairly easily, because top management feels committed to and presumably sold on the desirability of exploring the use of a computer in its operations.

More often, however, lower-level managers initiate interest because of a known need for using faster processing methods in their departments. In this case, communications flow upward first, and all data pertinent to the problem that would be helpful in gaining the approval of superiors must be presented. Success in gaining the approval of top management is related to a great extent to its members' attitudes and personalities and their relationship to lower management. If members of top management are young, progressive, and willing to risk investment of money in new methods to meet competition head-on, no great problem should arise in gaining their support. On the other hand, if members of top management are conservative and unimaginative, insist on presentation of all facts regardless of their value, and drag matters on unnecessarily, the job of selling them the idea of a new computer would be more difficult.

Preliminary Survey Phase

Given management's initial approval and cooperation, the first step in a feasibility study is to initiate a preliminary survey, as a basis for a later detailed study, to determine whether or not a particular computer system should be installed. One goal of the initial study is to allow management and its affiliated staff an opportunity to have an overview of electronic data processing (EDP) and how it would contribute to the organization's efforts. Some inexperienced firms rationalize their limited background in data-processing and conversion techniques by concerning themselves with two or three key applications for possible conversion and building their hopes on the false premise that, once they have a computer system, the knowledge gained from running these applications would eventually help in solving all other problems. *The role of the preliminary study team is to take a look at the organization's operations and find out whether there is justification for changes in existing methods.*

A preliminary survey is expected to determine (1) the company's data-processing requirements, and (2) the facility needed to fulfill these requirements. In determining the data-processing requirements, the preliminary survey team takes a short-range and long-range outlook into all (not just a few) applications that can possibly be computerized. Even for a small firm, a long-range outlook into this matter could mean a potential installation capable of serving both present and future needs. The question then arises whether existing applications should be computerized or, if they are already computerized, whether expanding their degree of computerization is feasible. Likewise, in the case of new applications, consideration must be made in terms of their potential for computerization, and whether they should be immediately computerized or gradually converted over a period of time.

Understanding the nature of the company's current data-processing activities is a prerequisite to identifying the operations that might potentially be computerized, and gives the team as a whole a more objective overview of the task under study. In searching for the problems that could easily be solved by a computer system, information regarding their solution must be based on a preestablished set of operating instructions rather than on instructions given by the employees now handling the job. The availability of operating instructions can be used later in developing a program for computer processing.

Once the applications and their data-processing requirements have been determined, the next step is to specify the type of data-processing facility that will best handle the job. The alternative facilities range from an improvement of the existing system to the introduction of a computer system, the size and level of sophistication depending on factors such as cost, volume of data, and complexity of applications. Since the overall objective of the team is a general evaluation of the potential use of a computer system, the team often indicates to management more than one alternative, such as the use of a service bureau or a time-sharing facility, for consideration. These alternatives are later evaluated in terms of their dollar-saving potential, the type of improvements to be expected, potential applications to be handled, and so on. Management, at this point, is in a better position to decide whether to pursue a detailed feasibility study.

PERSONNEL MAKEUP OF A FULL-SCALE FEASIBILITY STUDY

Project Team

The project team consists primarily of members who served on the preliminary survey team, selected key personnel representing various departments, and/or junior officers whose section might be affected by a computer system. The combined knowledge and diversified backgrounds of the team members should contribute in a positive way to carrying out the demands of the feasibility study. Attempting to conduct the study is not an easy task. The team's decisions have immediate and long-term implications. The team must consider many factors. Questions such as the following must be answered within the time constraints of the study: What is the basic objective of a computer system? Is it feasible to centralize operations and reduce costs? What applications can be economically run once an installation becomes operative? What applications have the potential of being converted after the installation of the system? Will supervisors and employees cooperate, especially those whose jobs might be affected by the new installation?

Most firms hope that when a computer is installed they will realize benefits related to *publicity, economy, accuracy,* and *speed.* A forward-looking, progressive company wants to identify itself with the latest equipment, impressing both customers and competitors. The computer installation is usually but not always viewed as a sign of efficiency, progress, and prosperity. Often, "computerized" organizations allow local citizens to visit the installation. Although the gesture is good *publicity* for the firm, it can be costly, as one or more company officials have to take time to show and explain the system to the visiting groups. Some companies hire guides whose sole job is taking groups on tours to explain the system and the applications it handles. This leaves a good impression on the local citizenry and has a favorable effect on the firm's employees as well. If employees are aware of the uses of and the benefits derived from the system, they tend to support it and, consequently, publicize it in their community to the best advantage of the firm.

Economy of operation and available space are also involved. For example, when clerical employees, bookkeepers, and other aides work behind desks, with calculators, adding machines, typewriters, pencils, and paper in a large room, a business firm that uses such manual processing methods generally experiences inefficient operation and high costs. By contrast, a computer operation is expected to produce better results and occupy little space for an average-sized installation designed to do the same job. Economy through efficiency in the use of available space and through rapid processing reduces the marginal cost of applications—especially "bread-and-butter" applications.

With a computer installation *accuracy* is also evident, due to minimum human intervention and the self-checking features built into the system. The project team should weigh the *speed* factor against its contribution to certain key applications. For example, in a retail store the credit department can use the computer for processing customer accounts with emphasis on the delinquent file. More prompt collection can be expected with high-speed computers than with any other mechanical method.

Authority and Responsibility of the Project Team. In conducting the feasibility study it is important that the project team have authority commensurate with the responsibility which it agrees to assume. Its members should be authorized to contact line managers as well as staff members for data acquisition. This cannot be done successfully unless top management is in full agreement with what the team is doing. By the same token, all findings should be reported to top management—preferably to the chief executive. In the case of a very large firm, an executive vice-president in charge of manufacturing or finance is often the person to whom the team reports.

Project Director. Regardless of the background and knowledge of the project team, its job can only be done well after a project director has been appointed to head the study and synchronize the work of the team. To protect the team from departmental pressures and to secure its independence, the director chosen is often a high-ranking management officer with special abilities and an awareness of the importance of the study. He is expected to be imaginative and able to size up a problem quickly, determine the alternatives, and adopt the one that can provide an effective solution. To do so, a wide background in business and specific knowledge in accounting and finance are essential, because most business applications involve knowledge based on these two fields. Knowledge of accounting helps him understand the accounting implications of an application and communicate more effectively with the personnel engaged in payroll, accounting, and other related departments. His finance background, on the other hand, helps him consider more seriously the matter of costs versus savings. Cost justification has to be sold to management before a new installation can be approved. A firm's vice-president in charge of finance may become the project director, and he is assumed to be objective in his special assignment, since his work and position are independent of any department or division of the organization. His function is simply to implement the goals of the study and find out how best to introduce an electronic data-processing system that will achieve these goals.

SENIOR MANAGEMENT COMMITTEE. In larger organizations, personnel selection for the study is usually headed by a *senior management committee* whose job is also to disseminate information and maintain communications among the various executives about the findings of the project team. The committee is also used in leveling off any misunderstanding about the prospective system and promoting enthusiasm and interest in future use of the computer by the departments. Without that effort and the cooperation of all departments, the project may collapse. The committee relays any information it receives (feedback) to the project team and keeps it informed about other matters of concern.

PERSONAL QUALIFICATIONS OF TEAM MEMBERS. A team member is expected to be knowledgeable in and guided by the concepts and policies that management uses in operating the company. He should seek whatever information is necessary to understand how these policies and concepts are worked out. Knowledge of company procedures provides the basis for analysis and evaluation of the flow and transformation of data through the organization by the existing system. Without this knowledge, it would be impossible to wisely select a computer tailored to solve the company's specific problems.

Above all, a project team member must be experienced in human relations, because he will be dealing with people at all times. His experience must guide him in communicating effectively to gain their cooperation and help in matters related to the study. Furthermore, he must be creative, because the flexibility of data-processing systems demands unique ways of doing things. Imagination, hard work, and patience are needed to make detailed charts and construct useful programs.

Part of the work of the project team involves the collection of cost figures on the present system. A team member should be unbiased, able to evaluate clerical and other related costs, and ready to utilize any other information that might help him arrive at a true and clear survey and evaluation report.

The attitude and interest of the team members are very important. When asked to serve on the team, some men may be reluctant to accept, for some of the following reasons:

1. They might be reluctant to learn a new and different field.
2. Some personnel fear that, once a computer system is installed, it

may fail to render the desired results they now get under the present system. They feel personally responsible for the substantial investment made in their department.

3. Some qualified officers might be reaching retirement or anticipating transfer to a better position within the company. For these reasons, the project team should probably consist of younger men who have been with the firm long enough to understand its functioning well and who have had experience in dealing with people effectively. There are, of course, exceptions to these generalities. In many cases, team members, regardless of age, have proved invaluable to the effective conduct of the study.

Once the team is formed, the project director, a leader with confidence and optimism, can alleviate further fears or reservations by first reducing as much as possible the amount of work team members have to do on their regular jobs. They would be in a better position if their regular duties were temporarily assigned to someone else, allowing them to concentrate freely on the project. Second, the pressure of a deadline can be eased; the director can emphasize a deadline for presenting findings to management only *after* the team has had a chance to become familiar with the total situation.

TECHNICAL QUALIFICATIONS OF TEAM MEMBERS. In addition to the personal qualifications described, project team members should possess adequate knowledge in data processing and a background in accounting and related fields. When a team includes members with specialized knowledge in one area only, problems are bound to occur. For example, members with competence in programming tend to overemphasize the technical aspects of a computer, such as speed and access time, overlooking the computer's wide applicability to the projects or the procedures used by the firm. On the other hand, members with an accounting background tend to stress the procedures but deemphasize the technical aspects of the computer. Either extreme can lead to confusion or to compromising the proper selection of a computer system. Hence, the need for balance in the team's makeup between these two types of "experts" is obvious.

A basic background in data processing is often inadequate for large-scale feasibility studies. Project team members are asked to take advanced EDP courses and gain first-hand experience by programming various applications. This education is available either in academic institutions or in the educaton centers of computer manufacturers. Many academic institutions of higher learning have a variety of courses at the undergraduate and graduate levels in computer data processing. Most curricula now include courses in data processing, programming, and data-processing management.

The other alternative for team members is to attend a computer manufacturer's educational school. Most manufacturers, of necessity, believe in the "sale-through-education" approach. Courses ranging from the basics of keypunching to advanced programming techniques for large-scale computers are available. The project team should utilize this opportunity by taking a series of courses suitable for its needs. One popular series progresses from the history of data processing through machine functions, flowcharting and block diagramming, programming basics and techniques, and coding, to the role of management in the field of EDP.

Role of the Consultant

Most firms find it necessary to seek the professional advice of a management or EDP consultant to guide the team on specialized matters. A presumably unbiased specialist, the consultant has experience that is valuable in providing a sound basis for the eventual selection of the new system. Despite his high fee ($250 to $400 per day), he is sought after for several reasons:

1. The project team is not skilled enough to do the survey well.
2. The consultant's leadership and experience in analyzing and solving problems can be invaluable during the critical phases of the study.
3. As an outsider, a consultant often settles technical arguments between members of the team and allows the study to continue with little interruption.
4. The idea of presenting a new system, verified and supported by a consultant, especially an EDP consultant, carries with it a psychological feeling of completeness and perfection.
5. An EDP consultant can be used after the study is completed to direct the training of programmers and to educate various levels of management on the overall features of the new system. He can also provide programmers and other technical help to operate the new installation until the company's own personnel are ready to take over.

Unfortunately, there are not many unbiased consultants or those with no outside interest in the outcome of the study. For these reasons, it is very important to be selective in deciding on the consultant or consulting firm to contact. Probably the best course is to hire a consultant for those phases of the study in which he can be neutral.

Other than EDP consultants, two sources of technical consultants can be considered: computer manufacturers' representatives and CPA (certified public accountant) firms. A manufacturer's representative brings with him a wealth of technical information on computer systems and their supportive hardware. He is well versed on the capabilities of each system, what it can do, and the applications it can handle. It should be noted, however, that heavy reliance on his judgment or recommendations poses the danger that, being sales-oriented, he might hurriedly recommend a system which might not be in accord with the specific needs of the organization. Reputable computer companies provide an adequate support staff, including systems analysts, to further analyze the problem and contribute to the selection of a sound, effective system.

Many CPA firms, especially the larger ones, have been specializing in business data processing. Their combined experience in accounting and EDP systems can prove invaluable to the functioning of the project team, especially in computer cost analysis. If the organization conducting the feasibility study is already a client of the CPA firm, its EDP specialist could very well be the consultant to hire. Smaller firms should also seek competent consulting help if the local CPA is ill-equipped to provide such service.

PROCEDURAL STEPS OF A FULL-SCALE FEASIBILITY STUDY

Management's decision to authorize a full-scale feasibility study indicates an interest in acquiring a computer installation, pending the recommendations of the study team. The team is expected to have in-depth information on how each potential EDP application is presently performed. The members gather all the relevant details on each available file and on the inflow and outflow of information affecting it. They inquire about the application's complexity, the number of times it is performed, the number of employees in charge of its operation, and the percentage of time it consumes. Based on these details, a proposed system can be drafted, followed by cost and hardware considerations and a final summary of findings to be considered by management.

Feasibility studies differ in the way they are conducted, depending on the size and scope of the study, the size of the firm, and so on. However, most studies follow an overall pattern that includes these key steps:

1. Preparation of a study plan.
2. Analysis of the present system.
3. Design of a proposed system.
4. New hardware and cost determination.
5. Evaluation of study findings.
6. Preparation of final recommendations to management.

Preparation of a Study Plan

Once management has authorized the establishment of a feasibility study and the formation of a project team to do the job, the next step is the preparation of a study plan that clearly points out the objectives of the study and the amount of time and funds allotted to it. A study plan provides direction and controls the moves made by the members of the team. It suggests that they carry out their survey and present final recommendations within a time constraint, which ranges from 2 weeks to several months, depending on the complexity of the study and the degree of familiarity the team has with the present applications. All activities must also be accomplished within a budget, with some flexibility for unexpected expenses or for additional research.

Analysis of the Present System

The next step in the feasibility study is analysis of the present system through interviews, data collection, and complete and accurate documentation of the data gathered. Documentation of current procedures involves careful study of the way these procedures are handled. The analysis includes the following:

1. A description of the documentation format.
2. The size of the file, and the frequency, source, and destination of the transactions making up the file.
3. The meaning of each transaction item and the amount of information it contains.
4. A description of the type and volume of all incoming and outgoing file data.
5. The number of employees involved and the amount of time they devote to each function.

The foregoing documented details, along with all other information gathered, are recorded for analysis in several ways. Among these are organization charts; layout and logic charts; charts depicting form distribution, equipment utilization, and work-load distribution; personnel statistics; and volume frequency tables. The ultimate contribution of these charts and tables is a complete description of the present system and how it relates to the company's activities, with emphasis on its cost of operation. Some authors call this phase *input–output analysis.*

In analyzing the present system, the team should be gearing its study around either a *special-purpose* or a *general-purpose* computer, whichever more nearly fits its particular needs. Briefly, a special-purpose computer is less flexible for running different applications than a general-purpose computer. When ordering a special-purpose computer, the firm placing the order bears the total cost of the design, which makes it quite expensive. Considering the higher cost, the team should be able to justify in detail the need for its use. A general-purpose computer, on the other hand, is more widely advertised and used, and much more flexible than a special-purpose computer. It can be used for different kinds of applications and is less costly, since it is a standard item with design cost spread among the thousands of units sold.

When considering size, the team should think in terms of present and future applications to be processed. In other words, the computer system under consideration should be capable of handling the present problems of the firm as well as those resulting from future growth.

The price paid for a computer is based on its size and the number of auxiliary components that are required. In purchasing an automobile, for example, a low-priced, fully equipped automobile can be as costly as a high-priced, luxury, stripped model. In ordering a computer, the project team should determine whether a small-sized computer with additional auxiliary components is more suitable than a basic medium-sized or large-scale installation. Size has a bearing on cost. The larger the computer, the more primary-storage capacity it has and the greater is its processing speed. Speed and the amount of storage space are the two chief factors that determine the cost of the basic computer. Also, input and output equipment and the speed with which they operate are used in determining the total cost of the system.

Another important consideration is *compatibility,* which means that a system's components operate in harmony and efficiently with one another. For instance, if the central processing unit has access time measured in microseconds, the use of punched paper tape for input would be incompatible, because the speed with which data are read from punched paper tape is not great enough to use the central processing unit to its best capacity. Some companies emphasize speed and accuracy, sacrificing economy. Others stress accuracy and economy in processing data, speed being a minor point. Still other firms stress accuracy only, with little consideration for speed or economy. A project team must weigh these factors in the light of what its firm needs and can afford.

Design of a Proposed System

This design phase is often carried out while documentation and various accompanying charts are being developed. The purpose of this step is to improve upon the present system and to set up the data requirements for selecting and determining the cost of the necessary hardware. The overall activities involved in designing a proposed system are

1. Listing and explaining the required files for the proposed system.
2. Laying out the volume of inputs and outputs of the proposed system.
3. Developing a flowchart of the entire system.
4. Indicating in some detail the number and frequency of required processing runs to be incorporated into the proposed system, with time estimates of each run.

With the foregoing information, the project team should now be in a position to determine the specifications and capabilities of the computer system that will process the company's operations. The system is organized around the *processor* and the *input–output storage devices.* The processor relates to the central processing sector where primary storage and calculations take place. Input–output storage devices cover peripheral devices (e.g., card readers and printers) and storage devices such as disk and magnetic-tape devices. The capacity and technical requirements for all the devices to be included in the proposed system should be clearly defined; questions such as the following must be answered:

How fast must the processor function?
What is its reserve capacity?
How easy is it to expand processor capacity?
What size core memory is needed?
How many sequential-access files are needed and how fast do they perform?
What type of input devices must be ordered?
What is the number and capacity of the input devices required?
What type of printer would be compatible with the processor and input devices?
How well does the proposed system accept remote-inquiry devices?
What type of remote-inquiry devices operate best with it?
What is the monthly cost of operating these devices?

At this phase the project team begins contacting various computer manufacturers to acquire data about specific systems. A round of meetings takes place, and often the representative of a particular computer manufacturer arranges for a live demonstration of selected systems to give a general view of their overall capabilities.

Like Ralph, who contacted several automobile dealers, project team members are interested in exploring available systems with no particular bias to any computer manufacturer or design. It has been contended that in concentrating on one particular set of equipment by a given manufacturer the team would be less confused, would gain access to testing various applications of its own, and might find it easier to finalize its decision than when viewing too many systems of essentially the same configuraton. Although this approach provides some benefits and saves time, the team can be "high-pressured" into adoption of the system, as is true in purchasing other items. The team therefore should consider each compatible system before deciding on one.

After meeting with manufacturers' representatives, the project team should receive a definite proposal consisting of the model numbers and detailed costs. Costs are quoted on a monthly rental basis or for direct purchase. Some proposals also include a maintenance contract for the system. Manuals of various components of the systems can be made available for the team's further study.

Purchase Versus Lease. After the project team has decided on the type and size of computer needed, it should determine whether to purchase or lease the system. Many firms lease a computer chiefly because of the technological obsolescence factor. New computers are put on the market every year. Manufacturers improve and modify their equipment constantly, and periodically they offer a new and improved generation of systems. Leasing also permits flexibility in adapting a new system to the firm's particular problems, whereas outright purchase may mean future system modifications updating to respond to the company's changing needs.

Maintenance and repair costs are additional considerations. Leasing usually includes maintenance and repair. The computer manufacturer generally provides his own personnel to service the equipment and to make sure it remains in good operating condition, relieving the user of any responsibility. If the system is purchased, however, the firm may need to contract with maintenance personnel to service the system. The manufacturer also can be called upon to do this for a charge. In any event, maintenance can be expensive to a firm that is responsible for servicing its own system.

The decision to lease a computer is often easier to make, because the project team would not be committing the company to a substantial investment with a lease, as it does with a purchase contract. If a computer is leased and later proves unsatisfactory, it can be returned to the manufacturer at little cost. However, this depends largely upon the terms of the lease agreement. Lease terms run between 12 and 48 months; the larger the system, the longer the contract period. A company bound by a 4-year lease policy, for example, may not find it as convenient to return a computer as would be the case with a 2-year lease contract.

Not only the terms of the lease, but also the cost of the leased system, should be considered. A company with a good cash position, expecting to use a particular computer for a long time, might find purchasing more profitable than renting. Purchasing gives the company the advantage of depreciating the cost as an asset—a tax advantage. The project team should consider this problem from the standpoint of the initial cost of acquisition as well as from that of operation. The rent is a fixed cost that will have to be paid whether or not the system is used at capacity. Rental charges plus daily operating costs constitute the total processing cost.

Some types of computer systems are available from large leasing companies. These companies operate independently and generally charge lower rates than the computer manufacturers. The system they lease depreciates over a longer period of time, goes through many hands, and therefore rents for less. One disadvantage of this type of leasing is that the kind of advice and assistance usually available with a manufacturer-leased system is not available from a leasing company. A company considering a lease plan should explore the extent of assistance offered prior to signing a contract.

COST ANALYSIS. After proposals and cost figures have been submitted by the manufacturers and acted upon by the project team, the project director should see that a cost estimate of the proposed computer system is made. The estimate should be compared with the present system to find out if any savings can be realized. Using an arbitrary 6-year projection, estimated savings are presented in Fig. 21-1.

On line 1, it is expected that the amount expended on the present system will decrease as the proposed system begins to handle more converted operations. On line 2, the amount expended in operating the proposed system will increase the more converted activities it handles. Line 3 shows conversion costs for each year. Total costs are shown on line 4. Net savings from the proposed system are computed by subtracting the projected recurring cost of the present system (line 5) from total costs. The breakeven point is some time during the third year of operation.

A company considering the adoption of a new computer system faces a number of costs associated with installation. Among others are

1. Site preparation.
2. Personnel training.
3. Systems design.
4. File conversion.
5. Program testing.
6. Miscellaneous costs.

FIGURE 21-1. *Evaluation of proposed system savings*

Item	*'74*	*'75*	*Annual Figures ($1000's)* *'76*	*'77*	*'78*	*'79*	*6-yr. Total ($100's)*
1. Estimated cost of operating *present* system	175	85	49	10	2	0	$321
2. Estimated cost of operating *proposed* system	10	50	75	85	100	113	433
3. Actual conversion costs	75	50	18	5	2	0	150
4. Total costs	260	185	142	100	104	113	904
5. *Present* system recurring costs	150	155	160	165	172	185	987
6. Net annual savings	(110)	(30)	18	65	68	72	$ 83

Site-preparation costs cover such factors as room design, extension of utility lines to areas where components will be located, installation of acoustical and other material to secure a quiet atmosphere, and provision of reserve space for possible addition to the system at a future date. Manuals and other site-preparation aids are usually provided by the manufacturer to help the prospective user prepare the site for the new system. The project team can obtain rough estimates from a local contractor experienced in this work.

Personnel training is the responsibility of the user. This involves training qualified personnel for systems design, programming, supervision, flowcharting and coding, assembly, and conversion techniques. These all require time, the amount depending on the complexity and flexibility of the system and the technical background of the present staff. The computer manufacturer usually undertakes the task of training the staff in machine operation, programming, and other related areas. Training-cost estimates are difficult to make, since they are mostly based on the complexity of the system and the ability of the staff to absorb the details of the training program.

Likewise, *systems design* costs cannot be precisely measured, since they also depend largely on the experience of the analyst and the requirements of the proposed system. However, *file conversion, program testing,* and *miscellaneous costs,* such as paper tape and punched cards, are relatively easy to compute, provided that some planning has been made as to the exact nature and extent of the work and materials involved.

One additional step the project team can take at this time is to program a typical application of the firm. After the program has been written, it should be tested to judge whether the specific computer produces the desired results. This brings up the question: What application should be selected? Should it be a brief, basic application where the results can be used as a speedy way of selecting a given computer or should it be the one application that must be processed regardless of the computer used? The latter alternative is preferred in most cases, provided that the steps in the application are organized and well presented. Such preparation makes the job of programming and testing the application as a whole less difficult.

Others argue that the application to be selected should involve the development of data that cannot be processed by the presently used system. In one respect, this would test the capability of a computer to produce results important to management for making better decisions. However, most of those experienced in feasibility studies concur that an application from the "brute-force area," where a large number of personnel and much clerical work are involved, would be the best to test. Economy and cost reduction are factors that induce many firms to convert to an EDP system. In manufacturing, such "bread-and-butter" applications include inventory control, product control, and factory scheduling. In banks, consumer credit loans and loan accounting are popular examples.

As indicated in Fig. 21-1, the project team can now evaluate the economic value of the proposed system by relating its total operating, installation, and preparatory costs to the operating costs of the present system. Assuming that net savings from the proposed system are significant enough to recommend its adoption, the next question is: Should the company purchase or lease the system?

To answer this question, the project team should develop a comparative cost table showing which alternative would be more economical. To illustrate, suppose that the decision has been made to order a computer system consisting of a processor, a card reader–punch, a line printer, three magnetic tape drives, and one magnetic disk unit. Assume also that the system has a salvage value of 10 percent of the purchase price at the end of a 6-year period. A hypothetical example of a comparative purchase–lease cost report is shown in Fig. 21-2.

Details related to the key terms in Fig. 21-2 are as follows:

1. **Lease:** Most leased systems carry a 2- to 4-year contract. The system can be used beyond an 8-hour shift without additional charges. Payments are made on a monthly basis or by whatever special arrangements the company makes with the leasing firm.
2. **Gross purchase price:** The amount paid for the hardware, taxes, insurance, delivery, and so forth.
3. **Salvage value:** The approximate value of the component or system over its life span (illustrated in Fig. 21-2 as 4 or 6 years).
4. **Net purchase cost:** The net amount that can be depreciated over the life of the system.
5. **Net cost:** The net purchase cost on an annual basis. The top figure of each component is the net purchase cost on a 4-year basis. The figure between parentheses is the net purchase cost on a 6-year basis.

FIGURE 21-2. Comparative purchase-lease report

System Components Quantity	Item	Lease Monthly	Lease Annually	Purchase: Gross purchase price	Salvage value 10%	Net purchase cost	Net cost[1] per year 4 yr. basis	Maintenance expense per yr.	Total purchase cost per year	Amount of savings favoring purchase[2]
1	processor	4,900	58,800	240,000	24,000	216,000	54,000 (36,000)	2,000	56,000 (38,000)	2,800 (20,800)
1	card R/P	800	9,600	40,000	4,000	36,000	9,000 (6,000)	800	9,800 (6,800)	200* (2,800)
1	printer	1,000	12,000	50,000	5,000	45,000	11,250 (7,500)	2,050	13,300 (9,550)	1,300* (2,450)
3	tapes	2,700	32,400	130,000	13,000	117,000	29,250 (19,500)	4,000	33,250 (23,500)	850* (8,900)
1	disk	500	6,000	25,000	2,500	22,500	5,625 (3,750)	1,050	6,675 (4,800)	675 (1,200)
	Totals	9,900	118,800	485,000	48,500	436,500	109,125 (72,750)	9,900	119,025 (82,650)	2,825 (36,150)

1 All figures between parentheses relate to data based on 6-year lease.
2 Asterisks denote savings in favor of lease.

6. **Maintenance expense:** This expense varies with each component, depending on its complexity and the frequency of repairs. The figures shown are averages.
7. **Total purchase cost:** The net purchase cost plus maintenance.
8. **Amount of savings favoring purchase:** This value is determined by subtracting the total purchase cost per year from the annual lease cost for that component.

In deciding whether to purchase or lease the $485,000 system presented in Fig. 21-2, it would hardly seem worthwhile to purchase the system with only $2,825 savings. The interest rate on borrowed funds and other indirect expenses would obviously make the lease plan more attractive. However, if the company believes that the system will probably be used for 6 or more years, then perhaps the purchase plan would be more profitable. On a 6-year basis, this would show a $36,150 savings over the lease plan.

Again, before a final decision is made to purchase the system, consideration of factors such as physical and technological obsolescence must be looked into.

Obsolescence can be costly and is inherent in the computer field. Computer design, speed, capacity, and so forth, change constantly. A computer that appeared to be ideal 2 years ago, for example, may not be as efficient today. So, the firm needs to take a close look at its procedures, its short- and long-range objectives, and its needs and systems requirements with regard to the data files and the way they must be processed. If the proposed system still meets all these conditions and saves enough money to justify the commitment, the company should proceed with an outright purchase.

Preparation of Final Recommendations to Management

Now that technical and purchase–lease figures have been gathered and evaluated, the project team's first step is to prepare a report to management recommending the purchase or lease of a particular computer system and accompanied by all pertinent details. The report, in essence, tells management what the team considers as the "best buy" and the one that will do the best job.

ELECTRONIC DATA PROCESSING VERSUS EMPLOYEES OF THE FIRM

During the analysis stage, employees should be informed of work being done on introducing a computer installation into the organization. Although they do not share in the selection process, the project team should investigate its effect upon them. Because the employees lack knowledge about computer technology, they may worry about their job security and could develop an "inferiority complex," believing that the computer will "tell them what to do." If this reaction is left unchecked, the net effect could be the employees' refusal to cooperate. They may begin to withhold information deliberately, contributing to the collapse of the entire system.

For these reasons, management cannot afford to ignore the feelings and attitudes of its employees. The matter becomes worse in a unionized firm when union officials enter the picture to protect the security of their members. To quiet replacement fears, management should publicize, educate, and distribute materials on the proposed system well in advance of the installation. The suggestion box is a useful safety valve that employees should be encouraged to use to air their grievances and to offer suggestions related to the installation. The grapevine is also an effective, though unofficial, line of communication. Since no executive can stop its use, it should be implemented to the best advantage of the firm by feeding needed information to lower-level employees, especially those whose jobs may be in question.

By presenting a proper profile of the uses and capabilities of a prospective computer system, employees can be sold on the following: (1) the use of a computer means relieving much physical as well as mental effort; (2) it is a tool to aid them in doing their jobs with greater efficiency, not to replace them; and (3) more and better opportunities are bound to arise of which they can take advantage. This includes opening a second, and possibly a third, shift, which will generate a new set of jobs for women, especially for housewives who find it difficult holding a job during the day.

CONVERSION PHASE

When top management approves the acquisition of the recommended computer system, some time will elapse before the system is installed—between 1 month and 2 years, depending on the complexity of the system and the availability of the components for delivery. Once the choice has been made, an order is placed with the computer manufacturer. The order lists the primary system configuration and other supportive hardware needed by the firm. When received, the manufacturer gives the firm a tentative delivery date to be confirmed at a later date. Meanwhile, the company can take several preparatory preinstallation steps. As outlined in Fig. 21-3, the primary steps are as follows:

1. **Planning the EDP department.** A management committee begins the task of appropriating funds and laying out the makeup of the new data-processing department, including the hiring of a manager and qualified staff.
2. **Hiring a data-processing manager.** A manager is hired to coordinate the procedural plans for the department with the committee.

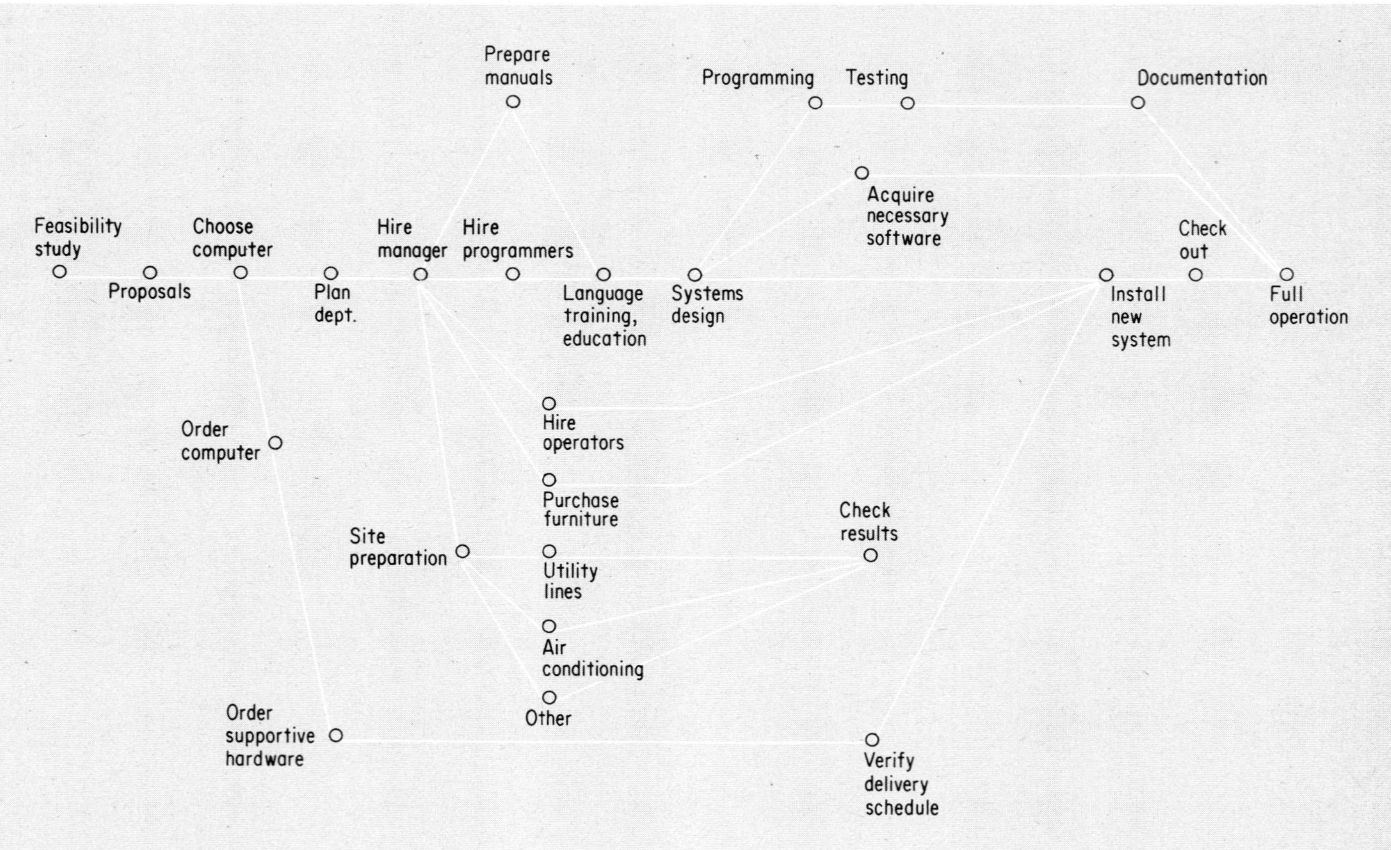

FIGURE 21-3. *Critical path schematic of installation of a computer system*

Depending on his experience and the extent of his authority, he begins to recruit new talent or implement the training of qualified members of the organization for console operation, programming, and other required tasks. Meanwhile, he supervises the preparation of the new quarters for the installation. This involves extending utility lines, installing air-conditioning units, and purchasing furniture and other necessary items.

3. **System design.** This phase can be quite critical. System analysts and other specialists lay out the system's requirements, implement the preparation of software, and write, test, and document the necessary programs. The manufacturer usually arranges for the company's programmers to have access to a compatible system for test runs.

Execution of the foregoing steps requires careful planning and timing. This is where an outside consultant can be extremely helpful. Not only can he implement the conversion process but he also provides temporary help in programming, systems design, and file conversion. Often, these short-term employees later become a part of the permanent staff. Some aspects of conversion that must be considered are:

1. **Standards.** This relates to developing a scale by which the performance of the new system can be evaluated for efficiency and economical operation.
2. **Systems analysis and design.** One of the more complex aspects of conversion is systems analysis. It involves gathering and recording data related to required reports, present procedures, and the like, for design of the new system. Once completed, the design phase establishes input–output and general operating routines for each department that may be using the new installation.
3. **Programming.** Programming follows systems design. It converts systems design into machine-readable instructions for computer processing.
4. **Testing.** Testing of the system's components and the written program is involved in this phase. The components are checked before they are integrated into the system as an entity. Likewise, programs are checked out for errors before they are released for future processing.
5. **Documentation.** Documentation relates to a detailed description of each program so that other program or systems analysts can alter or modify it in the future, if necessary. The detailed description of each program is documented in a special manual, which also includes copies of flowcharts and other pertinent information. Examples of manuals are *operators' manuals,* which explain the operation of the computer system, and *systems manuals,* which lay out the functions, procedures, and input–output details of the system.
6. **Training of operators.** Operators are trained in the procedures and knowledge required for proper handling of various components

of the system, including handling input data, loading the program, and setting up and controlling the system in general.

Once the new system is installed, it should be ready for full operation. Now that the company has a powerful tool for processing various types of applications, management should encourage the departments to find new applications and better ways of processing existing files. How well the system performs in the future depends, to a large extent, on how well company officials support and use the facility.

DURATION OF A FEASIBILITY STUDY

One question often asked is: "How long does it normally take to conduct a feasibility study?" The answer differs with the firm. Some of the factors that have a bearing on the time limit are:

1. **The competence of project team members and the extent of their knowledge about the problems and policies of their firm, as well as their general understanding of the computers available on the market.**
2. **The speed with which the team collects cost and other needed data for preparing its final report and forming an opinion as to whether a computer system should be installed.** If cost data, for example, are not available because of present inefficient methods, or because of a deliberate attempt on the part of employees to withhold such vital information, a great deal more time will be needed for the project team to form an opinion than would be the case if these conditions did not exist.
3. **The size of the firm doing the study.** The larger the firm, the more complex its operations are likely to be. These operations include systems, procedures, and people. For a project team to understand the systems and procedures that will be affected by a computer installation, detailed studies have to be made, which will be very time-consuming. The people consulted during the procedure can reduce this time by cooperating in making available the data sought by the team.
4. **The size of the computer installation under study.** Regardless of the size of a given computer, a firm needs time to get acquainted with its operation and requirements. However, smaller-sized computers, especially minicomputers, require less time for final decision than larger systems. Determining the need for a large system would involve lengthy surveys and substantial time to evaluate its usefulness in the many processing applications for which it is being considered.

In conclusion, a large firm needing a large-scale computer would generally require more time than a small firm needing a smaller-sized computer. This generality is not meant to imply that any connection necessarily exists between the size of the firm and the size of the computer needed. Computer size depends solely on processing needs rather than on firm size.

SUMMARY

Deciding on a computer installation is not an easy task. A traditional approach is for a company to form a team to review and evaluate the company's clerical and management information routines, the operations that can be converted to computer processing, the areas that can benefit most from a computer system, and the total expected costs of the proposed installation.

A feasibility study is initiated either by top management or by lower-level management, based on felt need for a more automated processing system. In either case, top management's approval and support is necessary. The project team is made up of key personnel representing various departments. The team determines the company's data-processing requirements and specifies the data-processing facility needed to fulfill these requirements. The procedure in a full-scale feasibility study involves preparation of a study plan, analysis of the present system, design of the proposed system, determination of new hardware and costs evaluation of findings, and preparation of a recommendation to management.

Considering the serious and technical nature of the project, it is expected that each team member be acquainted with company policies and procedures and have adequate background in data-processing fundamentals. Deficiencies in the latter area can be made up through formal courses offered by local educational institutions or through sessions with computer manufacturers' representatives. In the final analysis, professional competence is expected before the team can be in a position to justify a computer system useful to the organization.

QUESTIONS

1. What alternatives are available to a firm confronted with the installation of data-processing equipment? Explain.
2. What problems must top management decide on before data processing is introduced?
3. What factors characterize the firm that is likely to purchase a computer? Explain.
4. What major objectives can be realized from an EDP installation?

5. What factors determine the success of a feasibility study? Explain.
6. Who stimulates interest in a feasibility study? Why?
7. Who is usually appointed as a project team member? What is the project team's main function? Explain.
8. What qualifications (personal and technical) should a project director have? Explain.
9. Why are some team members reluctant to be on the team or unlikely to do a satisfactory job?
10. What are the desired qualifications of each of the project team members? Explain in detail.
11. What is your opinion with respect to companies pirating computer personnel from other firms?

SUGGESTED READING

Buckle, D. G. R., et al. "Computers and the Small Firm: 2," *The Computer Journal,* Feb. 1969, pp. 10–14.

Groobey, J. A. "Maximizing Return on EDP Investments," *Data Management,* Sept. 1972, pp. 28–32.

Schroeder, W. J. "The Part-Time Computers," *Business Automation,* Jan. 1971, pp. 18–22.

managing the data-processing department

22

MAKEUP AND ORGANIZATION OF THE DATA-PROCESSING STAFF

Data-Processing Management

Systems Analysis and Design

Programming

Computer Operations

What Can Be Done About Displaced Employees?

ORGANIZATION STRUCTURE

Line Organization

Line and Staff Organization

Functional Organization

LOCATION OF THE DATA-PROCESSING DEPARTMENT

Centralized Location Under One User

Centralized Location Independent of All Users

Centralized Location Above User Level

Decentralized Location

CONTROLLING DATA-PROCESSING OPERATIONS

Accuracy Factor

Fraud Factor

Security Factor

RESPONSIBILITY OF THE DATA-PROCESSING DEPARTMENT

Correct Procedures

Authority To Request Data Processing

Standardized Procedures

Installing a computer is not a simple task. Extremely technical in nature, the task must be specified in detail. Management must define the system's requirements and investigate the degree of its effective and economic use in the organization. Thus, its acquisition is much more difficult and perhaps requires more serious investigation than any other acquired asset in the organization.

Systems investigation was discussed in the preceding chapter in terms of a feasibility study resulting in computer selection. This chapter discusses three areas of implementation: (1) the makeup and organization of the data-processing staff, (2) the form of organization of the data-processing department, and (3) the location of the data-processing department in the organization. Each area requires planning in every detail and, considering the substantial investment in hardware and program development, the various functions and services must be staffed with qualified and well-trained personnel.

MAKEUP AND ORGANIZATION OF THE DATA-PROCESSING STAFF

A computer installation cannot be considered operative until various required positions have been defined, qualified personnel are hired, and steps are taken with respect to employees displaced as a result of the new installation.

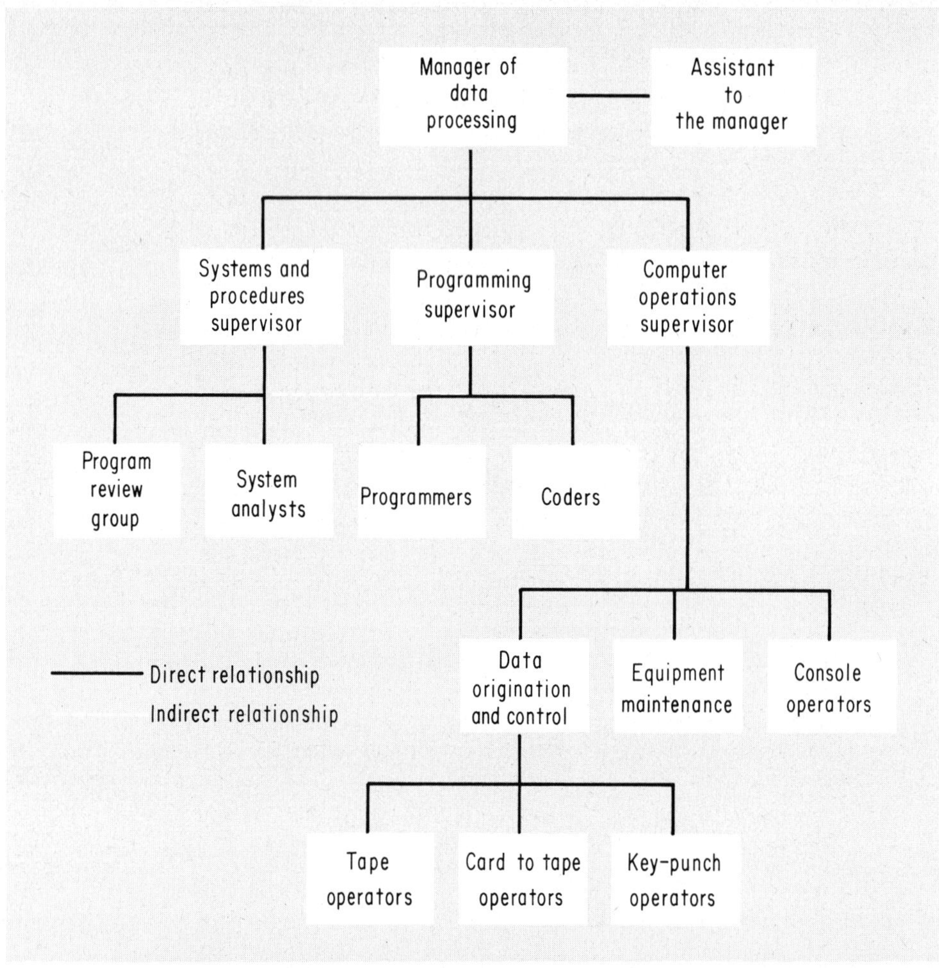

FIGURE 22-1. ***General organization structure of a data-processing center***

Data-processing positions are commonly divided as follows:

1. Management
2. Systems analysis and design
3. Programming
4. Operations

Each position entails certain prerequisites involving qualifications, training, and selection requirements. An overall organization chart is presented in Fig. 22-1.

Management is viewed as a social process. It is social because it deals with people. It is a process because it involves a specific way of doing things. The manager's role is dealing with people to achieve preplanned goals. He is directly responsible to the user for all work performed in his department. For him to function effectively and produce results on time, he should earn the respect of all concerned—the users as well as the data-processing staff. Broad knowledge of data processing and the ability to sell other department heads on the services of his department greatly enhance his visibility and strengthen his relations with them. In the final analysis, the manager needs to prove his worth by the actions he takes and the applications he implements. If the result of what he institutes is a sincere reflection on his ability to handle required tasks, management and his colleagues as well as his subordinates will accord him due respect.

In other words, a data-processing manager gains respect by the way he manages. Coping with people requires understanding and perception of their various needs, for needs are highly individualized and change constantly; what an employee needs today, he may not need tomorrow. Task-oriented needs can be satisfied by

1. Showing appreciation for honest effort.
2. Praising the employee for good work done.
3. Promoting an attitude of job security and opportunities for promotion and advancement.
4. Paying competitive wages and developing standards for regular salary increases.
5. Offering work that sustains interest and motivation.
6. Providing good working conditions.

If all these factors are earnestly considered, the dual goal of employee satisfaction and achievement of organizational goals will be accomplished.

The foregoing remarks suggest that a manager's real authority must be granted and recognized through his subordinates, since what they think of him as a leader is what makes him respected and effective. The authority he receives from his superior is not sufficient in and of itself, as his effectiveness comes from below upward, not from the top downward. When his employees report to work on time, are self-directed, self-motivated, and anxious to perform their job assignments, he is considered a good "boss," because people work *with* him rather than *for* him. If the opposite occurs, the result usually leads to confusion in the department, which certainly does not promote effective performance.

Types of Leadership. This discussion leads to the type of leadership that a data-processing manager should possess. There are three main types of leaders: the democratic, authoritarian, and free-rein types.

Democratic leadership emphasizes informal group participation and the desire to satisfy its members. A data-processing manager can expect to accomplish a great deal if he allows his subordinate supervisors, and, indirectly, his systems analysts and programmers, to participate in evaluating given projects and suggesting solutions. Naturally, the final decision rests with the manager. It is assumed that for a democratic-type leadership to succeed the employees must be competent, and that they have been briefed on the details of the project under discussion.

Authoritarian leadership states that leadership is a right given and approved from above and that this right should be exercised. In this approach, the manager assigns jobs to his subordinates, and only one-way communication takes place with regard to commands and the delegation of work assignments. This type of leadership can accomplish quick results, since it does not allow undue delays for consultations or group participation. On the other hand, if this approach causes individual employees to feel as though they are not a part of the group, they can make the manager's job unpleasant.

The free-rein approach regards the employees as competent, well-qualified members of the department who are able to function on their own. They are asked to make independent decisions on problems that affect their work and, as long as they accomplish results in a satisfactory manner, they are left largely unsupervised. This is advantageous in that it gives each employee a chance to think and to help arrive at decisions and solve problems. However, lack of supervision may cause unnecessary confusion in the department if the employees involved abuse their freedom. In this approach, the manager must be willing to take the final responsibility for the actions of his subordinates.

In summary, an ideal manager is a person who has knowledge of and understands his employees' various needs, who allows his subordinates to participate in discussing and evaluating a given project, but who reserves to himself final authority in the matter, and *earns* rather than *demands* support and respect.

TECHNICAL BACKGROUND. In addition to the key managerial and human-relations skills, a basic but significant qualification of a data-processing manager is a broad knowledge of data processing in general and an in-depth acquaintance with the particular installation. This combined background is required if he is to coordinate and implement the applications requested by the user.

A manager's technical knowledge is useful in two ways. First, by keeping abreast of current developments in the field he makes sure that the computer system is modified or periodically updated so that it does not suffer from technological obsolescence. Second, technical knowledge, especially in the area of programming and systems analysis, is desirable for handling staff problems. For instance, programmers or systems analysts often find it necessary to share a particular problem with their manager. If the manager shows poor judgment or makes limited contributions, he may soon find out that those subordinates will bypass him and seek consultation elsewhere.

TRAINING. A person with the foregoing qualifications is not easy to find. Many installations settle for less, and consequently compromise the overall effectiveness of the data-processing department. Others plan in advance by (1) selecting a man with imagination, organizational ability, tact, direct experience in supervision, and preferably a college degree, and (2) putting him through a management training program where he can acquire communications and human-relations skills and develop leadership ability to handle a group as specialized as the data-processing staff. In addition to the formal training program (usually conducted on the premises in large organizations or at a local university), the manager goes through on-the-job training under direct guidance of a senior member of management. How practical all this training is depends on the size of the data-processing department, the caliber of the staff, and the requirements set by management for the data-processing-manager's post.

OTHER MANAGERIAL POSITIONS. The size of the computer facility in large organizations often makes it necessary for the data-processing manager to have assistants, each holding a supervisory title. Among others are the following:

1. The **systems manager** directs the work done in systems analysis and design.
2. The **programming manager** is in charge of all phases of programming, testing, and maintenance.
3. The **operations manager** directs the activities and operation of the hardware, including auxiliary equipment. In a very large system, the operations manager often has a key-punch supervisor, as well as a scheduling supervisor who controls input–output activities and schedules source documents for processing.
4. The **education director** implements all activities with respect to training and educating new and current employees of the department. In some cases, he acts as a liaison in promoting EDP education.

SALARIES. Management salaries cover a wide range depending on (1) the type of organization (business, educational, etc.), (2) the size of the installation, (3) the size of the data-processing staff, (4) geographical location, (5) seniority, and (6) level of experience. Generally, experienced managers employed by industrial organizations having large installations and a sizable staff earn higher salaries than those who work in smaller installations. With the exception of a few large universities, educational institutions, on the average, pay their data-processing managers a relatively lower salary than either average-sized industrial firms or larger universities.

Compared to other managers in industry, however, data-processing managers generally receive higher salaries, because of the higher salary scale at the technical level. The pay may be as low as $11,500 in a small installation to a high of $50,000 in a super-sized installation.

Data-management talent is tapped either from without (through employment agencies, consultants, etc.) or from within the organization. A logical approach is continued upgrading of the overall salary structure, increasing with the steady demand for qualified data-processing managers. Of approximately 98,000 computer systems installed by the end of 1973, less than 62,000 were directed by full-time managers. With an expected accelerated increase in the number of installations in the coming years, an acute shortage of qualified managers will take place unless a large number of persons are trained in this area. Graduate schools of business and a few management associations have taken this shortage into consideration. It is conceivable that a new supply of management talent will soon be available to meet the current demand.

Systems Analysis and Design

Systems analysis is more complex than programming operations. A systems analyst must possess two key qualities: the ability to solve new problems and the ability to communicate effectively with the user. As a problem solver, he discovers what information must be provided to management and the ways in which it can be obtained. This involves frequent meetings with the user requesting the service, and without whose cooperation the problem cannot be adequately worked out. Thus, the systems analyst must have imagination and creativity for solving problems, and tact and negotiating ability for effectively communicating with the user.

In addition, an analyst is expected to have a college degree in one of the business areas—that is, production, finance, accounting, management, or marketing—as well as a basic background in mathematics and statistics. In installations where a systems analyst is expected to do some programming, experience in at least one language and in the functioning of a computer is also essential.

Larger data-processing departments often have a program review group consisting of systems analysts and selected senior programmers. The group evaluates and revises proposed data-processing procedures and, in smaller installations, may be required to develop mechanized procedures in addition to the regular assignments. The combined background of the group makes sure that all procedures and/or programs being evaluated are workable and efficient.

TRAINING. One major problem that business organizations face is the shortage of qualified systems analysts. With the exception of large organizations, business firms have failed to institute effective training programs for filling critical vacancies. In 1973, there were an estimated 130,000 qualified systems analysts for 200,000 openings. In order to satisfy a projected demand of 225,000 positions for the succeeding year, 95,000 more analysts must be trained. This high demand-supply ratio puts the qualified analyst in a favorable bargaining position and causes many firms to settle for less experienced applicants. Consulting firms, private business or technical schools, and universities have recently been active in offering formal systems analysis training programs, whose costs vary with the institution and the extent of course coverage. Among computer manufacturers, IBM is the only manufacturer offering users a 6-month systems training program, at a cost close to $6,000. Details regarding educational training and other prerequisites were covered in Chapter 14.

PROFESSIONAL ORIENTATION OF THE SYSTEMS ANALYST. Many organizations, including those offering full-fledged training programs, have been troubled by the high rate of turnover of their systems groups. This problem stems not only from the inadequate supply of systems analysts, but also from the professional orientation of this new breed of professionals.

A systems analyst enters the industrial organization with a professional self-image built by his achievement and not by any status bestowed upon him by the organization. He wants to grow, and because of his drive for continued professional growth, he tends to be less interested in becoming company-oriented. He often changes jobs at no significant increase in salary, seeking a new challenge.[1]

Although the demand for his unique services and talent offsets the traditional vulnerability of an employee doing a routine task as a salaried professional, the systems analyst's autonomy is threatened by the employing organization because it develops its own controls. He has supervisors, not colleagues. He has neither exclusive nor final responsibility for his task. His work can be expanded, tapered off, or terminated, and his salary is generally lower than the salary of the supervisor he serves.

Tension is caused by the conflict between the values and standards of the professional, project-oriented analyst, on the one hand, and the apparently divergent values of the organization on the other. The analyst seeks status through expertise, since he is oriented to look at his task as professional, and he is concerned with competent performance in a highly skilled area. Because of this orientation, he tends to work within the framework of his specialized field and proceeds systematically to solve

[1] The recession of the late 1960s was an exception in that most systems analysts felt the drop in the number of openings, forcing them to keep their jobs to weather the economic crisis.

various assigned problems. Management, on the other hand, operates within the framework of business and, of necessity, proceeds in a more opportunistic way to meet the challenging demands of the market upon the business. When that way does not fulfill the needs of the systems analyst, he becomes dissatisfied and may move. His view of his job as a temporary shelter and his willingness to go elsewhere in an attempt to grow professionally and seek new challenges indicate a lack of organizational loyalty and a low commitment to the employing organization's goals and needs.

Although it is unlikely to happen, systems analysts express a desire for increased autonomy, which would leave them free of direct administrative control. As professionals, they dislike being bothered by their supervisor and list, among others, the following needs as important: (1) independence on the job, (2) a fair and objective evaluation of work accomplished, (3) financial needs, (4) acknowledgment by the group supervisor of a job well done, and (5) professional guidance on the job, including advice on succession patterns in management.

Whether a company has a satisfactory relationship with the systems analyst depends on its point of view and philosophy. The analyst will have certain needs and motivations. How long he will stay on the payroll will depend on how well the company recognizes these needs, and how long it continues to provide appropriate challenges.

In acknowledging the high mobility rate and the demand for systems analysts, the organization should be expected to narrow whatever gap exists between its needs and expectations and those of the systems analyst. In doing so, organizations should see a leveling off of cultural conflict—that is, the conflict between the institutional subculture, which is built on loyalty to and belief in the organization, and the professional subculture of the systems analyst, which is geared to commitment to his profession.

Some of the steps that the data-processing manager can take to increase the loyalty of the systems analyst are

1. Promotions should be made from within, even though such attempts may stifle boldness and initiative. The social sentiments of the systems group can be encouraged to favor selection from within. Furthermore, selecting less qualified men and then training them as analysts is one way of minimizing the high cost of employee turnover. When highly trained analysts are hired from outside, they may feel unchallenged and leave once they have accomplished their work.
2. Salary schedules should be adjusted to be competitive with other organizations, with shorter intervals between raises and more frequent salary reviews.
3. The responsibility of the systems analyst needs to be commensurate with adequate authority. Implicit in delegating the analyst authority to attain a preplanned objective is that he assume re-

sponsibility for managing the details and achieving the results. If he is to feel a full sense of responsibility for the outcome, he needs to be delegated authority to take full charge of implementing the various aspects of his project. The problem here is that the analyst's authority ends with the completion of the project. His sense of responsibility will take longer to dissipate, making the relationship between the systems analyst and his line supervisor difficult throughout.

Programming

Generally, programming involves determining the type of output expected of the computer, flowcharting a set of instructions for the computer, coding the program, and debugging. In large organizations, programmers concentrate on the construction of flowcharts and tests, and on selecting the necessary utility routines for the system. The coder carries out the rest by converting the details of program logic into machine instructions to be used directly by the computer.

Programmers are often expected to code as well as flowchart and write the program. Coders do not have to know how to program in order to function as coders. In fact, their duties, in some cases, are performed by the use of devices that translate the program into machine-readable language.

Other types of programmers include maintenance and utility programmers. A *maintenance* programmer does some coding and some programming, but is not asked to handle totally new programs. A *utility* programmer's primary task is supplying programmers with any required special software subsystems. To do this task well, he is expected to be up-to-date on the company's data-processing and programming needs.

EDUCATION AND TRAINING. Business programmers are required to have at least a high school education and 1 or 2 years of college. A college degree is not as required of programmers as it is of systems analysts, except in such cases where the programmer also performs a systems analysis function. The single most important prerequisite of programmers is logical and writing abilities. Logical ability is needed for designing program logic in various forms; it can be measured by one of many tests offered by computer manufacturers and some private testing institutions. The Programming Aptitude Test (PAT) developed by IBM is available to users upon request.

Programmer training consists of formal and on-the-job training. Formal training lasts approximately 2 months and covers an introductory course in computer concepts, a symbolic language course and one advanced language course (COBOL, PL/1, etc.), including a series of problems and exercises. On-the-job training lasts as long as 1 year, depending on the aptitude of the programmer and the requirements of the employing organization. The programmer gains first-hand experience in logical analysis, coding, testing, and documentation techniques.

SALARIES. Compared to the systems analyst, the average business programmer commands a relatively low salary. Trainees start at around $6,900, usually with a substantial increase in salary upon completion of the training prescribed by the firm. Programmers who perform well and meet the standards of excellence could easily double their starting salary in 3 to 4 years. Typical salaries at that level range between $12,500 and $14,500 per year.

The demand for programming talent is almost as great as for systems analysts. In 1973, over 200,000 qualified programmers were available for a total market requirement of 225,000. With the increased availability of canned programs and advances in software and hardware, the need for additional programmers or for the "run-of-the-mill" programmer is questionable.

Computer Operations

Any duties involved in the preparation of data for input, in maintenance, and in the actual operation of the system are part of the computer-operations area. The bulk of the employees of the data-processing department are employed here. The group consists of *console operators, tape operators* (if any), *key-punch operators, job schedulers, control clerks,* and *facility librarians.* This is an area that requires close attention to details. The supervisor checks on the flow of data from the input stage to the processing stage to see that the data are completed satisfactorily. This will minimize any machine "downtime" or "idle time." The supervisor also makes sure that employees are cooperating with one another. For instance, in a card-oriented system, the console operator must rely on the key-punch operator for the initial punching of source data in cards before they can be processed on the computer. If any delay occurs, the console operator's job will also be delayed. Proper training for operative employees differs with the position. The key-punch operator normally is expected to have had some experience in the use of the key punch, either from a former employer, through courses taken in a private educational institution, or on the job. However, in the event that a firm is interested in retaining its own employees, they are sent to a manufacturer's training center, where they learn the concepts and operation of the key punch. When they return, an on-the-job training program supplements their formal training and gives them practice in operating the key punch.

Console operators follow the same procedure as key-punch operators except that more time is needed for a complete orientation in computer operation than in keypunching. A computer console consists of a number of buttons and switches that have to be manipulated and used in a given sequence if processing is to be done correctly. The depression of a button at the wrong time may prevent the loading of the program or the processing of input data. Manual dexterity and alertness on the job are required of a console operator. Alertness on the job means being able to detect and correct any machine malfunctioning and to handle emergencies during processing. A console operator should also have some programming background, so that he can correct minor errors on the spot. Some programmers begin as console operators and then gradually advance to the job of programmer.

The job of the employees who operate the equipment often becomes monotonous. Because employees usually produce less with increased monotony, it is desirable to rotate them on different jobs. For instance, in smaller installations the programmer can operate the console on one application and act as a coder on another application. A console operator with a programming background can develop a program on one application and code a program on another application. This will not only allow employees to gain broad experience, but will also act as a backup system in the event of illness, vacation, or the like. Employees can substitute for one another temporarily or as needed, giving flexibility to the operation of the data-processing department.

Keypunching also can become routine and boring, especially when a large volume of data is to be punched in the same location in thousands of cards. This monotony often results in a high labor turnover. The author had access to an installation that employed 11 key-punch operators. Within 1 year, only 2 of the original 11 operators were left. The other 9 were new and only partially experienced. Some of the reasons given by those leaving were (1) little incentive, (2) no challenge, (3) monotony and boredom on the job, (4) too much like a factory job, (5) no opportunity for advancement, (6) low pay and a heavy work load, (7) irregular and unsatisfactory raises, (8) limited social opportunity, and (9) little brainwork.

To avoid drudgery on the job, the supervisor should assign to key-punch operators duties that involve some decision making and a variety of tasks. For example, a key-punch operator could be asked to operate the sorter, load data or programs, operate the console, or to make suggestions as to better ways of designing a data card. Many key-punch operators have been found to be excellent in operating such machines. Management can be instrumental in reducing labor turnover by decreasing monotony, thus improving morale.

What Can Be Done About Displaced Employees?

Many firms feel pressured to retain employees whose jobs have been replaced by the new system, especially those who may be too old to learn but not ready to retire. Although their replacement would be appropriate in terms of maintaining an overall efficient system, there are social, human, and, in the case of unions, legal factors that often compromise rational judgment. Cognizant of these factors, many firms that choose to install a computer system conveniently neglect to take any action. In fact, the manager of the new data-processing department may choose the "lesser of two evils" by assigning trifling duties to "unfit" employees, thus retaining them on the company payroll. This move is sometimes taken to show the employee that the company is acting in good faith, although its real motive is to discourage him from remaining with the firm. The net effect is usually that the employee eventually finds his job so meaningless and himself so unwanted that he resigns and finds a more suitable position elsewhere, or he decides to stay on the job, a course which results in frustration for all concerned. If the former alternative is chosen, it happens to the company's relief. The latter alternative leaves much to be desired; both the company and the employee are unhappy about the status quo. The employee's morale suffers, as he continually anticipates the worst and hopes for the best. His presence in the department affects the morale of other employees as well.

Can a company realize significant savings in retaining employees who do not perform adequate service because of the new computer system? The answer depends on the circumstances leading to the decision to retain or displace them. Generally, the answer is "No." No company can or should retain employees who were formerly engaged in the operation of a replaced system and whose background offers little to the new system. Exceptions include the following:

1. **Those who are qualified and willing to be retrained for a new position.** For example, a typist whose job previously was typing statements can be retrained to operate a key-punch machine, filling a useful position at the data input phase. The employee's attitude and ability are very important. In one case, a 42-year-old production scheduling clerk was asked by his supervisor to improve his academic background by taking courses in mathematics at night school to prepare himself to program new applications. He refused on the basis that he could no longer compete with younger students because he had not been to school for a number of years. Mathematics was his weakest subject, and he felt that he could not possibly take the specific computer mathematics course recommended by the supervisor.
2. **Those who can be transferred to another department where, with a brief orientation, they can render useful service.** This is possible especially where the work of one department is similar to that of another department. In such a case, the possibility of employee transfer is worth investigating.

ORGANIZATION STRUCTURE

Given the availability of a qualified staff in the systems, programming, and operations areas, a formal set of relationships must exist for determining the pattern of communication among staff members and for clarifying who reports to whom and in what capacity. This set of relationships is typically depicted in the form of an organization chart based on (1) line, (2) line and staff, or (3) functional organization structures. Each form offers advantages and poses limitations. The data-processing department's structure is dependent in some respect on its location in the organization—that is, whether it is centralized, decentralized, or some combination of the two.

Line Organization

Most data-processing departments initially adopt a line form of structure in which systems, programming, and operations managers report directly to the data-processing manager. The second-line managers assume direct responsibility over the activities of the subordinates in their section. In smaller installations, other supervisors, such as key-punch, console, and programming supervisors, often report directly to the data-processing manager. Although this relatively broad span of management has the advantage of better control of the overall activities, it does prevent the manager from devoting a great deal of time to planning and/or discussing mutual problems with the user.

SPAN OF MANAGEMENT. There is a limit to the span of management or the number of subordinates a manager can effectively handle. In considering additions to the existing staff, a manager should keep in mind that adding one more subordinate to his staff will increase the total number of relationships by more than one. That is, when an additional employee is hired, he is hypothetically expected to establish *direct* relationship with his supervisor on task-oriented matters, *direct-group* relationships with the supervisor on matters involving the employee and the group he works with, and *cross* relationships in terms of interaction with his peers on task and other related matters. With this in mind, the total number of relationships resulting from one additional employee represents a significant addition to the manager's total responsibility. Thus, because of the specialized nature of the task performed in data processing, it is probably more practical to have a narrow span of management so that the manager has enough time to plan, organize, and control the overall activities of the department.

Line and Staff Organization

Data-processing managers whose departments have grown to the point where they can no longer effectively discharge their planning, organizing, and controlling functions find it necessary to add a number of staff assistants for handling such jobs as production scheduling, control of various projects, supervision of operating activities, training of EDP personnel, developing standards, and maintaining data files and software.

Compared to line personnel, staff personnel operate in an advisory capacity and report directly to the data-processing manager. Addition of the staff function allows the manager more time to work on user projects and to maintain the necessary relations with upper management. This form of structure is operational in large EDP departments.

Functional Organization

Line managers often encounter difficulty maintaining smooth relations with the EDP staff members. The traditional conflict that goes on between line and staff makes it difficult to accomplish certain goals as planned. Many organizations eventually decide to establish an organization structure built around the key functions of the department concerned. Thus, in the data-processing department, the structure would be organized around (1) the development function, which covers systems and programming activities; (2) operating functions, encompassing input preparation, computer operation, and auxiliary routines; and (3) control functions, which handle production control and such areas as training procedures and standards.

Functional organization is probably the most sophisticated type of organization, offering the advantage of improving relations between systems and programming personnel; in general, it combines personnel of like skills together for more efficient functioning.

For smaller installations, the functional form of structure offers the advantages of (1) having a narrow span of management, (2) allowing third-line supervisors to assume managerial responsibilities, and (3) adding one or more layers of management in the event of future installation expansion.

LOCATION OF THE DATA-PROCESSING DEPARTMENT

The exact location of a data-processing department differs in different firms. Some firms believe that the EDP facility should be under the "department of most use," or in the department where clerical costs are the highest and savings are the greatest. Others feel that it should be an independent department not tied directly to any other department. Thus, there are several alternative possibilities for locating the data-processing facility. No single alternative is ideal for all organizations, since the choice depends on the type of organization, the capabilities of the data-processing staff, the type of management involved in the final decision, and the traditions the organization follows. Some of the ways of locating the EDP department follow.

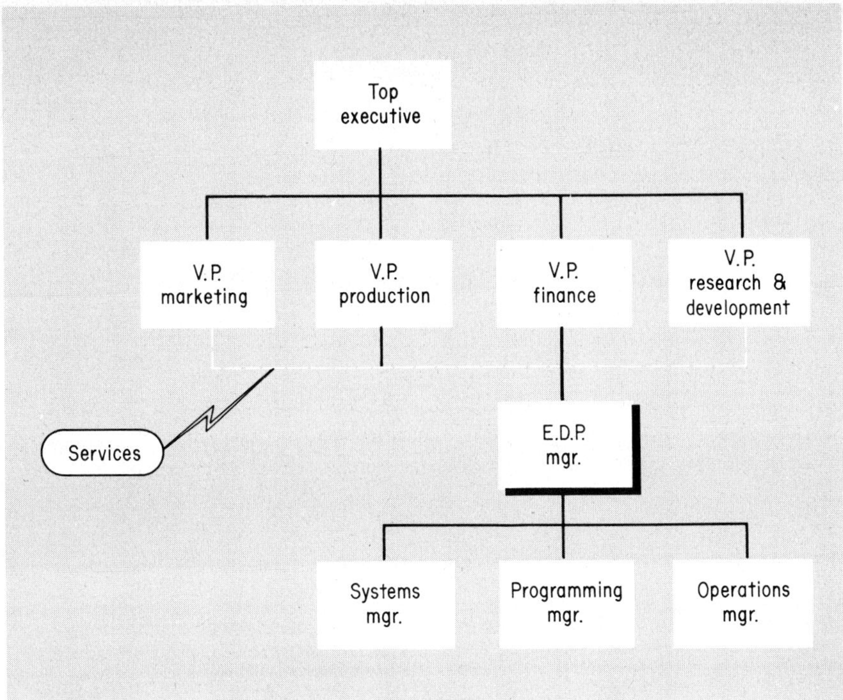

FIGURE 22-2. Organization chart showing a centralized EDP structure, reporting to the vice-president of finance

Centralized Location Under One User

The centralized-location-under-one-user structure is designed to serve all departments, but is directly under the largest user or the "department of most use"—usually the finance department (Fig. 22-2). This approach is likely to be a good choice when most of the applications to be processed belong to the sponsoring department. As far as the data-processing manager is concerned, his responsibility centers on satisfying the executive of that department.

One primary drawback of locating the firm's only EDP facility under one particular division is that other departments will have to cross organizational lines to get service. They are often viewed by the EDP staff as secondary users. Some organizations either limit the frequency of computer use by other departments or authorize the EDP manager to schedule them within the often already tight schedule committed to the primary department. In any case, the location of the system can erect barriers to other departments for effective use of the EDP system.

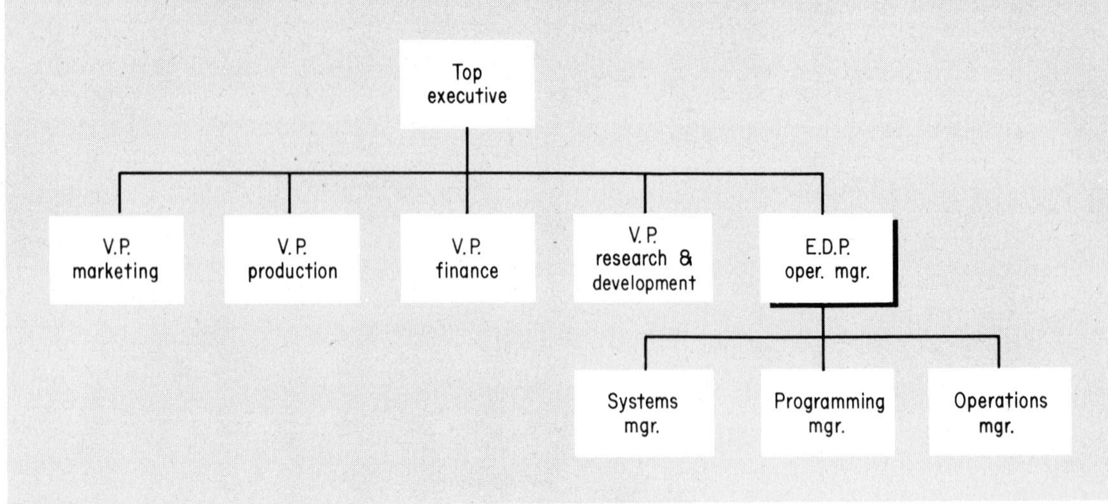

FIGURE 22-3. Organization chart showing a centralized autonomous EDP line structure

Centralized Location Independent of All Users

An independent centralized location provides equal service to all users, with no allegiance to any particular department. The EDP manager is at the same level as other department heads and reports directly to a top executive (Fig. 22-3). The cost of operating the EDP department is assumed by the company, although some plan is devised for billing each department for a portion of the total cost based on the extent of use or some other practical method.

From a managerial view, placing the EDP facility on the same level as any other department places the EDP manager in a position where he can negotiate projects with the user on an equal status. The user cannot very well impose his will or challenge any decisions the EDP manager makes. Furthermore, if all users have access to the same facility, the facility itself can work toward standardizing any related data-processing activities common to all departments and can make such data available upon request.

Centralized Location Above User Level

Placing a centralized data-processing department above the level of all departments gives its manager more power to determine how user applications will be implemented. This alternative location is acceptable in organizations that rely heavily on the operations of the EDP facility (Fig. 22-4).

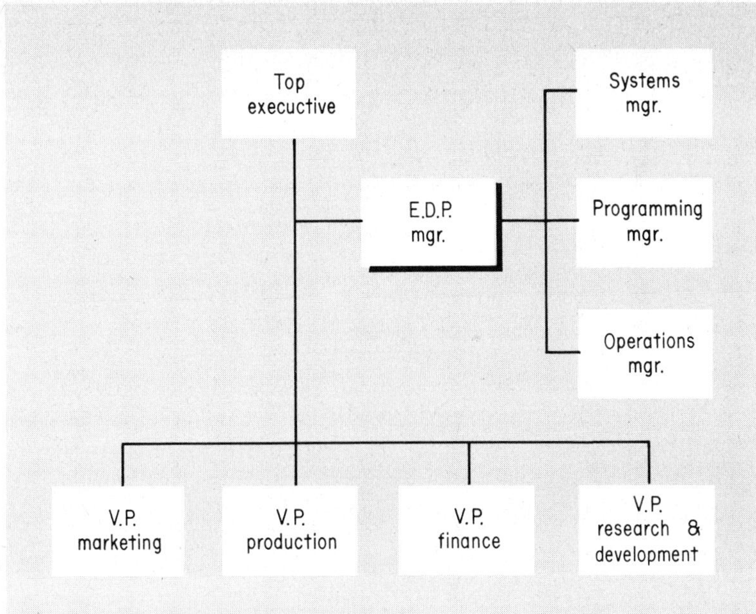

FIGURE 22-4. Organization chart showing a centralized EDP line structure above the departmental level

When the data-processing facility is made an independent center and at a higher level than other departments, the data-processing manager is expected to have a broader knowledge of company procedures and systems, because he will be serving the company in general. The independent organizational status of a computer center is most likely to reflect management's view that the center is a tool to aid in controlling the organization. This gives additional support to the need for the EDP manager to report directly to a top executive.

Decentralized Location

Some organizations, especially large industrial firms with scattered divisions, have a complete data-processing facility for each department or division. In this case, the data-processing manager reports to the division manager (Fig. 22-5). When this arrangement is assigned to heavy users, it permits full use of the facility without interruption from other users. Of course, operation costs have to be justified, and unless the EDP system is kept at optimal capacity it can be a very costly operation.

Other ways of locating a data-processing facility consist of some combination of the methods mentioned. For example, some organizations find it appropriate to decentralize operations and centralize systems and programming functions (Fig. 22-6), or to decentralize systems and pro-

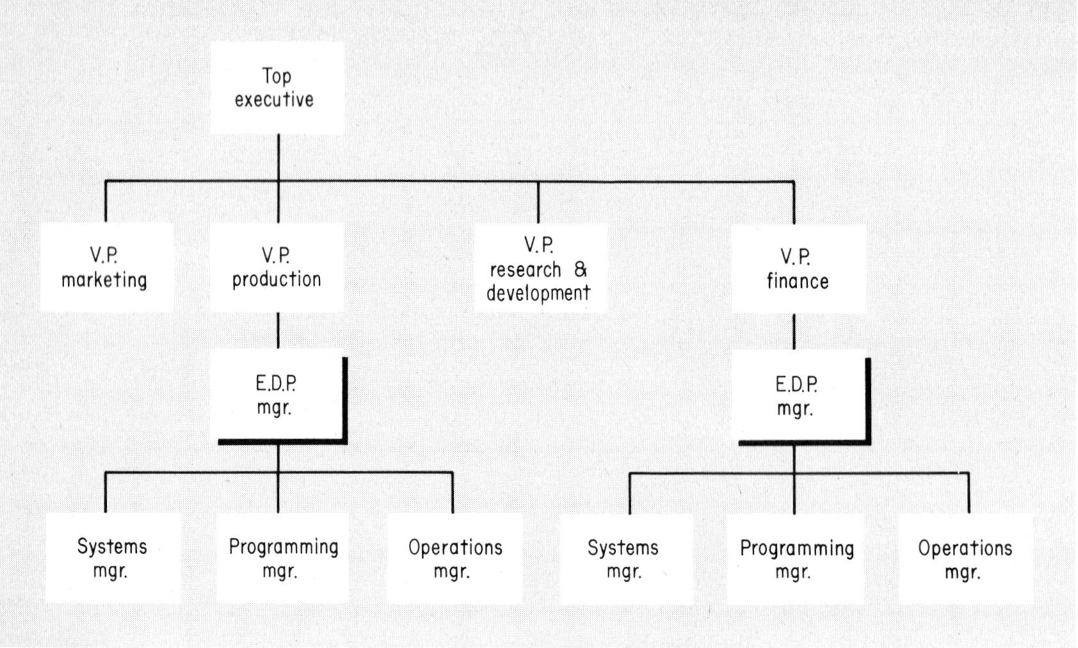

FIGURE 22-5. *Organization chart showing a decentralized data-processing line structure*

FIGURE 22-6. *Organization systems and programming chart showing a centralized system and program line structure and decentralized EDP operation*

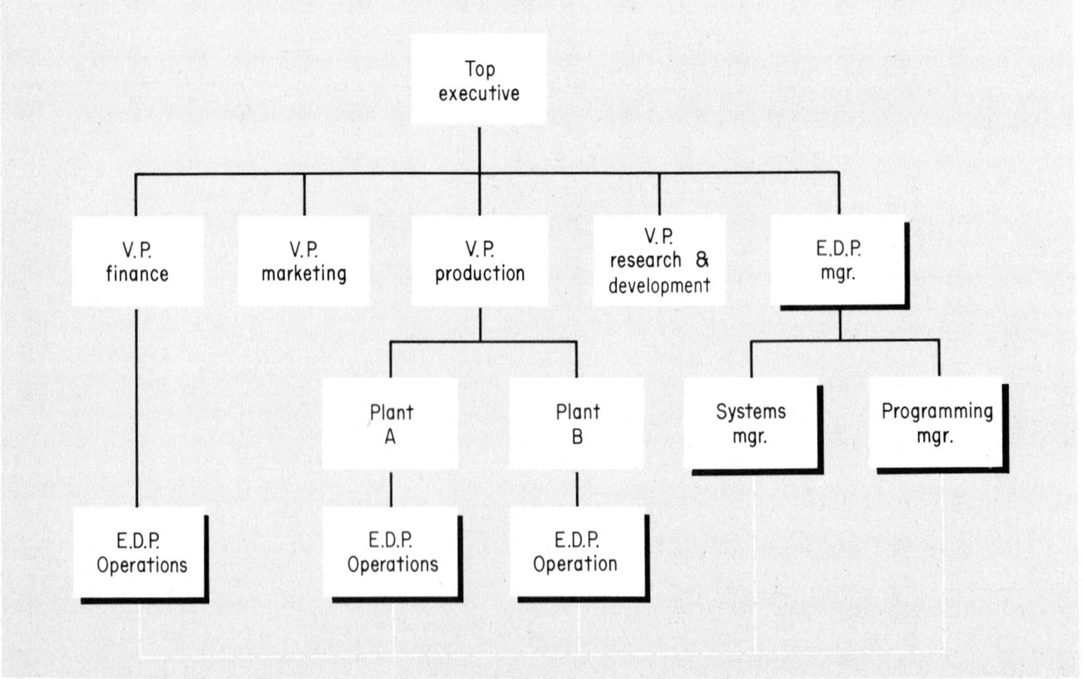

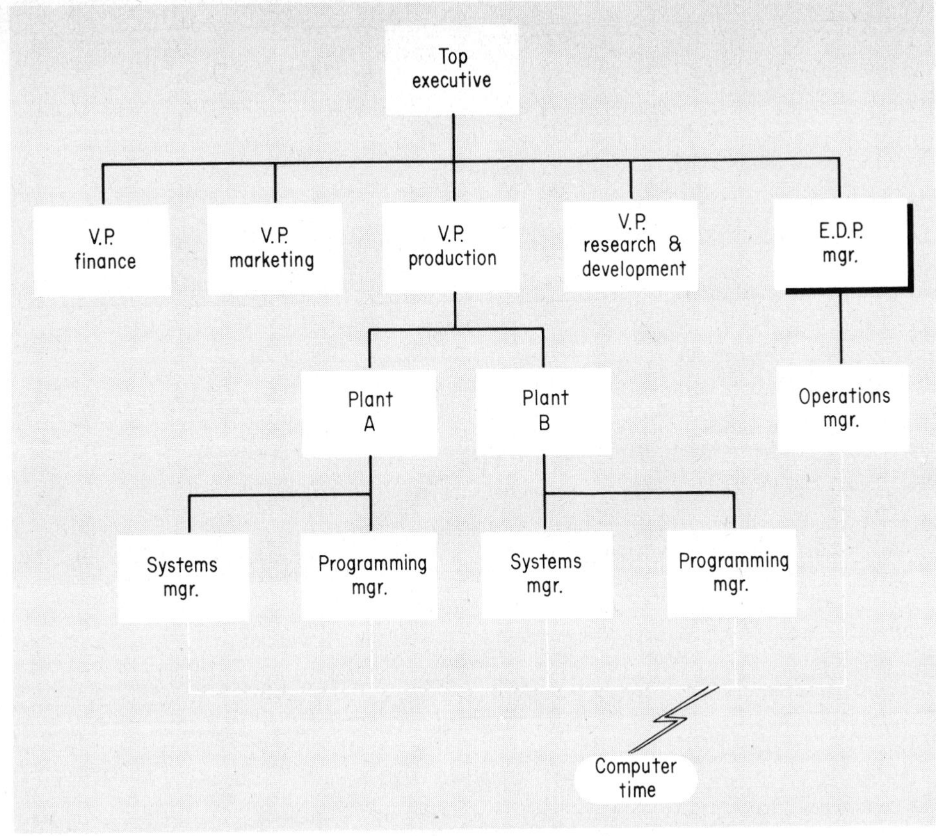

FIGURE 22-7. Organization chart showing a centralized operations structure and a decentralized system and programming operation

gramming, leaving operations at a centralized center (Fig. 22-7). Final choice rests with top management; considering company philosophy and objectives, it must decide which location of its EDP facility would best serve the users involved.

CONTROLLING DATA-PROCESSING OPERATIONS

Data-processing operations should be provided with control procedures for (1) ensuring accuracy of the processed results, (2) safeguarding data against fraud, and (3) securing data from unauthorized use. It is the data-processing manager's responsibility to handle the control functions and implement the necessary measures to make sure that both incoming and outgoing information remain valid and secure and are used within preplanned performance standards.

Accuracy Factor

Most decisions made by management are based on financial and other related reports generated by the data-processing department. Some of management's key financial decisions rely so heavily on the validity of the reports that one error can be extremely costly. Thus, the need for accuracy of processed information must be assured at all times. To help achieve effectiveness from the new system, all source documents must be debugged at the user's end and presented in a standardized, prescribed manner. This procedure makes it unnecessary for the input data staff to feed the data through a verifying phase or to question their accuracy. It is often said that the fewer the people, the greater the department's accuracy. Although this hypothesis might have validity, it is not easy to attain, because it would be difficult for a data-processing department to be completely automated. People will always be needed to perform needed tasks. This fact emphasizes the vital role of effective and clear communications. Clear instructions should be communicated to those employees preparing the source documents as well as to those who convert the documents into input. The latter employees must know exactly what is to be done and how they are to proceed. Naturally, when anything goes wrong, poor communications may not always be the reason. The reason may be incompetence among those doing the job.

Inadequate knowledge of a given job being performed by an employee can usually be detected easily. It should be remedied immediately, either by further training or by replacement. Before any hurried replacement is made, however, the supervisor should analyze the situation thoroughly to find out whether the problem arises from the user's poor presentation of the source documents, from the complex nature of the job, or from the incompetence of the person performing the task. In the first possibility, contact should be made with the user to call attention to and alleviate this problem. However, if the source document is properly presented but its contents are too involved, steps should be taken to convert them into appropriate media.

In addition to maintaining accurate incoming source data, the program that handles the data should be well debugged and validated, and the system used in processing must be guided by valid procedures. Once the data are received, various individuals must be assigned to perform different tasks. For example, the staff member assigned to handle the programming phase must not also be the one who loads the data or lists the results. That is, the operations group should be independent of the programming group to discourage collusion. In small installations, the system may be exposed to manipulation when one individual (e.g., the programmer) is assigned two or more separate tasks.

Fraud Factor

Protection against fraud is related to protection of accuracy. Several methods can be instituted to allèviate this problem. First, the user should keep a duplicate copy of all input information sent to the data-processing department to foil entry of unauthorized inputs by others. Second, each operations and programming supervisor can be instructed to report changes or errors in the data or the program directly to the data-processing manager. The purpose is to leave each group unaware of the activities of the other. Furthermore, any changes to be made must have advance approval from the manager. Third, in a centralized structure the data-processing department can be isolated so that it will not be directly subjected to undue pressure from a powerful or large user who wishes to make improper program runs. Any request for processing, especially one concerning funds or supplies, must be in writing and signed by an authorized executive. Unfortunately, smaller organizations cannot make effective use of this measure. On the other hand, smaller firms generally take a more direct interest in the effective operation of the overall data-processing system than do larger firms.

Security Factor

The data-processing department handles various types of information, some of which is vital to the very survival of the organization. For example, in organizations competing with one another for a surprise presentation of a new product, certain key output information is available only to a few top-level executives and cannot be allowed to fall into the hands of competitors or even unauthorized company personnel. The cost of accidental or intentional loss in this case can be very high.

One way to control confidential data is to retain them on tape, disk, or other media in a safe until they are needed for printout. This method protects the coded data against fire, theft, or easy access for duplication. To make a readable copy, the stored data must first be mounted on the proper output device for readout and listing. Access to the safe should be authorized only by the data-processing manager to a designated executive.

To minimize accidental loss of data during processing, several control steps can be taken:

1. Files should be clearly labeled to tell the operator their contents.
2. In the case of tape storage, a protective ring should be used to prevent the operator from accidentally writing (instead of reading) data on the data tape.
3. Duplicate (backup) copies of programs and vital files should be preserved for reference or substitution for lost or destroyed original sets.
4. Preventive measures are common in the large installations of corporations performing highly classified research for the government. Each member of the data-processing staff is initially given a battery of psychological tests to learn about his present personality and to predict what might be his future behavior. Screening out unstable

aspirants from the outset, regardless of their technical competence, often pays good dividends.

5. Insurance against fire or loss of replaceable equipment and supplies, as well as fidelity insurance to protect the organization from employees' dishonesty, should be taken. Although the number of losses resulting from dishonest employees is not large, concentration of a large amount of vital data under the jurisdiction of relatively few persons makes fidelity insurance necessary.

RESPONSIBILITY OF THE DATA-PROCESSING DEPARTMENT

As a service department, the data-processing center assumes the responsibility of providing various departments with accurate and meaningful reports based on the source data received. Before the data-processing department can assume this responsibility, the source documents it receives must be accurate and their processing approved by the proper official. This requires correct, standardized procedures, and authority to request data processing.

Correct Procedures

Other departments must follow correct procedures. Managers at different levels in the organization must first know what information they want. To illustrate, the general manager of the production department is responsible to the president for application of the broad policies adopted by the board of directors. The general manager would not be interested in the voluminous details generated in the departments of his subordinate supervisors. Unless exceptions occur, his way of managing is through reports and other condensed statements he receives concerning activities and operations. Likewise, the department head is responsible to the general manager for efficient operation of his department within the budget appropriated for that purpose. The department head, too, is not generally concerned with routine matters occurring at the lower level unless exceptions to the formulated policies and procedures occur. What each manager requires for managing his department determines the types of reports that must be prepared by the data-processing department. Unless the department managers are specific on this matter, the data-processing department is in no position to act on the data received.

Authority to Request Data Processing

The data to be processed must be forwarded by a department official who has the authority to request data processing. If a given department head. for instance, has complete autonomy over what goes on in his department, he should be the one to request the service of the data-processing center directly. If, on the other hand, his authority in this matter is limited, he should seek the approval of his immediate superior, who would then request the service. In the latter case, the data-processing manager should be informed of the circumstances.

Standardized Procedures

Those departments that are authorized to use the service must follow standardized procedures. For instance, before a payroll application can begin, the exact regular and overtime pay for each class of employees must be determined, and exceptions, such as sickness and vacations, with or without pay, must be systematized. Also, the time and frequency of payment of bonuses, commissions, and dividends should be determined. The data-processing department cannot process the payroll unless the amount and frequency of payments of the elements included in it are outlined by the department heads involved.

Once the type and number of reports are determined, the authority of each person requesting service is clarified, and procedures regarding basic input data are systematized, the data-processing department should be ready for effective operation. Accurate and timely results, however, can be ensured only if its manager devises proper procedures to systematize the service. The procedure begins with a request form and ends in the presentation of the finished results.

THE REQUEST FORM. Before any service is rendered, authorized personnel must first contact the data-processing manager, requesting service. This *can* be done over the telephone. However, to avoid any misunderstanding or misinterpretation, the request should be in writing. The data-processing staff should not accept or authorize the rendering of service to any department without prior approval of its manager. When a request form is presented, the data-processing manager is the proper person to act upon it. The form should include spaces for information, such as (1) the name of the department requesting service, (2) the names and titles of the persons filling out the form, (3) the type of data to be processed, (4) the form in which the results are to be presented (summary form or detailed form), (5) the sequence of the results to be presented, (6) the number of copies needed, (7) the frequency of processing (whether the application must be processed daily, weekly, or monthly), (8) the party that should receive the results, and (9) the signature of the party authorized to request service.

The department requesting the processing of a new application should arrange a meeting with the data-processing manager to discuss the problem from the standpoints of economy and workability of the application on the computer system. In larger systems, the systems analyst performs this function. Once a procedure is devised and the application prepared, further meetings are no longer necessary, as the application can be scheduled to run at the regular intervals requested.

Some of the advantages of a request form are

1. The data provided on the form help the data-processing manager to estimate the time that the application would take, permitting him to promise delivery of the results by a certain date. Use of the data-processing equipment is limited to the number of hours in a given shift. Considering other jobs to be done, the manager must check as to whether the application can fit into the schedule without disruption. Without the request form, confusion in scheduling could easily occur.
2. The request form serves as historical record of the completed application or of the services rendered. The manager can tell how much time is spent on each machine, the frequency of usage, and, consequently, the cost of each application. This machine cost, plus the portion of the data-processing employees' salaries charged to the completion of the application, would make up the basic cost of the application. This cost can be reported to the proper department so that it can absorb its share of the cost of operating the data-processing center. In a small firm, this procedure may not be necessary. If emergency requests for service are made, the data-processing department should have enough flexibility to handle them immediately. Effective communications in this regard are important. When they are verbal, the manager should "listen" and not just "hear." A story is told of a general manager who called the data-processing manager and inquired about the time when the regular trial balance would be ready. The processing manager answered, "Immediately," thinking that the general manager had telephoned because the trial balance had priority. This resulted in running the trial balance ahead of other equally important applications, causing complaints from other departments.

SCHEDULING. Once the request form is evaluated, a schedule is set up for running the application. The manager or his subordinate in charge of scheduling should promise a realistic delivery date, making proper allowance for the processing of other applications, machine breakdown, and unforeseeable problems. It is commendable of the manager to promise a deadline earlier than usual if he is sure it can be met. However, it would not be appropriate for him to do all or part of the work just to please the department requesting the service. In the event of emergencies, an overtime shift should be arranged. In this case, cost is a factor that should be weighed to see whether the emergency processing of the application is justified.

In small installations, a manager usually spends approximately 40 percent of his time operating the equipment and the remainder of his time managing the department. He often performs functions normally assigned to a machine operator. Some managers have limited authority, are overworked and underpaid and their departments are understaffed. Their authority is so limited in some cases that even the purchase of a professional book would require a superior's approval. This limited authority is unfortunate, since ideally a manager should spend his time planning the work of those in his department and getting things done through them. Naturally, he assumes final responsibility for the accuracy of the results and for their delivery to the proper user.

SUMMARY

A data-processing department is made up of a manager, a number of systems analysts, programmers, and an operations staff. A manager's primary task is to coordinate the activities of the department and promote an efficient operation throughout. To do the job well, he is expected to be knowledgeable in human relations and have an adequate technical background in computer processing. Lower managerial levels include a systems manager, a programming manager, and an operations manager.

Systems analysts are expected to be able to solve new problems and communicate effectively with users and programmers. Although the recession of the late 1960s put a damper on the mobility of most professionals, the demand for qualified systems analysts remains strong. Once hired, the company should make a special effort to keep them through competitive salaries, promotions, and the like.

Programmers, including maintenance and utility programmers, constitute a good percentage of the data-processing staff. Their activities range from flowcharting and coding to updating and debugging programs. Salary and educational requirements are not as high as those of the systems analysts. With recent advances in software and hardware, the demand for the "run-of-the-mill" programmer is in question.

The computer operations group prepares data for input and operates the system when needed. Compared to the programming or the systems group, it is a lower, but necessary, level in the department; obviously, this group commands lower pay.

Most EDP departments initially adopt a line structure in which subordinates report directly to the manager. Although this structure allows better control over the department's activities, it commits too much of the manager's time to the routine task of supervision and at the same time restricts the subordinates' freedom in making decisions on task-related matters. Thus, a line and staff or a functional structure eventually develops.

Among the alternative ways of locating the data-processing department are centralized location under one user, centralized location independent of all users, centralized location above user level, or a decentralized location with separate facilities for each division. Any data-processing system carries with it the need to safeguard data against fraud, ensure accuracy of the output, and secure data from unauthorized use. Final responsibility for proper control rests with the data-processing manager.

QUESTIONS

1. "The fewer the people, the greater the department's accuracy." Do you agree with this statement? Defend your answer.
2. Where should the computer be located? Under whose direction should it be? Why?
3. What are the qualifications of a data-processing manager? What are his duties and responsibilities?
4. What can a manager do to satisfy the needs and wants of his subordinates?
5. Explain the three types of leaders. Which type is preferred for data-processing management? Why?
6. What three main groups are under the manager's direct supervision?
7. What technical background should a manager possess? Explain.
8. What is the main function of a systems analyst? What qualifications should he have?
9. What steps are involved in programming? Which of these steps are considered the most pertinent to programming?
10. What types of positions are available in the area of computer operations? Explain.
11. How should displaced employees be handled?
12. Why do key-punch operators leave their jobs?
13. What factors are involved in controlling data-processing operations? Which factor is the most critical? Why?
14. Discuss the responsibilities of the data-processing department.
15. What purpose does a request form serve? What type of information does it contain?
16. Do you believe that a manager should spend a reasonable amount of his time operating equipment? Why?

SUGGESTED READING

COLEMAN, WILLIAM. "The Programmer as a Manager," *The Office*, May 1971, pp. 14–15.

COWIE, J. B. "Computer Systems Management," *The Computer Bulletin*, May 1969, pp. 148–152.

DAVIS, SIDNEY. "Internal Recruitment and Training of Data Processing Personnel," *Computers and Automation,* Sept. 1969, pp. 38–39.

GOTTERER, M. H. "Selection Techniques for Data Processing Personnel," *Data Management,* Sept. 1972, pp. 66–68.

IRVINE, E. H. "Personnel Management and Organizational Patterns and Techniques," *Data Management,* Sept. 1972, pp. 63–66.

MCMURRER, J. A., and J. R. PARISH. "How Can We Produce More People for the Computer Industry?," *Computers and Automation,* Sept. 1969, pp. 28–30.

NEWLIN, CLARKE, JR. "The Changing World of the Data Processing Administrator," *Data Management,* Feb. 1972, pp. 35–38.

APPENDICES

terms to learn

Abacus A manual calculating device that uses beads to represent decimal values.

Access Time (1) The time interval between the instant of which data are called for from a storage device and the instant delivery is completed; i.e., the read time. (2) The time interval between the instant at which data are requested to be stored and the instant at which storage is completed; i.e., the write time.

Accounting Machine (1) A keyboard-actuated machine that prepares accounting records. (2) A machine that reads data from external-storage media, such as cards or tapes, and automatically produces accounting records or tabulations, usually on continuous forms.

Accumulator A register in which the result of an arithmetic or logic operation is formed.

Action Entry Lower right quadrant of a decision table, specifying the action to be taken.

Action Stub Lower left quadrant of a decision table, listing every possible action that can be taken.

Adder A device whose output is a representation of the sum of the quantities represented by its inputs.

Address (1) An identification, as represented by a name, label, or number, for a register, location in storage, or any other data source or destination, such as the location of a station in a communications network. (2) Loosely, any part of an instruction that specifies the location of an operand for the instruction.

ADP Automatic Data Processing.

Analog Computer A computer that represents variables by physical analogies. Thus, any computer that solves problems by translating physical conditions such as flow temperature, pressure, angular position, or voltage into related mechanical or electrical quantities and uses mechanical or electrical equivalent circuits as an analog for the physical phenomenon being investigated. In general, a computer that uses an analog for each variable and produces analogs as output. Thus, an analog computer measures continuously, whereas a digital computer counts discretely.

Analytical Engine The first general-purpose computer, developed by Charles P. Babbage around 1833.

Array Variable A dimensioned variable that represents one or more memory cells specified in a dimensioned statement.

ASCII An acronym for American Standard Code for Information Interchange, used when transmitting data between computers.

Assemble To prepare a machine-language program from a symbolic-language program by substituting absolute operation codes for symbolic operation codes and absolute relocatable addresses for symbolic addresses.

Asynchronous Operating independently.

Automation (1) The implementation of processes by automatic means. (2) The theory, art, or technique of making a process more automatic. (3) The investigation, design, development, and application of methods of rendering processes automatic, self-moving, or self-controlling.

Auxiliary Storage A storage that supplements another storage.

Bar Printer A printing device that uses several type bars positioned side by side across the line. Printing data on a line involves activating specific bars to move vertically until the characters they contain are properly aligned. Then the data are printed simultaneously.

Basic An acronym of Beginners All-purpose Symbolic Instruction Code. A widely used time-sharing language developed by Professors Kemeny and Kurtz with a structure similar to that of Fortran.

Batch Processing A technique by which items to be processed must be coded and collected into groups prior to processing.

Batch Totals The sum of specific quantities (related to batches of source documents) used to verify the accuracy of later operations.

Baud A unit of signaling speed that amounts to 1 bit per second.

Binary (1) Pertaining to a characteristic or property involving a selection, choice, or condition in which there are two possibilities. (2) Pertaining to the number representation system with a radix of 2.

Binary-Coded Decimal Pertaining to a decimal notation in which the individual decimal digits are each represented by a group of binary digits; e.g., in the 8-4-2-1 binary-coded decimal notation, the number 23 is represented as 0010 0011, whereas in binary notation, 23 is represented as 10111.

Bit (1) An abbreviation of binary digit. (2) A single character in a binary number. (3) A single pulse in a group of pulses. (4) A unit of information capacity of a storage device.

Block A set of things, such as words, characters, or digits, handled as a unit.

Block Diagram Another name for a system flowchart.

Block Sorting An operation involving a sort of one or more of the most significant characters of a key to serve as a means of making workable-sized groups from a large volume of records to be sorted.

Blocking Combining two or more records into one block.

Branch A set of instructions that is executed between two successive decision instructions.

Buffer A storage device used to compensate for a difference in rate of flow of data, or time of occurrence of events, when transmitting data from one device to another.

Business Data Processing Data processing for business purposes; e.g., recording and summarizing the financial transactions of a business.

Business Organization A framework by means of which the activities of a business are tied together to provide for integrated performance. Also, a human relationship in group activity.

Byte A set of consecutive binary digits (usually, 8-bit set) operating as a unit.

Calculating Reconstructing or creating new data by compressing certain numeric facts.

Calculation Specification Form Used in determining the calculations required for obtaining the result.

Calculator (1) A device capable of performing arithmetic. (2) A calculator as in (1) that requires frequent manual intervention. (3) Generally and historically, a device for carrying out logic and arithmetic digital operations of any kind.

Card Control and File Description Form Specifies the input and output devices required in handling the data.

Card Stacker An output device that accumulates punched cards in a deck.

Cash Discount A fixed amount or a percentage deducted by the seller from the price of an item for inducing cash payment by the buyer.

Cathode Ray Tube Abbreviated CRT, it is an electronic vacuum tube which displays information by plotting data point by point on its screen.

Central Processing Unit (CPU) A major device containing the arithmetic unit, main memory, and control unit.

Chain Printer A device that uses a chain of several links, each of which contains alphabetic and numeric characters. The chain rotates horizontally at constant speed. Hammers from the back of the paper are timed to fire against selected characters on the chain, causing the printing of a line.

Channel A parallel track on a magnetic tape, a band on a magnetic drum, or a path along which information flows.

Character An elementary mark or event that is used to represent data. A character is often in the form of a graphic spatial arrangement of connected or adjacent strokes.

Classifying Arranging data in a specific form, usually by sorting, grouping, or extracting.

Clock A circuit in a synchronous computer that emits signals at equal intervals.

Closed Tables A decision table that consists of a set of rules which are accessed to by other decision tables for processing.

COBOL Common Business-Oriented Language: a procedural language developed for business data processing. The language is intended as a means for direct presentation of a business program to a computer with a suitable compiler.

Data Division The part of a COBOL program describing the data to be processed by the object program. It contains primarily a file section that describes the file(s) used and a working-storage section that reserves memory space for storage of results.

Environment Division The part of the program describing the physical characteristics of the equipment being used and the aspects of the problems that are dependent on the program. Its two main sections are the configuration and the input/output section.

Identification Division The part of the program that identifies the name of the programmer, the title of the COBOL program, and the compiler listing associated with it.

Procedure Division The part of the program that is programmer-defined and determines the operations that will perform the necessary processing of data. Its structure includes sections and paragraphs, as well as conditional, imperative, and compiler-directing classes of sentences/statements.

Word (Also called *reserved word.*) A word that holds a preassigned meaning in COBOL, to be used in its prescribed context.

Code Check A summation check for accuracy in which binary bits representing each character are converted and their sum maintained throughout a processing cycle.

Coding The translation of flow diagrams into the language of the computer.

Collator A device to collate or merge sets of cards or other documents into a sequence.

Compile To prepare a machine-language program from a computer program written in another programming language by making use of the overall logic structure of the program, generating more than one machine instruction for each symbolic statement, as well as performing the function of an assembler.

Composite Card A multipurpose data card, or a card that contains data needed in the processing of various applications.

Computer A calculating device that processes data represented by a combination of discrete (in digital computers) or continuous (in analog computers) data.

Computer-Assisted Instruction A concept that applies computers and specialized input/output display terminals directly to individualized student instruction.

Computer Word A sequence of bits or characters treated as a unit and capable of being stored in one computer location. Synonymous with *machine word.*

Condition Entry Upper right quadrant of a decision table, indicating all the possible combinations of conditions listed in the condition stub.

Condition Stub Upper left quadrant of a decision table, listing the conditions related to a particular problem.

Constant Any specific value (number) that does not change during program execution.

Control (1) The part of a digital computer or processor that determines the execution and interpretation of instructions in proper sequence, including the decoding of each instruction and the application of the proper signals to the arithmetic unit and other registers in accordance with the decoded information. (2) Frequently, in any mechanism, one or more of the components responsible for interpreting and carrying out manually initiated directions. Sometimes it is called *manual control.* (3) In some business applications, a mathematical check. (4) In programming, instructions that determine conditional jumps are often referred to as *control instructions,* and the time sequence of execution of instructions is called the *flow of control.*

Control Panel (1) A part of a computer console that contains manual controls. (2) Same as *plugboard.*

Control Punch A specific code punched in a card to cause the machine to perform a specific operation.

Control Statement A statement that serves to interrupt sequential execution of instructions by transferring control to a statement elsewhere in the program.

Counter A device, such as a register or storage location, used to represent the number of occurrences of an event.

Cram (Card Random-Access Memory) A mass-storage device that consists of a number of removable magnetic cards, each of which is capable of storing magnetic bits of data.

CRT See cathode-ray tube.

Cryogenics The study and use of devices utilizing properties of materials near the absolute zero in temperature.

Cycling Tape Creating a new tape file through an updating procedure.

Data Base A single file containing information in a format applicable to any user's needs and available when needed.

Data Communication Transmitting or receiving processed data, sound, or other bits of information over telephone wire, radio, or other electromagnetic means.

Data Inscriber A special key-to-tape input device which records input data in a 16-millimeter tape cartridge for direct computer processing.

Data Manipulation The performance of all necessary routines on input data.

Data Origination Determination of the nature (origin) of source data.

Data-Phone A device which facilitates data communication over telephone channels.

Data Processing Any operation or combination of operations on data.

Data-Processing Cycle The sequence of steps involved in manipulating business information.

Data Recorder A key-to-tape input device designed to encode data in seven-track or nine-track magnetic tape.

Data Word A word that may be primarily regarded as part of the information manipulated by a given program. A data word may be used to modify a program instruction, or to be arithmetically combined with other data words.

Debug To detect, locate, and remove mistakes from a routine or malfunctions from a computer. Synonymous with *troubleshoot.*

Decision Table A documentation format; a table of the contingencies to be dealt with in defining a problem and the actions to be taken.

Declarative Operation A coding sequence that involves writing symbolic labels and operation codes for data and constants. It is made up of a symbolic label, a declarative-operation code, and an operand.

Delayed Time Pertains to processing data at some time after they have been received.

Demodulator See *MODEM*.

Density The number of characters that can be stored in a given unit of length, such as an inch of magnetic tape.

Detail Printing (Listing) The printing of one line for each card read by the tabulator.

Difference Engine A special-purpose computer developed by Charles P. Babbage around 1812 to compute mathematical tables.

Digit-Punching Position The area on a punched card reserved to represent a decimal digit.

Digital Computer A computer that operates on discrete data by performing arithmetic and logic processes on these data. Contrast this with *analog computer*.

Dim Commonly used in array programming, a statement that establishes a dimensioned computer-memory area of a specific size for processing.

Direct-Access Storage (1) The process of obtaining information from or placing information into storage where the time required for such access is independent of the location of the information most recently obtained or placed in storage. (2) A device in which random access, as defined in (1), can be achieved without effective penalty in time.

Direct Address An address that specifies the location of an operand. Synonymous with *one-level address*.

Disbursements Payment of financial obligations (for example, invoices).

Disk Pack A device containing a set of magnetic disks for storing secondary information.

Document Card A special card form used in preparing a document such as a check, a purchase order, etc.

Documentation As a means of communication, a written record of a phase of a specific project; it establishes design and performance criteria for various phases of the project.

Drum Printer A printing device that uses a drum embossed with alphabetic and numeric characters. As the drum rotates, a hammer strikes the paper (from behind) at a time when the desired character on the drum passes the line to be printed. To complete printing a given line, further rotation of the drum containing the remaining characters is necessary.

Dual-Gap Read-Write Head A device used in magnetic tape data processing to insure the accuracy of recorded data on tape. A character written on tape is read immediately by a read head to verify its validity.

Dump A snapshot of the computer's internal storage.

Duplex A data channel that allows simultaneous transmission in both directions.

EBCDIC (Extended Binary-Coded Decimal Interchange Code) An 8-bit code first used with the IBM 360 system.

Editing The act of deciding on the kind of data to be processed and checking its validity and accuracy.

EDVAC Electronic discrete variable automatic computer, developed by the Moore School of Electrical Engineering as the first commercial electronic computer.

Electronic Data Processing The processing of data by an electronic device such as a computer.

Electrostatic Printer A device that prints an optical image on special paper. Spots of electricity are placed in matrix form on paper. When the paper is dusted with powdered-ink material, the particles cling to the electrically charged characters. Later, they are moved to a high temperature zone where the ink is melted and is permanently fixed to the paper.

Else Rule A catchall rule written in the right column of a decision table. It represents conditions that are not represented in the table.

End A statement that defines the end of a program.

End-of-File Indicator A code which indicates that the last record of a data file has been read.

End Printing performed by a reproducer where certain data punched in a card are printed across the end of the same card.

ENIAC Electronic numerical integrator and calculator (the first all-electronic general-purpose computer), built in the early 1940s by Prosper Eckert and John W. Mauchly while at the University of Pennsylvania.

Equalization A process by which a modem maintains the quality of a transmission line.

Extended Entry Table A decision table in which the statements written in the stub section are extended into the entry section.

Facsimile Involves transmission of images, messages, or diagrams over radio waves.

Feasibility Study A phase of project initiation; a proposal that describes the user's problem, the variables involved, and a tentative approach to its solution.

Feedback The part of a closed loop system that automatically brings back information about the condition under control.

Field A specified area of a record used for a particular category of data; e.g., a group of card columns used to represent a wage rate, or a set of bit locations in a computer word that are used to express the address of the operand.

Fixed-Word-Length Having the property that a machine word always contains the same number of characters or digits.

Floating Point Usually, representation of numbers and a method of performing arithmetic. The point is at a location defined by the number itself.

Flowchart A graphical representation for the definition, analysis, or solution of a problem, in which symbols are used to represent operations, data flow, and equipment.

For A statement that initiates a program loop.

Format Statement A nonexecutable statement that serves input/output statements to specify the arrangement of data in an external medium such as a punched card, a magnetic tape, or on printed paper.

Fortran (From *formula translations*) Any of several specific procedure-oriented programming languages.

Fortran IV A problem-oriented language, initially designed for scientific application, which allows the programmer to think in terms of the problem rather than the computer used in solving it. The language is quite convenient for many business applications.

Fourth-Generation Computers A new generation of computer systems characterized by (1) functionally modular hardware and software design, (2) real time execution of most processing, (3) optional use of communication interfaces, and (4) in-line data processing by on-line units.

Frequency The number of times a signal is repeated over a given period.

Full-Duplex Channel A channel that facilitates simultaneous transmission in both directions.

Group Printing A procedure whereby one line is printed for each group of punch cards.

General-Purpose Computer A computer that is designed to solve a wide class of problems.

Group Printing A procedure whereby one line is printed for each group of cards having similar characteristics.

Grouping Arranging a mass of data into related groups, each having common characteristics.

Hardware Physical equipment; e.g., mechanical, magnetic, electrical, or electronic devices. Contrast with *software*.

Help A system command that asks for system assistance in resolving errors and references information about the system.

Hexadecimal Relating to a number-representation system using base sixteen.

Hollerith A widely used system of encoding alphanumeric information onto cards, hence *Hollerith cards*, as synonymous with *punched cards*.

Hollerith Code See Hollerith.

Housekeeping For a computer program, the setting up of constants and variables to be used in the program.

Imperative Statement A statement that commands the computer's immediate execution of specific sequential statements following it. Imperative statements include the DO statement, CONTINUE statement, and the STOP and END statements.

Indirect Address An address that specifies a storage location that contains either a direct address or another indirect address Synonymous with *multi-level address*.

Information Retrieval A technique of classifying and indexing useful information in mass-storage devices, in a format that is amenable to interaction with the user.

Inhibit Wire One of four wires strung through a magnetic core. It is used in a write operation if it is decided that a given core is to represent a 0 state.

Input (1) The data to be processed. (2) The state or sequence of states occurring on a specified input channel. (3) The device or collective set of devices used for bringing data into another device. (4) A channel for impressing a state on a device or logic element. (5) The processes of transferring data from an external storage to an internal storage.

Input Device The mechanical unit designed to bring data to be processed into a computer; e.g., a card reader, a tape reader, or a keyboard.

Input Specification Form Identifies various types of cards within a given file and specifies their sequence.

Instruction A set of characters that defines the details of an operation.

Instruction Word A computer word that contains an instruction.

Integer Variable A series of alphanumeric characters with the first letter being I, J, K, L, M, or N.

Interpreter (1) A program that translates and executes each source-language expression before translating and executing the next one. (2) A device that prints on a punched card the data already punched in the card.

Interrecord Gap An interval of space or time deliberately left between recording portions of data or records. Such spacing is used to prevent errors through loss of data or overwriting and permits tape stop/start operations.

Interrupt A break in the normal flow of a program, usually caused by an external source. The interrupt causes the computer to handle a particular set of events before resuming the ordinary operation.

IOCS (Input/Output Control System) A standard set of routines designed to initiate and manipulate input and output operations.

Key Punch A keyboard-operated device that punches holes in a card to represent data.

Keyboard A group of marked levers operated manually for recording characters.

Label One or more characters used to identify an item of data. Synonymous with *key*.

Library Subroutine A set of tested subroutines available on file for use when needed.

Limited-Entry Table A widely used type of decision table requiring fixed information in each quadrant. Condition entries are limited to "Y," "N," or a blank, while condition stubs are answered with either "Y" or "N," with "X"s in the action entry, responding to each "Y" in the condition entry.

Line-At-A-Time Printer A device capable of printing one line of characters across a page—i.e., 100 or more characters simultaneously—as continuous paper advances line by line in one direction past type bars or a type cylinder that contains all characters in all positions.

Literal A true value defined by a programmer.

Load Point A tape marker, indicating the beginning of the usable portion of the tape when writing or reading is to begin.

Logic (1) The science dealing with the criteria or formal principles of reasoning and thought. (2) The systematic scheme that defines the interactions of signals in the design of an automatic data-processing system. (3) The basic principles and application of truth tables and interconnection between logical elements required for arithmetic computation in an automatic data-processing system.

Loop A sequence of instructions that is repeated until a terminal condition prevails.

Looping Executing repeatedly a set of computer instructions until a terminating condition is met.

Macro Instruction (1) An instruction consisting of a sequence of micro instructions that are inserted into the object routine for performing a specific operation. (2) A more powerful instruction that combines several operations in one instruction.

Magnetic Core A configuration of magnetic material that is, or is intended to be, placed in a spatial relationship to current-carrying conductors, and whose magnetic properties are essential to its use. It may be used to concentrate an induced magnetic field as in a transformer, induction coil, or armature, to retain a magnetic polarization for the purpose of storing data, or for its nonlinear properties as in a logic element. It may be made of such material as iron, iron oxide, or ferrite, and in such shapes as wires and tapes.

Magnetic Disk A rotating metal disk having two magnetized surfaces for storing data.

Magnetic Drum A right circular cylinder with a magnetic surface on which data can be stored by selective magnetization of portions of the curved surface.

Magnetic Tape A tape coated with magnetizable material, on which information may be recorded in the form of magnetically polarized spots.

Management Information System An all-inclusive system designed to provide instant information to management for effective and efficient business operation.

Manipulation The actual work performed on source-data processing.

Mark I A first-generation American computer (an automatic sequence-controlled calculator) developed by Howard G. Aiken of Harvard in May 1944.

Mark-Sensed Card A card designed to permit entering data on it with an electrographic pencil.

Mass-Storage File A type of temporary secondary storage that supplies the computer with the necessary data for an immediate, up-to-date report on a given account.

Matching A data-processing operation similar to a merge, except that instead of producing a sequence of items made up from the input, matched sequences are produced.

Match-Merging An operation combining the matching and merging functions in one routine. Matched pairs of cards merging in the middle pocket, whereas unmatched cards fall in separately designated pockets.

Matrix Printer A high-speed printer that prints character-like configurations of dots through the proper selection of wire ends from a matrix of wire ends, rather than conventional characters through the selection of typefaces. Synonymous with *wire printer*.

Memory (1) A device into which data can be entered, in which it can be held, and from which it can be retrieved at a later time. (2) Loosely, any device that can store data.

Merge To combine two or more sets of data into one, usually in a specified sequence.

MICR *Magnetic-Ink Character Recognition,* a technique involving the use of a device that senses characters printed with an ink containing magnetized particles and encodes them into a machine language.

Microprogram A sequence of pseudo-instructions that are translated by a micrologic subsystem of the computer.

Microsecond One millionth of a second.

Millisecond One thousandth of a second.

Minicomputer A low-cost, small, general-purpose, digital computer with a 4,000-basic-word memory and a price tag of less than $25,000, stripped down.

Mixed-Entry Table A decision table which consists of a combination of rows with extended entries and rows with limited entries.

MODEM (Modulator/Demodulator) A device designed to interface between the computer and the communication system.

Modularity Operating system programs which permit the user to expand the existing system to meet increased processing demands or to handle new applications.

Multiplex Making simultaneous use of a communication channel for transmitting a number of messages.

Multiplexing See multiplex.

Multiprocessing Relating to a system involving more than one arithmetic and logic unit for simultaneous use.

Multiprogramming Running two or more programs simultaneously by interleaving their operations.

Nanosecond One billionth of a second.

Napier's Bones A technique introduced by John Napier to aid multiplication through the use of data tables or rods.

9-Edge The bottom edge of a punched card.

Numeralization Representation of alphabetic data through the use of digits; a desired step in automatic data processing.

Object Program The program that is the ouput of an automatic coding system. Often the object program is a machine-language program ready for execution, but it may well be in an intermediate language.

Object Time The time span during which a stored program is in active control of a specific application.

OCR Optical Character Recognition.

Octal (1) Pertaining to a characteristic or property involving a selection, choice, or condition in which there are eight possibilities. (2) Pertaining to the number representation system with a radix of eight.

Off-Line Pertaining to equipment or devices not under direct control of the central processing unit.

On-Line Pertaining to peripheral equipment or devices in direct communication with the central processing unit.

On-Line Input A system in which the input device transmits certain data directly to (and under control of) the central processing unit.

On-Line Processing Data processing by means of a system, and of the peripheral equipment or devices in a system, in which the operation of such equipment is under control of the central processing unit, and in which information reflecting current activity is introduced into the data-processing system as soon as it occurs; thus, directly in line with the main flow of transaction processing.

On-Line, Real-Time Pertains to a system which receives input data, processes them, and returns results (output) fast enough to affect an ongoing process.

Open-End Table A decision table where the last action instruction transfers logic flow to another open-end table.

Operand That which is operated upon. An operand is usually identified by an addressed part of an instruction.

Operating System A set of routines for monitoring the operations of a computer system.

Operation Code A code that represents specific operations. Synonymous with *instruction code.*

Optical Character Recognition (OCR) A technique which relies on electronic devices and light to detect, and convert into machine language, characters which have been printed or written on documents in human-understandable form.

Optical Scanning Translation of printed or handwritten characters into machine language.

Origination Determination of the nature, type, and origin of some documents.

Output (1) Data that has been processed. (2) The state or sequence of states occurring on a specified output channel. (3) The device or collective set of devices used for taking data out of a device. (4) A channel for expressing a state of a device or logic element. (5) The process of transferring data from an internal storage to an external storage.

Output Device The part of a machine that translates the electrical impulses representing data processed by the machine into permanent results, such as printed forms, punched cards, and magnetic writing on tape.

Output-Format Specification Form Specifies that data desired on the report and other information pertaining to the fields used in the output file.

Packing Density The number of useful storage elements per unit of dimension; e.g., the number of bits per inch stored on a magnetic tape or drum track.

Parallel Printing One-line-at-a-time printing, a characteristic of the tabulator.

Parallel Processing Concurrent processing of two or more programs stored in memory.

Parallel Reading Row-by-row reading of a data card.

Parameter A variable that is given a constant value for a specific purpose or process.

Parity Check A check that tests whether the number of 1's (or 0's) in an array of binary digits is odd or even. Synonymous with *odd-even check.*

Payroll Register A record of employees to be paid, with the amount due to each.

PBX (Short for *Public Exchange Service*) A telephone system offered by various telephone companies.

Peripheral Equipment Components which work in conjunction with, but which are not a part of, the central processing system—for example, a card reader, a printer.

Phase The duration of signal in time.

Picosecond One thousandth of a nanosecond, or 10^{-12} seconds.

Picture A string of specified alphabetic, numeric, or alphanumeric characters which gives certain characteristics of data items

PL/1 (Programming Language/1) A new language with certain features similar to FORTRAN and some of the best features of other languages. It makes use of recent developments in computer technology and offers the programmer a relatively flexible problem-oriented language for programming problems that can best be worked out by using a combination of scientific and business compiling techniques.

> **Declare Statement** A statement used in deciding on the form of treating numeric quantities.
>
> **Delimiter** A character that specifies an elementary action, such as an arithmetic operation, and/or provides punctuation.
>
> **Expression** A sequence of constants and identifiers, separated by operators and parentheses, that describes a rule for calculating a value.
>
> **Get List Statement** A statement that provides data values to the computer.
>
> **Go To Statement** An unconditional branching statement that tells the computer to go directly to a statement with a specific label.
>
> **Identifier** A string of alphanumeric and break characters. It begins with a letter, cannot contain blanks, and must not exceed 31 characters.
>
> **Procedure Block** A block providing the link that allows the operating system to initiate execution of the object program. It begins with a PROCEDURE statement and terminates with an END statement.
>
> **Put Skip List Statement** A statement that permits a printout of all the values of the identifiers in it.

Plotter A visual display or board in which a dependent variable is graphed by an automatically controlled pen or pencil as a function of one or more variables.

Point-of-Sale (POS) Input System A technique geared to automating a collection of source data through on-line computer systems.

Polling A request to each available computer console for a message or for readiness to accept a reply.

Primary Storage An area or a device in the central processing unit where required data are stored until needed.

Problem-Oriented Language A machine-independent language requiring only statement of the problem (not the procedure) for proper solution.

Procedure-Oriented Language A machine-independent language designed to simplify stating the necessary procedures for solving the problem; e.g., FORTRAN and COBOL.

Process A general term covering such terms as *assemble, compile, generate, interpret,* and *compute.*

Processor The CPU; an assembler or a compiler translator routine.

Processor Program A programming aid that prepares an object program, first by reading symbolic instructions and then comparing and converting them into a suitable computer language.

Profit-and-Loss Statement A financial statement showing the company's earning capability during a specific period of time.

Program (Noun) (1) A plan for solving a problem. (2) Loosely, a routine. (Verb) (3) To devise a plan for solving a problem. (4) Loosely, to write a routine.

Program Card A coded card inserted in the program control unit of the key punch to control automatically operations such as skipping, duplicating, and shifting.

Program Flowchart A graphic representation of a computer problem, using symbols to represent machine instructions or groups of instructions.

Programming Preparing a logical sequence of events which the computer must follow and execute to solve a problem.

Program Specifications A list of the information requirements of the system, with emphasis upon the input and output specifications, existing files, and the processing details. Related to *systems specifications.*

Punched Card (1) A card punched with a pattern of holes to represent data. (2) A card as in (1) before being punched.

Punched-Card Data Processing The production of records and reports by means of machines (or systems) which use a punched card as a primary medium.

Punching Station The area on the key punch where a card is aligned for the punching process.

Purchase Order A requisition made by the purchasing department to a supplier for meeting the needs of a division or a department (e.g., production department) of the firm.

Quanta A slice of computer time, usually used in reference to computer time allocation.

Queuing A computer technique which involves lining up input instructions or messages from various terminals and processing them on a first-come, first-served basis or according to a priority system controlled by a multiplexor-programmed routine.

RAMAC (Random-Access Method of Accounting and Control) A mass-storage device that consists of a number of rotating disks stacked one on top of another to make up a data file.

Random Access Pertaining to a storage device in which the access time is effectively independent of the location of the data.

Read Check An inspection-type unit in an input or output component that ascertains the accuracy of the data handled.

Reading Station The area on the key punch where a data card is aligned for reading by a sensing mechanism to duplicate it automatically into another card located in the punching station.

Real Constant A number written with a decimal point.

Real-Time Pertains to the processing of information or transactions as they actually occur. It is actually a concurrent operation for computing and physical processing.

Real-Time Processing The processing of data as received and in time for the result to affect a decision.

Real Variable A series of alphanumeric characters with the first letter being any letter other than I, J, K, L, M, or N.

Record A collection of related items of data, treated as a unit.

Recording The process by which an input device facilitates the presentation of source data for processing.

Redundancy A situation where two or more rules in a decision table depict the same combination.

Register A device capable of storing a specified amount of data, such as one word.

Relational Test A test shown in a conditional statement, in which the subject operand is compared wth the object operand and some action is taken based on the relation that exists.

Reproducer A machine that reproduces a punched card by duplicating another similar card.

Reserved Word A COBOL word which represents a particular meaning to be used in prescribed context.

RPG Report Program Generator.

RPG II Report Program Generator II; designed to process files of records on the IBM System/3 computer system.

Secondary Storage An area or a device (other than the central processing unit) that stores relevant information until needed. Also called file *memory.*

Second-Generation Computer Refers to transistor-built (versus vacuum tube) computers, capable of processing data at millisecond and microsecond speeds with high-speed printers and readers (for example, the IBM 1401 computer system).

Selecting Extracting certain cards from a deck for a specific purpose without disturbing the sequence in which they were originally filed.

Self-Checking Code An error-detecting code.

Sense Wire One of four wires strung through a magnetic wire and used in a read operation to determine if a given core is in a 1-bit or an 0-bit state.

Sequence Checking An operation designed to determine whether the cards in a given file are in proper order.

Sequential Data Processing A technique by which items to be processed must be coded and collected into groups prior to processing.

Serial-Punching Principle A character-at-a-time punching of data in a card.

Serial Reading Column-by-column reading of a data card.

Simplex Transmission of information in one direction only.

Simulation Symbolic representation (in terms of a model) of the essence of a system for testing an idea or a product before operationalizing its full-scale production.

Simultaneous-Punching Principle Introduced by James Powers, a method whereby information to be punched is initially accumulated and then punched simultaneously in a card.

Single Master-Card Gang Punching A gang-punching operation related to a deck of cards, consisting of copying data from one master card into a group of succeeding cards.

Software (1) The collection of programs and routines associated with a computer; e.g., compilers, library routines. (2) All the documents associated with a computer; e.g., manuals, circuit diagrams. Contrasts with *hardware.*

Sorter A machine capable of sorting punched cards either alphabetically or numerically.

Sorting Arranging numeric or alphabetic data in a given sequence.

Source Document A document from which basic data is extracted.

Source Program A program written in a source language, a language that is an input to a given translation process.

Space Division Multiplexing A technique that provides separate physical channels for each signal being transmitted.

Special-Purpose Computer A computer that is designed to solve a restricted class of problems.

Standardization Establishment of specific procedural requirements for the efficient production of a large volume of goods or for automatic processing of data.

Storage The retention of data (source or finished) in memory until needed.

Storage Map A pictorial aid u ed by the programmer for estimating the proportion of storage capacity to be allocated to data.

Stored Program A series of instructions in storage to direct the step-by-step operation of the machine.

Stringing The stage in which an input file is read completely.

Stub A detachable portion of a paycheck, on which earnings and deductions are recorded for reference.

Stub Card A card containing a detachable stub to serve as a receipt for future reference.

Subroutine A routine that can be part of another routine.

Subsystem A component of a system (for example, in a punched-card data-processing system, the keypunch is a primary subsystem).

Summarizing Condensing a mass of data into a concise and meaningful form.

Summary Card A card summarizing data read from detail cards.

Summary Punch A card punch operating in conjunction with another machine, commonly a tabulator, to punch into cards data that have been summarized or calculated by the other machine.

Supervisory Program (Synonymous with *monitor routine*), a program which handles the loading and relocation of various program segments or runs.

Synchronous System A computer whose operations are handled in set time intervals fixed by pulses emitted by a clock.

System (1) An organized collection of parts united by regulated interaction. (2) An organized collection of men, machines, and methods required to accomplish a specific objective.

Systems Analysis The examination of an activity, procedure, method, technique, or business, to determine what must be accomplished and how the necessary operations may best be accomplished.

Systems Analyst A person skilled in the definition and development of techniques for the solving of a problem, especially those techniques for solutions on a computer.

System Command A keyword that causes prompt system action.

System Flowchart A graphic representation of a system in which data provided by a source document are converted into final documents.

System Study The detailed process of determining a system or set of procedures for using a computer for definite functions or operations, and establishing specifications to be used as a basis for the selection of equipment suitable to the specific needs.

System Synthesis The planning of the procedures for solving a problem. This may involve, among other things, the analysis of the problem, preparation of a flow diagram, preparing details, testing and developing subroutines, allocation of storage locations, specification of input and output formats, and the incorporation of a computer run into a complete data-processing system.

Table Look-Up A procedure for obtaining the function value corresponding to an argument from a table of function values.

TASI (Short for *Time Assigned Speech Interpolation*) A type of multiplexing that combines frequency division and time division multiplexing techniques.

Teleptype Printer A device that presents type in a square block. The type square moves from left to right and positions one character at a time. When this happens, a hammer strikes the character from behind, depressing it against the inked ribbon that faces the paper form.

Terminal An area or a device in a data-transmission system where messages can enter and/or exit.

Thin-Film Memory Primary-storage unit made up of layers of magnetic material, usually less than 1 micron thick.

"Thinking" Machine A term used colloquially to refer to electronic computers.

Throughput The total output during a given time period.

Time Card A card used for showing the number of hours an employee has worked.

Time Division Multiplexing Splitting of a transmission channel according to its "time" characteristics.

Time-Sharing A data processing technique where two or more terminals can concurrently utilize a central computer system for various routines.

Toggle (1) Same as *flip-flop*. (2) Any device having two stable states.

Total System Concept Relates to a management information system by stressing interrelationships between the system producing information and the system producing decisions.

Trailer Record A record that follows a group of records and contains pertinent data related to the group of records.

Turnaround Time The amount of time required for a given routine to reach the computer for processing and get back to the programmer in the form of desired output.

12-Edge The top edge of a punched card.

Unit Record (1) A separate record that is similar in form and content to other records; e.g., a summary of a particular employee's earnings to date. (2) Sometimes, a piece of nontape auxiliary equipment; e.g., card reader, printer, or console typewriter.

User's Request A statement of what a proposed system is expected to produce and whom it will accommodate, source of data input, desired output information, and anticipated deadline. A phase of project initiation.

Variable A name that is arbitrarily chosen to represent numbers and computer locations where the numbers are located.

Variable-Word-Length Having the property that a machine word may have a variable number of characters. It may be applied either to a single entry whose information content may be changed from time to time, or to a group of functionally similar entries whose corresponding components are of different lengths.

Verifier A device on which a record can be compared or tested for identity, character by character, with a retranscription or copy as it is being prepared.

Virtual Storage Managing the location of program and data by a combination of storage devices, paging, and software, such that a programmer is unaware of constraints on amount of available storage.

Wheel Printer A device similar in method of operation to the bar printer, except that the type bars are replaced by wheels around which all the necessary characters are embossed.

Wire-Matrix Printer A type of printer which uses a 5×7 configuration of small wires to print alphabetic or numeric characters.

Word An ordered set of characters that occupies one storage location and is treated by the computer circuits as a unit and transferred as such. Ordinarily, a word is treated by the control unit as an instruction, and by the arithmetic unit as a quantity. Word lengths may be fixed or variable depending on the particular computer.

Word Length The number of bits or other characters in a word.

X Punch A punch in the second row, one row above the zero row, on a Hollerith punched card.

Zone Punch A punch in the O, X, or Y row on a Hollerith punched card.

computer organizations

B

American Federation of Information Processing Societies (AFIPS), 345 East 47 Street, New York, N.Y. 10017.

Founded in May 1961, AFIPS represents an estimated 26,000 members of the information processing community. Its primary *purpose* is to advance understanding and knowledge of the information processing sciences through active engagement in various scientific activities and cooperation with state, national, and international (called IFPS) organizations on information processing.

The association's primary *activities* are the Spring and Fall joint computer conferences, traditionally held in the Eastern and Western parts of the country, respectively. *Proceedings* of each conference are published and made available to all members.

Association for Computing Machinery (ACM), 1130 Avenue of the Americas, New York, N.Y. 10036.

Founded in 1947, ACM has over 20,000 members in more than 160 chapters. Its *function* is to advance the design, development, and application of information processing and the interchange of such techniques between computer specialists and users.

ACM's primary *activities* are chapter and regional meetings and an annual conference (usually held in August). It sponsors various seminars and special-interest groups and *publishes Computing Reviews* (monthly), *Communications of the ACM* (monthly), and *Journal of the ACM* (quarterly).

Association for Educational Data Systems (AEDS), 1201 Sixteenth Street, N. W., Washington, D.C. 20036.

Founded in 1962 by professional educators, AEDS holds approximately 2,600 members interested in sharing information related to the effect of data processing on the educational process. It acts as a clearinghouse of such information, recommends professional consultants, and organizes workshops and seminars on educational data processing. AEDS' main *periodicals* are *Monitor* (monthly) and *Journal of Educational Data Processing* (quarterly).

Association of Data Processing Service Organizations (ADAPSO), 947 Old York Road, Abington, Pa. 19001.

An association of commercial institutions, ADAPSO offers data-processing services through systems its members operate on their own premises. A *directory* is published annually.

Association for Systems Management (ASM), 7890 Brookside Drive, Cleveland, Ohio 44138.

Founded in 1944, SPA holds approximately 7,000 members through 105 chapters in the United States, Mexico, Canada, Venezuela, and other foreign countries. Its *purpose* is to promote advanced management systems and procedures through seminars, professional education, and research.

SPA's primary *periodicals* are the monthly *Journal of Systems Management*, the *International Newsletter*, and *Annual Ideas for Management*. Its other publications include *Total Systems, Profile of a Systems Man: An Annotated Bibliography of the Systems Professional,* and *Guide to Office Clerical Standards.* In addition to chapter meetings, it also holds an annual international meeting in the United States.

Business Equipment Manufacturers Association (BEMA), 235 East 42 Street, New York, N.Y. 10017.

Founded in 1916, BEMA comprises the fifty-five companies which manufacture computing equipment and office machines. Its main *function* is to guide users in solving problems and applying information for general benefit, and to sponsor the setting of standards for computers and information processing. It *publishes* a weekly *News Bulletin* and an *Annual Report.*

Data Processing Management Association (DPMA), 505 Busse Highway, Park Ridge, Ill. 60068.

Founded in 1951 as the National Machine Accountants Association (the name was changed to DPMA in 1962), DPMA claims membership of over 22,000 in the United States, Canada, and Japan.

The primary *purpose* of DPMA is to develop and promote business methods and education in data processing and data-processing management. Through its chapters, it promotes a professional attitude among its members in understanding and applying data-processing techniques.

DPMA's primary *periodical* is the monthly *Data Management.* It also publishes proceedings of its annual conference (usually held in June) and *Research and Career Information.*

Since 1962, the Certificate in Data Processing has been given to establish professional standards in data processing. The Association also sponsors the "Registered Business Programmer" annual examination.

Other associations, especially those with an interest in data processing, include:

Administrative Management Society, Willow Grove, Pa. 19090.

American Documentation Institute, 2000 P Street, N. W., Washington, D.C. 20036.

American Management Association, 135 West 50 Street, New York, N.Y. 10020.

American Records Management Association, 738 Builders Exchange, Minneapolis, Minn. 55402.

American Society for Information Science, 2000 P Street, N. W., Washington, D.C. 20036.

Digital Equipment Computer Users Society, 146 Main Street, Maynard, Mass. 01754.

Federal Government Accountants Association, 1523 L Street, N. W., Washington, D.C. 20005.

Industrial Management Society, 330 South Wells Street, Chicago, Ill. 60606.

National Association of Accountants, 505 Park Avenue, New York, N.Y. 10022.

National Management Association, 333 West First Street, Dayton, Ohio 45402.

Society for Advancement of Management, 16 West 40 Street, New York, N.Y. 10018.

Society for Information Display, 654 North Sepulveda Boulevard, Suite 5, Los Angeles, Calif. 90040.

Special Library Association, 31 East 10 Street, New York, N.Y. 10003.

selected periodicals

Abstracts of Computer Literature, Burroughs Corporation Plant Library, 460 Sierra Madre Villa, Pasadena, Calif. 91109.

Bimonthly, 36-page review of literature on various aspects of computing (free).

Automation-Data in State and Local Government, Michigan Department of Education, Bureau of Educational Services, Library Division, 735 East Michigan Avenue, Lansing, Mich. 48913.

Monthly, 4-page review of published EDP articles (free).

Communications of the ACM, Association for Computing Machinery, 1130 Avenue of the Americas, New York, N.Y. 10036.

Monthly, 80-page journal covering technical articles and subjects of general interest.

Computer Characteristics Quarterly, Adams Associates, 128 The Great Road, Bedford, Mass. 01730.

Quarterly, 250-page presentation of data on key characteristics of computers and peripheral devices.

Computer Design, Computer Design Publishing Company, P.O. Box A, Winchester, Mass. 01890.

Monthly, 90-page coverage of subjects on circuitry (free to qualified subscribers).

Computer Education, Data Processing Horizons, Inc., P.O. Box 99, South Pasadena, Calif. 91030.

A monthly magazine covering the latest developments in the teaching of data processing. It also covers such aspects of educational interest as computer characteristics, profiles on schools, book reviews, films, correspondence courses, and seminars.

Computers and People, Berkeley Enterprises, Inc., 815 Washington Street, Newtonville, Mass. 02160.

Monthly, 75-page journal covering topics of general interest.

Computers and the Humanities, Queens College of the City University of New York, Flushing, N.Y. 11367.

A 65-page journal published five times each year, covering topics related to the humanities.

Computerworld, Computerworld, Inc., 129 Mt. Auburn Street, Cambridge, Mass. 02138.

A weekly newspaper covering various aspects and developments in the EDP field.

Computing Reviews, Association for Computing Machinery, 1130 Avenue of the Americas, New York, N.Y. 10036.

Monthly, 100-page journal presenting critical evaluation of books, articles, and films on various aspects of computing.

Computing Surveys: A quarterly publication of the ACM for tutorial and survey purposes.

Data Base: A quarterly publication of ACM's special interest group on Business Data Processing.

Data Processing, North American Publishing Company, 134 North 13th Street, Philadelphia, Pa. 19107.

Monthly, 75-page magazine covering topics of general interest in data processing.

Data Processing Digest, Data Processing Digest, Inc., 1140 South Robertson Boulevard, Los Angeles, Calif. 90035.

Monthly, 20-page coverage of general topics on data processing.

Data Processing for Education, American Data Processing, Inc., 4th Floor, Book Building, Detroit, Mich. 48226.

Monthly, 12-page coverage of general data-processing topics in education.

Datamation, F. D. Thompson Publications, Inc., 35 Mason Street, Greenwich, Conn. 06830.

Monthly, 140-page magazine, covering current and prospective developments in the data-processing field.

EDP Analyzer, 134 Escondido Avenue, Vista, Calif.

A highly regarded monthly periodical on specific topics.

IBM Systems Journal, International Business Machines Corporation, Armonk, N.Y. 10504.

A quarterly publication of technical articles by IBM authors.

Information Processing Journal, Cambridge Communication Corporation, 1612 K Street, N. W., Washington, D.C. 20006.

Quarterly, 215-page journal presenting a critical evaluation of articles and books on various aspects of electronic data processing.

Infosystems, Business Press International, Inc., 288 Park Avenue, West Elmhurst, Ill. 60126.

Monthly, 85-page journal on various EDP subjects. Free to educators in data processing and other qualified individuals.

Journal of the Association for Computing Machinery, Association for Computing Machinery, 1130 Avenue of the Americas, New York, N.Y. 10036.

A quarterly publication emphasizing technical papers (free to members).

Journal of Data Management, Data Processing Management Association, 505 Busse Highway, Park Ridge, Ill. 60068.

Monthly, 68-page magazine covering business-oriented data-processing topics (free to members).

Journal of Systems Management, Cleveland, Ohio.

A monthly publication of the ASM on analysis of information and management systems and procedures.

Other Periodicals of Interest:

Data Processing for Management, American Data Processing, Inc., 22nd Floor, Book Tower, Detroit, Mich. 48226.

Data Systems News, United Business Publications, P.O. Box 7387, Philadelphia, Pa. 19101.

Digital Computer Newsletter, Information Systems Branch, Office of Naval Research, Washington, D.C. 20360.

Honeywell Computer Journal, Honeywell, Inc., Electronic Data Processing Division, Wellesley Hills, Mass. 02181.

IBM Data Processor, IBM Corporation, Data Processing Division, 112 East Post Road, White Plains, N.Y. 10601.

Information Display, Information Display Publications, Inc., 647 North Sepulveda Boulevard, Los Angeles, Calif. 90049.

Journal of Computer and System Sciences, Academic Press, Inc., 111 Fifth Avenue, New York, N.Y. 10003.

Scientific and Control Computer Reports, Auerback Corporation, 121 North Broad Street, Philadelphia, Pa. 19107.

hexadecimal-decimal conversion table

Table 1, which follows on next page, is included as a quick reference to converting hexadecimal numbers (000-6FF) to decimal and decimal numbers (0000-1791) to hexadecimal.

To convert a given hexadecimal number to decimal, locate the two high-order hexadecimal digits in the left column and the low-order digit in the top row. The decimal equivalent is located at their intersection point. For example, the decimal equivalent of hexadecimal number 1F2 is determined by locating digits 1F in the left column of the conversion table and moving horizontally across that row to the value in the column headed by the low-order hexadecimal digit 2. This value, 0498, is the decimal equivalent of hexadecimal number 1F2.

Conversely, when the hexadecimal equivalent of a given decimal number is desired, the decimal number is first located in the body of the table. The low-order hexadecimal digit is represented by the top digit of the column containing the decimal number and the two remaining hexadecimal digits are located in the left column on the same line containing the decimal number. Thus, the hexadecimal 1F2 is the equivalent of decimal number 0498.

TABLE 1

Hexadecimal-Decimal Conversion Table

	0	1	2	3	4	5	6	7	8	9	A	B	C	D	E	F
00 —	0000	0001	0002	0003	0004	0005	0006	0007	0008	0009	0010	0011	0012	0013	0014	0015
01 —	0016	0017	0018	0019	0020	0021	0022	0023	0024	0025	0026	0027	0028	0029	0030	0031
02 —	0032	0033	0034	0035	0036	0037	0038	0039	0040	0041	0042	0043	0044	0045	0046	0047
03 —	0048	0049	0050	0051	0052	0053	0054	0055	0056	0057	0058	0059	0060	0061	0062	0063
04 —	0064	0065	0066	0067	0068	0069	0070	0071	0072	0073	0074	0075	0076	0077	0078	0079
05 —	0080	0081	0082	0083	0084	0085	0086	0087	0088	0089	0090	0091	0092	0093	0094	0095
06 —	0096	0097	0098	0099	0100	0101	0102	0103	0104	0105	0106	0107	0108	0109	0110	0111
07 —	0112	0113	0114	0115	0116	0117	0118	0119	0120	0121	0122	0123	0124	0125	0126	0127
08 —	0128	0129	0130	0131	0132	0133	0134	0135	0136	0137	0138	0139	0140	0141	0142	0143
09 —	0144	0145	0146	0147	0148	0149	0150	0151	0152	0153	0154	0155	0156	0157	0158	0159
0A —	0160	0161	0162	0163	0164	0165	0166	0167	0168	0169	0170	0171	0172	0173	0174	0175
0B —	0176	0177	0178	0179	0180	0181	0182	0183	0184	0185	0186	0187	0188	0189	0190	0191
0C —	0192	0193	0194	0195	0196	0197	0198	0199	0200	0201	0202	0203	0204	0205	0206	0207
0D —	0208	0209	0210	0211	0212	0213	0214	0215	0216	0217	0218	0219	0220	0221	0222	0223
0E —	0224	0225	0226	0227	0228	0229	0230	0231	0232	0233	0234	0235	0236	0237	0238	0239
0F —	0240	0241	0242	0243	0244	0245	0246	0247	0248	0249	0250	0251	0252	0253	0254	0255
10 —	0256	0257	0258	0259	0260	0261	0262	0263	0264	0265	0266	0267	0268	0269	0270	0271
11 —	0272	0273	0274	0275	0276	0277	0278	0279	0280	0281	0282	0283	0284	0285	0286	0287
12 —	0288	0289	0290	0291	0292	0293	0294	0295	0296	0297	0298	0299	0300	0301	0302	0303
13 —	0304	0305	0306	0307	0308	0309	0310	0311	0312	0313	0314	0315	0316	0317	0318	0319
14 —	0320	0321	0322	0323	0324	0325	0326	0327	0328	0329	0330	0331	0332	0333	0334	0335
15 —	0336	0337	0338	0339	0340	0341	0342	0343	0344	0345	0346	0347	0348	0349	0350	0351
16 —	0352	0353	0354	0355	0356	0357	0358	0359	0360	0361	0362	0363	0364	0365	0366	0367
17 —	0368	0369	0370	0371	0372	0373	0374	0375	0376	0377	0378	0379	0380	0381	0382	0383
18 —	0384	0385	0386	0387	0388	0389	0390	0391	0392	0393	0394	0395	0396	0397	0398	0399
19 —	0400	0401	0402	0403	0404	0405	0406	0407	0408	0409	0410	0411	0412	0413	0414	0415
1A —	0416	0417	0418	0419	0420	0421	0422	0423	0424	0425	0426	0427	0428	0429	0430	0431
1B —	0432	0433	0434	0435	0436	0437	0438	0439	0440	0441	0442	0443	0444	0445	0446	0447

1C —	0448	0449	0450	0451	0452	0453	0454	0455	0456	0457	0458	0459	0460	0461	0462	0463
1D —	0464	0465	0466	0467	0468	0469	0470	0471	0472	0473	0474	0475	0476	0477	0478	0479
1E —	0480	0481	0482	0483	0484	0485	0486	0487	0488	0489	0490	0491	0492	0493	0494	0495
1F —	0496	0497	0498	0499	0500	0501	0502	0503	0504	0505	0506	0507	0508	0509	0510	0511
20 —	0512	0513	0514	0515	0516	0517	0518	0519	0520	0521	0522	0523	0524	0525	0526	0527
21 —	0528	0529	0530	0531	0532	0533	0534	0535	0536	0537	0538	0539	0540	0541	0542	0543
22 —	0544	0545	0546	0547	0548	0549	0550	0551	0552	0553	0554	0555	0556	0557	0558	0559
23 —	0560	0561	0562	0563	0564	0565	0566	0567	0568	0569	0570	0571	0572	0573	0574	0575
24 —	0576	0577	0578	0579	0580	0581	0582	0583	0584	0585	0586	0587	0588	0589	0590	0591
25 —	0592	0593	0594	0595	0596	0597	0598	0599	0600	0601	0602	0603	0604	0605	0606	0607
26 —	0608	0609	0610	0611	0612	0613	0614	0615	0616	0617	0618	0619	0620	0621	0622	0623
27 —	0624	0625	0626	0627	0628	0629	0630	0631	0632	0633	0634	0635	0636	0637	0638	0639
28 —	0640	0641	0642	0643	0644	0645	0646	0647	0648	0649	0650	0651	0652	0653	0654	0655
29 —	0656	0657	0658	0659	0660	0661	0662	0663	0664	0665	0666	0667	0668	0669	0670	0671
2A —	0672	0673	0674	0675	0676	0677	0678	0679	0680	0681	0682	0683	0684	0685	0686	0687
2B —	0688	0689	0690	0691	0692	0693	0694	0695	0696	0697	0698	0699	0700	0701	0702	0703
2C —	0704	0705	0706	0707	0708	0709	0710	0711	0712	0713	0714	0715	0716	0717	0718	0719
2D —	0720	0721	0722	0723	0724	0725	0726	0727	0728	0729	0730	0731	0732	0733	0734	0735
2E —	0736	0737	0738	0739	0740	0741	0742	0743	0744	0745	0746	0747	0748	0749	0750	0751
2F —	0752	0753	0754	0755	0756	0757	0758	0759	0760	0761	0762	0763	0764	0765	0766	0767
30 —	0768	0769	0770	0771	0772	0773	0774	0775	0776	0777	0778	0779	0780	0781	0782	0783
31 —	0784	0785	0786	0787	0788	0789	0790	0791	0792	0793	0794	0795	0796	0797	0798	0799
32 —	0800	0801	0802	0803	0804	0805	0806	0807	0808	0809	0810	0811	0812	0813	0814	0815
33 —	0816	0817	0818	0819	0820	0821	0822	0823	0824	0825	0826	0827	0828	0829	0830	0831
34 —	0832	0833	0834	0835	0836	0837	0838	0839	0840	0841	0842	0843	0844	0845	0846	0847
35 —	0848	0849	0850	0851	0852	0853	0854	0855	0856	0857	0858	0859	0860	0861	0862	0863
36 —	0864	0865	0866	0867	0868	0869	0870	0871	0872	0873	0874	0875	0876	0877	0878	0879
37 —	0880	0881	0882	0883	0884	0885	0886	0887	0888	0889	0890	0891	0892	0893	0894	0895
38 —	0896	0897	0898	0899	0900	0901	0902	0903	0904	0905	0906	0907	0908	0909	0910	0911
39 —	0912	0913	0914	0915	0916	0917	0918	0919	0920	0921	0922	0923	0924	0925	0926	0927
3A —	0928	0929	0930	0931	0932	0933	0934	0935	0936	0937	0938	0939	0940	0941	0942	0943
3B —	0944	0945	0946	0947	0948	0949	0950	0951	0952	0953	0954	0955	0956	0957	0958	0959

Reprinted courtesy of the IBM Corporation.

TABLE 1 ***(Continued)***

Hexadecimal-Decimal Conversion Table

	0	1	2	3	4	5	6	7	8	9	A	B	C	D	E	F
3C —	0960	0961	0962	0963	0964	0965	0966	0967	0968	0969	0970	0971	0972	0973	0974	0975
3D —	0976	0977	0978	0979	0980	0981	0982	0983	0984	0985	0986	0987	0988	0989	0990	0991
3E —	0992	0993	0994	0995	0996	0997	0998	0999	1000	1001	1002	1003	1004	1005	1006	1007
3F —	1008	1009	1010	1011	1012	1013	1014	1015	1016	1017	1018	1019	1020	1021	1022	1023
40 —	1024	1025	1026	1027	1028	1029	1030	1031	1032	1033	1034	1035	1036	1037	1038	1039
41 —	1040	1041	1042	1043	1044	1045	1046	1047	1048	1049	1050	1051	1052	1053	1054	1055
42 —	1056	1057	1058	1059	1060	1061	1062	1063	1064	1065	1066	1067	1068	1069	1070	1071
43 —	1072	1073	1074	1075	1076	1077	1078	1079	1080	1081	1082	1083	1084	1085	1086	1087
44 —	1088	1089	1090	1091	1092	1093	1094	1095	1096	1097	1098	1099	1100	1101	1102	1103
45 —	1104	1105	1106	1107	1108	1109	1110	1111	1112	1113	1114	1115	1116	1117	1118	1119
46 —	1120	1121	1122	1123	1124	1125	1126	1127	1128	1129	1130	1131	1132	1133	1134	1135
47 —	1136	1137	1138	1139	1140	1141	1142	1143	1144	1145	1146	1147	1148	1149	1150	1151
48 —	1152	1153	1154	1155	1156	1157	1158	1159	1160	1161	1162	1163	1164	1165	1166	1167
49 —	1168	1169	1170	1171	1172	1173	1174	1175	1176	1177	1178	1179	1180	1181	1182	1183
4A —	1184	1185	1186	1187	1188	1189	1190	1191	1192	1193	1194	1195	1196	1197	1198	1199
4B —	1200	1201	1202	1203	1204	1205	1206	1207	1208	1209	1210	1211	1212	1213	1214	1215
4C —	1216	1217	1218	1219	1220	1221	1222	1223	1224	1225	1226	1227	1228	1229	1230	1231
4D —	1232	1233	1234	1235	1236	1237	1238	1239	1240	1241	1242	1243	1244	1245	1246	1247
4E —	1248	1249	1250	1251	1252	1253	1254	1255	1256	1257	1258	1259	1260	1261	1262	1263
4F —	1264	1265	1266	1267	1268	1269	1270	1271	1272	1273	1274	1275	1276	1277	1278	1279
50 —	1280	1281	1282	1283	1284	1285	1286	1287	1288	1289	1290	1291	1292	1293	1294	1295
51 —	1296	1297	1298	1299	1300	1301	1302	1303	1304	1305	1306	1307	1308	1309	1310	1311
52 —	1312	1313	1314	1315	1316	1317	1318	1319	1320	1321	1322	1323	1324	1325	1326	1327
53 —	1328	1329	1330	1331	1332	1333	1334	1335	1336	1337	1338	1339	1340	1341	1342	1343
54 —	1344	1345	1346	1347	1348	1349	1350	1351	1352	1353	1354	1355	1356	1357	1358	1359
55 —	1360	1361	1362	1363	1364	1365	1366	1367	1368	1369	1370	1371	1372	1373	1374	1375
56 —	1376	1377	1378	1379	1380	1381	1382	1383	1384	1385	1386	1387	1388	1389	1390	1391
57 —	1392	1393	1394	1395	1396	1397	1393	1399	1400	1401	1402	1403	1404	1405	1406	1407

58 —	1408	1409	1410	1411	1412	1413	1414	1415	1416	1417	1418	1419	1420	1421	1422	1423
59 —	1424	1425	1426	1427	1428	1429	1430	1431	1432	1433	1434	1435	1436	1437	1438	1439
5A —	1440	1441	1442	1443	1444	1445	1446	1447	1448	1449	1450	1451	1452	1453	1454	1455
5B —	1456	1457	1458	1459	1460	1461	1462	1463	1464	1465	1466	1467	1468	1469	1470	1471
5C —	1472	1473	1474	1475	1476	1477	1478	1479	1480	1481	1482	1483	1484	1485	1486	1487
5D —	1488	1489	1490	1491	1492	1493	1494	1495	1496	1497	1498	1499	1500	1501	1502	1503
5E —	1504	1505	1506	1507	1508	1509	1510	1511	1512	1513	1514	1515	1516	1517	1518	1519
5F —	1520	1521	1522	1523	1524	1525	1526	1527	1528	1529	1530	1531	1532	1533	1534	1535
60 —	1536	1537	1538	1539	1540	1541	1542	1543	1544	1545	1546	1547	1548	1549	1550	1551
61 —	1552	1553	1554	1555	1556	1557	1558	1559	1560	1561	1562	1563	1564	1565	1566	1567
62 —	1568	1569	1570	1571	1572	1573	1574	1575	1576	1577	1578	1579	1580	1581	1582	1583
63 —	1584	1585	1586	1587	1588	1589	1590	1591	1592	1593	1594	1595	1596	1597	1598	1599
64 —	1600	1601	1602	1603	1604	1605	1606	1607	1608	1609	1610	1611	1612	1613	1614	1615
65 —	1616	1617	1618	1619	1620	1621	1622	1623	1624	1625	1626	1627	1628	1629	1630	1631
66 —	1632	1633	1634	1635	1636	1637	1638	1639	1640	1641	1642	1643	1644	1645	1646	1647
67 —	1648	1649	1650	1651	1652	1653	1654	1655	1656	1657	1658	1659	1660	1661	1662	1663
68 —	1664	1665	1666	1667	1668	1669	1670	1671	1672	1673	1674	1675	1676	1677	1678	1679
69 —	1680	1681	1682	1683	1684	1685	1686	1687	1688	1689	1690	1691	1692	1693	1694	1695
6A —	1696	1697	1698	1699	1700	1701	1702	1703	1704	1705	1706	1707	1708	1709	1710	1711
6B —	1712	1713	1714	1715	1716	1717	1718	1719	1720	1721	1722	1723	1724	1725	1726	1727
6C —	1728	1729	1730	1731	1732	1733	1734	1735	1736	1737	1738	1739	1740	1741	1742	1743
6D —	1744	1745	1746	1747	1748	1749	1750	1751	1752	1753	1754	1755	1756	1757	1758	1759
6E —	1760	1761	1762	1763	1764	1765	1766	1767	1768	1769	1770	1771	1772	1773	1774	1775
6F —	1776	1777	1778	1779	1780	1781	1782	1783	1784	1785	1786	1787	1788	1789	1790	1791

Reprinted courtesy of the IBM Corporation.

TABLE 2

Base Two (Binary)

n	2^n	2^{-n}
0	1	1.0
1	2	0.5
2	4	0.25
3	8	0.125
4	16	0.062 5
5	32	0.031 25
6	64	0.015 625
7	128	0.007 812 5
8	256	0.003 906 25
9	512	0.001 953 125
10	1,024	0.000 976 562 5
11	2,048	0.000 488 281 25
12	4,096	0.000 244 140 625
13	8,192	0.000 122 070 312 5
14	16,384	0.000 061 035 156 25
15	32,768	0.000 030 517 578 125
16	65,536	0.000 015 258 789 062 5
17	131,072	0.000 007 629 394 531 25
18	262,144	0.000 003 814 697 265 625
19	524,288	0.000 001 907 348 632 812 5
20	1,048,576	0.000 000 953 674 316 406 25
21	2,097,152	0.000 000 476 837 158 203 125
22	4,194,304	0.000 000 238 418 579 101 562 5
23	8,388,608	0.000 000 119 209 289 550 781 25
24	16,777,216	0.000 000 059 604 644 775 390 625
25	33,554,432	0.000 000 029 802 322 387 695 312 5
26	67,108,864	0.000 000 014 901 161 193 847 656 25
27	134,217,728	0.000 000 007 450 580 596 923 828 125

index

A

B

C

D

E

F

G

H

I

N

O

P

S

T

U

V

W

XYZ